Employment Law

Fourth edition

Malcolm Sargeant and David Lewis

FT Prentice Hall

FINANCIAL TIMES

An imprint of **Pearson Education**

Harlow, England • London • New York • Boston • San Francisco • Toronto • Sydney • Singapore • Hong Kong
Tokyo • Seoul • Taipei • New Delhi • Cape Town • Madrid • Mexico City • Amsterdam • Munich • Paris • Milan

Pearson Education Limited

Edinburgh Gate
Harlow
Essex CM20 2JE
England

and Associated Companies throughout the world

Visit us on the World Wide Web at:
www.pearsoned.co.uk

First published 2001
Second edition published 2003
Third edition published 2006
Fourth edition published 2008

ISBN: 978-1-4058-5868-7

British Library Cataloguing-in-Publication Data
A catalogue record for this book is available from the British Library

Library of Congress Cataloging-in-Publication Data
A catalog record for this book is available from the Library of Congress

10 9 8 7 6 5 4 3 2 1
11 10 09 08

Typeset in 10/12.5pt Minion by 35
Printed in Great Britain by Henry Ling Ltd, at the Dorset Press, Dorchester, Dorset

The publisher's policy is to use paper manufactured from sustainable forests.

Contents

Supporting resources

Visit **www.mylawchamber.co.uk/sargeant** to find valuable online resources

Companion Website for students

■ Practice exam questions to test yourself on each topic throughout the course.
■ Regular updates on major changes in the law to make
  sure you are ahead of the game by knowing the latest developments.
■ Web links to help you read more widely around the subject, and really impress
  your lecturers.

For more information please contact your local Pearson Education sales
representative or visit **www.mylawchamber.co.uk/sargeant**

Guided tour

1

The Study of Employment Law

1.1 Introduction

The subject of employment law is the regulation of the relationship between employer and worker or, put in another way, the relationship between the user of labour and the supplier of labour. This regulation takes place at an individual level and at a collective level. At an individual level the law takes the view that the contract of employment is like any other contract, namely a legally binding agreement that two equal parties have voluntarily entered into. At a collective level workers and employers have banded together into trade unions and employers' associations in order, partly, to give themselves greater bargaining power with each other.

The sources of this regulation are diverse and include:

(1) primary and secondary legislation initiated or supported by Government;
(2) the EU Treaty and legislation, usually, but not always, in the form of Directives;
(3) the decisions of the courts, including the High Court, employment tribunals and the Employment Appeal Tribunal, but especially, as in other fields of law, decisions of the Court of Appeal and the House of Lords;
(4) the decisions of international courts, especially the European Court of Justice and the European Court of Human Rights;
(5) codes of practice and guidance issued by Ministers of the Crown and by individual bodies authorised by statute to do so. These latter include the Health and Safety Commission and the Commission for Equality and Human Rights;
(6) the Advisory, Conciliation and Arbitration Service (ACAS) and the Central Arbitration Committee (CAC), which have been given a special role by governments in the field of dispute resolution between workers and employers, both individually and collectively.

A concern for students of employment law is how to access the large amount of information available in the most efficient and effective way. Books like this one are one source of information, but further study means accessing the law and its sources directly. The purpose of this chapter is to provide some information on accessing employment law and to show that a large amount of information is available free from the organisations mentioned above and others, much of which is accessible via the Internet.

1.2 Primary and secondary legislation

The Acts of Parliament most often referred to in this book are the Trade Union and Labour Relations (Consolidation) Act 1992 (TULRCA 1992) and the Employment Rights Act 1996

'The Study of Employment Law' chapter provides a comprehensive introduction to the main sources of employment legislation, and the best ways of accessing them.

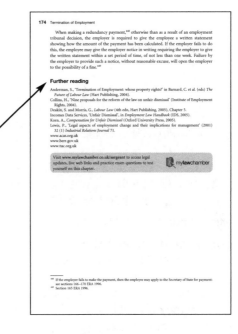

174 Termination of Employment

When making a redundancy payment,[168] otherwise than as a result of an employment tribunal decision, the employer is required to give the employee a written statement showing how the amount of the payment has been calculated. If the employer fails to do this, the employee may give the employer notice in writing requiring the employer to give the written statement within a set period of time, of not less than one week. Failure by the employer to provide such a notice, without reasonable excuse, will open the employer to the possibility of a fine.[169]

Further reading

Anderman, S., 'Termination of Employment: whose property rights?' in Barnard, C. et al. (eds) *The Future of Labour Law* (Hart Publishing, 2004).
Collins, H., 'Nine proposals for the reform of the law on unfair dismissal' (Institute of Employment Rights, 2004).
Deakin, S. and Morris, G., *Labour Law* (4th edn, Hart Publishing, 2005), Chapter 5.
Incomes Data Services, 'Unfair Dismissal', in *Employment Law Handbook* (IDS, 2005).
Korn, A., *Compensation for Unfair Dismissal* (Oxford University Press, 2005).
Lewis, P., 'Legal aspects of employment change and their implications for management' (2001) 32 (1) *Industrial Relations Journal* 71.
www.acas.org.uk
www.berr.gov.uk
www.tuc.org.uk

Visit www.mylawchamber.co.uk/sargeant to access legal updates, live web links and practice exam questions to test yourself on this chapter.   mylawchamber

---

[168] If the employer fails to make the payment, then the employee may apply to the Secretary of State for payment: see sections 166–170 ERA 1996.
[169] Section 165 ERA 1996.

Concise **Further reading** lists direct you to the most relevant resources with which to supplement your study.

124 Termination of Employment

dismissal takes place. The first of these is when a contract of employment, under which the individual is employed, is terminated by the employer. Where there is a dispute as to whether a dismissal has taken place, the onus of proof is on the employee. Thus it is vitally important not to confuse a warning of impending dismissal – for example, through the announcement of a plant closure – with an individual notice to terminate.[112] For the giving of notice to constitute a dismissal at law the actual date of termination must be ascertainable. Where an employer has given notice to terminate, an employee who gives counter-notice indicating that he or she wishes to leave before the employer's notice has expired is still to be regarded as dismissed.[113]

There are occasions when there is a dispute as to whether the individual has been dismissed or whether they have resigned. This was so in *Morris v London Iron and Steel Co Ltd*[114] where the employee claimed that he had been dismissed and the employer claimed that there had been a resignation. The employment tribunal was unable to decide which was the truth after hearing evidence. Bearing in mind that the onus of proof was on the employee, the complaint was dismissed. This approach was approved in the Court of Appeal:

. . . the judge should at the end of the day look at the whole of the evidence that has been called before him, drawing inferences where appropriate, and ask himself what has or has not been shown on the balance of probabilities, and then, bearing in mind where the onus of proof lies, decide whether the plaintiff or the defendant, or both, succeeds.

A radical alteration to an employee's contract of employment may amount to a withdrawal of that contract and a conclusion that the employee was dismissed. *Hogg v Dover College*[115] was a drastic example of this. A teacher was informed by his employer that he would no longer be head of department, that he would be employed on a part-time basis only and his salary was to be halved. The EAT concluded that:

. . . both as a matter of law and common sense, he was being told that his former contract was from that moment gone . . . It is suggested on behalf of the employers that there was a variation, but again, it seems to us quite elementary that you cannot hold a pistol to somebody's head and say 'henceforth you are to be employed on wholly different terms which are in fact 50% of your previous contract'.

This was not a variation of the contract which might give the employee the opportunity to accept or reject a potential repudiation, but amounted to an express dismissal by the employer. This approach was applied in *Alcan Extrusions v Yates*[116] where the imposition of a continuous rolling shift system in place of a traditional shift system, contained in the employees' contracts of employment, also amounted to an express dismissal by the employer. Alternatively, the unilateral variation of an employee's contractual working hours might amount to a breach of a fundamental term entitling the employee to resign and claim constructive dismissal. In *Greenaway Harrison Ltd v Wiles*[117] the threat to end the

---

[112] See *Doble v Firestone Tyre Co Ltd* [1981] IRLR 300.
[113] Section 95(2) ERA 1996.
[114] [1987] IRLR 182 CA.
[115] [1990] ICR 39.
[116] [1996] IRLR 327.
[117] [1994] IRLR 380.

Short extracts from legislation and legal judgements ensure that you have access to primary material in all key areas.

Clear headings and sub headings keep you firmly focused and constantly aware of the context and structure of each chapter.

Trade Unions **361**

11.5 Rights in relation to trade union membership and discipline

Until the Industrial Relations Act 1971 there was little statutory regulation limiting a trade union's powers to admit, discipline or expel a member.[35] Section 65 of this Act introduced rules against arbitrary exclusions or expulsions and unfair or unreasonable disciplinary action. Although this section was repealed in 1976, it was reintroduced in the Employment Act 1980 as part of the Government's attack on the closed shop.

11.5.1 Exclusion and expulsion

Currently an individual may not be excluded or expelled from a trade union, except for four specific reasons.[36] (Note that exclusion means not being admitted to membership.[37]) These are:

(1) if the individual does not satisfy an enforceable membership requirement;
(2) if the individual does not qualify for membership on the grounds that the union only operates in a particular part or parts of Great Britain;
(3) if the union's purpose is to regulate the relations with one particular employer, or a number of particular employers, and the individual no longer works for any of those employers;
(4) if the exclusion or expulsion is entirely attributable to the individual's conduct (other than 'excluded conduct') and the conduct to which it is wholly or mainly attributable is not 'protected conduct'.

In the first of these exceptions, the 'enforceable membership requirement' means a restriction on membership as a result of employment being in one specific trade, industry or profession; or of an occupational description such as a particular grade or level; or of the need for specific trade, industrial or professional qualifications or work experience. 'Excluded conduct' means:

(i) being or ceasing to be, or having been or ceased to be, a member of another trade union or employed by a particular employer or at a particular place;
(ii) conduct to which section 65 TULRCA 1992 applies.

'Protected conduct' consists of the individual being or ceasing to be, or having been or ceased to be, a member of a political party. However, activities undertaken as a member of a political party are not protected.

These rules necessitated a revision of the 'Bridlington Principles'. These were a set of recommendations agreed at the 1939 Trades Union Congress which were designed to minimise disputes over membership questions.[38] They laid down the procedures by which the TUC dealt with complaints by one trade union against another and were designed to

---

[35] The Trade Union Act 1913 had established a requirement that a trade union could not refuse admission or discipline solely because of a refusal to contribute to the political fund.
[36] Section 174 TULRCA 1992.
[37] See *NACODS v Gluchowski* [1996] IRLR 252.
[38] For an example of a TUC disputes committee attempting to resolve issues under the Bridlington Principles, see *Rothwell v APEX* [1975] IRLR 375 CA.

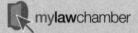 **my**law**chamber**

Visit the *Employment Law*, 4th Edition, **Mylawchamber** site at www.mylawchamber.co.uk/ sargeant to access:

■ **Companion website support:** Use the practice exam questions and answer guidance to test yourself on each topic throughout the course. The site includes updates to major changes in the law to make sure you are ahead of the game, and web links to help you read more widely around the subject.

Preface

In recent years there have been many developments in employment law and regulation. All these developments are reflected in this edition.

The book is intended to be a comprehensive and supportive text for those studying employment law, whether they are law students or others. It emphasises the importance of the European Union in shaping employment protection in this country and other Member States of the Community. It also tries to reflect the continuing changes that are taking place in the subject and includes new developments in information and consultation of employees and new areas of discrimination law. Mostly it will provide the reader with a good understanding of employment law and, hopefully, encourage them to further study and research.

Malcolm Sargeant
David Lewis

Abbreviations

AC	Appeal Cases
ACAS	Advisory, Conciliation and Arbitration Service
All ER	All England Law Reports
AMRA	Access to Medical Reports Act 1988
ASTMS	Association of Supervisory, Technical and Managerial Staffs
AUEW	Amalgamated Union of Engineering Workers
CA	Court of Appeal
CAC	Central Arbitration Committee
CBI	Confederation of British Industry
CEEP	European Centre of Enterprises with Public Participation
CHR	European Convention on Human Rights
CMLR	Common Market Law Reports
CO	Certification Officer
CPSA	Civil and Public Services Association
CRE	Commission for Racial Equality
DDA	Disability Discrimination Act 1995
DfEE	Department for Education and Employment
DRC	Disability Rights Commission
DRCA	Disability Rights Commission Act 1999
DTI	Department of Trade and Industry
EA	Employment Act 2002
EADR	Employment Act (Dispute Resolution) Regulations 2004
EAT	Employment Appeal Tribunal
EC	European Community
ECHR	European Court of Human Rights
ECJ	European Court of Justice
ECR	European Court Reports
EEA	European Economic Area
EEC	European Economic Community
EES	European Employment Strategy
EHRR	European Human Rights Reports
EIRR	European Industrial Relations Report
EOC	Equal Opportunities Commission
EPA	Equal Pay Act 1970
ERA	Employment Rights Act 1996
ERELA	Employment Relations Act 1999
ETA	Employment Tribunals Act 1996
ETEJO	Employment Tribunals Extension of Jurisdiction Order 1994

ETUC	European Trade Union Confederation
ETUI	European Trade Union Institute
EU	European Union
EWC	European Works Council
GCHQ	Government Communications Headquarters
GMBATU	General, Municipal, Boilermakers and Allied Trades Union
HASAWA	Health and Safety at Work etc. Act 1974
HC	House of Commons
HL	House of Lords
HMSO	Her Majesty's Stationery Office
HRA	Human Rights Act 1998
HSCE	Health and Safety (Consultation with Employees) Regulations 1996
ICE	The Information and Consultation of Employees Regulations 2004
ICR	Industrial Cases Reports
IRLR	Industrial Relations Law Reports
LBPIC	Telecommunications (Lawful Business Practice) (Interception of Communications)
MHSW	Management of Health and Safety at Work
MP	Member of Parliament
MPL	Maternity and Parental Leave etc. Regulations
NALGO	National Association of Local Government Officers
NEC	National Executive Committee
NGA	National Graphical Association
NIRC	National Industrial Relations Court
NMW	National Minimum Wage
NMWA	National Minimum Wage Act 1998
NUM	National Union of Mineworkers
NURMTW	National Union of Rail, Maritime and Transport Workers
OJ	Official Journal
ONS	Office for National Statistics
PTW	Part-time workers
QB	Queen's Bench
RIP	Regulation of Investigatory Powers Act 2000
RRA	Race Relations Act 1976
SDA	Sex Discrimination Act 1975
SE	Societas Europae
SI	Statutory Instrument
SNB	Special Negotiating Body
SOGAT	Society of Graphical and Allied Trades
SRA	Standard Retirement Age
TGWU	Transport and General Workers Union
TICE	Transnational Information and Consultation of Employees
TUC	Trades Union Congress
TULRCA	Trade Union and Labour Relations (Consolidation) Act 1992
TUPE	Transfer of Undertakings (Protection of Employment) Regulations 1981

UEAPME	Union Européene de l'Artisant et des Petites et Moyennes Entreprises
ULR	Union Learning Representative
UNICE	Union of Industrial Employers' Confederations of Europe
WLR	Weekly Law Reports
WT	Working time

Table of Cases

Table of Statutes

Table of Statutory Instruments

Table of European Legislation

Table of International Legislation

1

The Study of Employment Law

1.1 Introduction

The subject of employment law is the regulation of the relationship between employer and worker or, put in another way, the relationship between the user of labour and the supplier of labour. This regulation takes place at an individual level and at a collective level. At an individual level the law takes the view that the contract of employment is like any other contract, namely a legally binding agreement that two equal parties have voluntarily entered into. At a collective level workers and employers have banded together into trade unions and employers' associations in order, partly, to give themselves greater bargaining power with each other.

The sources of this regulation are diverse and include:

(1) primary and secondary legislation initiated or supported by Government;
(2) the EU Treaty and legislation, usually, but not always, in the form of Directives;
(3) the decisions of the courts, including the High Court, employment tribunals and the Employment Appeal Tribunal, but especially, as in other fields of law, decisions of the Court of Appeal and the House of Lords;
(4) the decisions of international courts, especially the European Court of Justice and the European Court of Human Rights;
(5) codes of practice and guidance issued by Ministers of the Crown and by individual bodies authorised by statute to do so. These latter include the Health and Safety Commission and the Commission for Equality and Human Rights;
(6) the Advisory, Conciliation and Arbitration Service (ACAS) and the Central Arbitration Committee (CAC), which have been given a special role by governments in the field of dispute resolution between workers and employers, both individually and collectively.

A concern for students of employment law is how to access the large amount of information available in the most efficient and effective way. Books like this one are one source of information, but further study means accessing the law and its sources directly. The purpose of this chapter is to provide some information on accessing employment law and to show that a large amount of information is available free from the organisations mentioned above and others, much of which is accessible via the Internet.

1.2 Primary and secondary legislation

The Acts of Parliament most often referred to in this book are the Trade Union and Labour Relations (Consolidation) Act 1992 (TULRCA 1992) and the Employment Rights Act 1996

(ERA 1996). Both of these have been much amended by other statutes. There are other important Acts, such as the Equal Pay Act 1970, the Sex Discrimination Act 1975, the Race Relations Act 1976, the Disability Discrimination Act 1995 and the National Minimum Wage Act 1998. There are also a large number of statutory instruments which form an important source of employment law. For example, much EU legislation is introduced via regulations under section 2(2) European Communities Act 1972.

Study sources for both Acts of Parliament and secondary legislation are:

(1) Office of Public Sector Information (OPSI) – The Stationery Office, which is the official publisher to Parliament, prints copies for sale of all primary and secondary legislation. These can be expensive but are often available in libraries. All such legislation since, and including, 1988 is available on the OPSI web site at:

   www.opsi.gov.uk

   Click on 'Legislation' and you will be taken to a site from which you can access new legislation made available in the previous two weeks. If you then click on 'UK' under the heading 'Legislation' you will be taken to a further page which will enable you to access all Acts of the UK Parliament adopted since 1988. If you click onto 'Statutory Instruments' you will be able to access subordinate legislation. Bear in mind that there are several thousand statutory instruments adopted each year, so it will help you if you know the year and the number that you are looking for, for example, SI 1998/1833 will lead you to statutory instrument number 1833 adopted in 1998, which will take you to the Working Time Regulations 1998.

(2) Houses of Parliament – *Hansard* is the full verbatim report of debates in the Houses of Parliament and is kept by many libraries in microfiche format. There is also a large amount of information available on Parliament's web site at:

   www.parliament.uk

   If you click on this, you will be able to choose between the House of Commons or the House of Lords and explore at your leisure. Click on 'House of Commons' and you will see a section on 'Research Papers'. If you click on these you will be able to explore all the recent research papers written by House of Commons research staff. This will include papers on employment law issues and Bills before Parliament.

   Alternatively, if, at the Parliament Home Page, you click on 'Site Map' this will give you access to the entire work of Parliament, including copies of Bills before Parliament and the current work of the House of Commons and the House of Lords. It will usefully give you access to the Committee System and the reports that Select Committees of both Houses have made. For example, you might follow this through to the Education and Employment Committee or the Trade and Industry Committee.

   The Government Department that has the most relevance to the study of employment law is the Department for Business, Enterprise and Regulatory Reform (formerly the Department of Trade and Industry (DTI)). Its web site can be found at:

   www.berr.gov.uk

   The site has copies of all the consultations that have been carried out concerning the introduction of many EU measures in the field of employment law. Both sites carry guidance to current legislation.

(3) Other sources of statute will be as for other law subjects studied, such as *Halsbury's Statutes*, LEXIS and LAWTEL.

1.3 The EU Treaty and legislation

Six countries adopted the Treaty of Rome in 1957 but the European Community has grown to 27 Member States at the time of writing. The scope of the Community's activities has also grown from being concerned with a number of primarily economic objectives to a Community that has an important social dimension as well as an economic one (see Chapter 2).

As a result of this, there is a large amount of EU material available and it seems to increase at a rate that alarms even specialist students of Community law. Ways of accessing this information will include:

(1) European Documentation Centres – a large number of libraries contain European Documentation Centres, which will normally have a specialist librarian in charge. These keep paper copies of both current and historical EU material. They are most useful if you know what you are looking for rather than starting a cold search.
(2) The EU has a web site with an enormous amount of material. It is not the easiest site to navigate but will reward those who know which document they are looking for or those with patience. It can be found at:

> www.europa.eu.int

> Once you have clicked on the language you require the next page provides a subject list of what the European Union does. Click on 'Employment and Social Affairs' and you will come across a page divided into two sections which are 'Latest developments' and 'A comprehensive guide to European Law'. Useful sites on this page include 'Employment and Social Affairs' which will take you to the page of the Directorate General that has responsibility for these matters. You might also try the 'European Foundation for the Improvement of Living and Working Conditions' which has extensive information about what is going on in the EU and individual Member States. Lastly you might also click on the page headed 'Legislation in Force' in order to be able to access the piece of legislation that you are interested in.

(3) A good library will have other sources, such as those contained on various CD-ROMs, as well as access to relevant information via other commercial bodies.

1.4 The courts

1.4.1 Employment tribunals and the EAT

Section 1(1) Employment Rights (Dispute Resolution) Act 1998 renamed industrial tribunals as employment tribunals so this is how they are referred to in this book. Unlike many other courts, employment tribunals and the Employment Appeal Tribunal (EAT) are created by statute[1] as is the subject matter in which they deal.[2] The composition of

---

[1] See sections 1 and 20 Employment Tribunals Act 1996.
[2] Sections 2–3 and 21 Employment Tribunals Act 1996.

employment tribunals is set out in the Employment Tribunals Act 1996.[3] An interesting issue with regard to tribunals and the Human Rights Act 1998 was raised in *Smith v Secretary of State for Trade and Industry*.[4] Article 6(1) of the European Convention on Human Rights gives everyone the right to an 'independent and impartial' tribunal. The question raised was whether employment tribunals which were appointed by the Secretary of State could adjudicate in claims against the Secretary of State and still be an independent and impartial tribunal.

The work of employment tribunals is increasing partly because of new legislation on employment rights giving individuals the opportunity to make a complaint to an employment tribunal. Appeals from employment tribunals, on a point of law, are normally to the EAT, which sits in Edinburgh and London. The table below provides a breakdown of employment tribunal claims in 2006/7:[5]

Subject matter	Number and percentage of applications	
Unfair dismissal	44,467	24.6%
Wages Act	28,248	15.7%
Breach of contract	24,002	13.3%
Redundancy pay	7,000	3.9%
Sex discrimination	12,175	6.7%
Race discrimination	3,742	2.1%
Disability discrimination	5,444	3.0%
Equal pay	27,497	15.2%
Working Time Directive	14,960	8.3%
Flexible working	225	0.1%
Age discrimination (from October 2006)	739	0.4%
National minimum wage	739	0.4%
Others	211,182	6.2%
Total	180,420	100%

1.4.2 Case reports

Paper reports of proceedings at the EAT, the Court of Appeal (CA) and the House of Lords (HL) are published in:

Industrial Cases Reports (ICR), and
Industrial Relations Law Reports (IRLR).

Wherever possible, these are the sources used in this book. Both carry good summaries of the cases in question. Cases may also be reported in non-specialist law reports, such as

---

[3] Sections 4 and 22–25 Employment Tribunals Act 1996.
[4] [2000] IRLR 6.
[5] See ACAS Annual Report 2006/7.

the All England Law Reports (All ER), the Weekly Law Reports (WLR), or in Appeal Cases (AC).

Other more comprehensive, sources are:

(1) www.employmentappeals.gov.uk (the EAT);
(2) www.courtservice.gov.uk (the High Court and the Court of Appeal);
(3) www.parliament.uk/parliament/sitemap.htm (the House of Lords).

Apart from the EAT, these sources are not restricted to employment law cases only and can be found via a number of other links. The advantage of all these sites over the paper reports is that the judgment of the court is reported in full on all cases. The Employment Tribunals Service web site also contains a lot of useful information and statistics. It can be found at:

www.ets.gov.uk

1.4.3 International courts

For the purposes of this subject, the two most important courts are the European Court of Justice (ECJ) and the European Court of Human Rights (ECHR). Significant and relevant cases in both are reported in the ICR and IRLR, but they both have their own paper and electronic reports. These are:

European Case Reports (ECR) for the European Court of Justice; and
European Human Rights Reports (EHRR) for the European Court of Human Rights.

Again, these reports cover all the work of the courts and will include a large number of cases which are not directly relevant to the study of employment law. In addition, both courts have web sites which will provide access to their judgments of the court. These sites are:

(1) www.curia.eu.int (the ECJ)
(2) www.echr.coe.int (the ECHR).

1.5 Advisory, Conciliation and Arbitration Service

The Advisory, Conciliation and Arbitration Service (ACAS) was established by statute in 1975 to promote the improvement of industrial relations.[6]

It operates as an independent publicly funded body and is not subject to direct ministerial control. It is run by a committee of 12 individuals, which is made up of leading figures from business, unions, independent sectors and academics. ACAS operates in four key areas of activities. These are:

(1) preventing and resolving disputes by means of collective conciliation and advisory mediation;
(2) conciliating in actual and potential complaints to employment tribunals;

---

[6] See now section 209 TULRCA 1992.

(3) providing information and advice;

(4) promoting good practice and training.

Examples of its success are:

(1) 835 collective cases were completed in 2006/7,[7] of which 33 were subsequently withdrawn. Of the rest, conciliation was successful in 758 cases and unsuccessful in 44.

(2) In the same period 73,869 applications to employment tribunals were dealt with. Of these 22,545 were withdrawn and 28,403 settled, and only 20,073 made it to a tribunal hearing.

The ACAS annual report is a good source of statistical information and is free from its web site. It also produces a wide range of publications which focus on good practice and explain the legal obligations of practitioners. Of considerable importance is its handbook on *Discipline at Work* (see Chapter 5) and its Codes of Practice on:

- Disclosure of information to trade unions for collective bargaining purposes 1997;
- Time off for trade union duties and activities 2003; and
- Disciplinary and grievance procedures 2004.

ACAS has authority to issue these codes of practice under sections 199–202 TULRCA 1992. Section 207 TULRCA 1992 provides that the contents of these codes will be taken into account at hearings before employment tribunals, courts or the Central Arbitration Committee (CAC). ACAS has a very useful web site, which contains consultation and proposals on matters such as new codes of practice. It can be found at:

www.acas.org.uk

1.6 Central Arbitration Committee

The Central Arbitration Committee (CAC) is a permanent independent body with a number of roles:[8]

(1) to adjudicate on applications relating to the statutory recognition of trade unions for collective bargaining purposes (see Chapter 12);

(2) to determine disputes between employers and trade unions over the disclosure of information for collective bargaining purposes (see Chapter 12);

(3) to determine claims and complaints regarding the establishment and operation of European Works Councils in Great Britain (see Chapter 10);

(4) to provide voluntary arbitration in trade disputes, in certain circumstances.

In the period 2006/7 the CAC did not receive any applications concerning voluntary arbitration or European Works Councils. It did, however, receive 11 applications concerning disclosure of information and 64 concerning trade union recognition.

The Committee consists of a chair, 11 deputy chairs together with 55 members experienced as representatives of employers or workers. Any determinations of the

---

[7] See annual report available on the ACAS web site, www.acas.org.uk.
[8] See sections 259–265 TULRCA 1992.

Committee are made by the chair, or deputy chair, plus two members The CAC has a useful web site at:

www.cac.gov.uk

This web site contains information about the CAC and its statutory powers. It also contains information about decisions of the CAC and details about individual cases.

1.7 Certification Officer

The Certification Officer is appointed[9] to carry out particular functions[10] (see Chapter 12):

(1) maintaining a list of trade unions and employers' associations and determining their independence;
(2) dealing with complaints from trade union members that their union has failed to keep certain accurate records;
(3) dealing with complaints from members that their trade union has failed to comply with statutory requirements concerning secret postal ballots for electing its officers and executive;
(4) ensuring observance of the rules on political funds and ballots by trade unions;
(5) ensuring that the statutory procedures for union amalgamations and changes are complied with;
(6) dealing with members' complaints concerning breaches of their rules by trade unions.

The Certification Officer produces a detailed and useful annual report, which contains lists of all employers' organisations and trade unions certified as independent. The report and other material can be seen on the web site at:

www.certoffice.org

1.8 Information Commissioner

The Office of the Information Commissioner (previously known as the Data Protection Commissioner) was established by the Data Protection Act 1998, much of which came into effect on 1 March 2000.[11] The Commissioner oversees and enforces compliance with the Data Protection Act 1998 and the Freedom of Information Act 2000. It does this by, amongst other means,

(1) publishing guidance to assist with compliance;
(2) providing a general enquiry service;
(3) encouraging the development of Codes of Practice;
(4) maintaining the public register of data controllers under the Data Protection Act 1998 and the list of public authorities with approved publication schemes under the Freedom of Information Act 2000;
(5) prosecuting persons in respect of offences under the legislation.

---

[9] Sections 254–255 TULRCA 1992.
[10] Part I TULRCA 1992.
[11] Section 6(1) Data Protection Act 1998.

There is an excellent web site at:

www.informationcommissioner.gov.uk

This site provides legal guidance and compliance advice as well as links to the Data Protection Act 1998, codes of practice and consultation documents, including the code of practice on the use of personal data in employer/employee relationships.

1.9 Commission for Equality and Human Rights (CEHR)

The Commission for Equality and Human Rights was established by section 1 of the Equality Act 2006. In addition to assuming responsibility for the work of the previous anti-discrimination Commissions (i.e. the Equal Opportunities Commission, the Commission for Racial Equality and the Disability Rights Commission), it has the duty to combat unlawful discrimination on the grounds of sexual orientation, religion or belief and age.

Section 8 Equality Act 2006 provides that the CEHR must:

(a) promote understanding of the importance of equality and diversity,
(b) encourage good practice in relation to equality and diversity,
(c) promote equality of opportunity,
(d) promote awareness and understanding of rights under the equality enactments,
(e) enforce the equality enactments,
(f) work towards the elimination of unlawful discrimination, and
(g) work towards the elimination of unlawful harassment.

It must also monitor the effectiveness of equality and human rights legislation and report on progress made every three years.[12] As part of its general powers the CEHR can provide advice and information, produce codes of practice, conduct inquiries, carry out investigations and issue unlawful act notices.[13]

The CEHR web site is located at:

www.equalityhumanrights.com

1.10 Other useful web sites

Some sites are useful because they provide good links to other legal sites, such as:

University of Kent	http://library.ukc.ac.uk/library/lawlinks
Industrial Law Society	www.industriallawsociety.org.uk

Other useful sites include:

British Employment Law	www.emplaw.co.uk
Cabinet Office	www.cabinet-office.gov.uk
Chartered Institute of Personnel and Development	www.cipd.co.uk
Confederation of British Industry	www.cbi.org.uk

---

[12] Sections 11–12 Equality Act 2006.
[13] Sections 13–16, 20–21 Equality Act 2006.

Employers Forum on Age	www.efa.org.uk
European Industrial Relations Observatory	www.eiro.eurofound.ie
European Trade Union Confederation	www.etuc.org
European Trade Union Institute	www.etuc.org/etui
Federation of Small Businesses	www.fsb.org.uk
Health and Safety Executive	www.hse.gov.uk
Incomes Data Services	www.incomesdata.co.uk
International Labour Organisation	www.ilo.org
Labour Research Department	www.lrd.org.uk
Low Pay Commission	www.lowpay.gov.uk
National Statistics	www.statistics.gov.uk
Times Law Reports	www.timesonline.co.uk
Trades Union Congress	www.tuc.org.uk
UK Law Journals Directory	www.elj.warwick.ac.uk/juk/directory.html
UK Official Publications	www.official-documents.co.uk
UNICE (European employers' organisation)	www.unice.org
Unison	www.unison.org.uk

Further reading

Collins, H., Ewing, K. and McColgan, A., *Labour Law: Text and Materials* (Hart Publishing, 2005), Chapter 1.

Deakin, S. and Morris, G., *Labour Law* (4th edn, Hart Publishing, 2005), Chapter 2.

Visit **www.mylawchamber.co.uk/sargeant** to access legal updates, live web links and practice exam questions to test yourself on this chapter.

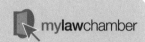

2
European Labour Law

2.1 Historical background

The Treaty of Rome, which established the European Economic Community in 1957, was minimalist in its approach when dealing with social policy. Article 2 of the original treaty outlined the purpose of the Community as essentially an economic one. The only suggestion of a social dimension was contained in the inclusion of a reference to 'an accelerated raising of the standard of living' as one of the objectives. In comparison, Article 2 of the present Treaty includes much more and refers to such objectives as 'a high level of employment and social protection', 'equality between men and women', and 'the raising of the standard of living and the quality of life'.

In addition, Article 3 of the 1957 EEC Treaty established the Social Fund with limited objectives and Article 119 provided for the principle of equal pay between men and women. Article 119 EC (now 141) has subsequently played an important role in the jurisprudence of the ECJ on the issue of equal pay, but, at the time, its motivations were competition ones, as the French Government, it is said, was concerned about competition for its textile industry from low-paid female workers elsewhere.

One of the early major initiatives concerning social policy came at the Heads of Government meeting in Paris in 1972. The meeting declared that the Member States:

> attach as much importance to vigorous action in the social field as to the achievement of economic union.

This encouraging statement resulted in the Social Action Programme of 1974,[1] which defined the social aims of the European Community. These were:

(1) full and better employment at all levels;
(2) the improvement of living and working conditions; and
(3) increased involvement of management and labour in the economic and social decisions of the Community, and of workers in the life of undertakings.

A justification for a European Community role in developing a social dimension to what was essentially a Community which started with economic and political objectives arising out of the devastation created by the Second World War, was stated in *Defrenne v Sabena (No 2)*.[2] This case, one of a series brought under Article 141 EC on equal pay, was about an airline hostess who was forced to retire at the age of 40 years, in contrast to male

---

[1] Bulletin of the European Communities, Supplement 2/74.
[2] Case 43/75 [1976] ECR 455 ECJ.

cabin crew who could work until normal retirement age and thus have entitlement to a full pension. During its judgment the ECJ defined the aim of Article 141 EC as being twofold:

(1) To avoid a situation where one Member State, which had implemented the principle of equal pay, should be at a competitive disadvantage with another Member State that had not.

(2) The provision was part of the social policy of the Community which was intended to ensure social progress and the constant improvement of the living and working conditions of the people.

Thus there were two objectives which were still linked to economic aims, namely the creation of a level playing field between Member States and the improvement of living and working conditions. One of the results of the 1974 Social Action Programme was Directives concerned with the protection of workers in situations of transfers of undertakings,[3] collective redundancies[4] and insolvent employers[5] (see Chapter 10).

The early 1980s seemed to be a period of relative inactivity, although this changed from 1985 onwards with, first, the development of the social dialogue (see below) and, secondly, the drawing up of a declaration of the social principles of the European Community. This was entitled the Charter of the Fundamental Social Rights of Workers, which was adopted by 11 of the 12 Member States at the Strasbourg summit in 1989.[6] The Charter included many of the fundamental beliefs underlying the post-Second World War western European welfare states. It included rights to social protection for workers, children, adolescents, the elderly and the disabled; freedom of association and collective bargaining; consultation and participation at work; access to vocational training; equal treatment for men and women; and an equitable wage for workers sufficient for them to have a decent standard of living. The Commission followed this declaration with an action plan. The United Kingdom refused to sign the Charter because it seemed to give to the Community the right to intervene in matters that the United Kingdom felt ought to be left to national governments. The Secretary of State for Employment at the time stated that:

> . . . the effect of accepting the Charter as it stands would be to concede that the Community had competence to deal with these subjects and that it should take action in any event. That runs entirely contrary to the principle of subsidiarity . . . subjects such as holidays and hours should not be regulated from Brussels.[7]

Initiatives that followed this declaration included Directives on working time,[8] protection for pregnant workers[9] and the protection of young workers at work.[10] Thereafter

---

[3] Council Directive 77/187/EEC, now amended by Directive 98/50/EC and consolidated by Directive 2001/23/EC, on the approximation of the laws of the Member States relating to the safeguarding of employees' rights in the event of transfers of undertakings, businesses or parts of undertakings or businesses OJ L201/88 17.7.98.

[4] Now consolidated into Council Directive 98/59/EC on the approximation of the laws of the Member States relating to collective redundancies OJ L225/21 12.8.98.

[5] Council Directive 80/987/EEC on the approximation of the laws of the Member States relating to the protection of employees in the event of the insolvency of their employer OJ L283/23 28.10.80.

[6] COM (89) 22.11.89.

[7] *Hansard* HC vol 162 col 724.

[8] Council Directive 93/104/EC concerning certain aspects of the organisation of working time OJ L307/18 13.12.93.

[9] Council Directive 92/85/EEC on the introduction of measures to encourage improvements in the safety and health of pregnant workers and workers who have recently given birth or are breastfeeding OJ L348/1 28.11.92.

[10] Council Directive 94/33/EC on the protection of young people at work OJ L216/12 20.8.94.

this Social Agreement was attached to the Treaty of European Union 1992. The United Kingdom remained outside its scope but allowed the Community's institutions to be used for its purposes. Under this process the Community adopted Directives on European Works Councils[11] and parental leave,[12] to which the United Kingdom ultimately agreed to be bound after the general election of 1997.

In 2000 the Community adopted the Charter of Fundamental Rights which was a further and comprehensive statement of the social rights of individuals within the Community, many of which affect the individual at work. It also adopted two major anti-discrimination measures, relying upon Article 13 of the Treaty (see below).

2.2 The influence of European and EU labour law on national law

As is shown throughout this book, much of the employment law in the United Kingdom is underpinned by the policies of the institutions of the European Community. The major and relevant sources of EU labour law considered here are:

- the EU Treaty;
- Community legislation;
- the Social Dialogue;
- the European Court of Justice (ECJ);
- the European Employment Strategy and the Lisbon Agreement.

2.2.1 The Social Policy Agenda

In June 2000 the European Commission issued a Communication on the subject of the Social Policy Agenda.[13] One of the main justifications had been that social policy has enabled the Community to make acceptable the structural change in the economies of the Member States. Ever since the Social Action Programme of 1974 the Community has been concerned that the development of the single market would, by a process of Europeanisation of the economies of Member States, lead to adverse consequences for workers. There would be growing numbers of workers who would be affected by the changes and this was a rationale for introducing social protection. The development of the single market itself would also require a process of harmonisation in those areas of social policy that influenced the competitiveness of different economies.

In the future, according to the Communication:

> modernising the European social model and investing in people will be crucial to retain the European social values of solidarity and justice while improving economic performance.

---

[11] Council Directive 94/45/EC on the establishment of a European Works Council or a procedure in Community-scale undertakings and Community-scale groups of undertakings for the purposes of informing and consulting employees OJ L254/64 30.9.94.

[12] Council Directive 96/34/EC on the Framework Agreement on parental leave OJ L145/4 19.6.96.

[13] COM (2000) 379 28.6.2000.

A key feature of this process is the combining of good social conditions with high productivity and high quality goods and services. The result of this, importantly, is that:

> This new Social Policy Agenda does not seek to harmonise social policies. It seeks to work towards common European objectives and increase co-ordination of social policies in the context of the internal market and the single currency.

Thus co-ordination is set to become as important as the harmonisation of social policy. Such open policy co-ordination involves establishing policy guidelines, setting benchmarks and concrete targets and a monitoring system to evaluate progress. This is the means by which the European Employment Strategy has been developed. This does not mean that there will not be any legislation. The Communication states that standards should be developed or adapted to ensure respect for fundamental social rights. These standards can be achieved through legislation or through agreement between the social partners.

In 2005 the Commission issued a further Communication on the Social Agenda. It stated that its motto for the period up to 2010 was to be:

> A Social Europe in the global economy: jobs and opportunities for all.

The task now was to improve the implementation of measures based on certain principles which were to:

– pursue an integrated European approach guaranteeing positive interplay between economic, social and employment policies;
– promote quality – of employment, social policy and industrial relations – which, in return, should make it possible to improve human and social capital;
– modernise systems of social protection by adapting them to the current requirements of our societies, on the basis of solidarity and by strengthening their role as a productive factor;
– take account of the 'cost of the lack of social policy'.

The Social Agenda adopted a two-pronged approach. First, it is concerned with strengthening citizens' confidence. This confidence is seen to be essential for managing the change process and encouraging economic growth. Secondly, measures are to be presented under two major headings, which are employment and equal opportunities and inclusion.

2.3 The consolidated Treaty

A summary of those parts of the EC Treaty that are relevant to the study of employment law follows.

2.3.1 Articles 2 and 3 basic principles

Article 2 lists the purposes of the Community. Amongst this list are a number of social objectives. These are:

(1) to promote a high level of employment and social protection;
(2) equality between men and women;

(3) protection and improvement of the environment;
(4) the raising of the standard of living and quality of life;
(5) the economic and social cohesion and solidarity amongst Member States.

These high ideals are partly to be achieved by the activities defined in Article 3. These activities include measures concerning the entry and movement of persons as provided for in Title IV,[14] the promotion of co-ordination between employment policies of the Member States, the European Social Fund, the strengthening of economic and social cohesion, and a high level of health protection. In all these activities the Community will aim to eliminate inequalities and promote equality between men and women.[15]

2.3.2 Article 13 anti-discrimination

Article 13 is a wide-ranging Article which allows the Council of Ministers, acting unanimously, on a proposal from the Commission, to take action to combat discrimination based on sex, racial or ethnic origin, religion or belief, disability, age or sexual orientation. One of the important omissions prior to the Treaty of Amsterdam 1998 was the Community's inability to take action in the field of race discrimination[16] in the way that it has, to its credit, tackled sex discrimination issues. Since the new Treaty of Amsterdam took effect the Council has adopted a Directive on equal treatment irrespective of racial or ethnic origin[17] as well as adopting a Directive on establishing a general framework for equal treatment in employment and occupation (see Chapters 6 and 7).[18]

2.3.3 Articles 39–42 freedom of movement

Article 39 is concerned with securing the freedom of movement of workers within the Community. It provides for the abolition of discrimination in employment based upon nationality. Subject to limitations resulting from 'public policy, public security or public health', Community workers have the right to:

(1) accept offers of employment;
(2) move freely within the territory of Member States for this purpose;
(3) stay in a Member State for the purposes of employment and to remain in the State after having worked there, although Article 39(4) excludes the public sector from these provisions.

Article 40 allows the Council to adopt measures, acting on a qualified majority vote, to bring about this freedom of movement. Article 42 provides the Council with the same powers to adopt measures in relation to migrant workers and their dependants[19] with regard to social security, but in this case the Council must act unanimously.

---

[14] Title IV concerns visas, asylum, immigration and other policies related to the free movement of persons.
[15] Article 3(2) EC.
[16] Although Article 6 of the old EC Treaty had permitted action on discrimination on the grounds of nationality.
[17] Council Directive 2000/43/EC on the implementation of the principle of equal treatment between persons irrespective of racial or ethnic origin OJ L180/22 17.7.2000.
[18] Council Directive 2000/78/EC, OJ L303/16 2.12.2000.
[19] See also Regulation 1612/68/EEC on freedom of movement for workers within the Community OJ L257/2 19.12.68.

The freedom of movement of labour is one of the fundamental principles of the European Community and can have far-reaching and, sometimes, unexpected effects: for example, *Union Royal Belge des Sociétés de Football Association ASBL v Bosman*[20] concerned a footballer who brought a complaint against both his own club and the national football association that the transfer regulations between football clubs inhibited the freedom of movement of workers. The ECJ agreed and, as a result, transfer fees for footballers at the end of their contracts were abolished throughout the EU.

2.3.4 Articles 125–130 employment

Article 125 provides that the Member States and the Community shall work towards developing a co-ordinated strategy for employment and particularly work 'for promoting a skilled, trained and adaptable workforce and labour markets responsive to economic change'.

These Articles are concerned with the responsibilities of the Member States and the Community towards achieving these goals. The Council of Ministers has the responsibility, acting on a qualified voting majority, to draw up guidelines each year for the Member States to 'take into account in their employment policies'.[21] The role of the Community is a co-ordinating and encouraging one, but 'the competences of the Member States shall be respected'.[22]

2.3.5 Articles 136–145 social provisions

Article 136 provides the objectives. Taking into account the European Social Charter 1961, and the Charter of Fundamental Social Rights of Workers 1989, the objectives of the Community and the Member States are:

> the promotion of employment, improved living and working conditions, so as to make possible their harmonisation while the improvement is being maintained, proper social protection, dialogue between management and labour, the development of human resources with a view to lasting high employment and the combating of exclusion.

Article 137 deals with those measures that are within the competence of the EU to take action whether by a qualified majority vote or a unanimous vote in the Council of Ministers, and those measures which are not within its competence. First, Article 137(1) recognises that there are matters which are within the shared competence of the EU and the Member States. The Community is permitted, therefore, to take actions 'which support and complement the activities of the Member States in certain fields'. These fields include:

(1) the improvement of the working environment to protect workers' health and safety;
(2) working conditions;
(3) social security and protection of workers;
(4) protection of workers where their employment contract is terminated;
(5) information and consultation of workers;

---

[20] Case I-415/93 [1995] ECR-I 4921 ECJ.
[21] Article 128(2) EC.
[22] Article 127(1) EC.

(6) representation and collective defence of the interests of workers and employers;
(7) integration of people excluded from the labour market;
(8) equality between men and women with regard to labour market opportunities and treatment at work;
(9) the combating of social exclusion.

The scope of these areas is very large. The subjects covered include health and safety, collective consultation, social exclusion and equality of opportunity and treatment between men and women. Measures adopted concerning these provisions require only a qualified majority vote in the Council of Ministers, after due consultation with the European Parliament. This will be especially significant in those areas of controversy, especially with regard to the extension of consultation rights for workers.

There are a number of these subject areas, however, where the Council can only adopt measures with the unanimous agreement of the Council of Ministers. These are listed in Article 137(1). The issues include:

(1) social security and social protection of workers;
(2) protection of workers where their employment is terminated;
(3) representation and collective defence of the interests of workers and employers.

These measures, requiring unanimity, perhaps represent the greater sensitivities of Member States to decisions concerning them.

Lastly, there are a number of issues, contained in Article 137(5), from which the EU is excluded. These are the issues that Member States have reserved for their exclusive competence and are concerned with:

(1) pay;
(2) the right of association;
(3) the right to strike;
(4) the right to impose lock-outs.

Thus issues directly concerned with trade union membership and the taking of industrial action by workers or employers are reserved for the Member State.

Articles 138 and 139 are concerned with promoting the consultation of management and labour at Community level (see below for a discussion of the Social Dialogue).

Notwithstanding these provisions, but without prejudice to them, Article 140 provides the Commission with a duty to encourage co-operation and facilitate their co-ordination in the social field, but especially with respect to matters relating to employment, labour law and working conditions, vocational training, social security, occupational accidents, diseases and hygiene, and with the right of association and collective bargaining between employers and workers. The Commission is therefore encouraged to carry out studies, deliver opinions and arrange consultations on these matters.

Article 141[23] provides that each Member State shall ensure that the principle of equal pay for male and female workers for equal work or work of equal value is applied.[24]

---

[23] See Chapter 6 on sex and race discrimination.
[24] Article 142 deals with paid holiday schemes; Article 144 provides that the Commission may be given the task of implementing certain common measures on social security, with regard to migrant workers; Articles 143 and 145 concern reports to be written and published.

The principle of equality between the sexes has been described, by the ECJ,[25] as one of the fundamental principles of Community law. Article 141(3) allows the Council, acting on a qualified majority vote, to adopt measures to ensure the application of the principles of equal opportunities and equal treatment of men and women in employment. These principles shall not, however,

> prevent any Member State from maintaining or adopting measures providing for specific advantages in order to make it easier for the underrepresented sex to pursue a vocational activity or to prevent or compensate for disadvantages in professional careers.[26]

2.4 European Community legislation

2.4.1 Meaning of the term 'worker'

There are wide differences between Member States of the EU in the proportion of the workforce that is treated as self-employed. Self-employment ranges from 8.4% in Denmark and 9.4% in Germany to 24.5% in Italy, 25.8% in Portugal and 33.8% in Greece.[27] It is unlikely that these differences can just be explained by differences in the way that different economies are structured. A partial explanation is the way that EU Directives are written and the approach of the ECJ. The result is that Directives aimed at employment protection will have different levels of coverage in different Member States, depending upon whom they treat as employees for the purposes of Community legislation.

The lack of uniformity of application is compounded by the English-language versions of the various Directives, which appear to sometimes use the term 'worker' and sometimes to use the term 'employee'. The Collective Redundancies Directive,[28] the Health and Safety Directive[29] and the Working Time Directive[30] all refer to the term workers; whilst the Acquired Rights Directive,[31] the Insolvency Directive[32] and the European Works Council Directive[33] all refer to employees. In contrast the French language versions of all these Directives use only the term *travailleur*, except in the case of the Insolvency Directive where the more specific term of *travailleur salarié* is used. The term *travailleur* has perhaps a more general meaning than the term employee and can apply to an employment relationship not having a contract of employment.

Despite these differences of approach, the ECJ has decided that the meaning of employee and worker should be left to the Member States, except where there is a Community use of the term. Thus, in *Hoekstra*,[34] there was a consideration of various terms, including

---

[25] See Case 13/94 *P v S and Cornwall County Council* [1996] IRLR 347 ECJ.
[26] Article 141(4) EC; although in Case 407/98 *Abrahamsson and Anderson v Fogelqvist* [2000] IRLR 732, the ECJ limited the potential effect of this Article (see Chapter 6).
[27] Figures from Directorate General for Employment, Industrial Relations and Social Affairs, *Employment in Europe 1996*, COM (96) 485.
[28] Note 4 above.
[29] Directive 89/391/EEC on the introduction of measures to encourage improvements in the safety and health of workers at work OJ L183/1 29.6.89.
[30] Note 8 above.
[31] Note 3 above.
[32] Note 5 above.
[33] Note 11 above.
[34] Case 75/63 *Hoekstra (née Unger) v Bestuur der Bedrijfsvereniging voor Detailhanden en Ambachten* [1964] ECR 177 ECJ.

'assimilated worker' and 'wage earner', which arose out of a social security regulation. The ECJ concluded that if the definition of worker were a matter of competence for national law, it might be possible for each Member State to modify the concept of 'migrant worker' and eliminate some of the protection offered to such individuals.[35] The ECJ also stated that 'it follows from the Treaty . . . that the protected worker is not exclusively one who is currently employed'. Thus the term 'worker' not only has a Community meaning but one that is wider than the term 'employee'.

Levin[36] was concerned with a British national with a non-EEC husband applying for residence in the Netherlands. The Dutch Government argued that workers needed to perform work in the fullest sense of the word to contribute to the economic development of the Community. The ECJ stated that:

> The terms 'worker' and 'activity as an employed person' may not be defined by reference to the national laws of the Member States but have a Community meaning. If that were not to be the case, the Community rules on freedom of movement for workers would be frustrated, as the meaning of those terms could be fixed and modified unilaterally, without any control by the Community institutions, by national laws which would thus be able to exclude at will certain categories of persons from the benefit of the Treaty.

Later the Court defined the employment relationship as:

> for a certain period of time a person performs services for and under the direction of another person in return for which he receives remuneration.[37]

In *Sylvie Lair*[38] the ECJ held that 'migrant workers are guaranteed certain rights linked to the status of worker even when they are no longer in an employment relationship' and, in *Raulin*,[39] it held that 'the nature of the legal relationship between the employee and the employer is of no consequence as regards the status of the worker'.

This very broad definition of worker in situations affecting Community law is in contrast to the ECJ's approach when considering other employment protection measures. When considering measures which might not have this Community impact, the Court has concluded that only partial harmonisation of the laws of Member States is required, i.e. that existing employment protection rights should be extended to include the new protection. This means that only those currently protected, as employees for example, would receive the benefit of the extra protection. The case for the adoption of a Community definition for the term 'employee' was argued by the European Commission in *Mikkelson*,[40] which concerned the application of the Acquired Rights Directive.[41] The ECJ, however, decided that the Community had not intended to establish a uniform level of protection throughout the Community on the basis of some common criteria. The

---

[35] Article 39 EC provides for the principle of freedom of movement within the Community for workers; the ECJ reasoned that if each State could define the meaning of worker, for the purposes of this principle, then each State would be able to inhibit the freedom of movement, hence the need for a Community definition.

[36] Case 53/81 *DM Levin v Staatssecretaris van Justitie* [1982] ECR 1035 ECJ.

[37] Case 66/85 *Deborah Lawrie-Blum v Land Baden-Württemberg* [1986] ECR 2121 ECJ.

[38] Case 39/86 *Sylvie Lair v Universitat Hannover* [1988] ECR 3161 ECJ.

[39] Case 357/89 *VJM Raulin v Minister van Onderwijs en Wetenschappen* [1992] ECR 1027 ECJ.

[40] Case 105/84 *Foreningen af Arbejdsledere i Danmark v Danmols Inventar, in liquidation* [1985] ECR 2639 ECJ.

[41] Note 3 above.

Directive was to be interpreted as only aimed at partial harmonisation by extending the existing protection guaranteed to workers by the laws of the Member States. In *Rask*,[42] the ECJ repeated its conclusion:

> It [the Directive] is not intended to establish a uniform level of protection throughout the Community on the basis of common criteria. Thus the Directive can only be relied upon to ensure that the employee concerned is protected . . . under the legal rules of the Member State concerned.

This approach has been developed in the national courts so that a wider definition of worker may apply to the implementation of other areas of Community law. In *Perceval-Price v Department of Economic Development*[43] the Northern Ireland Court of Appeal held that certain office holders were entitled to be regarded as workers for the purposes of Article 141 EC on equal pay. The Court of Appeal stated:

> The object of Community legislation, protection against inequality of treatment or discrimination, seems to us to require the inclusion within the definition of all persons who are engaged in a relationship which is broadly that of employment rather than being called self-employed or independent contractors.

2.4.2 Scope of Community legislation and subsidiarity

It is important to appreciate the influence of the EU on modern day employment law in the United Kingdom. Community law, mostly in the form of Directives,[44] underpins much legislation on this issue.[45] Examples of the diversity of this European intervention are Directives on:

- Safeguarding employees' rights in transfers of undertakings.[46]
- Rights to consultation in collective redundancies.[47]
- Protection of employees in the event of their employer's insolvency.[48]
- Employer's obligation to inform employees of conditions applicable to the contract of employment.[49]
- Organisation of working time.[50]
- Protection of young people at work.[51]
- Establishment of European Works Councils.[52]
- Protection of pregnant employees and those who have recently given birth.[53]

---

[42] Case 209/81 *Rask and Christensen v ISS Kantineservice A/S* [1993] IRLR 133 ECJ.
[43] [2000] IRLR 380 CA.
[44] Although not exclusively Directives, e.g. see Regulation 1612/68 referred to above; it does, however, appear to be the current main channel of such legislation.
[45] Article 241 EC provides for the different types of action that the institutions may take part in.
[46] Note 3 above.
[47] Note 4 above.
[48] Note 5 above.
[49] Council Directive 91/533/EEC.
[50] Note 8 above.
[51] Note 10 above.
[52] Note 11 above.
[53] Note 9 above.

- Parental leave.[54]
- Rights of part-time workers.[55]
- Measures on equal treatment and equal pay.[56]
- Protection of workers on fixed-term contracts.[57]

This is, of course, not a comprehensive list, but is illustrative of the variety of subject matter covered. In addition, from time to time, the Council of Ministers and the European Commission also issue guidance in the form of Recommendations for good practice. Two examples of this are Council Recommendation 86/397/EEC on the employment of disabled people in the Community[58] and Commission Recommendation 92/131/EEC on the protection of the dignity of women and men at work.[59]

The role of the Community has at times been controversial, especially with regard to the United Kingdom. One of the major issues for the United Kingdom has been the question of who has competence in the field of employment law. There is a potential conflict between the requirements of the Community to harmonise legislation in this area, in order to aid the development of the single market, and the demands of the national State to regulate its own labour market. This argument about subsidiarity, or the correct level for legislation to be enacted, was a feature of the relations between the United Kingdom and the European Community during the Conservative Governments of 1979 to 1997. The conflict was illustrated in *United Kingdom v Council of Ministries of the European Union*.[60] This case concerned a challenge by the United Kingdom against the implementation of the Working Time Directive.[61] This Directive was adopted by the Council of the EC in November 1993. It was adopted as a health and safety measure under, then, Article 118a of the EC Treaty (now 137). This meant that only a qualified majority vote was required for its adoption. The United Kingdom argued that it should have been adopted under, then, Article 100 or 235 (now 94 or 308), which required a unanimous vote in the Council of Ministers, thus enabling the United Kingdom to block its adoption.

Part of the argument concerned the issue of subsidiarity. The United Kingdom argued that there was no justification for a wide-ranging Directive aimed at harmonising the practices of Member States, which varied considerably. It argued that:

> the Community legislature neither fully considered nor adequately demonstrated that there were transnational aspects which could not be satisfactorily regulated by action by Member States, that action by Member States alone or lack of Community action would conflict with the requirements of the EC Treaty . . . or that action at Community level would provide clear benefits compared with action at Member State level.

This argument was not accepted by the ECJ, which pointed out, in its judgment, that the harmonisation of national legislation to improve the level of health and safety of workers

---

[54] Note 12 above.
[55] Council Directive 97/81/EC concerning the Framework Agreement on part-time work concluded by UNICE, CEEP and ETUC OJ L14/9 20.1.98.
[56] Council Directives 75/117/EEC on equal pay and 76/207/EEC on equal treatment.
[57] Council Directive 99/70/EC concerning the Framework Agreement on fixed-term work OJ L175/43 10.7.99.
[58] OJ L225/43 12.8.86; see Chapter 6 and 7.
[59] OJ L49/1 24.2.92; see Chapter 6.
[60] Case 84/94 [1997] IRLR 30 ECJ.
[61] Note 8 above.

was a requirement of Article 118a (now 137). Such harmonisation necessarily presupposed Community-wide action.

Article 5 EC now provides for the principle of subsidiarity:

> In areas which do not fall within its exclusive competence, the Community shall take action, in accordance with the principle of subsidiarity, only if and insofar as the objectives of the proposed action cannot be sufficiently achieved by the Member States and can, therefore, by reason of the scale or effects of the proposed action, be better achieved by the Community.

The issue of where the competence for action lies, with the Community or with the Member State, is an ongoing feature of United Kingdom and EU relations. It can be illustrated by the Community's involvement with ensuring the consultation of workers in certain situations. There seemed no dispute about its competence in adopting measures concerned with transnational consultation,[62] but there were more doubts about its proposals to ensure consultation and information within the Member States.[63] Employment policy is one where there is a shared competence between the Community and the Member State. It is not clear where the dividing line is.

2.5 The Social Dialogue

The Social Dialogue at Community level is a method of involving the representatives of employers and trade unions in the process of decision making on matters connected with social and employment policy. It began when the then President of the European Commission, Mr Jacques Delors, invited the chairs and secretaries of all the national organisations affiliated to the European private employers organisation UNICE,[64] the European public employers organisation CEEP[65] and the trade union organisation ETUC[66] to a meeting at Val Duchesse on 31 January 1985. These organisations, also known as the social partners, began a process of dialogue, setting up working parties and reaching their first 'joint opinion' on 6 November 1986.

This process was given formal recognition in the Single European Act, introduced in 1987. Article 118b stated:

> The Commission shall endeavour to develop the dialogue between management and labour at European level which could, if the two sides considered it desirable, lead to relations based on agreement.

This process was taken a further step forward at the Palais d'Egmont on 12 January 1989, when a steering group, consisting of the social partners and the Commission, was set up. One of their subsequent actions was to establish an ad hoc committee to consider their role. The outcome of these deliberations formed part of the Protocol on Social Policy attached to the Treaty of European Union.

These measures are now contained in Article 138. The Commission is given the task of promoting the consultation of management and labour at Community level. To this end

---

[62] Council Directive 94/45/EC, note 11 above.
[63] OJ L80/29 23.3.2002.
[64] Union of Industrial Employers' Confederations of Europe.
[65] European Centre of Enterprises with Public Participation.
[66] European Trade Union Confederation.

the Commission must, before submitting proposals in the social policy field, consult the social partners. This may involve these partners submitting joint recommendations or opinions of their own. If they wish the social partners may inform the Commission that they desire to initiate a period of consultation as contained in Article 139 EC. If this happens the effect is to stop the Commission going forward until the social partners, now in the form of a social dialogue committee, have tried to come to an agreement on the issue concerned. They have nine months in which to do this, unless all the parties and the Commission agree to extend the period.[67] If they fail to reach agreement the Commission is free to press ahead with its own proposals. If they succeed, they may present their proposals to the Commission for the purposes of adoption by the Council of Ministers.

An interesting question raised by this whole process is to what extent the social partners, UNICE, CEEP and the ETUC, are representative of management and labour in the EU and whether the now institutionalised consultation that takes place with them should really take place with more democratic and accountable bodies such as the European Parliament. In 1993 the Commission put forward three criteria for deciding on the representativeness of the social partners at European level.[68] These were that the social partners should:

(1) be cross-industry or relate to specific sectors or categories and be organised at European level;
(2) consist of organisations which are themselves an integral and recognised part of the Member States' social partner structures;
(3) have adequate structures to ensure their effective participation in the consultation process.[69]

There remains the associated question of whether other organisations should be involved in this formal process. When, for example, the social partners were negotiating on issues related to parental leave, should not other interest groups such as parents' organisations be involved in the formal body that negotiates legislative measures, rather than just be consulted by the Commission? This was the issue in *UEAPME*[70] *v Council of Ministers.*[71] This organisation represented the interests of small and medium-sized undertakings at European Community level. The application was a request for an annulment of the Parental Leave Directive,[72] or, alternatively, an annulment of the Directive's application to small and medium-sized enterprises. This Directive had resulted from a framework agreement made between the three social partner organisations, UNICE, CEEP and ETUC. Although UEAPME had been consulted by the Commission it claimed that it ought also to have been part of the negotiation process. The claim was rejected by the Court of First Instance on the grounds that it was not for the Commission to decide on who takes part in the negotiations between management and labour. This was an issue for those taking part.

---

[67] Article 138.4 EC.
[68] See Commission Communication on adapting and promoting the Social Dialogue at Community level COM (98) 322.
[69] This is still the approach of the Commission; see Directorate General for Employment and Social Affairs, *Industrial Relations in Europe* (2000).
[70] Union Européene de l'Artisant et des Petites et Moyennes Entreprises.
[71] Case 135/96 [1998] IRLR 602 CFI.
[72] Note 12 above.

The Court held, however, that the Commission does have a responsibility to verify whether those parties taking part are sufficiently representative, bearing in mind the content of the agreement in question. This, according to the Court, was an issue of democracy. There needed to be care with this as the process bypassed the European Parliament altogether. The claim was still lost, because the Court decided that UNICE also represented small and medium-sized enterprises.

There are also a wide range of other bodies, with representatives of management and labour, who are consulted on social policy issues. A detailed examination is not included here, but they include the Economic and Social Committee, which is a consultative assembly of the European Communities and consists of 222 members who represent employers, workers and other interest groups. In addition to the central social dialogue process there are a number of sectoral committees covering a wide range of sectors, such as agriculture and transport. There are also cross-industry advisory committees and an Employment Committee.

This process has resulted in framework agreements on parental leave, part-time work and fixed-term contracts. These have resulted in Directives being adopted on these subjects. The Directives consist of a preamble followed by three or four articles followed by the framework agreement reached by the social partners. The purpose of the Directives is to turn the social partners' framework agreements into Community law.[73] This may be a process and a concept that is difficult for observers from the United Kingdom, where there is little institutionalised consultation with the social partners, to appreciate. The process has also had its failures with a lack of agreement on issues such as the organisation of working time and proposals for mandatory consultation within Member States.

2.6 European Court of Justice

The purpose of the ECJ is to ensure that, in the interpretation and application of the EC Treaty, the law is observed.[74] It must ensure that Community law is not interpreted differently or applied differently in each Member State. Community law is an independent legal order[75] which takes precedence over that of the Member State.[76] The effect of these decisions has been as profound on employment law issues as other matters. Apart from the judgments which interpret the Treaty, employment law in the United Kingdom has been affected by the ECJ through a variety of means. These include the Commission taking action against Member States for a failure to transpose Community legislation adequately into national law, national courts referring matters to the ECJ for an interpretation of Community law, and by the establishment and use of the principle of direct effect.

Since 1952, when it was first created, more than 15,000 cases have been brought before the ECJ and, in order to help with the increasing workload, the Court of First Instance was created in 1989. The ECJ consists of 27 judges and eight advocates general, all of whom

---

[73] See, e.g., Council Directive 97/81/EC concerning the Framework Agreement on part-time work, note 55 above.
[74] Article 220 EC.
[75] See Case 26/62 *NV Algemene Transporten Expeditie Onderneming van Gend en Loos v Nederlandse Administratie der Belastingen* [1963] ECR 1 ECJ.
[76] See Case 6/64 *Flaminio Costa v ENEL* [1964] ECR 585 ECJ.

hold office for a renewable term of six years. In 2006, the Court completed 546 cases[77] and received a further 537 cases.[78]

2.6.1 Failure to fulfil Treaty obligations[79]

On the whole Member States are quite good in fulfilling their obligations to transpose Directives into national law. As at 2003, the EU average was 96.58% of Directives being transposed. The best performers were Denmark with 97.87%, Spain with 97.54% and Sweden with 97.29%. The United Kingdom was the worst performer with 95.76%, accompanied by Austria on 95.77% and Italy on 95.87%.[80]

An example of such an action in the employment law field, two cases entitled *Commission v United Kingdom*[81] concerned the implementation of the Collective Redundancies Directive and the Acquired Rights Directive.[82] The Commission argued that there had been a failure to correctly transpose these Directives in a number of ways, one of which was the requirements for consultation. At the time the UK legislation only required consultation with representatives of independent and recognised trade unions. Trade union recognition was itself entirely voluntary. The result of this was that consultation only needed to take place when a trade union was recognised and such recognition was at the discretion of the employer. The Commission argued that the United Kingdom had failed in its responsibilities by not providing for representation of employees in situations where the employer refused to recognise representatives. The ECJ rejected all of the United Kingdom's arguments and held that United Kingdom law frustrated the protection for employees provided by the Directives. As a result regulations were introduced to allow for the consultation with employee representatives in situations where there were no trade unions.[83]

2.6.2 References to the ECJ

Under Article 234 EC the ECJ is able to give preliminary rulings on the interpretation of the Treaty and the validity and interpretation of the acts of the institutions of the Community. These references will come from the courts and tribunals in each Member State, when needing an interpretation of Community law in order to help reach a judgment in a particular case. In 2000 there were a total of 215 such referrals from the United Kingdom.

---

[77] Joined cases are treated as one.

[78] This includes two Article 227 references from other Member States.

[79] The United Kingdom did not, of course, join the Community until 1972, although Greece did not join until 1985.

[80] All of these figures can be found on the ECJ web site, www.europa.eu.int. All these figures are to be treated with caution, however, as they are only a snapshot at a particular time.

[81] Cases 382/92 and 383/92 [1994] IRLR 392 ECJ and [1994] IRLR 412 ECJ.

[82] Council Directive 75/129/EEC and Council Directive 2001/23/EC: see Chapter 10.

[83] Collective Redundancies Transfer of Undertakings (Protection of Employment) (Amendment) Regulations 1995, SI 1995/2587; subsequently amended again in 1999 by SI 1999/1925.

Here are three examples of the usage of this Article 234, illustrating the variety of topics and the variety of courts that may make references:

(1) *Attridge Law v Coleman*[84] was a reference from an Employment Tribunal to the ECJ relating to an interpretation of the Disability Discrimination Act 1995. The complainant in the case was not herself disabled but needed a lot of time off work to care for her disabled son. She argued that the Framework Directive on Equal Treatment in Employment and Occupation[85] provided protection 'on the grounds of disability' and thus meant that the DDA 1995 should be interpreted as applying to cover discrimination against those who are associated with a disabled person. The matter was referred to the Court of Justice to discover the Court's view on whether the Directive applied to only disabled people or whether others were also covered by it.

(2) *R v Secretary of State for Trade and Industry, ex parte TUC*[86] was a reference from the High Court to the ECJ, resulting from a challenge to the Government by the Trades Union Congress. Regulation 13(3) of the Maternity and Parental Leave etc. Regulations 1999, SI 1999/3312 provides that 'An employee is not entitled to parental leave in respect of a child born before 15 December 1999.' The exception to this was a child placed with the employee for adoption purposes on or after that date. The TUC brought judicial review proceedings claiming that the exclusion of the right in respect of children, under the age of five years, born before 15 December 1999 was not a correct interpretation of the Parental Leave Directive. This regulation excluded some 2.7 million parents who might otherwise have qualified for parental leave. The Government estimated that to change the rule would cost employers an additional £58 million. The High Court refused to grant an interim injunction to protect these parents, but did refer the question to the ECJ for a decision.

(3) *Lawrence v Regent Office Care Ltd*[87] concerned school catering and cleaning staff whose work was contracted out by North Yorkshire County Council. Prior to the contracting out they had won an equal value claim when compared in a job evaluation exercise to certain other council employees. After the outsourcing exercise the employees were asked to work on lower rates than those rates paid by the County Council to their employees. The employees argued that Article 141 EC could be relied upon by them to establish pay parity with local government employees with whom they had previously been compared. The Court of Appeal referred the matter to the ECJ and asked the Court to decide whether employees who were now employed by private contractors could rely on Article 141 to compare themselves with current employees of the Council.

2.7 Direct effect

Direct effect provides individuals, under certain circumstances, with the ability to rely on directly and enforce Community law in the national courts.[88] It aids the individual who

---

[84] [2007] IRLR 88.
[85] Directive 2000/78/EC.
[86] [2000] IRLR 565.
[87] [2000] IRLR 608 CA.
[88] See Case 26/62 *Van Gend en Loos* [1963] ECR 1 ECJ and Case 6/64 *Costa v ENEL* [1964] ECR 585 ECJ.

wishes to exercise a right under Community law which the State has failed to transpose, or has inadequately transposed, into national law. The extension of the doctrine of direct effect to include Directives, rather than just Articles of the Treaty and Regulations,[89] was of importance as most employment legislation comes from the Community in the form of Directives.[90] In *Pubblico Ministero v Ratti*[91] the ECJ held that:

> It follows that a national court requested by a person who has complied with the provisions of a directive not to apply a national provision incompatible with the directive not incorporated into the internal legal order of a defaulting Member State, must uphold that request if the obligation in question is unconditional and sufficiently precise.

Apart from the restrictions contained in this statement the ECJ has held that Directives have vertical effect and not horizontal effect. The action, relying upon Community law, could be taken against the State, but not against an individual.[92] The definition of the State was stretched in *Foster v British Gas*[93] to include those carrying out a service on behalf of the State pursuant to a statutory power. This meant that ex-nationalised utilities such as British Gas plc, at the time, were emanations of the State and could have actions taken against them to enforce Community law.

Kampelmann[94] concerned, amongst other matters, the late implementation by the German Government of Directive 91/533/EEC on proof of the employment relationship.[95] The ECJ held that the provisions of the Directive were sufficiently precise and unconditional, even though the State had a choice about what information should be required of an employer. Despite there being this choice, it was possible to ascertain the minimum content of the information to be supplied to an employee. The Court then explained that the scope of vertical direct effect had been widened beyond merely the State to include decentralised bodies and 'organisations or bodies . . . subject to the control or authority of the state'.[96] This also included regional authorities, municipal utilities and bodies under their control.

This results in a discrepancy between the rights of employees of 'public' enterprises or the State and employees of private undertakings. The former can rely upon their ability to take action against their employer for failure to implement a piece of Community legislation, whilst the employee of the private undertaking may not be able to. They can rely, however, on the principle of 'indirect effect', which means that the courts have an obligation to interpret national law so that it complies with Community law.[97]

Gibson v East Riding of Yorkshire Council[98] concerned the failure of the United Kingdom Government to transpose the Working Time Directive into national law in sufficient time. The Directive was adopted in 1993 and Member States were given three years in which to

---

[89] See Article 249 EC.
[90] See Case 41/74 *Van Duyn v Home Office* [1974] ECR 1337 ECJ.
[91] Case 148/78 [1979] ECR 1629 ECJ.
[92] Case 152/84 *Marshall v Southampton and South West Hampshire Area Health Authority* [1986] ECR 723 ECJ.
[93] Case 188/89 [1990] IRLR 353 ECJ.
[94] Case 253/96 *Kampelmann v Landschaftsverband Westfalen-Lippe* [1998] IRLR 334 ECJ.
[95] Note 49 above.
[96] See *Marshall*, note 92 above.
[97] Case 14/83 *Von Colson and Kamann v Land Nordrhein-Westfalen* [1984] ECR 1891 ECJ.
[98] [2000] IRLR 598 CA.

implement it. The United Kingdom Government introduced the Working Time Regulations[99] to take effect from 1 October 1998, some two years late. Ms Gibson, who did not receive paid holidays, claimed that the provisions of the Directive in relation to holidays had direct effect and that her employer was an emanation of the State. As a result she claimed to be able to rely upon the Directive, even though it was not part of British law. The employment tribunal rejected this claim, but the EAT[100] held that the provisions of the Directive did have direct effect against an emanation of the State. Morrison J summarised the principles of law which govern the enforcement of Community law in the United Kingdom:

(1) A provision of the Treaty or of a Directive may only have direct effect if it is sufficiently precise and unconditional.[101]
(2) A Directive remains sufficiently precise even if its precise scope would require the ECJ to interpret its provisions.
(3) In the employment field, the test of conditionality is met if the provisions of the Directive identify:
  (a) the beneficiaries of the right;
  (b) the person under a duty to give effect to the right; and
  (c) the nature and extent, or content, of the right.[102]
(4) The fact that the Directive permits precise derogations from its terms by Member States does not of itself render the Directive conditional. A provision is unconditional if there is no need for further action by Community institutions or by Member States in order to define its contents.
(5) The courts are under a duty to ensure the fulfilment of obligations arising under a Directive. Although Directives have direct effect, this is only with regard to employees of an emanation of the State.
(6) Where the United Kingdom has introduced legislation to give effect to a Directive, then the courts will take a purposive approach to avoid a conflict between the statute and the Directive, even to the extent of adding words to make the two compatible.[103] This will have the result of giving the Directive horizontal direct effect.

Although the EAT held that the provisions of the Directive relating to holidays were sufficiently clear and unambiguous, the Court of Appeal disagreed. The court held that there were a number of ambiguities in the provisions which did not make them sufficiently precise and unconditional. These included:

the absence of a precise definition of 'working time' upon which the entitlement to leave depends, the absence of criteria to assess entitlement during the first year, or part year, of employment, or where there is more than one employer, or part-time work or work on a commission basis.[104]

As a result the Court of Appeal concluded that this aspect of the Directive did not have direct effect.

[99] SI 1998/1833.
[100] [1999] IRLR 358.
[101] Morrison J gave a number of examples of provisions which have or have not been held to be sufficiently precise and unconditional.
[102] See Case 6/90 *Francovich v Italy* [1992] IRLR 84 ECJ.
[103] As in *Litster v Forth Dry Dock and Engineering Ltd* [1989] IRLR 161 HL.
[104] *Gibson v East Riding of Yorkshire Council* [2000] IRLR 598 CA.

2.8 The Lisbon Agreement and the European Employment Stategy

In March 2000 the EU Council of Ministers agreed at the Lisbon Spring Council Meeting to adopt a strategy aimed at raising the rate of growth and employment. This was partly a result of a concern about the poor performance of the EU economy compared to the USA and the emerging economies of Asia.

The EU set itself the target of becoming:

> The most competitive and dynamic knowledge-based economy in the world, capable of sustainable economic growth with more and better jobs and greater social cohesion.

The perceived challenges were global competition, enlargement and the ageing population. Europe was much more likely to be successful if its Members worked together rather than as individual States. It was a policy of combining economic growth with a concern to advance social cohesion. The EU wanted to have a high productivity, high value added, high employment economy in order to maintain its commitment to social and environmental Europe. This progress was to be achieved by a combination of Community measures and an open method of co-ordination in areas which were within the fields of national competence.

This strategy was designed to increase employment levels and encourage social cohesion. As part of this the Commission set itself the target of achieving an EU employment rate of 70% and to increase the participation levels of women in the workforce by 2010.

The **Stockholm European Council** held in March 2001 added two intermediate and one additional target: the employment rate should be raised to 67% overall by 2005, 57% for women by 2005 and 50% for older workers by 2010. The **Barcelona Council** in March 2002 confirmed that full employment was the goal of the EU and called for a strengthened employment strategy to underpin the Lisbon strategy.[105]

In 2005 the Kok report[106] revealed that many countries would not reach their targets on employment and the Commission launched a new Communication in 2005 which included a complete revision of the European Employment Strategy (EES).

In terms of more jobs, the EU needs to create some 22 million jobs in order to reach the 2010 Lisbon target.[107] Creating those better jobs may not be easy. The unemployment rate varies enormously. Overall the figure was 8.8% in 2004, with the highest levels being in Poland (18.8%) and Slovakia (16.4%) and the lowest being in Ireland (4.3%), the UK (4.6%) and the Netherlands (4.8%).

Looking at this from a different perspective, the full employment rate in the EU25 was 63.8% in 2005[108] compared to the Lisbon target of 70% by 2010. Only four Member States, Denmark, Netherlands, Sweden and the UK, had achieved this target, although another five were not far off. Looking at these results one might conclude that the target of full

---

[105] For further information on this see the EU website at: http://ec.europa.eu/employment_social/employment_
strategy/index_en.htm (the source of this information).
[106] *Facing the challenge: the Lisbon Strategy for growth and Employment*: Report from the High Level Group chaired by Wim Kok, November 2004.
[107] *Annual Review of working conditions in the EU 2005/06* (2006) European Foundation for the Improvement of Living and Working Conditions.
[108] See Eurostat website for *EU Labour Force Survey; Principal Results 2005*.

employment is some way off and it is unlikely that it will be achieved by 2010. There are almost 20 million unemployed people in the EU.

If one looks at the specific groups for whom Lisbon set targets, then the picture is equally varied. The majority of Member States are far behind the Lisbon target rate of 60% for female participation in the labour market. Nine Member States had exceeded the target by 2005[109] but the Member States with the lowest female participation rate in the EU25 were Malta (33.7%) and Italy with an employment rate of 45.3%. Some Member States (in 2004) actually had declining female employment rates. This took place in Slovakia, the Czech Republic, Lithuania and Poland (where female participation rates fell by 5%).

With regard to older workers, the Lisbon jobs agenda was to be achieved by, first, increasing employment rates for those in the 55–64 years range, with a target of 50%. In 2005 there were eight Member States which exceeded the target rate of 50% employment.[110] There were, however, nine Member States with 33% or less of the 55–64-year-old workforce employed. Again these Member States are unlikely to reach the 50% target.

The EES is designed to be the main method for ensuring co-ordination of the employment policy priorities for Member States at EU level. The components of the EES are as follows:

- *Integrated Employment Guidelines*: following a proposal from the Commission, the European Council agrees every year on a series of guidelines setting out common priorities for Member States' employment policies.
- *National Reform Programmes*: every Member State draws up a programme in which it describes how these Guidelines are going to be implemented nationally.
- *Joint Employment Report*: the Employment chapter of the annual progress report is adopted by the Council to form the Joint Employment Report.
- *Recommendations*: the Council may decide, by qualified majority, to issue country-specific Recommendations upon a proposal by the Commission.
- *EU annual progress report*: the Commission reviews progress made at both national and Community level, based on regular monitoring of the actions listed in the Community Lisbon Programme and on an evaluation of the implementation of the Member States' national programmes.[111]

Further reading

Barnard, C., *EC Employment Law* (3rd edn, Oxford University Press, 2006), Chapter 1.
Steiner, J., Woods, L. and Twigg-Fleisner, C., *EU Law* (9th edn, Oxford University Press, 2006), Part 1.
http://ec.europa.eu/employment_social/employment_strategy/index_en.htm for material on the Lisbon strategy.
http://ec.europa.eu/employment_social/labour_law/index_en.htm for material on EC labour law.
http://ec.europa.eu/index_en.htm for exploring the European Commission website.

Visit **www.mylawchamber.co.uk/sargeant** to access legal updates, live web links and practice exam questions to test yourself on this chapter.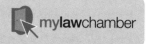

[109] The highest rates of such participation are in Denmark, Sweden, the Netherlands, the UK and Finland.
[110] These were Denmark, Estonia, Ireland, Cyprus, Portugal, Finland, Sweden and the UK.
[111] See the Commission web site mentioned above.

3

The Employment Relationship

3.1 Introduction

The purely contractual approach to the employment relationship is unsatisfactory because it suggests that there are two equal parties agreeing the terms of a contract and entering into an equal bargain. The contractual approach was adopted by the courts in the 1870s, but it is still, in reality, an unequal relationship. One party uses the labour or talents of another in return for providing remuneration. The payment of that remuneration, except in unusual circumstances, creates a labour force which is dependent upon the employer's goodwill and desire to continue with that relationship. It may be made less unequal by statutes which limit the freedom of employers to take action against workers and may be made more equal by collective bargaining arrangements between employers and trade unions. In 1897 the Webbs wrote that:

> Individual bargaining between the owner of the means of subsistence and the seller of so perishable a commodity as a day's labour must be, once and for all, abandoned. In its place, if there is to be any genuine freedom of contract, we shall see the conditions of employment adjusted between equally expert negotiators acting for corporations reasonably comparable in strength.[1]

This was a call for effective collective bargaining with trade unions being able to bargain with employers as equals.

Otto Kahn-Freund[2] described contracts of employment as concealing the realities of subordination behind the conceptual screen of contracts considered as concluded between equals. The reality, he concluded, was that such contracts were between institutions and individuals. Freedom of contract is seen as a voluntary act of submission by the individual.[3] Later Lord Wedderburn suggested that:

> The lawyer's model of a freely bargained individual agreement is misleading. In reality, without collective or statutory intervention, many terms of the 'agreement' are imposed by the more powerful party, the employer, by what Fox has called 'the brute facts of power'.[4]

Despite these limitations, the courts have not allowed the power of the employer to overcome the freedom that the parties have to enter freely into contractual relations. *Nokes v Doncaster Collieries*[5] concerned an individual miner working for Hickleton Main Colliery

---

[1] Sidney Webb and Beatrice Webb, *Industrial Democracy* (1897).
[2] Professor Otto Kahn-Freund, who died in 1979, was an eminent and influential labour law academic.
[3] See Paul Davies and Mark Freedland, *Kahn-Freund's Labour and the Law* (Stevens, 1983).
[4] Lord Wedderburn of Charlton, *The Worker and the Law* (Sweet & Maxwell, 1986), Ch 2.
[5] *Nokes v Doncaster Amalgamated Collieries Ltd* [1940] AC 1014 HL.

Ltd who was apparently unaware that the company had been dissolved by a court order and that his contract of employment had been transferred to Doncaster Amalgamated Collieries Ltd. The issue was whether, in the circumstances, the contract automatically transferred to the new employer, even though the employee was unaware of the change. Lord Atkin stated:

> My Lords, I should have thought that the principle that a man is not to be compelled to serve a master against his will . . . is deep seated in the common law of this country.

The employee needed to have knowledge of the employer and to have given consent to the transfer. Without such knowledge and consent it would not be possible to say that the employee had freely entered into a contractual relationship with the employer.[6]

Discussion about the importance of the contractual relationship also perhaps conceals the complexity and variety of working relationships that now exist. It is not enough to describe a model of an employer/worker relationship consisting of a full-time employer and a full-time worker. Apart from the distinction between the employed and the self-employed, which in itself may be at times a difficult distinction (see below), contractual relationships will include those on part-time contracts, fixed-term contracts, zero hours contracts, casual contracts and so on.

The contract of employment is also an unsatisfactory way of describing the employment relationship because it does not reflect the often informal relationship between employers and workers. This informal relationship is reflected, for example, in the number of hours that are worked in the United Kingdom, which are longer than elsewhere in the EU (see Chapter 8). The hours that many people work are clearly in excess of their contractual obligations and suggest that there is an informal expectation that this level of work is required. Similarly it is difficult to incorporate quality and quantity of effort into a contract. During peak periods of work, employees may perform at a much more demanding level than in normal periods in order to cope with the extra work demands. The contract of employment is not able to describe or incorporate this aspect of the employer/worker relationship.

3.2 Parties to the contract – employers

3.2.1 Employers' associations

Employers' associations are potentially important in their role as:

(1) A representative of a particular industrial or commercial sector, such as the Engineering Employers' Association, or as a representative of a particular type of employer, such as the Federation of Small Businesses, or as representatives of different employers working with common interests, such as the Business Services Association.[7]

(2) A social partner, when they might be consulted by Government on proposed policies or legislation. They may also have an international role as a result of which they can influence EU decisions. One example of this is the Confederation of British Industry

---

[6] For the statutory approach to employee rights during transfers, see Chapter 10.
[7] Representing contracting businesses working in a variety of sectors.

(CBI) which is a member of UNICE, the European private employers' organisation, which is, in turn, a member of the Social Dialogue Committee in the EU (see Chapter 2).

(3) A negotiator with trade unions on behalf of the members that they represent. It is perhaps less common than previously, with the decline in membership of trade unions, to have industry or sector-wide agreements on pay and conditions. They are more common in the public sector than the private one. Where they exist, of course, they may regulate the pay and conditions of large numbers of employees, such as in the education or health service sectors. There is also a likelihood that such agreements will be incorporated into individuals' contracts of employment.[8]

Part II TULRCA 1992 is concerned with the regulation of employers' associations. They are defined as temporary or permanent organisations which consist mainly or wholly of either employers or individual owners of undertakings; or consist of constituent bodies or affiliated organisations, which are, in themselves, collections of employers or owners of undertakings; whose principal purposes include the regulation of relations between employers and workers or trade unions.[9] The Certification Officer has an obligation to keep lists of employers' associations and make them available for public inspection at all reasonable hours, free of charge.[10] It is not mandatory, however, for associations to apply for listing.[11] According to the Certification Officer's annual report for 2006–7, there were 81 listed and 70 unlisted employers' associations at the end of March 2007. Combined they had a total membership of 241,398 with total assets of £486,395,000.[12] The listed members range from the Engineering Employers' Federation and the Electrical Contractors' Association to, perhaps, less obvious associations, such as the England and Wales Cricket Board.

An employers' association may be either a body corporate or an unincorporated association.[13] If the latter, it will still be capable of making contracts, suing and being sued, as well as being capable of having proceedings brought against it for alleged offences committed by it or on its behalf.[14] As for trade unions (see Chapter 11), the purposes of employers' associations, in so far as they relate to the regulation of relations between employers and workers, are protected from action for restraint of trade.[15]

3.2.2 Identifying the employer

Section 295(1) TULRCA 1992 defines an employer, in relation to an employee, as 'the person by whom the employee is (or, where the employment has ceased, was) employed'.

---

[8] For examples of such incorporation, see *Gascol Conversions v Mercer* [1974] IRLR 155 and *Whent v T Cartledge* [1997] IRLR 153.

[9] Section 122(1) TULRCA 1992.

[10] Section 123(1) and (2) TULRCA 1992; for information about the Certification Officer, see Chapter 1.

[11] The process for applying to have a name entered on the list, removing it from the list and appealing against the Certification Officer's decisions are contained in sections 124–126 TULRCA 1992.

[12] The figures for membership and assets relate to employers' associations' returns for 2005–6.

[13] Section 127(1) TULRCA 1992.

[14] Section 127(2) TULRCA 1992. See *Barry Print v (1) The Showmen's Guild of Great Britain; (2) Bob Wilson & Sons (Leisure) Ltd*, unreported, 27 October 1999 where an unincorporated association was held to be without legal personality, save for section 127(2) TULRCA 1992.

[15] Section 128 TULRCA 1992; issues related to the property of and to the administration of employers' associations are contained in sections 129–134 TULRCA 1992.

Section 296(2) offers a similar definition in relation to workers.[16] In this case the employer is 'a person for whom one or more workers work, or have worked or normally work or seek to work'. These definitions are repeated elsewhere, such as in section 54 National Minimum Wage Act 1998.[17] The differences between employees and workers are important and are discussed below.

The employer may be an individual, but is more likely to be a partnership or a business with limited liability. In equity partnerships the individual partners are likely to retain personal responsibility for the actions of the partnership. In a business with limited liability there may be a separation of identity between the management of a company or business and the legal person that is that company or business. Thus, in some situations, management may make decisions affecting an employee, who will then have recourse against the business itself. The contract of employment or statement of particulars of employment will normally identify the employer.[18]

It is possible for the natural or legal person who is the employer to be changed if there is a transfer of the contract of employment. As will be explained in Chapter 10, the Transfer of Undertakings (Protection of Employment) Regulations 2006[19] enable the identity of the employer to be changed in such a manner that the employee will retain continuity of employment.[20] Unlike the case of *Nokes v Doncaster Collieries*[21] this may happen, in situations protected by these regulations, even without the employee's knowledge.[22]

3.2.3 Employers as employees

The separation of the identity of management and the owners of an undertaking has some consequences for employees. The courts are reluctant to lift the veil of incorporation to look into, perhaps, the reality of that which lies behind it. In *Catherine Lee v Lee's Air Farming Ltd*[23] the controlling shareholder was also the company's sole employee. The court decided that:

> There appears no greater difficulty in holding that a man acting in one capacity can give orders to himself acting in another capacity than there is in holding that a man acting in one capacity can make a contract with himself in another capacity. The company and the deceased[24] were separate legal entities.

Thus it is possible for a controlling shareholder to be an employee of the same organisation. The Court of Appeal considered such a situation in *Secretary of State v Bottrill*[25]

---

[16] See also section 230(4) ERA 1996.
[17] See Chapter 8.
[18] Section 1(3)(a) ERA 1996.
[19] SI 2006/1057.
[20] See also section 218 ERA 1996 in relation to continuity of employment in certain changes of employer; discussed further below.
[21] [1940] AC 1014 HL.
[22] See *Secretary of State for Trade and Industry v Cook* [1997] IRLR 151 CA, which overturned a previous decision in *Photostatic Copiers (Southern) Ltd v Okuda* [1995] IRLR 12, and confirmed that such knowledge was not an essential prerequisite.
[23] [1961] AC 12.
[24] The applicant was the widow of the controlling shareholder and sole employee.
[25] *Secretary of State for Trade and Industry v Bottrill* [1999] IRLR 326 CA.

where an individual was appointed managing director of a company and, temporarily at least, held all the share capital. At the same time the individual signed a contract of employment, which set out the duties of the post, the hours to be worked, holiday and sickness entitlement and details of remuneration. The issue was whether such a person was really an employee. The court did not accept a previous EAT decision which had concluded that a 50% shareholder,[26] who was also a director, was not an employee. The EAT had concluded that a controlling shareholder could not be an employee because such a person would be able to control decisions that affected his or her own dismissal and remuneration and that there was a difference between an individual running a business through the device of a limited liability company and an individual working for a company subject to the control of a board of directors. The EAT stated that, in the context of employment protection legislation, *Lee's Air Farming* could not be relied upon to support the pro-position that a shareholder with full and unrestricted control over a company could also be employed under a contract of service. The Court of Appeal, however, stated that all the factors that indicated an employer/employee relationship, or otherwise, needed to be examined. The fact that the person was a controlling shareholder was only one of those factors, albeit a potentially decisive one. Other factors to be considered were whether there was a genuine contract between the shareholder and the company; the reasons for the contract coming into existence and what each party actually did in carrying out their contractual obligations. The issue of control was important in deciding whether there was a genuine employment relationship, for example, were there other directors and to what extent did the employee become involved in decisions affecting them as employees.[27] Lord Woolf MR stated:

> We recognise the attractions of having in relation to the ERA a simple and clear test which will determine whether a shareholder or a director is an employee for the purposes of the Act or not. However, the Act does not provide such a test . . . we do not find any justification for departing from the well-established position in the law of employment generally . . . If an individual has a controlling shareholding, that is certainly a fact which is likely to be significant in all situations, and in some cases it may prove decisive. However, it is only one of the factors which are relevant and is certainly not to be taken as determinative without considering all the relevant circumstances.

3.2.4 Associated, superior and principal employers

One of the concerns of employment protection legislation is to ensure that, when necessary, two or more associated employers are treated as if they were one employer. This is especially important where there are exemptions for small employers, such as in the

---

26 *Buchan v Secretary of State for Employment* [1997] IRLR 80; the Court of Appeal preferred the decision of the Court of Session in *Fleming v Secretary of State for Trade and Industry* [1997] IRLR 682 where the court concluded that whether a person was an employee or not was a matter of fact and all the relevant circumstances needed to be looked at, rather than adopting a general rule of law.

27 See also *Sellars Arenascene Ltd v Connolly* [2001] IRLR 222 CA which also considered the position of a controlling shareholder of a business that had been taken over. The court held that the tribunal had placed too much reliance upon the individual's interest as a shareholder rather than as an employee. The fact that he would gain if the company prospered applied to employees as well as shareholders.

requirements for statutory recognition of trade unions[28] and the application of the right to return to work provisions of the Maternity and Parental Leave etc. Regulations 1999.[29]

Section 297 TULRCA 1992 and section 231 ERA 1996 define any two employers as associated if one is a company of which the other has, directly or indirectly, control or if both are companies of which a third person, either directly or indirectly, has control.[30] This is a convenient definition when adding up numbers of employees to decide whether an employer or a group of employers cross a numbers threshold. It is important not to assume that groups of associated employers are to be treated as one employer for employment protection purposes in all situations. Each employer retains its distinct legal personality. In *Allen v Amalgamated Construction*,[31] for example, the ECJ held that a relevant transfer[32] of employees took place between two companies, who were distinctive legal entities, but who were part of the same group and would probably, in the statutory definitions, be seen as associated employers.

A superior employer, according to section 48 National Minimum Wage Act 1998, is deemed to be the joint employer, with the immediate employer, of the worker concerned. This occurs where the immediate employer of a worker is in the employment of some other person and the worker is employed on the premises of that other person. This is a definition that seems to be aimed at stopping workers being sub-contracted to other workers in order that the superior employer is liable for ensuring that the national minimum wage is paid.

Section 12(1) DDA 1995 makes it unlawful for a principal, in relation to contract work, to discriminate against a disabled person. Section 12(4) describes a principal as:

a person (A) who makes work available for doing by individuals who are employed by another person who supplies them under a contract made with A.

There are similar provisions, aimed at making the hirer, rather than the recruitment agency or intermediary, liable for discrimination against contract workers, contained in section 9(1) Sex Discrimination Act 1975 and section 7(1) Race Relations Act 1976. *Abbey Life Assurance Co Ltd v Tansell*[33] concerned a computer contractor who hired himself out via a company he had established for that purpose. He was placed as a contractor by an agency, so that there were two organisations between him and the ultimate hirer. The Court of Appeal held that the ultimate hirer was still the principal for the purposes of the DDA 1995, as Parliament had probably intended that it should be the ultimate hirer who should be liable, rather than the agency.

---

[28] See Schedule A1 Part I, paragraph 7 TULRCA 1992 and Chapter 12.

[29] SI 1999/3312; see regulation 20(6).

[30] See also section 82(1) Sex Discrimination Act 1975.

[31] Case C-234/98 *GC Allen v Amalgamated Construction Co Ltd* [2000] IRLR 119 ECJ; see also *Michael Peters Ltd v (1) Farnfield; (2) Michael Peters Group plc* [1995] IRLR 190 where the Group chief executive failed to persuade the EAT that the chief executive's post transferred with a number of subsidiaries to the transferee employer.

[32] In relation to the Transfer of Undertakings Regulations 1981, SI 1981/1794, replaced by new Regulations in 2006; see Chapter 10.

[33] [2000] IRLR 387 CA.

3.3 Parties to the contract – employees

3.3.1 Dependent labour

One of the features of employment law in the United Kingdom is the distinction between employees and workers. The latter tends to have a wider meaning. Section 230(1) ERA 1996 defines an employee as 'an individual who has entered into or works under (or, where the employment has ceased, worked under) a contract of employment'. Section 230(2) then defines a contract of employment, for the purposes of the Act, as meaning 'a contract of service or apprenticeship, whether express or implied, and (if it is express) whether oral or in writing'. The meaning of worker can be the same, but it can also have a wider meaning, i.e. an individual who has entered into, or works under, a contract of employment or

> any other contract, whether express or implied and (if it is express) whether oral or in writing, whereby the individual undertakes to do or perform personally any work or services for another party to the contract whose status is not by virtue of the contract that of a client or customer of any profession or business undertaking carried on by the individual.[34]

Thus there are some individuals who will not be under a contract of employment to a particular employer, but are under a contract to perform personally any work or services for an employer. Often these latter will be treated as self-employed, which means, for example, that they would not receive the benefits of employment protection measures attributable to employees. Nevertheless, these workers may be as dependent on one employer as that same employer's employees.

In *Byrne Brothers (Formwork) Ltd v Baird*[35] the EAT held that the intention[36] was to create an intermediate class of protected worker who, on the one hand, is not an employee and, on the other hand, cannot be regarded as carrying on a business. In this case the EAT concluded that self-employed sub-contract workers in the construction industry fitted into this category. The court stated:

> There can be no general rule, and we should not be understood as propounding one; cases cannot be decided by applying labels. But typically labour-only sub-contractors will, though nominally free to move from contractor to contractor, in practice work for long periods for a single employer as an integrated part of his workforce.

Not all the self-employed are people engaged in business on their own account and one way of distinguishing between the two is to ask what is the dominant purpose of the contract.[37] Is the contract to be located in the employment field or is it in reality a contract between two independent businesses?

By way of contrast, in *Inland Revenue v Post Office Ltd*[38] the EAT decided that sub-postmistresses and sub-postmasters were not workers for the purposes of the National Minimum Wage Act 1998 because they had a choice whether or not to do the work themselves.

---

[34] Section 230(3) ERA 1996.
[35] [2002] IRLR 96.
[36] This case was concerned with the definition of worker in regulation 2(1) of the Working Time Regulations 1998, which is identical to that contained in section 230(3) ERA 1996.
[37] See *James v Redcats (Brands) Ltd* [2007] IRLR 296.
[38] [2003] IRLR 199.

The numbers of self-employed workers has grown significantly in the last 20 years and, in 2007, amounted to approximately 3.8 million people, compared to over 25 million employees.[39] Over two-thirds of the self-employed have no employees themselves and are dependent upon using their own skills and labour.[40] For some workers, self-employment is an illusion. They will be dependent upon one employer for their supply of work and income, but may be lacking in certain employment rights because of their self-employed status. One study of freelancers in the publishing industry, for example, concluded that:

> Freelancers in publishing are essentially casualised employees, rather than independent self-employed . . . in objective terms they are disguised wage labour.[41]

There is then a real difficulty in distinguishing between those who are genuine employees and those who are self-employed, especially if they have the same dependence on one employer as do employees. To some extent this is recognised by the Government when certain employment protection measures are applied to workers and others to employees only. The Working Time Regulations 1998,[42] for example, refer, in regulation 4(1), to a 'worker's working time', whilst the Maternity and Parental Leave etc. Regulations 1999 apply only to employees (see table on p 41).[43]

3.3.2 The distinction between the employed and the self-employed

There are a number of reasons why it is important to establish whether an individual is an employee or self-employed:

(1) Some employment protection measures are reserved for employees, although there are measures which refer to the wider definition of worker, including the Working Time Regulations 1998,[44] the Sex Discrimination Act 1975 and the Race Relations Act 1976 (see below). An example of the protection offered to employees is contained in *Costain Building & Civil Engineering Ltd v Smith*,[45] where a self-employed contractor was appointed by the trade union as a safety representative on a particular site. The individual had been placed as a temporary worker with the company through an employment agency. After a number of critical reports on health and safety he was dismissed by the agency at the request of the company. He complained that he had been dismissed, contrary to section 100(1)(b) ERA 1996, for performing the duties of a health and safety representative. In the course of the proceedings he failed to show that he was other than self-employed. This proved fatal to the complaint, as the relevant regulations only allowed trade unions to appoint safety representatives from amongst

---

[39] Information supplied by the Office for National Statistics; see www.statistics.gov.uk.

[40] Julie Bevan, *Barriers to Business Start Up: A Study of the Flow into and out of Self Employment*, Department of Employment Research Paper no 71.

[41] Celia Stanworth and John Stanworth, 'The Self Employed without Employees – Autonomous or Atypical?' (1995) 26(3) *Industrial Relations Journal*, September.

[42] SI 1998/1833.

[43] SI 1999/3312. See regulation 13(1) where employees with one year's continuous service, and responsibility for a child, are entitled to parental leave.

[44] See, e.g., *Quinnen v Hovells* [1984] IRLR 227, where the EAT concluded that the definition of employment contained in section 82(1) Sex Discrimination Act 1975 enlarged the ordinary meaning of employment to include individuals outside the master/servant relationship.

[45] [2000] ICR 215.

its members who were employees.[46] As the EAT concluded that there was not a contract of employment in existence between the agency and the individual, he did not come within the protection offered to trade union health and safety representatives.

(2) Self-employed persons are taxed on a Schedule D basis, rather than the Schedule E basis for employed earnings. This allows the self-employed person to set off business expenses against income for tax purposes. A good example of the effect of this was shown in *Hall v Lorimer*.[47] Mr Lorimer had been employed as a vision mixer working on the production of television programmes. He decided to become freelance and built up a circle of contacts. He worked on his own and was used by a large number of companies for a short period each. He worked on their premises and used their equipment. The Inland Revenue had assessed his income as being earned under a series of individual contracts of service and thus chargeable to Schedule E income tax. He claimed that he was self-employed and should have been taxed under Schedule D. It was important to him financially. In his first year his gross earnings were £32,875 and he had expenses of £9,250. If assessed under Schedule E he would need to pay tax on the gross amount. If assessed under Schedule D he would be able to offset his expenses and only be liable for tax on £23,625. In the event Mr Lorimer was successful and the Court of Appeal held that he was self-employed.

(3) Employers are vicariously liable for the actions of their employees, rather than for independent contractors. Lord Thankerton summed up the test for vicarious liability at that time:

> It is clear that the master is responsible for acts actually authorised by him; for liability would exist in this case even if the relation between the parties was merely one of agency, and not one of service at all. But a master, as opposed to the employer of an independent contractor, is liable even for acts which he has not authorised, provided they are so connected with acts which he has authorised that they may rightly be regarded as modes – although improper modes – of doing them.[48]

This liability of the employer has been extended so that it continues even for acts of intentional wrongdoing which the employer could not have approved. The employer of a school house warden who sexually abused boarders at a school for maladjusted and vulnerable boys, for example, was held to be vicariously liable for the actions of the employee.[49] The House of Lords held that the correct test for deciding whether an employee's wrongful act had been committed during the course of employment, so as to make the employer vicariously liable, is to examine the relative closeness of the connection between the nature of the employment and the employee's wrongdoing. In this case the employee's position as warden and the close contact with the boys that this entailed created a sufficiently close connection between the acts of abuse and the work

---

[46] Regulation 3(1) Safety Representatives and Safety Committees Regulations 1977, SI 1977/500; employee is defined by reference to section 53(1) HASAWA 1974, which defines employee as a person who works under a contract of employment.

[47] *Hall (HM Inspector of Taxes) v Lorimer* [1994] IRLR 171 CA.

[48] *Canadian Pacific Railway Co v Lockhart* [1942] AC 591 at p 599 PC.

[49] *Lister v Hesley Hall Ltd* [2001] IRLR 472 HL.

which he had been employed to carry out.[50] Applying this test, the Court of Appeal has ruled that a club owner was vicariously liable for an act of violence committed by a security guard away from the club premises.[51] The House of Lords has subsequently stated that there is no relevant distinction between performing an act in an improper manner and performing it for an improper purpose or by improper means. Thus the mere fact that employees were acting dishonestly or for their own benefit is likely to be insufficient to show that they were not acting in the course of employment.[52]

(4) The employer will also owe a duty of care to employees as shown in *Lane v Shire Roofing*[53] where the claimant was held to be an employee (see below) rather than a self-employed contractor. As a result of this damages were awarded, after a work-related accident, in excess of £100,000, which would not have been awarded if the claimant had been carrying out work as an independent contractor.[54] In *Waters v Commissioner of Police of the Metropolis*[55] a police constable complained that the Commissioner of Police had acted negligently in failing to deal with her complaint of sexual assault by a colleague and the harassment and victimisation resulting from making the complaint. The House of Lords held that:

> If an employer knows that acts being done by employees during their employment may cause physical or mental harm to a particular fellow employee and he does nothing to supervise or prevent such acts, when it is in his power to do so, it is clearly arguable that he may be in breach of his duty to that employee. It seems that he may also be in breach of that duty if he can foresee that such acts will happen . . .

Thus the employer owes a duty of care to employees who may be at physical or mental risk or for whom it is reasonably foreseeable that there may be some such harm.[56]

3.4 Identifying the employee

The common law has developed a number of tests for distinguishing those who have a contract of employment from those who are self-employed contractors. It is important, perhaps, not to see these tests as mutually exclusive, but rather developments in the law as a result of the courts being faced with an increasingly complex workplace and a greater variety of types of work situations.

---

[50] See also *Balfron Trustees Ltd v Peterson* [2001] IRLR 758 where an employee of a firm of solicitors acted dishonestly; the crucial factor, according to the High Court, relying on *Lister*, was whether the employer owed some form of duty or responsibility towards the victim; if the answer was yes, then the employer cannot avoid liability because the duty or responsibility was delegated to an employee who failed to follow the employer's instructions.

[51] *Dubai Aluminium v Salaam* [2003] IRLR 608.

[52] *Mattis v Pollock* [2003] IRLR 603.

[53] *Lane v Shire Roofing Co (Oxford) Ltd* [1995] IRLR 493 CA.

[54] See also *Makepeace v Evans Brothers (Reading)* [2001] ICR 241 CA where a main site contractor was held not to have a duty of care to a contractor's employee who injured himself using equipment supplied by the main site contractor; responsibility rested with the employer alone.

[55] [2000] IRLR 720 HL.

[56] See also, e.g., *Spring v Guardian Assurance plc* [1994] IRLR 460 HL on the duty of care owed on employment references and *Wigan Borough Council v Davies* [1979] IRLR 127 on bullying and harassment by fellow employees.

Employment protection rights of employees and workers[57]

Employment right	Employees only	All workers (including employees)
Written statement of employment particulars	X	
Itemised pay statement	X	
Protection against unlawful deductions from wages		X
Guarantee payments	X	
Time off – for public duties, to look for work or arrange training in redundancy, antenatal care, dependants, pension trustees, employee reps, for young person to study or train, for members of EWCs	X	
Ordinary or additional maternity leave	X	
Parental leave, paternity leave, adoption leave	X	
Right to notice	X	
Written statement of reasons for dismissal	X	
Unfair dismissal	X	
Right to be accompanied		X
Right to a redundancy payment	X	
Right to an insolvency payment	X	
Protection by the Transfer Regulations	X	
Protection by the Fixed-term Work Regulations	X	
Right to be informed and consulted about collective redundancies	X	
Right to national minimum wage		X
Right to rest breaks, paid annual leave and maximum working time		X
Protection by Part-time Workers Regulations		X
Rights connected with belonging to a trade union or time off for trade union duties and activities	X	
Right to dispute resolution procedures	X	

3.4.1 The control test

An early test developed by the courts was the control test. In *Walker v Crystal Palace*[58] a professional footballer was held to have a contract of service with the club. He was paid £3 10s (£3.50) per week for a year's contract, in which he was expected to provide his playing services exclusively to Crystal Palace Football Club. He was given detailed rules about training and under whose direction he was during that training. He was also expected

---

[57] Adapted from a DTI table contained in its 2002 discussion paper on employment status; available on the web site www.berr.gov.uk; the Department for Trade and Industry (DTI) was renamed the Department for Business, Enterprise and Regulatory Reform in 2007.
[58] *Walker v The Crystal Palace Football Club Ltd* [1910] 1 KB 87.

to be available for training and matches. The club argued that he did not have a contract of service because, it asserted, it was essential that in such a relationship the master should have the power to direct how work should be done. In *Yewens v Noakes* Bramwell J had defined a servant as:[59]

> a person subject to the command of his master as to the manner in which he shall do his work.

It was argued that this definition could not be applied to a professional footballer who was hired to display their talents and skills. The control of the club is limited to deciding whether the player is picked for the team or not. Farewell J dismissed this argument on the basis that many workmen displayed their own initiative, like footballers, but were still bound by the directions of their master. In this case the player had agreed to follow detailed training instructions and to obey his captain's instructions on the field:

> I cannot doubt that he is bound to obey any directions which the captain, as the delegate of the club, may give him during the course of the game – that is to say, any direction that is within the terms of his employment as a football player.[60]

It is difficult now, perhaps, to comprehend the attempts to fit a professional footballer into this concept of control.

The problem with this test is that it is limited in its application in distinguishing the employed from the self-employed. Employers, subject to statutory and common law restraints, are able to exercise considerable control over employees. This was recognised in *Market Investigations*[61] where the issue was whether a market research interviewer was employed under a contract of service (see below).

This test recognises the reality of many employment relationships and the level of control may still be a factor in deciding whether a person is working under a contract of employment or a contract for services. In *Lane v Shire Roofing Company* the Court of Appeal recognised this:[62]

> First, the element of control will be important; who lays down what is to be done, the way in which it is to be done, the means by which it is to be done, and the time when it is to be done? Who provides (ie hires and fires) the team by which it is to be done, and who provides the material, plant and machinery and tools used?

Although the concept of control is only one of a number of factors which might influence the final decision as to whether a person is an employee or not, it can still be crucial. In *Clifford v UDM*[63] the Court of Appeal approved the approach of an employment tribunal in deciding that in situations that lack clarity, then control may be an important factor. The control exercised need not be done directly. *Motorola Ltd v Davidson*[64] concerned an individual who was engaged by an agency to work at Motorola's premises. The individual was dismissed by the agency at the request of the company. This level of

---

[59] [1880] 6 QB 530 at p 532.
[60] [1910] 1 KB 87 at p 93.
[61] *Market Investigations Ltd v Minister of Social Security* [1968] 3 All ER 732.
[62] [1995] IRLR 493 at p 495.
[63] *Clifford v Union of Democratic Mineworkers* [1991] IRLR 518 CA.
[64] *Motorola Ltd v (1) Davidson; (2) Melville Craig Group Ltd* [2001] IRLR 4.

control, even though exercised via a third party, was sufficient to establish an employment relationship between the company and the individual.

3.4.2 The integration test

Early reliance on the control test alone proved inadequate, especially when considering more complex employment relationships. These relationships occur when there are highly skilled individuals carrying out work which, except in the most general sense, cannot be subject to any close control by an employer. Such examples might be a ship's captain[65] or the medical staff in a hospital, as in *Cassidy v Ministry of Health*.[66]

It is not entirely clear when a person is integrated into an organisation and when they are not. It was stated in *Stevenson, Jordan & Harrison v McDonald and Evans*[67] that:

> One feature that seems to run through the instances is that, under a contract of service, a man is employed as part of the business, and his work is done as an integral part of the business; whereas, under a contract for services, his work, although done for the business, is not integrated into it but is only accessory to it.

If an individual is integrated into the organisational structure the individual is more likely to be an employee. The less the integration, the more likely the individual is to be self-employed. In *Beloff v Pressdram Ltd*[68] Lord Widgery CJ approved Denning LJ's statement in *Stevenson, Jordan & Harrison*[69] and stated:

> The test which emerges from the authorities seems to me, as Denning LJ said, whether on the one hand the employee is employed as part of the business and his work is an integral part of the business, or whether his work is not integrated into the business but is only accessory to it, or, as Cooke J expressed it, the work is done by him in business on his own account.

It is difficult to understand where the dividing line may be: for example, what of the dependent contractor? If a person is self-employed, but works continuously for one organisation, are they to be treated as integrated into the organisation or not? Much work is now the subject of outsourcing. To what extent, for example, is the catering assistant who works for an outsourced company to be treated as an integrated part of the organisation in which he or she is located?

The integration test seemed to be an attempt to cope with the difficulties posed by the growth of technical and skilled work which may not be the subject of close control by an employer. Although it may be used as an indicator of a person under a contract of service, it cannot be conclusive. Indeed the problem of this test and the control test is that they do not sufficiently distinguish between the employed and the self-employed. It is arguable that it is possible for workers without a contract of employment to be closely integrated into an organisation and closely controlled by that organisation. To some extent this has been recognised by the Court of Appeal in *Franks v Reuters Ltd*.[70] In this case it was held that a

---

[65] See *Gold v Essex County Council* [1942] 2 KB 293.
[66] [1951] 2 KB 343 CA.
[67] [1952] 1 TLR 101, *per* Denning LJ.
[68] [1973] 1 All ER 241.
[69] [1952] 1 TLR 101.
[70] [2003] IRLR 423.

person who had worked for Reuters on a full-time permanent basis for more than four years on an assignment from an employment agency could be an employee of Reuters. It is consistent with general legal principles that dealings between parties over a period of years are capable of generating an implied contractual relationship (see *Dacas v Brook Street Bureau* below).

3.4.3 The economic reality test

This test is considered in *Market Investigations Ltd v Minister of Social Security*,[71] where the court not only considered the amount of control exercised over a part-time market researcher, but also the question as to whether she was in business on her own account. The case concerned a market researcher who was employed to carry out specific and time limited assignments. The issue was whether the researcher was employed under a contract of service or a contract for services. The court cited the case of *Ready Mixed Concrete*[72] in which MacKenna J stated that a contract of service existed if three conditions were fulfilled. These were:

(1) whether the servant agreed that they would provide their own work and skill in return for a wage or other remuneration;
(2) the individual agreed, expressly or impliedly, to be subject to the control of the master; and
(3) that the other provisions of the contract were consistent with a contract of service.

It was also stated that an 'obligation to do work subject to the other party's control is a necessary, though not always a sufficient, condition of a contract of service'. In *Market Investigations* the court held that further tests were needed to decide whether the contract as a whole was consistent or inconsistent with there being a contract of service. The company argued that the researcher performed a series of contracts and that a master and servant relationship was normally continuous. This view was rejected by the court which doubted

> whether this factor can be treated in isolation. It must, I think, be considered in connection with the more general question whether Mrs Irving could be said to be in business on her own account as an interviewer.

It was concluded that she was employed by the company under a series of contracts of service. She was not in business on her own account, even though she could work for other employers (although she did not). She did not provide her own tools or risk her own capital, nor did her opportunity of profit depend in any significant degree on the way she managed her work.

This test of economic reality, i.e. looking at the contract as a whole to decide whether the individual was in business on his or her own account, was an important development of the approach towards distinguishing between those employed under a contract of service from others. The element of control is still important, but there is a need to take

---

[71] [1968] 3 All ER 732.
[72] *Ready Mixed Concrete (South East) Ltd v Minister of Pensions and National Insurance* [1967] 2 QB 497.

into account the other factors that make up the contract of employment. This is often so regardless of whether the parties to the contract have labelled it a contract for services or a contract of service (see below). There is, as Cooke J pointed out in *Market Investigations*, no exhaustive list of factors which can be taken into account in determining the relationship. Perhaps, more importantly, this test recognises the fact that the parties to the contract are independent individuals. The employee is not necessarily seen as merely someone under the control of another.

Thus a person who works for a number of different employers may be seen as an employee[73] or a self-employed contractor.[74] The economic reality test builds upon the control and integration tests and will consider such matters as investment in the business or the economic risk taken as important considerations.

3.4.4 The multiple factor test

This test is a further recognition that there is no one factor that can establish whether a contract of service exists. In different situations, different factors can assume greater or lesser importance. It is really a test that *Ready Mixed Concrete*[75] and *O'Kelly*[76] tried to come to terms with. In the first case the court identified five factors which were inconsistent with there being a contract of service. In *O'Kelly* the court identified 17 possible factors which might influence the decision. More recently, the important factor has appeared to be that of mutuality of obligation (see below). MacKenna J[77] illustrated the complexity of the decision:

> An obligation to do work subject to the other party's control is a necessary, though not always a sufficient, condition of a contract of service. If the provisions of the contract as a whole are inconsistent with it being a contract of service, it will be some other kind of contract, and the person doing the work will not be a servant. The judge's task is to classify the contract . . . he may, in performing it, take into account other matters than control.

The problem with this approach, which may be insoluble without a more precise statutory definition, is that it can lead to inconsistencies of approach. It is employment tribunals that will decide what weight is to be given to specific factors in particular circumstances. It is not always clear whether such a decision is a question of fact or law, which, in turn, affects the appeal courts opportunities to intervene in tribunal decisions to create a uniformity of approach (see below).

3.4.5 Mutuality of obligation

One important factor the courts have examined in order to decide whether a contract of service exists or not is that of mutuality of obligation between employer and individual. In *O'Kelly v Trust House Forte plc*[78] a number of 'regular casual' staff made a claim for unfair

---

[73] See *Lee v Chung and Shun Shing Construction & Engineering Co Ltd* [1990] IRLR 236.
[74] See *Hall (HM Inspector of Taxes) v Lorimer* [1994] IRLR 171 CA.
[75] [1967] 2 QB 497.
[76] *O'Kelly v Trust House Forte plc* [1983] IRLR 369 CA.
[77] *Ready Mixed Concrete (South East) Ltd v Minister of Pensions and National Insurance* [1967] 2 QB 497 at p 517.
[78] [1983] IRLR 369.

dismissal. In order to be permitted to make this claim they needed to show that they were working under a contract of service. The tribunal had identified a number of factors which were consistent, or not inconsistent, with the existence of a contract of employment. These included performing the work under the direction and control of the appellants and, when they attended at functions, 'they were part of the appellants' organisation and for the purpose of ensuring the smooth running of the business they were represented in the staff consultation process'. These elements of control and integration were, however, not enough. One of the factors on which the tribunal had placed 'considerable weight' was a lack of mutuality of obligation between the two parties. The employer was under no obligation to provide work and the individuals were under no obligation to perform it.

In *Carmichael*,[79] the House of Lords approved the conclusion of an employment tribunal, which had held that the applicant's case 'founders on the rock of the absence of mutuality'. The case concerned the question as to whether two tour guides were employees under contracts of employment and therefore entitled under section 1 ERA 1996 to a written statement of particulars of the terms of their employment. The House of Lords accepted that they worked on a casual 'as and when required' basis. An important issue was that there did not exist a requirement for the employer to provide work and for the individual to carry out that work. Indeed the court heard that there were a number of occasions when the applicants had declined offers of work. There was an 'irreducible minimum of mutual obligation' that was necessary to create a contract of service. There needed to be an obligation to provide work and an obligation to perform that work in return for a wage or some form of remuneration. Part-time home workers, for example, who had been provided with work, and had performed it, over a number of years could be held to have created this mutual obligation.[80] The obligation upon the employer is to provide work when it is available, not to provide work consistently. Thus a person who worked as a relief manager and had a contract which stated that there would be times when no work was available and he would not be paid on these occasions was still entitled to be treated as having a contract of employment. There was an obligation upon the employer to provide work when it was available.[81]

When this mutual obligation is absent in either party, then a contract of service, in some extreme cases, will not exist. In *Express and Echo Publications Ltd v Tanton*[82] the Court of Appeal stated that the test was a contractual one. It was necessary to look at the obligations provided, rather than what actually occurred. In this case an individual's contract enabled them to arrange, at their own expense, for their duties to be performed by another person when they were unable or unwilling to carry out their work. Such a term was incompatible with a contract of service, as it meant that the individual lacked the obligation to work

---

[79] *Carmichael v National Power plc* [2000] IRLR 43 HL.

[80] *Nethermere (St Neots) Ltd v Gardiner* [1984] ICR 612 CA; see also *Clark v Oxfordshire Health Authority* [1998] IRLR 125 CA where the position of a nurse in the staff bank was considered and it was held that there was an absence of mutuality of obligation.

[81] *Wilson v Circular Distributors Ltd* [2006] IRLR 38.

[82] [1999] IRLR 367 CA. See also *Stevedoring and Haulage Services Ltd v Fuller* [2001] IRLR 627 where the documentation expressly provided that the individuals were being engaged on an ad hoc and casual basis with no obligation on the company to offer work and no obligation on the applicants to accept it.

themselves in return for the remuneration. The obligation to work personally for another is, according to the EAT in *Cotswold Developments*,[83] at the heart of the relationship. This approach is somewhat qualified in *Byrne Brothers (Formwork) Ltd v Baird*[84] which concerned labour only sub-contractors in the construction industry, with a contract that allowed the worker to provide a substitute in limited and exceptional circumstances. This more qualified right was not inconsistent with an obligation of personal service. This approach was also held not to apply to gymnasts working for a local authority who were able to provide substitutes for any shift that they were able to work.[85] The difference in approach resulted from the fact that the local authority paid the substitutes directly and that the gymnasts were only able to be replaced by other gymnasts on the Council's approved list.[86]

Subsequently the Court of Appeal stressed that both 'mutuality of obligation' and 'control' are the irreducible minimum legal requirements for the existence of a contract of employment. *Montgomery v Johnson Underwood Ltd*[87] concerned a temporary agency worker who, despite being on a long-term temporary assignment of over two years, wished to show that she was employed by the agency which had placed her. She failed because the court held that there was little or no control or supervision of her by the agency, so that one of the essential prerequisites was missing.

On the other hand, in *Consistent Group Ltd v Kalwak*[88] the EAT found that there was sufficient mutuality of obligation between the worker and the agency to establish that the workers concerned were employees of the Agency. Consistent Group Ltd provided staff from Poland to work in hotels and food processing. The recruits were given contracts headed 'Self-employed sub-contractor's contract for services'. It contained clauses which stated that the sub-contractor was not an employee of the agency and was not entitled to sick pay, holiday pay or pension rights. The sub-contractor was able to work for others provided that the agency did not believe that it would interfere with any work provided by the agency; the sub-contractor agreed to provide services personally and, if he or she could not, had to inform Consistent and find an approved replacement. Despite all this, the EAT warned that tribunals must be alive to the fact that armies of lawyers will simply place substitution clauses, or clauses denying any obligation to accept or provide work in employment contracts, as a matter of form, even where such terms do not begin to reflect the real relationship.

The reality was that these workers had come from Poland expecting to work for the agency and their accommodation depended upon doing such work. There was no realistic chance of them working elsewhere whilst the agency required their services. Although they were able to provide substitutes rather than do the work personally, this only arose if they

---

[83] *Cotswold Developments Construction Ltd v Williams* [2006] IRLR 181.
[84] [2002] IRLR 96.
[85] *MacFarlane v Glasgow City Council* [2001] IRLR 7.
[86] See *Ready Mixed Concrete*, note 77 above, where the High Court had held that occasional and limited delegation was not inconsistent with a contract of service.
[87] [2001] IRLR 269 CA.
[88] [2007] IRLR 560.

were unable to work, not if they did not wish to accept the work.[89] The contract, therefore, bore no relationship to the reality and there was sufficient mutuality of obligation to establish that an employment relationship existed.

3.5 Question of fact or law

Appeals from an employment tribunal may be based either on a question of law, or against a decision that was so unreasonable as to be perverse. This means:

> that the primary facts as found by the fact-finding tribunal must stand, but also that the inferences of fact drawn by the tribunal from the primary facts can only be interfered with by an appellate court if they are insupportable on the basis of the primary facts so found.[90]

This reluctance of the appeal courts to interfere unless there is a point of law or a perverse decision may possibly lead to inconsistencies between different employment tribunals. It seems rather odd that the EAT, which is composed of one lawyer and two experienced lay people, should be confined to appeals on the question of law. The problem of inconsistencies between the approaches of different employment tribunals was highlighted in *O'Kelly*[91] where the Court of Appeal stated:

> Without the Employment Appeal Tribunal being entitled to intervene where in its view the employment tribunal has wrongly evaluated the weight of a relevant consideration then it will be open to employment tribunals to reach differing conclusions, so long as they are reasonably maintainable, on essentially the same facts.

In such cases, the court concluded, it is only where the weight given to a particular factor shows a mis-direction in law that an appellate court can interfere.

It is not always clear whether an issue is a question of law or a question of fact. In *Carmichael*,[92] for example, the Court of Appeal had held that the employment tribunal should have decided as a matter of law that an exchange of letters constituted an offer and acceptance which gave rise to a contract of employment in writing. The House of Lords disagreed[93] and stated that the employment tribunal was entitled to find, as a fact, that the parties did not intend the letters to be the sole record of their agreement. The oral exchanges could also be taken into account. This difference in interpretation allowed the Court of Appeal to reverse the decision of the employment tribunal and the House of Lords to restore it.

In *Lee v Chung*[94] the Privy Council had suggested that the decision as to whether a person was employed under a contract of service or not was often held to be a mixed question of fact and law. It distinguished between those cases where the issue is dependent

---

[89] This distinction between someone who was unable to work, as opposed to someone who was unwilling to work, was also considered in *James v Redcats (Brands) Ltd* [2007] IRLR 296; if the requirement is to provide a substitute when the individual was unable to work, this does not appear to suggest that there is no obligation to perform the work personally.
[90] *Nethermere (St Neots) Ltd v Gardiner* [1984] ICR 612 at 631, *per* Dillon LJ.
[91] [1983] IRLR 369.
[92] [1998] IRLR 301 CA.
[93] [2000] IRLR 43 HL.
[94] [1990] IRLR 236.

on the true construction of a written document[95] and those where the issue is dependent upon an investigation of factual circumstances in which the work is performed. This latter situation makes the decision a question of fact, in which the appeal courts should not interfere.

This seems to be the approach adopted in *Carmichael*, by the House of Lords, except that in this case one of the differences with the Court of Appeal rested on whether one should rely on a construction of the written documents (a question of law) or on the factual circumstances surrounding the agreement (a question of fact). One can appreciate that there might be a public policy issue related to allowing appeals on any issue other than a legal one, which might result in increased numbers of appeals. It is difficult, however, to escape the conclusion that the issue is flexible and that, if an appeal court feels strongly enough, it will find ways of reviewing an employment tribunal's conclusions.

3.6 The intentions of the parties

What is the effect of the parties to the contract deciding that, for whatever reason, it should be a contract for services, rather than a contract of service? This clearly happens in different occupations, where there is an acceptance that individuals are to be treated as self-employed contractors, rather than employees. One study of the construction industry concluded that some 58% of the workforce, excluding local government, was treated as self-employed. This was some 45% of the total workforce. The author concluded that there 'is the strongest indication that self-employment, as an employment status, is an economic fiction'.[96] In *Ferguson v Dawson & Partners*[97] the court considered an individual who worked on a building site as a self-employed contractor. He had no express contract of any kind, although the court came to accept that implied terms of a contract did exist. Although the label of self-employment, as agreed by the parties, was a factor to be considered, it could not be decisive if the evidence pointed towards a contract of employment.[98]

In the financial services industry, sales people are traditionally treated as self-employed, yet they have targets to meet and meetings to attend and cannot sell policies from businesses that compete with their employing company. In these industries, as in others, the parties have come to an arrangement based upon a particular employment relationship. In *Massey v Crown Life Assurance*[99] a branch manager with an insurance company changed his employment status from employee to self-employment, although he continued in the same job. Two years later, the company terminated the agreement and he

[95] See *Davies v Presbyterian Church of Wales* [1986] IRLR 194 HL.
[96] Mark Harvey, *Towards the Insecurity Society: The Tax Trap of Self-employment*, Institute of Employment Rights (1995) October.
[97] [1976] 1 WLR 1213 CA.
[98] See also *Young & Woods Ltd v West* [1980] IRLR 201 CA and *Lane v Shire Roofing Company (Oxford) Ltd* [1995] IRLR 493 CA where the courts relied upon the test in *Market Investigations Ltd*, note 61 above, to decide that the applicants in both cases were employees, even though treated as self-employed for tax purposes.
[99] [1978] 1 WLR 676 CA.

brought a claim for unfair dismissal. He could only make this claim, of course, if he were an employee. Lord Denning MR summed up the Court of Appeal's approach:

> If the true relationship of the parties is that of master and servant under a contract of service, the parties cannot alter the truth of that relationship by putting a different label on it . . . On the other hand, if the parties' relationship is ambiguous and is capable of being one or the other, then the parties can remove that ambiguity, by the very agreement itself which they make with one another.[100]

Thus, the parties' views as to their relationship can be important if there is any ambiguity.

The House of Lords has held[101] that the intentions of the parties can be relevant, rather than a more limited concentration on the written documentation, where this is not decisive, although the meaning of documents should be that which would be conveyed to a reasonable man.[102]

3.7 Continuity of employment

Continuity of employment is important as a number of statutory rights, such as the right to be protected from unfair dismissal and the right to receive written reasons for a dismissal, depend upon having continuous employment with an employer. The period of continuous employment required was reduced from two years to one year in 1999.[103] Other rights such as the right to take parental leave and the right to additional maternity leave also depend upon the employee having one year's continuous employment with an employer.[104] The employment concerned must relate to employment with one employer,[105] although this can include associated employers. The test for control amongst such employers is normally decided by looking at who has the voting control, but there might be, in exceptional circumstances, a need to look at who has de facto control.[106]

3.7.1 Continuity and sex discrimination

The question of whether such a rule can amount to indirect sex discrimination or whether it can be objectively justified was considered in *R v Secretary of State for Employment, ex parte Seymour-Smith and Perez (No 2)*.[107] This case was brought when the qualifying period was two years and the complainants were individuals who were stopped from bringing a complaint for unfair dismissal because they did not have the necessary two years' continuous service. They complained that the proportion of women who could comply with the two-year qualifying period was considerably smaller than the proportion of men.

---

[100] Ibid at p 679.
[101] *Carmichael v National Power plc* [2000] IRLR 43 HL.
[102] See *Investors Compensation Scheme Ltd v Hopkin & Sons* [1998] IRLR 896 HL.
[103] Unfair Dismissal and Statement of Reasons for Dismissal (Variation of Qualifying Period) Order 1999, SI 1999/1436.
[104] Maternity and Parental Leave etc. Regulations 1999, SI 1999/3312.
[105] Section 218(1) ERA 1996.
[106] *Payne v Secretary of State for Employment* [1989] IRLR 352.
[107] [2000] IRLR 263 HL.

The House of Lords referred a number of questions to the ECJ.[108] The ECJ replied[109] that the entitlement to compensation and redress for unfair dismissal came within the scope of Article 119 EC (now 141) and the Equal Treatment Directive,[110] but that the national court must verify whether the statistics showed that the measure in question has had a disparate impact between men and women. It is then up to the Member State to show that the rule was unrelated to any discrimination based upon sex and reflected a legitimate aim of its social policy. This case began with the dismissal of the applicants in 1991 and finally returned to the House of Lords for a decision in 2000. The court accepted that the qualification period did have a disparately adverse effect on women. In the period between 1985 and 1991 the number of men and women who qualified for protection was in the ratio of 10:9. The court held that objective justification had to be determined as at 1985, when the amendment was introduced, and at 1991, when the individuals made their complaint. The court held that the onus was on the Member State to show:

(1) that the alleged discriminatory rule reflected a legitimate aim of its social policy;
(2) that this aim was unrelated to any discrimination based on sex; and
(3) that the Member State could reasonably have considered that the means chosen were suitable for attaining that aim.

The Government argued that the extension of the qualifying period should help reduce the reluctance of employers to take on more people. The court was sympathetic to the Government's case and accepted objective justification:

> The burden placed on the government in this type of case is not as heavy as previously thought. Governments must be able to govern. They adopt general policies, and implement measures to carry out their policies. Governments must be able to take into account a wide range of social, economic and political factors . . . National courts, acting with hindsight, are not to impose an impracticable burden on governments which are proceeding in good faith.

It was perhaps ironic that the judgment was arrived at after a new Government had reduced the qualifying period to one year.

3.7.2 Continuity and the start date

An employee's period of continuous employment begins on the day on which the employee starts work, although any period before an individual's 18th birthday does not count for the purposes of redundancy payments.[111] In *The General of the Salvation Army v Dewsbury*[112] a part-time teacher took on a new full-time contract which stated that her employment began on 1 May. As 1 May was a Saturday and the following Monday was a Bank Holiday, she did not actually commence her duties until the Tuesday, 4 May. She was subsequently dismissed with effect from 1 May in the following year. The issue was whether she had one year's continuous employment. The EAT held that the day on which

---

[108] [1997] IRLR 315 HL.
[109] [1999] IRLR 253 ECJ.
[110] Directive 76/207/EEC; see Chapter 6.
[111] Section 211(1) and (2) ERA 1996.
[112] [1984] IRLR 222.

an employee starts work is intended to refer to the beginning of the employee's employment under the relevant contract of employment and that this may be different to the actual date on which work commences.

There is a presumption that an individual's period of employment is continuous, unless otherwise shown.[113] Thus the onus is on those who wish to challenge the presumption to show that there was not continuous service within the definition in the Act. It is likely, however, that the presumption of continuity only applies to employment with one employer, unless the tribunal accepted that a transfer of the business and, therefore, the contract of employment, had taken place.[114]

Section 212(1) ERA 1996 states that:

> Any week during the whole or part of which an employee's relations with his employer are governed by a contract of employment counts in computing the employee's period of employment.

A week is defined, in section 235(1) ERA 1996 as a week ending with Saturday or, for a weekly paid employee, a week ends with the day used in calculating the week's remuneration. Thus if a contract of employment exists in any one week, using these formula, then that week counts for continuity purposes. In *Sweeney v J & S Henderson*[115] an employee resigned from his employment on a Saturday and left immediately to take up another post. The individual regretted the decision and returned to the original employer the following Friday, to recommence work. The employee was held to have continuity of employment as a result of there not being a week in which the contract of employment did not apply. This was despite the fact that the employee worked for another employer during the intervening period.[116] The employee worked under a contract of employment with the employer during each of the two weeks in question and thus fulfilled the requirements of section 212(1) ERA 1996.

Where there is a period in the employment where the contract is tainted by illegality, continuity may not be preserved. In *Hyland v JH Barker (North West) Ltd*[117] an employee was paid a tax-free lodging allowance even though the employee did not stay away from home. The period of four weeks in which this happened did not count towards continuity of employment. Unfortunately for the employee, as this period fell within the 12-month period prior to dismissal, he was held not to have the necessary continuity of service to make a complaint of unfair dismissal. The EAT stated that 'continuously employed' meant 'continuously employed under a legal contract of employment'.

3.7.3 Continuity and absences from work

Absence from work means not performing in substance the contract that previously existed between the parties. Such a definition applied to a coach driver whose work was

---

[113] Section 210(5) ERA 1996.
[114] See *Secretary of State for Employment v Cohen and Beaupress Ltd* [1987] IRLR 169.
[115] [1999] IRLR 306.
[116] In *Carrington v Harwich Dock Co Ltd* [1998] IRLR 567 an employee resigned on a Friday and was re-employed on the following Monday. Despite a letter from the employer stating that, by resigning voluntarily, the employee's continuity of service was broken, the EAT held that there was continuity.
[117] [1985] IRLR 403.

greatly reduced by the miners' strike in 1984. A substantial part of the individual's work was removed, but the employee was able to claim a temporary cessation of work (see below).[118]

There are a number of reasons for which a person can be absent from work without breaking their statutory continuity of employment. These are:

(1) If the employee is incapable of work as a result of sickness or injury.[119] Absences of no more than 26 weeks under this category will not be held to break continuity.[120] There needs to be a causal relationship between the absence and the incapacity for work in consequence of sickness or injury. The absence from work also needs to be related to the work on offer. If an injured employee were offered different work, for which they were suitable, from that which they normally do, the tribunal would have to decide whether the employee was absent from that newly offered work as a result of the sickness or injury.[121]

(2) If there is a temporary cessation of work. According to section 212(3)(b) ERA 1996, absence from work on account of a temporary cessation[122] of work will not break continuity of employment. The word 'temporary' indicates a period of time that is of relatively short duration when compared to the periods of work. The decision as to whether the cessation is temporary is not a mathematical one, however, only to be achieved by comparing an individual's length of employment with the length of unemployment in a defined period.[123] Although it was possible to look back over the whole period of an individual's employment in order to come to a judgment, temporary still was likely to mean a short time in comparison with the period in work. Thus seasonal workers who were out of work each year for longer than they actually worked could not be considered to have continuity of employment.[124] Other seasonal workers who were regularly out of work for long periods were in the same position, even though, at the beginning of the next season, it was the intention of both parties that they should resume employment.[125] In contrast an academic who was employed on regular fixed-term contracts to teach was held to have continuity, even though the individual was not employed during August and September each year. During this

---

[118] *GW Stephens & Son v Fish* [1989] ICR 324; the miners' strike lasted for about one year; the employee in this case had the normal duty of driving miners to work each day.

[119] Section 212(3)(a) ERA 1996.

[120] Section 212(4) ERA 1996; see also *Donnelly v Kelvin International Services* [1992] IRLR 496, where an employee who resigned on the grounds of ill health, but was then re-employed some five weeks later, was held to have continuity even though they had worked for another employer during the period.

[121] See *Pearson v Kent County Council* [1993] IRLR 165; see also *Byrne v City of Birmingham District Council* [1987] IRLR 191 CA where the employer created a pool of casual employees to share the work; the absence then was not because of a cessation of work, but because the employee was not offered any.

[122] Cessation of work means that work has temporarily ceased to exist; it does not mean that the work has been temporarily or otherwise re-allocated to another employee, thus continuing: see *Byrne v City of Birmingham* above.

[123] See *Ford v Warwickshire County Council* [1983] IRLR 126 HL.

[124] *Berwick Salmon Fisheries Co Ltd v Rutherford* [1991] IRLR 203; see also *Flack v Kodak Ltd* [1986] IRLR 255 CA, where a group of seasonal employees in a photo finishing department tried to establish their continuity of employment.

[125] *Sillars v Charrington Fuels Ltd* [1989] IRLR 152 CA.

time the employee prepared for the coming year's teaching and the EAT decided that this amounted to a temporary cessation of work.[126]

(3) Absence from work in circumstances that, by custom or arrangement, the employee 'is regarded as continuing in the employment of his employer for any purposes'.[127] In *Curr v Marks and Spencer plc*[128] the Court of Appeal ruled that a four-year absence under a child break scheme broke continuity because the ex-employee was not regarded by both parties as continuing in the employment of the employer for any purpose. Similarly, in *Booth v United States of America*[129] the employees were employed on a series of fixed-term contracts with a gap of about two weeks between each contract. On each return to work they were given the same employee number, the same tools and equipment and the same lockers. Despite the employees arguing that this arrangement was designed to defeat the underlying purpose of the legislation, the EAT could not find an arrangement which would require, in advance of the break, some discussion and agreement that continuity could be preserved. It was clear that the employers did not want such an arrangement. Neither is it likely that an agreement made subsequent to the absence could be used to preserve continuity. Section 212(3)(c) ERA 1996 envisages the arrangement being in place when the employee is absent, so an agreement between an employer and an employee that a break in work would not affect continuity could not be supported because it was made after the employee's return.[130]

3.7.4 Continuity and industrial disputes

A week does not count for the purposes of computing continuity of service if during that week, or any part of it, the employee takes part in a strike.[131] In contrast, periods when the employee is subject to a lock-out do count for continuity purposes. However, in neither case is continuity itself broken.[132] *Bloomfield v Springfield Hosiery Finishing Co Ltd*[133] concerned a dispute which resulted in a strike by employees. They were summarily dismissed and the employer began to recruit replacement employees. As a result the strike ended and the employees returned to work. Subsequently the employees were dismissed for reasons of redundancy. Their claims for redundancy payments were rejected because, it was said, they did not have sufficient continuity of employment, as a result of being dismissed during the strike. The court held, however, that the term 'employee' should be given a wide meaning and that the strikers continued to be employees during the strike or until the employer engaged other persons or permanently discontinued the work that they were employed to do.

---

[126] *University of Aston in Birmingham v Malik* [1984] ICR 492; see also *Ford v Warwickshire County Council* [1983] IRLR 126 HL.
[127] Section 212(3)(c) ERA 1996.
[128] [2003] IRLR 74.
[129] [1999] IRLR 16.
[130] *Morris v Walsh Western UK Ltd* [1997] IRLR 562; see now *London Probation Board v Kirkpatrick* [2005] IRLR 443.
[131] Section 216(1) ERA 1996.
[132] Section 216(2) ERA 1996.
[133] [1972] ICR 91.

3.7.5 Continuity and change of employer

Although the continuity provisions normally apply to employment by one employer,[134] there are situations where a transfer from one employer to another can preserve continuity of employment.[135] One such situation is when there is a relevant transfer under the Transfer of Undertakings (Protection of Employment) Regulations 1981[136] (see Chapter 10). The Transfer of Undertakings Regulations create a situation where it is as if the original contract of employment was agreed with the new employer. Thus an employee's period of service will transfer to the new employer.

Where the trade, business[137] or undertaking is transferred to a new employer, then continuity is also preserved by section 218(2) ERA 1996 and the employee's length of service moves to the new employer, although, as pointed out in *Nokes v Doncaster Collieries*,[138] this is likely to require the knowledge and consent of the employee. There have been difficulties in defining when a business has transferred, rather than a disposal of assets taking place. *Melon v Hector Powe Ltd*[139] concerned the disposal, by the employer, of one of two factories to another company. The disposal included the transfer of the work in progress and all the employees in the factory. The court held that there was a distinction between a transfer of a going concern, which amounted to a transfer of a business which remains the same business, but in different hands, and the disposal of part of the assets of a business.[140] It is employees in the former situation who are able to rely on section 218 ERA 1996. There are a number of specific situations where continuity is preserved:[141]

(1) if a contract of employment between a corporate body and an employee is modified by an Act of Parliament so that a new body is substituted as the employer;

(2) if on the death of an employer, an employee is taken into employment by the personal representatives or trustees of the deceased;

(3) if there is a change in the partners, personal representatives or trustees that employ a person;[142]

(4) if the employee is taken into the employment of another employer who is an associated employer of the employee's current employer;[143]

(5) if an employee of the governors of a school maintained by a local education authority is taken into the employment of the authority, or vice versa;

(6) if a person in relevant[144] employment with a health service employer is taken into such relevant employment by another such employer.

---

[134] Section 218(1) ERA 1996.
[135] See section 218(2)–(10) ERA 1996.
[136] SI 1981/1794.
[137] Business is defined in section 235 ERA 1996 as including a trade or profession and includes any activity carried on by a body of persons (whether corporate or unincorporated).
[138] [1940] AC 1014 HL.
[139] [1980] IRLR 477 HL.
[140] The court cited a speech to this effect by Lord Denning in *Lloyd v Brassey* [1969] ITR 199.
[141] Section 218(3)–(10) ERA 1996.
[142] See *Stevens v Bower* [2004] IRLR 957.
[143] See *Hancill v Marcon Engineering Ltd* [1990] IRLR 51; a transfer from an American company to one in the UK, where both were controlled by a Dutch company, was enough to ensure that the employee had transferred to an associate employer.
[144] 'Relevant' means those undergoing professional training who need to move employers for that training; section 218(9) ERA 1996; section 218(10) defines health service employers.

Section 219 ERA 1996 provides that the Secretary of State may make provisions for preserving continuity of employment. The current regulations are the Employment Protection (Continuity of Employment) Regulations 1996,[145] which serve, in regulation 2, to protect continuity of employment, in relation to a dismissal, where an employee is making a complaint about dismissal or making a claim in accordance with a dismissal procedures agreement.[146] Continuity is also protected, in relation to a dismissal, as a result of any action taken by a conciliation officer or the making of a compromise agreement (see Chapter 5).

3.8 Specific types of employment relationship

3.8.1 Agency staff

The employment agency industry is an important part of the United Kingdom economy. It grew from an industry that merely supplied domestic staff to the current-day one that supplies individuals on a wide range of skills and levels. It is estimated that about 1 million temporary staff go out on assignments each week and that the employment/recruitment industry has annual sales of about £23 billion.[147]

3.8.1.1 The draft Directive

In March 2002 the European Commission published its latest proposal for a Directive on the working conditions for temporary agency workers[148] after the failure of the social partners to come to an agreement on the issue in May 2001. This is the latest stage of a long saga beginning when the Commission published its first proposal more than 25 years ago in 1982. One of the purposes of the initiative is to raise the status of temporary work. It is regarded as an important element in the new flexible economy which the EU hopes will create more and better jobs in the future.

The purpose of the Directive, as described, is to be twofold (Article 2). First, the principle of non-discrimination is to be applied to temporary workers in order to improve the quality and status of such work. Interestingly, nowhere in the Directive is the word 'temporary' defined, so it would presumably apply equally to a very short-term posting of a few hours and a longer-term placement which could be over a number of years. It is an interesting thought that part of the objective of the Fixed-term Work Directive was concerned to stop the abuse of fixed-term contracts by limiting the number of such contracts before a person would be assumed to be a permanent employee. In comparison there is no such issue with temporary agency work. Indeed temporary work is to be encouraged and its status improved. Why is there this difference? The second purpose contained in Article 2 is that the Directive aims to establish a suitable framework for the use of temporary work 'to contribute to the smooth functioning of the labour and employment market'.

---

[145] SI 1996/3147.
[146] See section 210 ERA 1996.
[147] See the web site of the Recruitment and Employment Confederation, www.rec.uk.com.
[148] COM (2002) 149.

Article 1(1) specifies that it applies to the contract of employment or the employment relationship which exists between a temporary agency and the worker who is posted to a user undertaking to work under its supervision. The final definition as to who will be covered is, as usual, left to the Member State, as a worker is defined as someone who is protected as such under national law. It is perhaps unlikely that some agency temporary workers will be covered. It may be difficult to show an employment relationship with those that work under the guise of a limited liability company. An example of such a complex, but not unusual, employment situation is found in *Hewlett-Packard Ltd v O'Murphy*.[149] Here the individual concerned formed a private limited company which then entered into a contract with the agency which in turn had a contract with Hewlett-Packard. This case concerned the relationship between the worker and the user company. He failed to show that there was an employment relationship between the two, but the relationship with the agency must also be unclear.

Article 3(2) does specify that people may not be excluded solely on the basis that they are part-time workers or on fixed-term contracts within the meaning of the Directives on part-time work and fixed-term contracts.

The temporary worker is to receive at least as favourable treatment in terms of basic working and employment conditions, including seniority in the job, as the comparable worker in the user enterprise. Basic working and employment conditions are those relating to working time, rest periods, night work, paid holidays, public holidays and pay. They also relate to work done by pregnant women, nursing mothers, children and young people, as well as any action taken to combat discrimination on other grounds. This seems an important list of terms, but there are some significant omissions. There is no mention of any notice period, so temporary staff can still, subject to any other issues, be removed at short notice. Neither is there any opportunity for any disciplinary or grievance appeals procedure. Presumably this is an issue that is assumed to be between the worker and the agency employer, even though any disciplinary or grievance matters are likely to be between the individual and the user enterprise. Lastly there is no mention of pension arrangements. The exclusion of these would make any attempt to lift the status of temporary agency workers to the same status as permanent workers meaningless.

There are three categories of temporary worker mentioned in the Directive. They may each receive differing levels of protection. The first is the worker who has a permanent contract of employment with an agency, so that they continue to be paid between assignments. Member States may exclude such workers from the principle of non-discrimination. This is regardless of the pay of such people. Permanent employees of the agency will not therefore have the opportunity to compare themselves with comparable workers from client businesses when they are working on a posting. The second category are those who are on a posting, or postings with the same employer, of less than six weeks. Member States are to be permitted to exclude these temporary workers from protection against discrimination on the grounds that they are a temporary worker. This will exclude large numbers of people. In France and Spain, as mentioned earlier, some 80% of temporary staff work on assignments of less than one month and all could be excluded. In

---

[149] [2002] IRLR 4.

a survey done by the UK Recruitment and Employment Confederation in early 2002, the responding agencies estimated that 64.4% of their temporary agency workers would be able to accumulate six weeks' or more employment with one employer. This would leave over one-third of all such staff in the United Kingdom excluded in this category. The final category appears to be everyone else, i.e. those posted on an assignment, or assignments, lasting for more than six weeks and who do not have a permanent contract of employment with the agency through which they work.

It is this issue that caused the negotiations between the social partners to break down. The employers' organisations were opposed to the idea that a temporary agency worker should be treated as favourably as employees in the host undertaking. This is despite the fact that relative experience is to be taken into account, which will mean, presumably, that the permanent member of staff will nearly always have more experience. It was even suggested that the comparison should be with permanent members of staff of the employment agency, the effect of which would be to neuter the aims of the Directive. If one is to have such a Directive and if one of its objectives is to increase the quality and status of temporary workers, there is no one realistically with whom they can be compared except with comparable staff in the host organisation.

The complexities of doing such comparisons do, however, appear to be considerable, especially in the commercial sector rather than the industrial sector. If all the comparators were earning a simple hourly rate, then the comparison would be relatively easy. It is when all the comparators are on a salary scale, as many are in the public sector, that the matter becomes complicated. Each temporary agency worker will need to have their experience assessed in order to arrive at the correct pay for the work concerned. Perhaps employers will be tempted to arrange the work done by temporary staff in such a way as to ensure that there are no comparable workers occupying an 'identical or similar post' (Article 3(1)).

Like the Directive and Regulations concerning part-time work, temporary agency workers are to be notified of permanent vacancies in the user enterprise to give them the opportunity to find permanent employment (Article 6). In addition measures will need to be taken to improve access to training both in the agency employer and in the user enterprise.

3.8.1.2 Agency/worker relationship

One of the questions for the courts has been to identify the employer of the staff concerned. Although the particular facts of each case will be important, the possible options are:

(1) whether the individual is working under a contract for services;
(2) whether there is a global contract of employment between the individual and the agency, covering all the assignments on which a temporary worker may be sent;
(3) whether there is a contract of employment for each individual assignment.

McMeechan v Secretary of State for Employment[150] concerned a temporary worker who completed a series of individual assignments through an employment agency. He was given a job sheet and a standard written statement of terms and conditions for each assignment. The statement specified that he was providing services as a self-employed

---

[150] [1997] IRLR 353.

worker and was not operating under a contract of service, although the agency did deduct tax and national insurance contributions. When the agency became insolvent, the individual made a claim to the Secretary of State for wages owed. The claim was refused because, it was argued, the individual was not an employee of the insolvent company. The Court of Appeal examined two aspects of the relationship between the agency and the individual. The first was the general relationship covering the whole period during which the individual was used by the agency and the second was the relationship during any specific engagement on which the agency had used the individual. The court considered[151] *Wickens v Champion Employment*[152] which looked at the general relationship and concerned an attempt to show that all temporary staff of an agency were working under contracts of employment. This failed because:

> the relationship between the employers and the temporaries seems to us wholly to lack the elements of continuity, and care of the employer for the employee, that one associates with a contract of service.

The question for the court on the individual assignment was whether this could amount to a contract of service or not. The arguments for there being a contract for services were that there was an express statement that the individual was self-employed and the freedom which the worker had to work for a particular client on a self-employed basis. On the side of there being a contract of service were the reserved power of the agency to dismiss for misconduct, the power to bring any assignment to an end, the establishment of a grievance procedure and the stipulation of an hourly rate of pay, which in turn was subject to deductions for unsatisfactory timekeeping, work, attitude or misconduct. The court concluded that:

> when those indications are set against each other, and the specific engagement is looked at as a whole in all its terms, the general impression which emerges is that the engagement involved in this single assignment gave rise, despite the label put on it by the parties, to a contract of service between the temporary worker and the contractor.

In *Dacas v Brook Street Bureau*[153] it was stated that formal written contracts between a woman and an agency and between that agency and the end user relating to the work to be done for the end user did not necessarily preclude the implication of a contract of employment between the woman and the end user. As a matter of law, when an issue is raised about the status of an applicant in unfair dismissal proceedings, an employment tribunal is required to consider whether there is an implied contract between the parties who have no express contract with one another. This view was supported by the Court of Appeal in *Cable & Wireless plc v Muscat*.[154] The court stated that in cases involving a triangular relationship consisting of a worker, an employment agency and an end user, the tribunal should consider the possibility of an implied contract between the worker and the end user. In this case such a contract was held to exist as the individual had been employed

---

[151] The court contrasted the judgments in *McLeod v Hellyer Brothers Ltd* [1987] IRLR 232, which concerned Hull trawlermen who worked on periodic agreements, and *Nethermere (St Neots) Ltd v Gardiner* [1984] ICR 612, which concerned home workers with no fixed hours who were paid by results.

[152] [1984] ICR 365.

[153] [2004] IRLR 358.

[154] [2006] IRLR 355.

and then, at the employer's request, become a contractor via an employment agency. The court held that the end user was under an obligation to provide work and the worker was under an obligation to attend their premises and do the work, subject to their control and supervision. According to the EAT, in *James v London Borough of Greenwich*,[155] it will, however, be unusual to find a contract of employment in such a situation, the important feature being that the end user cannot insist on the agency providing a particular worker.[156] It is not necessary to look for a contract between the end user and the worker providing that the arrangements are genuine. This will be even less likely if the worker already has an express contract of employment with the agency. In such a situation the employee will have protection from unfair dismissal and there is no good policy reason for extending that protection to a second employer.[157]

3.8.1.3 Employment agencies and businesses

The private employment industry has been regulated since 1973 when the Employment Agencies Act 1973 came into force. This contained a system for licensing and regular inspections by the Department of Employment. The implementation of this Act was changed by the Conduct of Employment Agencies and Employment Businesses Regulations 2003,[158] which came into effect in April 2004.

The 1973 Act and the 2003 Regulations distinguish between employment businesses and employment agencies. Employment businesses are those that are concerned with the supply of temporary staff, whilst employment agencies are those that are concerned with the supply of work seekers to fill permanent vacancies with client organisations.[159] Many organisations are both employment businesses and employment agencies.

The main provisions of the Act and the Regulations are:

(1) Neither an employment agency nor employment business may charge fees to work seekers for finding them work, or seeking to find them work. Neither an agency nor an employment business may make help to a work seeker conditional upon using other services which require a fee. There is a limitation on the terms in contracts between employment businesses and hirers preventing temporary workers from taking up permanent jobs unless a fee is paid to the employment business first.

(2) An employment business may not introduce a work seeker to a hirer to perform the normal tasks carried out by a worker who is taking part in an industrial dispute or other industrial action, unless it is an unofficial strike or industrial action, i.e. one that does not take place within the rules governing such actions contained in the Trade Union and Labour Relations (Consolidation) Act 1992.

(3) Employment businesses are not able to withhold pay due to a temporary worker just because the worker has not obtained a signed worksheet from the hirer.

---

[155] [2007] IRLR 168.

[156] Most people working in the agency business or Human Resource Management might disagree with this statement.

[157] This was the situation in *Cairns v Visteon UK Ltd* [2007] IRLR 175 where the worker had a contract of employment with the agency, but tried to establish that she also had one with the end user.

[158] SI 2003/3319.

[159] See section 13(1)–(3) Employment Agencies Act 1973.

(4) When an agency or business first offers to provide services to a work seeker, then the agency or business must provide the work seeker with details of their terms of business and fees, if any. The agency or business will obtain the agreement of the work seeker about fees, if any, and the type of work the agency or business will try to find for the work seeker.

(5) Employment businesses must agree whether the work seeker is, or will be, employed under a contract of service or a contract for services (see above). The work seeker will also be given an undertaking that the business will pay him or her for the work that he or she does, regardless of whether the business is paid by the hirer. Other terms of business will include the rate of remuneration paid to the work seeker and the minimum rate of remuneration to be paid to the employment business, details of any entitlements to holidays and to payment in respect of holidays.

(6) Similar requirements are imposed upon employment agencies to explain to work seekers what services will be provided and details of any fees to be paid to the agency for work finding services, although fees may only be charged to work seekers wanting work in such areas as sport, music, dance and theatre.

(7) Agencies and businesses are required to keep documentation showing the work seeker's agreement to the terms of business and any changes to them. Neither an agency nor a hirer may introduce or supply a work seeker unless the agency or business has sufficient information about the hirer, the dates on which the work seeker is required and the duration of the work, the position to be filled and the experience, training and qualifications necessary to work in the position, including the rate of remuneration to be paid to the work seeker. There are similar conditions concerning the finding out of information about a work seeker before that person can be introduced to a hirer. Agencies and employment businesses must obtain references on job seekers wishing to work with vulnerable persons.

(8) Every advertisement must carry the full name of the agency or business and state the nature of the work, its location and the minimum qualifications necessary when advertising rates of pay.

(9) Employment agencies must not introduce an employer to a young person under the age of 18 years if that person is attending school or has just left school, unless that person has received vocational guidance from their local careers service.

(10) There are strict rules on record keeping.

Generally the Act and the Regulations regulate the relationship between the hirer and the agency or business and the relationship between the job seeker and the agency or business. They set down the requirements for communicating of information between all the parties involved and the terms of the agreements between each of the parties.

Anyone who contravenes the prohibition on charging fees to work seekers, fails to comply with regulations to secure the proper conduct of the agency or business, falsifies records or fails, without reasonable excuse, to comply with a prohibition order, will be guilty of an offence and subject to a fine not exceeding £5,000. There is a further fine of up to £1,000 for obstructing any officer from carrying out enforcement functions.

An employment tribunal may make an order prohibiting a person (or company) from carrying on, or being concerned with, an employment agency or business for up to ten years on the grounds of the person being unsuitable because of misconduct or any other sufficient reason. In addition, terms of contracts with hirers or work seekers which are invalid in terms of the Act or Regulations will be, of course, unenforceable. Any contravention of the Act or Regulations which causes damage, including death or injury, will be actionable in civil law.

3.8.1.4 Gangmasters

Gangmasters is a term used to refer to individuals or groups of individuals who hire out 'gangs' of workers for the completion of certain tasks, most commonly in the agricultural and parts of the fisheries sector. Their activities have fallen outside the regulatory controls covering employment agencies and businesses. It appears that the individuals making up these gangs are often immigrant workers, sometimes illegal, who work long hours for low pay and are generally exploited. The worst incident in recent times was the drowning of 21 Chinese cockle pickers in Morecambe Bay in 2004. It has been estimated that there are up to 60,000 such workers living on very low pay in the United Kingdom.

In response to these issues the Government adopted the Gangmasters (Licensing) Act 2004. This Act makes provision for the licensing of activities concerning the supply of workers involved in:

- agricultural work;
- gathering shellfish;
- processing or packaging agricultural produce or shellfish or fish products.

The Act established the Gangmasters Licensing Authority which will issue licences to gangmasters and keep under review the activities of persons acting as gangmasters. A person or organisation may not be a gangmaster without a licence issued by the Authority. A register of licences is to be established which will be accessible to members of the public.

Persons who act as gangmasters without a licence or with false documents are guilty of an offence and can be fined plus imprisoned for up to 12 months. Similarly a person may not knowingly use an unlicensed gangmaster. Such a person will also be liable to a fine and imprisonment for a period up to 51 weeks. The Act also allows the Government minister to appoint enforcement officers who will ensure that only licensed gangmasters are operating. These officers will have wide powers to inspect records and obtain information. Obstruction of such officers is a criminal offence, allowing fines and imprisonment of the obstructors.

3.8.2 Fixed-term contracts

The number of employees on fixed-term contracts increased by over 100,000 between 1994 and 2001 and the Labour Force Survey for Spring 2001 estimated that the total was then 1,396,000 individuals. This figure includes significant numbers of seasonal and casual workers. The majority of those working on fixed-term contracts are women (some 55%), which is reflected in the rest of the European Community. There are also some discrepancies related to ethnic origin: some 5.5% of white employees are on such contracts, compared to 7% of black employees and 8–9% of those employees of an Indian/Pakistani/Bengali ethnic origin. Of no surprise to those that work in the public sector is the fact that over half of all employees on fixed-term contracts are in that sector. More disappointingly is that some 70% of all those who have been on fixed-term contracts for more than two years are in the public sector. Perhaps reflecting the nature of charity funding, there are also some 60,000 employees of charities who are on these types of contract.

Fixed-term work makes up a significant amount of work in the EU, with approximately 12.2% of its working population being employed on such contracts. On 18 March 1999 the Social Partners at European Community level (see Chapter 2) concluded a Framework Agreement on fixed-term work. This in turn became Directive 99/70/EC on fixed-term work.[160] This Directive comes after a lengthy period of the European Commission attempting to obtain agreement amongst the Member States. Proposals were first introduced in 1990 and, until 1999, only one measure had been adopted.[161]

The purposes of the Framework Agreement are to:

(a) improve the quality of fixed-term work by ensuring the application of the principle of non-discrimination;
(b) establish a framework to prevent abuse arising from the use of successive fixed-term employment contracts or relationships.[162]

A fixed-term worker is defined by clause 3 of the Agreement as:

A person having an employment contract or relationship entered into directly by an employer and a worker where the end of the employment contract or relationship is determined by objective conditions such as reaching a specific date, completing a specific task, or an occurrence of specific event.

The Agreement introduces a principle of non-discrimination against fixed-term workers,[163] with stricter controls over the renewal of such contracts.

That such workers need to be protected is illustrated in *Booth v United States of America*.[164] Despite arguing that the arrangement for two-week breaks between contracts was designed to defeat the legislation, the applicants were unsuccessful in their claim for a redundancy payment, even though, apart from three two-week breaks, they had some five years' service. One of the concerns of the Fixed-Term Work Directive is to encourage some objective justification for continuing fixed-term contracts of employment.

Section 18 Employment Relations Act 1999 was a first step by the Government in implementing the requirements under the Fixed-term Work Directive. It removed section 197(1) and (2) ERA 1996, which allowed individuals with a fixed-term contract of one year or more to opt out of the unfair dismissal provisions contained in Part X ERA 1996.[165]

---

[160] Council Directive 99/70/EC of 28 June 1999 concerning the Framework Agreement on fixed-term work OJ L175/43 10.7.99.
[161] Council Directive 91/383/EEC supplementing the measures to encourage improvements in the safety and health at work of workers with a fixed duration employment relationship or a temporary employment relationship OJ L206 29.7.91.
[162] Clause 1 Framework Agreement.
[163] Clause 4 Framework Agreement.
[164] [1999] IRLR 16.
[165] See Employment Relations Act 1999 (Commencement No 2 and Transitional and Savings Provisions) Order 1999, SI 1999/2830.

Section 45 Employment Act 2002 provided the authority for the introduction of the Fixed-term Employees (Prevention of Less Favourable Treatment) Regulations.[166] They define a fixed-term contract as either a contract of employment which is made for a specific term, or a contract that terminates automatically on the completion of a particular task, or the occurrence or non-occurrence of any specific event except one resulting from the employee reaching normal retirement age or such conduct of the employee that might entitle an employer to summarily dismiss that employee.[167] The ability of the parties to give notice to terminate does not prevent the contract from being one for a fixed term.[168]

The scope of the unfair dismissal provisions in the ERA 1996 has been widened to include these 'task' contracts of employment.[169] The ending of these contracts will be regarded as a dismissal for the purposes of the Act. As a result an individual on such a contract will gain a number of statutory rights which are currently enjoyed by permanent employees. These include the right not to be unfairly dismissed, the right to a written statement of reasons for dismissal and the right to statutory redundancy payments. The ERA 1996 is also to be amended so that those on 'task' contracts of less than three months will have the right to minimum notice periods in the same way as permanent employees.

A number of important decisions have been taken about which individuals are to be protected and about which are to be excluded. The Government has decided to apply the regulations to employees only. The approach is different from that taken by Part-time Workers Regulations. Those who are not treated as employees are to be excluded. Whilst recognising the problems associated with including non-employees, the decision does have the result of excluding significant numbers of individuals who work on fixed-term contracts and who, apart from their employment status, are indistinguishable from permanent employees or employees on fixed-term contracts.

The definition of the comparator uses the same approach as that used by the Part-time Workers Regulations. The individual with whom a fixed-term worker is to be compared is someone who, at the time when the alleged treatment takes place, is employed by the same employer and is engaged on the same or broadly similar work, having regard for whether they have similar skills and qualifications, if this is relevant. The comparable permanent employee must work or be based at the same establishment, although other locations will be considered if there is no one appropriate at the same establishment.[170]

The Regulations provide that a fixed-term employee has the right not to be treated by the employer less favourably than a comparable permanent employee with regard to the terms of the contract or by being subject to any other detriment related to being a fixed-term employee.[171] This includes less favourable treatment in relation, first, to any period of service qualification related to a condition of service, secondly, to training opportunities and, thirdly, to the opportunity to secure permanent employment in the establishment.

---

[166] The Fixed-term Employees (Prevention of Less Favourable Treatment) Regulations 2002, SI 2001/2034, which came into force on 1 October 2002.

[167] Regulation 1(2).

[168] *Allen v National Australia Group Ltd* [2004] IRLR 847.

[169] For these purposes they are referred to as limited term contracts.

[170] Regulation 2.

[171] Regulation 3. In *Department of Work and Pensions v Webley* [2005] IRLR 288, the Court of Appeal ruled that termination by simple effluxion of time cannot, of itself, constitute less favourable treatment.

Importantly, however, the Government has decided to include less favourable treatment in relation to pay and pensions. As a result, the rules on statutory sick pay, rights to guarantee payments and payments on medical suspension are amended to ensure that fixed-term employees and comparable permanent employees are treated in the same way. Similarly, where there are qualifying rules for membership of pension schemes, then these rules should be the same for fixed-term and comparable permanent employees, unless the different treatment can be objectively justified. The Government believes that this will help reduce pay inequalities because the majority of fixed-term employees are women, so the inclusion of pay and pensions will help the reduction of inequalities between the sexes.

There is a defence of objective justification to the provisions of the Regulations.[172] Interestingly, the Government has opted to allow the 'package' approach, as an alternative to the 'item by item' approach, when deciding whether an individual has been treated less favourably on the grounds of being a fixed-contract employee. It will not be necessary to compare each part of the terms of employment and ensure that each individual part is comparable to the permanent employee, unless the employer so wishes. Such treatment is objectively justifiable if the terms of the fixed-term employee's contract of employment, as a whole, are at least as favourable as the permanent comparator. This presumably means that it will be permissible to, say, pay a higher salary in compensation for other benefits such as holidays and pensions, so long as the value of the 'package' overall is equivalent or better than that of the permanent employee.

If an employee considers that he or she has been treated less favourably on the grounds of being a fixed-term employee, which is not objectively justifiable, then the employee is entitled to request a written statement giving particulars of the reasons for the treatment. This must be provided by the employer within 21 days of the request. Such a statement will be admissible in any future employment tribunal proceedings.[173] A dismissal connected to enforcing an employee's rights under the Regulations will be treated as an unfair dismissal.[174]

Unfortunately, the Regulations seem unlikely to stop the repeated use of fixed-term contracts, which seems a rather strange outcome. Where there is a succession of fixed-term contracts resulting in the employee being continuously employed for four years or more, then the contract will automatically be deemed a permanent contract, unless there is objective justification suggesting otherwise.[175] The problem comes in the definition of continuous employment contained in the ERA 1996. Any week during which a contract of employment exists will count towards continuity of employment (section 212(1) ERA 1996).[176] Thus any sort of substantial break not covered by section 212(3) ERA 1996 is likely to break continuity and make the Regulations ineffective. There is an issue with this provision following the case of *Adeneler*[177] at the European Court of Justice. This case concerned a number of workers employed by the Greek Milk Organisation, ELOG, who had been employed on a number of fixed-term contracts. One of the issues in the case was

---

[172] Regulation 4.
[173] Regulation 5.
[174] Regulation 6.
[175] Regulation 8.
[176] See *Sweeney v J & S Henderson Ltd* (1999) IRLR 306.
[177] Case C-21/204 *Adeneler v Ellinikos Organismos Galaktos* [2006] IRLR 716.

that Greek legislation provided that continuity was broken if there was a gap of more than 20 days. The Court of Justice recognised that the decision as to what constituted continuity had been left to the Member State to decide. It held, however, that this discretion could not be exercised in such a way as to compromise one of the aims of the Directive, namely to prevent the misuse of fixed-term contracts. It therefore held that a gap of 20 days allowed such misuse to continue and was not in accord with the aims of the Directive.

If an employee considers that he or she has become a permanent employee because of the rules, then the employee may request a written statement from the employer stating that he or she is now a permanent employee or, if not, the reasons why the individual is to remain a fixed-term employee. This statement must be given within 21 days and is admissible in future employment tribunal proceedings.[178]

Provision is made for some flexibility as the maximum period can be varied by collective or workforce agreements. This opportunity for flexibility may, however, be of limited benefit. The agreement will be reached with employee representatives, the majority of whom are likely to be permanent employees. This may not be a problem for situations where the employees are represented by a trade union and reach a collective agreement on the issue. It might be a problem where employees elect their own representatives, the majority of whom will not be affected. It is more likely to be a problem if the workforce agreement is reached by a majority vote of the workforce (this can be done where there are fewer than 20 employees). It is perhaps questionable whether employees in such situations will resist management demands for a more flexible approach if the majority are unaffected by the proposals.

Employees will be able to claim unfair dismissal if they are dismissed with regard to their rights under the Regulations. They will take their claim for less favourable treatment to an employment tribunal which will have the right to award compensation to the claimant and recommend action for the employer to take, within a specific period, to obviate or reduce the adverse effect complained of. The compensation is to be limited, however, as the tribunal is specifically forbidden from awarding damages for injury to feelings (although such claims will still be possible if the individual was dismissed for exercising their rights under the Regulations). The matters that will be taken into account will be the loss of benefit arising from the infringement and any reasonable expenses of the complainant as a result of the infringement.

3.8.3 Part-time contracts

The European Directive on part-time work[179] was adopted as a result of a Framework Agreement reached by the social partners as part of the Social Dialogue process (see Chapter 2).

---

[178] Regulation 9.
[179] Directive 97/81/EC of 15 December 1997 concerning the Framework Agreement on part-time work concluded by UNICE, CEEP and ETUC OJ L14/9 20.1.98.

3.8.3.1 Discrimination against part-time workers

The treatment of part-time workers is a discrimination issue, because the great majority of part-time workers are female.[180] In the United Kingdom, women represent 33% of all those working full-time and 81% of all those working part-time. Some 44% of women in employment work part-time.[181] Evidence given by the Equal Opportunities Commission to the Education and Employment Committee of the House of Commons contained examples of how part-time workers were disadvantaged. Over 75% of female part-timers, for example, earn less than the average hourly wage. About 54% of male part-timers and 42% of female part-timers work for employers who do not have a pension scheme, compared with 25% of full-time employees. Part-time work also is still mostly confined to the low paid in a relatively narrow range of occupations. There appear to be limited opportunities for part-time employees to be promoted.

According to the Equal Opportunities Commission,[182] some considerable progress was made as a result of the Employment Protection (Part-time Employees) Regulations 1995.[183] These regulations removed the rule that employees were required to work a minimum number of hours before they were entitled to certain employment protection rights already enjoyed by full-timers. They followed the decision of the House of Lords in *R v Secretary of State for Employment, ex parte Equal Opportunities Commission*,[184] which held that aspects of the minimum number of hours rule were incompatible with Article 119 EEC (now 141), the Equal Pay Directive[185] and the Equal Treatment Directive.[186] The 1995 Regulations extended protection to an estimated 689,000 part-time employees, of whom 574,000 (83%) were female.

3.8.3.2 The Framework Agreement on part-time work

The purpose of the Agreement, according to clause 1, is to provide for the removal of discrimination against part-time workers and to improve the quality of part-time work, as well as to facilitate the development of part-time work on a voluntary basis. A part-time worker is defined in clause 3.1 as:

> An employee whose normal hours of work, calculated on a weekly basis or on average over a period of employment of up to one year, are less than the normal hours of work of a comparable full-time worker.

The justification for the measure is contained in the preamble to the Agreement. It is a measure that:

- promotes both employment and equal opportunities for men and women;
- helps with the requirements of competition by creating a more flexible organisation of working time;

---

[180] See *R v Secretary of State, ex parte Equal Opportunities Commission* [1994] IRLR 176 HL.
[181] See Office for National Statistics, 'Women in the Labour Market', *Labour Market Trends*, March 1999, p 103.
[182] *Hansard* HC vol 2 col 346, session 1998–99.
[183] SI 1995/31.
[184] [1994] IRLR 176 HL.
[185] Directive 75/117/EEC.
[186] Directive 76/207/EEC.

- facilitates access to part-time work for men and women in preparation for retirement;
- reconciles professional and family life;
- facilitates the take-up of education and training opportunities.

The Agreement applies to part-time workers, but there is an express provision (clause 2.2) permitting Member States to exclude casual part-time workers for objective reasons.

The comparable full-time worker has a narrow definition. It is someone who is a full-time worker in the same establishment, having the same type of employment or employment relationship and who is engaged on the same or similar work as the part-timer. Due regard is to be given to other considerations which include seniority, qualifications and skill. Where there is no full-time comparator, there is still a comparison to be made. It is to be done with reference to:

> the applicable collective agreement or, where there is no applicable collective agreement, in accordance with national law, collective agreements or practice.

It is perhaps difficult to give this any meaning in the United Kingdom where consultation with the social partners takes place less often than in many other countries in the European Community. Importantly, however, there is no suggestion that there should be a situation where there are no comparators. The Agreement states that the comparison should be with the full-time comparator and, if there is no such person, then in accordance with national law, collective agreements or practice. It does not appear to suggest that, in the absence of a full-time comparator, there should be no comparison at all.

Clause 4 establishes the principle that part-time workers should not be treated less favourably than their full-time comparators merely because they work part-time, unless the difference in treatment can be objectively justified. Objective justification presumably will mean a reason for the difference in treatment that is not related to the individual working part-time. In *Bilka-Kaufhaus*[187] the ECJ considered the position of part-time shop sales assistants who were excluded from an occupational pension scheme when full-time shop assistants were included. The Court concluded that an employer may be able to justify the exclusion of part-timers, in relation to a sex discrimination claim, where it represents a real need on the part of the undertaking, and the means chosen to meet this need are appropriate to achieving that objective.

Where appropriate the principle of *pro rata temporis* should apply and, after consultation with the social partners, Member States may, where justified by objective reasons, make access to particular conditions of employment subject to periods of service, time worked or earnings.

Opportunities for part-time work are to be encouraged. This includes the removal of obstacles to part-time work and giving consideration to requests from workers to transfer from full-time to part-time work and vice versa. A worker's refusal to transfer from full-time to part-time work, or vice versa, is not to be treated as a valid reason for termination of that worker.

---

[187] Case 170/84 [1986] IRLR 317 ECJ.

3.8.3.3 The Part-time Workers Regulations

The Part-time Workers (Prevention of Less Favourable Treatment) Regulations (the PTW Regulations) came into force on 1 July 2000.[188]

The Regulations and, perhaps, the Directive represent an attempt to improve the situation of part-time workers. The Department of Trade and Industry's press release that accompanied the Regulations quoted the Secretary of State as saying that:

> The proposals I am putting forward today will ensure that part-timers are no longer discriminated against. This revised package safeguards the position of part-timers whilst avoiding unnecessary burdens on business.

In an attempt to achieve these two somewhat contradictory aims the Secretary of State stated that:

> ... the regulations will be introduced with a light touch by ensuring that comparisons can only be made between part-time and full-time workers with the same type of contract.

The effect of this is seen in the DTI's summary of the Regulatory Impact Assessment which accompanied the Regulations. The Assessment stated that there are some 6 million part-time employees in Great Britain. Of these the DTI estimates that 1 million have a comparable full-time employee against whom it is necessary to compare the terms and conditions of part-timers. Of these, it is estimated, some 400,000 will benefit from the equal treatment provisions. Large numbers of low-paid part-time workers will be excluded because there are no full-time comparators. It is difficult to understand how this justifies the Secretary of State's assertion that the regulations will 'ensure that part-timers are no longer discriminated against'.

Regulation 2(1) of the PTW Regulations identifies a full-time worker as someone who is paid wholly or partly by reference to the time worked, and, having regard to the custom and practice of the employer in relation to their other workers, is identifiable as a full-time worker. Regulation 2(2) has the same definition for part-time workers as this, except that they must be identifiable as part-time workers. The definition for a full-time comparator follows closely the definition in the Directive, although, in terms of defining where the comparator needs to be based, it does have a wider definition. Full-timers, in relation to the part-timers, need:

(1) to be employed by the same employer under the same type of contract;
(2) to be engaged in the same or broadly similar work having regard, where relevant, to whether they have similar levels of qualifications, skills and experience;
(3) to be based at the same establishment or, if there is no full-time comparator at the same establishment, at a different establishment.

Matthews v Kent Fire Authority[189] concerned a claim by part-time retained fire fighters that they were treated less favourably than full-time fire fighters. The Court of Appeal had concluded that although they were employed under the same type of contract they did not carry out the 'same or broadly similar work'. The House of Lords disagreed and stated

---

[188] SI 2000/1551.
[189] [2006] IRLR 367.

that in making the assessment particular attention should be given to the extent to which the work was exactly the same and to the importance of that work to the enterprise as a whole. If a large component of the work was the same, then the issue was whether the differences were so important that the work could not be regarded as the same or broadly similar. If part-time and full-time employees carry out the same work, but the full-timers do extra duties, this does not necessarily mean that the work is not the same or broadly similar.

It is a very demanding test for establishing whether an individual's job can be used as a comparator on which to base a claim for discrimination. The first issue, of course, is what happens if there is no full-time person who can meet the criteria. Where a workforce is made up entirely of part-time employees in a particular category, the regulations will be of no assistance in enabling them to claim discrimination on the basis of being a part-time worker.[190] One example might be a contract cleaning operation. All the employees concerned with cleaning might be part-time and all the supervisory, management and administration employees might be full-time. The result is that there is no full-time comparator on whom the cleaning staff can base a claim. These employees may be low paid because they are part-time and, perhaps, because they are not organised collectively, but they are unable to base a claim using the PTW Regulations. Although there may be a *prima facie* case for showing discrimination, it could not be a case based upon the PTW Regulations. Even the Government's own figures suggest that 80% of part-time workers will not have a full-time comparator available to them.

Regulations 3 and 4 provide an exception to the need for such a comparator. Where a full-time worker, following the termination or variation of the contract of employment, works fewer hours, the worker will be able to use him or herself in the previous full-time position as the comparable full-timer, for the purpose of deciding whether there has been less favourable treatment of a part-time worker. The same rule applies if a full-time worker returns to work and works fewer hours in the same job or a job at the same level, for the same employer, after an absence of less than 12 months. This is regardless of whether the absence followed a termination of employment or not.[191]

Regulation 5 establishes the principle of non-discrimination. A part-time worker has the right not to be treated less favourably than the employer treats a comparable full-time worker as regards the terms of the contract or by being subject to detriment by any act, or failure to act, by the employer. The right only applies if the treatment is on the grounds that the worker is part-time and that the treatment cannot be justified on objective grounds. In determining whether a part-timer has been treated less favourably, the principle of *pro rata temporis* applies. The one exception to this concerns overtime. Not paying overtime rates to a part-time worker until they have at least worked hours comparable to the basic working hours of the comparable full-time worker is not to be treated as less favourable treatment. *McMenemy v Capita Business Services Ltd*[192] concerned

---

[190] In *Wippel v Peek & Cloppenburg Gmbh* [2005] IRLR 211 the European Court of Justice suggested that a part-time casual worker might be covered by the Framework Agreement. However, Ms Wippel could not find a full-time comparator who worked on a casual basis.

[191] See also the provisions of flexible working contained in the EA 2002 – Chapter 9.

[192] [2007] IRLR 400.

a part-time worker who worked on Wednesdays, Thursdays and Fridays only at a call centre. The call centre operated seven days a week. All employees had a contract of employment which entitled them to time off in lieu when statutory holidays coincided with one of their working days. This meant that Mr McMenemy was not entitled to time off for statutory holidays that occurred on Mondays. Other colleagues who worked full-time did receive this time off. He complained that as a result he was being treated less favourably than a comparable full-time worker. He failed in his claim because the court held that the reason why he was not given time off for Monday statutory holidays was not solely because he was a part-time worker, but because he did not work on Mondays. In order to show less favourable treatment he had to show that the employer intended to treat him less favourably solely because he was a part-time worker. The reason here for the less favourable treatment was that he had agreed not to work on Mondays. A full-time worker who worked from Tuesday to Saturday would also not be entitled to the benefit of statutory holidays that fell on a Monday.

In the Government's compliance guidance, accompanying the PTW Regulations, the following examples are some of those given as arising from the principle of non-discrimination:

- previous or current part-time status should not of itself constitute a barrier to promotion;
- part-time workers should receive the same hourly rate as full-time workers;
- part-time workers should receive the same hourly rate of overtime pay as full-time workers, once they have worked more than the normal full-time hours;
- part-time workers should be able to participate in profit sharing or share option schemes available for full-time workers;
- employers should not discriminate between full-time and part-time workers over access to pension schemes;
- employers should not exclude part-timers from training simply because they work part-time;
- in selection for redundancy part-time workers must not be treated less favourably than full-time workers.

These examples apply, of course, only if the employer cannot objectively justify a distinction in treatment or if there is no full-time comparator, meeting the criteria provided, with whom the employees can relate.

3.8.3.4 Remedies

As with other discrimination measures, the employer or agent of the employer will be liable for anything done by an employee in the course of their employment.[193] There is a defence of having taken all reasonable steps to prevent the worker doing the act in the course of their employment.[194] There is the right not to be dismissed or suffer detriment as a result of exercising any rights under the regulations.[195] Interestingly, before a complainant brings a case to an employment tribunal they may request in writing from the employer the

---

[193] Regulation 11(1) PTW Regulations 2000.
[194] Regulation 11(3) PTW Regulations 2000.
[195] Regulation 7 PTW Regulations 2000.

reasons for the less favourable treatment. The worker is entitled to a reply within 21 days and that reply, or lack of it, is admissible in tribunal proceedings.[196] There may be conciliation by ACAS which will try to arrange a settlement.[197] The tribunal can award compensation, although not for injury to feelings, and make a recommendation for action by the employer to correct the fault.

3.8.4 Apprentices

Section 230(2) ERA 1996 defines a contract of employment as a contract of service or apprenticeship. The purpose of a contract of apprenticeship is to 'qualify the apprentice for his particular trade or calling'.[198] The execution of work for the employer is secondary.[199] It is distinct from an ordinary contract of employment because:

> although a contract of apprenticeship can be brought to an end by some fundamental frustrating event or repudiatory act, it is not terminable at will as a contract of employment is at common law.[200]

Edmunds v Lawson QC[201] was a case that was of great interest to law students wishing to progress to the Bar. It concerned the question as to whether a person who was offered and accepted an unfunded pupillage with a barrister's chambers was under a contract of apprenticeship with the chambers. If this were so, then the consequence would be that the pupil would be entitled to be paid at least to the level of the national minimum wage.[202] It was accepted that there was an offer of a pupillage and an acceptance of the offer. Consideration was held to be the claimant's promise to come as a pupil. This was held to be of value not only to the pupil, but also to the chambers and the individual pupil masters. The last requirement to establish a contractual relationship was an intention to enter legal relations. The High Court, in the absence of any express provisions, implied this intention from the subject matter of the agreement. There is a distinction between agreements which regulate business relations and those which regulate social arrangements. The former were likely to have legal consequences.[203] An offer, as in this case, to provide professional training was therefore likely to be a business relationship, thus establishing the necessary intent. The Court of Appeal agreed with the views of the High Court, except that, despite all this, it held that the resulting contract was not a contract of apprenticeship. The pupil could not therefore be defined as a worker in terms of the National Minimum Wage Act 1998. Such a relationship would require a mutual obligation on the part of the pupil master

---

[196] Regulation 6 PTW Regulations 2000.

[197] Introduced by the Part-time Workers (Prevention of Less Favourable Treatment) Regulations 2001, SI 2001/1107 as an amendment to section 18(1) ETA 1996 and section 203(2)(f) ERA 1996; Regulation 8 PTW Regulations 2000.

[198] *Wiltshire Police Authority v Wynn* [1981] 1 QB 95 CA. See *Flett v Matheson* [2005] IRLR 412 on the status of modern apprenticeship agreements.

[199] See *Wallace v CA Roofing Services Ltd* [1996] IRLR 435.

[200] *Ibid* at p 436.

[201] [2000] IRLR 391 CA.

[202] Section 54(2) and (3) National Minimum Wage Act 1998 offers a definition of worker and a contract of employment for the purposes of the Act.

[203] See, for further consideration of this, *Rose and Frank Company v JR Crompton Brothers Ltd* [1925] AC 445.

to provide training and on the part of the pupil to serve and work for the master and carry out all reasonable instructions. This latter obligation was missing from the relationship.

Further reading

Deakin, S. and Morris, G. *Labour Law* (4th edn, Hart Publishing, 2005), Chapter 3.

Painter, R. and Holmes, A., *Cases and Materials on Employment Law* (6th edn, Oxford University Press, 2006), Chapter 2, Sections 1–3.

Wynn, M. and Leighton, P., 'Will the real employer please stand up? Agencies, Client Companies and the employment status of the temporary agency worker' (2006) 35(3) *Industrial Law Journal* 301.

http://www.hmrc.gov.uk/employment-status/index.htm for the view on employment status of HM Revenue & Customs.

http://www.direct.gov.uk/en/Employment/Employees/EmploymentContractsAndConditions/index. htm for the official page on employment contracts, including employment status.

Visit **www.mylawchamber.co.uk/sargeant** to access legal updates, live web links and practice exam questions to test yourself on this chapter.

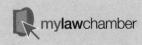

4

The Contract of Employment

4.1 Express terms

The Contracts of Employment Act 1963 required employers to give each employee a written statement setting out certain particulars of the employee's terms of service. This Act, subsequently amended and now contained in the ERA 1996, preceded an EEC Directive[1] on this issue and, rather unusually, the adoption of European legislation required little change in domestic law. The Directive required Member States to ensure that all employees received information 'of the essential aspects of the contract or employment relationship'.[2]

The express terms of a written contract will normally be conclusive in the event of a dispute. In *Gascol Conversions Ltd v JW Mercer*[3] the Court of Appeal held that:

> it is well settled that where there is a written contract of employment, as there was here, and the parties have reduced it to writing, it is the writing which governs their relations. It is not permissible to say they intended something different.

In this case the employees had signed a written statement accepting a new contract of employment. By way of contrast, in *Systems Floors (UK) Ltd v Daniel*,[4] the EAT concluded that a statement of terms and conditions of employment, given to the employee as a result of the employer's statutory obligations,[5] was only evidence of a contract of employment. In this case the employees had signed a document which, it was held, was an acknowledgement of the receipt of the statutory statement. The EAT concluded that this statement did not constitute a written contract between the parties. It was merely a document that stated the employer's views of the terms. It may provide strong *prima facie* evidence of what the terms of the contract are but it is not conclusive of the terms of the employment contract. However, it will place a heavy burden on the employer to show that the actual terms of the contract are different to the terms of the statement.

Article 2(2)(c) of the Directive specifies that the information given to the employee must include the title, grade or nature of the post and give a brief specification or description of the work. The ECJ has held that this provision is sufficiently precise and

---

[1] Council Directive 91/533/EEC on an employer's obligation to inform employees of the conditions applicable to the contract or the employment relationship OJ L288/32 18.10.91.
[2] *Ibid* article 2(1).
[3] [1974] IRLR 155 at p 157 CA.
[4] [1981] IRLR 475.
[5] Now section 1 ERA 1996.

unconditional to allow individuals to rely on it before the national courts (see Chapter 2 on direct effect). Although the written statement of terms is important evidence, employers must be allowed to provide evidence that they have made a mistake and provided incorrect terms.[6]

4.2 The statutory statement

Section 1 ERA 1996 provides that employees should receive a written statement of the particular terms of employment not later than two months after the beginning of employment. This statement may be given in instalments but must be complete not later than the two months, even if the employment ends within that period.[7] If a person, before the two months has passed, is to work outside the United Kingdom for a period of at least one month, then the statement must be given to them before they leave the country to commence work.[8]

The EA 2002[9] inserted new sections 7A and 7B into the ERA 1996. These provide that employers need not give a separate statement if they give employees a letter of engagement or a contract of employment containing the information that would have been given if it were contained in such a statement.[10] This document still needs to be given within the two-month period or it can be given in the form of a letter of engagement prior to the start of employment. In such a case the effective date of the document will be the date on which employment begins.[11]

Section 11 ERA 1996 allows an employee to make a reference to an employment tribunal if a statutory statement or an alternative document is not received, if the one received is incomplete, the employer has failed to provide a statement of any changes that take place.[12] If the employment has ceased, the reference must be made within three months of the cessation or such further time as the employment tribunal thinks was reasonably practicable. If the lack of, or incompleteness of, a statutory statement or alternative document becomes evident upon a claim being made under certain employment tribunal jurisdictions such as unfair dismissal or disability, sex or race discrimination, then the tribunal is required to increase the compensation awarded by an amount equivalent to between two and four weeks' pay.[13] Where compensation is not awarded the employment tribunal must award a minimum of two to four weeks' pay.[14]

The ERA 1996 provides the following minimum list of contents for the statement of terms and conditions.

---

[6] Joined cases C-253/96 to 258/96 *Kampelmann v Landschaftsverband Westfalen-Lippe* [1998] IRLR 334 ECJ.
[7] Section 2(6) ERA 1996.
[8] Section 2(5) ERA 1996.
[9] Section 37 EA 2002.
[10] The information contained in sections 1(3), 4(a)–(c), (d)(i), (f) and (h).
[11] Section 7B ERA 1996.
[12] Section 4(1) ERA 1996.
[13] Section 38 EA 2002; the complete list of such jurisdictions is contained in Schedule 5 to the Act; it includes, apart from those mentioned above, a wide range of issues such as those relating to the national minimum wage, working time and redundancy payments.
[14] Subject to the maximum for a week's pay specified in section 227 ERA 1996.

4.2.1 Names and addresses of employer and employee[15]

The identity of the employer may be the subject of dispute. This may be true of individuals who are placed by one employer to work in the premises, and under the control of, another employer, such as employment agency staff.[16] It may also be true of changes resulting from a reorganisation or a transfer of employees between employers. However, a transfer of a contract of employment needs the employee's knowledge and, at least, implied consent.[17] In a case where two disabled employees were sponsored by Royal British Legion Industries to work in a 'host' organisation and remained there for nine years,[18] there was a dispute as to the identity of the employer. The EAT concluded that the correct approach was to start with the written contractual arrangements and decide whether these represented the true intentions of the parties. If they did, then the tribunal needed to discover if the situation had changed and when. There was a need to look at the reality of the situation in order to come to a correct conclusion.[19]

4.2.2 Date when employment began[20]

The date when employment begins can be important in establishing whether an employee has the minimum length of continuous service required for entitlement to various employment protection measures (see Chapter 3). For example, those individuals who are employed as temporary staff via an employment agency and are then employed on a permanent basis by the host company at which they work may need to clarify the precise start date of the new employment. The *Systems Floors*[21] case centred around a difference between the employee and the employer about the actual start date for that employee. The employee's opportunity to make an unfair dismissal claim depended upon the outcome of this argument.

4.2.3 Date on which continuous employment began[22]

For the purposes of assessing length of service, a person 'starts work' when their contract of employment commences rather than the date when they first undertook duties. This principle is likely to have a particular impact when the first day of the month is a Bank Holiday.[23] There is a requirement to take into account employment with a previous employer if that employment counts towards continuous employment. If there is a change of employer and a transfer of employment in accordance with section 218 ERA 1996 or a relevant transfer takes place in accordance with the Transfer of Undertakings (Protection

---

[15] Section 1(3)(a) ERA 1996.
[16] See *Dacas v Brook Street Bureau* [2004] IRLR 359 (Chapter 3 above).
[17] See *Bolwell v (1) Redcliffe Homes Ltd; (2) O'Connor* [1999] IRLR 485 CA.
[18] *Secretary of State for Education and Employment v Bearman* [1998] IRLR 431.
[19] See *Clifford v Union of Democratic Mineworkers* [1991] IRLR 518 CA.
[20] Section 1(3)(b) ERA 1996.
[21] [1981] IRLR 475.
[22] Section 1(3)(c) ERA 1996.
[23] See section 211(1) ERA 1996 and *General of the Salvation Army v Dewsbury* [1984] IRLR 222.

of Employment) Regulations 2006,[24] then all the employment with the previous employer is likely to be added to the period of service with the new employer (see Chapter 10).

4.2.4 Remuneration[25]

The statement will need to contain information on the scale or rate of remuneration or the method of calculating it and the intervals at which it is paid. Remuneration can have a wider meaning than the payment of wages, although the term 'wages' itself is capable of a broad definition. It need not be confined to the payment of regular wages, but may include payment relating to work done.[26] Wages, according to section 27(1) ERA 1996, means 'any sums payable to the worker in connection with his employment' (see below).[27]

Employees also have the right to receive a written itemised pay statement from the employer. This is to be given before or at the time of payment and must contain information about the gross[28] amount of wages or salary, the amount of any variable or fixed deductions and the purpose for which they are made, the net amount of wages payable and, where different parts are payable in different ways, the amount and method of each part-payment.[29] The employer may give the employee a statement which contains an aggregate amount of fixed deductions, provided that the employer has given, at or before the time at which the pay statement is given, a standing statement of fixed deductions.[30] Such a standing statement must be in writing and contain details of the amount and purpose of each deduction and the intervals at which the deduction will be made. The statement can be amended in writing by the employer and must be renewed with amendments at least every 12 months.[31]

An employer may not receive payments from one of their workers, in their capacity as an employer, unless there is already existing a contractual agreement for such payments to be made, or there is a statutory provision authorising such payment.[32] The exceptions to this rule are contained in section 16 ERA 1996. These exceptions are:

(1) any payments that are a reimbursement of overpayment of wages or expenses paid to the worker;
(2) a payment made by a worker as a consequence of any disciplinary proceedings resulting from a statutory provision;
(3) any payments required by the employer as a result of the worker taking part in industrial action;

---

[24] SI 2006/246.
[25] Section 1(4)(a) ERA 1996.
[26] See *New Century Cleaning Co Ltd v Church* [2000] IRLR 27 CA.
[27] Section 27(1) ERA 1996 lists a number of items that are included in the term wages, such as statutory sick pay and statutory maternity pay; section 27(2) lists a number of items that are excluded from the definition, such as payments for expenses and redundancy pay.
[28] Gross amount is defined in section 27(4) ERA 1996 as the total amount of wages before deductions of whatever nature.
[29] Section 8 ERA 1996.
[30] Section 9(1) ERA 1996.
[31] Section 9(2)–(5) ERA 1996.
[32] Section 15 ERA 1996.

(4) a payment whose purpose is the satisfaction of an order of a court or tribunal requiring the payment to the employer.[33]

The employer does not have complete freedom to regulate remuneration as there is statutory regulation of wages. For example, the National Minimum Wage Regulations 1999[34] provide for a statutory minimum wage; the Equal Pay Act 1970 attempts to stop discrimination in pay between women and men; and the Maternity and Parental Leave etc. Regulations 1999[35] define remuneration during maternity leave. Other sources of regulation may include collective agreements incorporated into the contract of employment as well as custom and practice within a particular industry.

4.2.5 Hours of work[36]

Any terms and conditions relating to hours of work, including those relating to normal hours of work, need to be included.[37] Normal working hours are where there is a fixed number or a minimum number of hours stated.[38] Where there are no normal working hours, there is a formula for calculating a week's wage for statutory purposes. This involves averaging over 12 weeks, although weeks in which remuneration is not due are excluded from this period.[39]

An example of the problems that might happen when there is a lack of clarity on working hours occurred in *Ali v Christian Salvesen Food Services Ltd*,[40] which concerned a dispute over an annualised hours contract of employment. Employees were paid on a notional 40-hour week, but were not entitled to overtime until they had worked 1,824 hours in one year. The problem arose for employees who were terminated during the course of the year and wanted payment for hours they had worked in excess of the notional 40 hours per week. The Court of Appeal refused to imply a term to fill the gap to deal with this issue, because there was a likelihood that such a term had been deliberately left out of the agreement on the annualised contracts.

The Working Time Regulations 1998[41] also have an important bearing on the hours worked (see Chapter 8). An employee is given a contractual right to not be required to work more than a maximum of 48 hours work per week, averaged over a reference period, unless there has been agreement otherwise in writing. Thus, in *Barber v RJB Mining (UK) Ltd*[42] the High Court issued a declaration that the employees, who had been required to work in excess of this during the reference period, were not required to work again until the average fell to the maximum permitted.

---

[33] Section 16 ERA 1996.
[34] SI 1999/584.
[35] SI 1999/3312.
[36] Section 1(4)(c) ERA 1996.
[37] According to the ECJ in Case 350/99 *Lange v Georg Schünemann GmbH* [2001] IRLR 244, Directive 91/533 on proof of the employment relationship requires employers to notify employees of any term which obliges the employees to work overtime.
[38] Section 234 ERA 1996; this is concerned with the calculation of a week's pay as in Part XI ERA 1996.
[39] Section 224 ERA 1996.
[40] [1997] IRLR 17 CA.
[41] SI 1998/1833 as amended by the Working Time Regulations 1999, SI 1999/3372.
[42] [1999] IRLR 308.

The Part-time Workers (Prevention of Less Favourable Treatment) Regulations 2000[43] raise an important issue with regard to working time. They introduced the principle of non-discrimination between part-time workers and full-time comparators. Regulation 5 establishes the principle of non-discrimination (see Chapter 3). A part-time worker has the right not to be treated less favourably than the employer treats a full-time comparator. The principle of *pro rata temporis* applies, so a part-timer should receive a proportion of the benefits enjoyed by the full-time comparator in relation to hours worked. However, the one exception to this concerns overtime. Part-timers are not entitled to premium overtime rates until they have at least worked hours which are the same as the basic full-time hours of the comparable full-timer.

4.2.6 Entitlement to holidays and holiday pay[44]

The statement of terms and conditions must enable the employee to calculate any entitlement to accrued holiday pay on termination of employment. The minimum amount of holidays is regulated by the Working Time Regulations 1998 (see Chapter 8).[45] Regulation 13 provides for a minimum of 4.8 weeks' paid[46] leave during a leave year.[47] The Regulations also contain detailed provisions for dealing with individuals who terminate their employment during the year, enabling the employee to receive payment for leave not taken.[48]

4.2.7 Sickness, injury and pensions[49]

Employees are entitled to know the arrangements for absence through sickness and incapacity, including sickness pay. This information can be included in a separate document, as can information about pension schemes.[50] The statement of terms and conditions need merely direct individuals to the appropriate document, which must be 'reasonably accessible to the employee'.[51] There is no requirement for the employer to provide information about pensions if the employee's pension rights derive from any statutory provision, when those statutory provisions provide for another body or authority to give the employee information about pension rights.[52]

In *Mears v Safecar Security Ltd*[53] the written terms of employment did not contain any reference to sick pay. The Court of Appeal concluded that where there was a gap in the terms of employment and the tribunal had insufficient information to fill that gap, then the question should be settled in favour of the employee. However, in this case the court

---

[43] SI 2000/1551.
[44] Section 1(4)(d)(i) ERA 1996.
[45] Note 41 above.
[46] Regulation 16 Working Time Regulations 1998 concerns payment for periods of leave.
[47] This will rise to 5.6 weeks in April 2009.
[48] Regulation 14 Working Time Regulations 1998.
[49] Section 1(4)(d)(ii) ERA 1996.
[50] Section 1(4)(d)(iii) ERA 1996.
[51] Section 2(2) ERA 1996.
[52] Section 1(5) ERA 1996.
[53] [1982] ICR 626 CA.

held that, taking into account all the circumstances and evidence, there had been no intention to provide pay during periods of absence through sickness and that such a term should have been included in the written terms of employment.

4.2.8 Length of notice[54]

The statement needs to reflect the notice that the employee is required to give and is entitled to receive on termination of employment. Minimum periods of notice to which an employee and an employer are entitled are contained in section 86 ERA 1996. These are related to the length of continuous employment. After one month's employment an individual with less than two years' continuous service is entitled to a week's notice. Thereafter one week is added for each year of service up to and including 12 years (see Chapter 5).

4.2.9 Title of job or job description[55]

There is a need to provide the job title or a brief job description of the work to be done by the employee. The reliance that can be placed upon this job title or brief description was tested before the ECJ in *Kampelmann*.[56] Here the employers realised that a mistake had been made in the job information. The ECJ held that the job title or description could be factual evidence of the job duties, but that proof of the essential aspects of the relationship cannot depend solely upon the employer's notification. Employers must therefore be allowed to bring evidence to the contrary by showing that the notification is wrong.

4.2.10 Temporary contracts[57]

Where a position is not intended to be permanent, there is an obligation to include the period for which it is expected to continue and the date, if it is a fixed-term contract, upon which the contract is expected to end. This type of contract can include employment agency workers, who may be engaged on a week-to-week or even day-to-day basis, as well those individuals who are employed directly on fixed-term contracts. Issues arise for the latter when either the term is extended or the contract is not renewed (see Chapter 3).

4.2.11 Place of work[58]

The location of the place of work needs to be written down. If the employee is required or permitted to work at various locations, then there needs to be a note to this effect, together with the address of the employer. The precise place of work can be extremely important. For example, the consultation requirements for collective redundancies depend upon the

---

[54] Section 1(4)(e) ERA 1996.
[55] Section 1(4)(f) ERA 1996.
[56] Joined cases C-253/96 to 258/96 *Kampelmann v Landschaftsverband Westfalen-Lippe* [1998] IRLR 334 ECJ.
[57] Section 1(4)(g) ERA 1996.
[58] Section 1(4)(h) ERA 1996.

number of employees to be dismissed 'at one establishment'.[59] Many employers will have a requirement for flexibility[60] and a requirement for the employee to be mobile written into the contract of employment. In *Aparau v Iceland Frozen Foods plc*[61] an employee was transferred to another branch after having several disagreements with the store manager. The employee disputed the employer's right to insist on the transfer and resigned, claiming constructive dismissal. The question was whether a mobility clause had become incorporated into the contract of employment. The EAT held that it had not and that it was not necessary to imply such a term. In certain occupations there may be an implication that mobility is necessary, but not in the contract of employment of a cashier working in a shop, where the nature of the work did not make such a clause necessary.[62]

4.2.12 Collective agreements[63]

Any collective agreements which directly affect the terms and conditions of employment are to be included in the statement. This includes, where the employer is not a party to the agreement, the identities of the parties by whom the agreement is made. This latter requirement will concern collective agreements that are, for example, reached by employers' associations and trade unions. It is apparent from section 2(3) ERA 1996, which allows reference to a collective agreement on periods of notice, that the terms of the collective agreement should be reasonably accessible to the employee (for issues concerning the incorporation of collective agreements into contracts of employment, see below).

4.2.13 Periods working outside the United Kingdom[64]

If an employee is to work outside the United Kingdom for a period of more than one month, the statement will need to contain information about the period they are to be working outside the country, the currency in which they are to be paid, any additional remuneration payable and any terms and conditions relating to their return to the United Kingdom. This information was of particular importance when certain rights, such as those connected with making a claim for unfair dismissal, were dependent upon whether a person ordinarily worked outside Great Britain or not. Although this requirement no longer applies, the courts still expect an employee to be working in Great Britain at the time of dismissal.[65]

The Government introduced Regulations[66] to implement the Posted Workers Directive[67] in 1999. The purpose of the Directive was to ensure that any legislation concerning the

---

[59] Section 188(1) TULRCA 1992 and see Chapter 10.
[60] See *Deeley v British Rail Engineering Ltd* [1980] IRLR 147.
[61] [1996] IRLR 119 EAT.
[62] See also *Jones v Associated Tunnelling Co Ltd* [1981] IRLR 477 and *White v Reflecting Roadstuds Ltd* [1991] IRLR 331.
[63] Section 1(4)(j) ERA 1996.
[64] Section 1(4)(k) ERA 1996.
[65] See *Lawson v Serco Ltd* [2006] IRLR 289.
[66] Equal Opportunities (Employment Legislation) (Territorial Limits) Regulations 1999, SI 1999/3163.
[67] Council Directive 96/71/EC concerning the posting of workers in the framework of the provision of services OJ L18/1 21.1.97.

employment relationship in a Member State should be extended to include workers posted to that State. This protection is in relation to maximum working hours, paid holidays, minimum pay rates, rules on temporary workers, health and safety at work, the protection of pregnant women and provisions for ensuring equality of treatment between men and women. In the United Kingdom the Government amended the Sex Discrimination Act 1975, the Race Relations Act 1976 and the Disability Discrimination Act 1995 by ensuring that they cover all individuals apart from those who work wholly outside Great Britain.[68]

4.2.14 General provisions

If there are no particulars to be described under any of these headings,[69] there needs to be a statement to that effect.[70] All of the information needs to be contained in a single document with the exception of: section 1(4)(d)(ii) and (iii) relating to incapacity for work, including sick pay provisions, and pension schemes; section 1(4)(e) relating to periods of notice; section 1(4)(g) relating to temporary contracts; section 1(4)(j) relating to collective agreements; and section 1(4)(k) on employment outside the United Kingdom. Thus these matters can be dealt with in separate documents. In relation to incapacity for work, pensions, periods of notice and the impact of collective agreements, all there needs to be is a reference to some other document which is readily accessible to the employee.[71]

4.2.15 Disciplinary and grievance procedures[72]

The statement also needs either to specify the disciplinary and dismissal[73] rules and procedures relevant to an individual or refer them to a reasonably accessible document containing the rules and procedures. For the purposes of statutory statements, reasonably accessible means that the employee has reasonable opportunities to read the documents in the course of employment, or the documents being made reasonably accessible to the employee in some other way.[74] There also needs to be a reference to a person to whom the employee may apply if dissatisfied with any disciplinary or dismissal decision relating to him or her. Additionally any rules concerning the steps necessary for the purpose of seeking redress of any grievance need to be stated as well as specifying the person to whom the employee should address grievances. The disciplinary, dismissal or grievance requirements do not apply if the complaint relates to health and safety at work.

A failure to provide and/or implement a procedure may amount to a breach of contract entitling the employees to make a claim for constructive dismissal. In *W A Goold (Pearmak) Ltd v McConnell*,[75] two sales people had their method of remuneration changed. This resulted in a substantial drop in their income. There was no established procedure for

---

[68] Section 10 SDA 1975, section 8 RRA 1976 and section 68(2) DDA 1995.
[69] Under section 1(3) or (4) ERA 1996.
[70] Section 2(1) ERA 1996.
[71] Section 2(2) and (3) ERA 1996.
[72] Section 3 ERA 1996. On the impact of statutory disputes procedures see Chapter 5 below.
[73] Section 3(1)(aa) ERA 1996.
[74] Section 6 ERA 1996.
[75] [1995] IRLR 516.

dealing with such grievances, but they talked to their manager initially. Nothing was done as a result of this. They then approached a new managing director, with whom they had a number of discussions. They were promised that something would be done, but nothing happened immediately. They then sought an interview with the chairman of the company, but were told that such interviews could only be arranged through the managing director. As a result they resigned and claimed constructive dismissal. Having considered Parliament's intentions in requiring employers to provide information as to whom employees might approach if dissatisfied with a disciplinary matter or any grievance, the EAT concluded that the employer was in breach of the implied term to afford promptly a reasonable opportunity to obtain redress for a grievance.

Similarly an attempt to use different procedures to those contractually agreed may entitle the employee to seek an injunction to stop the employer's action.[76] In *Raspin v United News Shops Ltd*[77] an employee was dismissed after the failure of the employer to follow agreed disciplinary procedures. The employee was awarded compensation by the employment tribunal to compensate for the period that would have been worked if the procedure had been followed.[78]

4.3 Implied terms

There are a number of other sources of terms. These include: collective agreements, workforce agreements, custom and practice and works rules.

Guidance about the implication of terms was given in *Mears v Safecar Security Ltd*.[79] First, one needs to see if there is an express term agreed. If not, one should decide if there was a term which can be said to have been agreed by implication. If this is not the case, then one looks to see whether such a term can be derived from all the circumstances, including the actions of the parties during the period in which the employment lasted. Finally, if none of this is possible, the employment tribunal may be required to invent a term. This last point was strongly disagreed with by the Court of Appeal in *Eagland v British Telecommunications plc*.[80] The case concerned a part-time cleaner who disputed her statement of terms and conditions. It omitted any terms relating to paid holidays, pay during absence for sickness and membership of a pension scheme which were included in the contracts of other part-time cleaners. The court held that it was not the task of employment tribunals to invent terms which had not been agreed between the parties. It distinguished between those terms which were mandatory and those which were non-mandatory. Amongst the latter are arrangements for disciplinary rules, pensions and sick pay schemes. Included in the former would be those legal necessities that arise out of a contract of employment, for example minimum periods of notice. Although the employment tribunal will have the opportunity to include those terms arising out of legal necessities, they have no power to impose non-mandatory terms where there is no evidence of the parties' intentions.

---

[76] See *Peace v City of Edinburgh Council* [1999] IRLR 417 and *Deadman v Bristol City Council* [2007] IRLR 888.
[77] [1999] IRLR 9.
[78] See also *Harper v Virgin Net Ltd* [2004] IRLR 390.
[79] [1982] ICR 626 CA.
[80] [1992] IRLR 323 CA.

4.3.1 Terms implied by statute

The provisions on statutory statements have been described above and it follows that the same legislation affects the terms of a contract of employment. One group of statutes and regulations are those concerned with non-discrimination. The most overt example of such implication of a term is contained in section 1(1) Equal Pay Act 1970, which states that:

> If the terms of a contract under which a woman is employed at an establishment in Great Britain do not include (directly or by reference to a collective agreement or otherwise) an equality clause they shall be deemed to include one.

Other pieces of legislation will impose a non-discrimination requirement which may influence many other terms of the contract. These will include the Sex Discrimination Act 1975, the Race Relations Act 1976, the Disability Discrimination Act 1995, the Part-time Workers (Prevention of Less Favourable Treatment) Regulations 2000 and the Employment Equality (Age) Regulations 2006.[81] All these pieces of legislation are concerned, in part, with preventing discrimination in employment against particular groups of workers.

A second group of statutes and regulations are concerned with specific terms and with setting minimum standards. These include the Working Time Regulations 1998,[82] which, for example, impose rules concerning maximum working hours and holiday entitlement, and the NMWA 1998 which requires minimum rates of pay for certain workers.

The third category is concerned with allowing statutory bodies to influence the contents of the contract. This will include the Central Arbitration Committee (CAC), which has powers under section 185 TULRCA 1992 to deal with disputes over disclosure of information. The CAC may require the employer to observe certain terms and conditions that it specifies. The CAC also has extensive powers to require collective bargaining arrangements between employers and trade unions in relation to the contents of certain aspects of the contract of employment.

4.3.2 Terms implied in fact

These are intended to determine the true intentions of the parties. It is not a matter of law, but a matter of fact which the parties intended to be included in the contract. The two standard tests used to decide whether a term can be implied are the business efficacy test[83] and the officious bystander test, although these may be used as one. In *Shirlaw v Southern Foundries*[84] McKinnon LJ suggested that a term could be implied where it was so obvious that 'it goes without saying':

> If, while the parties were making their bargain, an officious bystander were to suggest some express provision for it in the agreement, they would testily suppress him with a common 'Oh, of course'.

---

[81] See Chapters 6 and 7 below.
[82] SI 1998/1833.
[83] See *The Moorcock* (1889) 14 PD 64.
[84] [1939] 2 KB 206 CA.

Lord Wright in *Luxor (Eastbourne) Ltd v Cooper*[85] suggested that these tests allowed the implication of a term:

> of which it can be predicated that 'it goes without saying', some term not expressed but necessary to give to the transaction such business efficacy as the parties intended.

One example in the employment context is *Jones v Associated Tunnelling Co Ltd*,[86] where there was a dispute about whether an employee was required to work at a particular location. Browne-Wilkinson J stated that, in order to achieve business efficacy, the starting point must be that a contract of employment cannot simply be silent on the place of work:

> in such a case, it seems to me that there is no alternative but for the tribunal or court to imply a term which the parties, if reasonable, would probably have agreed if they had directed their minds to the problem.[87]

In *Ali v Christian Salvesen Food Services Ltd*[88] the court refused to imply a term into an annualised hours contract, even though there was an apparent gap, because the parties may have intended to leave that gap in the agreement. The Court of Appeal concluded:

> The importation of an implied term depends, in the final analysis, upon the intention of the parties as collected from the words of the agreement and the surrounding circumstances.

The giving of effect to the intentions of the parties was also illustrated in *Aspden v Webb Poultry & Meat Group (Holdings) Ltd*.[89] Here an employer introduced a generous permanent health scheme for employees, allowing incapacitated employees to receive an amount equivalent to 75% of their annual salary, beginning 26 weeks after the start of the incapacity. The employee was dismissed during a prolonged absence as a result of a serious illness. He claimed that there was an implied term in his contract of employment that he would not be dismissed during incapacity for work as this would frustrate the benefits of the health insurance scheme. Although there was an express term in the contract allowing the employer to dismiss as a result of prolonged incapacity, the court implied a term that a dismissal would not take place to stop an employee benefiting from the health scheme. This was because the contract was not written with the scheme in mind and if the parties had stopped to consider the issue it would have been their mutual intention not to frustrate the operation of the health scheme.[90]

4.3.3 Terms implied by law

These differ from terms implied in fact because they are not the result of identifying the intentions of the parties. In *Scally v Southern Health and Social Services Board*[91] the House of Lords stated:

> A clear distinction is drawn . . . between the search for an implied term necessary to give business efficacy to a particular contract and the search, based on wider considerations, for a term which the law will imply as a necessary incident of a definable category of contractual relationship.

---

[85] [1941] AC 108.
[86] [1981] IRLR 477.
[87] See also *Courtaulds Northern Spinning Ltd v Sibson* [1988] IRLR 276 CA, which also concerned a change of work base for an employee.
[88] [1997] IRLR 17 CA, see text to note 40 above.
[89] [1996] IRLR 521. See also *Briscoe v Lubrizol Ltd* [2002] IRLR 607.
[90] See also *Takacs v Barclays Ltd* [2006] IRLR 877.
[91] [1991] IRLR 522 HL.

In *Malik and Mahmud v BCCI*[92] the court stated that such implied terms operated as 'default rules'.

Such implication is intended to fill a clear gap in the contract and is dependent upon its being a term that neither party has addressed. This test derived from a decision in *Liverpool City Council v Irwin*[93] which concerned a group of tenants living in a block of flats. Their agreement with the local authority did not include much information about the landlord's responsibilities, especially with regard to the maintenance of the common parts. The House of Lords decided that it was possible to imply a term so that the landlord was responsible for keeping the common parts in repair. This was on the basis that it was a sufficiently common type of agreement and that such agreements would normally include such a term; that the agreement was clearly incomplete; and that it was reasonable to include such a term, given the expectations of the parties.

4.4 Duties of the employer

4.4.1 Duty of mutual trust and confidence

There is a duty on the part of both the employer and the employee not to act in a manner which jeopardises an implied term of mutual trust and confidence which enables the contract of employment to continue in the manner envisaged.[94] In *United Bank Ltd v Akhtar*[95] an employee had a mobility clause in his contract of employment, which provided that he could be transferred to any place in the United Kingdom, in which the bank operated, at short notice and with only the prospect of a discretionary relocation payment. He was asked to move to Birmingham from Leeds with less than one week's notice, although he had difficult personal circumstances. The court held that this amounted to a fundamental breach of the implied term that employers will not conduct themselves in such a manner that will harm or destroy the relationship of confidence and trust between employer and employee. It was possible to imply a term which controls the exercise of discretion in a contract of employment. In this case there was an implied requirement that reasonable notice should be given in exercising the power to relocate the bank's employees.

An extreme example of employer behaviour can be found in the cases concerning ex-employees of the Bank of Credit and Commerce. This bank collapsed in 1991 after a period of trading insolvently and corruptly. In a series of cases, ex-employees claimed that the bank had been in breach of an implied term not to operate their business in a corrupt and dishonest manner.

---

[92] [1997] IRLR 462 HL.
[93] [1977] AC 239 HL.
[94] See, for example, *Bliss v South East Thames Regional Health Authority* [1985] IRLR 308 CA, where the requirement that a consultant undergo a psychiatric examination was described by the court as an act which was calculated to destroy the relationship of confidence and trust which ought to exist between employer and employee.
[95] [1989] IRLR 507; see also *Woods v WM Car Services (Peterborough) Ltd* [1982] IRLR 413 CA, where continual attempts to change an employee's terms and conditions of employment amounted to a breach of the duty of trust and confidence.

The House of Lords, in *Malik*,[96] accepted this argument and stated that:

> The conduct must, of course, impinge on the relationship in the sense that, looked at objectively, it is likely to destroy or seriously damage the degree of trust and confidence the employee is reasonably entitled to have in his employer.

Here the House of Lords concluded that the manner in which the bank conducted itself impinged on the relationship and that the employees were able to treat the employer's conduct as a repudiatory breach of the contract of employment, enabling them to leave and claim constructive dismissal. The court then went on to approve a claim for what became known as 'stigma' damages. The employees' job prospects had been so damaged that they were entitled to compensation for the damage done to their job prospects elsewhere.

Many ex-employees of BCCI had signed compromise agreements[97] excluding further claims against the employer. However, the House of Lords would not allow the employer to rely upon these agreements in order to exclude claims for stigma damages. The agreements were signed some eight years before the House of Lords held that such claims were sustainable and the parties could not have intended to provide for the release of rights which they could never have contemplated as possible.[98]

Malik was further considered in *Johnson v Unisys Ltd*,[99] where an employee claimed damages for loss allegedly suffered as a result of the manner in which he was dismissed. The House of Lords stated that a common law right concerning the manner in which an employee is dismissed could not co-exist alongside the statutory right not to be dismissed. It was not possible to imply a separate term into the contract of employment that a power of dismissal would be exercised fairly and in good faith. Thus the employee could not rely upon the fact that he was dismissed without a fair hearing and in breach of the employer's disciplinary procedure to establish a claim for a breach of the implied term of trust and confidence. The court also stated that it was not appropriate to apply this implied term to dismissals, because it was about preserving the relationship between employer and employee and not about the way that the relationship is terminated.[100] Although it has a number of undesirable consequences, for example requiring courts and tribunals to decide whether an employer's wrongful conduct formed part of the process of dismissal, this approach was followed in *Eastwood v Magnox Electric plc*.[101] In this case the claimants alleged that they had been victims of their employer's campaign to deprive them of their jobs by fabricating evidence and encouraging other employees to give false statements for the purpose of disciplinary proceedings. The House of Lords held that in these circumstances the employees were not excluded from bringing common law claims for psychiatric injury based on a breach of trust and confidence prior to dismissal.

---

[96] Consolidated cases *Malik v Bank of Credit and Commerce International SA, in liquidation; sub nom Mahmud v Bank of Credit and Commerce International SA* [1997] IRLR 462 HL.
[97] See Chapter 5.
[98] *Bank of Credit and Commerce International v Ali* [2001] IRLR 292 HL.
[99] [2001] IRLR 279 HL.
[100] See *Addis v Gramophone Company Ltd* [1909] AC 488 HL, which prevents an employee in a case of wrongful dismissal from recovering damages for injured feelings, mental distress or damage to reputation arising out of the manner of the dismissal.
[101] [2004] IRLR 733.

The issue then is whether the employer acted in a manner which was serious enough to be a fundamental breach of the contract of employment by breaching an implied term of mutual trust and confidence. Lord Steyn, in *Malik*,[102] stated:

> It is true that the implied term adds little to the employee's obligations to serve his employer loyally and not act contrary to his employer's interests. The major importance of the implied duty of trust and confidence lies in its impact on the obligations of the employer[103] . . . and the implied obligation as formulated is apt to cover the great diversity of situations in which a balance has to be struck between an employer's interest in managing his business as he sees fit and the employee's interest in not being unfairly and improperly exploited.

The affected employees still needed to establish that the bank's wrongdoing had placed a stigma on them which hindered their prospects of finding suitable alternative employment. In a subsequent decision,[104] the Court of Appeal held that the question to be asked was: but for the breach of duty, what would the prospective employer have done and what would have been the result for the employee? This might mean looking at the whole history of a person's search for new employment, such as considering how many jobs have been applied for, how many interviews obtained and what the results were. It is for the claimant to show causation, but the judge should look at the whole picture in reaching a conclusion.

In *French v Barclays Bank plc*[105] the action of the employer in stopping an interest-free bridging loan to a relocated employee, as a result of the length of time it took to sell the employee's old house, was held to be serious enough to be a breach of this implied term. This was even though the giving of the loan was at the discretion of the employer. Similarly the giving of a reference to a potential employer revealing information about which the employee was unaware is also likely to be a breach. In *TSB Bank plc v Harris*,[106] when a prospective employer approached the current employer for a reference, the current employer revealed that 17 customer complaints had been made about the employee. It was the employer's practice not to discuss these with the employee concerned, which meant that the information, as a result of which a job offer was withdrawn, was unknown to the individual at the time of the reference. This failure to inform the employee and to discuss the complaints with her prior to revealing the information to a prospective employer amounted to a breach of the implied term of mutual trust and confidence.

This implied term is dependent upon the alleged conduct of the employer being without reasonable and proper cause. Thus if an employer has justifiable suspicions that an employee was dishonest, it would not be a breach of trust and confidence to remove responsibilities for cash from the employee's duties. This was the case in *Hilton v Shiner Ltd*,[107] where the EAT stated that there was a two-stage process for consideration. First, whether there had been acts which seem likely to seriously damage or destroy the relationship of trust and confidence. Secondly, whether there is no reasonable or proper cause for those acts.

---

[102] [1997] IRLR 462 at p 468.
[103] The court cited Douglas Brodie, 'The Heart of the Matter: Mutual Trust and Confidence' (1996) 25 ILJ 121.
[104] *Bank of Credit and Commerce International SA v Ali (No 3)* [2002] IRLR 460 CA.
[105] [1998] IRLR 646 CA.
[106] [2000] IRLR 157; see also cases under duty of care below.
[107] [2001] IRLR 727.

Sexual harassment by a senior male employee against a female employee is also likely to amount to a breach of the implied term. If the actions were such that, over a period of time, an employee came to find the workplace intolerable and felt that they had to resign over the unwanted harassment, the employee may then be entitled to make a claim for constructive dismissal because of the breach.[108] More generally, the contract of employment engages obligations in connection with self-esteem and dignity. Thus the use of foul and abusive language could also be a breach of trust and confidence.[109]

The process by which an employer deals with an employee against whom there is to be an investigation can itself lead to a breach of mutual trust and confidence. Thus the suspension of a care worker, pending an inquiry, on the grounds that there was to be an investigation about allegations of sexual abuse against a child in her care, was interpreted as a breach of the implied term of trust and confidence.[110] The court held that because an investigation was to take place about allegations, it did not follow automatically that the employee must be suspended. The court described the employer's response as a 'knee-jerk reaction'.

It remains to be seen how far the duty of trust and confidence imposes positive obligations on employers to ensure that employees are treated fairly. For example, the House of Lords has accepted that in certain circumstances it will be necessary to imply an obligation on an employer to take reasonable steps to bring a contractual term to the employee's attention.[111] Similarly, in *Transco v O'Brien*[112] the Court of Appeal held that there was a breach of trust and confidence when, without reasonable excuse, an employee was denied the opportunity given to everyone else of signing a revised contract with enhanced redundancy payments. On the other hand, a failure to warn an employee who was proposing to exercise pension rights that the way he was proposing to act was not the most financially advantageous was not seen as breaching trust and confidence.[113]

Employees who believe that their employer has breached a duty of trust and confidence must decide what course of action to take. A resignation, which amounts to an acceptance of the employer's breach and the ending of the contract, may give rise to a claim for constructive dismissal. To continue to work and receive pay does not entitle the employee to disregard lawful and legitimate instructions from the employer made in accordance with the contract of employment. The obligation to carry out work and obey instructions is not dependent upon the employer's performance of their obligations under an implied term.[114] If the employee resigns, the likely remedy for a successful claim will be compensation. Where there is a breakdown in mutual trust and confidence it may be difficult for a tribunal to order reinstatement or re-engagement of the employee. In *Wood Group Heavy*

---

[108] See *(1) Reed; (2) Bull Information Systems Ltd v Stedman* [1999] IRLR 299.
[109] See *Horkulak v Cantor Fitzgerald* [2003] IRLR 756.
[110] *Gogay v Hertfordshire County Council* [2000] IRLR 703 CA. See also *King v University Court of the University of St Andrews* [2002] IRLR 252, where the Court of Session confirmed that the duty of trust and confidence subsisted during an investigation into allegations of misconduct which might result in the employee's dismissal.
[111] *Scally v Southern Health Board* [1991] IRLR 522.
[112] [2002] IRLR 444.
[113] *University of Nottingham v Eyett* [1999] IRLR 87. See also *Outram v Academy Plastics* [2000] IRLR 499.
[114] See *Macari v Celtic and Athletic Football Club Ltd* [1999] IRLR 787 at p 795.

Industrial Turbines Ltd v Crossan[115] an employee was dismissed for a genuine belief by the employer that the employee had been dealing in drugs at the workplace. The employment tribunal ordered re-engagement in the belief that the employers had not carried out sufficient investigations. The EAT allowed the employer's appeal against this remedy because it decided that:

> it is difficult to see how the essential bond of trust and confidence that must exist between an employer and an employee, inevitably broken by such investigations and allegations, can be satisfactorily repaired by re-engagement. We consider that the remedy of re-engagement has very limited scope and will only be practical in the rarest cases where there is a breakdown in confidence as between the employer and the employee.

4.4.2 Duty to provide work and pay

In *Beveridge v KLM UK Ltd*[116] an employee informed her employers that, after a long period of absence through sickness, she was fit to return to work. However, they refused to allow her to return until their own doctor had certified her fitness to do so. This process took six weeks, during which she was not allowed to work and was not paid. When she claimed that that this amounted to an unauthorised deduction from her wages, the employment tribunal held that the employer was under no obligation to pay her as there was no express term of the contract to this effect. However, the EAT ruled that an employee who offers services to her employer is entitled to be paid unless there is an express provision of the contract providing otherwise. There was no such term in this case and the employee could do no more than attempt to fulfil her side of the contract.

There is also an issue as to whether there is an implied term in the contract of employment that the employer has a duty to provide work, as well as pay. The traditional common law view was stated in *Collier v Sunday Referee Publishing Co Ltd.*[117] Here a newspaper sub-editor was retained by his original employer after the newspaper for which he worked was taken over by another organisation. When he was not given any work to do, he claimed that his employer had breached his contract. Asquith J illustrated the general point graphically:

> Provided I pay my cook her wages regularly she cannot complain if I choose to take any or all of my meals out.

However, the court recognised that there were exceptions, including this one, when there was an obligation to provide work. Examples given were where individuals earned their income from commission and where publicity is part of the bargain, for example, in the case of actors or singers.[118]

This is particularly important when employers seek to insist on employees serving out lengthy periods of notice whilst keeping them idle, in order to stop them going to work for

---

[115] [1998] IRLR 680.
[116] [2000] IRLR 765.
[117] [1940] 2 KB 647.
[118] See also *Breach v Epsylon Industries Ltd* [1976] IRLR 180 which emphasised that it was necessary to look at the background to the contract to consider how it should be construed, in order to decide whether there was a term to be implied concerning the provision of work.

what is perceived to be a rival organisation.[119] The purpose may be to stop the competitor taking advantage of the individual's abilities and expertise but is more likely to stop the employee going to a rival company with up-to-date knowledge of the existing employer's business. This period of enforced idleness is sometimes referred to as 'garden leave'. It particularly affects individuals who are reliant upon continuing to work in order to maintain their skills or stay in the public eye. In *Provident Financial Group plc and Whitegates Estate Agency Ltd v Hayward*[120] there was a specific term in the contract of employment which provided that the employer need not provide work. Taylor LJ stated that:

> the employee has a concern to work and a concern to exercise his skills. That has been recognised in some circumstances concerned with artists and singers who depend on publicity, but it applies equally I apprehend, to skilled workmen and even to chartered accountants.

Thus the need to exercise and maintain skills could be widely interpreted as including those who are experts in their field. In *William Hill Organisation Ltd v Tucker*[121] an employee was put on six months' 'garden leave'. The individual concerned held a unique position with specialist skills. In this case the court decided that the contract was capable of being construed so as to give rise to an obligation on the employer to allow the employee to carry out his duties. This was not only because the individual held a 'specific and unique post' and needed to practise his skills regularly, but also because the terms of the contract pointed towards this conclusion; especially the obligation which required the employee to work the hours necessary to carry out the duties of the post in a full and professional manner.

4.4.3 Duty of care

This is a duty that might cover a variety of responsibilities by the employer and the employee. There are certain statutory requirements relating to health and safety matters. Section 2(1) HASAWA 1974 requires an employer 'to ensure, so far as is reasonably practicable, the health, safety and welfare at work of all his employees'. Similarly there is an obligation on employees to inform the employer, or any other person responsible for health and safety, of any work situation which might present a 'serious and imminent danger to health and safety'.[122]

There is an implied duty in every contract of employment that an employer will take all reasonable steps to provide and maintain a safe system of work so as not to expose the employee to unnecessary risks of injury. In *Wilsons and Clyde Coal Co Ltd v English*[123] Lord Thankerton listed a number of duties of the master towards the servants:

> If the master retains control, he has a duty to see that his servants do not suffer through his personal negligence, such as (1) failure to provide proper and suitable plant, if he knows, or ought to

---

[119] The court is unlikely to give injunctive relief to an employer if the restriction stops the employee on 'garden leave' taking up employment with a non-competing organisation; see *Provident Financial Group plc and Whitegates Estate Agency Ltd v Hayward* [1989] IRLR 84 CA.
[120] *Ibid.*
[121] [1998] IRLR 313 CA.
[122] Regulation 14(2) Management of Health and Safety at Work Regulations 1999, SI 1999/3242.
[123] [1938] AC 57 HL; see also *Morris v Breaveglen Ltd* [1993] IRLR 350 CA.

have known, of such failure; (2) failure to select fit and competent servants; (3) failure to provide a proper and safe system of working; and (4) failure to observe statutory regulations.

This duty extends to responsibility for actions taken by employees and agents of the employer. The employer may be liable even if, centrally, it had taken all precautions as were 'reasonably practicable', but this had not been done by its employees elsewhere.[124] This general duty extends to persons not in the direct employ of the employer.[125] However, providing that the employer had taken all steps that are reasonably practicable, they should not be held liable for the acts of their careless or negligent employees or agents. In *R v Nelson Group Services (Maintenance) Ltd*[126] gas fitters had not completed their tasks correctly and had thereby exposed customers to danger to their health and safety. The Court of Appeal allowed an appeal from the High Court on the grounds that the judge's directions had not allowed the employer's defence of reasonable practicability to be decided by the jury.

Section 2(2)(e) HASAWA 1974 states that an employer has a duty to provide and maintain a working environment that is, as far as is reasonably practicable, safe and without risk to health. This is the starting point for an implied term in every contract of employment that employers have a duty to provide and monitor, as far as is reasonably practicable, a working environment which is reasonably suitable for the performance by them of their contractual duties. This includes the right of an employee not to be required to work in a smoke-filled atmosphere, as in *Waltons & Morse v Dorrington*.[127] In this case a secretary objected to working in poorly ventilated accommodation with a number of smokers. Although the employer took some measures, they proved inadequate to solve the problem and the employee was able to resign and successfully claim unfair constructive dismissal. In *Dryden v Greater Glasgow Health Board*[128] the introduction of a no-smoking policy by the employer, after consultation, had an adverse effect on a nurse who smoked 30 cigarettes a day. The EAT concluded that where a rule is introduced for a legitimate purpose the fact that it has an adverse effect on an employee does not enable that employee to resign and claim constructive dismissal. There was no implied term in the employee's contract of employment which entitled her to continue smoking.

The employer's duty of care is owed to the individual employee and not to some unidentified ordinary person. This is especially true in relation to psychiatric illness caused by stress at work. The stages in deciding whether employers have carried out their responsibilities are: first, whether the harm was foreseeable; secondly, what the employer did and should have done about it; and, thirdly, where a breach has been shown, whether there is a causal relationship between the breach and the harm.

According to the House of Lords,[129] the best statement of general principle remains that of Swanwick J in *Stokes v GKN Ltd*:[130]

---

[124] *R v Gateway Foods Ltd* [1997] IRLR 189 CA.
[125] Section 3(1) HASAWA 1974 and *R v Associated Octel Co Ltd* [1997] IRLR 123 HL.
[126] [1999] IRLR 646 CA.
[127] [1997] IRLR 488. See the Smoke-free (Premises and Enforcement) Regulations 2006, SI/2006 3368 which came into force in England and Wales on 1 July 2007.
[128] [1992] IRLR 469.
[129] *Barber v Somerset County Council* [2004] IRLR 475.
[130] [1968] 1 WLR 1776.

The overall test is the conduct of the reasonable and prudent employer taking positive thought for the safety of his workers in the light of what he knows or ought to know.

The test is the same whatever the employment. It is not the job that causes harm but the interaction between the individual and the job. There needs to be some indication to the employer that steps need to be taken to protect an employee from harm. Thus if an employee returns to work after a period of illness and does not make further explanation or disclosure, then the employee is implying that he or she is fit to return to work. The employer is then entitled to take this at face value unless there is reason to think the contrary.[131]

Factors that are relevant to the question of foreseeability are questions such as: the nature and workload of the job; is the workload more than normal for that job?; is the work particularly demanding for the employee?; are there signs of stress amongst others doing the same job?; is there a high level of absenteeism? The next stage is to consider whether there are signs of impending harm for the individual employee concerned, such as whether there are frequent or prolonged absences and whether the employee or his or her doctor has warned the employer about the risk of harm.[132]

Once harm is assessed as being foreseeable, the question is what the employer should have done about it.[133] The actions that are reasonable will depend upon the employer's size and resources. It is then necessary to show that the breach was at least partly responsible for the harm. It is not enough to show that occupational stress caused the harm.[134]

The duty of care does not extend to medical practitioners who carry out health assessments on behalf of employers seeking to recruit new staff. In *Baker v Kaye*[135] a medical practitioner concluded that an applicant was likely to consume excessive amounts of alcohol in a stressful work-related context. The employer withdrew a conditional offer of employment after receiving the medical report. Unfortunately for the applicant, he had already resigned from his previous post, as he had not anticipated any problems with the report of the medical examination. The High Court was asked to consider whether there was a duty of care owed by the doctor to the applicant. The court relied upon *Caparo Industries*[136] and *Hedley Byrne & Co Ltd v Heller & Partners Ltd*[137] to come to the conclusion that it was clear that economic loss was a foreseeable consequence of a breach of this duty and that there was a sufficient proximity between the parties to give rise to a duty of care. However, in this case the court concluded that the defendant was not in breach of that duty. In a subsequent decision the Court of Appeal disagreed with this conclusion and held that there was no duty of care owed by a medical practitioner to a job applicant in these circumstances, even though the applicant might suffer economic loss as a result of a careless error in a doctor's report.[138] There was not sufficient proximity, as the duty of care

---

[131] See *Young v Post Office* [2002] IRLR 660 and compare *Green v DB Group Ltd* [2006] IRLR 764.
[132] See *Hone v Six Continents Ltd* [2006] IRLR 764 and *Intel Corporation v Daw* [2007] IRLR 355CA.
[133] See *Pratley v Surrey County Council* [2003] IRLR 794.
[134] See *Marshall Ltd v Osborne* [2003] IRLR 672.
[135] [1997] IRLR 219.
[136] *Caparo Industries plc v Dickman* [1990] 2 AC 605 HL.
[137] [1964] AC 465 HL.
[138] *Kapfunde v Abbey National plc* [1998] IRLR 583 CA.

will generally be owed to the person who commissions the report, not the subject of it. A medical practitioner is likely to be viewed, therefore, as an agent of the employer.[139]

In *Spring v Guardian Assurance plc*,[140] the House of Lords held that an employer was under a duty of care to a former employee when providing a reference to a prospective employer. The duty was derived from the previous contractual relationship between the employer and the ex-employee. In this case the applicant sought damages for economic loss as a result of a failure to obtain work resulting from a reference written by a former employer. The question was whether the employer owed a duty of care to the applicant in the preparation of an employment reference. The House of Lords decided that the employee did have a remedy in negligence if they could establish that the inaccurate reference was a result of the employer's lack of care. This duty of care does not mean that every reference needs to be full and comprehensive. In *Bartholomew v London Borough of Hackney*[141] the Court of Appeal needed to weigh up the duty of the employer to the individual to provide a reference and a duty to the potential employer to provide a reference without being misleading or unfair.[142] The court accepted that a reference must not give 'an unfair or misleading impression overall, even if its discrete components are factually correct'. According to the High Court in *Kidd v Axa Equity & Law Life Assurance Society plc*,[143] it was not in the public interest to impose an obligation on employers to provide a full, frank and comprehensive reference. The court further held that to show a breach of the duty of care the claimant needed to show:

(1) that the information provided in the reference was misleading;
(2) that the provision of such misleading information was likely to have a material effect on the mind of a reasonable recipient of the reference to the detriment of the claimant;
(3) that the defendants were negligent in providing such references.

The employer providing the reference is also under an obligation to carry out any necessary inquiries into the factual basis of any statements made in the reference. Unfavourable statements should be confined to matters which had been investigated and for which there were reasonable grounds for believing that they were true.[144]

Finally, if the employee has a safety grievance, there is an implied term that employers will act promptly and provide a reasonable opportunity for employees to obtain redress. This view was put forward in *Waltons & Morse v Dorrington*,[145] where a non-smoker's attempts to have grievances about a smoky work atmosphere were frustrated.

---

[139] See *London Borough of Hammersmith & Fulham v Farnsworth* [2000] IRLR 691, where the doctor's knowledge of an individual's disability was held to be enough for the employer to be held to have such knowledge.
[140] [1994] IRLR 460 HL.
[141] [1999] IRLR 246 CA.
[142] The reference needs actually to have been given to a third party: see *Legal and General Assurance Ltd v Kirk* [2002] IRLR 124 CA.
[143] [2000] IRLR 301.
[144] *Cox v Sun Alliance Life Ltd* [2001] IRLR 448 CA.
[145] [1997] IRLR 488.

4.5 Duties of employees

4.5.1 Duty of obedience and co-operation

There is an implied duty to obey an employer's lawful and reasonable instructions and an employee's failure to follow such an instruction might lead to a fundamental breach of the contract of employment.[146] However, it is possible for the failure to obey an unlawful instruction to result in a fair dismissal, for example, when an employer reasonably but mistakenly believed that they were giving a lawful instruction.[147] Certainly a belief by the employee that the employer has breached an implied term is not justification for failing to obey other lawful and legitimate instructions.[148] This duty to obey might include the need to adapt to new technology. For example, in *Cresswell v Board of the Inland Revenue*[149] the introduction of computers into the administration of the PAYE system was held not to fall outside the job descriptions of the employees concerned. More recently, the EAT has ruled that there can be an implied term that an employee may be obliged to perform duties which are different from those expressly required by the contract or to perform them at a different place. However, it is likely to be legitimate to find an implied obligation to undertake a duty which is outside the express terms only where: the circumstances are exceptional; the requirement is plainly justified; the work is suitable; the employee suffers no detriment in terms of contractual benefits or status; and the change is temporary.[150]

The implied term to serve the employer faithfully according to the contract of employment also applies to managers who supervise others and exercise discretion in the carrying out of their duties. If the employee exercises that discretion in order to disrupt the work of the employer, then there may be a breach of this implied term. In *Ticehurst v British Telecom*,[151] as part of an industrial dispute, a supervisor refused to sign a declaration that she would work normally. This was seen as an intention not to perform the full range of duties and amounted to a breach of the implied term to serve the employer faithfully. In *Wiluszynski v London Borough of Tower Hamlets*[152] local authority employees took partial industrial action and refused to answer queries from Members of the Council. Despite warnings, the employees carried on attending the place of work and fulfilled all their other duties. The employer refused to pay them for the period when they were not fulfilling all their contractual duties. The Court of Appeal held that the employees were in repudiatory breach of their contracts, but that the employer had alternatives to accepting the breach and dismissing the employees. One of these alternatives was to tell the employees that they would not be paid during the period when they failed to carry out all the terms of their contracts.

This obligation to carry out duties in a full and professional manner was an issue in *Sim v Rotherham Metropolitan Borough Council*.[153] The National Union of Teachers instructed

---

[146] See *Laws v London Chronicle Ltd* [1959] 2 All ER 285 CA.
[147] *Farrant v The Woodroffe School* [1998] IRLR 176.
[148] See *Macari v Celtic and Athletic Football Club Ltd* [1999] IRLR 787.
[149] [1984] IRLR 190.
[150] *Luke v Stoke City Council* [2007] IRLR 305 and 777 CA.
[151] [1992] IRLR 219 CA.
[152] [1989] IRLR 259 CA.
[153] [1986] IRLR 391.

its members not to provide cover for absent colleagues. The Union claimed that the system had operated on the basis of goodwill only. The High Court rejected this argument and stated that the teachers had a professional obligation which they owed to their pupils and the school in which they worked. The court accepted that there was no statement in the teachers' contracts which identified this duty but held that this was not to be expected in professional contracts of employment. Such contracts specified the nature of the work and these extra duties were simply part of the professional obligations of teachers.

4.5.2 Duty of fidelity

There are two aspects of the duty of fidelity owed by employees to their employer. The first is the implied duty not to compete with the employer and the second is not to disclose certain confidential information, except under certain circumstances. A further issue is the use of restrictive covenants by employers to deter employees from working for competing businesses and using the knowledge and skills gained while in their employment.

4.5.2.1 Not competing

There is no general rule which, in the absence of an express term, restricts ex-employees from competing with their previous employer. If the previous employer had not included an express term restricting the employees' activities in the contract of employment, then they are unlikely to be able to claim that there is any sort of implied term that achieves the same result.[154] The position is more complicated when considering existing employees who are contemplating or actively setting up a business to compete with their present employer. In *Lancashire Fires Ltd v SA Lyons & Co Ltd*,[155] the Court of Appeal cited, with approval, a judgment of Lord Greene MR[156] in which he warned against the danger of 'laying down any general proposition and the necessity for considering each case on its facts'. However, the High Court has recently ruled that where a contact address list is maintained on the employer's email system and is backed-up by the employer that information belongs to the employer. Thus it cannot be removed or copied by employees for use outside.[157]

The obligations may be more extensive for some types of employees than others. In *Lancashire Fires* the younger brother of the company owner had obtained a loan from the company's principal supplier to set up in a competitive business. He had also started to purchase the necessary premises and equipment. As a result he was held to have been in breach of the duty of fidelity. An individual does not breach an implied term of loyalty if merely indicating an intention to set up in business to compete with the employer, especially if any of the steps taken are in their own time and not that of the employers. Thus two employees who wrote to a limited number of customers suggesting that they were about to start a competitive business were held not to be in breach of such an implied term.[158] Other employers might find this a strange decision and understand why the

---

[154] *Wallace Bogan & Co v Cove* [1997] IRLR 453 CA.
[155] [1997] IRLR 113 CA.
[156] *Hivac Ltd v Park Royal Scientific Instruments Ltd* [1946] Ch 169.
[157] *Pennwell Publishing Ltd v Ornstien* [2007] IRLR 700.
[158] See *Laughton and Hawley v Bapp Industrial Supplies Ltd* [1986] IRLR 245 and *Helmet Systems Ltd v Tunnard* [2007] IRLR 126.

employer in this case, having heard about the letter, dismissed the employees concerned. In *Adamson v B & L Cleaning Services Ltd*[159] an employee asked a customer to be put on a tendering list for a contract on which they were working when it was due for renewal. The EAT held that the actions of the individual amounted to a breach of the implied duty of fidelity.

Related to the issue of not competing is the making of secret profits from an individual's employment. Such action may lead to a breach by the employee of the implied term of mutual trust and confidence. Thus if an employee acts in such a way that the employer loses their trust and confidence in the employee, summary dismissal may be justified. In *Neary and Neary v Dean of Westminster*[160] the claimants were dismissed for using their positions in the organisation to make secret profits. This conduct was held to undermine fatally the relationship of trust between the employer and the employees. In *Nottingham University v Fishel*[161] the court distinguished between an individual's fiduciary duty and the individual's obligation towards maintaining trust and confidence. This case concerned the earnings of a university academic from organisations other than his employer. A feature of a fiduciary relationship is the duty to act in the interests of another. This is not necessarily the case in an employment relationship, where there is no obligation for the employee to pursue the employer's interests above the individual's own.[162] To decide on whether the employment relationship and the fiduciary relationship coincide requires an examination of the particular circumstances. In this case the individual did not have this fiduciary relationship because there was no contractual obligation to seek work on behalf of the university, rather than for himself.[163]

4.5.2.2 Restrictive covenants

The approach to the justification of restraints of trade was summarised by Lord Parker in *Herbert Morris v Saxelby Ltd*,[164] when he stated:

> . . . two conditions must be fulfilled if the restraint is to be held valid. First, it must be reasonable in the interests of the contracting parties, and, secondly, it must be reasonable in the interests of the public. In the case of each condition [there is] a test of reasonableness. To be reasonable in the interests of the parties, the restraint must afford adequate protection to the party in whose favour it is imposed; to be reasonable in the interests of the public it must in no way be injurious to the public.
>
> With regard to the former test, I think it is clear that what is meant is that for a restraint to be reasonable in the interest of the parties it must afford *no more than* adequate protection to the party in whose favour it is imposed.

The court also drew the distinction between 'objective knowledge', which is the property of the employer, and 'subjective knowledge', which is the property of the employee.

---

159 [1995] IRLR 193; see also *Marshall v Industrial Systems & Control Ltd* [1992] IRLR 294, where a company director making plans, and inducing another to join in those plans, to deprive their employer of their best customer, was held to have breached the duty of loyalty.
160 [1999] IRLR 288.
161 [2000] IRLR 471.
162 On the duty of employees to disclose their own misconduct see *Item Software Ltd v Fassihi* [2004] IRLR 928.
163 However, he did have such a relationship in relation to other employees of the university out of whose work he made a profit. See also *Shepherd Investments v Walters* [2007] IRLR 110.
164 [1916] AC 688 at p 707 HL; see now *TFS Derivatives Ltd v Morgan* [2005] IRLR 246.

This latter might consist of information in a person's memory, rather than confidential information kept by the employer. Even this subjective knowledge is capable of being protected, although the court will look at each case on its own facts. The names and addresses of customers may be legitimate information to be protected, even if it is innocently remembered by the ex-employee, rather than deliberately taken from the employer.[165]

However, there is a distinction between those covenants against competition which follow a sale of a business, including its goodwill, and those covenants designed to prevent ex-employees entering into competition with their previous employers.[166] Covenants concerning the latter are more likely to be interpreted strictly by the courts.

This concept of a restraint clause in a contract providing no more protection than is necessary is illustrated in *TSC Europe (UK) Ltd v Massey*.[167] In this case an ex-employee was subject to a clause that stopped the inducement of employees to leave the company. The clause was held to be unreasonable and unenforceable for two reasons. First, it applied to all employees and not just those who had particular skills or knowledge that were important to the business. Secondly, it applied to any employee who joined the company during the prohibited period, including those who joined after the plaintiff had left. The test of reasonableness is applied by considering the substance, and not the form, of the transaction, and by reference to all the facts and surrounding circumstances.[168] In this case, it was held to be too wide[169] and, therefore, unenforceable.[170]

The same approach is taken with respect to contractual clauses which limit an individual's ability to compete with their ex-employer. According to the Court of Appeal, the employer needs to establish that at the time the contract was made the nature of the employment was such as to expose the employee to the kind of information capable of protection beyond the term of the contract.[171] Thus a clause which, on its true construction, prohibited an employee engaging in any business in the same industry, rather than from any business competing with the ex-employer, was wider than necessary to protect the legitimate interests of that employer. It should also be noted that it is only possible to remove an offending part of a covenant if it is a separate obligation to that which can be enforced.[172]

---

[165] See *SBJ Stephenson Ltd v Mandy* [2000] IRLR 233.

[166] See *Office Angels Ltd v Rainer-Thomas* [1991] IRLR 214.

[167] [1999] IRLR 22; see also *Wincanton Ltd v (1) Cranny; (2) SDM European Transport Ltd* [2000] IRLR 716 CA.

[168] Reasonableness must be interpreted in accordance with what was in the contemplation of the parties at the date the contract was made: *Allan Janes LLP v Johal* [2006] IRLR 599.

[169] By way of contrast, a similar clause was held to be reasonable in *SBJ Stephenson Ltd v Mandy* [2000] IRLR 233, because the protection of the levels of investment in training employees and the stability of the workforce was a legitimate subject for a restrictive covenant.

[170] See also *Dawnay, Day & Co Ltd v de Braconier d'Alphen* [1997] IRLR 442 CA where a clause which purported to stop the solicitation of employees of all sorts, including junior staff, was held to be too wide to be enforceable.

[171] *Thomas v Farr plc* [2007] IRLR 419.

[172] *Scully UK Ltd v Lee* [1998] IRLR 259 CA; see also *Hollis & Co v Stocks* [2000] IRLR 712 CA, where a restriction on an employee not to work within ten miles of the ex-employer's office (a firm of solicitors) was interpreted as a restriction on working as a solicitor, rather than any employment, and was therefore not an unreasonable restraint of trade.

In *Rock Refrigeration*[173] a restrictive covenant which had effect upon the ending of the contract of employment 'howsoever arising' was not necessarily unreasonable. Nevertheless, in the event of the termination resulting from the employer's repudiatory breach of the contract, the employee would be released from their obligations under the contract. Similarly, a covenant which 'restricts individuals from competing in any aspect of a company's business being carried on at the date of the termination in which the employees were actually involved during their employment' was held to be reasonable.[174] A non-solicitation clause which prevented an ex-employee from dealing even with potential clients who were negotiating with the employer at the time the individual left employment was also held not to be too vague to be relied upon. This was the situation in *International Consulting Services (UK) Ltd v Hart*,[175] where an ex-employee approached a potential customer who had held some preliminary discussions about the provision of services. In this context, the discussions were held to be negotiations and were caught by the non-solicitation clause.

4.5.2.3 Confidential information

In *Faccenda Chicken*[176] employees set up a business delivering chickens to butchers, supermarkets and catering operations and competed directly with their previous employer who had an identical operation. None of the employees had a restrictive covenant in their previous contracts of employment. The Court of Appeal considered the apparent contradiction between the duty of an employee not to disclose confidential information which had been obtained in the course of employment with the *prima facie* right of any person to exploit the experience and knowledge which they have acquired for the purpose of earning a living. Neil LJ set out the following legal principles:

(1) where the parties were, or had been, linked by a contract of employment, then the obligations of the employee are to be determined by that contract;
(2) in the absence of express terms, the obligations of the employee with respect to the use of information are the subject of implied terms;
(3) whilst the employee remains in the employment of the employer, these obligations are included in the implied term of good faith or fidelity;[177]
(4) the implied term which places an obligation on the employee as to conduct after the ending of employment is more restricted in its application than that which imposes a general duty of good faith;[178]

---

[173] *Rock Refrigeration Ltd v Jones and Seward Refrigeration Ltd* [1996] IRLR 675 CA.
[174] *Turner v Commonwealth & British Minerals Ltd* [2000] IRLR 114 – the fact that the employees were paid extra in return for agreeing to the restrictive covenant is not decisive, but is a legitimate factor to be taken into account; see also *Ward Evans Financial Services Ltd v Fox* [2002] IRLR 120 CA.
[175] [2000] IRLR 227.
[176] *Faccenda Chicken Ltd v Fowler* [1986] IRLR 69 CA.
[177] The duty of good faith will be broken if the employee makes, copies or memorises a list of the employer's customers for use after the end of employment.
[178] The court relied upon the judgments in *Printers & Finishers Ltd v Holloway* [1965] RPC 253 and *E Worsley & Co Ltd v Cooper* [1939] 1 All ER 290 to distinguish between those secrets which are really trade secrets and not to be revealed and those matters which are confidential whilst the employment subsists.

(5) in order to decide whether a particular item of information falls within an implied term to prevent its use or disclosure after employment has ceased, it is necessary to consider all the circumstances of the case.

In considering what all the circumstances of the case are, a number of issues can be taken into account. First, the nature of the employment: if it is one that habitually uses confidential information there may be a higher standard of confidentiality required. Secondly, the nature of the information itself: only information that can be regarded as a 'trade secret' can be protected, rather than looking at the 'status' of the information. Thirdly, the steps that the employer had taken to impress upon the employee the confidentiality of the information. Finally, whether the relevant information can be isolated from other information which the employee is free to disclose or use.

For information to be classified as a trade secret, and therefore not to be disclosed, it is not incumbent upon an employer to point out to an employee the precise limits of what is sought to be made confidential, although the closer an employee is to the 'inner circles' of decision making, the more likely they are to know that information is confidential.[179] This issue presents particular problems for employees who wish to change employers. There is a distinction between that knowledge which an employer can show to be a trade secret and therefore the employer's property and that information which is the result of the skill, experience and know-how accumulated by an employee in the course of their employment. The information needs to be precise and specific enough for a separate body of objective knowledge to be identified, rather than a general claim to an accumulated body of knowledge which an employer claims to be confidential.[180]

By way of contrast, an employer may be able to enforce an obligation of confidentiality against an employee who has made an unauthorised disclosure and used documents acquired in the course of employment. In *Camelot v Centaur Publications Ltd*[181] a copy of the draft accounts of the company which ran the National Lottery was sent by an unknown employee to an interested journalist. The information revealed, amongst other matters, increases in remuneration for some of the company's directors. The company asked the court to ensure that the leaked documents were returned, so that they could identify the employee who caused the leak. The Court of Appeal accepted that the case was not a whistleblowing one and held that it was in the public interest to enable the employer to discover a disloyal employee in their midst.

4.5.2.4 Public Interest Disclosure Act 1998
The Public Interest Disclosure Act 1998 amended ERA 1996 to provide some protection to those who disclose information about certain matters. Section 43J ERA 1996 makes void any provision in an agreement, including a contract of employment, which attempts to stop the worker from making a protected disclosure. Section 43A of the ERA 1996 provides that a 'protected disclosure' is a 'qualifying disclosure', as defined in section 43B, which is

---

[179] As in *Lancashire Fires Ltd v SA Lyons & Co Ltd* [1997] IRLR 113 CA.
[180] See *FSS Travel and Leisure Systems Ltd v Johnson* [1998] IRLR 382 CA and *Brooks v Olyslager OMS (UK) Ltd* [1998] IRLR 590 CA.
[181] [1998] IRLR 80 CA.

made in accordance with sections 43C–43H. The qualifying disclosures defined in section 43B are information about criminal offences, failure to comply with a legal obligation,[182] a miscarriage of justice, a danger to health and safety and damage to the environment. A likelihood of any of these events occurring is also a qualifying disclosure, as well as any information about concealment, or attempts to conceal, such information.

These disclosures must normally be made in 'good faith'[183] to an individual's employer or to some other person who has responsibility for the matter disclosed. The disclosure needs to be to these persons, to a legal adviser or to a prescribed person.[184] Sections 43G and 43H ERA 1996 impose strict rules about making disclosures in other circumstances. For example, apart from making the disclosure in good faith, the worker must reasonably believe that the information is true and not make disclosures for private gain. It must also be reasonable for the worker to make the disclosure.

Protection is given to a wide group of workers as defined in section 43K ERA 1996. Those who make a protected disclosure have the right not to be subject to detriment by any act, or failure to act, on the part of the employer by reason of the individual making the disclosure.[185] A dismissal for the same reason will be automatically unfair[186] as will selection for redundancy for this reason.[187] One of the problems for workers seeking to rely on this legislation is that there are a number of hurdles which have to be overcome, including showing that one is acting in good faith[188] and had a reasonable belief in the existence of wrongdoing.[189]

4.6 Other sources of terms

4.6.1 Custom and practice

It is possible for terms to become incorporated into the contract of employment as a result of long-term custom and practice. In *Sagar v Ridehalgh & Sons Ltd*[190] a weaver challenged a long-accepted practice in the textile industry of deducting pay for poor work. The weaver failed in the complaint because the court held that the practice had prevailed at the place of work for over 30 years. The practice was judged to be 'reasonable, certain and notorious' and, therefore, to have legal effect. There is a question of whether the practice can have

---

[182] See *Parkins v Sodexho Ltd* [2002] IRLR 109 and *Babula v Waltham Forest College* [2007] IRLR 346.

[183] See section 43C ERA 1996.

[184] See sections 43D–43F ERA 1996 and the Public Interest Disclosure (Prescribed Persons) Order 1999, SI 1999/1549.

[185] Section 47B ERA 1996. On the vicarious liability of employers see *Cumbria County Council v Carlisle-Morgan* [2007] IRLR 314. On compensation for injury to feelings see *Virgo Fidelis School v Boyle* [2004] IRLR 268.

[186] In *Miklaszewicz v Stolt Offshore Ltd* [2002] IRLR 344 an individual was dismissed, after the legislation came into effect, for making a disclosure some six years before. He was still held to be protected as the court held that it was the date of dismissal that triggered the employee's entitlement to protection, not the date of the disclosure.

[187] See sections 103A and 105(6A) ERA 1996; Public Interest Disclosure (Compensation) Regulations 1999, SI 1999/1548 on the level of awards that may be given; there is no maximum figure set for compensation in such cases.

[188] See *Street v Derbyshire Unemployed Workers Centre* [2004] IRLR 687.

[189] See *Bolton School v Evans* [2007] IRLR 140.

[190] [1931] 1 Ch 310 CA.

effect unless the individual is aware of its existence. In *Sagar*, the court found it difficult to believe that the complainant did not know of its existence.

In *Duke v Reliance Systems Ltd*[191] it was held that a management policy could not become incorporated into a contract of employment on the grounds of custom and practice unless it had been shown that the policy has been drawn to the employees' attention and had been followed without exception for a 'substantial period'. These factors were later referred to as 'to be among the most important circumstances to be taken into account', but that all the other circumstances needed to be looked at. These included whether the 'substantial' period should be looked at in relation to these other circumstances to justify the inference that the policy had achieved the status of a contractual term. Additionally the issue of communication with the employees was one of the circumstances in which it was made to support the inference that the employers intended to become contractually bound by it.[192]

The need for the custom and practice to be reasonable, certain and notorious was further illustrated in *Henry v London General Transport Services*.[193] In this case the trade union came to an agreement with the employers about changes to terms and conditions of employment in preparation for a management buy-out. These changes resulted in reductions in pay and other less advantageous terms and conditions. There had been a tradition of at least annual negotiations between the employer and the trade union and agreement on changes to terms and conditions. However, there was no express agreement that changes would automatically be incorporated into employees' individual contracts of employment. A number of employees, unhappy at the reductions, claimed unlawful deductions from their wages. The EAT held that, once the reasonableness, certainty and notoriety of the custom and practice was established it was to be presumed that the term represented the wishes and intentions of the parties concerned. This was not undermined by the fact that some individuals did not know of the practice or did not support it. Thus, in this case, the agreement was held to have become incorporated into the employees' individual contracts of employment.

4.6.2 Collective and workforce agreements

Collective agreements are defined in section 178(1) TULRCA 1992 as 'any agreement or arrangement made by or on behalf of one or more trade unions and one or more employers or employers' associations' concerning matters listed in section 178(2) TULRCA 1992 (see Chapter 12). The first item on the list, in section 178(2)(a), includes terms and conditions of employment. Collective agreements are presumed not to be legally enforceable contracts unless the agreement is in writing and contains a provision to that effect.[194] The result is that the vast majority of such agreements are not legally binding in

---

[191] [1982] IRLR 347.
[192] *Quinn v Calder Industrial Materials Ltd* [1996] IRLR 126.
[193] [2001] IRLR 132.
[194] Section 179(1) TULRCA 1992.

themselves (see Chapter 12). However, they achieve legal effect if they become incorporated into the contract of employment. If the contract states, for example, that:

> The basic terms and conditions of your employment by this company are in accordance with and subject to the provisions of relevant agreements made between and on behalf of the Engineering Employers' Federation and the trade unions . . .[195]

then this is likely to be interpreted as an express provision incorporating the collective agreements negotiated between the employers and the trade unions (this issue is further considered in Chapter 12).[196]

Workforce agreements appear to be an alternative strategy for dealing with a need to create a mechanism for consulting and negotiating with employees when there is no trade union recognised for collective bargaining purposes (see Chapter 12). Specifically, the requirements for reaching such agreements are contained in the Working Time Regulations 1998[197] and the Maternity and Parental Leave etc. Regulations 1999.[198] In both cases they are aimed at creating an opportunity for the parties to agree a more flexible approach to the implementation of the requirements of the regulations.

A workforce agreement[199] must apply to all the relevant members of a workforce or group and the agreement needs to be signed by all the individual members of the workforce or the group, or their representatives. The exception being in the case of smaller employers with 20 or fewer employees. In this case the agreement can be signed either by the appropriate representatives or by the majority of the workforce. There is no suggestion that such an agreement should not be legally enforceable, although it is interesting to contemplate how an agreement signed by a small employer and the majority of the workforce can bind a minority who might be opposed to the agreement.

4.7 Variations in terms

Section 4 ERA 1996 provides rules for notifying changes in the section 1 ERA 1996 statement of terms and conditions. The employer is required to give the employee a written statement of the changes at the earliest opportunity and, in any event, not later than one month after the change.[200] Section 4(3)(b) ERA 1996 provides for this to be done earlier if the person is required to work outside the United Kingdom for a period of more than one month. If the change relates to a change of employer and continuity of employment is not broken, then the new employer is not required to give a new statement, but merely to inform the employee of the change in circumstances,[201] specifying the date on which continuous employment began.[202]

---

[195] Quoted in *Alexander v Standard Telephones & Cables Ltd* [1991] IRLR 286.
[196] Collective agreements can be arrived at, and incorporated into the contract of employment, by individual employers or by employers' associations negotiating with individual trade unions or groups of unions; see, e.g., *Hamilton v Futura Floors Ltd* [1990] IRLR 478.
[197] SI 1998/1833.
[198] SI 1999/3312.
[199] See Schedule 1 Maternity and Parental Leave etc. Regulations 1999.
[200] Section 4(3)(a) ERA 1996.
[201] Section 4(6) ERA 1996.
[202] Section 4(8) ERA 1996.

There are a number of ways in which an employer may seek to change the terms of a contract of employment. The most straightforward would be to achieve mutual agreement to the changes with the employees and/or their representatives. If an employer is unable or unwilling to obtain this agreement, they may attempt to do so unilaterally. One way is to dismiss the employees and then offer them new contracts of employment containing the new terms. The employer will have satisfied their common law obligations if they give the contractually required period of notice of termination to their employees. The danger with this approach is that employers may leave themselves open to claims for unfair dismissal and redundancy and a lack of consultation concerning potential redundancies (see Chapter 10). In *GMB v Man Truck & Bus UK Ltd*[203] the respondent company had been formed by a merger of two other businesses. In order to harmonise terms and conditions the employees were given notice of dismissal and then offered immediate re-employment on the new harmonised terms and conditions. The EAT held that the employer had failed to consult as required by section 188 TULRCA 1992, which applies where there are collective dismissals.[204]

If the employer seeks to impose new terms then this may be interpreted as a repudiatory breach of contract, which the employee may decide to accept or not. One exception to this would be if the employer has a contractual right, by virtue of a document incorporated into the contract of employment, to make unilateral changes.[205] In *Farrant v The Woodroffe School*[206] the employer tried to alter the job description of an employee on the mistaken advice that they were entitled to do so under the terms of the contract of employment. Even though the advice, from the education department of the local authority, was mistaken, the subsequent dismissal of the employee was held to be fair because it was not unreasonable for the employer to act on the advice that they had been given.[207] A second exception might be if the courts were willing to imply a term into the contract which permitted the employer to make a change. In *Jones v Associated Tunnelling Co Ltd*[208] the EAT concluded that there was an implied term to the effect that the employer had the right to change the employee's place of work to another location within reasonable daily commuting distance. The nature of the work required this change and the term was implied in order to give the contract business efficacy.

In *Jones*,[209] the employer also unsuccessfully claimed that the employee had assented to the change in the contract by continuing to work for another 12 months and not objecting. This argument was also used in *Aparau v Iceland Frozen Foods plc*,[210] where the EAT adopted the same approach. There was a need for:

> great caution in reaching the conclusion that an employee has, by merely continuing an employment without any overt change or overt acceptance of terms which the employer is seeking to impose, truly accepted those terms so as to vary the contract.

---

[203] [2000] IRLR 636.
[204] See Chapter 10.
[205] See *Airlie v City of Edinburgh District Council* [1996] IRLR 516.
[206] [1998] IRLR 176.
[207] See also *Port of Sheerness Ltd and Medway Ports Ltd v Brachers* [1997] IRLR 214, where the employer's legal advisers were held liable for giving negligent advice on handling redundancies.
[208] [1981] IRLR 477.
[209] *Ibid.*
[210] [1996] IRLR 119 EAT; see also [2000] IRLR 196 CA on a separate point.

This case concerned a shop worker who was issued with a new contract containing a mobility clause, which was not activated for a further 12 months. It could not be said that the employee accepted the change by continuing performance when the impact of the change was some time away. Similarly, continuing to work under protest should not be construed as acceptance.[211]

In cases of pressing financial need the employer may be justified in changing the employees' terms and conditions. In *Catamaran Cruisers Ltd v Williams*[212] a company was in financial difficulties and wished to reduce employees' terms and conditions. The EAT thought that they were able to do this, but the lay members of the panel were obviously concerned about the outcome and stated that they wished:

> to record that much of recent employment law has been to protect employees against arbitrary changes of their terms and conditions of employment and that this, as a principle, must stand . . . and that an employer must demonstrate . . . if he dismisses an employee for failing to accept changes of their terms and conditions of employment his actions must fall within the bounds of reasonableness.

Sometimes employers make changes which are the result of management policy rather than a change in the contract of employment. If an employer has a code of practice on staff sickness which, for example, included procedures for monitoring different types of absence, a decision to alter the procedure so that there were more frequent checks might amount to a change of policy which the employer could carry out unilaterally.[213] Lord Woolf summed up the approach:[214]

> The general position is that contracts of employment can only be varied by agreement. However, in the employment field an employer or for that matter an employee can reserve the ability to change a particular aspect of the contract unilaterally by notifying the other party as part of the contract that this is the situation. However, clear language is required to reserve to one party unusual power of this sort. In addition, the Court is unlikely to favour an interpretation which does more than enable a party to vary contractual provisions with which that party is required to comply.

Further reading

Barmes, L., 'The Continuing Conceptual Crisis in the Common Law of the Contract of Employment' (2004) 67(3) *Modern Law Review* 435.
Collins, H., Ewing, K. and McColgan, A., *Labour Law: Text and Materials* (Hart Publishing, 2005), Chapter 2.
Deakin, S. and Morris, G., *Labour Law* (4th edn, Hart Publishing, 2005), Chapter 4.
Freedland, M., *The Personal Employment Contract* (Oxford University Press, 2003).
www.acas.org.uk
www.berr.gov.uk/

Visit **www.mylawchamber.co.uk/sargeant** to access legal updates, live web links and practice exam questions to test yourself on this chapter.

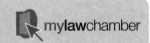

---

[211] *Rigby v Ferodo Ltd* [1987] IRLR 516 HL.
[212] [1994] IRLR 386.
[213] *Wandsworth London Borough Council v D'Silva* [1998] IRLR 193 CA.
[214] *Ibid* at p 197.

5

Termination of Employment

5.1 Introduction

There are a number of ways in which a contract of employment, like any other contract, can be brought to an end. It can occur because the performance of the contract becomes impossible or because either of the parties brings it to an end, in accordance with the contract. This may be done by voluntary notice given by the employee or by the employee's employment being terminated, by notice or otherwise, by the employer. In addition, statute provides some protection for employees who are dismissed, even when that dismissal is in accordance with the contract of employment.

5.2 Termination of the contract not resulting from dismissal

5.2.1 Frustration

The common law doctrine of frustration is concerned with situations where, as a result of some event outside the control of the parties, the contract becomes impossible to perform, at least in the way that the parties intended. This view was stated by Lord Radcliffe in *Davies Contractors Ltd v Fareham Urban District Council:*[1]

> . . . frustration occurs whenever the law recognises that without default of either party a contractual obligation has become incapable of being performed because the circumstances in which performance is called for would render it a thing radically different from that which was undertaken by the contract.

In *Paal Wilson & Co v Partenreederei Hannah Blumenthal*[2] the court held that there were two essential factors which must be present to frustrate a contract. These were that:

(1) there must be some unforeseen change in the outside or extraneous circumstances, not provided for by the parties, which stopped the performance of the contract;
(2) the outside or extraneous event should have occurred without the fault or default of either party to the contract.

Such a situation might be a custodial sentence. In *FC Shepherd & Co Ltd v Jerrom*[3] a contract of apprenticeship was held to be frustrated when an individual was sentenced to

---

[1] [1956] AC 696 HL at p 728.
[2] [1983] 1 AC 854 HL.
[3] [1986] IRLR 358 CA; see also *Four Seasons Healthcare Ltd v Maughan* [2005] IRLR 324.

a period in a young offenders' institution for his part in a motorcycle gang fight. This was an event that was capable of rendering the performance of the contract impossible. The fact that the frustration must have occurred without the fault of either party means, according to the court, that the party who asserts that the performance of the contract has been frustrated must show that the frustration was not caused by his or her own act, and the person against whom frustration is asserted cannot rely on his or her own misconduct as an answer.

A number of principles can be derived from these and other cases.[4] These are:

(1) The court must guard against too easy an application of the doctrine.
(2) Although it is not necessary to decide that frustration occurred on a particular date, it may help the court to decide on whether there was a true frustration situation.
(3) There were a number of factors which may help to decide the issue.[5] These were the length of the previous employment; how long the employment would have continued;[6] the nature of the job; the nature, effect and length of the illness or disabling event; the needs of the employer for the work to be done and the need for a replacement to do it; the risk to the employer of incurring obligations related to redundancy or unfair dismissal of the replacement employee; whether wages have continued to be paid; the acts of the employer in relation to the employment, including dismissal of the employee; and whether in all the circumstances an employer could be expected to wait any longer.
(4) The party alleging frustration should not be able to rely on that frustration if it were caused by that party.[7]

Long-term sickness of an employee is capable of frustrating the operation of the contract of employment, although care needs to be taken as to whether the long-term incapacity has become a disability, thus providing the individual with protection under the Disability Discrimination Act 1995 (see Chapter 7). If, however, there are provisions in the contract of employment concerning rules for long-term sickness, it may be difficult to argue that the incapacity is an unforeseen event,[8] although it is unlikely that a total incapacity arising from an illness could have been foreseen.[9] The frustration of a contract takes place because of events that have happened. It is not possible to argue that a contract has been frustrated by the likelihood of an event happening in the future. Thus when an employee returns to work after a heart attack, it is not possible to argue frustration on the grounds that the same employee might have a second heart attack in the future.[10]

---

[4] See *Williams v Watson Luxury Coaches Ltd* [1990] IRLR 164.
[5] Some of which derive from *The Egg Stores (Stamford Hill) v Leibovici* [1976] IRLR 376, which considered the issues connected with the fairness of dismissing absentees.
[6] This is not to say that short-term contracts are not capable of being frustrated; see *Hart v RN Marshall & Sons (Bulwell) Ltd* [1977] IRLR 50.
[7] Diplock described this as 'the fundamental and moral rule that a man should not be allowed to take advantage of his own wrong' in *Hongkong Fir Shipping Co v Kawasaki Kishen Kaisha* [1962] 2 QB 26.
[8] See *Villella v MFI Furniture Centres Ltd* [1999] IRLR 468.
[9] *Nottcutt v Universal Equipment Co (London) Ltd* [1986] IRLR 218 CA.
[10] *Converform (Darwen) Ltd v Bell* [1981] IRLR 195.

5.2.2 Death of the employer

The death of either party may serve to frustrate a contract, but certain tribunal proceedings may continue and be defended by the personal representative of the deceased employer.[11] These proceedings include those for itemised pay statements, guarantee payments, protection from detriment, time off work,[12] maternity rights, the right to a written statement of reasons for dismissal and those rights relating to unfair dismissal, redundancy payments and insolvency protection.[13] Where a right under these headings accrues after the death, then it will be treated as a liability of the deceased employer and as having accrued before the death.[14]

5.2.3 Voluntary resignation

This refers to a situation where the employee voluntarily resigns with or without notice.[15] It is not always clear whether an employee has resigned voluntarily or as a result of pressure from the employer.[16] As was held in *Sheffield v Oxford Controls Co Ltd*,[17] there is a principle of law which states that:

> where an employee resigns and that resignation is determined upon by him because he prefers to resign rather than be dismissed (the alternative having been expressed to him by the employer in the terms of the threat that if he does not resign he will be dismissed) the mechanics of the resignation do not cause that to be other than a dismissal.

This approach was followed by the Court of Appeal in *Jones v Mid-Glamorgan County Council*,[18] which described it as a 'principle of the utmost flexibility which is willing . . . to recognise a dismissal when it sees it'.[19] There was not a dismissal, however, in *International Computers Ltd v Kennedy*,[20] which also involved a redundancy situation. Advice to employees to make every effort to find other jobs as quickly as possible was not equivalent to a statement which said 'resign or be dismissed'. The invitation to resign was too imprecise in relation to the ultimate dismissal of individuals. It would also appear that there is no dismissal when an employee resigns on terms offered by an employer's disciplinary subcommittee. In *Staffordshire County Council v Donovan*[21] the EAT stated:

> It seems to us that it would be most unfortunate if, in a situation where the parties are seeking to negotiate in the course of disciplinary proceedings and an agreed form of resignation is worked

---

[11] See article 9 Employment Tribunals (Extension of Jurisdiction) Order 1994, SI 1994/1623.

[12] Excluding sections 58–60 ERA 1996 for time off for occupational pension trustees.

[13] Section 206(1) ERA 1996.

[14] Section 207 ERA 1996.

[15] This may, in certain circumstances, amount to constructive dismissal: see below.

[16] See *Martin v MBS Fastenings (Glynwed) Distribution Ltd* [1983] IRLR 198 CA; this was not the issue at the Court of Appeal, but in the lower courts there was a question as to whether the employee had resigned in anticipation of the result of a disciplinary hearing or had been invited to resign by the employer.

[17] [1979] IRLR 133 at p 135. See now *Sandhu v Jan de Rijk Transport Ltd* [2007] IRLR 519 CA.

[18] [1997] IRLR 685 CA; [1997] ICR 815 CA.

[19] See also *Allders International Ltd v Parkins* [1981] IRLR 68, where an employee was given the option of resigning or the employer calling in the CID to investigate allegations of theft.

[20] [1981] IRLR 28.

[21] [1981] IRLR 108.

out by the parties, one of the parties should be able to say subsequently that the fact that the agreement was reached in the course of disciplinary proceedings entitles the employee thereafter to say that there was a dismissal.

Two issues here are to what extent the employee must make clear their decision to resign and whether the employer has any obligations arising out of the decision. Often contracts of employment require a resignation to be done in a certain way, for example, by putting it in writing or directing it to a certain individual. *Ely v YKK Fasteners*[22] concerned an employee who was considering emigrating to Australia. The employee told his employer of his plans and that he had applied for a job there. Eventually the employer took steps to replace him. When the individual decided not to emigrate he informed his employers. By then he had been replaced and the employer regarded the individual's employment as being at an end. The question was whether there had been a resignation or a dismissal. It was held that there was a dismissal and that the reason for this was the employee's late notification to the employer that he had changed his mind about resigning. This dismissal was for 'some other substantial reason' (see below) within the meaning of section 98(1)(b) ERA 1996.

Sometimes employees resign on the spur of the moment because they have become angry or discontented about some actions of the employer. This occurred in *Kwik-Fit (GB) Ltd v Lineham*[23] where, after an argument, the employee threw his keys down on to a counter and walked out. The EAT held that there was no ambiguity in the words used by the employee. When a resignation occurs there is no obligation, except in special circumstances, for the employer to do anything but accept the employee's decision. Words spoken in the heat of the moment or as a result of pressure on an employee may, however, amount to special circumstances. Where there are such special circumstances the employer should allow a day or two to elapse before accepting the resignation at face value. During this time information may arise as to whether the resignation was really intended. Not to do such an investigation may open the employer to the risk of new facts coming out at an employment tribunal hearing which may cast doubt on the intention to resign. Where there are no special circumstances arising out of a decision made in the heat of the moment or as a result of employer pressure, the employer is entitled to take the employee's words at face value and is not required to look behind the words and interpret them as a 'reasonable employer' might. Thus, in *Sothern v Franks Charlesly & Co*,[24] the words 'I am resigning' could be taken at face value, but in *Barclay v City of Glasgow District Council*,[25] the resignation by an employee with learning difficulties was held to constitute a special circumstance even though unambiguous words of resignation had been used.[26]

5.2.4 Termination by agreement

Termination by mutual consent is an important concept that has been widely used by employers in order to reduce the number of employees. It will usually take the form of

---

[22] [1993] IRLR 500 CA.
[23] [1992] IRLR 156.
[24] [1981] IRLR 278 CA.
[25] [1983] IRLR 313.
[26] See also *Sovereign House Security Services Ltd v Savage* [1989] IRLR 115 CA, where the words 'jacking the job in' spoken in a heated moment were held not to be a resignation.

a financial inducement in excess of any statutory entitlement to make it attractive for employees to resign. One common form is that of early retirement, where older workers are induced to leave the workforce by the offer of enhanced retirement packages. This was the situation in *Birch and Humber v The University of Liverpool*[27] where the employer invited applications for early retirement as part of a staff reduction exercise. The two applicants were amongst those who applied and were accepted. Subsequently they applied for redundancy payments. The employment tribunal was first faced with the question of whether they had been dismissed. It was held that, because the retirement of any individual was subject to the employer's approval, then it was that approval which amounted to a dismissal, i.e. when the employer wrote to the employees stating when their employment would end, a dismissal took place. The appeal to the EAT against this decision was successful and was supported by the Court of Appeal, which held that there had been a mutual agreement to terminate the contract of employment. The acceptance of the applications could not be divorced from the formal applications to retire. Purchas LJ stated that 'in my judgment, dismissal . . . is not consistent with free, mutual consent, bringing a contract of employment to an end'.

The important question is whether the employer and the employee have freely agreed to end the contract of employment. *Igbo v Johnson Matthey Chemicals Ltd*[28] concerned a clause in a contract which an employer required an employee to sign before extended leave was granted. The clause stated that a failure to return on the due date would lead to the contract of employment being automatically terminated. The employee was ill at the time she was due to return and, despite the submission of a medical certificate, the employer took the view that the failure did indeed terminate the contract. It was argued that there was no dismissal, but a consensual termination. The Court of Appeal rejected this because of its impact on (now) section 203(1) ERA 1996, which provides that any agreement designed to exclude or limit the operation of the Act or stopping an individual from bringing proceedings before an employment tribunal was void. The clause that the employee had been required to sign attempted to limit her potential claim for unfair dismissal under the ERA 1996.[29] *Logan Salton v Durham County Council*[30] concerned an employee who, after he became aware that a report to his employer recommended his summary dismissal, negotiated a written leaving agreement with the employer. He subsequently claimed that this agreement was done under duress. The EAT refused to accept this and distinguished the case from *Igbo* by holding that the agreement was not part of the contract of employment or a variation of it, but a separate contract that was entered into willingly, without duress and after proper advice and for good consideration.

---

[27] [1985] IRLR 165 CA; see also *Scott v Coalite Fuels and Chemicals Ltd* [1988] IRLR 131 which also concerned individuals taking voluntary early retirement; the EAT followed *Birch and Humber* in holding that the decision as to whether someone had been dismissed was a question of fact for the employment tribunal to decide.

[28] [1986] IRLR 215 CA.

[29] See also *Tracey v Zest Equipment Co Ltd* [1992] IRLR 268, where the clause stated that 'the company will assume that you have terminated your employment with us' if there was a failure to return to work on the due date; this was held to be too imprecise to be legally binding.

[30] [1989] IRLR 99.

5.3 Termination of the contract by dismissal

5.3.1 Meaning of dismissal

For statutory purposes section 95 ERA 1996 provides that a person is dismissed by the employer if:

(1) the contract under which the individual is employed is terminated by the employer with, or without, notice;
(2) the person is employed under a limited term contract which terminates by virtue of the limiting event without being renewed under the same contract (see Chapter 4). There are three categories of limiting event: the expiry of a fixed term; the performance of a specific task; or the occurrence of an event or failure of an event to occur;[31]
(3) the employee terminates the contract, with or without notice, as a result of the employer's conduct. This last situation is commonly referred to as constructive dismissal.

As with issues concerning voluntary resignation and mutual agreement (see above), employment tribunals may be asked to decide whether words used by an employer constitute dismissal. In *Tanner v DT Kean*,[32] for example, an employer used the words 'That's it, you're finished with me.' The employee claimed that this was a dismissal, but the employment tribunal held that the words were an expression of annoyance and a reprimand. They considered what a reasonable employee would take the words to mean in the circumstances. The EAT stated that, in order to arrive at the correct meaning of the words, one could look at events that preceded the words spoken as well as the events which followed, in order to determine whether the employer's words were intended to bring the contract to an end.

5.3.2 Wrongful dismissal

The common law concept of wrongful dismissal may not be a fruitful avenue for employees to follow, unless, as in *Clark v BET plc*,[33] the individual is entitled to a long period of notice.[34] This is because, as most employers will have a contractual right to give notice, damages will be limited to those losses arising out of the breach of contract, i.e. the loss of the notice period, although this may include the loss of benefits that might have accrued during that notice period. In *Silvey v Pendragon plc*[35] the employee was dismissed for reasons of redundancy some 12 days before his 55th birthday, when certain pension rights would have accrued to him. Although the employee was given 12 weeks' pay in lieu of notice there was no provision for such a payment in his contract of employment. The failure to give him 12 weeks' notice was held to be a repudiatory breach of the contract. The court held that he was not only entitled to damages consisting of wages or salary, but

---

[31] 'Limited term contracts' and 'limiting event' are defined in section 235(2A) and (2B) ERA 1996 respectively.
[32] [1978] IRLR 110.
[33] [1997] IRLR 348; the notice entitlement was three years.
[34] See also *University of Oxford v (1) Humphries; (2) Associated Examining Board* [2000] IRLR 183 CA, which was a case where a university employee had a tenured post which would continue until he retired.
[35] [2001] IRLR 685 CA.

also of the value of any pension rights which would have accrued during the period of notice. There was no difference in principle between lost pension rights and lost pay. Secondly, any entitlement to non-contractual damages will be limited by the common law duty to mitigate one's losses. It may, however, be the only action possible if an employee has less than one year's continuous employment and is debarred from pursuing a claim for unfair dismissal in accordance with Part X ERA 1996.

It is not entirely clear what the effect of an employer's breach is. The alternatives seem to be, first, that it results in an automatic termination of the contract of employment. This might seem reasonable as a breach which consists of a wrongful dismissal is likely to have the effect of destroying the basis of mutual trust and confidence between the employer and employee. The problem with this approach is that it makes wrongful dismissal a special case when compared to the way that the law of contract would normally treat a breach of contract. This 'normal' route is the second alternative, which is that it is the innocent party's choice as to whether to accept the repudiation and terminate the contract. In *Sanders v Ernest A Neale Ltd*[36] it was explicitly held that a repudiation of the contract of employment was an exception to the 'normal rule' that an unaccepted repudiation did not discharge the contract. Dismissal, which was a breach by an employer of the employee's contract of employment, terminated the contract without the need for acceptance by the employee.

Although an employee might refuse to accept that the contract is at an end, the reality is that they may have little choice in the matter. This dilemma was exemplified in *Gunton v London Borough of Richmond upon Thames*,[37] where it was accepted that the employer had repudiated the contract of employment and a wrongful dismissal had taken place. The Court of Appeal accepted that the individual ought to be able to decide whether to accept the repudiation of the contract, but stated that:

> this practical basis for according an election to the injured party has no reality in relation to a contract of service where the repudiation takes the form of an express and direct termination of the contract in contravention of its terms. I would describe this as a total repudiation which is at once destructive of the contractual relationship.

The problem for the wronged individual is that the court will not allow them to claim pay for work not done, i.e. after their contract has been repudiated.[38] If the individual then claims damages the contract must, by implication, be treated as being at an end, because the court could not reinstate the individual by an order for specific performance. Moreover the claim for damages for wrongful dismissal cannot continue beyond the time when, under the contract of employment, the employer could lawfully have brought the contract to an end.[39] This contrasts with the approach of the courts when an employer unilaterally varies a term of the contract of employment, such as a reduction of wages. Such an event is likely to be a repudiatory action by the employer. In *Rigby v Ferodo Ltd*[40] an employee elected to continue working after the employer reduced his wages. Although the

---

[36] [1974] ICR 565.
[37] [1980] IRLR 321 CA.
[38] See *Alexander v Standard Telephones and Cables Ltd* [1991] IRLR 286.
[39] See Ralph Gibson LJ in *Boyo v London Borough of Lambeth* [1995] IRLR 50 CA.
[40] [1987] IRLR 516 HL.

employer's action was a repudiatory breach of the contract of employment, the contract did not automatically end unless the employee accepted the breach as a repudiation. The employee had made known his objections and so it could not be held that there was an implied acceptance of the breach. Unlike cases of outright dismissal and an employee walking out, there was no reason why the contract of employment should be treated any differently to any other contract. Generally an unaccepted repudiation leaves the contractual obligations of the parties unaffected.

5.3.3 Notice

At common law employment is liable to be determined by 'reasonable' periods of notice.[41] If there is no express term to that effect in the contract of employment then it may be implied.[42]

Statute has limited the freedom of action of employers in giving, or not giving, notice of dismissal to their employees. The employee has certain statutory rights to a minimum notice period to be given by the employer.[43] These are an entitlement to at least one week's notice for employees who have been continuously employed for at least one month and with less than two years' continuous employment, with an extra week for each year of continuous employment up to not less than 12 weeks' notice for continuous employment of 12 years or more. By way of contrast, employers are entitled to at least one week's notice of termination of employment from employees who have been continuously employed for at least one month.[44] Additionally, any requirements for consultation with employees or their representatives, in redundancy or transfer situations (see Chapter 10), may inhibit the employer from giving notice until the appropriate time. None of this affects more generous contractual arrangements or the rights of either party to treat the contract as terminated without notice as a result of the other's conduct.[45]

The contract of employment continues to subsist during the notice period. The statutory rules contemplate the contract being brought to an end by one of the parties. It follows, therefore, that the ending of the contract through the doctrine of frustration, which occurs through no fault or design of the parties, will exclude any rules relating to notice periods.[46] Employees have the right to be paid during their notice period even if there is no work for them, provided that they are ready and willing to work. Pay is also protected if the notice period coincides with absence from work because of sickness, pregnancy, childbirth, parental leave or holiday leave.[47] An employer is not required, however, to pay for absences due to time off taken in accordance with Part VI ERA 1996,[48] or for trade union duties and activities, as in sections 168 and 170 TULRCA 1992, or for

---

[41] See *McClelland v Northern Ireland Health Services Board* [1957] 2 All ER 129 HL.
[42] See, e.g., *Masiak v City Restaurants (UK) Ltd* [1999] IRLR 780.
[43] Section 86(1) ERA 1996.
[44] Section 86(2) ERA 1996.
[45] Section 86(6) ERA 1996.
[46] *GF Sharp & Co Ltd v McMillan* [1998] IRLR 632.
[47] Sections 88–89 ERA 1996. See *Burlo v Langley* [2007] IRLR 145.
[48] Such as time off for public duties, looking for work and care of dependants.

taking part in strike action during the notice period, if it is the employee that has given notice.[49]

The ERA 1996 does not prevent an employee from accepting a payment in lieu of notice but an employer must have contractual authority for insisting on such a payment. Without such authority a payment in lieu of notice will be construed as damages for the failure to provide proper notice.[50] Thus a payment in lieu can properly terminate a contract of employment if the contract provides for such a payment or the parties agree that the employee will accept a payment in lieu, provided the payment relates to a period no shorter than that of the notice to which the employee would be entitled either under the contract of employment or section 86(1) ERA 1996.[51] The date of termination at common law is the day notice expires or the day wages in lieu are accepted.

5.3.4 Summary dismissal

The right to dismiss summarily, i.e. without giving notice, may be an express or an implied term of the contract of employment. If it is an express term then the reason for the dismissal needs to come within the contractual definition of conduct leading to such dismissal. Thus, in *Dietman v London Borough of Brent*,[52] a clause in the contract of employment defined gross misconduct, for which instant dismissal would result, as 'misconduct of such a nature that the authority is justified in no longer tolerating the continued presence at the place of work of the employee who commits the offence'. After an inquiry the employee was found grossly negligent in her duties. The court held, however, that gross negligence did not come within the contractual definition of gross misconduct and that, therefore, the employee had been wrongfully dismissed.

The fact that a dismissal is without notice, or without sufficient notice, does not in itself render it unfair in statutory terms, but the lack of notice may render it a breach of the terms of the contract and a wrongful dismissal.[53] It is likely that the summary nature of the dismissal can only be justified as a response to actions which breach an important term of the contract in such a way as to undermine the employment relationship, including the duty of mutual trust and confidence. In *Laws v London Chronicle (Indicator Newspapers) Ltd*[54] Lord Evershed MR stated that the question was 'whether the conduct complained of is such as to show the servant to have disregarded the essential conditions of the contract of service'. A more modern view was expressed in *Neary and Neary v Dean of Westminster*[55] where Lord Jauncey stated that:

> conduct amounting to gross misconduct justifying dismissal must so undermine the trust and confidence which is inherent in the particular contract of employment that the master should no longer be required to retain the servant in his employment.

---

[49] Section 91(1)–(2) ERA 1996.
[50] *Cerberus v Rowley* [1981] IRLR 160.
[51] *Ginsberg Ltd v Parker* [1988] IRLR 483.
[52] [1988] IRLR 299 CA.
[53] See *BSC Sports & Social Club v Morgan* [1987] IRLR 391.
[54] [1959] 2 All ER 285 CA.
[55] [1999] IRLR 288.

The conduct affecting the basis of mutual trust and confidence between the parties needs to be serious[56] and perhaps more than a one-off incident. A situation where an employee appeared to be provoked into swearing at an employer and was then dismissed was held to be a wrongful dismissal, because the employer had already decided to dismiss the employee prior to the incident.[57] An example of where the courts have held a summary dismissal for gross misconduct to be acceptable is when an employee accesses confidential information, to which they are not entitled, for illegitimate purposes. In *Denco Ltd v Joinson*[58] an employee, who was a trade union representative, obtained information relating to the employer's business and other employees' salaries. The EAT held that this was no different to going into an office, for which he had no authorisation, picking up a key off the desk and unlocking a filing cabinet to take out confidential information.

If employers do not invoke the right to end the contract within a reasonable period, they will be taken to have waived their rights and can only seek damages. What is a reasonable period will depend on the facts of the particular case. In *Allders International v Parkins*[59] it was held that nine days was too long a period to be allowed to pass in relation to an allegation of stealing before deciding what to do about the alleged repudiatory conduct.

Finally, there may be an issue as to whether an individual is entitled to payment in lieu of notice after an instant dismissal. In *T & K Home Improvements Ltd v Skilton*[60] a contractual term entitled the employer to terminate an employee's contract of employment 'with immediate effect' if he failed to reach his sales targets in any one month. However, such a phrase was held not to deprive the employee of the right to the three months' notice to which the contract entitled him. There was evidence elsewhere in the contract of terms which specifically deprived him of the right to a payment in lieu in certain situations, but these did not apply in this case.

5.3.5 Remedies for wrongful dismissal

A wrongful dismissal is a dismissal without notice or with inadequate notice in circumstances where proper notice should have been given. The expression also covers dismissals which are in breach of agreed procedures. Thus where there is a contractual disciplinary procedure, an employee may be able to obtain an injunction (interdict) or declaration from the courts so as to prevent a dismissal or declare a dismissal void if the procedure has not been followed.[61] However, an injunction will only be granted if the court is convinced that the employer's repudiation has not been accepted, that the employer has sufficient trust and confidence in the employee, and that damages would not be an adequate remedy.[62]

The problem with seeking an injunction to stop an employer taking steps which might lead to a repudiatory breach is that it might have the same effect as an order for specific

---

[56] The gross misconduct must be examined in relation to the particular job and does not necessarily mean that the employee could not be employed elsewhere: see *Hamilton v Argyll and Clyde Health Board* [1993] IRLR 99.
[57] *Wilson v Racher* [1974] ICR 428 CA.
[58] [1991] IRLR 63.
[59] [1981] IRLR 68.
[60] [2000] IRLR 595 CA.
[61] See *Jones v Gwent County Council* [1992] IRLR 521.
[62] See *Dietman v London Borough of Brent* [1988] IRLR 299.

performance. The stopping of certain actions by an employer might have the same effect as ordering the employer to take alternative actions. This did not stop the granting of an interlocutory injunction in *Peace v City of Edinburgh Council*.[63] This case concerned a teacher who was subject to a disciplinary procedure. The employer was stopped from introducing a new procedure which would have been in breach of the contract of employment. The court concluded that they were intervening in a choice between alternative schemes, rather than enforcing mutual co-operation. The individual was suspended, but the employment contract remained in existence.[64] *Anderson v Pringle of Scotland Ltd*[65] concerned an employer's desire to change the method of selecting individuals for redundancy from a 'last in first out' basis to a more discretionary one. The 'last in first out' formula had been part of a collective agreement which was incorporated into the employees' contracts of employment. The court showed itself willing to grant an interim interdict (injunction) prohibiting the employers from using any other method for selection. The court recognised the issue of specific performance, but held that the employment relationship continued and the decision was about the mechanisms of dismissal, rather than the principle of dismissal. Lord Prosser stated that:

> In the contemporary world, where even reinstatement is a less inconceivable remedy, intervention before dismissal must in my view be seen as a matter of discretion, rather than an impossibility.[66]

Since the courts are reluctant to enforce a contract of employment, in the vast majority of cases the employee's remedy will lie in damages for breach of contract. A person who suffers a wrongful dismissal is entitled to be compensated for such loss as arises naturally from the breach and for any loss which was reasonably foreseeable by the parties as being likely to arise from it. Hence an employee will normally recover only the amount of wages lost between the date of the wrongful dismissal and the date when the contract could lawfully have been terminated.[67]

The principle that damages resulting from a breach of contract by wrongful dismissal should put an individual in the same position as if the contract had been performed does not apply in a situation where the failure to give contractual notice results in the loss of opportunity to claim unfair dismissal.[68] If an employer has the option of paying for the notice period whilst it is being worked or paying a sum of money in lieu of notice, then the employer is able to pay this, even if it means that the employee will be stopped from having enough continuous employment to qualify to make a claim.[69] The courts will make the assumption that the employer will choose to perform the contract in the least burdensome way and that, had the contract been performed lawfully, the employee would have been dismissed at the earliest opportunity.[70] There would not be a concern, when looking at the

---

[63] [1999] IRLR 417.
[64] See also *Robb v London Borough of Hammersmith* [1991] IRLR 72.
[65] [1998] IRLR 64.
[66] *Ibid* at p 67. See also *Irani v Southampton and South West Hampshire Health Authority* [1985] IRLR 203, where an interlocutory injunction was granted to restrain the employer from implementing an employee's notice before they had followed the disputes procedure.
[67] See *Marsh v National Autistic Society* [1993] IRLR 453.
[68] See *Harper v Virgin Net Ltd* [2004] IRLR 390.
[69] *Morran v Glasgow Council of Tenants Associations* [1998] IRLR 67.
[70] *Lavarack v Woods of Colchester Ltd* [1967] 1 QB 278 CA.

failure to follow a disciplinary procedure, as to whether an employee would have been dismissed or not, if those disciplinary procedures had been followed, but for how much longer the employee would have been employed before the employer could contractually give notice. It is this that will decide whether there has been a loss of opportunity or not.[71]

Damages are not awarded for distress or hurt feelings. In *Bliss v South East Thames Regional Health Authority*[72] Dillon LJ stated the general principle:

> The general rule laid down by the House of Lords[73] is that where damages fall to be assessed for breach of contract rather than in tort it is not permissible to award general damages for frustration, mental distress, injured feelings or annoyance caused by the breach. Modern thinking tends to be that the amount of damages recoverable for a wrong should be the same whether the cause of action is laid in contract or tort. But in *Addis* Lord Loreburn regarded the rule that damages for injured feelings cannot be recovered in contract for wrongful dismissal as too inveterate to be altered.

It was argued, in *French v Barclays Bank plc*,[74] that a loan contract providing low-interest mortgage facilities should fall within the exceptions. Thus, when an employer varied the terms of the loan, it was argued, there ought to be damages awarded for anxiety and stress. This argument was not accepted by the court who felt constrained by the authorities, such as *Addis* and *Bliss*.[75]

Employees have a duty to mitigate their losses, although there should be no set-off against any sums to which they are contractually entitled. This issue was considered in *Cerberus Software Ltd v Rowley*.[76] The contract of employment provided for the termination of the contract upon the giving of either side of six months' notice. The contract also allowed that the employer *may* make a payment in lieu of notice to the employee. In the event the employee was dismissed without notice or payment in lieu. After five weeks he obtained alternative work at a higher salary. He then brought an application claiming damages for wrongful dismissal. One issue was whether he was entitled to six months' pay in lieu of notice as a contractual right or whether the measure of damages was the amount that the employee would have earned if the contract had continued. In the latter case the employee would have a duty to mitigate losses. The court held that the contract gave the employer a choice of whether to make the payment in lieu or not, so the employee did not have a contractual right to the six months' pay and the normal rules concerning minimising losses should apply.[77] The distinction between a claim for payments due under the contract and those which are damages for wrongful dismissal is important. In the former situation the court or tribunal is being asked to set a sum to be paid to the claimant, irrespective of any damage suffered as a consequence of the breach.[78] Where there is a failure to mitigate, the court will deduct a sum it feels the employee might reasonably have been expected to earn. As regards state benefits, it would appear that any benefit received by the dismissed employee should be deducted only where not to do so would result in a

---

[71] See *Janciuk v Winerite Ltd* [1998] IRLR 63.
[72] [1985] IRLR 308 CA.
[73] In *Addis v Gramophone Company Ltd* [1909] AC 488 HL.
[74] [1998] IRLR 646 CA.
[75] See also *Johnson v Unisys Ltd* [2001] IRLR 279.
[76] [2001] IRLR 160 CA.
[77] See also *Gregory v Wallace* [1998] IRLR 387 CA.
[78] See *Abrahams v Performing Rights Society* [1995] IRLR 486 CA.

net gain to the employee.[79] Finally, the first £30,000 of damages is to be awarded net of tax, but any amount above this figure will be awarded gross since it is taxable in the hands of the recipient.

Proceedings may be brought before an employment tribunal in respect of:[80]

(1) damages for a breach of contract of employment or other contract connected to employment;[81]
(2) a claim for a sum due under such a contract;[82] and
(3) a claim for the recovery of any sum, in pursuance of any enactment relating to the performance of such a contract.[83]

Provided the claim arises or is outstanding on the termination of the employee concerned, such actions can be taken by both the employer and the employee.[84] Certain breach of contract claims which are excluded.[85] These are terms of the contract which:

(1) require the employer to provide living accommodation for the employee;
(2) impose an obligation on the employer or the employee in connection with the provision of living accommodation;
(3) relate to intellectual property;[86]
(4) impose an obligation of confidence;
(5) are a covenant in restraint of trade.

Employees must present their claim to the employment tribunal within three months of the effective date of termination of employment, or, if there is no such date, the last day on which the employee worked in the terminated employment. The tribunal has discretion to lengthen this period if it decides that it was not reasonably practicable for the employee to present their complaint in time.[87] It is not possible to bring a complaint for a breach of contract to an employment tribunal before the effective date of termination. An employment tribunal will only have jurisdiction to hear the complaint if, unless otherwise agreed by the tribunal, the complaint is made between two fixed points, i.e. the start date (the effective date of termination) and the end date (the end of the period of three months beginning with the contract termination date).[88]

Anyone wishing to bring a claim must first submit a statement of grievance to their employer.[89]

---

[79] See *Westwood v Secretary of State* [1984] IRLR 209.
[80] Excluding those related to personal injuries (articles 3 and 4 ETEJO 1994).
[81] This includes the ability to enforce compromise agreements on terms connected with the end of employment: see *Rock-It Cargo Ltd v Green* [1997] IRLR 581.
[82] In *Sarker v South Tees Acute Hospitals NHS Trust* [1997] IRLR 328 an employee was dismissed before she commenced work, but the court held that she was still entitled to make a claim for damages as the contractual relationship had come into existence.
[83] Section 3(2) Employment Tribunals Act 1996.
[84] Articles 3 and 4 ETEJO 1994. See *Peninsula Ltd v Sweeney* [2004] IRLR 49 and *Miller Ltd v Johnston* [2002] IRLR 386.
[85] Article 5 ETEJO 1994.
[86] Defined as including copyright, rights in performance, moral rights, design rights, registered designs, patents and trade marks (article 5 ETEJO 1994).
[87] Article 7 ETEJO 1994.
[88] *Capek v Lincolnshire County Council* [2000] IRLR 590.
[89] On the statutory procedures see Schedule 3 Employment Act 2002 and regulation 15 EADR Regulations 2004 which extends the normal time limit by a further three months in specified circumstances.

5.4 Unfair dismissal

The statutory concept of unfair dismissal was first introduced in the Industrial Relations Act 1971 and the right to claim is now contained in Part X ERA 1996. Section 94(1) ERA 1996 states that employees have the right not to be unfairly dismissed by their employer. In looking at the question of whether a dismissal is unfair, a number of stages need to be gone through. These are concerned with, first, establishing the individual's eligibility for protection; secondly, showing that a dismissal has taken place and determining the effective date of termination; thirdly, looking at the reasons for the dismissal; and, lastly, the question of reasonableness.

5.4.1 Eligibility

Before individuals can make a complaint of unfair dismissal they need to qualify for the right by overcoming some initial hurdles. These relate to their employment status and length of continuous service. Also considered here are contracts which have an unlawful purpose.

5.4.1.1 Only employees qualify

Section 94(1) provides that it is employees that have the right. An employee is an individual who works under a contract of employment.[90] With an increasing number of rights accruing to workers[91] it may seem less logical for those working under a contract to perform services personally to continue to be excluded from Part X ERA 1996.[92] Issues concerning employment status are considered in Chapter 3, but see *Connolly v Sellers Arenascene Ltd,*[93] where it was held that the position of a controlling shareholder in a company was not incompatible with being an employee for the purposes of an unfair dismissal claim.

5.4.1.2 Illegality

As has been stated before, the general rules of contract apply equally to contracts of employment and there is a general principle that the courts will not enforce an illegal contract, the *ex turpi causa non oritur actio* rule.[94] This rule is not only about whether the contract of employment is in itself legal or not, but looks at the purpose of the contract. If the contract has an illegal purpose, then it may not be relied upon. In *Colen v Cebrian Ltd,*[95] Waller, LJ summarised the position as follows:

> an analysis needs to be done as to what the parties' intentions were from time to time. If the contract was unlawful at its formation or if there was an intention to perform the contract unlawfully

---

[90] Section 230(1)–(2) ERA 1996.
[91] Section 230(3) ERA 1996.
[92] There are specific groups excluded from the right: these are the police (section 200 ERA 1996) and share fishers (section 199(2)) as well as those affected by a little-used opportunity to opt out of the provisions and replace them with a dismissal procedure agreement; see section 110.
[93] [2001] ICR 760.
[94] Action is not available on an illegal contract.
[95] [2004] IRLR 210; see also *Wheeler v Quality Deep* [2005] ICR 265.

as at the date of the contract, then the contract will be unenforceable. If at the date of the contract the contract was perfectly lawful and it was intended to perform it lawfully, the effect of some act of illegal performance is not automatically to render the contract unenforceable. If the contract is ultimately performed illegally and the party seeking to enforce takes part in the illegality, that *may* render the contract unenforceable at his instigation. But not every act of illegality in performance even participated in by the enforcer, will have that effect. If the person seeking to enforce the contract has to rely on his illegal action in order to succeed then the court will not assist him. But if he does not have to do so, then in my view the question is whether the method of performance chosen and the degree of participation in that illegal performance is such as to 'turn the contract into an illegal contract'.

Knowledge of the illegality does not always appear to be relevant. In *EuroDiam Ltd v Bathurst*[96] the Court of Appeal indicated that the defence of *ex turpi causa* should be approached pragmatically and with caution, especially where the defendant's conduct in participating in an illegal contract was so reprehensible, in comparison with the plaintiff, that it would be wrong to allow the defendant to rely upon it. Such a situation occurred in *Hewcastle Catering Ltd v Ahmed and Elkamah*.[97] This case concerned a number of employees who were dismissed after co-operating with HM Customs & Excise in an investigation of a fraud about VAT on customers' bills, for which their employer was prosecuted. The employees had participated in the fraud but only the employer had benefited. The court concluded that it would be wrong to allow the employer to rely on the argument that the fraud made the employees' contracts of employment illegal and prevented them bringing unfair dismissal claims.[98]

Thus the consequences of a strict application of the *ex turpi causa* rule can be severe. *Salvesen v Simmons*[99] involved an employee who, at his request, was paid partly through an annual salary, with all the normal deductions for income tax and national insurance contributions, and partly through a consultancy which he operated with his wife. These latter payments were made without deductions. When a change of employer occurred, the new employer declined to continue with this arrangement. This was one of the issues that led the individual to resign and claim constructive dismissal. The EAT held that the contract had an illegal purpose, namely to defraud the Inland Revenue of tax. The result was that the employee was unable to rely upon it for the purposes of his claim, which further resulted in a loss of rights even though, as was stated, the amount of tax lost to the Inland Revenue was small.[100] In *Hyland v JH Barker (North West) Ltd*[101] the giving of a tax-free lodging allowance for four weeks, whilst the employee commuted daily, was enough to taint the contract of employment with illegality. As a result the employee was unable to establish a sufficient length of continuous employment to make an unfair dismissal claim.

---

[96] [1988] 2 All ER 23 CA.
[97] [1991] IRLR 473 CA.
[98] See also *Broaders v Kalkare Property Maintenance Ltd* [1990] IRLR 421, where the EAT stated that a fraud against an employer was quite different to one concerned with fraud against the tax authorities. The former did not make the contract illegal, even though the employee was receiving unofficial payments without the employer's knowledge.
[99] [1994] IRLR 52.
[100] On the argument that the European Convention on Human Rights is infringed in these circumstances see *Soteriou v Ultrachem Ltd* [2004] IRLR 870.
[101] [1985] IRLR 403.

However, there is a difference between tax evasion and tax avoidance. Thus in *Lightfoot v D & J Sporting Ltd*[102] an arrangement to pay part of the salary to the employee's wife was held to be legitimate tax avoidance and did not make the employee's contract of employment illegal.

It seems that such payments need to be part of an individual's regular remuneration and be more than occasional one-off payments without deductions. In *Annandale Engineering v Samson*[103] the occasional tax-free payments to a kennel hand by a greyhound trainer, made whenever one of their dogs won a race, could not be classified as part of the kennel hand's regular remuneration. The employer was not able to rely on the defence of illegality.

An exception to this approach was established in relation to claims for unlawful sex discrimination. In *Leighton v Michael*[104] an ex-employee in a fish and kebab bar made a claim for sex discrimination. She had taken on extra work and payment for this was made gross, i.e. without any deductions for income tax and National Insurance contributions. The employment tribunal had decided that it could not make a decision on sexual harassment claims because the contract of employment was tainted with illegality. In the employment tribunal's view the employee needed to show that the discrimination was in the field of employment. In order to do this the claim had to be founded on the contract of employment, which was tainted. The EAT distinguished between actions based on dismissal, including constructive dismissal, and those based on discrimination. The former claims were concerned with enforcing rights based upon the contract of employment and in order to rely on the statutory rights the claimant had to establish not only that they were an employee, but also that they had been dismissed on the termination of a contract. By way of contrast, in a sex discrimination case, although there needs to be a reference to the contract to show that the claimant was employed, the right not to suffer unlawful discrimination does not involve relying upon, or basing a claim upon, the contract of employment. It is conferred by statute on persons who are employed.[105]

This distinction may seem artificial. Indeed, in *HM Prison Service v Miss M Chilton*,[106] which concerned another sex discrimination claim, Judge Peter Clark observed:

> We have grave reservations as to the correctness of *Leighton*. We are unable to appreciate the distinction between statutory claims of unfair dismissal and sex discrimination for the purpose of applying the public policy doctrine of illegality. Both statutory causes of action depend upon the contract as a prerequisite for the claim.

Despite this, because they had not heard full argument on the issue, the EAT again followed *Leighton*.

Hall v Woolston Hall Leisure Ltd[107] concerned an employee who, it was held, was dismissed on the grounds of pregnancy and therefore had a claim under the Sex Discrimination Act 1975. She was paid part of her salary without the deduction of tax or national

---

[102] [1996] IRLR 64.
[103] [1994] IRLR 59.
[104] [1995] ICR 1091.
[105] Rights to protection in employment under the Sex Discrimination Act 1975 accrue to the wider definition of workers, rather than just employees; see Chapter 6.
[106] Employment Appeal Tribunal judgment delivered on 23 July 1999; not reported.
[107] [2000] IRLR 578 CA.

insurance contributions and she was aware of this illegality. The Court of Appeal confirmed the approach in *Leighton* and held that public policy grounds, that she should not be able to rely on the contract because of her knowledge of the illegality, were insufficient to defeat her claim. The court stated that it was undoubtedly correct that, where the complaint is of sex discrimination by dismissing an employee, the employee must establish that she was employed and was dismissed from that employment, so that reliance must be placed on the contract of employment. It further stated:

> It is the sex discrimination that is the core of the complaint, the fact of the employment and the dismissal being the particular factual circumstances which Parliament has prescribed for the sex discrimination complaint to be capable of being made . . . and the awareness of the employee that the employer was failing to deduct tax and NIC and to account to the Revenue does not of itself constitute a valid ground for refusing jurisdiction.

More recently, the EAT has stated that it does not consider that the authorities

> support the proposition that if the arrangements *have the effect* of depriving the Revenue of tax to which they were in law entitled then this renders the contract unlawful . . . there must be some form of misrepresentation, some attempt to conceal the true facts of the relationship, before the contract is rendered illegal. . . .[108]

5.4.1.3 Continuous employment

Normally employees must be continuously employed for a period of not less than one year, ending with the effective date of termination,[109] in order to qualify for the right not to be unfairly dismissed.[110] However, this qualification does not apply if the reason or principal reason for dismissal was automatically unfair (see below). The length of this qualifying period has changed on a number of occasions. Initially, in 1971, the period was two years. It then became one year and subsequently six months. The Employment Act 1980 lengthened the period to two years again for smaller employers.[111] In 1985 this was extended to all employers and remained at this level until 1999. Continuity is to be calculated up to the effective date of termination in accordance with sections 210–219 ERA 1996 (see Chapter 3).

5.4.2 The dismissal

5.4.2.1 Whether a dismissal has taken place

Having established that an individual is an employee with at least one year's continuous service and not otherwise excluded, progress can be made to the next stage, i.e. to establish that a dismissal has taken place. This is also a prerequisite in order to qualify for a redundancy payment. Section 95 ERA 1996 specifies the circumstances in which a

---

[108] *Enfield Technical Services Ltd v Payne* [2007] IRLR 840.
[109] Subject to the provisions in section 97 ERA 1996 on the effective date; see section 213(1) on continuity being preserved in accordance with that section.
[110] Section 108(1) ERA 1996 as amended by the Unfair Dismissal and Statement of Reasons for Dismissal (Variation of Qualifying Period) Order 1999, SI 1999/1436.
[111] Those employing fewer than 20 employees.

dismissal takes place. The first of these is when a contract of employment, under which the individual is employed, is terminated by the employer. Where there is a dispute as to whether a dismissal has taken place, the onus of proof is on the employee. Thus it is vitally important not to confuse a warning of impending dismissal – for example, through the announcement of a plant closure – with an individual notice to terminate.[112] For the giving of notice to constitute a dismissal at law the actual date of termination must be ascertainable. Where an employer has given notice to terminate, an employee who gives counter-notice indicating that he or she wishes to leave before the employer's notice has expired is still to be regarded as dismissed.[113]

There are occasions when there is a dispute as to whether the individual has been dismissed or whether they have resigned. This was so in *Morris v London Iron and Steel Co Ltd*[114] where the employee claimed that he had been dismissed and the employer claimed that there had been a resignation. The employment tribunal was unable to decide which was the truth after hearing evidence. Bearing in mind that the onus of proof was on the employee, the complaint was dismissed. This approach was approved in the Court of Appeal:

> . . . the judge should at the end of the day look at the whole of the evidence that has been called before him, drawing inferences where appropriate, and ask himself what has or has not been shown on the balance of probabilities, and then, bearing in mind where the onus of proof lies, decide whether the plaintiff or the defendant, or both, succeeds.

A radical alteration to an employee's contract of employment may amount to a withdrawal of that contract and a conclusion that the employee was dismissed. *Hogg v Dover College*[115] was a drastic example of this. A teacher was informed by his employer that he would no longer be head of department, that he would be employed on a part-time basis only and his salary was to be halved. The EAT concluded that:

> . . . both as a matter of law and common sense, he was being told that his former contract was from that moment gone . . . It is suggested on behalf of the employers that there was a variation, but again, it seems to us quite elementary that you cannot hold a pistol to somebody's head and say 'henceforth you are to be employed on wholly different terms which are in fact 50% of your previous contract'.

This was not a variation of the contract which might give the employee the opportunity to accept or reject a potential repudiation, but amounted to an express dismissal by the employer. This approach was applied in *Alcan Extrusions v Yates*[116] where the imposition of a continuous rolling shift system in place of a traditional shift system, contained in the employees' contracts of employment, also amounted to an express dismissal by the employer. Alternatively, the unilateral variation of an employee's contractual working hours might amount to a breach of a fundamental term entitling the employee to resign and claim constructive dismissal. In *Greenaway Harrison Ltd v Wiles*[117] the threat to end the

[112] See *Doble v Firestone Tyre Co Ltd* [1981] IRLR 300.
[113] Section 95(2) ERA 1996.
[114] [1987] IRLR 182 CA.
[115] [1990] ICR 39.
[116] [1996] IRLR 327.
[117] [1994] IRLR 380.

contracts of employment, if the change of hours was not accepted, amounted to an anticipatory breach giving rise to a constructive dismissal.

If an employer acts as a result of a genuine, but mistaken, belief that an employee has resigned, it may not be enough to prevent the conduct from amounting to a constructive dismissal. In *Brown v JBD Engineering Ltd*[118] an employer appointed a new employee and told customers that the previous employee was no longer employed by the employer, in the mistaken belief that the employee had left as a result of an agreement. The mistake might be a relevant factor, but could not be enough to prevent the employee claiming that a dismissal had taken place.

5.4.2.2 Limited term contracts
See 5.3.1 above and Chapter 3 on fixed-term contracts.

5.4.2.3 Constructive dismissal
Section 95(1)(c) ERA 1996 provides that an employee is to be treated as dismissed if the employee terminates the contract of employment as a result of the employer's conduct. This is known as constructive dismissal or discharge by breach. Lord Denning[119] provided a clear definition:

> If the employer is guilty of conduct which is a significant breach going to the root of the contract of employment; or which shows that the employer no longer intends to be bound by one or more of the essential terms of the contract; then the employee is entitled to treat himself as discharged from any further performance. If he does so, then he terminates the contract by reason of the employer's conduct. He is constructively dismissed.

Lord Denning went on to state that the employer's conduct must be sufficiently serious so as to entitle the employee to leave at once.[120] An example of serious conduct which amounted to a repudiatory breach is shown in *Weathersfield v Sargent*.[121] The employee was given instructions to discriminate against ethnic minority customers. She was so upset by this policy that she telephoned the employer and told them that she was resigning, although she did not explain why. It was argued, on behalf of the employer, that this failure to give a reason amounted to a failure to accept any repudiatory breach by the employer and so there could not be a constructive dismissal. The Court of Appeal did not accept this argument and held that it was quite clear as to what the real reason for the employee's departure was and the fact that the employee left for this reason amounted to an acceptance of the employer's repudiation.[122]

The Court of Appeal has accepted that a series of acts can cumulatively amount to a breach of the implied duty of trust and confidence and thus a constructive dismissal. The 'final straw', however, does not have to be of the same character as earlier acts. It must

---

[118] [1993] IRLR 568.
[119] *Western Excavations (ECC) Ltd v Sharp* [1978] IRLR 27 CA.
[120] See also *Woods v WM Car Services (Peterborough) Ltd* [1981] IRLR 413 CA, which followed *Western Excavations* in this respect.
[121] [1999] IRLR 95 CA.
[122] In *Moores v Bude-Stratton Town Council* [2000] IRLR 676 a local authority councillor's abusive conduct towards an employee of the authority amounted to a breach of the duty of trust and confidence, such as to justify the employee resigning and claiming constructive dismissal.

contribute something to the breach, but what it adds may be relatively insignificant so long as it is not utterly trivial. In *London Borough of Waltham Forest v Omilaju*,[123] the complainant was employed by a local authority and issued five sets of proceedings alleging race discrimination and victimisation. These were heard in July and August 2001 but the employer refused to pay Mr Omilaju his full salary when he was absent without leave in order to attend the employment tribunal. It was the authority's rule that employees in his position were required to apply for special unpaid leave or annual leave. In September 2001 Mr Omilaju resigned and claimed unfair dismissal. The Court of Appeal upheld the employment tribunal's decision that the refusal to pay for the time attending the tribunal could not be regarded as the 'final straw' in a series of actions which together amounted to a breach of trust and confidence. According to the Appeal Court, a 'final straw' does not have to be of the same character as earlier acts. However, it must contribute something to the breach of the implied term even if what it adds may be relatively trivial.

It is not necessary for an employee to leave immediately in order to show that the leaving is as a result of an employer's breach of contract. However, there is a need to establish that the breach (or breaches) was the effective cause of the employee leaving. In *Jones v F Sirl & Son (Furnishers) Ltd*[124] the employee left some three weeks after the final breach of a number of breaches of contract by her employer. She had obtained another job and left to take up the new position. The EAT concluded that the main cause of her leaving was the employer's actions, not because it had been prompted by finding another position to go to. A delay also occurred in *Waltons & Morse v Dorrington*[125] where the employer was held to be in breach of implied terms to provide a safe working environment and that the employer would reasonably and promptly afford employees a reasonable opportunity to obtain redress for any grievances.[126] In this case the employee strove to establish the right to sit in a smoke-free environment at work. The failure of the employers to deal with her grievance on the issue led to the employee leaving and claiming constructive dismissal. She continued to work until she found alternative employment and it was argued that she had affirmed her contract in doing so. In rejecting the view that a delay in leaving negated the constructive dismissal resulting from the employer's breach, the EAT took into account her length of service and the fact that she needed to earn an income.[127] Similarly, continuing to work is not necessarily an affirmation of contractual changes. In *Aparau v Iceland Frozen Foods plc*[128] new contracts of employment were issued which contained a mobility clause. Some 18 months later the employee was given instructions to move to another branch. The employee denied that the employer had the right to issue such an instruction and successfully claimed that she had been constructively dismissed. The EAT had accepted that the mobility clause had not been incorporated into the contract of employment and a summary instruction to relocate was a repudiatory breach. In contrast,

---

[123] [2005] IRLR 35.
[124] [1997] IRLR 493 EAT.
[125] [1997] IRLR 488.
[126] See also *WA Goold (Pearmak) Ltd v McConnell* [1995] IRLR 516.
[127] In contrast, *Dryden v Greater Glasgow Health Board* [1992] IRLR 469 concerned an employer's introduction of a no-smoking policy; the EAT held that there was no implied duty to provide facilities for smokers and no breach as a result of which the employee could claim constructive dismissal.
[128] [1996] IRLR 119 EAT.

White v Reflecting Roadstuds Ltd[129] concerned the transfer of an employee to an area of work where he earned less income. The employee resigned and claimed that he had been constructively dismissed. The claim failed because the EAT held that there was an express flexibility clause which permitted the employer to do this. There was no necessity to imply a reasonableness term into the clause as this would introduce a reasonableness test into the area of constructive dismissal.

An employer is not entitled to alter the formula whereby wages are calculated but whether a unilateral reduction in pay or fringe benefits is of sufficient materiality as to entitle the employee to resign is a matter of degree. A failure to pay an employee's salary or wage is likely to constitute a fundamental breach if it is a deliberate act on the part of the employer rather than a mere breakdown in technology. In *Gardner Ltd v Beresford*,[130] where the employee resigned because she had not received a pay increase for two years while others had, the EAT accepted that in most cases it would be reasonable to infer a term that an employer will not treat employees arbitrarily, capriciously or inequitably in relation to remuneration. However, if a contract makes no reference at all to pay increases, it is impossible to say that there is an implied term that there will always be a pay rise.[131]

The conduct complained about does not need to be taken by the employer. In *Hilton International Hotels (UK) Ltd v Protopapa*[132] a supervisor was severely reprimanded by her immediate superior in front of other employees. She resigned and claimed constructive dismissal. On appeal, the employer argued that there could not be a constructive dismissal because the immediate superior had no authority to sack her. The EAT did not accept this and re-affirmed the principle that an employer is to be held liable for the actions of employees for acts done in the course of their employment.[133] Finally, it should be noted that it is possible for an employer's repudiatory breach to be the result of the behaviour of the employee. In *Morrison*,[134] for example, the employer suspended an employee without pay as a result of the employee's behaviour. They had no contractual authority to suspend the employee who resigned and successfully claimed that she had been constructively dismissed. The employment tribunal decided that there should be a 40% reduction in her compensation, because she had provoked the employer's unlawful reaction.

5.4.2.4 The effective date of termination of employment

The date on which a contract of employment terminates is important not just for reasons of calculating payments due but also for calculating the effective start of the three-month period in which employees must make their complaint to an employment tribunal.[135] The common law approach to the date of termination is that this will be the date that the notice given by the employer or employee expires, or the date that payment in lieu of notice is

---

[129] [1991] IRLR 331.
[130] [1978] IRLR 63.
[131] See *Murco Petroleum v Forge* [1987] IRLR 50.
[132] [1990] IRLR 316.
[133] See also *Warnes v The Trustees of Cheriton Oddfellows Social Club* [1993] IRLR 58, where an invalid resolution passed at a club's annual general meeting took away the secretarial duties of the club steward. Despite the invalidity of the resolution, this act amounted to a fundamental breach of contract allowing a claim for constructive dismissal.
[134] *Morrison v Amalgamated Transport and General Workers Union* [1989] IRLR 361 CA.
[135] See below for the impact of statutory disciplinary and grievance procedures.

accepted. If an employer has given notice to an employee and, during the notice period, the employee resigns with the intention of leaving at an earlier date, the employee will still be taken as being dismissed,[136] but the effective date on which the contract ends will be that indicated by the employee's notice.[137]

Section 97(1) ERA 1996 provides a definition of the 'effective date of termination' in differing circumstances:

(1) When a contract of employment is terminated by notice, the effective date is the date on which the notice expires. In *Hutchings v Coinseed Ltd*[138] an employee resigned and was told by her employer that she would not be required to work during her period of notice. She then started work for a competitor employer at a higher salary. The court rejected the employer's claim that this amounted to a repudiatory breach of contract entitling them not to pay the employee during the notice period, given the fact that they had not required her to do work for them during this period. Where there is a mutual variation of the notice to terminate, the notice and the contract of employment expire on the new date.[139]

(2) Where a contract of employment is terminated without notice, then the effective date is the date on which the termination takes effect.[140] This is regardless of whether the employer followed correctly all the contractual procedures to which the employee was entitled[141] or whether the dismissal was done in the correct manner.[142] The Court of Appeal has held that where an employee is dismissed and no longer has the right to work under the contract of employment and where the employer no longer has the obligation to pay the individual, then the contract of employment is at an end, unless there is a contractual provision to continue the employment relationship during any appeal proceedings.[143] *Drage v Governors of Greenford High School*[144] concerned the dismissal of a school teacher. The question at issue was whether the effective date of termination was the date when he was told of the initial decision to dismiss him or the date when he was notified that his appeal against dismissal had failed. The Court of Appeal held that:

> The critical question arising is this, as in any similar case where contractual provision is made for an internal appeal, is whether during the period between the initial notification and the outcome of the appeal the employee stands (a) dismissed with the possibility of re-instatement or (b) suspended with the possibility of the proposed dismissal not being confirmed and the suspension thus being ended.

---

[136] Section 95(2) ERA 1996.
[137] See *Thompson v GEC Avionics Ltd* [1991] IRLR 488, where an employee was given notice that her employment would cease on 9 November and she subsequently resigned and gave notice terminating her employment on 21 September, which was held to be the effective date of termination.
[138] [1998] IRLR 190 CA.
[139] See *Palfrey v Transco plc* [2004] IRLR 916.
[140] *BMK Ltd and BMK Holdings Ltd v Logue* [1993] IRLR 477 considered the effective date of termination in constructive dismissals; the question to be asked is when did the termination take effect?
[141] See *Batchelor v British Railways Board* [1987] IRLR 136 CA.
[142] See *Robert Cort & Son Ltd v Charman* [1981] IRLR 437, which considered a summary dismissal without the contractual notice being given.
[143] See *Savage v J Sainsbury Ltd* [1980] IRLR 109 CA.
[144] [2000] IRLR 315 CA.

Thus if a contract is held to have been suspended during the appeals procedure, then the effective date will be the notification ending that procedure. The terms of the initial notification are likely to be important, therefore, although not necessarily decisive.[145]

Even if the employee was contractually entitled to further payments, this may not delay the effective time or date of termination. Thus if an employee, as in *Octavius Atkinson & Sons Ltd v Morris*,[146] was summarily dismissed during the day, the effective time of the dismissal was when it was communicated to him. This was so even though the employee was entitled to further payments for travel to and from work.

(3) Where there is a limited term contract which terminates as a result of the limiting event without being renewed under the same contract, the effective date is the date on which the termination takes effect.

Where the notice period is shorter than that required by section 86 ERA 1996,[147] then, for the purposes of the qualifying length of service required to claim unfair dismissal and for the purpose of calculating the basic award for unfair dismissal,[148] the effective date of termination will be at the end of the period stipulated by section 86 ERA 1996.[149]

Whether in a particular case the words of dismissal evince an intention to terminate the contract at once or an intention to terminate it only at a future date depends on the construction of those words. Such construction must not be technical but reflect what an ordinary, reasonable employee would understand by the language used. Moreover, words should be construed in the light of the facts known to the employee at the time of notification. If the language used is ambiguous, it is likely that tribunals will apply the principle that words should be interpreted most strongly against the person who uses them. It should also be observed that where a dismissal has been communicated by letter, the contract of employment does not terminate until the employee has actually read the letter or had a reasonable opportunity of reading it. Thus in *McMaster v Manchester Airport*,[150] the employer had posted a letter of dismissal to the applicant and had presumed that it was received and read. This was not an altogether unreasonable assumption, given that the employee was absent from work through sickness and might reasonably have been expected to be at home where the dismissal letter was sent. In fact he was away on a day trip to France and did not read the letter until the next day. The court held that it was the day that the employee read the letter which was the effective date of termination.

---

[145] See *Chapman v Letherby & Christopher Ltd* [1981] IRLR 440, where the EAT held that the construction to be put on a letter of dismissal should not be a technical one, but one which an ordinary, reasonable employee would understand by the words used.

[146] [1989] IRLR 158 CA.

[147] The minimum periods of notice required; see above.

[148] Sections 108(1) and 119(1) ERA 1996.

[149] Section 97(2)–(5) ERA 1996; in *Lanton Leisure Ltd v White and Gibson* [1987] IRLR 119 two employees were dismissed without notice for gross misconduct and, consequently, failed to have enough continuous service to qualify for making an unfair dismissal claim. The employees claimed that they were entitled to the protection of (now) section 97(2) ERA 1996. The EAT concluded that the employment tribunal had a duty to consider first whether there had been conduct warranting a dismissal for gross misconduct, which had the effect of removing the employees' contractual rights to notice.

[150] [1998] IRLR 112.

5.4.3 The reasons for dismissal

Having established that a dismissal has taken place and when it took effect, the next stage is to decide whether the reasons for the dismissal can be treated as coming within those permitted by the ERA 1996, or whether they can be regarded as unfair.

5.4.3.1 Statement of reasons for dismissal

If an employer gives an employee notice of dismissal or terminates the employee's contract of employment without notice, then the employee is entitled to be given a written statement giving particulars of the reasons for the dismissal. Employees employed under a limited term contract which expires without being renewed under the same contract are also entitled to such a statement.[151] There are a limited number of conditions attached to this right:

(1) it only applies to employees, so a worker who is not an employee will have no such right to a statement if the employer terminates that worker's contract;

(2) the employee must, at the effective date of termination,[152] have been continuously employed for a period of one year;[153]

(3) the employee is entitled to the statement only if the employee requests it. Once requested, the statement must be provided within 14 days of the request.[154]

It is acceptable for the statement to refer unambiguously to other letters already sent which contain the reasons for dismissal.[155] Special provision is made for women who are pregnant or who are on maternity or adoption leave, if this leave is brought to an end by the dismissal. If they are dismissed, there is no continuous service requirement threshold to be reached before they are entitled to a statement, neither do they need to request it.[156] Written statements provided by the employer are admissible in evidence in subsequent legal proceedings.[157]

An employee may make a complaint to an employment tribunal if the employer unreasonably fails to provide the requested written statement or if the reasons given are inadequate or untrue.[158] The obligation on employers is to state what they genuinely believe to be the reason or reasons for the dismissal. There is no requirement for the employment tribunal to decide whether they were good reasons or justifiable ones.[159] This would happen at a later stage if unfair dismissal proceedings were brought. If the employment tribunal finds the complaint well founded, then it may make a declaration as to what it considers the employer's reasons for dismissing were and also make an award

---

[151] Section 92(1) ERA 1996.
[152] Section 92(6)–(8) ERA 1996 describes the meaning of effective date of termination; these provisions are identical to those in section 97(1)–(2) described above.
[153] Section 92(3) ERA 1996.
[154] Section 92(2) ERA 1996.
[155] See *Kent County Council v Gilham* [1985] IRLR 16 CA.
[156] Section 92(4)–(4A) ERA 1996.
[157] Section 92(5) ERA 1996.
[158] Section 93(1) ERA 1996.
[159] *Harvard Securities plc v Younghusband* [1990] IRLR 17.

that the employer must pay the employee a sum equal to two weeks' pay.[160] Somewhat bizarrely this right to complain only relates to letters that have been requested. If the employer gives the ex-employee an unrequested letter stating the reasons for the dismissal, then the employee is unlikely to be able to complain about the adequacy or truthfulness of such a letter.[161]

5.4.3.2 Automatically unfair reasons

Dismissals for certain reasons do not require an employee to have worked continuously for a period of one year.[162] These dismissals are for reasons which are automatically unfair. They are dismissals relating to such matters as the following:[163]

(1) Family reasons[164] – these are reasons relating to the Maternity and Parental Leave etc. Regulations 1999[165] and include reasons related to (a) pregnancy, childbirth or maternity, (b) paternity, parental or adoption leave. They also include the right to time off for dependants contained in section 57A ERA 1996.

(2) Health and safety matters[166] – where the reason for dismissal was that the employee:
- carried out, or proposed to carry out, activities designated by the employer in connection with preventing or reducing risks to the health and safety of employees;
- performed, or proposed to perform, any of his or her functions as a safety representative or a member of a safety committee;
- took part or proposed to take part in consultation with the employer pursuant to the Health and Safety (Consultation with Employees) Regulations 1996 or in an election of representatives of employee safety within the meaning of those Regulations;
- where there was no safety representative or committee or it was not reasonably practicable to raise the matter in that way, brought to the employer's attention, by reasonable means, circumstances connected with his or her work which he or she reasonably believed were harmful or potentially harmful to health and safety;
- left or proposed to leave, or refused to return to (while the danger persisted), his or her place of work or any dangerous part of the workplace, in circumstances of danger which he or she reasonably believed to be serious and imminent and which he or she could not reasonably have been expected to avert;
- took, or proposed to take, appropriate steps to protect himself or herself or other persons, in circumstances of danger which he or she reasonably believed to be serious and imminent. Whether those steps were 'appropriate' must be judged by reference to all the circumstances, including the employee's knowledge and the facilities and advice available at the time. A dismissal will not be regarded as unfair

---

[160] Section 93(2) ERA 1996; see Part XIV Chapter 2 ERA 1996 for the meaning of a week's pay; considered below.

[161] See *Catherine Haigh Harlequin Hair Design v Seed* [1990] IRLR 175, where the EAT held that an employment tribunal could not hear a complaint about just such an unrequested letter.

[162] Section 108(2)–(3) ERA 1996.

[163] This should not be taken as a comprehensive list; the number of automatically unfair reasons seems to grow with each new piece of employment legislation.

[164] Section 99 ERA 1996.

[165] SI 1999/3312.

[166] Section 100 ERA 1996. See *Balfour Fitzpatrick v Acheson* [2003] IRLR 683.

if the employer can show that it was, or would have been, so negligent for the employee to take the steps which he or she took, or proposed to take, that a reasonable employer might have dismissed on these grounds.

(3) Protected shop workers and betting shop workers[167] who refuse to work on Sundays.

(4) Working time[168] – where the reason for the dismissal is that an employee has refused to comply with instructions contrary to the provisions of the Working Time Regulations 1998,[169] refused to give up any rights under these Regulations, failed to sign a workforce agreement or is performing, or proposing to perform, the duties of an employee representative in relation to Schedule 1 to those Regulations.

(5) Pension scheme trustees[170] – performing, or proposing to perform, the duties of a trustee of a relevant occupational pension scheme, which relates to the individual's employment.

(6) Employee representatives[171] – being, or taking part in the elections for, an employee representative for the purposes of consultation on collective redundancies[172] or transfers of undertakings.[173]

(7) Protected disclosures[174] – an employee dismissed for making a protected disclosure (see 4.5.2.4 above).

(8) Assertion of a statutory right[175] – where an employee brings proceedings to enforce a statutory right or alleges that an employer has infringed a statutory right. These are rights associated with bringing complaints to an employment tribunal; rights to minimum notice;[176] matters concerned with deductions from pay, union activities and time off for trade union duties and activities;[177] matters connected with the right to be accompanied at disciplinary or grievance hearings;[178] and rights conferred by the Working Time Regulations 1998.[179] It is irrelevant whether the employee has the right or whether it has been infringed, as long as the employee acts in good faith.

(9) The national minimum wage[180] – any action taken by, or on behalf of, an employee in connection with enforcing rights relating to the national minimum wage. Again it is irrelevant whether the employee has the right or whether it has been infringed, so long as the employee is acting in good faith.

(10) Working family tax credits or disabled persons tax credits[181] – any action taken, or proposed to be taken, by or on behalf of the employee in connection with rights requiring employers to make payments and requiring employers to provide employees with information.

---

[167] Section 101 ERA 1996.
[168] Section 101A ERA 1996. See *McClean v Rainbow Ltd* [2007] IRLR 15.
[169] SI 1998/1833.
[170] Section 102 ERA 1996.
[171] Section 103 ERA 1996.
[172] Part IV Chapter 2 TULRCA 1992.
[173] Transfer of Undertakings Regulations 2006, SI 2006/246.
[174] Section 103A ERA 1996.
[175] Section 104 ERA 1996. See *Mennell v Newell & Wright* [1997] IRLR 519.
[176] Section 86 ERA 1996.
[177] Sections 68, 86, 146, 168–170 TULRCA 1992; see also section 152 TULRCA 1992.
[178] Section 12(3) ERELA 1999.
[179] SI 1998/1833.
[180] Section 104A ERA 1996.
[181] Section 104B ERA 1996; see Schedule 3 Tax Credits Act 1999.

(11) Participation in protected industrial action[182] – where an employee took part in protected industrial action and is dismissed within the protected period. This protection does not extend to those who take part in unofficial industrial action (see Chapter 12).

(12) Part-time work – where employees bring proceedings to enforce their rights under the Part-time Workers (Prevention of Less Favourable Treatment) Regulations 2000.[183]

(13) Redundancy[184] – where the principal reason for a dismissal is redundancy and it is shown that the same circumstances apply to other employees in the same undertaking in similar positions and who have not been dismissed and it is shown that any of (1) to (12) apply.

(14) Spent offences – where a conviction of less than two-and-a-half years is spent[185] the employee is not under an obligation to disclose it. Section 4 of the Rehabilitation of Offenders Act 1974 stops employers from dismissing someone for not revealing the information to them. Certain sensitive occupations, such as nurses, police and social service workers are excluded from these provisions.[186]

(15) Transfers of undertakings – regulation 7(1) of the Transfer of Undertakings Regulations 2006[187] makes a dismissal by reason of relevant transfer automatically unfair, unless the reason for the dismissal was an economic, technical or organisational one.[188]

(16) Fixed-term work – where employees do anything to act on their rights under the Fixed-term Employees (Prevention of Less Favourable Treatment) Regulations 2002.

(17) Flexible work – section 104C ERA 1996 provides protection for a qualifying employee who applies, in accordance with section 80F ERA 1996,[189] to change their hours, times or place of work to enable the employee to care for a child.

(18) A statutory dismissal and disciplinary procedure has not been completed and this is wholly or mainly attributable to the failure by the employer to comply with its requirements.

Other instances of automatically unfair dismissal are those which constitute discrimination made unlawful by the Sex Discrimination Act 1975,[190] the Race Relations Act 1976[191] and the Disability Discrimination Act 1995.[192]

---

[182] Section 238A(2) TULRCA 1992. See 12.14.3 below.
[183] SI 2000/1551; see regulation 7.
[184] Section 105 ERA 1996.
[185] Meaning a period of time since the sentence was served; the length of this period depends upon the severity of the sentence.
[186] See *Wood v Coverage Care Ltd* [1996] IRLR 264 which was about an employee, whose post was redundant, being refused alternative work because of a conviction which excluded her from the social work alternative positions.
[187] SI 2006/246.
[188] Regulation 7(2) Transfer of Undertakings Regulations 2006; see *Wilson v St Helens Borough Council* [1998] IRLR 706 HL.
[189] Inserted by section 46 EA 2002.
[190] Section 6(2)(b) SDA 1975.
[191] Section 4(2) RRA 1976.
[192] Section 4(2)(d) DDA 1995.

5.4.3.3 Fair or unfair reasons for dismissal

Having established that a dismissal has taken place, it is then for the employer to show that the reason for the dismissal was fair.[193] This is to be done, first, by showing that the reason, (or the principal reason if there is more than one), for the dismissal is that:

(1) it relates to the capability or qualifications of the employee for performing work of the kind for which the employee was employed to do;
(2) it relates to the conduct of the employee;
(3) it is the retirement of the employee;
(4) the employee was redundant;
(5) the employee could not continue to work in the position for which the employee was employed without breaching a duty or restriction imposed by an enactment.[194]

There is perhaps a distinction between the first two of these reasons and the last three. It is a distinction, defined by the EAT, as that between the language of actuality and that of relationship. In *Shook v London Borough of Ealing*[195] the EAT considered this distinction:

> Two of them are couched in the language of actuality: the employee must be redundant or engaged under an unlawful contract, as the case may be. The other two are expressed in the language of relationship: the reason must *relate* to the capability for performing the work of the relevant kind or must *relate* to the conduct of the employee, as the case may be.

If the reason, or principal reason, does not fall into one of these categories it may still be fair if the dismissal takes place for:

> some other substantial reason of a kind such as to justify the dismissal of an employee holding the position which the employee held.[196]

It follows that where no reason is given by the employer, a dismissal will be unfair simply because the statutory burden has not been discharged. Equally, if a reason is engineered in order to effect dismissal because the real reason would not be acceptable, the employer will fail because the underlying principal reason is not within section 98(1) or (2) ERA 1996.[197]

No account is to be taken of any pressure exerted upon an employer to dismiss unfairly. If the employer is subject to pressure resulting from threats of, or actual, industrial action to dismiss an employee this will not be taken into account. The employment tribunal will consider the matter of the fairness of the reason or the reasonableness of the employer as if there was no such pressure.[198] The exception to this rule is where an employer has been pressurised to dismiss an individual for not joining a trade union. In such a case the employer may request the tribunal to add the person whom it is alleged exercised the pressure as a party to the proceedings. The effect of this is that the tribunal may order that part of any compensation due is paid by the third party.[199]

---

[193] Section 98(1) ERA 1996.
[194] Section 98(2) ERA 1996.
[195] [1986] IRLR 46.
[196] Section 98(1)(b) ERA 1996.
[197] See *ASLEF v Brady* [2006] IRLR 76.
[198] Section 107 ERA 1996.
[199] Section 160 TULRCA 1992.

The reason for the dismissal is to be the one known to employers at the time of the dismissal. It is not acceptable for the employment tribunal to take into account matters which were not known to the employer at the time of the dismissal.[200] In *W Devis & Sons Ltd v Atkins*[201] the employer attempted to introduce new evidence of a dismissed employee's serious misconduct. This failed because it was information that came to light after the dismissal had taken place for another reason, namely a failure to obey instructions. The court approved the approach taken in *Abernethy v Mott, Hay & Anderson*[202] where it was ruled that:

> A reason for the dismissal is a set of facts known to the employer, or it may be of beliefs held by him, which cause him to dismiss the employee. If at the time of the dismissal the employer gives a reason for it, that is no doubt evidence, at any rate as against him, as to the real reason.

Any extra information could, however, be taken into account when assessing compensation. The exception to this rule is information that may become available during an internal appeals procedure, although this material must relate to the original decision. To exclude this information would be to ignore important parts of the case, either in favour of the employer or the employee. Lord Bridge stated in *West Midlands Co-operative Society Ltd v Tipton*:[203]

> The apparent injustice of excluding . . . misconduct of an employee which is irrelevant to the real reason for dismissal is mitigated . . . by the provisions relating to compensation in such a case. But there is nothing to mitigate the injustice to an employee which would result if he were unable to complain that his employer, though acting reasonably on the facts known to him when he summarily dismissed the employee, acted quite unreasonably in maintaining his decision to dismiss in the face of mitigating circumstances established in the course of the domestic appeals procedure . . .[204]

Consideration of the fairness of the reasons for a dismissal is closely connected to the reasonableness of the employer's action in treating it as a sufficient reason for dismissal. Section 98(4)(a) ERA 1996 provides that once the employer has satisfied the requirements for showing that the reason for the dismissal comes within the terms of section 98(1) or (2), then the issue for the tribunal is whether the employer acted reasonably or unreasonably in treating it as a sufficient reason for dismissing the employee. This will partly depend upon the size and administrative resources of the employer's undertaking[205] and will be decided upon 'in accordance with equity and the substantial merits of the case'.[206]

5.4.3.4 Capability or qualifications

Capability is assessed by reference to skill, aptitude, health or any other physical or mental quality.[207] Assessing capability may well be subjective and an employer will need to be able

---

[200] This includes considering the reasons throughout the notice period: see *Parkinson v March Consulting Ltd* [1997] IRLR 308 CA.

[201] [1977] AC 931 HL.

[202] [1974] IRLR 213.

[203] [1986] IRLR 112 HL.

[204] Similarly defects in the disciplinary or dismissal procedures can be remedied on appeal: see *Whitbread & Co v Mills* [1987] IRLR 18.

[205] Section 98(4)(a) ERA 1996.

[206] Section 98(4)(b) ERA 1996.

[207] Section 98(3)(a) ERA 1996.

to show that they had reasonable grounds for their belief. In *Taylor v Alidair Ltd*,[208] which concerned the competence of an airline pilot, Lord Denning MR stated:

> In considering the case, it must be remembered that . . .[the Act] contemplated a subjective test. The tribunal have to consider the employer's reason and the employer's state of mind. If the company honestly believed on reasonable grounds that the pilot was lacking in proper capability to fly aircraft on behalf of the company, that was a good and sufficient reason for the company to determine the employment then and there.

There are, of course, special considerations concerning competence when the individual could put people's safety at risk, but the question as to when it is fair to dismiss an incompetent employee is an important one for employers.

(a) Incompetent employees

The employer has a right not to have their business harmed by an incompetent employee, but the employee also has a right to be treated fairly. In *Whitbread & Co v Thomas*[209] three employees were dismissed as a result of their lack of competence in failing to prevent stock losses. This was done despite the fact that the employer did not know which of the three might be responsible for the losses. The employer had, however, done everything possible to prevent the losses, including issuing warnings and transferring, temporarily, the staff to other locations. The EAT accepted that the employer had fulfilled three necessary conditions. These were, first, that if the act had been committed by an identified individual it would have led to dismissal. Secondly, that the act was committed by one or more of the individuals in the group and, thirdly, that there had been a proper investigation to try to identify the person or persons responsible for the act.[210] Treating an employee fairly does not necessarily mean not dismissing them because they have many years of service. In *Gair v Bevan Harris Ltd*[211] a foreman was dismissed for unsatisfactory performance of his duties. This dismissal was held to be fair, even though the employee had 11 years' service with the employer. An unreasonable procedural delay, however, might turn an otherwise fair dismissal into an unfair one.[212]

Paragraphs 18–19 of the ACAS Code of Practice on Disciplinary and Grievance Procedures[213] provide that:

> It is normally good practice to give employees at least one chance to improve their conduct or performance before they are issued with a final written warning. However, if an employee's misconduct or unsatisfactory performance – or its continuance – is sufficiently serious, for example because it is having, or is likely to have, a serious harmful effect on the organisation, it may be appropriate to move directly to a final written warning . . .

---

[208] [1978] IRLR 82 CA.

[209] [1988] IRLR 43.

[210] See *Monie v Coral Racing Ltd* [1980] IRLR 464 CA where this principle was established in situations of dishonesty. The EAT, in *Whitbread*, suggested that it would apply to situations concerning incompetence only exceptionally.

[211] [1983] IRLR 368.

[212] See *RSPCA v Cruden* [1986] IRLR 83, where an employee was dismissed for what was described, by the employment tribunal, as 'gross misjudgment and idleness quite incompatible with the proper performance of his duties'. The dismissal was unfair, however, because of a long delay in instituting proceedings.

[213] Originally introduced in 1977, the current Code was brought into force on 1 October 2004. Section 207 TULRCA 1992 provides for the code to be taken into account by employment tribunals. See 5.4.5 below.

Following the meeting, an employee who is found to be performing unsatisfactorily should be given a written note setting out:

- the performance problem;
- the improvement that is required;
- the timescale for achieving this improvement;
- a review date; and
- any support the employer will provide to assist the employee.

However, the Code of Practice allows for the situation where, through negligence, the worker commits a single error which has serious consequences. In such circumstances warnings may not be appropriate, but the disciplinary procedure should have indicated that summary dismissal may take place in such circumstances.[214]

(b) Ill health and absenteeism

A second and important aspect of capability is how employers deal with employees who are absent from work as a result of ill health.[215] Paragraphs 37–40 of the same Code of Practice make the following recommendations about dealing with absence:

> . . . it is important to determine the reasons why the employee has not been at work. If there is no acceptable reason, the matter should be treated as a conduct issue and dealt with as a disciplinary matter.
>
> If the absence is due to genuine (including medically certified) illness, the issue becomes one of capability, and the employer should take a sympathetic and considerate approach. When thinking about how to handle these cases, it is helpful to consider:
>
> - how soon the employee's health and attendance will improve;
> - whether alternative work is available;
> - the effect of the absence on the organisation;
> - how similar situations have been handled in the past; and
> - whether the illness is the result of disability, in which case the provisions of the Disability Discrimination Act 1995 will apply.
>
> The impact of long-term absences will nearly always be greater on small organisations, and they may be entitled to act at an earlier stage than large organisations.
>
> In cases of extended sick leave both statutory and contractual issues will need to be addressed and specialist advice may be necessary.

According to the EAT, responsibility for the ill health is not a concern of the employment tribunal, only the question as to whether the employer was reasonable in dismissing the employee because of their unfitness for work. Thus even when the employer may have some responsibility for the employee's lack of fitness for work, the matter is not relevant when considering whether the dismissal was fair on the grounds of capability.[216] Subsequently, this view was disagreed with in *Edwards v Governors of Hanson School*,[217] which concerned the dismissal of a school teacher after a period of ill health which, he alleged, was due to the headmaster's treatment of him. Here the EAT expressed the view

---

[214] Paragraph 56 ACAS Code of Practice 2004.
[215] Paragraphs 38–40 ACAS Code of Practice 2004.
[216] See *McAdie v Royal Bank of Scotland* [2007] IRLR 895 CA.
[217] [2001] IRLR 733.

that the requirement for the employment tribunal to take such action as is 'just and equitable' may require that tribunal to take into account the conduct of both the employer and the employee. This, in turn, may require the employment tribunal to inquire into any allegations of misconduct, provided that the award remains as compensation for the employee, rather than punishment of the employer.

It is likely that a dismissal for ill health will not be a fair dismissal if the employee concerned has not been consulted. Discussions and consultation with the employee may bring out new facts which may influence the employer's decision. This is so even where the employer has received an independent medical report on the employee's state of health.[218] There is a contrast between those situations where an employee becomes permanently unfit to carry out duties required by their post and those occasions when the employer decides to dismiss an employee as a result of a poor attendance record.

The issue of an individual becoming permanently unfit for work may also be an issue under the Disability Discrimination Act 1995 (DDA 1995) (see Chapter 7).[219] In *Seymour v British Airways Board*,[220] for example, a registered disabled person was dismissed after the employer prepared and implemented a policy in relation to 'non-effective' staff, who might be restricted in their work for medical reasons. The EAT held that, although the disabled person was entitled to special consideration, this was not sufficient to give them priority over others during a redundancy situation. After the passing of the DDA 1995, much has changed. In *Kent County Council v Mingo*[221] a disabled employee was held to have been discriminated against because priority was given to other redundant or potentially redundant employees who were not so disadvantaged. The unfitness for work needs to be in relation to the particular work for which the individual was employed to undertake. Even where a contract of employment gives the employer the right to transfer an employee to any other work at a similar level, the fitness of the employee needs to be assessed in relationship to the particular kind of work.[222]

Continued periodic absences may be a considerable problem for some employers. It is important that the employee is aware of the possible consequences of their absenteeism record. Formal warnings may not always be appropriate, neither, necessarily, will medical evidence where it is not possible to provide an accurate prognosis for the future. In *Lynock v Cereal Packaging*[223] the EAT held that the approach of the employer must be based upon 'sympathy, understanding and compassion'. Each case must depend upon its own facts and important factors will be:

> The nature of the illness; the likelihood of recurring or some other illness arising; the length of the various absences and the spaces of good health between them; the need of the employer for the work done by the particular employee; the impact of the absences on others who work with the employee . . . the important emphasis on a personal assessment in the ultimate decision and,

---

[218] See *East Lindsey District Council v GE Daubney* [1977] IRLR 181.
[219] *Eclipse Blinds Ltd v Wright* [1992] IRLR 133 is an example of a case, prior to the DDA 1995, which concerned a disabled person with deteriorating health.
[220] [1983] IRLR 55.
[221] [2000] IRLR 90.
[222] See *Shook v London Borough of Ealing* [1986] IRLR 46.
[223] [1988] IRLR 510.

of course, the extent to which the difficulty of the situation and the position of the employee has been made clear to the employee.

Trico-Folberth Ltd v Devonshire[224] concerned an employee who received a formal warning about the number of absences from work due to ill health. After further monitoring showed no improvement in attendance she was dismissed, initially because of an unacceptable attendance record. During the internal appeal procedure, an appellate body changed the reason for dismissal on compassionate grounds to one of being medically unfit to work. The employment tribunal stated that a dismissal for the original reason may well have been held to be fair, but not on grounds of being medically unfit. There had been insufficient investigation of the medical condition and insufficient consultation with the employee to justify dismissal on these grounds.[225] Consultation with the employee is necessary, so that the matter can be discussed with that individual. Only in the rarest of circumstances is a dismissal on the grounds of capability related to health likely to be fair if there has not been adequate consultation between the employer and the employee.[226]

(c) Qualifications

Qualifications means any degree, diploma or other academic, technical or professional qualification that is relevant to the position held.[227] The qualifications need to be construed in the light of the particular position that the employee held, so, depending upon the circumstances, even a failure to pass an aptitude test can be a reason for a dismissal under this heading.[228] Such qualifications might include the need for a driving licence as in *Tayside Regional Council v McIntosh*.[229] When the local authority advertised for vehicle mechanics they stipulated, in the advertisement, that applicants should have a clean driving licence, although this was not mentioned in the written offer of employment. The successful applicant met this criterion, but, three years later, was disqualified from driving as a result of a motoring offence. The employer dismissed him as there was no alternative work available. Despite the lack of an express term in the contract of employment, the EAT held that ownership of a licence could be inferred and that it was an essential and continuing condition of the individual's employment.

5.4.3.5 Conduct

There may, of course, be a relationship between competence and conduct, for example poor attendance at work might be seen as a lack of competence or a reflection of the conduct of an employee.[230] In *Whitbread & Co v Thomas*[231] recurring stock losses in an off-licence raised issues about both the employees' competence in controlling the stock and

---

[224] [1989] IRLR 396 CA.
[225] See also *Grootcon (UK) Ltd v Keld* [1984] IRLR 302 for a further case where lack of medical evidence was important and where the real reason for dismissal may have been the insistence of a major customer.
[226] See *East Lindsey District Council v GE Daubney* [1977] IRLR 181 for a fuller discussion of consultation requirements in such situations; this case was followed in *A Links & Co Ltd v Rose* [1991] IRLR 353.
[227] Section 98(3)(b) ERA 1996.
[228] See *Blackman v The Post Office* [1974] IRLR 46 NIRC.
[229] [1982] IRLR 272.
[230] See, e.g., *Trico-Folberth Ltd v Devonshire* [1989] IRLR 396 CA.
[231] [1988] IRLR 43.

the employees' conduct in relation to their honesty or otherwise. Prior to the employment tribunal considering whether the employer acted reasonably in treating a reason as sufficient for dismissing an employee, it must first establish what the reason for dismissal was.[232] Issues about employee conduct are also issues about how an employer reacts to that conduct, so employee awareness of the conduct that is expected of them is important in establishing the reasonableness of the employer in dismissing the employee for this reason. *Lock v Cardiff Railway Co Ltd*[233] involved the dismissal of a train conductor who asked a teenage boy to leave the train when it was discovered that he had no ticket or money to pay for one. In this case the employer had failed to follow the ACAS Code of Practice by not making it clear which offences would be regarded as gross misconduct justifying summary dismissal.

As a general rule, if an order is lawful, a refusal to obey it will be a breach of contract and amount to misconduct even though similar refusals have been condoned in the past. Nevertheless, in disobedience cases the primary factor to be considered is whether the employee is acting reasonably in refusing to carry out an instruction.[234] Another area where there might be grounds for a fair dismissal is when a worker is dishonest in relation to their employment. In *British Railways Board v Jackson*[235] a train buffet supervisor was dismissed because the employer believed that he was about to take his own goods on board the train to sell to buffet car customers, thus depriving the employer of revenue. There were no tills on train buffet cars, so the employer relied upon the honesty of its employees. The employer's action was held to be reasonable and the employer was entitled to take into account the prevalence of this type of dishonesty amongst employees and whether the dismissal would be a deterrent to others from following the same course. Dishonesty by employees against the employer is likely to be a breach of the fundamental relationship of mutual trust and confidence and certainly a repetition of such a breach might lead to dismissal being regarded as coming within the range of reasonable responses of an employer (see below).[236] Providing the evidence of the employee's dishonesty may be a problem for the employer, but if the employer has reasonable grounds for sustaining a genuine belief about the employee's guilt, after carrying out an investigation, this is likely to be sufficient.[237] Such an inquiry need not be a quasi judicial one in which the accused has an opportunity to question witnesses.[238]

It may not be immediately apparent to an employee that their actions are dishonest. Using an employer's telephone to make personal calls, for example, may be viewed as dishonest by an employer, but not by an employee. There may be a need for a proper investigation as to the purpose and circumstances of such calls. In *John Lewis plc v Coyne*[239]

---

[232] See *Wilson v Post Office* [2001] IRLR 834.
[233] [1998] IRLR 358.
[234] See *UCATT v Brain* [1981] IRLR 224.
[235] [1994] IRLR 235 CA.
[236] See *Conlin v United Distillers* [1994] IRLR 169 CA where a repeated act of dishonesty led to such a dismissal.
[237] See *British Leyland (UK) Ltd v Swift* [1981] IRLR 91 CA and *British Home Stores Ltd v Burchell* [1978] IRLR 379, considered further below.
[238] See *Ulsterbus Ltd v Henderson* [1989] IRLR 251 CA, which concerned a bus conductor accused of not issuing tickets in exchange for money who unsuccessfully appealed against dismissal on the grounds that he had not been able to question customers who were witnesses; see also *Santamera v Express Cargo Ltd* [2003] IRLR 273.
[239] [2001] IRLR 139.

the court seemed to prefer a subjective approach rather than any absolute definition of dishonesty. An employee was dismissed for breaching company rules on the use of telephones, but the lack of a sufficient investigation by the employer made it an unfair dismissal. The court considered that there was a two-stage process in judging whether dishonesty had occurred.[240] The first was that it must be decided whether, according to the ordinary standards of reasonable and honest people, what was done was dishonest. The second stage was to consider whether the person concerned must have realised that what he or she was doing was, by those standards, dishonest.

There is a distinction between dishonesty at work in relation to an employer and dishonesty outside work, often with no relationship to work or the employer. What, for example, is the position of an employer who has an employee facing criminal charges? In *Lovie Ltd v Anderson*[241] an employee was charged by the police with two separate offences of indecent exposure. It might be natural for an employer not to wish to have an employee facing such distasteful charges, but there is still an important obligation for the employer to carry out some sort of investigation and to give the employee an opportunity to state their case. Similarly, in *Securicor Guarding Ltd v R*[242] an employee was charged with sex offences against children, which he denied. The employer was concerned about the reaction of important customers to such a situation and, after a disciplinary hearing, the employee was dismissed. The dismissal was held to be unfair, partly because the employer had not considered other options, such as suspension with full pay, in accordance with the company's own disciplinary code, or moving the individual to less customer-sensitive work. By way of contrast, an assistant schools groundsman who pleaded guilty to a sexual offence against his daughter was dismissed because of the possible risk to other children. According to the Court of Appeal, the employer had no choice but to dismiss the employee despite the lack of further investigation. The plea of guilty and the nature of the job was sufficient.[243] In *Mathewson v RB Wilson Dental Laboratories Ltd*[244] a dental technician was arrested during his lunch break and charged with being in possession of cannabis. The employers were held to have acted reasonably in treating this as a sufficient reason for dismissal, even though the offence was unconnected with his work. The employer argued that it was not appropriate to employ someone who was using drugs on highly skilled work, and that there was concern about the effect of continuing to employ him on younger members of staff. A conviction itself, unless for a trivial or minor matter, would normally be sufficient to provide the employer with sufficient grounds for believing that the employee had committed the offence and might be sufficient to dismiss the individual.[245]

---

[240] This was a summary of the views put forward in *R v Ghosh* [1982] QB 1053 CA.

[241] [1999] IRLR 164.

[242] [1994] IRLR 633.

[243] *P v Nottinghamshire County Council* [1992] IRLR 362 CA; compare *ILEA v Gravett* [1988] IRLR 497, where the lack of a sufficient investigation was sufficient to render a dismissal unfair. The employee was a swimming instructor accused of a sexual offence against a girl, but the police decided to take no action.

[244] [1988] IRLR 512.

[245] See *Secretary of State for Scotland v Campbell* [1992] IRLR 263, where a prison officer who was also treasurer of the officer's social club was found guilty of embezzling the club; this verdict was sufficient to justify his dismissal.

Examples of misconduct at work include those that involve relationships with colleagues. *Hussain v Elonex*[246] concerned an alleged head-butting incident and was part of a number of incidents between the complainant and another employee. This was considered grounds for dismissal, although there was an appeal on procedural grounds. The same result occurred in *Fuller v Lloyds Bank plc*[247] where, after an employer's investigation into an incident at a Christmas party that involved smashing a glass into another employee's face, the complainant was dismissed.

An employer is entitled to expect an employee not to compete for customers or contracts (see Chapter 4 on implied duties of the contract of employment). Such competition may amount to a sufficient reason for dismissal. In *Adamson v B & L Cleaning Services*[248] a foreman for a contract cleaning firm refused to agree that he could not try to compete for a cleaning contract with his employer. The EAT distinguished between competing with the employer, which is more likely to be a sufficient reason, and merely indicating an intention to compete in the future,[249] or applying for a job with a competitor. The extent to which the plans for competing have reached may well be important for the employment tribunal in reaching a decision. Thus a managing director who had formed a plan with another senior manager and attempted to induce another employee to join them was held to have gone beyond merely indicating a plan to compete in the future and was held to have been fairly dismissed.[250]

5.4.3.6 Retirement (see Chapter 7 below)

5.4.3.7 Redundancy

In *Williams v Compair Maxam Ltd*[251] the EAT laid down some principles that a reasonable employer might accept if they were planning to dismiss employees on the grounds of redundancy. The EAT pointed out that these were not principles of law, but standards of behaviour. The approach has, however, been widely followed, even if the judgment now appears to reflect a period of industrial relations that no longer seems to exist. The EAT held that a reasonable employer might act in accordance with a number of principles. These were that:

(1) the employer would try to give as much warning as possible, to employees and their representatives, of impending redundancies;
(2) the employer would consult the employees' representatives and agree criteria for selection;
(3) the criteria for selection would not, as far as possible, depend upon the personal opinion of the individual making the selection, but more on objective criteria;
(4) the employer would seek to ensure that the selection is made fairly against these criteria;
(5) the employer would try to offer alternative employment, rather than dismissal.

In selecting employees for redundancy a senior manager is entitled to rely on the assessments of employees made by those who have direct knowledge of their work.

---

[246] [1999] IRLR 420.
[247] [1991] IRLR 336.
[248] [1995] IRLR 193.
[249] See *Laughton and Hawley v Bapp Industrial Supplies Ltd* [1986] IRLR 245 where the EAT held that an employee did not breach his duty of loyalty by indicating a future intention to compete.
[250] *Marshall v Industrial Systems & Control Ltd* [1992] IRLR 294.
[251] [1982] IRLR 83.

Employers may need to show, however, that their method of selection was fair and applied reasonably. An absence of adequate consultation with the employees concerned or their representatives might affect their ability to do this (consultation issues are considered below). It will not always be possible to call evidence subsequently to show that adequate consultation would not have made a difference to the decision about selection for redundancy. If the flaws in the process were procedural, it might be possible to reconstruct what might have happened if the correct procedures had been followed. If, however, the tribunal decides that the flaws were more substantive, such a reconstruction may not be possible.[252]

Thus reasonableness will normally require a warning to and consultation with affected employees and/or their representatives, the establishment of a fair selection procedure and an attempt to avoid or minimise the redundancies. A defect in this process is not necessarily fatal to the employer. In *Lloyd v Taylor Woodrow Construction*,[253] for example, there was failure to inform the employee of the selection criteria before the decision to dismiss was taken. This defect was corrected at the appeal stage when the employee was given the opportunity to challenge the criteria. This was held to be sufficient for the EAT to agree that the dismissal had not been unfair. In *John Brown Engineering Ltd v Brown*[254] an employer agreed the selection criteria with the employees' representatives, but then refused to publish the marks allocated to each employee. This was held to make the appeals procedure a sham, as individuals could not appeal against their selection without knowing their marks. This failure led to the dismissals being held to be unfair.

An employer will normally be expected to provide evidence as to the steps taken to select the employee for redundancy, the consultation that has taken place with the employee or the employee's representatives and the attempts to find alternative employment. Similarly, an employment tribunal would be expected to consider all these issues when reaching a decision on the reasonableness of the employer's action in dismissing for reasons of redundancy.[255]

'Last-in, first-out' is still used as a criterion for selection and it is assumed to be based on periods of continuous rather than cumulative service.[256] Arguably, this form of selection indirectly discriminates against women and needs to be objectively justified. Selecting employees on part-time and/or fixed-term contracts may also be potentially discriminatory. Section 105 ERA 1996 makes it unfair to select for redundancy on a variety of impermissible grounds (see 5.4.3.2 above). In addition, section 152 TULRCA 1992 offers special protection to those who are members of a trade union or take part in its activities.[257] Section 153 TULRCA 1992 provides that where the reason, or the principal reason, for the dismissal of an employee was redundancy, but the circumstances constituting the redundancy applied equally to other employees holding similar positions and those employees have not been selected for redundancy, and the reason, or the principal reason,

---

[252] See *King v Eaton (No 2)* [1998] IRLR 686.
[253] [1999] IRLR 782.
[254] [1997] IRLR 90.
[255] See *Langston v Cranfield University* [1998] IRLR 172.
[256] *International Paint Co v Cameron* [1979] IRLR 62.
[257] This section also covers those who wish to make use of a union's services and those not wishing to be members or take part in the union's activities; see Chapter 11.

was that the employee was a member of an independent trade union, or taking part in its activities, then that dismissal will be unfair. In *O'Dea v ISC Chemicals Ltd*[258] it was argued that an employee who spent half his time on trade union activities was in a special position and that, as a result, there were no other employees in a similar position with whom he could be compared in order to establish whether he had been unfairly selected for redundancy. The Court of Appeal held that the trade union activities should be ignored when deciding whether the circumstances of the redundancy applied equally to others in a similar position.

It is well established that employers have a duty to consider the alternatives to compulsory redundancy. According to ACAS;

> the measures for minimising or avoiding compulsory redundancies may include:
> - natural wastage
> - restrictions on recruitment
> - retraining and redeployment to other parts of the organisation
> - reduction or elimination of overtime
> - introduction of short-time working or temporary lay off (where this is provided for in the contract of employment or by an agreed variation of its terms)
> - retirement of those employees already beyond normal retirement age
> - seeking applicants for early retirement or voluntary redundancy . . .[259]

As regards alternative employment, 'the size and administrative resources' of the employer will be a relevant consideration here. Nevertheless, only in very rare cases will a tribunal accept that a reasonable employer would have created a job by dismissing someone else.

Consultation may be directly with the employees concerned or with their representatives (see Chapter 10 for specific requirements in relation to collective redundancies). In *Mugford v Midland Bank plc*[260] the EAT held that a dismissal on the grounds of redundancy was not unfair because no consultation had taken place with the employee individually, only with the recognised trade union. The EAT described the position with regard to consultation as follows:

- Where no consultation about redundancy has taken place with either the trade union or the employee, the dismissal will normally be unfair, unless the reasonable employer would have concluded that the consultation would be an utterly futile exercise.
- Consultation with the trade union over the selection criteria does not of itself release the employer from considering with the employee individually his being identified for redundancy.
- It will be a question of fact and degree for the tribunal to consider whether the consultation with the individual and/or the trade union was so inadequate as to render the dismissal unfair.

---

[258] [1995] IRLR 599 CA.
[259] Advisory Handbook on Redundancy Handling 2005.
[260] [1997] IRLR 208.

The overall picture must be viewed at the time of termination for the tribunal to decide whether the employer acted reasonably or not. The consultation must be fair and proper, which means that there must be:

- consultation when the proposals are still at a formative stage;
- adequate information and adequate time to respond;
- a conscientious consideration by the employer of the response to consultation.[261]

Although proper consultation may be regarded as a procedural matter, it might have a direct bearing on the substantive decision to select a particular employee, since a different employee might have been selected if, following proper consultation, different criteria had been adopted. It is not normally permissible for an employer to argue that a failure to consult or warn would have made no difference to the outcome in the particular case. It is what the employer did that is to be judged, not what might have been done. Nevertheless, if the employer could reasonably have concluded in the light of the circumstances known at the time of dismissal that consultation or warning would be 'utterly useless', he or she might well have acted reasonably. While the size of an undertaking might affect the nature or formality of the consultation, it cannot excuse lack of any consultation at all. Finally, it should be noted that the EAT has taken the view that warning and consultation are part of the same single process of consultation, which should commence with a warning that the employee is at risk.[262]

5.4.3.8 Contravention of an enactment

An example of a statutory ban on employment might be the rules contained in the Asylum and Immigration Act 1996. Section 8 precludes employers from employing an individual who has not been granted leave to enter or stay in the United Kingdom, or if his or her stay has conditions attached, which stops them from taking up employment. However, a dismissal for the reason that the employer could not lawfully continue to employ someone without contravening a restriction under an enactment, is not necessarily fair.[263]

5.4.3.9 Some other substantial reason

Section 98(1)(b) ERA 1996 includes a sixth potentially fair reason for dismissal. This is:

Some other substantial reason of a kind such as to justify the dismissal of an employee holding the position which the employee held.

This provides flexibility to employers to introduce reasons other than the specific ones provided for in the Act. In *RS Components Ltd v RE Irwin*,[264] which concerned the dismissal of a sales person who refused to accept a new contract of employment containing a restrictive covenant, the court held:

There are not only legal but also practical objections to a narrow construction of 'some other substantial reason'. Parliament may well have intended to set out . . . the common reasons for a dismissal but can hardly have hoped to produce an exhaustive catalogue of all the circumstances in which a company would be justified in terminating the services of an employee.

---

[261] *King v Eaton* [1996] IRLR 199.
[262] See *Elkouil v Coney Island Ltd* [2002] IRLR 174.
[263] *Sandhu v (1) Department of Education and Science; (2) London Borough of Hillingdon* [1978] IRLR 208.
[264] [1973] IRLR 239 NIRC. See now *Willow Oak Ltd v Silverwood* [2006] IRLR 607.

Thus 'some other substantial reason' is a general category which enables the courts to accept reasons that are not related to those in section 98(2) ERA 1996 as potentially fair. In Irwin's case the court was sympathetic to the employer's desire to protect its business by introducing non-competition covenants for its sales staff. The burden is on the employer to show a substantial reason to dismiss. The law is designed to deter employers from dismissing employees for some 'trivial or unworthy' reason,[265] but if an employer can show that there was a fair reason in the employer's mind at the time the decision was taken, and that the employer genuinely believed it to be fair, then this might make it a dismissal for some other substantial reason.[266]

This desire to help business make difficult decisions for sound business reasons has typified the approach of the courts. *St John of God (Care Services) Ltd v Brooks*[267] involved a charity-owned hospital whose National Health Service funding was reduced. As a result the employer proposed to cut pay and benefits to staff in order to make the necessary savings to stop them getting into financial trouble. The proposals were eventually accepted by 140 of the 170 employees. The complainants were four of those who did not accept the changes and were dismissed. The EAT held that it was insufficient to look at the proposals alone. They were only one factor and the reasonableness of the employer's actions had to be looked at in the context of sound business reasons and other factors, for example, that the majority of the employees accepted the changes. The employees were, therefore, dismissed for some other substantial reason.[268] The acceptance of new terms and conditions by the majority of employees was also a factor in *Catamaran Cruisers Ltd v Williams*.[269] In this case the employers wished to make substantial changes to improve safety and efficiency. The EAT held that:

> We do not accept as a valid proposition of law that an employer may only offer terms which are less or much less favourable than those which pre-existed if the very survival of his business depends upon acceptance of the terms.

The EAT remitted the matter back to the employment tribunal with an instruction that it should not look solely at the advantages and disadvantages to the employees – it was also necessary to look at the benefit to the employer of imposing the changes in the new contract of employment. In *Farrant v The Woodroffe School*[270] an employee was dismissed for refusing to accept organisational changes. The employer mistakenly believed that the employee was obliged to accept a new job description and that the dismissal was therefore lawful. The EAT held that dismissal for refusing to obey an unlawful order was not necessarily unfair. Of importance was not the lawfulness or otherwise of the employer's instructions but the overall question of reasonableness. In this case it was not unreasonable for the employer to act on professional advice, even if that advice was wrong.

---

[265] *Kent County Council v Gilham* [1985] IRLR 16 CA.
[266] On the removal of an incumbent chief executive following a takeover see *Cobley v Forward Technology* [2003] IRLR 706.
[267] [1992] IRLR 546.
[268] The EAT followed the approach adopted by the Court of Appeal in *Hollister v National Farmers' Union* [1979] IRLR 238 CA.
[269] [1994] IRLR 386.
[270] [1998] IRLR 76.

5.4.3.10 Reasonableness

According to section 98(4) ERA 1996, the employment tribunal will need to decide whether in the circumstances the employer acted reasonably or unreasonably, having regard to the size and administrative resources of the employer, in treating the reason as sufficient to dismiss the employee. This is to be determined 'in accordance with equity and the substantial merits of the case'. At this stage the burden of proof is neutral.[271] However, section 98A ERA 1996 provides that, if the requirements of the statutory dismissal procedure have been met, the failure to follow a more sophisticated procedure will not be treated 'as by itself making the employer's action unreasonable if he shows that he would have dismissed the employee if he had followed the procedure'.

As a matter of law, a reason cannot be treated as sufficient where it has not been established as true or that there were reasonable grounds on which the employer could have concluded that it was true. Under section 98(4) ERA 1996, tribunals must take account of the wider circumstances. In addition to the employer's business needs, attention must be paid to the personal attributes of the employee – for example, previous work record. Thus when all the relevant facts are considered, a dismissal may be deemed unfair notwithstanding the fact that the disciplinary rules specified that such behaviour would result in immediate dismissal. Conversely, employers may act reasonably in dismissing even though they have breached an employee's contract. In appropriate cases the test of fairness must be interpreted, so far as possible, compatibly with the European Convention on Human Rights.[272]

Employers will be expected to treat employees in similar circumstances in a similar way. The requirement that the employer must act consistently between all employees means that an employer should consider truly comparable cases which were known about or ought to have been known about. Nevertheless, the overriding principle seems to be that each case must be considered on its own facts and with the freedom to consider both aggravating factors and mitigating circumstances. The words 'equity and the substantial merits' also allow tribunals to apply their knowledge of good industrial relations practice and to ensure that there has been procedural fairness (see below).

In *Polkey v AE Dayton Services Ltd*[273] Lord Bridge stated that there might be exceptional circumstances where an employer could reasonably take the view that these normal procedural steps would be futile and could not have altered the decision to dismiss. In such circumstances the test of reasonableness may have been satisfied.[274] This approach did not imply that the employer must take a deliberate decision not to consult.[275] The test of

---

[271] See *Boys and Girls Welfare Society v McDonald* [1996] IRLR 129 which concerned a residential social worker who allegedly hit a boy in his care, and emphasised the error of placing the burden of proof on the employer.

[272] See *X v Y* [2004] IRLR 561 on Article 8 and respect for private life.

[273] [1987] IRLR 503 HL.

[274] In *Warner v Adnet Ltd* [1998] IRLR 394 CA a failure to consult as a result of the appointment of a receiver, the dire financial straits of the company and the need to find a buyer urgently made the normal requirement to consult unnecessary; consultation could not have made a difference.

[275] In *Ferguson v Prestwick Circuits Ltd* [1992] IRLR 266 the employers took a deliberate decision not to consult, claiming that the workforce had stated a preference for this approach after a previous redundancy exercise; this was held not to be a sufficient reason for failing to consult.

reasonableness was based on what the employers knew at the time of the dismissal, whether the decision not to consult was a deliberate decision or not.[276]

British Home Stores v Burchell[277] concerned the dismissal of an employee for allegedly being involved in acts of dishonesty with a number of other employees. The EAT provided some guidance on the steps that need to be taken by employers who suspect one or more employees of misconduct:

> First of all, there must be established by the employer the fact of that belief; that the employer did believe it. Secondly, that the employer had in his mind reasonable grounds upon which to sustain that belief. And thirdly . . . that the employer, at the stage at which he formed that belief on those grounds, at any rate at the final stage at which he formed that belief on those grounds, had carried out as much investigation into the matter as was reasonable in all the circumstances of the case.

This three-step test has been used extensively since this judgment.[278] In *Linfood Cash & Carry Ltd v Thomson*,[279] for example, two employees were dismissed on suspicion of theft. The dismissals were held to be unfair because, applying the *Burchell* test, the court concluded that even though the employer genuinely believed in the employees' guilt, they had no reasonable grounds for that belief and had not carried out a sufficient investigation.[280]

Having taken these steps the test is then whether it was reasonable for the employer to dismiss the employee. *British Leyland UK Ltd v Swift*[281] concerned an employee dismissed after being found guilty in a magistrates' court of fraudulently using a road fund licence belonging to a company vehicle on his own car. The question was whether a reasonable employer would have dismissed the employee. The court stated:

> It must be remembered that in all these cases there is a band of reasonableness, within which one employer might reasonably take one view; another quite reasonably take a different view . . . If it was quite reasonable to dismiss him, then the dismissal must be upheld as fair; even though some employers may not have dismissed him.

Thus there developed a test relating to a band of reasonable responses. This approach was supported in *Iceland Frozen Foods v Jones*[282] which concerned the dismissal of a night-shift foreman at a warehouse.[283] The employee had failed to secure the premises after the shift and was held responsible by the employer for slow production on the shift. The employment tribunal held that the dismissal was unfair both for the reasons and on procedural grounds. At the EAT Browne-Wilkinson J summarised the legal position:

(1) the starting point should always be the words of the statute;

(2) in applying the statute the tribunal must consider the reasonableness of the employer's conduct, not simply whether the members of the tribunal thought the dismissal fair;

(3) in considering the reasonableness of the employer's conduct, the tribunal must not substitute its own decision as to what was the right course for the employer to take;[284]

---

[276] See *Duffy v Yeomans & Partners Ltd* [1994] IRLR 642 CA.
[277] [1978] IRLR 379.
[278] It was approved by the Court of Appeal in *Weddel v Tepper* [1980] ICR 286 CA.
[279] [1989] IRLR 235.
[280] See *Sainsburys Ltd v Hitt* [2003] IRLR 23 CA.
[281] [1981] IRLR 91 CA.
[282] [1982] IRLR 439.
[283] See also *Neale v Hereford and Worcester County Council* [1986] IRLR 168 CA.
[284] See *Anglian Homes Improvements Ltd v Kelly* [2004] IRLR 793.

(4) in many cases there was a band of reasonable responses to the employee's conduct with one employer taking one view and another employer a different view;

(5) the function of the tribunal is to decide whether the decision to dismiss the employee fell within a band of reasonable responses which a reasonable employer might have adopted. If the dismissal falls within such a band then it is fair.

This approach was questioned in part by the EAT in *Haddon*,[285] *Wilson*[286] and *Midland Bank*.[287] The defects identified by the EAT were twofold. First, the expression 'range of reasonable responses' had become a mantra, so that nothing short of a perverse decision would be outside such a range. Secondly, it prevented members of employment tribunals from approaching the test of reasonableness by reference to their own experience in deciding what should be done. However, in *Post Office v Foley*,[288] the Court of Appeal re-affirmed the previous approach. The range of reasonable responses test does not become one of perversity because the behaviour of an employer has to be extreme before it falls outside the range. There are cases where it will not apply and the court gave two examples. First, where an employee, without good cause, sets fire to the factory, burns it down and is dismissed. Secondly, where an employee says good morning to the line manager and is dismissed. In these cases there is unlikely to be a need to use the range of reasonable responses test as the first dismissal would be reasonable and the second not. It is in the range between these two examples that there is the possibility of disagreement about what action a reasonable employer would take. That is when the employment tribunal must apply the test. As for the suggestion that the members of the tribunal ought to be able effectively to substitute their own views about what was the reasonable decision, the court held that:

> It was also made clear in *Iceland Foods* that the members of the tribunal must not simply consider whether they personally think that the dismissal is fair and they must not substitute their decision as to what was the right course to adopt for that of the employer. Their proper function is to determine whether the decision to dismiss the employee fell within the band of reasonable responses which a reasonable employer might have adopted.[289]

5.4.4 Procedural fairness (1): statutory dismissal, disciplinary and grievance procedures

The EA 2002 introduced, for the first time in the United Kingdom, a statutory dismissal and disciplinary procedure and a statutory grievance procedure. Section 98A(1) ERA 1996 provides that an employee who is dismissed without the relevant statutory procedure being completed will be regarded as unfairly dismissed if this is wholly or mainly because of the employer's failure to comply with its requirements. In an attempt to make employment

---

[285] *Haddon v Van den Bergh Foods Ltd* [1999] IRLR 672.
[286] *Wilson v Ethicon* [2000] IRLR 4.
[287] *Midland Bank plc v Madden* [2000] IRLR 288.
[288] *Post Office v Foley; HSBC plc (formerly Midland Bank) v Madden* [2000] IRLR 827 CA; see also *Beedell v West Ferry Printers Ltd* [2000] IRLR 650.
[289] On the approach to be taken when human rights issues are raised see *X v Y* [2004] IRLR 625 and *McGowan v Scottish Water* [2005] IRLR 167.

tribunals disregard procedural errors outside this minimum standard, a dismissal will not be held to be unfair if there are procedural errors outside the statutory framework or if the employer has failed to follow procedures beyond those in the statutory procedure. This is on the condition that following such additional procedures would have had no effect upon the outcome.[290] In effect these statutory procedures set a minimum standard and a failure by an employer to follow them may be fatal to the employer's case.

The standard protocol for both the dismissal and disciplinary procedure and the grievance procedure are the same.[291] There are three steps which need to be taken.[292] These are the statement, the meeting and the appeal steps:

(1) The statement: in a disciplinary or dismissal procedure the employer must set out in writing the employee's alleged conduct or characteristics or other circumstances which have led the employer to contemplating taking dismissal or disciplinary action.[293] A copy of this statement must be sent to the employee who is then invited to attend a meeting to discuss the matter (see the 'right to be accompanied' below).[294] In a grievance procedure, the employee must set out his or her grievance in writing and send a copy to the employer.[295] However, there need not be any express intention to raise a grievance.[296]

(2) The meeting: in a disciplinary or dismissal procedure, there is an obligation for the meeting to take place before any action is taken, except where the action to be taken is suspension. The employee must take all reasonable steps to attend the meeting,[297] after which the employer must inform the employee of the decision. The employee must also be notified of his or her right of appeal if not happy with the decision. Similarly, in a grievance procedure, the employer must invite the employee to at least one meeting to discuss the grievance. The employee must take all reasonable steps to attend and, after the meeting, be notified of the outcome and the right to appeal.[298]

(3) The appeal: if the employee wishes to appeal, then he or she must inform the employer,[299] after which the employee is to be invited to attend a further meeting. This meeting need not take place before the dismissal or disciplinary action takes effect, so the employee may have already been punished even before the appeal against that

---

[290] See *Kelly-Madden v Manor Surgery* [2007] IRLR 17.
[291] See Schedule 2 EA 2002 and the Employment Act (Dispute Resolution) Regulations 2004, SI 2004/752 (EADR Regulations 2004) which came into force 1 October 2004: Regulation 3(1) and (2) state when the standard and modified dismissal and disciplinary procedures apply; regulation 6 specifies when the standard and modified grievance procedures apply.
[292] Regulations 4, 8 and 11 EADR Regulations 2004 state the circumstances in which the statutory procedures do not apply or are treated as complied with. See Annex E of the ACAS Code of Practice.
[293] See *Alexander v Bridgen Ltd* [2006] IRLR 422. Regulation 2(1) excludes constructive dismissal from the definition of dismissal and specifies that 'relevant disciplinary action' is 'action short of dismissal, which the employer asserts to be based wholly or mainly on the employee's conduct or capability, other than suspension on full pay or the issuing of warnings (whether oral or written)'.
[294] EA 2002 Schedule 2 paragraph 1. See *YMCA Training v Stewart* [2007] IRLR 185.
[295] EA 2002 Schedule 2 paragraph 6. Regulation 2(1) EADR Regulations 2004 defines 'grievance' as 'a complaint by an employee about action which his employer has taken or is contemplating taking in relation to him'.
[296] See *Warner Ltd v Aspland* [2006] IRLR 87. On the modified procedure see *City of Bradford MDC v Pratt* [2007] IRLR 192.
[297] See EA 2002 Schedule 2 paragraph 7 and regulation 13 EADR Regulations 2004 on failure to attend a meeting.
[298] See EA 2002 Schedule 2 paragraph 7.
[299] See *Masterfoods Ltd v Wilson* [2007] ICR 370.

action has occurred. Again, the employee must take all reasonable steps to attend the meeting, after which he or she must be told by the employer of the final decision.[300] The same stages apply in the event of an employee appealing against a decision in the grievance disputes procedure. An appeal meeting is to be arranged to which the employee must take all reasonable steps to attend. After the appeal meeting the employee must be informed by the employer of the final outcome.[301]

There is also a modified procedure for both disciplinary and dismissal situations and also grievance situations which miss out the meeting stage and consist entirely of the statement and appeal stages outlined above.

There are some other requirements applicable to both procedures.[302] These are that:

- each step and action in the procedures should be taken without unreasonable delay;
- the timing and locations of meetings must be reasonable;
- the meetings must be conducted in a manner that enables both employer and employee to explain their cases; and
- in the case of appeal meetings, which are not the first meeting, the employer should, as far as is reasonably practicable, be represented by a more senior manager than attended the first meeting.

There are specific penalties for not using the statutory disciplinary and dismissal procedure (as well as with the statutory grievance procedure) which apply to the jurisdictions listed in Schedule 3 EA 2002.[303] If the failure to complete the procedure was the fault of the employer, the employment tribunal may increase the award by between 10% and 50% unless the result was viewed as unjust and inequitable. The reverse is true if the fault lies with the employee. In such a case the employment tribunal could reduce the award by a similar amount, provided that it was just and equitable to do so. Most large employers have their own formal procedures which will contain all the elements provided of the statutory procedures. Thus they are unlikely to be affected, except for penalties for not completing the procedure. The greatest effect will probably be on small and medium-sized employers.

5.4.5 Procedural fairness (2): ACAS Code of Practice

The Code was first introduced in 1977 and the current version came into effect on 1 October 2004. It was issued under section 201 TULRCA 1992, which provides for the revision of the code to bring it into line with statutory developments. Failure to observe the Code will not in itself render an employer liable to any proceedings.[304] However, it will be admissible in proceedings before employment tribunals and the Central Arbitration Committee and any relevant parts will be taken into account.[305] This would seem a

---

[300] See EA 2002 Schedule 2 paragraph 3.
[301] See EA 2002 Schedule 2 paragraph 8.
[302] Set out in Part 3 Schedule 2 EA 2002.
[303] Such as sex, race or disability discrimination, unfair dismissal, national minimum wage and the Working Time Regulations; see section 31 EA 2002.
[304] Section 207(1) TULRCA 1992.
[305] Section 207(2)–(3) TULRCA 1992; see also the ACAS advisory handbook on discipline and grievances at work.

sufficient incentive for employers to take note of the Code's recommendations. The Code covers disciplinary and grievance procedures and the right to be accompanied (see below).

According to the Code, management is responsible for maintaining discipline and setting standards of performance within the organisation, although this should be achieved by involving workers and their representatives.[306] In relation to disciplinary rules and procedures, the Code makes the following provision:

(1) It is unlikely that any set of rules could cover all the circumstances that may arise. Subjects that they would be expected to cover include misconduct, sub-standard performance, harassment or victimisation, misuse of company facilities including computer facilities such as e-mail and the Internet, poor timekeeping and unauthorised absences.[307]

(2) Workers should be made aware of the likely consequences of breaking disciplinary rules or failing to meet performance standards. They should, in particular, be given a clear indication of the type of conduct that will result in dismissal without notice. The Code suggests a number of such types of conduct ranging from theft and fraud, to serious bullying and harassment and serious infringement of health and safety rules.[308] An example of the dangers of not ensuring that employees know of all such types of conduct occurred in *W Brooks & Son v Skinner*.[309] After problems at a Christmas party for employees at which a number became drunk, the employer and the trade union concerned negotiated an agreement that in future such behaviour would result in instant dismissal. Although normally such a collective agreement would be enough to show that the information had been communicated to the employees, it was not held to be so in this case. The following Christmas some employees became drunk again and the complainant was dismissed. The dismissal was held to be unfair because the complainant did not know of the agreement and it did not relate to conduct which any reasonable employee would realise would result in dismissal.[310]

(3) Disciplinary procedures should not be seen as primarily a means of imposing sanctions, but rather a way of helping and encouraging an improvement in performance.[311] If the procedures are contractual, then the employee has the right to all the stages set out in the arrangements. In *Stoker v Lancashire County Council*[312] an employee was entitled to two appeal hearings but was only allowed one. This was sufficient for the Court of Appeal to remit the case back to an employment tribunal to reconsider the claim for unfair dismissal.

Regard should also be had for the rules of natural justice. This means that workers should be informed in advance of any disciplinary hearing of the allegations that are being made against them, together with supporting evidence. They should have the

---

[306] Paragraph 52 ACAS Code of Practice.
[307] Paragraph 54 ACAS Code of Practice.
[308] Paragraphs 56–57 ACAS Code of Practice.
[309] [1984] IRLR 379.
[310] Unlike that in the contrasting case of *Gray Dunn & Co Ltd v Edwards* [1980] IRLR 23.
[311] Paragraph 58 ACAS Code of Practice.
[312] [1992] IRLR 75 CA.

opportunity to challenge the allegations and evidence before a decision is reached and should have the right of appeal against any decisions taken.[313] *Hussain v Elonex*[314] concerned an employee who was involved in a number of incidents with another employee. In one of those incidents, the complainant was alleged to have head-butted the other employee and was dismissed. Prior to a disciplinary hearing, statements were taken from other employees, but the existence of these statements was not disclosed to the complainant. The court held that there was no requirement of natural justice that copies of the statements should be handed over. The complainant knew the allegations made against him and was given a full opportunity to respond. This was sufficient to meet the demands of natural justice.[315] In contrast, in *Spink v Express Foods Group Ltd*[316] an employee was deliberately not told of the accusations against him until the disciplinary hearing took place. This was held to be a breach of a fundamental tenet of fairness.[317] The employee's guilt, which led to the dismissal, was a matter that could be dealt with at the time of assessing compensation.

(4) In certain circumstances, for example where the case involves gross misconduct, where relationships have broken down or where there are considered to be risks to property, a brief period of suspension with pay should be considered. It should be made clear that this is not a disciplinary action.[318]

(5) Before a decision is reached there should be a disciplinary hearing at which the worker can state their case. There should be a formal procedure, especially when the statutory procedure applies, which includes oral and written warnings.[319] Care needs to be taken with warnings. In *Bevan Ashford v Malin*,[320] for example, a written warning was given to an employee that any future incidents would lead to dismissal. The warning was to last for one year, but there was some ambiguity as to when the year commenced. The EAT held that a written warning that was ambiguous would be construed strictly against the employer who drafted it and in favour of the employee who received it.

(6) When deciding on a disciplinary penalty, regard should be had to the need to act reasonably.[321] Relevant factors might include the extent to which standards have been

---

[313] Paragraph 59 ACAS Code of Practice. These are also ingredients of the statutory procedure discussed above. See *Ramsay v Walkers Snack Food Ltd* [2004] IRLR 754.

[314] [1999] IRLR 420; see also *Fuller v Lloyds Bank plc* [1991] IRLR 336, where witness statements after an employer's investigation were not disclosed to the complainant.

[315] Compare *Louies v Coventry Hood & Seating Co Ltd* [1990] IRLR 324, where an employer's failure to give the employee copies of two witness statements was held to be contrary to the rules of natural justice; the employers had only given a broad outline of the charges.

[316] [1990] IRLR 320.

[317] The EAT also expressed the view that the reference to the fact that not every procedural flaw was fatal to the employer's case in *Polkey v AE Dayton Services Ltd* [1987] IRLR 503 HL was a reference in the context of dismissal on the grounds of redundancy.

[318] Paragraph 39 ACAS Code of Practice.

[319] Paragraphs 21–24 ACAS Code of Practice.

[320] [1995] IRLR 360.

[321] See *Tower Hamlets v Anthony* [1989] IRLR 394 CA, where an employee was dismissed whilst an appeal against a formal warning on another incident was still being processed. The question was whether it was reasonable to wait for that appeal or not before dismissing and the court held that this might depend upon the timescale involved.

breached; precedent; the worker's general record, position, length of service;[322] and special circumstances which might be appropriate to adjust the penalty.[323]

Finally, we must consider the impact of appeal procedures. In *West Midlands Co-op v Tipton*[324] the House of Lords confirmed that a dismissal is unfair if an employer unreasonably treats the reason for dismissal as sufficient, either when the original decision to dismiss is made or when that decision is maintained at the conclusion of an internal appeal. A dismissal may also be unfair if the employer refuses to comply with the full requirements of an appeal procedure.[325] Whether procedural defects can be rectified on appeal will depend on the degree of unfairness at the original hearing.[326]

5.4.6 Procedural fairness (3): the right to be accompanied

Section 10 Employment Relations Act 1999 (ERELA 1999) introduced the right for workers[327] who are required or invited by the employer to attend a disciplinary or grievance hearing to be accompanied by a single companion if the worker reasonably requests, in writing, to be accompanied. Paragraph 103 of the ACAS Code of Practice on Disciplinary and Grievance Procedures 2004 points out that there is no test of reasonableness in this regard and that it will be a matter for the courts to decide. However, the Code also suggests that it would not be appropriate to insist on being accompanied by someone whose presence might prejudice the proceedings or who might have a conflict of interest. It further suggests that it would not be appropriate to invite someone from a remote location when there is someone suitable at the same site.

A disciplinary hearing, according to section 13(4) ERELA 1999, is a hearing that could result in:

- the administration of a formal warning to a worker by the employer;
- the taking of some other action in respect of a worker by his employer;
- the confirmation of a warning issued or some other action taken.[328]

Paragraph 99 of the ACAS Code of Practice states that the right to be accompanied depends upon the nature of the hearing. It does not extend to more informal interviews which will not result in a formal warning. In *Harding v London Underground*,[329] where the employee had received an 'informal oral warning', the EAT ruled that a disciplinary warning becomes a formal warning if it becomes part of the employee's disciplinary record.

---

[322] See *Strouthos v London Underground* [2004] IRLR 636 where the employee had 20 years' service with no previous warnings.

[323] Paragraph 17 ACAS Code of Practice.

[324] [1986] IRLR 112.

[325] See *Tarbuck v Sainsburys Ltd* [2006] IRLR 664.

[326] See *Taylor v OCS Ltd* [2006] IRLR 613.

[327] With the exception of those in the security services, which includes the Security Service, the Secret Intelligence Service and Government Communications Headquarters: section 15 ERELA 1999.

[328] A grievance hearing is one which concerns the performance of a duty by the employer in relation to a worker: section 13(5) ERELA 1999. On redundancy meetings see *Heathmill Ltd v Jones* [2003] IRLR 856.

[329] [2003] IRLR 252; see also *Skiggs v South West Trains Ltd* [2005] IRLR 459.

The right applies to workers, who are defined[330] as including those that come within the meaning of section 230(3) ERA 1996 plus agency workers, home workers,[331] persons in Crown employment, excluding those in the naval, military, air or reserve forces, and relevant members of the staff of the Houses of Parliament. Where a worker exercises this right, the employer must permit the worker to be accompanied at the hearing by a single companion who is chosen by the worker. The companion is to be permitted to address the hearing and confer with the worker during it. However, the employer does not have to allow the companion to: answer questions on behalf of the worker; address the hearing if the worker indicates that they do not wish the companion to do so; or use their position in a way that prevents the employer from explaining its case or prevents another person from making a contribution to the hearing.[332] Thus the companion is more than a witness to the proceedings but less than an advocate. There are rules as to who can be the companion. It can be:

(1) an individual who is employed by a trade union and is an official[333] of that union;
(2) an individual who is an official of a trade union whom the union has reasonably certified in writing as having experience of, or having received training in, acting as a worker's companion at such hearings;
(3) another of the employer's workers.[334]

An employer must also permit a worker to take paid time off during working hours for the purpose of accompanying another of the employer's workers to a hearing.[335] In addition, a worker has the right not to be subjected to detriment from the employer for exercising the right to ask for a companion or to be a companion. Any dismissal resulting from the assertion of these rights will be an automatically unfair dismissal, within Part X ERA 1996 (see above).[336] A worker may present a complaint to an employment tribunal if the employer fails, or threatens to fail, to comply with these provisions. This complaint must be made within three months beginning with the date of the failure or threat, unless the tribunal is satisfied that it was not reasonably practicable to do so. If the employment tribunal finds the complaint well-founded, it may order the employer to pay compensation to the worker, not exceeding two weeks' pay.[337]

5.4.7 Claiming unfair dismissal

An employee wishing to complain of unfair dismissal must first submit a statement of grievance to their employer.[338] Unless the 'time limit escape clause' applies,[339] claims must

---

[330] Section 13(1) ERELA 1999.
[331] Further definition of agency and home workers is provided in section 13(2) and (3) ERELA 1999.
[332] Section 10(2B)–(2C) ERELA 1999.
[333] Within the meaning of sections 1 and 119 TULRCA 1992.
[334] Section 10(3) ERELA 1999; section 10(4) provides an obligation on the employer to arrange alternative times for hearings if the companion has difficulties in attending.
[335] Section 10(6) ERELA 1999. See ACAS Code of Practice paragraph 109.
[336] Section 12(1)–(6) ERELA 1999.
[337] Section 11(1)–(6) ERELA 1999.
[338] See section 32 EA 2002 and *Basingstoke Press Ltd v Clarke* [2007] IRLR 588.
[339] Section 111(2) ERA 1996. See also paragraphs 6 and 9 Schedule 2 EA 2002 and regulation 15 EADR Regulations 2004 which extend the normal time limit for a further three months in specified circumstances.

normally arrive at an employment tribunal within three months of the effective date of termination. A complaint can also be presented before the effective date of termination provided it is lodged after notice has been given. This includes notice given by an employee who is alleging constructive dismissal.[340] What is or is not reasonably practicable is a question of fact, and the onus is on the employee to prove that it was not reasonably practicable to claim in time. The meaning of 'reasonably practicable' lies somewhere between reasonable and reasonably capable of physically being done.[341] The tribunal will look at the issue of reasonableness against all the surrounding circumstances.

The courts have dealt with this jurisdictional point on several occasions and have taken the view that since the unfair dismissal provisions have been in force for many years tribunals should be fairly strict in enforcing the time limit. Nevertheless, the issue of reasonable practicability depends upon the awareness of specific grounds for complaint, not upon the right to complain at all. Thus there is nothing to prevent an employee who is precluded by lapse of time from claiming on one ground from proceeding with a second complaint under another ground raised within a reasonable period. According to the Court of Appeal, if employers want to protect themselves from late claims presented on the basis of newly discovered information they should ensure that the fullest information is made available to the employee at the time of dismissal.[342]

5.4.8 Conciliation, arbitration and compromise agreements

ACAS has an important role in conciliation and arbitration (see Chapter 1). In 2006/7, 38% of unfair dismissal applications[343] to employment tribunals were settled before reaching the stage of a formal tribunal hearing. These are not all a response to the intervention of ACAS, but clearly the organisation plays a significant part in reducing the burden on employment tribunals. Rule 22 of the Employment Tribunals (Constitution and Rules of Procedure) Regulations 2004[344] introduced a fixed period during which the parties are given the opportunity to reach an ACAS conciliated settlement. A standard procedure of 13 weeks applies to unfair dismissal and redundancy claims. However, this can be extended by two weeks if ACAS considers it probable that proceedings will be settled during the further period.

Copies of unfair dismissal applications and subsequent correspondence are sent to an ACAS conciliation officer who has the duty to promote a settlement of the complaint:

- if requested to do so by the complainant and the employer (known as the respondent), or
- if, in the absence of any such request, the conciliation officer considers that he or she could act with a reasonable prospect of success.

---

[340] Section 111(4) ERA 1996.
[341] *Palmer v Southend Borough Council* [1984] IRLR 119. On the effect of the advice received see *Marks & Spencer plc v Williams-Ryan* [2005] IRLR 562.
[342] See *Marley Ltd v Anderson* [1996] IRLR 163.
[343] See ACAS Annual Report 2006/7.
[344] SI 2004/1861.

In *Moore v Duport Furniture*[345] the House of Lords decided that the expression 'promote a settlement' should be given a liberal construction capable of covering whatever action by way of such promotion is appropriate in the circumstances. Where the complainant has ceased to be employed, the conciliation officer must seek to promote that person's re-employment (i.e. reinstatement or re-engagement) on terms that appear to be equitable. If the complainant does not wish to be re-employed, or this is not practicable, the conciliation officer must seek to promote agreement on compensation.[346] In addition, section 18(3) Employment Tribunals Act 1996 (ETA 1996) requires conciliation officers to make their services available before a complaint has been presented if requested to do so by either a potential applicant or a respondent.

Where appropriate, a conciliation officer is to 'have regard to the desirability of encouraging the use of other procedures available for the settlement of grievances', and anything communicated to a conciliation officer in connection with the performance of the above functions is not admissible in evidence in any proceedings before a tribunal except with the consent of the person who communicated it.[347] It should be noted that an agreement to refrain from lodging a tribunal complaint is subject to all the qualifications by which an agreement can be avoided at common law – for example, on grounds of economic duress.

Section 203(1) ERA 1996 provides that any provision in any agreement is void in so far as it attempts to exclude the operation of any part of the ERA 1996 or stops a person from bringing any proceedings under the Act.[348] Exceptions to this are found in section 203(2) and include a provision that any agreement to refrain from instituting or continuing proceedings has been reached where an ACAS conciliation officer has taken action under section 18 ETA 1996.[349] If an agreement is reached with the help of the conciliation officer, then it will be treated as an exception to section 203(1) ERA 1996. Another exception is where an agreement to refrain from instituting or continuing proceedings has been reached in accordance with the conditions regulating compromise agreements.[350] These provisions are contained in section 203(3), (3A), (3B) and (4) ERA 1996. The conditions regulating compromise agreements are:

(1) the agreement must be in writing;
(2) the employee or worker must have received advice from an independent adviser;
(3) there must be an insurance policy in force to cover any claims from the complainant or the employer in respect of any losses in consequence of the advice;
(4) the agreement must identify the adviser;[351]

[345] [1982] IRLR 31.
[346] Section 18(4) ETA 1996.
[347] Section 18(6)(7) ETA 1996.
[348] In *Sutherland v Network Appliance Ltd* [2001] IRLR 12 the EAT held that it was only those parts of the agreement that were in contravention of section 203(1) ERA 1996 that would be void; not necessarily the whole agreement.
[349] Section 203(2)(e) ERA 1996.
[350] Section 203(2)(f) ERA 1996.
[351] See *Gloystarne & Co Ltd v Martin* [2001] IRLR 15, where the individual concerned denied having appointed a trade union official as his representative or agreeing to the compromise reached.

(5) the agreement must state that these conditions regulating compromise agreements have been satisfied.

A person is an independent adviser if he or she is a qualified lawyer;[352] an officer, official, employee or member of an independent trade union who has been certified by the trade union as authorised and competent to give advice; an advice centre worker who is similarly certified by the advice centre or some other persons identified by the Secretary of State. The effect of following this procedure is to stop any further proceedings and is something that employers may use if they wish to take action that might otherwise end up in a complaint to an employment tribunal. According to the Appeal Court, the requirement that in order to constitute a valid compromise an agreement must 'relate to the particular proceedings' should be construed as requiring the particular proceedings to be clearly identified. Although one document can be used to compromise all the proceedings, it is insufficient to use the expression 'all statutory rights'.[353]

Section 212A TULRCA 1992 is an attempt to provide an alternative to employment tribunals in unfair dismissal disputes. It allows ACAS to devise a scheme for arbitration in such cases.[354] The characteristics of the scheme are:

(1) the arbitrators are independent individuals, at least some of whom will not be lawyers;
(2) parties to a dispute would both need to agree to go to arbitration;
(3) in so agreeing, they would give up all their rights to go to an employment tribunal;
(4) the parties would submit their cases in writing and legal representation would be discouraged at the hearing, which would take place locally;
(5) the decision of the arbitrator, who would have all the relevant powers of an employment tribunal, are to be binding, with no appeal to the EAT.

The arbitrators will be heavily influenced by the ACAS Code of Practice on Discipline and Grievance Procedures as well as the requirements of the statutory procedures outlined above. The advantage of the scheme is that it should, if used, speed up the process and be less formal than employment tribunals have become. However, in 2006/7 there were only three unfair dismissal applications under the scheme.[355]

5.4.9 Remedies

The remedies following a finding of unfair dismissal by an employment tribunal are reinstatement, re-engagement or compensation. There is also the opportunity for an employee to obtain interim relief.

---

[352] Section 203(4) ERA 1996 contains further definition of who is a qualified lawyer. On legal executives see Compromise Agreements (Description of Person) Order 2004 (Amendment) Order 2004, SI 2004/2515.
[353] *Hinton v University of East London* [2005] IRLR 552.
[354] See ACAS Arbitration Scheme (Great Britain) Order 2004, SI 2004/753.
[355] ACAS Annual Report 2006/7.

5.4.9.1 Interim relief

An employee may apply for interim relief[356] if they have presented a claim for unfair dismissal by virtue of:

(1) dismissal on the grounds of trade union membership or activities;[357]
(2) being a designated employee to carry out activities connected with health and safety, or being a health and safety representative;[358]
(3) being an employee representative, or a candidate to be such a representative, for the purposes of the Working Time Regulations 1998;[359]
(4) being a trustee of an occupational pension scheme relating to the individual's employment;[360]
(5) being an employee representative for the purposes of consultation on collective redundancies or transfers of undertakings;[361]
(6) being a reason connected with obtaining or preventing recognition of a trade union;[362]
(7) being a reason connected with making a protected disclosure.[363]

The application to the tribunal needs to be made within seven days immediately following the effective date of termination and the employer will be given seven days' notice of the hearing together with a copy of the application.[364] If it appears to the employment tribunal that it may, after a proper hearing, make a declaration of unfair dismissal, it will ask the employer if the employer is willing to reinstate or re-engage the employee. If the employer refuses or the employee reasonably refuses an offer of alternative employment,[365] the employment tribunal is able to make an order for the continuation of the contract of employment.[366] It will stipulate the level of pay to be given to the employee, based on what the employee would normally have expected to earn in the period, but will take into account any payments already made by the employer as payments in lieu of notice or by way of discharging the employer's liabilities under the contract of employment.[367] Section 132 ERA 1996 enables the employment tribunal to award compensation if the employer does not comply with an order for continuation.

5.4.9.2 Reinstatement or re-engagement

If the employment tribunal finds the complaint well founded, it will explain to the complainant about its power to make an order for reinstatement or re-engagement and ask whether the complainant wishes the tribunal to make such an order. If the complainant

---

[356] Section 128 ERA 1996.
[357] Section 161(1) TULRCA 1992.
[358] Section 100(1)(a)–(b) ERA 1996.
[359] Section 101A(d) ERA 1996.
[360] Section 102(1) ERA 1996.
[361] Section 103 ERA 1996.
[362] Section 161(2) and Schedule A1 TULRCA 1992.
[363] Section 103A ERA 1996.
[364] Section 128(2) and (4) ERA 1996.
[365] Section 129 ERA 1996. There are issues about what terms and conditions might be offered on re-engagement.
[366] Section 130(1) ERA 1996, but not an order that ensures the employee actually goes back to work.
[367] Section 130(2)–(7) ERA 1996; this includes any payments made as damages for breach of contract.

expresses a wish for such an order, the tribunal will consider it.[368] An order for reinstatement is an order that the employer treat the employee as if that employee had never been dismissed. Thus the employee will return to the same job on the same terms and conditions as if there had been no interruption. The employer will pay any amounts due, less any amounts already paid to the employee in connection with the dismissal.[369] An order for re-engagement is an order that the employee be taken back by the employer into a position comparable to that from which the employee was dismissed, or other suitable employment. The employment tribunal will specify the terms and conditions upon which the employee will return.[370]

If at least seven days before the hearing the employee has expressed a wish to be re-employed but it becomes necessary to postpone or adjourn the hearing because the employer does not, without special reason, adduce reasonable evidence about the availability of the job from which the employee was dismissed, the employer will be required to pay the costs of the adjournment or postponement.[371] In addition, section 116(5) ERA 1996 states that where an employer has taken on a permanent replacement, this shall not be taken into account unless the employer shows either:

- that it was not practicable to arrange for the dismissed employee's work to be done without engaging a permanent replacement, or
- that a replacement was engaged after the lapse of a reasonable period without having heard from the dismissed employee that he or she wished to be reinstated or re-engaged, and that when the employer engaged the replacement it was no longer reasonable to arrange for the dismissed employee's work to be done except by a permanent replacement.

The employment tribunal has considerable discretion about making such orders and there are tests of practicability and justice. The tribunal will take into account the complainant's wishes and whether it is practicable for the employer to comply with an order for reinstatement. It will also take into account whether such an order would be just in circumstances where the employee contributed towards the dismissal.[372] In *Rao v Civil Aviation Authority*[373] an employee with an extremely poor attendance record was dismissed. The dismissal was held to be unfair on procedural grounds and the employment tribunal refused to order reinstatement or re-engagement because there was no evidence that, if he were re-employed, his absences would not continue, he would require re-training and his return might not be welcomed by his fellow employees. The EAT approved this decision and stated that 'practicable' is not the same as 'possible' or 'capable' and that the task of the employment tribunal was to look at what had happened and at what might happen and reach a decision on the basis of what would be fair and just for all parties. The

---

[368] Sections 112–113 ERA 1996.
[369] Section 114 ERA 1996.
[370] Section 115 ERA 1996; the tribunal will, as far as is reasonably practicable, specify terms as favourable as reinstatement, the exception being where there is contributory fault by the employee (section 116(4) ERA 1996).
[371] Section 13(2) ETA 1996.
[372] Section 116 ERA 1996.
[373] [1992] IRLR 303 EAT; the finding of the new tribunal on compensation was appealed at *Rao v Civil Aviation Authority* [1994] IRLR 240 CA.

issue of practicability was considered in *Port of London Authority v Payne*,[374] which involved a number of dock workers who had been unfairly selected for redundancy because of their trade union activities. The employers claimed that it was not practicable for them to comply with the orders for re-engagement because they were going through a period of large-scale redundancies and there were no available job vacancies.[375] The court held:

> The employment tribunal, though it should carefully scrutinise the reasons advanced by the employer, should give due weight to the commercial judgment of the management . . . The standard [for re-engagement] must not be set too high. The employer cannot be expected to explore every possible avenue which ingenuity might suggest.

Wood v Crossan[376] concerned an employee who was suspected of various offences, including dealing in drugs. The employers formed a genuine belief that he was guilty of the allegations and, after an investigation, the employee was dismissed. The employment tribunal held that the dismissal was unfair because of an inadequate investigation and other procedural defects. The complainant's job had disappeared, so there was no possibility of reinstatement. Taking into account that the individual had 16 years' service and that there was no apparent animosity between him and the employer, the employment tribunal ordered that the complainant be re-engaged at the same salary. The appeal against this was allowed by the EAT, who held that the employer's belief in the guilt of the employee resulted in a breakdown of mutual trust and confidence. Without this bond the employment relationship could not exist. The EAT further concluded:

> We consider that the remedy of re-engagement has very limited scope and will only be practical in the rarest cases where there is a breakdown in confidence as between the employer and the employee. Even if the way the matter is handled results in a finding of unfair dismissal, the remedy, in that context, invariably to our mind will be compensation.

Where a person is reinstated or re-engaged as the result of a tribunal order but the terms are not fully complied with, a tribunal must make an additional award of compensation of such amount as it thinks fit, having regard to the loss sustained by the complainant in consequence of the failure to comply fully with the terms of the order.[377] It is a matter for speculation how long re-employment must last for it to be said that an order has been complied with. If a complainant is not re-employed in accordance with a tribunal order, he or she is entitled to enforce the monetary element at the employment tribunal.[378] Compensation will be awarded together with an additional award unless the employer satisfies the tribunal that it was not practicable to comply with the order.[379] According to section 117(3)(b) ERA, the additional award will be of between 26 and 52 weeks' pay. The employment tribunal has discretion as to where, within this range, the additional compensation should fall, but it must be exercised on the basis of a proper assessment of the factors involved. One factor would ordinarily be the view taken of the employer's

---

[374] [1994] IRLR 9 CA.
[375] See *Clancy v Cannock Chase Technical College* [2001] IRLR 331, where the EAT confirmed a tribunal decision to decline to make a re-engagement order because of a worsening redundancy situation with the employer.
[376] *Wood Group Heavy Industrial Turbines Ltd v Crossan* [1998] IRLR 680.
[377] Section 117(2) ERA 1996.
[378] Section 124(4) ERA 1996.
[379] Section 17(3)–(4) ERA 1996.

conduct in refusing to comply with the order. Conversely, employees who unreasonably prevent an order being complied with will be regarded as having failed to mitigate their loss. Finally, if the employer has failed to complete a statutory dismissal procedure, an award of four weeks' pay must be included in a re-employment order unless this would cause injustice.

5.4.9.3 Compensation

Compensation for unfair dismissal is divided into two parts. The first is a basic award which, like redundancy payments, is related to age, length of service and pay. The second is a compensatory award, which is related to the actual loss suffered.

The basic award is arrived at by calculating the number of years of continuous service and allowing the appropriate amount for each year. This appropriate amount is:

- one and a half weeks' pay for each year of employment in which the employee was not below 41 years of age;
- one week's pay for each year of employment in which the employee was not below the age of 22 years;
- half a week's pay for each year of employment in which the employee was not within either of the above.

Only 20 years' service can be taken into account, which results in a statutory maximum of 30 weeks' pay. A week's pay is to be calculated in accordance with Part XIV Chapter II ERA 1996 (see Chapter 8).[380] In certain cases there is a minimum award of £4,200.[381] These are in cases of unfair selection for redundancy or for dismissal related to one of a number of reasons that are the same as those listed above for being eligible for interim relief. The basic award can be reduced by such proportion as the tribunal considers just and equitable on two grounds:

- the complainant unreasonably refused an offer of reinstatement (such an offer could have been made before any finding of unfairness);
- any conduct of the complainant before the dismissal, or before notice was given.

This does not apply where the reason for dismissal was redundancy unless the dismissal was regarded as unfair by virtue of section 100(1)(a) or (b), 101A(d), 102(1) or 103 ERA 1996. In that event the reduction will apply only to that part of the award payable because of section 120 ERA 1996.[382] If there is a failure on the part of the employer to follow the statutory dismissal procedure, then the employment tribunal may award a minimum basic award for unfair dismissal (see below) of four weeks' pay, provided that this does not cause an injustice to the employer.[383]

A compensatory award is that which a tribunal 'considers just and equitable in all the circumstances having regard to the loss sustained by the complainant in consequence of

[380] Section 119 ERA 1996; the maximum week's pay in 2007 is £310, so the maximum basic award would be £9,300.
[381] Section 120 ERA 1996; the amount is for 2007.
[382] Section 122 ERA 1996.
[383] Section 112(5) ERA 1996.

the dismissal insofar as that loss is attributable to action taken by the employer'.[384] Thus tribunals will normally have to assess how long the claimant would have been employed but for the dismissal.[385] In *Dench v Flynn & Partners*[386] an assistant solicitor was able to claim compensation for unemployment after a subsequent short-term job because it was attributable to the original dismissal. However, the mere fact that the employer could have dismissed fairly on another ground arising out of the same factual situation does not render it unjust or inequitable to award compensation.[387]

Section 123(3) ERA 1996 specifically mentions that an individual whose redundancy entitlement would have exceeded the basic award can be compensated for the difference, while a redundancy payment received in excess of the basic award payable goes to reduce the compensatory award. The compensatory award can be reduced in two other circumstances: where the employee's action caused or contributed to the dismissal, and where the employee failed to mitigate his or her loss. Before reducing an award on the ground that the complainant caused or contributed to the dismissal, a tribunal must be satisfied that the employee's conduct was culpable or blameworthy – i.e. foolish, perverse or unreasonable in the circumstances. Thus there could be a finding of contributory fault in a case of constructive dismissal on the basis that there was a causal link between the employee's conduct and the employer's repudiatory breach of contract.[388]

In deciding whether to reduce compensation the tribunal must take into account the conduct of the complainant and not what happened to some other employee – for example, one who was treated more leniently. Not all unreasonable conduct will necessarily be culpable or blameworthy; it will depend on the degree of unreasonableness. Although ill-health cases will rarely give rise to a reduction in compensation on grounds of contributory fault, it is clear that an award may be reduced under the overriding 'just and equitable' provisions.[389] Having found that an employee was to blame, a tribunal must reduce the award to some extent, although the proportion of culpability is a matter for the tribunal. According to the Court of Appeal, tribunals should first assess the amount which it is just and equitable to award because this may have a very significant bearing on what reduction to make for contributory conduct.[390] The percentage amount of reduction is to be taken from the total awarded to the employee before other deductions, such as offsetting what has already been paid by the employer.

Clearly, complainants are obliged to look for work but there are stages that the tribunal must go through before it can decide what amount to deduct for an employee's failure to mitigate his or her loss.[391] These are:

- to identify what steps should have been taken by the applicant to mitigate loss;
- to find the date on which such steps would have produced an alternative income;

---

[384] Section 123 ERA 1996.
[385] See *Software 2000 Ltd v Andrews* [2007] IRLR 568.
[386] [1998] IRLR 653.
[387] See *Devonshire v Trico-Folberth* [1989] IRLR 397.
[388] See *Polentarutti v Autokraft Ltd* [1991] IRLR 457.
[389] See *Slaughter v Brewer Ltd* [1990] IRLR 426.
[390] See *Rao v Civil Aviation Authority* [1994] IRLR 240.
[391] See *Savage v Saxena* [1998] IRLR 102.

- thereafter, to reduce the amount of compensation by the amount of income which would have been earned.

The onus is on the employer to prove that there was such a failure. While acknowledging that the employee has a duty to act reasonably, the EAT has concluded that this standard is not high in view of the fact that the employer is the wrongdoer.[392]

If the relevant statutory dismissal procedure was not completed before the unfair dismissal proceedings were commenced, and this was wholly or mainly attributable to a failure by the employer, the tribunal is required to increase the level of the compensatory award. Similarly, if the non-completion of the procedure was wholly or mainly caused by the employee's failure to comply with its requirements, or exercise a right of appeal under it, the tribunal must reduce the award.[393]

Section 123(5) ERA 1996 stipulates that no account is to be taken of any pressure that was exercised on the employer to dismiss the employee and section 155 TULRCA 1992 provides that compensation cannot be reduced on the grounds that the complainant:

- was in breach of (or proposed to breach) a requirement that he or she: must be, or become, a member of a particular trade union or one of a number of trade unions; ceases to be, or refrains from becoming, a member of any trade union or of a particular trade union or of one of a number of particular trade unions; would not take part in the activities of any trade union, of a particular trade union or of one of a number of particular trade unions; would not make use of union services;
- refused, or proposed to refuse, to comply with a requirement of a kind mentioned in section 152(3)(a) TULRCA 1992;
- objected, or proposed to object, to the operation of a provision of a kind mentioned in section 152(3)(b) TULRCA 1992;
- accepted or failed to accept an offer made in contravention of section 145A or 145B TULRCA 1992 (see Chapter 11).

The maximum compensatory award is £60,600 in 2007, but it should be noted that this figure is linked to the retail price index. The limit applies only after credit has been given for any payments made by the employer and any deductions have been made,[394] but any 'excess' payments made by the employer over that which is required are deducted after the amount of the compensatory award has been fixed. As regards deductions, normally an employer is to be given credit for all payments made to an employee in respect of claims for wages and other benefits. Where an employee has suffered discrimination as well as unfair dismissal, section 126 ERA 1996 prevents double compensation for the same loss.

It is the duty of tribunals to inquire into the various grounds for compensation, but it is the responsibility of the aggrieved person to prove the loss. The legislation aims to reimburse the employee rather than to punish the employer. Hence employees who appear to have lost nothing – e.g. where it can be said that, irrespective of the procedural unfairness which occurred, they would have been dismissed anyway – do not qualify for

---

[392] *Fyfe v Scientific Furnishings Ltd* [1989] IRLR 331.
[393] Section 124A ERA 1996.
[394] Section 124(5) ERA 1996.

a compensatory award. However, if the employee puts forward an arguable case that dismissal was not inevitable, the evidential burden shifts to the employer to show that dismissal was likely to have occurred in any event.[395] Additionally, a nil or nominal award may be thought just and equitable in a case where misconduct was discovered subsequently to the dismissal.

The possible heads of loss have been divided into the following categories:

(1) *Loss incurred up to the date of the hearing*

Here attention focuses on the employee's actual loss of income, which makes it necessary to ascertain the employee's take-home pay. Thus, tax and National Insurance contributions are to be deducted, but overtime earnings and tips can be taken into account. Similarly, any sickness or incapacity benefits received may be taken into account. It should also be noted that the loss sustained should be based on what the employee was entitled to, whether or not he or she was receiving it at the time of dismissal.[396] As well as lost wages, section 123(2) ERA 1996 enables an individual to claim compensation for the loss of other benefits – e.g. a company car or other perks. Similarly, 'expenses reasonably incurred' are mentioned in the statute – so, for example, employees will be able to recover the cost of looking for a new job or setting up their own business. However, complainants cannot be reimbursed for the cost of pursuing their unfair dismissal claims.

(2) *Loss flowing from the manner of dismissal*

Compensation can be awarded only if the manner of dismissal has made the individual less acceptable to potential employers. There is nothing for non-economic loss, e.g. hurt feelings. However, economic loss may arise where the person is not fit to take up alternative employment as early as he or she would otherwise have done (or ever); or where by virtue of stigma damage, loss of reputation or embarrassment no suitable employer was prepared to engage him or her, at any rate on terms that would not cause continuing loss.[397]

(3) *Loss of accrued rights*

This head of loss is intended to compensate the employee for the loss of rights dependent on a period of continuous service, but because the basic award reflects lost redundancy entitlement, sums awarded on these grounds have tended to be nominal. Nevertheless, tribunals should include a sum to reflect the fact that dismissed employees lose the statutory minimum notice protection that they have built up.

(4) *Loss of pension rights*

There are two types of loss: the loss of the present pension position and the loss of the opportunity to improve one's pension position with the dismissing employer. When an employee is close to retirement, the cost of an annuity which will provide a sum equal to the likely pension can be calculated. In other cases the starting point will be the contributions already paid into the scheme, and, in addition to having their own contributions returned, employees can claim an interest in their employer's contributions, except in cases of transferred or deferred pensions. However, in assessing

---

[395] See *Britool Ltd v Roberts* [1993] IRLR 481.
[396] For example, the minimum wage: see *Pagetti v Cobb* [2002] IRLR 861.
[397] See *Dunnachie v Hull City Council* [2004] IRLR 727.

future loss the tribunal must take into account a number of possibilities – for example, future dismissal or resignation, early death, and the fact that a capital sum is being paid sooner than would have been expected. Although employment tribunals have been given actuarial guidelines on loss of pension rights, in each case the factors must be evaluated to see what adjustment should be made or whether the guidelines are safe to use at all.[398]

(5) *Future loss*

Where no further employment has been secured, tribunals will have to speculate how long the employee will remain unemployed. Here the tribunal must utilise its knowledge of local market conditions as well as considering personal circumstances. According to the EAT, employees who have become unfit for work wholly or partly as a result of unfair dismissal are entitled to compensation for loss of earnings, at least for a reasonable period following the dismissal, until they might reasonably have been expected to find other employment.[399] If another job has been obtained, tribunals must compare the employee's salary prospects for the future in each job and see as best they can how long it will take the employee to reach in the new job the salary equivalent to that which would have been attained had he or she remained with the original employer. Where the employee is earning a higher rate of pay at the time compensation is being assessed, the tribunal should decide whether the new employment is permanent, and, if so, should calculate the loss as between the date of dismissal and the date the new job was secured.

Finally, mention must be made of the Employment Protection (Recoupment of Jobseeker's Allowance and Income Support) Regulations 1996,[400] which were designed to remove the state subsidy to employers who dismiss unfairly. Such benefits had the effect of reducing the losses suffered by dismissed persons. These Regulations provide that a tribunal must not deduct from the compensation awarded any sum which represents jobseeker's allowance received, and the employer is instructed not to pay immediately the amount of compensation which represents loss of income up to the hearing (known as the 'prescribed element'). The National Insurance Fund can then serve the employer with a recoupment notice which will require him or her to pay the Fund from the prescribed element the amount which represents the jobseeker's allowance paid to the employee prior to the hearing. When the amount has been refunded by the employer, the remainder of the prescribed element becomes the employee's property. It is important to note that private settlements do not fall within the scope of these Regulations.

5.5 Redundancy payments

Dismissal as a result of redundancy is a common feature of economies which are constantly changing and developing. Some 200,000 people are dismissed for this reason in the United

---

[398] See *Port of Tilbury v Birch* [2005] IRLR 92.
[399] See *Kingston upon Hull City Council v Dunnachie (No 3)* [2003] IRLR 843.
[400] SI 1996/2439.

Kingdom each year, although this figure will clearly fluctuate according to the health or otherwise of the economy or part of it.[401] This suggests that about 4% of the workforce experience redundancy each year. About twice as many men as women are made redundant[402] and those aged 50 years and over consistently account for between 20% and 25% of all redundancies.

Statutory protection for redundant workers was first introduced by the Redundancy Payments Act 1965 and was seen as a way of encouraging mobility of labour. This Act provided for the establishment of the Redundancy Fund and for employees, with sufficient continuity of employment, to be entitled to a redundancy payment. The Employment Protection Act 1975 also introduced collective consultation requirements as a result of the newly adopted EEC Directive on consultation in situations of collective redundancies (see Chapter 10). The provisions concerning the right to a redundancy payment are now contained in Part XI Chapter I ERA 1996.

Subject to various provisions (see below) an employer is obliged to pay a redundancy payment to any employee who is dismissed by reason of redundancy or is eligible for a redundancy payment by reason of being laid off or kept on short-time.[403] Dismissal, for redundancy purposes, has essentially the same meaning as in cases of unfair dismissal[404] and includes the death of the employer.[405] A prerequisite to a claim for a payment is that there has been a dismissal and the reason for it is redundancy. In *Birch and Humber v The University of Liverpool*[406] the employer invited staff to apply for early retirement as a means of reducing employee numbers. The employees in this case applied and were accepted. They subsequently claimed that they had been dismissed for reasons of redundancy. The act of acceptance of their application for early retirement, they claimed, was an act of dismissal. The Court of Appeal did not agree that the acceptances could be isolated from the formal applications to retire. There had not been a dismissal but a mutual determination of the contracts of employment, even though the situation might conveniently be called a redundancy situation.

Once notice has been given by the employer, the relevant date can be postponed by agreement without prejudicing the original reason for dismissal. Thus, in *Mowlem Northern Ltd v Watson*[407] an employee was given notice of dismissal by reason of redundancy, but was then kept on for a further three months on a temporary basis in order to help try to win another contract. When this failed the employee left and the employer denied liability for making a redundancy payment on the grounds that the employee had resigned. The EAT held that the employee was entitled to the payment as the delay in leaving had been a result of a mutual agreement to postpone the date of termination by reason of redundancy.

---

[401] These and the following statistics come from Bénédicte Terryn, 'Redundancies in the United Kingdom', *Labour Market Trends*, May 1999, p 251.
[402] This may be a result of the preponderance of male employment in declining industries.
[403] Section 135(1) ERA 1996.
[404] See section 136 ERA 1996.
[405] Section 136(5) ERA 1996.
[406] [1985] IRLR 165 CA.
[407] [1990] IRLR 500.

According to section 139(1) ERA 1996, employees are to be regarded as being redundant if their dismissals are attributable wholly or mainly to:

- the fact that the employer has ceased, or intends to cease, to carry on the business[408] for the purposes for which the employees were employed, or
- the fact that the employer has ceased, or intends to cease, to carry on that business in the place where the employees were so employed, or
- the fact that the requirement of that business for employees to carry out work of a particular kind, or for employees to carry out work of a particular kind in the place where they were so employed, has ceased or diminished or is expected to cease or diminish.

In this context 'cease' or 'diminish' means either permanently or temporarily and from whatever cause.[409]

In *High Table Ltd v Horst*[410] three waitresses worked for an agency and were capable of being transferred to a variety of locations to work. In practice they worked for some years at one location. When a redundancy situation arose at that location, the employees sought to rely on their mobility clauses to argue that they were unfairly selected for redundancy. The Court of Appeal held that it defied common sense to expand the meaning of the place where an employee was employed. As these waitresses had worked permanently at that one location, that was their place of employment.

Lord Irvine LC, in *Murray v Foyle Meats Ltd (Northern Ireland)*,[411] stated:

> [The statutory definition of redundancy] asks two questions of fact. The first is one of whether one or other of various states of economic affairs exists. In this case, the relevant one is whether the requirements of the business for employees to carry out work of a particular kind have diminished. The second question is whether the dismissal is attributable, wholly or mainly, to that state of affairs. This is a question of causation. In the present case, the Tribunal found as a fact that the requirements of the business for employees to work in the slaughter hall had diminished. Secondly, they found that that state of affairs had led to the appellants being dismissed. That, in my opinion, is the end of the matter.

This case concerned the fact that some meat operatives from one part of the business were to be considered for dismissal for reasons of redundancy and not meat operatives from the other parts which were less affected by the situation. The House of Lords approved the EAT decision in *Safeway Stores plc v Burrell*,[412] which had considered different approaches to whether a dismissal for redundancy had taken place, specifically the 'function test' and the 'contract test'.

The question arises as to whether there is a need to identify specific individuals, the requirements for whose work has ceased or diminished, or whether it is sufficient to state that there has been a reduction in the need for the numbers of employees needed. This latter approach might mean dismissing some employees whose work continues.

The function test required the tribunal to look at the work that the employee was required to do, and actually did, in order to decide whether or not the job has disappeared.

---

[408] 'Business' is defined in section 235(1) ERA 1996.
[409] Section 139(6) ERA 1996.
[410] [1997] IRLR 513 CA.
[411] [1999] IRLR 562 HL.
[412] [1997] IRLR 200.

The contract test required the tribunal to consider whether there was a diminishing need for the work which the employee could be required to do under the contract of employment. In *Safeway Stores* the EAT concluded that both these approaches were incorrect. There was a three-stage process:

- The first question was: was the employee dismissed?
- If so the second question was: had the requirements of the employer's business for employees to carry out work of a particular kind ceased or diminished?
- If so the third question was: was the dismissal of the employee caused wholly or mainly by that state of affairs?

The third stage is then one of causation and in this case the court approved a system of selection known as 'bumping'. For example, if a fork-lift driver who was delivering materials to six production machines on the shop floor, each with its own operator, is selected for dismissal on the basis of 'last in, first out', following a decision of the employer that only five machine operators were required, and one machine operator with longer service is transferred to driving the fork-lift truck, the truck driver is dismissed for redundancy. This is the case even though the job of driving the fork-lift truck continues. There has been a diminished need for employees to carry out work of a particular kind and the dismissal of the employee was caused by this state of affairs.

The expiry of a limited term contract may be a dismissal for reasons of redundancy. Thus the lecturers in *Pfaffinger v City of Liverpool Community College*,[413] who were employed during each academic year only, were dismissed for redundancy at the end of each academic term. Business re-organisations can lead to dismissals which are related to redundancy. Alternatively, they might be dismissals for 'some other substantial reason'.[414] An employer cannot, however, argue a case based on redundancy and then introduce a justification of some other substantial reason, when the first argument fails.[415]

5.5.1 Qualifications and exclusions

In order to qualify for a right to a redundancy payment an employee must have been continuously employed for two years at the relevant date.[416] There are a number of situations where employees will lose their right to a redundancy payment:

(1) Employees who are dismissed with or without notice for reasons connected to their conduct.[417]
(2) If an employee gives notice to the employer terminating the employment with effect from a date prior to the date upon which the employer's notice of redundancy is due to

---

[413] [1996] IRLR 508.
[414] See *Murphy v Epsom College* [1984] IRLR 271 CA for an example of a situation where a dismissal as a result of new technology might have been for reasons of redundancy or for some other substantial reason.
[415] *Church v West Lancashire NHS Trust (No 2)* [1998] IRLR 492.
[416] Section 155 ERA 1996. In most cases the relevant date is to be ascertained in the same way as the effective date of termination for unfair dismissal purposes (see above). However, where a statutory trial period has been served (see below), for the purpose of submitting a claim in time the relevant date is the day that the new or renewed contract terminated.
[417] Section 140(1) ERA 1996; section 140(2)–(3) provides protection for those dismissed, in certain circumstances, as a result of the employee taking part in a strike.

expire, then the employee may lose their right to a redundancy payment.[418] This is provided that the employer serves a notice on the employee requiring the employee to withdraw their notice and to stay in employment until the employer's notice expires and warning the employee that they will lose their right to a payment.[419] An employee may ask an employment tribunal to decide whether it should be just and equitable to receive a payment, taking into account the reasons for which the employee seeks to leave early and the reasons for which the employer requires the employee to continue.[420]

(3) If, before the ending of a person's employment, the employer or an associated employer makes an offer, in writing or not, to renew the contract or to re-engage under a new contract which is to take effect either on the ending of the old one or within four weeks thereafter, then section 141 ERA 1996 has the following effect:

- if the provisions of the new or renewed contract as to the capacity and place in which the person would be employed, together with the other terms and conditions, do not differ from the corresponding terms of the previous contract, or
- the terms and conditions differ, wholly or in part, but the offer constitutes an offer of suitable employment, and
- in either case the employee unreasonably refuses that offer, then he or she will not be entitled to a redundancy payment.

The burden is on an employer to prove both the suitability of the offer and the unreasonableness of the employee's refusal. Offers do not have to be formal, nor do they have to contain all the conditions which are ultimately agreed. However, supplying details of vacancies is not the same as an offer of employment[421] and sufficient information must be provided to enable the employee to take a realistic decision.

The suitability of the alternative work must be assessed objectively by comparing the terms on offer with those previously enjoyed. A convenient test has been whether the proposed employment will be 'substantially equivalent' to that which has ceased. Merely offering the same salary will not be sufficient but the fact that the employment will be at a different location does not necessarily mean that it will be regarded as unsuitable. By way of contrast, in adjudicating upon the reasonableness of an employee's refusal, subjective considerations can be taken into account – e.g. domestic responsibilities. In *Spencer and Griffin v Gloucestershire County Council*[422] the employees had refused offers of suitable employment on the grounds that they would not be able to do their work to a satisfactory standard in the reduced hours and with reduced staffing levels. The Court of Appeal held that it was for employers to set the standard of work they wanted carried out but it was a different question whether it was reasonable for a particular employee, in all the circumstances, to refuse to work to the standard which the employer set. This is a question of fact for the tribunal.

---

[418] If the employee leaves early by mutual consent, then the redundancy entitlement will not be affected; see *CPS Recruitment Ltd v Bowen* [1982] IRLR 54.

[419] Section 142(1)–(2) ERA 1996.

[420] Section 142(3) ERA 1996.

[421] See *Curling v Securicor Ltd* [1992] IRLR 548.

[422] [1985] IRLR 393.

If the new or renewed contract differs in terms of the capacity or place in which the employee is employed or in respect of any other terms and conditions of employment, then the employee is given a trial period of up to four weeks in which to decide whether to accept the new or renewed contract.[423] If the employee or the employer terminates this new or renewed contract, then the entitlement to a redundancy payment under the original dismissal remains.[424] The four-week trial period is to be taken as four calendar weeks and not necessarily four 'working' weeks. Thus if public or other holidays come within the four-week period they do not serve to lengthen that period.[425] This trial period can be extended by agreement if a period of retraining is necessary, provided that the agreement is in writing and specifies the date on which the retraining ends and the terms and conditions which will apply at the end of the retraining.[426] If the employee unreasonably refuses the offer of suitable alternative employment or unreasonably terminates their employment during the trial period, then they may lose their right to a payment.[427] *Cambridge & District Co-operative Society Ltd v Ruse*[428] concerned a long-serving employee who managed a butcher's shop, which was eventually closed. The employee was then offered the position of butchery department manager in a larger store. He refused because he considered this to be a loss of status and therefore not suitable alternative employment. The argument was whether this was an unreasonable refusal. The EAT accepted that the offer of employment was to be assessed objectively but the reasonableness of an employee's refusal was more subjective and depended upon personal factors important to that employee. The reasons did not necessarily need to be connected with the employment itself.

(4) If an employee takes part in strike action after having received notice of termination, the employer is entitled to issue a notice of extension. This notice, which must be in writing and indicate the employer's reasons, may request the employee to agree to extend the contract of employment beyond the termination date by a period equivalent to the number of days lost through strike action. Failure by the employee to agree to this extension, unless they have good reasons such as sickness or injury, may justify the employer withholding a redundancy payment.[429]

(5) The Secretary of State may make an exemption order excluding certain employees from any right to a redundancy payment. These are employees who, under an agreement between one or more employers and one or more trade unions or their associations, have the right to a payment on the termination of their contracts of employment.

---

[423] See *Elliot v Richard Stump Ltd* [1987] IRLR 215 in which an employer's mistaken refusal to consider a four-week trial period was sufficient to enable an employee to reject an offer of alternative employment and claim an unfair dismissal on the grounds of redundancy.

[424] Section 138(2)–(4) ERA 1996.

[425] See *Benton v Sanderson Kayser Ltd* [1989] IRLR 19 CA, where an employee lost their right to a redundancy payment because they gave their notice after a four-week period had ended, even though the period had included a seven-day Christmas break.

[426] Section 138(6) ERA 1996.

[427] Section 141 ERA 1996.

[428] [1993] IRLR 156.

[429] Sections 143–144 ERA 1996.

The Secretary of State may act after receiving an application from all the parties to an agreement that an order be made. A condition of such orders is that any disputes about the right of an employee to a payment on the termination of employment, or a dispute about the amount of such payment, should be submitted to an employment tribunal for resolution.[430]

(6) Section 158 ERA 1996 enables the Secretary of State to exclude those receiving a pension from the right to redundancy payments.[431] Those employees who have a right or a claim to periodical payments or lump sums resulting from pensions, gratuities or superannuation allowances, which are paid with reference to the employment or on the leaving of the particular employment, can be excluded.[432]

5.5.2 Lay-offs and short-time

For the purposes of the legislation a person is taken to be laid off for a week if they work under a contract of employment where the remuneration depends upon work being provided by the employer and the employer does not provide any work during the week in question.[433] An employee is taken to be kept on short-time for a week if they earn less than half a week's pay as a result of a diminution of work provided by the employer during that week.[434] Employees are entitled to a redundancy payment by reason of being laid off or being kept on short-time if they are laid off or kept on short-time for a period of four consecutive weeks or for a series of six or more weeks within a period of 13 weeks.[435] In order to claim the employee must resign[436] and give notice of the intention to claim a redundancy payment. An employer may resist the claim by issuing a counter-notice to the employee within seven days of receiving the notice of intention from the employee. In such circumstances the matter will be decided by an employment tribunal.[437]

5.5.3 Time off[438]

Section 52 ERA 1996 provides that an employee, with at least two years' service, who is given notice of dismissal by reason of redundancy is entitled to time off to look for new employment or to make arrangements for training for future employment (see Chapter 8). An employee who is permitted such time off is entitled to be paid at the appropriate hourly rate.[439]

---

[430] Section 157 ERA 1996.
[431] See Redundancy Payments (Pensions) Regulations 1965, SI 1965/1932.
[432] Sections 159–161 ERA 1996 also exclude the right to redundancy payments in respect of certain public offices, service in overseas government employment and certain domestic servants.
[433] Section 147(1) ERA 1996.
[434] Section 147(2) ERA 1996.
[435] Section 148 ERA 1996.
[436] Section 150 ERA 1996.
[437] Section 149 ERA 1996; if there is a likelihood of full employment for a period of at least 13 weeks within four weeks of the employee's notice, then there is no entitlement to a redundancy payment: section 152 ERA 1996.
[438] See Chapter 8 on working time.
[439] Section 53 ERA 1996.

5.5.4 Level of payments

For those entitled to payment, once the number of years' service has been calculated[440] the 'appropriate amount' is calculated by allocating a certain sum of money to each of those years' service. The formula to be applied is:

(1) one and a half weeks' pay for each year of employment in which the employee was not below the age of 41 years;

(2) one week's pay for each year of employment (not in (1)) in which the employee was not below the age of 22 years;

(3) half a week's pay for each year of employment not within (1) or (2).[441]

This calculation is subject to a number of restrictions. First, there is a maximum amount to a week's pay as defined in section 227 ERA 1996.[442] This amount is £310 per week in 2007. There is also a maximum of 20 years' service to be taken into account.[443] Thus the maximum amount that can be claimed for a redundancy payment in 2007 is £9,300.

Any questions as to the right of an employee to a redundancy payment, or the amount of such payment, are to be referred to an employment tribunal. There is a presumption in any such case that the employee has been dismissed by reason of redundancy.[444] An employee does not have any right to a redundancy payment unless, before the end of a period of six months beginning with the relevant date:[445]

(1) the payment has been agreed and paid or the employee has made a claim for the payment by notice in writing given to the employer;

(2) a question as to the employee's right to, or the amount of, the payment has been referred to an employment tribunal or a complaint has been made to an employment tribunal for unfair dismissal under section 111 ERA 1996.[446]

The written notice to the employer does not have to be in a particular form. The test is whether it is of such a character that the recipient would reasonably understand in all the circumstances that it was the employee's intention to seek a payment. In this context the words 'presented' and 'referred' seem to have the same meaning – i.e. an application must have been received by the employment tribunal within the six-month period. Nevertheless, if any of the above steps are taken outside this period but within 12 months of the relevant date, a tribunal has the discretion to award a payment if it thinks that it would be just and equitable to do so. In such a case a tribunal must have regard to the employee's reasons for failing to take any of the steps within the normal time limit.[447] As with unfair dismissal, an employee wishing to claim a redundancy payment must first submit a statement of grievance to their employer.

---

[440] Section 162(1) ERA 1996.
[441] Section 162(2) ERA 1996.
[442] See Chapter 8 for further discussion on the concept of a week's pay.
[443] Section 162(3) ERA 1996.
[444] Section 163 ERA 1996.
[445] See section 145 ERA 1996 for the meaning of the relevant date.
[446] Section 164(1) ERA 1996.
[447] Section 164(2) ERA 1996.

When making a redundancy payment,[448] otherwise than as a result of an employment tribunal decision, the employer is required to give the employee a written statement showing how the amount of the payment has been calculated. If the employer fails to do this, the employee may give the employer notice in writing requiring the employer to give the written statement within a set period of time, of not less than one week. Failure by the employer to provide such a notice, without reasonable excuse, will open the employer to the possibility of a fine.[449]

Further reading

Anderman, S., 'Termination of Employment: whose property rights?' in Barnard, C. et al. (eds) *The Future of Labour Law* (Hart Publishing, 2004).

Collins, H., 'Nine proposals for the reform of the law on unfair dismissal' (Institute of Employment Rights, 2004).

Deakin, S. and Morris, G., *Labour Law* (4th edn, Hart Publishing, 2005), Chapter 5.

Incomes Data Services, 'Unfair Dismissal', in *Employment Law Handbook* (IDS, 2005).

Korn, A., *Compensation for Unfair Dismissal* (Oxford University Press, 2005).

Lewis, P., 'Legal aspects of employment change and their implications for management' (2001) 32 (1) *Industrial Relations Journal* 71.

www.acas.org.uk

www.berr.gov.uk

www.tuc.org.uk

Visit **www.mylawchamber.co.uk/sargeant** to access legal updates, live web links and practice exam questions to test yourself on this chapter.

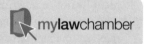 **my**law**chamber**

---

[448] If the employer fails to make the payment, then the employee may apply to the Secretary of State for payment: see sections 166–170 ERA 1996.

[449] Section 165 ERA 1996.

6

Discrimination on the Grounds of Race, Sex, Religion or Belief, and Sexual Orientation

6.1 Introduction

Article 13 EU Treaty states:

> Without prejudice to the other provisions of this Treaty and within the limits of the powers conferred by it upon the Community, the Council, acting unanimously on a proposal from the Commission and after consulting the European Parliament, may take appropriate action to combat discrimination based on sex, racial or ethnic origin, religion or belief, disability, age or sexual orientation.

This principle of non-discrimination in Community law is both an underlying principle and one that receives expression in a number of places in the Treaty. Article 12 EC prohibits any discrimination on the grounds of nationality and Articles 39 to 43 EC provide for the free movement of workers[1] and the right of establishment for self-employed workers in Member States. A number of Articles also provide for the principle of equality between men and women, namely Articles 2 and 3(2) EC and Articles 137 and 141 EC.

Following on from the achievements in Amsterdam the European Commission put forward proposals to implement the principle of equal treatment. These initiatives included:

(1) Council Directive 2000/78/EC establishing a general framework for equal treatment in employment and occupation.[2] The purpose of the Directive is to put into effect in the Member States:

> the principle of equal treatment as regards access to employment and occupation . . . of all persons irrespective of racial or ethnic origin, religion or belief, disability, age or sexual orientation.[3]

Sex discrimination is dealt with elsewhere, in the Equal Treatment Directive.[4] Article 2 of this Directive defines direct and indirect discrimination and contains a

---

[1] See *Bossa v Nordstress Ltd* [1998] IRLR 284 for an example of Article 39 affecting the decision of the EAT in a case concerning an Italian national, interviewed in England, applying for a job working for a company in Hong Kong, but based in Italy.

[2] OJ L303/16 2.12.2000.

[3] Article 1 of the Directive.

[4] Directive 2006/54/EC on the implementation of the principle of equal opportunities and equal treatment of men and women in matters of employment and occupation OJ L204/23 26.7.2006; this Directive recast seven previous sex equality Directives, including the Equal Pay Directive 75/117, the Equal Treatment Directive 76/207 as amended by Directive 2002/73 and the Burden of Proof Directive 97/80, into one consolidated Directive from 15 August 2009, although the consolidated Directive itself must be transposed into national law by 15 August 2008.

provision, in Article 2(3), for dealing with harassment. Harassment is defined as something which has the effect of 'creating an intimidating, hostile, offensive or disturbing environment'. The scope of the equal treatment measures are in Article 3 and include conditions for access to employment; access to vocational guidance and training; employment and working conditions, including dismissals and pay; and membership of any workers' or employers' organisations.

(2) Council Directive 2000/43/EC implementing the principle of equal treatment between persons irrespective of racial or ethnic origin.[5] This helps bring to an end the imbalance in the EU's anti-discrimination programme. In contrast to the EU's action on sex discrimination, it has taken few initiatives to combat race discrimination. It was not until the Amsterdam Treaty and the adoption of the new Article 13 (see above) that the Community had the authority to take such action. In its guide to the Directive the European Commission accepts that racial discrimination is widespread in everyday life and that legal measures are of 'paramount importance for combating racism and intolerance'.[6]

The purpose of the Directive, contained in Article 1, is:

> to lay down a framework for combating discrimination on the grounds of racial or ethnic origin, with a view to putting into effect in the Member States the principle of equal treatment.

Article 2 is concerned with the meaning of direct and indirect discrimination and follows the Equal Treatment in Employment and Occupation Directive closely, including the addition of harassment. Its scope, of course, is wider than just employment, but those areas that are related to employment are also similar to the Equal Treatment in Employment Directive. Article 8 also provides that the burden of proof rests with the respondent.

The Community has a long and effective record of measures combating sex discrimination and promoting equal treatment and equal pay. The original treaty establishing the European Economic Community, signed in Rome in March 1957, contained Article 119 which committed each Member State to the principle of 'equal remuneration for the same work as between male and female workers'. This was undoubtedly a far-reaching principle to have adopted in the 1950s. This commitment is now contained in Article 141 EC and includes the adoption of the principle of equal pay for male and female workers for equal work or for work of equal value. It also provides for the Community:

> to adopt measures to ensure the application of the principle of equal opportunities and equal treatment of men and women in matters of employment and occupation, including the principle of equal pay for equal work or work of equal value.[7]

The Equal Opportunities and Equal Treatment Directive provides, in Article 1, that its purpose is:

> to ensure the implementation of the principle of equal opportunities and equal treatment of men and women in matters of employment and occupation.

---

[5] OJ L180/22 17.7.2000.
[6] See also Council Regulation 1035/97 establishing a European Monitoring Centre on Racism and Xenophobia OJ L151 10.6.97.
[7] Article 141(3) EC.

Article 2 states that, for the purposes of this Directive, discrimination includes:

- harassment and sexual harassment, as well as any less favourable treatment based on a person's rejection of or submission to such conduct,
- instruction to discriminate against persons on grounds of sex,
- any less favourable treatment of a woman related to pregnancy or maternity leave within the meaning of Directive 92/85/EC.

The extent to which the social objectives of Article 141 EC and, consequently, the Equal Treatment Directives, could influence the development of equal opportunities has been considered by the ECJ. One issue was whether this included positive discrimination in favour of women in terms of access to work. This was tested in *Marschall*,[8] where the complainant was a male comprehensive school teacher who had applied for promotion to a higher grade. He was told that an equally qualified female applicant would be given the position as there were fewer women than men in the more senior grade. The ECJ considered previous judgments[9] which concluded that the Equal Treatment Directive did not permit national rules which enabled female applicants for a job to be given automatic priority. Article 2(4) of the the Equal Treatment Directive 76/207, however, provided that the Directive should be 'without prejudice to measures to promote equal opportunity for men and women' and the ECJ considered whether this could alter the outcome. It distinguished between those measures which were designed to remove the obstacles to women and those measures which were designed to grant them priority simply because they were women. The latter measures, as in *Kalanke* and *Marschall*, conflicted with the Directive. There was a difference between measures concerned with the promotion of equal opportunity and measures imposing equal representation. This situation appears unchanged despite Article 141(4) EC introduced by the Treaty of Amsterdam, which states:

> With a view to ensuring full equality of practice between men and women in working life, the principle of equal treatment shall not prevent any Member State from maintaining or adopting measures for providing for specific advantages in order to make it easier for the under-represented sex to pursue a vocational activity or to prevent or compensate for disadvantages in professional careers.

In *Abrahamsson and Anderson v Fogelqvist*[10] the ECJ held, somewhat disappointingly, that this did not permit measures positively to discriminate in favour of women in a selection process. Preference could not be given to one sex merely because they were under-represented. There had to be an objective assessment of the relative qualifications for the job in question in order to establish that the qualifications of the two sexes were similar before any preference could be given to one sex over the other.[11]

Article 3 of the Equal Opportunities and Equal Treatment Directive now states simply that:

> Member States may maintain or adopt measures within the meaning of Article 141(4) of the Treaty with a view to ensuring full equality in practice between men and women in working life.

---

[8] Case C-409/95 *Marschall v Land Nordrhein-Westfalen* [1998] IRLR 39 ECJ.
[9] See Case C-450/93 *Kalanke v Freie Hansestadt Bremen* [1995] ECR 660 ECJ and Case C-312/86 *Commission v France* [1998] ECR 6315 ECJ.
[10] Case 407/98 [2000] IRLR 732 ECJ.
[11] See Case 158/97 *Application by Badeck* [2000] IRLR 432 ECJ.

The cumulative effect of Article 141 EC and the Equality Directives has been to influence considerably the decisions of the courts in the United Kingdom when interpreting its anti-discrimination legislation. Two of the principal statutes concerned with discrimination are the Sex Discrimination Act 1975 (SDA 1975) and the Race Relations Act 1976 (RRA 1976).[12] They are considered together as the approach and, often, the wording of each statute is similar.

6.1.1 Types of discrimination

6.1.1.1 Direct discrimination

In relation to discrimination in the employment field and vocational training, direct discrimination is described in section 1(2)(a) SDA 1975. A person discriminates against a woman if:

> On the ground of her sex he treats her less favourably than he treats or would treat a man.

Section 2(1) SDA 1975 provides that this discrimination can be reversed, so that men are discriminated against if treated less favourably than women on the grounds of their sex. This is qualified in section 2(2) so that any special treatment given to women in connection with childbirth or pregnancy should not be taken as being discriminatory against men (see Chapter 9).

Thus the two essential features of direct discrimination, in the SDA 1975, are, first, that it takes place on the grounds of sex and, secondly, that it takes place when a person is treated less favourably than a person of the other sex. Thus a comparative model of justice is used. The treatment given to A is relative to the treatment given to the comparator B.

The 'less favourable treatment test' also applies in situations of gender re-assignment[13] and discrimination against married women and civil partners in the field of employment.[14]

The question to be asked under section 1(1)(a), according to the House of Lords, is:

> Would the complainant have received the same treatment from the defendant but for his or her sex?[15]

This test can be applied where the treatment given derives from the application of gender-based criteria and where the treatment given results from the selection of the complainant because of his or her sex. Thus, when a local authority gave free use of its swimming pools to persons of pensionable age, then a male of 61 years who has not reached pensionable age is discriminated against in comparison with a woman who reached it at the age of 60 years.[16] There need be no intention to discriminate and motives are not relevant. In *R v Birmingham City Council, ex parte Equal Opportunities Commission*[17] the local authority offered more places in selective secondary education to boys rather than

---

[12] Two other important statutes are considered separately; these are the Equal Pay Act 1970 and the Disability Discrimination Act 1995.
[13] Section 2A(1) SDA 1975. See 6.1.2.4 below.
[14] Section 3(1) SDA 1975.
[15] *James v Eastleigh Borough Council* [1990] IRLR 288 HL.
[16] *Ibid.*
[17] [1989] IRLR 173 HL.

girls. This was held to be treating those girls less favourably on the grounds of their sex and the fact that the local authority had not intended to discriminate was not relevant.

In the absence of an actual comparator the court will need to construct a hypothetical one, in order for the complainant to show that she was treated less favourably than the hypothetical male. Inferences as to how this hypothetical male would have been treated can be gained from the surrounding circumstances and other cases which might not be exactly the same but would not be wholly dissimilar. An exact comparator is not, of course, needed as it might be impossible to prove less favourable treatment, especially in isolated cases, if this were the case.[18]

The provisions on direct discrimination are mirrored in the RRA 1976, so that interpretations of provisions in one Act, by the courts, can lead to the same interpretation being applied to the other Act. Section 1(1)(a) RRA 1976 provides that a person discriminates against another if, on racial grounds, they treat that person less favourably than they would treat another person. Thus here there is also a twofold test to be applied. The first is that the discrimination should be on racial grounds and the second is that the person concerned is treated less favourably than another person. This is not to suggest that there is a hypothetical reasonable employer who treats employees reasonably, so that it is possible to identify those treated less reasonably on racial grounds. In *Zafar v Glasgow City Council*[19] Lord Browne-Wilkinson stated that:

> In deciding that issue, the conduct of a hypothetical reasonable employer is irrelevant. The alleged discriminator may or may not be a reasonable employer. If he is not a reasonable employer, he might well have treated another employee in just the same unsatisfactory way as he treated the complainant, in which case he would not have treated the complainant less favourably for the purposes of the Act of 1976.

Thus if an employer behaves in the same unreasonable way to all their employees it may not be possible for one individual to say that they have been treated less favourably, no matter how unreasonably they were treated. This situation also occurred in *Laing v Manchester City Council*[20] where a white supervisor was held not to have acted appropriately in her supervisory role to a subordinate who was black and of West Indian origin. The claimant failed to establish a *prima facie* case of discrimination because the supervisor's behaviour was not the result of any bias against the employee or other black employees, but was the result of her lack of experience, which resulted in her treating all employees in the same manner.

The test to be applied in race discrimination cases is the same as that applied in sex discrimination claims. The court will need to ask the question whether the complainants would have received the same treatment but for their race. This question needs to be asked when a choice is to be made between a non-racial explanation offered and a racial explanation offered by the complainant.

---

[18] See *Balamoody v UK Central Council for Nursing* [2002] IRLR 288 CA.
[19] [1998] IRLR 36 HL.
[20] [2006] IRLR 748.

6.1.1.2 Indirect sex and race discrimination

In relation to sex discrimination in the employment field and vocational training, indirect discrimination is described in section 1(2)(b) SDA 1975. A person discriminates against a woman if:

> He applies to her a provision, criterion or practice which he applies or would apply equally to a man, but –
> (i) which is such that it would be to the detriment of a considerably larger proportion of women than of men, and
> (ii) which he cannot show to be justifiable irrespective of the sex of the person to whom it is applied, and
> (iii) which is to her detriment.

This revised definition became effective in October 2001.[21]

The previous definition still applies to discrimination on the grounds of colour and nationality.[22] A person discriminates against another if:

> He applies to that other a requirement or condition which he applies or would apply equally to persons not of the same racial group as that other but –
> (i) which is such that the proportion of persons of the same racial group as that other who can comply with it is considerably smaller than the proportion of persons not of that racial group who can comply with it; and
> (ii) which he cannot show to be justifiable irrespective of the colour, race, nationality or ethnic origins of the person to whom it is applied; and
> (iii) which is to the detriment of that other because he cannot comply with it.

In relation to race, ethnic or national origins, indirect discrimination occurs where a provision, criterion or practice applies or would apply to persons not of the same race, ethnic or national origins but such people would be put at a particular disadvantage and this cannot be shown to be a proportionate means of achieving a legitimate aim.[23]

The process for deciding whether indirect sex discrimination has taken place is, therefore, to examine the 'provision, criterion or practice' and assess, first, whether it would be to the detriment of a considerably larger proportion of women than of men and, secondly, whether it is to the individual's detriment.[24] This is provided that the application of the 'provision, criterion or practice' cannot be shown to be justifiable irrespective of the sex of the person to whom it is applied. Each situation needs to be looked at on its own merits. Just because a policy might be gender-neutral in some situations, it does not follow that it will be so in all situations. *Whiffen v Milham Ford Girls' School*,[25] for example, concerned a school which followed its local educational authority's model redundancy policy. This required that the non-renewal of temporary fixed-term contracts should be the

---

[21] Sex Discrimination (Indirect Discrimination and Burden of Proof) Regulations 2001, SI 2001/2660. This gives effect to Article 2(2) of Council Directive 97/80/EC on the burden of proof in cases of discrimination based on sex OJ L14/6 20.1.98.

[22] Section 1(1)(b) RRA 1976.

[23] Section 1(1A) RRA 1976.

[24] As with direct discrimination, section 2(1) SDA 1975 enables this provision to be reversed in order to provide similar protection for men.

[25] [2001] IRLR 468 CA.

first step to be taken. In this particular case, however, the result was indirectly to discriminate against female employees because 100% of men could satisfy the condition that an employee needed to be on a permanent contract in order not to be terminated early, but only 77% of female employees could satisfy this condition.

A 'requirement or condition' (provision, criterion or practice) can be the necessity for previous management training or supervisory experience,[26] a contractual requirement that required employees to serve in any part of the United Kingdom at the employer's discretion,[27] or the imposition of new rostering arrangements for train drivers.[28] One might conclude that merely the imposition of such requirements under these circumstances would be sufficient for an employee to show that the employee had suffered a detriment, but there is a need for a detriment to be shown. In *Shamoon*,[29] for example, a female chief inspector was stopped from doing staff appraisals after some complaints about the manner in which she carried them out. When she complained of sex discrimination, the House of Lords ruled that a detriment occurs if a reasonable worker would or might take the view that they had been disadvantaged in the circumstances in which they had to work. However, it is not necessary to demonstrate some physical or economic consequence.

In *Seymour-Smith*[30] the House of Lords gave judgment in a long-running case that had begun with the dismissal of the applicants in 1991. The House of Lords had referred the case to the ECJ for guidance, amongst other matters, on the legal test:

> for establishing whether a measure adopted by a Member State has such a degree of disparate effect as between men and women as to amount to indirect discrimination for the purposes of Article 119 [now 141] of the EC Treaty unless shown to be based on objectively justified factors other than sex.

The ECJ responded[31] by stating that the first question, when attempting to establish whether there was indirect discrimination, was to ask whether the measure in question had a more unfavourable impact on women than on men. After this it is a question of statistics. This means considering and comparing the respective proportions of men and women that were able to satisfy the requirement of the two-year rule. The ECJ further stated:

> it must be ascertained whether the statistics available indicate that a considerably smaller percentage of women than men is able to satisfy the condition of two years' employment required by the disputed rule. That situation would be evidence of apparent sex discrimination unless the disputed rule were justified by objective factors unrelated to any discrimination based on sex.

In this case the House of Lords decided that the statistics did not indicate a significant difference, although it was accepted that such measures should be reviewed from time to time.[32] The Government argued, as objective justification for the measure, that it would

---

26 *Falkirk City Council v Whyte* [1997] IRLR 560 where in practice the need for such experience became obligatory rather than desirable as at the beginning of the selection for promotion process.

27 *Meade-Hill and National Union of Civil and Public Servants v British Council* [1995] IRLR 478 CA.

28 *London Underground v Edwards* [1998] IRLR 364 CA.

29 *Shamoon v Chief Constable of the RUC* [2003] IRLR 285.

30 *R v Secretary of State for Employment, ex parte Seymour-Smith and Perez (No 2)* [2000] IRLR 263 HL.

31 Case C-167/97 [1999] IRLR 253 at p 278.

32 The need to assess provisions periodically in the light of social developments was made by the ECJ in *Commission v United Kingdom* [1984] IRLR 29.

encourage recruitment as some employers were reluctant to employ new staff because of the lack of such a rule. This argument appeared to be accepted by the court, although it is somewhat ironic that the final decision was given some time after the qualifying period was reduced to one year with little apparent effect on recruitment. In *Rutherford v Secretary of State (No 2)*[33] the issue of statistics was considered in a case where a man complained that the inability to claim unfair dismissal and redundancy payments[34] after retirement age were indirectly discriminatory on grounds of sex. His argument was that a considerably higher proportion of men worked after the age of 65 years compared to women and that, therefore, these rules indirectly discriminated against men. The Court of Appeal followed the approach taken in *Seymour-Smith* by insisting that the employment tribunal should have primarily compared the respective proportions of men and women who could satisfy the age requirement.

Although these cases concern sex discrimination, the same rules apply in cases of racial discrimination. The justification for any measure needs to be irrespective of the colour, race, nationality or ethnic or national origins of the persons concerned. In *JH Walker Ltd v Hussain*[35] an employer had banned employees from taking non-statutory holidays during its busy period of May, June and July. Their justification for this was a business-related one. About half the company's production workers were Muslims of Indian ethnic origin. The holiday period ban coincided with an important religious festival when many of the employees traditionally took time off. Seventeen employees took the day off despite the ban. When they returned to work they were given a final written warning. The 17 employees successfully complained of indirect racial discrimination. The employment tribunal and the EAT held that the rule was discriminatory and that the business justification put forward was not adequate (on religious discrimination see Chapter 6).

6.1.1.3 Victimisation

Section 4 SDA 1975 provides that a person is discriminated against (victimised), in respect of any provisions in the Act, if the person victimised is treated less favourably than other persons would be treated in those circumstances, and the reason that the person is victimised is because that person has:

(1) brought proceedings under the SDA 1975, the Equal Pay Act 1970[36] or sections 62–65 Pensions Act 1995;[37]
(2) given evidence in such proceedings;
(3) done anything else with reference to these Acts in relation to the discriminator;
(4) alleged that the discriminator has committed an act which contravenes any of these pieces of legislation.

The RRA 1976 also provides protection from victimisation on the same basis in section 2. Both the SDA 1975 and the RRA 1976 remove this protection, however, in the treatment

---

[33] [2004] IRLR 892. This conclusion, for different reasons, was subsequently upheld by the House of Lords; [2006] IRLR 551.
[34] Sections 109 and 156 ERA 1996.
[35] [1996] IRLR 11.
[36] See *St Helens MBC v Derbyshire* [2004] IRLR 851.
[37] These sections introduce an equal treatment rule into occupational pension schemes.

of a person who makes allegations that are false or not made in good faith.[38] A complaint of victimisation on sex or race grounds is different to a complaint of sex or race discrimination. The latter is about showing less favourable treatment on the grounds of sex or race, whilst a victimisation claim is about showing less favourable treatment as a result of doing a protected act.[39]

Conscious motivation by the employer to treat someone less favourably as a result of their previous actions was not necessary, which was the situation in *Nagarajan v London Regional Transport*,[40] where an applicant for a post claimed victimisation when the application was unsuccessful. The individual concerned had made a number of previous complaints against London Regional Transport. The House of Lords held that the reason why a person is discriminated against on racial grounds is not relevant when deciding whether an act of racial discrimination has occurred. There was, therefore, no good reason for adopting a different approach to motivation when applying section 1(1)(a) or section 2(1) RRA 1976.

This approach appeared to be somewhat qualified by the House of Lords in *Chief Constable of West Yorkshire Police v Khan*.[41] In this case a sergeant in the police applied for promotion in another force at the same time as having an outstanding employment tribunal application alleging racial discrimination by his employer. The employer refused to give a reference until the proceedings were completed. The employee then complained that he had been unlawfully victimised contrary to section 2 RRA 1976. The court acknowledged that such references were normally given on request, but decided that in this case the reference had not been withheld because the employee had brought proceedings. It had been withheld so that the employer's position could be protected with regard to the proceedings. This was a legitimate action for the employer, acting honestly and reasonably, and should not result in a charge of victimisation. In contrast, the failure of an employer to provide a reference to an ex-employee who had settled a complaint of sex discrimination after alleging that she had been dismissed because of her pregnancy was entitled to bring a complaint of victimisation against her previous employer.[42]

In *St Helens Metropolitan Borough Council v Derbyshire*[43] a number of staff had brought an equal pay claim. About two months before the equal pay claims were due to be heard the employers sent letters to the staff stating that they were concerned about the impact of the claim on staff. The House of Lords agreed with the court in *Khan* (see above) that employers acting honestly and reasonably ought to be able to take steps to preserve their position in discrimination proceedings, but it emphasised that it was primarily from the perspective of the alleged victim that one decides whether any detriment has been suffered, not from the perspective of the alleged discriminator.

---

[38] Section 4(2) SDA 1975 and section 2(2) RRA 1976.
[39] See *(1) Air Canada; (2) Alpha Catering Services v Basra* [2000] IRLR 683, where a complainant was not allowed to raise the question of victimisation during the employment tribunal hearing of her race discrimination complaint; she was subsequently able to start completely fresh proceedings on the victimisation complaint.
[40] [1999] IRLR 572 HL.
[41] [2001] IRLR 830 HL.
[42] *Coote v Granada Hospitality Ltd (No 2)* [1999] IRLR 452. See now section 20A SDA 1975 and section 27A RRA 1976 on discrimination after the employment relationship has ended.
[43] [2007] IRLR 540.

6.1.1.4 Harassment

Section 3A RRA 1976 defines harassment on the grounds of race, ethnic or national origins. This occurs when a person engages in 'unwanted conduct which has the purpose or effect of violating that other person's dignity, or creating an intimidating, hostile, degrading, humiliating or offensive environment'. However, conduct will only be regarded as having this effect if 'having regard to all the circumstances, including in particular the perception of that other person, it should reasonably be considered as having that effect'. In relation to, sex, gender reassignment, colour and nationality, harassment is not defined by legislation and the behaviour complained about will have to be treated as a form of detriment or dismissal.

In *Reed and Bull v Stedman*[44] the bullying behaviour of a manager towards a secretary was held to amount to sexual harassment in breach of section 6(2) SDA 1975. This behaviour resulted in, according to the EAT, a breakdown of mutual trust and confidence. When the secretary was forced to leave her employment as a result of this breach, she was entitled to make a claim for constructive dismissal, resulting from discrimination within the meaning of section 6(2) SDA 1975. The EAT considered that sexual harassment was a form of 'shorthand for describing a type of detriment'. The question to be asked was whether the applicant had been the subject of a detriment and whether this detriment was on the grounds of sex. Motive and intention is not essential, although it may be relevant, but lack of intent is not a defence. The EAT held that:

> The essential characteristic of sexual harassment is that it is words or conduct which are unwelcome to the recipient and it is for the recipient to decide for themselves what is acceptable to them and what they regard as offensive. A characteristic of sexual harassment is that it undermines the victim's dignity at work. It creates an 'offensive' or 'hostile' environment for the victim and an arbitrary barrier to sexual equality in the workplace.

It follows from this that because a tribunal would not find an action or statement offensive, but that the applicant does, the complaint should not be dismissed. There still needs to be evidence of the harassment however. In a one-to-one counselling interview between a male manager and a female clerical officer, it was alleged that the manager was sexually aroused and that she was effectively trapped in the interview room with him.[45] She claimed that this amounted to sexual harassment. The employment tribunal accepted that the manager was not sexually aroused, but decided that the atmosphere at the interview was sexually intimidating. There was, for example, only one copy of the appraisal report, so that it had to be read jointly. The EAT allowed the appeal. Proof of sexual harassment would cause a detriment, but having rejected the evidence on which the claim was made, i.e. that the manager was sexually aroused, it could not be said that there was sexual harassment. The EAT did not think that it was necessary or desirable for all female employees to be required to have a female chaperone every time they had an interview with a male manager.

---

[44] *(1) Reed; (2) Bull Information Systems Ltd v Stedman* [1999] IRLR 299.
[45] *British Telecommunications plc v Williams* [1997] IRLR 668.

Driskel v Peninsula Business Services Ltd[46] provides a useful summary by the EAT of the approach to be taken by employment tribunals. Having adopted the categorisation of sexual harassment in *Reed and Bull* the EAT then stated:

(1) A finding of less favourable treatment leading to 'detriment' was one of fact and degree, and a single act may justify such a complaint.[47]
(2) Although the ultimate judgment is an objective one, the employment tribunal can take into account the employee's subjective perception of the subject matter of the complaint as well as the understanding, motive and intention of the alleged discriminator. Thus an isolated incident, without complaints, may not amount to harassment, but taken together with other such incidents may amount to discrimination.[48]
(3) The employment tribunal should not lose sight of the significance of the sex of the complainant and the alleged discriminator; there is a difference in banter between heterosexual males and between persons of opposite sexes.
(4) Reliance should be placed on *King v The Great Britain-China Centre*[49] in that sex discrimination may well be covert and not readily admitted, as in race discrimination cases.

Employers are likely to be held liable for subjecting their employees to detriment if they fail to take action, or permit harassment of employees where they had the ability to control the situation. This happened in one particularly distasteful case where two waitresses were subjected to racial and sexual abuse whilst they were clearing tables during an after dinner speech by a well-known comedian.[50] There is still, however, a need to show that the employer treated the employee less favourably than they would have treated a man or a person from a different racial group in similar circumstances.[51] The word 'subjecting' in section 4(2)(c) RRA 1976 implies control. A person subjects another to detriment if they cause or allow that detriment to happen in circumstances where they can control whether it happens or not. If the abuse or harassment comes from a third party, the question for a tribunal is whether the event or situation was sufficiently under the control of the employer that good employment practice could have eliminated or reduced the detriment. In this case it was clear that the management should have withdrawn the employees from their waitressing duties in order to protect them from racial abuse and harassment.

6.1.2 Sex discrimination – the subject matter

Overall employment rates for working age males and females have shown a similar development over recent years. The employment rate for males rose from 76.5% in 1995 to 79.1% in 2005. In the same period the female employment rate rose from 66.1% to

---

46 [2000] IRLR 151.
47 See also *Insitu Cleaning Co Ltd v Heads* [1995] IRLR 4.
48 See *Moonsar v Fiveways Transport Ltd* [2005] IRLR 9.
49 [1991] IRLR 513 CA.
50 See *Burton and Rhule v De Vere Hotels* [1996] IRLR 596.
51 See *Home Office v Coyne* [2000] IRLR 838 CA, where the fact that the employer regarded the harassment as the female employee's fault was not something that could be related to her sex as opposed to her relations with some other employees.

70.4%.[52] The gender gap in pay has slowly been decreasing. Between 1975 and 2005 the full-time gender gap has fallen by 12 percentage points from over 29% to 17.1%. In 2005 average hourly earnings for women working full-time were £11.67 and for men £14.08. The part-time gender gap has decreased much less, falling by a little over 3% in the same period. In 2005 part-time women earned £8.68 on average, compared to the male average full-time earnings of £14.02. This left a part-time gender gap of some 38.4%.[53]

In all ethnic groups men have higher average hourly earnings than women. When the national minimum wage was introduced, it was estimated that between 1.9 million and 2.4 million employees in the United Kingdom over the age of 18 years had earnings below the minimum wage and that 70% of these employees were women.[54]

6.1.2.1 Women and men

Although the SDA 1975 has, as a primary purpose, the removing of gender imbalances between men and women, it does not necessarily require the same treatment as between men and women. The aim is to ensure that one gender is not treated less favourably than another. One area of contention in the employment field has been the imposition of dress codes that might have the effect of discriminating against one particular sex. In *Smith v Safeway plc*,[55] for example, a male employee was dismissed because his ponytail grew too long to keep under his hat. The store had a code which required men to have hair not below shirt collar level, but female employees were permitted to have hair down to shoulder length. Phillips LJ stated that:

> I can accept that one of the objects of the prohibition of sex discrimination was to relieve the sexes from unequal treatment resulting from conventional attitudes, but I do not believe that this renders discriminatory an appearance code which applies a standard of what is conventional.

The result was that the court held that the employer was imposing a dress code that reflected a conventional outlook and that this should not be held to be discriminatory. The effect of such a decision was, however, that a male employee was dismissed because of the length of his hair, which would have been permissible in a female employee.[56]

6.1.2.2 Married people

Section 3(1) SDA 1975 provides substantially the same definition of direct and indirect discrimination as section 1(2). In this case, however, the rules protect married people and those in civil partnership from discrimination on the grounds of their marital status. This is so unless, of course, any action can be shown to be justifiable irrespective of the marital status of the person to whom it is applied.

This may be a rule mainly designed to stop discrimination against married women in employment, although it also applies to men.[57] However, there is no corresponding rule

---

[52] Figures from the Office for National Statistics; www.statistics.gov.uk
[53] Figures from the Equal Opportunities Commission publication *Women and Men at Work*, 2006; available at www.equalityhumanrights.com.
[54] Equal Opportunities Commission, *Figures from Women and Men in Great Britain: Pay and Income*, 1999.
[55] See *Smith v Safeway plc* [1996] IRLR 457 CA.
[56] In *Burrett v West Birmingham Health Authority* [1994] IRLR 7 female nurses were required to wear caps but male nurses were not. The EAT held that the important issue was that they both had to wear uniforms, not that those uniforms differed. See also *Department for Work & Pensions v Thompson* [2004] IRLR 348.
[57] Section 3(2) SDA 1975.

that states that it is unlawful to discriminate against people because they are unmarried.[58] *Bavin v NHS Pensions Trust Agency*[59] considered issues concerned with the rights of transsexuals (see below), but was primarily concerned with the entitlement of dependants on the death of a member of a pension scheme. The rules stated that only widows or widowers were entitled to benefits. This excluded all other dependants who were not married, for whatever reason, to the deceased pension scheme member. The issue of discrimination for this reason did not even arise in the case.

Section 3 also acts to stop discrimination in favour of single parents. In *Training Commission v Jackson*[60] a married mother was refused a child care payment to help her take up a place on an employment training scheme. She was refused on the basis that the scheme was intended to help lone parents attend such a scheme. The Training Commission relied upon the defence, in section 3(1)(b)(ii), that the restriction was justifiable. It was argued that lone parents were a particularly disadvantaged group in the labour market and that this was the best use of limited resources. The EAT dismissed an appeal against the employment tribunal's decision that this reason was insufficient to justify the indirect discrimination against married people.

In considering issues between a married couple, outdated assumptions that the man is the breadwinner might also amount to unlawful discrimination against the woman in the marriage. In *Coleman v Sky Oceanic Ltd*,[61] for example, two competing travel firms employed one member each of what became a married couple. There was a concern about confidentiality of each business's information. The two companies consulted and decided to dismiss the female because the man was assumed to be the breadwinner. Such an assumption, according to the Court of Appeal, was an assumption based upon sex and amounted to discrimination under the SDA 1975. *Chief Constable of the Bedfordshire Constabulary v Graham*[62] also concerned a married couple. Inspector Margaret Graham had a promotion rescinded by the Chief Constable because she was married to a chief superintendent in the same division. It was considered that there would be difficulties arising from having the couple working together at these levels. The EAT upheld the employment tribunal's decision that the complainant was treated less favourably than a single person would have been, for reasons connected to her marital status. Interestingly, the EAT also supported the tribunal's view that there was also indirect discrimination. This was because there were a higher proportion of female officers in relationships than men.

6.1.2.3 Pregnancy and maternity

The period during pregnancy and maternity leave is a specially protected one. The dismissal of a female worker on account of pregnancy can only affect women and therefore constitutes direct discrimination.[63] Article 10(1) Pregnant Workers Directive[64] provides

---

[58] Although one might argue that Article 2(1) Equal Treatment Directive might provide protection to single people when it requires there to be no discrimination 'by reference in particular to marital or family status'.

[59] [1999] ICR 1192.

[60] [1990] ICR 222.

[61] [1981] IRLR 398 CA. On assumed ethnic characteristics see *Bradford NHS Trust v Al-Shahib* [2003] IRLR 4.

[62] [2002] IRLR 239.

[63] See, e.g., Case C-177/88 *Dekker v Stichting Vormingscentrum voor Jonge Volwassen* [1991] IRLR 27 ECJ and Case C-32/93 *Webb v EMO Air Cargo (UK) Ltd* [1994] IRLR 482 ECJ.

[64] Directive 92/85/EEC on the introduction of measures to encourage improvements in the safety and health of pregnant workers and workers who have recently given birth or are breastfeeding OJ L348/1 28.11.92.

that dismissal should be prohibited during the period from the beginning of pregnancy to the end of maternity leave, save in exceptional circumstances unrelated to the worker being pregnant, breastfeeding or having recently given birth.

Section 3A[65] SDA 1975 is concerned with discrimination on the grounds of pregnancy or maternity leave. It states that a person discriminates against a woman if:

> (a) at a time in a protected period, and on the ground of the woman's pregnancy, the person treats her less favourably than he would treat her had she not become pregnant.

This wording was criticised by the High Court in *Equal Opportunities Commission v Secretary of State for Trade and Industry.*[66] The court stated that this section impermissibly introduces a requirement for a non-pregnant comparator and that the statute needed to be recast to remove this requirement. The court also criticised aspects of section 6A which is concerned with 'exceptions relating to terms and conditions during maternity leave'.[67] In particular this section provides that, subject to exceptions, it is not unlawful 'to deprive a woman who is on additional maternity leave of any benefit from the terms and conditions of her employment'. The court stated that this part needed to be recast so that there was no difference between ordinary statutory maternity leave and additional statutory maternity leave.[68]

This protection does not just apply to permanent employees, but will also apply to others. In *Patefield v Belfast City Council,*[69] for example, a contract worker was replaced by a permanent employee whilst she was on maternity leave. The fact that the employer could have replaced her at any time when she was actually working was not relevant. Of importance was that she was replaced whilst on maternity leave and the employer was, therefore, guilty of direct sex discrimination. Similarly a loyalty bonus scheme introduced to keep people at work until an office closed down was held to be discriminatory when it was paid to only those employees that attended work, thus excluding two employees on maternity leave.[70]

In *Brown v Rentokil Ltd*[71] the ECJ considered the dismissal of a female employee who was absent through most of her pregnancy and was dismissed under a provision of the contract of employment which allowed for dismissal after 26 weeks' continuous absence through sickness. The court held that Articles 2(1) and 5(1) of the Equal Treatment Directive:

> preclude dismissal of a female worker at any time during her pregnancy for absences due to incapacity for work caused by an illness resulting from that pregnancy.

Absences after pregnancy and maternity leave are to be treated in the same way as any other sickness is treated under the employee's contract of employment. Measures which impose length of service conditions before an employee is eligible for promotion, when

---

[65] Inserted by the Employment Equality (Sex Discrimination) Regulations 2005, SI 2005/2467.
[66] [2007] IRLR 327.
[67] Also inserted by the Employment Equality (Sex Discrimination) Regulations 2005, SI 2005/2467.
[68] The court relied upon the case of *Land Brandenburg v Sass* at the ECJ, Case C-284/02 [2005] IRLR 147.
[69] [2000] IRLR 664.
[70] *Gus Home Shopping Ltd v Green and McLaughlin* [2001] IRLR 75.
[71] Case C-394/96 [1998] IRLR 445 ECJ.

time spent on maternity leave is excluded from the calculations as to that length of service, will also be excluded by Article 2(3) Equal Treatment Directive.[72] The Directive will allow national provisions which give women specific rights because of pregnancy,[73] but the provision of such rights is intended to ensure the principle of equal treatment.

> Therefore, the exercise of the rights conferred on women under Article 2(3) cannot be the subject of unfavourable treatment regarding their access to employment or their working conditions. In that light, the result pursued by the Directive is substantive, not formal, equality.[74]

Thus the refusal to appoint a pregnant woman to a permanent position because there was a statutory restriction on her employment in that position during her pregnancy amounted to sex discrimination. This was the situation in *Mahlberg v Land Mecklenburg-Vorpommern*[75] where a pregnant woman was refused an appointment as an operating theatre nurse because German law banned pregnant women from being employed in areas where they would be exposed to dangerous substances. The financial loss that the employer might suffer because they could not employ the woman in the position for the duration of her pregnancy was not an acceptable reason for the unfavourable treatment. Similarly, in *P & O Ferries Ltd v Iverson*[76] a woman was stopped from going to sea once she reached week 28 of her pregnancy. Pregnancy was one of a number of lawful reasons for stopping an individual going to sea, but it was the only one for which, with this employer, there was no pay. All the other reasons, including sickness, resulted in suspension with pay. The fact that this was not available to pregnant women was held to be discriminatory.[77] Whether the employee concerned is on a permanent contract or a fixed-term contract is of no consequence. In *Tele Danmark A/S*,[78] for example, the ECJ held that Article 5 of the Equal Treatment Directive and Article 10 of the Pregnant Workers Directive precludes a worker who was recruited for a fixed period who failed to inform her employer that she was pregnant even when she was aware of this when recruited, and then was unable to work during much of the period because of her pregnancy, from being dismissed on the grounds of her pregnancy. Expiry of the fixed term would not amount to a dismissal, according to the ECJ, but a non-renewal of the fixed-term contract on the grounds of pregnancy would.[79]

6.1.2.4 Gender reassignment

Gender reassignment is defined in section 82(1) SDA 1975:

> Gender reassignment means a process which is undertaken under medical supervision for the purpose of reassigning a person's sex by changing physiological or other characteristics of sex, and includes any part of such a process.

---

[72] Case C-136/95 *Caisse Nationale d'Assurance Vieillesse des Travailleurs Salariés v Thibault* [1998] IRLR 399 ECJ.
[73] See Case C-179/88 *Handels og Kontorfunktionærernes Forbund i Danmark (acting for Herz) v Dansk Arbejdsgiverforening (acting for Aldi Marked A/S)* [1991] IRLR 31 ECJ.
[74] Note 72 above at p 406. On the consequences of failing to notify a woman on maternity leave of a vacancy for which she would have applied see *Visa v Paul* [2004] IRLR 42.
[75] Case 207/98 [2000] IRLR 276 ECJ.
[76] [1999] ICR 1088.
[77] See also *British Airways (European Operations at Gatwick) Ltd v Moore and Botterill* [2000] IRLR 296 for a similar approach in relation to air crew grounded because of pregnancy.
[78] Case 109/100 *Tele Danmark A/S v Kontorfunktionærernes Forbund i Danmark* [2001] IRLR 853 ECJ.
[79] Case 438/99 *Jiménez Melgar v Ayuntamiento De Los Barrios* [2001] IRLR 848 ECJ.

Section 2A SDA 1975[80] provides that a person A discriminates against person B and treats person B less favourably than they would other persons, on the grounds that B intends to undergo, is undergoing or has undergone gender reassignment.[81] This section was added after the ECJ decision in *P v S and Cornwall County Council*.[82] This concerned an employee who informed the employer of an intention to undergo gender reassignment. The first part of this was to undertake a 'life test' which consisted of spending a year living in the manner of the proposed gender. Whilst on sick leave for initial surgery, the employee was dismissed. The employment tribunal decided that the individual had been dismissed because of the gender reassignment, but decided that the SDA 1975 did not apply to these circumstances. They referred the matter to the ECJ with the question as to whether the Equal Treatment Directive provided for this situation. The ECJ held that the Directive sought to safeguard the principle of equality and applied, although not exclusively, to discrimination on the grounds of sex. The court held that discrimination on the basis of gender reassignment was to treat a person less favourably than persons of the sex to which the individual had been deemed to belong before the gender reassignment and was therefore contrary to Article 5(1) Equal Treatment Directive.[83] The Gender Recognition Act 2004 now gives transsexuals the opportunity to obtain legal recognition of their acquired gender.

Section 2A(2)–(4) SDA 1975 also provide that a person is treated less favourably if the reason concerns any arrangements[84] or absences concerned with the reassignment and there is an obligation not to treat the absences less favourably than absences through sickness or injury. In *Chessington World of Adventures Ltd v Reed*[85] an individual announced a change of gender from male to female and, as a result, was subjected to continuous harassment from her work colleagues. She eventually was absent through sickness and then dismissed. The EAT confirmed the employment tribunal's view that the employer, who had known of the harassment, was directly liable for the sex discrimination that had taken place.

6.1.3 Race discrimination – the subject matter

The ethnic minority population of Great Britain has grown during the post-war period. In 1984 there were 2.3 million people classified as ethnic minorities. By 2006 this had grown to 4.7 million. There was a growth in the white population, during the same period, from 51 million to 52.5 million.[86]

---

[80] Inserted by the Sex Discrimination (Gender Reassignment) Regulations 1999, SI 1999/1102.
[81] Section 2A(1) SDA 1975 provides that this is in relation to employment; sections 35A and 35B SDA 1975 concerning discrimination by, or in relation to, barristers or advocates; and discrimination in other fields in so far as it relates to vocational training. See *Gender Reassignment – A Guide for Employers*, www.womenandequalityunit.gov.uk
[82] Case 13/94 [1996] IRLR 347 ECJ.
[83] See *A v Chief Constable of West Yorkshire Police* [2004] IRLR 573.
[84] On access to toilet facilities see *Croft v Royal Mail Group* [2003] IRLR 592.
[85] [1997] IRLR 556.
[86] Equal Opportunities Commission *Facts about Men and Women in Great Britain 2004 and 2006* – see now www.equalityhumanrights.com.

Any consideration of the Race Relations Act 1976 must take into account the fact that race discrimination (as with sex discrimination) continues to exist, despite the fact that the Act was adopted almost 30 years ago. Unemployment remains higher amongst black and ethnic minority groups, when compared to the white population.[87] In 2002, for example, employment rates for all ethnic groups was 69%, including for black African people 49% and for Pakistani workers 24%, as compared to 71% for white people.[88] This discrimination extends to earnings, especially with regard to Pakistani/Bangladeshi male workers who, according to one report, earned about two-thirds of the earnings of their white counterparts.[89] Nor is it entirely possible to isolate the effects of the Act from the effects of other legislation, especially successive Immigration Acts which have been aimed at restricting the rights of immigrants (ethnic minorities) from entering Great Britain.[90] The first Race Relations Act was enacted in 1965, but did not include employment or the concept of indirect discrimination. There was a further Race Relations Act in 1968, which was eventually followed by the 1976 Act, which distinguished between direct and indirect discrimination.

6.1.3.1 Racial grounds

Section 1 RRA 1976 provides that discrimination can take place on racial grounds or against persons of a racial group. Section 3(1) defines racial grounds as meaning 'colour, race, nationality or ethnic or national origins'.[91] It also defines racial group as a group of persons 'defined by reference to colour, race, nationality or ethnic or national origins'. *Mandla v Dowell Lee*[92] resulted from a school refusing to change its school uniform policy to allow the wearing of turbans. This stopped a boy's application to join the school, because his father wished him to be brought up as a practising Sikh, which in turn required the wearing of a turban. The boy's father complained to the Commission for Racial Equality (CRE) which took up the case which finally went to the House of Lords to consider. In order to establish that racial discrimination had taken place, in terms of the Act, it was necessary for Sikhs to be defined as a racial group. The argument centred on whether they were an ethnic group. The court decided that there were a number of conditions to be met before a group could call itself an ethnic group. Lord Fraser stated:

> The conditions which appear to me to be essential are these: – (1) a long, shared history, of which the group is conscious as distinguishing it from other groups, and the memory of which it keeps alive; (2) a cultural tradition of its own, including family and social customs and manners, often but not necessarily associated with religious observance. In addition to those two essential characteristics the following characteristics are, in my opinion, relevant; (3) either a common geographical origin, or a descent from a small number of common ancestors; (4) a common language, not necessarily peculiar to the group; (5) a common literature peculiar to the group; (6) a common

---

[87] Although there is considerable variation as between ethnic groups.
[88] Labour Force Survey 2001/02; see Office for National Statistics web site – www.statistics.gov.uk.
[89] Figures drawn from CRE publications.
[90] Such as the Commonwealth Immigrants Acts 1962 and 1968; the latter was aimed at restricting the immigration of East African Asians.
[91] Discrimination on the grounds of race, ethnic or national origins is now treated differently to colour and nationality as a result of the Race Relations Act 1976 (Amendment) Regulations 2003, SI 2003/1626.
[92] [1983] IRLR 209 HL.

religion different from that of neighbouring groups or from the general community surrounding it; (7) being a minority or being an oppressed or a dominant group within a larger community.

Such a group could include converts to it or persons who have married into it. Thus the term ethnic could have a wide meaning.

Surprisingly, this definition did not extend to Rastafarians (discrimination on the grounds of religion or belief is discussed at Section 6.2 below). In *Dawkins*[93] an applicant for a job was turned away because he was a Rastafarian and would not comply with a requirement for short hair. His complaint of discrimination was rejected by the Court of Appeal on the grounds that Rastafarians could not be defined as a racial group within the definition of section 3(1) RRA 1976. They did not fulfil the criteria laid down in *Mandla v Lee* because they did not have a long shared history,[94] and could not be compared as a racial group to the Jamaican community or the Afro-Caribbean community in England. By way of contrast, the Scots and English could be held to be separate racial groups as defined by reference to their national origins, as both Scotland and England had been separate nations in the past,[95] although an attempt to define English-speaking Welsh people as a separate ethnic group from Welsh-speaking Welsh persons failed. This was because it was insufficient to identify a separate group on the basis of language alone.[96]

It is possible for a person to be unfavourably treated on racial grounds even if the claimant is not a member of the group being discriminated against. In *Weathersfield v Sargent*[97] a person of white European ancestry was instructed to discriminate against black and Asian people in the hiring out of vehicles. She resigned and claimed constructive dismissal on the grounds that she had been unfavourably treated on racial grounds. The Court of Appeal held that it was appropriate to give a broad meaning to the expression 'racial grounds'. It was an expression that should be capable of covering any reason or action based on race. In *Redfearn v SERCO Ltd*[98] a white man was employed as a bus driver and escort for children and adults with special needs. It emerged that he was a candidate for the British National Party at the local elections. Membership of this party was restricted to white people only. Some 70–80% of the bus passengers were of Asian origin and also some 35% of the employer's workforce in this instance. He was dismissed on health and safety grounds because of the feared reaction of other employees and passengers. The Court of Appeal supported the view that he had not been dismissed on racial grounds, although it did state that discrimination on racial grounds is not restricted to less favourable treatment on the grounds of the colour of the applicant. White persons could be treated less favourably than other white persons on the grounds of colour, e.g. in the case of a white person being dismissed after marrying a black person or a white publican refusing to admit or serve a white customer on the grounds that he or she is accompanied by a black person. The court also held that although the circumstances leading to the dismissal included racial considerations, this did not necessarily mean that the dismissal itself was 'on racial grounds'.

---

[93] *Dawkins v Department of the Environment; sub nom Crown Suppliers PSA* [1993] IRLR 284 CA.
[94] Only 60 years was suggested by the court.
[95] See *Northern Joint Police Board v Power* [1997] IRLR 610; applied in *BBC Scotland v Souster* [2001] IRLR 150 CS.
[96] *Gwynedd County Council v Jones* [1986] ICR 833.
[97] [1999] IRLR 94 CA.
[98] [2006] IRLR 623.

6.1.3.2 Segregation

Segregation is deemed to be less favourable treatment. Section 1(2) RRA 1976 provides that segregating a person from other persons on racial grounds is to treat that person less favourably than the others were treated. The segregation, it seems, needs to be more than accidental. In *Furniture, Timber and Allied Trades Union v Modgill*,[99] for example, the paint shop in a factory was entirely composed of workers from an ethnic minority. This had resulted from a policy of recruiting by word of mouth amongst the present employees. The paint shop had originally been mixed, but, because of this policy, came to consist entirely of individuals of Asian ethnic origin. Some of the employees made a complaint about this segregation, but the court held:

> Had there been evidence of a policy to segregate, and of the fact of segregation arising as a result of the company's acts, that might well have constituted a breach of the legislation; but it does not seem to us that there was evidence to support this position. We do not consider that the failure of the company to intervene and to insist on white or non-Asian workers going into the shop, contrary to the wishes of the men to introduce their friends, itself constituted the act of segregating persons on racial grounds, within the meaning of section 1(2).

6.1.3.3 Asylum and immigration

The rules on employing those who are subject to immigration control and who do not have permission to stay and work in the United Kingdom are strict. Section 15 of the Immigration, Asylum and Nationality Act 2006 provides that it is not permitted to employ an adult subject to immigration control if the person has not been given leave to enter or remain in the United Kingdom; or the person's leave is invalid, ceased to have effect or is subject to a condition preventing him or her from accepting employment. An employer will be liable to a penalty if they break this rule. An employer may be excused the penalty if he or she can show that he or she has complied with the prescribed requirements in relation to the employment of such persons. An employer who knew, at any time during the period of employment, that the person was subject to the limitations in section 15 cannot be excused the penalty.

Section 21 of the Act provides that a person who employs another knowing that the individual concerned is subject to immigration control and has not been given leave to enter or remain in the United Kingdom; or the individual's leave is invalid, ceased to have effect or is subject to a condition preventing him or her from accepting employment will be subject to the possibility of both a fine and a term of imprisonment. It is important, however, to treat all candidates in the same way in order to avoid any actions that might constitute unlawful discrimination.

6.1.4 The general duty to promote racial equality and gender equality

The Race Relations (Amendment) Act 2000 came into effect in April 2001. It amended the 1976 Act and, amongst other matters, it placed a statutory duty on a wide range of public authorities to promote racial equality and to prevent racial discrimination. This duty is now contained in section 71(1) RRA 1976, which states that:

---

[99] [1980] IRLR 142.

Every body or other person specified in Schedule 1A or of a description falling within that Schedule shall, in carrying out its functions, have due regard to the need –
(a) to eliminate unlawful and racial discrimination; and
(b) to promote equality of opportunity and good relations between persons of different racial groups.

Similarly, the Equality Act 2006[100] inserted sections 76A to 76E into the SDA 1975. Section 76A(1) provides that a public authority, in carrying out its functions, shall have due regard for the need:

(a) to eliminate unlawful discrimination and harassment, and
(b) to promote equality of opportunity between men and women.

This came into effect on 6 April 2007.

The Schedules each contain a large list of public authorities. The CRE published a statutory Code of Practice to give guidance to authorities in carrying out their duty.[101] Failure to observe the provisions of the Code may be admissible in evidence in legal proceedings.[102] Paragraph 3.2 of the Code provides that there are four guiding principles that should govern the implementation of this duty. These are:

(1) Promoting race equality is obligatory for all public authorities listed in the Schedule. It is a general duty that will underpin all policy and practice.
(2) Public authorities must meet the duty to promote race equality in all relevant functions. Relevance is about how much a function affects people, as members of the public or as employees of the authority.
(3) The weight given to race equality should be proportionate to its relevance. Section 71(1) RRA 1976 (above) states that authorities must have 'due regard' to its duty to promote race equality. This means that the weight given to race equality must be proportionate to its relevance to a particular function.
(4) The elements of the duty are complementary, which means that the duties to eliminate unlawful racial discrimination, promote equality of opportunity and promote good relations between people of different racial groups are all necessary to fulfil an overall duty.

Section 71(2) and (3) RRA 1976 enable the Secretary of State to impose specific duties to ensure the better performance of the public authorities in fulfilling their duties. The Race Relations Act 1976 (Statutory Duties) Order 2001[103] required the listed bodies to produce a Race Equality Scheme by May 2002. Such a scheme must state the functions and policies which the organisation has decided are relevant to its performance of its duty and include arrangements for consulting, monitoring, publishing results and training staff.[104]

If the CEHR is satisfied that a person has failed to comply with its duty, it can issue a compliance notice instructing the organisation to comply and report its actions back to the

---

[100] Sections 84–86.
[101] Statutory Code of Practice on the duty to promote race equality (CRE, 2002); now the Commission for Equality and Human Rights.
[102] Section 71C(11) RRA 1976.
[103] SI 2001/3458.
[104] Ibid regulation 2.

Commission. Failure to comply with this may result in the Commission's gaining a County Court Order to force the body to supply the information.[105]

The Equal Opportunities Commission also published a Code of Practice on the Gender equality Duty[106] describing it as the biggest change in legislation since the Sex Discrimination Act itself over 30 years ago. The effect of this duty is similar to that of the race equality duty. There is a further duty in relation to disability (see Chapter 7).

6.1.5 Discrimination in employment

Parts II SDA 1975 and RRA 1976 are concerned with discrimination in the employment field. Employment is defined in section 82(1) SDA 1975 and section 78(1) RRA 1976 as meaning employment under a contract of service or apprenticeship or a contract personally to execute any work or labour. However, in *Allonby v Accrington & Rossendale College*[107] the ECJ decided that the word 'worker' in Article 141 has a Community meaning and cannot be defined by Member States. According to the ECJ, for these purposes a 'worker' is a person who, for a certain period of time, performs services for and under the direction of another for which they receive remuneration. Except for those who do not qualify, such as those who work wholly outside Great Britain, there are no restrictions imposed, such as a minimum length of continuous service[108] or an upper age limit, to stop an individual making a complaint of discrimination.

In a rather strict interpretation of sex discrimination in recruitment advertising, the Court of Appeal held that an act of discrimination had taken place when a magazine refused to accept an advertisement for a housekeeper/cook based in Tuscany.[109] The advertisement was placed in the magazine by a single man. The journal's reason for refusing was that it only accepted advertisements for overseas positions where the employer was a woman and that this was a way of protecting young females from exploitation. The court decided that this approach was unacceptable. The motive, in accordance with the decision in *James v Eastleigh Borough Council*,[110] was not a valid justification for discrimination.

Section 4(1) RRA 1976[111] makes it unlawful for a person, in relation to employment at an establishment in Great Britain,[112] to discriminate:

(1) in the arrangements that are made for the purpose of determining who should be offered employment;[113]

---

[105] Sections 71D and 71E RRA 1976.
[106] See now www.equalityhumanrights.com.
[107] [2004] IRLR 224.
[108] For example, in *Weathersfield v Sargent* [1999] IRLR 94, the employee left work on her second day of employment.
[109] *Bain v Bowles* [1991] IRLR 356.
[110] [1990] IRLR 288 HL.
[111] Also section 6(1) SDA 1975.
[112] Section 10 SDA 1975 and section 8 RRA 1976 state that employment is to be regarded as in an establishment in Great Britain unless the employee does their work wholly outside Great Britain. Prior to the Equal Opportunities (Employment Legislation) (Territorial Limits) Regulations 1999, SI 1999/3163, which transposed the Posted Workers Directive (Directive 96/71/EC), the exclusion was those who worked wholly or mainly outside Great Britain; see *Carver v Saudi Arabian Airlines* [1999] ICR 991 CA.
[113] In *Rihal v London Borough of Ealing* [2004] IRLR 642 the Court of Appeal held that the employment tribunal had been entitled to take into account its finding that a 'glass ceiling' operated in the housing department.

(2) in the terms that are offered in that employment;

(3) by refusing or deliberately omitting to offer employment.[114]

6.1.6 Burden of proof

One of the problems with discrimination cases is the ability of the complainant to show that discrimination has actually taken place. According to the Court of Appeal, very little direct discrimination is overt or deliberate. There is a need to look at the surrounding circumstances which may demonstrate that an apparently fair-minded act or decision was or was not influenced by racial bias.[115] Often the employment tribunal will need to draw inferences as to the conduct of individuals in a particular case. In *King v The Great Britain-China Centre*[116] an applicant who was Chinese, but educated in Britain, failed to be short-listed for a post of deputy director of the Centre, even though her qualifications on paper seemed to meet the selection criteria. In such a situation the tribunal was entitled to look to the employer for an explanation. In this case none of the five ethnic Chinese candidates was selected for interview and the Centre had never employed a person with such an ethnic background. The Court of Appeal supported the approach of the employment tribunal in inferring that there was discrimination on racial grounds.[117] In *King*, Neill LJ set down some principles and guidance that could be obtained from the authorities.[118] These were that:

(1) it is for the applicant who complains of racial discrimination to make out his or her case;

(2) it is unusual to find direct evidence of racial discrimination;

(3) the outcome of a case will therefore usually rely upon what inferences it is possible to draw from the primary facts as found by the tribunal;

(4) there will be some cases where it is possible to draw the inference of discrimination and in such cases the tribunal is entitled to look to the employer for an explanation;

(5) it is unnecessary to introduce shifting evidential burdens of proof. Having adopted this approach then it is open to the tribunal to reach a conclusion based on the balance of probabilities.

Whether it is possible to draw an inference of discrimination on the basis of sex or race depends upon whether it is possible to show that a person has been subject to less favourable treatment than another person of a different sex or different racial group. In *Martins v Marks & Spencer plc*[119] an applicant of Afro-Caribbean ethnic origin applied, unsuccessfully, four times for a post as a trainee manager with Marks & Spencer. She settled a race discrimination claim on the last occasion and as part of the arrangement was allowed to take a selection test and was given an interview. She failed her selection

---

[114] Section 14 RRA 1976 and section 15 SDA 1975 apply these provisions to employment agencies except for where the agency reasonably relies upon an employer's statement that the discrimination is lawful.

[115] See *Anya v University of Oxford* [2001] IRLR 377 CA, where a black Nigerian resident in the United Kingdom complained of racial discrimination when he was rejected, following an interview, in favour of a white candidate.

[116] [1991] IRLR 513 CA.

[117] See *Igen Ltd v Wong* [2005] IRLR 258.

[118] See now section 63A SDA 1975 and section 54A RRA 1976.

[119] [1998] IRLR 326 CA.

interview with poor marks. The employment tribunal had found the selection panel 'biased' in its treatment of the candidate. This, the Court of Appeal decided, was not a meaningful conclusion. The real question was whether they were treating this candidate less favourably than they would treat another candidate in the same circumstances, and, secondly, whether one could infer that this less favourable treatment was on racial grounds. The Court of Appeal found that there was insufficient evidence for this. The employer had established a defence under section 32(3) RRA 1976.[120]

There is a need to establish a causal relationship between the detriment and the racial or sexual discrimination. Mummery J discussed causation in *O'Neill*:[121]

> The basic question is: what, out of the whole complex of facts before the tribunal, is the 'effective and predominant cause' or the 'real or the efficient cause' of the act complained of? As a matter of common sense not all the factors present in a situation are equally entitled to be treated as a cause of the crucial event for the purpose of attributing legal liability for consequences.

The tribunal's approach to the question of causation should be 'simple, pragmatic and commonsensical', although this approach needs to be qualified by the fact that the event complained of need not be the only or the main cause of the result complained of.

Section 4(2) RRA 1976[122] states that it is unlawful for a person to discriminate against an individual employed by them:

(1) in the terms of employment given;
(2) in the way that access to opportunities for promotion, transfer or training is afforded;
(3) by dismissing them or subjecting them to any detriment.

In relation to discrimination on the grounds of race, ethnic or national origins, dismissal specifically includes the non-renewal of a limited term contract or a constructive dismissal.[123] Additionally, where there has been a dismissal involving unlawful harassment or discrimination on the grounds of sex, race, ethnic or national origins, it is unlawful to inflict further harassment or discrimination if it 'arises out of and is closely connected to the employment relationship'.[124]

Issues related to promotion and development are important for removing both race and sex discrimination in employment. Jobs which require previous supervisory or management experience[125] can be indirectly discriminatory simply because there may be many fewer opportunities for women to obtain this sort of experience. In *British Gas plc v Sharma*[126] an employee with an MA was employed in a junior clerical post and was, apparently, unable to obtain promotion. She made a claim for race discrimination when she was not selected for two posts that carried a requirement for GCE 'O' levels.[127] In the event neither of the successful candidates had this level of education. The employment tribunal was entitled to draw an inference of race discrimination as a result of the

---

[120] See also section 41(3) SDA 1975.
[121] *O'Neill v Governors of St Thomas More Roman Catholic Voluntarily Aided Upper School* [1996] IRLR 372.
[122] See also section 6(2) SDA 1975.
[123] Section 4(4A) RRA 1976.
[124] Section 20A SDA 1975, section 27A RRA 1976.
[125] As in *Falkirk City Council v Whyte* [1997] IRLR 560.
[126] [1991] IRLR 101.
[127] A predecessor of GCSEs.

employer's changing of the selection criteria during the interviewing process. One of the remedies available is that under section 56(1)(c) RRA 1976.[128] An employment tribunal is able to make a recommendation for action within a specified period, which appears to be practicable, to obviate or reduce the adverse effect of the act of discrimination. The EAT held, however, that a recommendation by the tribunal that the applicant should be promoted at the next available opportunity was outside their powers as it might be seen as an act of positive discrimination. There may have been better qualified applicants at the next promotion opportunity.

In order to make the task for complainants of sex discrimination less onerous Council Directive 97/80/EC on the burden of proof in cases of discrimination based on sex[129] was adopted by the other Member States in 1997. It was adopted by the United Kingdom, via an extension Directive,[130] in 1998. The purpose of the Directive is summarised in Article 1:

> The aim of this Directive shall be to ensure that the measures taken by the Member States to implement the principle of equal treatment are made more effective, in order to enable all persons who consider themselves wronged because the principle of equal treatment has not been applied to them to have their rights asserted by judicial process after possible recourse to other competent bodies.

The Directive took effect in national law in October 2001.[131] Section 63A was inserted into the SDA 1975. It provides that where, on a hearing of the complaint, the complainant proves facts from which the tribunal could conclude, in the absence of an adequate explanation, that the respondent:

(1) has committed an unlawful act of discrimination against the complainant, and
(2) is someone who is to be treated as having committed such an act against the complainant,[132]

then the employment tribunal will uphold the complaint unless the respondents prove that they did not commit such an act, or that they should not be treated as having committed it.

Subsequently the Race Relations Act was amended[133] so that similar provisions apply in cases covered by that Act.

Igen Ltd v Wong[134] was a case where the Court of Appeal considered a number of questions in relation to the interpretation of the statutes concerning the shifting of the burden of proof. The court held that the provisions required an employment tribunal to go through a two-stage process. The first stage is for the applicant to prove facts from which the tribunal could conclude, in the absence of an adequate explanation, that the respondent has committed an act of discrimination against the applicant. The second stage, which only comes into effect if the complainant has proved these facts, requires the

---

[128] See also section 65(1)(c) SDA 1975.
[129] OJ L14/6 20.1.98 (Burden of Proof Directive).
[130] Council Directive 98/52/EC OJ L205/66 22.7.98.
[131] The Sex Discrimination (Indirect Discrimination and Burden of Proof) Regulations 2001, SI 2001/2660.
[132] Sections 41 and 42 SDA 1975 refer to the liability of employers and principals as well as those aiding such unlawful acts.
[133] In relation to employment tribunals section 54A was inserted into the RRA 1976 by the Race Relations Act 1976 (Amendment) Regulations 2003, SI 2003/1626.
[134] [2005] IRLR 258.

respondent to prove that he or she did not commit the unlawful act. This case actually contains a 13-point guidance to the decision-making process in relation to the burden of proof. It includes:

(1) the claimant must prove on the balance of probabilities facts so that, in the absence of an adequate explanation, the tribunal could conclude that the act of discrimination had taken place against the applicant;
(2) it is unusual to find evidence of direct discrimination;
(3) it could mean that at this stage the tribunal does not have to have reached a final conclusion;
(4) the respondent must prove, on the balance of probabilities, that the treatment was in no way whatsoever on a discriminatory ground.

It is not always necessary to go through this two-stage procedure. In *Brown v LB of Croydon*[135] the court held that it was not obligatory, but good practice to do so. In some circumstances it was possible to go straight to the second stage. In this case the emphasis was on the reasons for the treatment, so it was natural to do so.

The importance of shifting the burden of proof to the respondent once a *prima facie* case of discrimination has been established is of great importance. In *Madarassy v Nomura International plc*[136] the Court of Appeal stated:

> I do not underestimate the significance of the burden of proof in discrimination cases. There is probably no other area of civil law in which the burden of proof plays a larger part than in discrimination cases.

The burden of proof, however, does not shift just by showing that there was a difference in status (sex in this case) and a difference in treatment. 'Could conclude' means that 'a reasonable tribunal could properly conclude' from all the evidence put before it. This could include evidence from the complainant and evidence from the respondent contesting the complaint. The absence of an adequate explanation is not at this stage relevant as to whether there is a *prima facie* case of discrimination. It only becomes relevant if a *prima facie* case is proved. Thus the *prima facie* case has still to be shown.

6.1.7 In the course of employment

According to section 32(1) RRA 1976,[137]

> anything done by a person in the course of his employment shall be treated for the purposes of this Act . . . as done by the employer as well as him, whether or not it was done with the employer's knowledge or approval.

In *Jones v Tower Boot Co Ltd*[138] the employer argued that the acts of racial harassment were outside the normal course of employment. The employment tribunal took the view that this would amount to saying that no act could become the liability of the employer

---

[135] [2007] IRLR 259.
[136] [2007] IRLR 246.
[137] Section 41(1) SDA 1975.
[138] [1997] IRLR 168 CA.

unless it was expressly authorised by the employer. The Court of Appeal supported this approach and took the view that the words ought to be given their everyday meaning. In *Sidhu*[139] the event, which consisted of a racially motivated assault on an employee by another employee, took place at a family day out organised by the employers. This was held not to be 'in the course of employment', but subjecting a female police officer, by a male police officer, to inappropriate sexual behaviour during an after work gathering of police officers in a pub and during a leaving party for a colleague, amounted to actions done in the course of employment.[140] When there is a social gathering of work colleagues, it is for the employment tribunal to decide whether the gathering was an extension of employment. Whether a person was, or was not, on duty and whether the events occurred on the employer's premises are just two indicators that need to be considered. In this case the two police officers could not have been said to be merely socialising with each other.[141]

6.1.8 Taking all steps that are reasonable and practicable

Section 32(3) RRA 1976 and section 41(3) SDA 1975 provide an opportunity for employers to deny liability. The employer needs to show that they have taken such steps as are reasonably practicable to prevent the employee from doing the act or other acts of a similar description. In *Martins v Marks & Spencer plc*[142] (see above) the Court of Appeal held that:

> There can be no doubt that Marks & Spencer made out the defence on the findings of fact about the effective arrangements made for the 'special interview' to ensure that the members of the panel had no knowledge of the reason for the interview; their equal opportunities policy; their compliance with the Code of Practice issued by the Commission for Racial Equality in relation to selection procedures, criteria and interviewing; and their selection of the interviewing panel to include Mr Walters as a person with an interest in recruiting from ethnic minorities.

All these actions amounted to a sufficient defence for the employer. It is no defence to say that all possible steps were not taken because the taking of those steps would not have made any difference. This might be true in some extreme forms of harassment such as the sexual assault that took place in *Canniffe v East Riding of Yorkshire Council*.[143] Even though there may have been little the employers could have done to stop this action, the fact that they did not take further possible measures was enough to stop them being able to rely on section 41(3) SDA 1975. The proper approach for the employment tribunal, according to the EAT, was:

(1) to identify whether the respondent had taken any steps at all to stop the employee from committing the act or acts complained of and then,
(2) having identified what steps, if any, had been taken, to decide whether there were any further steps that could have been taken which were reasonably practicable.

Whether these further steps would have stopped the acts is not decisive.

---

[139] *Sidhu v Aerospace Composite Technology Ltd* [2000] IRLR 602 CA.
[140] *Chief Constable of the Lincolnshire Police v Stubbs* [1999] IRLR 81.
[141] The matter was also considered in *Waters v Commissioner of Police of the Metropolis* [2000] IRLR 720 HL where an alleged sexual assault in a section house was deemed to be in the course of employment; see also *Lister v Hesley Hall Ltd* [2001] IRLR 472 HL, Chapter 3.3.2.
[142] [1998] IRLR 326 CA.
[143] [2000] IRLR 555.

6.1.9 Aiding unlawful acts

Section 42(1) SDA 1975 and section 33(1) RRA 1976 provide that a person who knowingly aids another to do an act which is made unlawful by the SDA or RRA will be treated as if they committed that act themselves. This includes an employee or an agent for whose acts the employer is liable.[144] The exception to this is when a person reasonably relies upon a statement made by the other person that the acts which are being aided are not unlawful.[145]

The concept of 'knowingly aiding' was considered in *Anyanwu and Ebuzoeme v South Bank Students Union*.[146] This concerned two black students who were elected as paid officers of the students' union. They were subsequently expelled from the university for other reasons and barred from the students' union building. This led to the termination of their employment with the students' union. They complained that, amongst other matters, their employer had discriminated against them in terminating their employment. They also complained that the university had knowingly aided this unlawful act. The House of Lords held that the word 'aids' did not have any special or technical meaning in this context and that there was an arguable case that the university had 'knowingly aided' the students' dismissal from employment by the students' union. The university had brought about a state of affairs in which the employment contracts were bound to be suspended. In *Gilbank v Miles*[147] a pregnant hairdresser was subject to a campaign of bullying and discrimination which led to the salon manager being made jointly and severally liable with the company employer as she had helped create the growth of a discriminatory culture.

In *Hallam v Cheltenham Borough Council*[148] the police had concerns about a wedding reception that was to be held at a council-owned hall. The father of the bride was of Romany origin. The Council reacted by imposing new contractual conditions, including admittance only to those with pre-issued tickets. The hirer treated this as repudiatory conduct and held the reception elsewhere. The Council were subsequently found to be guilty of racial discrimination. One further question was whether the police officers concerned had knowingly aided the Council in this discriminatory act. The House of Lords held that each situation should be looked at on its merits. In this case the police officers had not been a party to, neither had they been involved in, the Council's decision. There were a number of ways in which the Council could have reacted to the information, some of which would have been lawful, so more than a general attitude of helpfulness and co-operation was required.

6.1.10 Genuine occupational qualification or requirement

Both the SDA 1975 and the RRA 1976 provide for a situation where being of a particular sex or of a particular racial group is a genuine occupational qualification.[149] There are certain situations where it is permissible to use sex or racial origin as a criterion in the

---

[144] Section 42(2) SDA 1975 and section 33(2) RRA 1976. See *Yeboah v Crofton* [2002] IRLR 634.
[145] Section 42(3)–(4) SDA 1975 and section 33(3)–(4) RRA 1976.
[146] *Anyanwu and Ebuzoeme v South Bank Students Union and South Bank University* [2001] IRLR 305 HL.
[147] [2006] IRLR 538.
[148] [2001] IRLR 312 HL.
[149] Section 7 SDA 1975 and section 5 RRA 1976.

selection of an applicant or in providing access to promotion and training. The SDA provides a listing in section 7(2) of those situations where being a man may be a genuine occupational qualification. These exceptions apply where only some of the duties of a job fall within the categories, as well as when all the duties do so.[150] These are:

(1) Where 'the essential nature of the job would be materially different if carried out by a woman'. These can be situations where a man is needed for physiological reasons, although reasons related to strength and stamina are excluded. There is no further elaboration except for the specific exception of dramatic performances or other entertainment where there is a requirement for authenticity reasons.

(2) Where there are decency reasons for a job to be held by a man such as those involving physical contact with men where they might reasonably object to the job being carried out by a woman or where the men are likely to be in a state of undress or using sanitary facilities. Such a situation arose in *Lasertop Ltd v Webster*[151] where a male applicant failed to obtain an interview for a sales/trainee manager position with a women-only health club. The job entailed showing potential members around the club, including the changing rooms, saunas, sun-bed room and toilet. The EAT concluded that the club could rely upon a genuine occupational qualification defence in such circumstances.

(3) Where the job concerns working in, or living in, a private home and the job needs to be held by a man because of the degree of physical or social contact and the knowledge of the intimate details of a person's life.[152]

(4) Where the nature or location of the establishment make it impracticable for the job holder to live anywhere but on the premises supplied by the employer and there are no separate sleeping or sanitary provisions for men and women, nor is it reasonable to expect the employer to provide them.

(5) Where the nature of the establishment, or the part in which work is done, requires the job holder to be a man. This can be a single sex hospital, prison or other establishment for persons requiring special care and attention, where it would not be reasonable for the job to be done by a woman.

(6) Where the job holder provides individuals with personal services promoting their welfare or education, or similar services, and this can best be done by a man.

(7) Where the job needs to be done by a man because it is likely to involve the performance of some of the work in a country where a woman would not be able to effectively perform the duties.

(8) Where the job is one of two held by a married couple.

If there are already sufficient numbers of male employees who are capable of carrying out these duties, and whom it would be reasonable to employ on these duties, without causing the employer undue inconvenience, then the exceptions would not apply.[153] Rather than recruit a new employee using a genuine occupational qualification exception, the employer would be expected to cover these duties with existing employees. In *Lasertop Ltd*

---

[150] Section 7(3) SDA 1975.
[151] [1997] IRLR 498.
[152] This provision was added by the Sex Discrimination Act 1986.
[153] Section 7(4) SDA 1975.

v *Webster*[154] the applicant claimed that the employer could not rely on the genuine occupational qualification defence for this reason. It was a new women-only health club. The EAT held that the relevant time for section 7(4) SDA 1975 to operate was at the time when the discrimination takes place. As this was a new club recruiting staff, the position envisaged by section 7(4) could not exist, as there were few existing employees at the time. The EAT was concerned that this would create a lacuna in the law, but still held that the employer could rely unhindered on the genuine occupational qualification defence.

Section 7A SDA 1975 provides similar rules to be applied in situations relating to gender reassignment and section 7B provides that there is a further genuine occupational qualification concerning those who are planning a gender reassignment or are undergoing the process of gender reassignment. This exception includes jobs that are concerned with, first, being called upon to conduct intimate searches; secondly, living or working in a private home; thirdly, where the location or establishment require the person to live on the premises and there are not separate facilities for preserving decency and privacy; and, finally, where the job holder is providing personal services to vulnerable individuals, promoting their welfare or similar and where the employer decides that the services cannot be provided by someone undergoing gender reassignment.

Under the RRA 1976 there are fewer situations in which a genuine occupational qualification applies. These are:

(1) where authenticity in drama or other entertainment requires a person of a particular racial group;
(2) where the production of visual imagery in art or photography requires a person from a particular racial group for reasons of authenticity;
(3) where the job involves working in a place where food and drink is served to the public and membership of a racial group is required for authenticity;
(4) where the job holder provides persons of that racial group with personal services promoting their welfare, and where those services can be most effectively performed by a person of that racial group.

In relation to (4), it should be noted that the test is whether the services can 'most effectively' be performed by a person from a particular racial group. It is not where they 'must be' or 'can be' provided by such a person. In *Tottenham Green Under Fives' Centre v Marshall (No 2)*[155] the EAT held that the 'desirable extra' of having a nursery worker being able to read and talk in dialect was sufficient to justify a genuine occupational qualification exception. Secondly, the services need to be performed personally. This means that employers filling managerial positions might find it more difficult to establish a genuine occupational qualification. When considering two management positions in a local authority housing department, Balcombe LJ stated:

> The critical questions may be put thus: 'Would the holders of these two jobs provide persons of the particular racial group with personal services promoting their welfare?' The Industrial Tribunal found not. The EAT found that they did not. The reason for the finding was quite

---

[154] [1997] IRLR 498.
[155] [1991] IRLR 162.

fundamental, that is that the holders of managerial posts in the housing benefits service did not provide a personal service at all. Their contact with members of the public was either negligible or non-existent.[156]

The concept of a genuine occupational requirement was introduced to the statute book in 2003. This applies where, 'having regard to the nature of the employment or the context in which it is carried out', being of a particular race, ethnic or national origin is a 'genuine and determining occupational requirement'. It must also be proportionate to apply the requirement and either the person to whom it is applied does not meet it or 'the employer is not satisfied, and in all the circumstances it is not reasonable for him to be satisfied, that that person meets it'.[157]

6.1.11 Discrimination by other bodies

Section 12 SDA 1975 and section 11 RRA 1976[158] provide that it is unlawful for:

> an organisation of workers, an organisation of employers, or any other organisation whose members carry on a particular profession or trade for the purposes of which the organisation exists

to discriminate on the grounds of sex or racial grounds against those applying for membership in the terms for admittance or in refusing or omitting to accept the application for membership. Similarly, in section 12(3) SDA 1975 and section 11(3) RRA 1976, discrimination against members by depriving them of access to membership benefits or of membership itself or some other detriment is made unlawful.

The words 'organisation of employers' is to be given its ordinary and natural meaning. Thus an organisation like the National Federation of Self-employed and Small Businesses would qualify as an employer's organisation. This despite the organisation's own claims that it did not qualify on the grounds that a minority of members were self-employed, rather than employers, and their purposes were not related to their members as employers, but rather to their interests as business people.[159] Section 13 SDA 1975 and section 12 RRA 1976 make it unlawful for bodies which can confer an authorisation or qualification which is needed for engagement in a particular trade or profession to discriminate. In *Arthur v Attorney General*[160] it was held that the body which sifted recommendations to the Lord Chancellor on appointments to become Justices of the Peace did not fall within the terms of section 12 RRA 1976, because it only provided a filtering function, rather than conferring approval. Neither were Justices of the Peace an 'occupation' within the definition of 'profession' as defined in section 78(1)[161] RRA 1976. *Tattari v Private Patients Plan Ltd*[162] distinguished between those bodies which granted qualifications or recognition for the purposes of practising a profession and those which stipulated a particular qualification

---

[156] *London Borough of Lambeth v Commission for Racial Equality* [1990] IRLR 231 at p 235 CA.
[157] Section 4A(1)–(2) RRA 1976.
[158] Section 11 SDA 1975 and section 10 RRA 1976 provide that discrimination is unlawful for partnerships, in relation to arrangements for appointing a person as a partner in the firm; in section 10(1) RRA 1976, however, the partnership needs a minimum of six or more partners before this aspect of the legislation applies.
[159] *National Federation of Self-employed and Small Businesses v Philpott* [1997] ICR 518.
[160] [1999] ICR 631. See also *Patterson v Legal Services Commission* [2004] IRLR 153.
[161] Section 82(1) SDA 1975. In both statutes 'profession' is defined as including any vocation or occupation.
[162] [1997] IRLR 586 CA.

for the purpose of its commercial agreements. In *Triesman v Ali*[163] the Court of Appeal held that the Labour Party was not a body within the meaning of section 11 RRA 1976. However, there might be a remedy under section 25 RRA 1976 which deals with associations not within section 11.

The issues become more complicated when there is a dispute between members of an organisation. In *Fire Brigades Union v Fraser*[164] one member accused another of sexual harassment. In this case the trade union decided to represent the harassed woman, rather than the man accused of harassment. The employment tribunal compared the treatment received by the man with that of the woman concerned. The EAT accepted that the trade union had failed to provide an explanation for the difference in treatment, so that the employment tribunal had been correct in inferring sex discrimination contrary to section 12(3) SDA 1975. The responsibilities in section 12(2) SDA 1975 and section 11(2) RRA 1976, concerning organisations of trade unions, employers and others, to non-members relate only to questions of admission or non-admission to the organisation. In another case concerning a trade union[165] an ex-member complained that they had been victimised and subjected to detriment by the union and three of its officials. The complaints referred to alleged verbal abuse and physical threats when the individual crossed a picket line and to the alleged dissemination of misinformation about the individual's conduct by the trade union. The claim failed because the individual was no longer a member and was unable to pursue a complaint that extended beyond admission and non-admission matters.

Discrimination against contract workers by a person other than the one with whom they have a contract is also unlawful where the contract worker is doing work for the other person (the principal) under a contract arranged between the principal and the contract worker's employer.[166] The Court of Appeal gave this a wide interpretation where an employee of a concessionaire in Harrods store was dismissed because the store withdrew its approval of her for reasons that she did not comply with the store's dress code. She made a successful claim of racial discrimination against the store.[167] The court held that section 7 RRA 1976 is not limited to cases where those doing the work are under the direct management or control of the principal. It also applies when an individual is doing work for their employer, but also work done for the principal. In this case it was held that the concessionaire was supplying employees under the terms of its contract with Harrods to do work for Harrods in accord with section 7 RRA 1976.

6.1.12 Remedies

Article 6 Equal Treatment Directive provides that all individuals have the right to obtain an effective remedy in a competent court against measures that infringe on the right to equal treatment between men and women.

---

[163] [2002] IRLR 489.
[164] [1997] IRLR 671.
[165] *Diakou v Islington Unison 'A' Branch* [1997] ICR 121.
[166] Section 9 SDA 1975 and section 7 RRA 1976.
[167] *Harrods Ltd v Remick* [1997] IRLR 583 CA. See also *Jones v Friends Provident* [2004] IRLR 783.

Section 63 SDA 1975[168] provides that individuals may bring a complaint of discrimination, in relation to Part II of the Act, to an employment tribunal. This will be subject to the statutory dispute and grievance procedures (see Chapter 5). The complaint may be as a result of discrimination by the other party or because the other party is liable under sections 41 and 42 SDA 1975.[169] Such liability may be as a result of things done in the course of employment (see above) or as a result of a person knowingly aiding another person to do something that is unlawful under the Act.[170] An employment tribunal will not consider the complaint unless it is presented within a period of three months of when the act complained of was done,[171] unless the tribunal 'considers that it is just and equitable to do so'.[172] A broad approach was shown in *Derby Specialist Fabrication Ltd v Burton*,[173] where an employee resigned after a period of racial abuse and harassment. Although the discriminatory acts took place before this constructive dismissal, the EAT approved of the tribunal's decision that the three-month period ran from the date of the resignation. If the employee is making a complaint as a result of suffering a detriment from the employer, then the three months commences from when he or she heard of the detriment.[174] Where an employment tribunal finds that a complaint was well founded, then it has a choice of what action to take:

(1) it may make an order declaring the rights of the claimant and the respondent in relation to the act complained of;
(2) it may make an order requiring the respondent to pay compensation to the claimant;
(3) it may make a recommendation that the respondent takes action, within a specified period of time, for the purpose of obviating the adverse effect on the complainant of any act of discrimination to which the complaint relates.[175]

In *Prestcold Ltd v Irvine*[176] it was held that actions (2) and (3) above were exclusive. The first should take care of losses of wages, whilst the second is concerned with taking steps other than payment of wages in order to obviate or reduce the adverse effects of discrimination. If the respondent fails, without reasonable justification, to comply with the recommendation, then the tribunal may increase the level of compensation.[177] It is important to observe that there is no upper limit on compensation that can be awarded.

---

[168] Section 54 RRA 1976.
[169] The provisions concerning the liability of employers and principals for acts done in the course of employment and the liability of a person who aids another person in carrying out an unlawful act under the SDA 1975; see also sections 32 and 33 RRA 1976.
[170] See *Anyanwu and Ebuzoeme v South Bank Students Union and South Bank University* [2000] IRLR 305 HL.
[171] Section 76(1) SDA 1975 and section 68(1) RRA 1976. On acts extending over a period see section 76(6) SDA 1975, section 68(7) RRA 1976 and *Hendricks v Commissioner of Police for the Metropolis* [2003] IRLR 96.
[172] Section 76(5) SDA 1975 and section 68(6) RRA 1976. Note also that employees must first submit a statement of grievance to their employer: EA 2002 Schedule 2 paragraphs 6 and 9.
[173] [2001] IRLR 69.
[174] Delays in internal procedures do not necessarily justify delaying the presentation of the complaint to an employment tribunal: it is one factor that will be taken into account; see *Robinson v Post Office* [2000] IRLR 804.
[175] Section 65(1) SDA 1975 and section 56(1) RRA 1976.
[176] [1980] IRLR 267.
[177] Section 65(3)(1) SDA 1975 and section 56(4)(a) RRA 1976.

In *Essa v Laing Ltd*[178] the Court of Appeal ruled that a victim of racial abuse was entitled to be compensated for the loss which arises naturally and directly from the wrong. It was not necessary for the particular type of loss to be reasonably foreseeable. Individuals can recover for both physical and psychiatric injury[179] and obtain aggravated damages.[180] In relation to injury to feelings, the Court of Appeal has suggested that there are three broad bands of compensation – the minimum sum being £5,000 and the maximum being £25,000.[181]

Section 76 SDA 1975 provides for various time limits in which an employment tribunal may consider a complaint under the Act (see below). Proceedings in *Mills and Crown Prosecution Service v Marshall*[182] commenced after the decision in *P v S and Cornwall County Council*[183] and were out of time. These proceedings concerned an individual who was offered a post in the Crown Prosecution Service. The offer was withdrawn after the applicant informed the Director of Public Prosecutions that they were intending to reassign their gender. The Court of Appeal approved the approach of the employment tribunal in hearing the case out of time. They held that the wording in section 76(5), which allowed the tribunal to hear such cases if it was 'just and equitable to do so', should be given the widest possible meaning as they were different from the words used in allowing tribunals discretion to hear complaints of unfair dismissal out of time.[184]

As an aid to complainants, section 74 SDA 1975[185] permits the Secretary of State to prescribe a means by which a respondent can be questioned about the reasons for doing any relevant act.[186] The answers will be admissible in the tribunal proceedings and a failure to respond, or the giving of evasive or equivocal answers, will enable the tribunal to draw inferences that it considers just and equitable to reach, including an inference that the respondent committed an unlawful act.[187] Additionally a complainant may apply to the Commission for Equality and Human Rights for assistance, which may include giving advice, trying to procure a settlement, arranging legal advice or representation.[188]

6.1.13 Codes of Practice

The Commission for Equality and Human Rights (CEHR)[189] may issue Codes of Practice whose purpose is the elimination of discrimination in the field of employment or for the promotion of equality in that field between, first, men and women and, secondly, for

---

[178] [2004] IRLR 313.
[179] See *Sheriff v Klyne Tugs* [1999] IRLR 481.
[180] See *British Telecom plc v Reid* [2004] IRLR 327.
[181] *Vento v Chief Constable of West Yorkshire Police (No 2)* [2003] IRLR 102.
[182] [1998] IRLR 494.
[183] Case 13/94 [1996] IRLR 347 ECJ.
[184] See also *Afolabi v London Borough of Southwark* [2003] IRLR 220; *Apelogun-Gabriels v London Borough of Lambeth* [2002] IRLR 116.
[185] Section 65 RRA 1976.
[186] Sex Discrimination (Questions and Replies) Order 1975, SI 1975/2048; see also the Race Relations (Questions and Replies) Order 1977, SI 1977/842.
[187] On the drawing of inferences generally see the Court of Appeal's decision in *Madden v Preferred Technical Group Ltd* [2005] IRLR 46.
[188] Section 75 SDA 1975 and section 66 RRA 1976.
[189] Similar provisions existed for the EOC and CRE under Part VII RRA 1976.

persons intending to undergo, or who have undergone, gender reassignment.[190] The Code of Practice for the elimination of racial discrimination and the promotion of equality of opportunity in employment was first issued by the Commission for Racial Equality in 1983[191] and finally updated in 2006. It is now the Code of Practice on Racial Equality in Employment and came into force on 6 April 2006.[192] Similarly, the Code of Practice on sex discrimination, equal opportunities policies, procedures and practices in employment was first issued by the EOC in 1985.[193] The purpose of the Code, stated in its introduction, is the elimination of discrimination in employment; to give guidance as to what steps employers should take; and to promote equality of opportunity.

Section 56A(10) SDA 1975[194] provides that a failure on the part of any person to observe the provisions of the Code will not, in itself, render them liable to proceedings. The failure will, however, be admissible as evidence in any proceedings before an employment tribunal and may be taken into account in determining the question. The CEHR is also entitled to conduct formal investigations[195] and make recommendations. Sections 67–73 SDA 1975 provide for the issue and enforcement of non-discrimination notices by the CEHR in relation to Part IV of the Act, which deals with discriminatory practices.

6.2 Discrimination on the grounds of religion or belief, or sexual orientation

Regulations forbidding discrimination on these grounds in employment were introduced in 2003. They were subsequently amended in 2006 by the Equality Act which extended the provisions to include goods, services and facilities.

6.2.1 Religion or belief

Religious discrimination can be closely linked to racial discrimination, but it was not expressly made unlawful until 2003. A good example was the case *Ahmad v ILEA*.[196] This concerned a Muslim school teacher who required a short time off on Friday afternoons to attend prayers at a nearby mosque. He resigned and claimed unfair dismissal when his employers refused him paid time off. They had offered him a part-time position working $4\frac{1}{2}$ days per week. The United Kingdom had not at the time incorporated the European Convention on Human Rights into national law, but, as Lord Denning stated in this case, 'we will do our best to see that our decisions are in conformity with it'. In this case it still

---

[190] Section 56A(1) SDA 1975; in addition, the European Commission has issued guidance from time to time, e.g. Commission Recommendation 92/131/EEC and Code of Practice on the protection of the dignity of women at work OJ L249/1 24.2.92.

[191] The Code of Practice was made under section 47 RRA 1976 and came into effect on 1 April 1984; see the Race Relations Code of Practice Order 1983, SI 1983/1081.

[192] See now www.equalityhumanrights.com.

[193] The Code of Practice was made under section 56A SDA 1975 and came into effect on 30 April 1985 by the Sex Discrimination Code of Practice Order 1985, SI 1985/387.

[194] Also section 47(10) RRA 1976.

[195] See Sex Discrimination (Formal Investigations) Regulations 1975, SI 1975/1993; also sections 48–52 RRA 1976.

[196] [1977] ICR 490.

meant rejecting the claim as it would give the Muslim community 'preferential treatment'. The court held that Article 9(2) of the Convention did not give an employee the right to absent him- or herself from work in breach of the contract of employment. Lord Scarman dissented, stating that the issue began, but did not end, with the law of contract. The judgment would mean that any Muslim, who took their religious duties seriously, could never be employed on a full-time contract as a teacher. This is an old case and one must doubt whether the same decision would be reached today. It does, however, illustrate how it is possible to penalise someone for carrying out the activities and ritual connected to their religious beliefs. Another example is *Mandla v Lee*[197] where the Sikhs were identified as an ethnic group, and were thus protected under the Race Relations Act 1976.

The 2001 census asked a question about religion. It was a voluntary question and over 4 million people did not answer it. Of those that did, their professed religious loyalty was as follows:

Religious affiliations 2001 census

Christian	42,079,417
Muslim	1,591,126
Hindu	558,810
Sikh	336,149
Jewish	266,740
Buddhist	151,816
Other	178,837
No religion/religion not stated	13,626,299

There are wide geographical differences. The highest proportion of Christians in England was the north-east with 80.1%. In London this figure fell to 58%. In the Borough of Tower Hamlets, 36% gave their religion as Muslim as well as 24% of the population of the London Borough of Newham. The London Borough of Harrow had 19.6% who stated that they were Hindu and in Barnet the figure for the Jewish population was 14.8%. On a lighter note, at the time of the census there was a campaign to persuade people to answer the religious question with 'Jedi Knight'. As a result some 370,000 people (0.7% of the population) declared their religion as Jedi Knight![198]

The Framework Directive was transposed into national law by the Employment Equality (Religion or Belief) Regulations 2003 (hereafter the Religion or Belief Regulations).[199] These Regulations were amended by Part 2 of the Equality Act 2006, which, importantly, extended the scope of non-discrimination on this ground to goods, facilities and services.

Religion or belief is defined as 'any religion, religious belief, or similar philosophical belief'.[200] This is not a helpful definition as it provides no meaning to the terms religion

---

[197] [1983] IRLR 209.
[198] This will only mean something to those who have watched the *Star Wars* movies.
[199] SI 2003/1660.
[200] Regulation 2(1).

or belief. It has been deliberately left to the courts, relying on Article 9 ECHR,[201] to decide whether any particular religion or belief meets this definition. The Government guidance on these Regulations[202] states that this definition is a broad one and will clearly include those religions that are widely recognised, such as Christianity, Islam, Hinduism and Judaism. Equally it will apply to groups within religions, such as Roman Catholics and Protestants.

The reference to religious belief is likely to include a belief that is based in a religion. It is interesting that the philosophical belief must be a 'similar' philosophical belief. Humanism will presumably be protected by the Regulations, but to what extent is it a belief similar to religious belief? The Government guidance suggests that it means that the philosophical belief should be profound and affect a person's way of life or perception of the world. An absence of belief may also be protected. Thus an employer who is of a particular faith but does not employ someone because they are not of the same faith is likely to be guilty of direct discrimination. It is not because the rejected applicant belongs to another religion that he or she is being discriminated against, but because he or she is not of the same religion as the employer.[203] What is clear is that other beliefs, such as political beliefs, are not protected by the Religion or Belief Regulations.

6.2.2 Sexual orientation

In order to meet its obligations under the Equal Treatment on Employment and Occupation Directive,[204] the Government adopted the Employment Equality (Sexual Orientation) Regulations 2003 (the Sexual Orientation Regulations).[205] These came into force on 1 December 2003. Prior to these Regulations there were few provisions protecting gay people at work from being discriminated against because of their sexual orientation.

The European Court of Justice concluded in *Grant v South-West Trains Ltd*[206] that discrimination based on sexual orientation was not contrary to Community law. The complaint was that the employer gave travel concessions to employees plus their spouses or partners of the opposite sex, but refused them to a long-term partner of the same sex as an employee. The ECJ held that there was no discrimination under Article 119 EEC (now 141 EC) or the Equal Pay Directive. The problem was that a condition such as this applied to male and female employees. The court considered the judgment arrived at in *P v S*[207] and accepted that the decision in that case had been based upon gender discrimination. In *Grant*, however, a female same sex partner would apparently have been treated in the same way as a male same sex partner, so there could be no discrimination between the two. This

---

[201] Article 9 of the European Convention on Human Rights states: 'Everyone has the right to freedom of thought, conscience and religion, this right includes the freedom to change his religion or belief . . .'.

[202] Explanatory Notes for the Employment Equality (Religion or Belief) Regulations 2003 (DTI, 2003).

[203] See *Kokkanikis v Greece* (1994) 17 EHRR 397.

[204] Directive 2000/78/EC.

[205] SI 2003/1661; the Government estimates that between 1.3 and 1.9 million people are affected by the Regulations.

[206] Case 249/96 [1998] IRLR 206 ECJ.

[207] *P v S and Cornwall County Council* Case 13/94 [1996] IRLR 347 ECJ.

approach meant that a person subjected to homophobic abuse and dismissal would not have been able to sustain a claim based upon sex discrimination or harassment.[208]

Until the Government relaxed its approach in 2000 this absence of protection posed a particular problem for members of the armed services. The Court of Appeal refused to construe the Equal Treatment Directive in order to include sexual orientation and suggested that any proscription of discrimination on the grounds of sexual orientation might need to be achieved by a specific Directive.[209] The Government's change of approach occurred after the European Court of Human Rights reached a decision in *Smith and Grady*.[210] Prior to this decision the policy of the Ministry of Defence had been that 'homosexuality, whether male or female, is considered incompatible with service in the armed forces'.[211] After the European Court of Human Rights held that the rights of the individuals under Article 8 (right to privacy) and Article 13 (right to an effective domestic remedy) of the European Convention on Human Rights had been violated, the ban on homosexuals in the armed forces was lifted. The Ministry of Defence issued a new Code of Social Conduct[212] which banned unacceptable social conduct, which applied to heterosexuals as well as homosexuals. The 'service test' was introduced to determine when it was necessary to intervene in the personal lives of employees. This test consists of the commanding officer considering whether:

> the actions or behaviour of an individual adversely impacted or are likely to impact on the efficiency or operational effectiveness of the service.

There is a distinction between discrimination against homosexuals on the grounds of their sexuality and discrimination on the grounds of their sex. In *Smith v Gardner Merchant Ltd*[213] a male homosexual complained that he was subjected to threatening and abusive behaviour by a female colleague. He was subsequently dismissed and the employment tribunal decided that it did not have jurisdiction to hear claims of discrimination on grounds of sexual orientation. The appeal was won at the EAT and upheld by the Court of Appeal who concluded that such discrimination against a male homosexual could amount to discrimination against him as a male. In this case the correct comparator, under section 5(3) SDA 1975,[214] in relation to the treatment by the work colleague could be with a homosexual woman and whether she would have been treated in the same way. For comparison concerning a complaint about the employer's handling of the situation, the female colleague could be used as the comparator. This approach did not help a lesbian school teacher who was subject to homophobic verbal abuse by pupils at the

---

[208] See *Smith v Gardner Merchant Ltd* [1998] IRLR 510 CA where a bar person was subjected to such abuse prior to dismissal.

[209] See *R v Secretary of State for Defence, ex parte Perkins (No 2)* [1998] IRLR 508 where a medical assistant was discharged from the Royal Navy because of his sexual orientation; see also *Secretary of State for Defence v MacDonald* [2001] IRLR 431 CS, which concerned a member of the RAF who was excluded because of his sexual orientation.

[210] *Smith and Grady v United Kingdom* [1999] IRLR 734 ECHR.

[211] *Ministry of Defence Guidelines on Homosexuality*, December 1994.

[212] *The Armed Forces Code of Social Conduct: Policy Statement*, 1999.

[213] [1999] IRLR 510 CA.

[214] Section 5(3) SDA 1975 provides that a comparison of persons of different sex or marital status or of the cases of discrimination and gender reassignment must be such that the relevant circumstances in the one case are the same, or not materially different, as in the other.

school. *Pearce v Governing Body of Mayfield Secondary School*,[215] followed the approach in *Smith v Gardner Merchant Ltd* to conclude that it could not be said that she had received less favourable treatment than a hypothetical homosexual male teacher, as there was no evidence that such a teacher would have been treated any differently.

Regulation 2(1) of the Sexual Orientation Regulations defines sexual orientation as a sexual orientation towards:

- persons of the same sex; thus covering both gay men and gay women;
- persons of the opposite sex; which provides for heterosexual relationships;
- persons of the same sex and opposite sex; which covers bisexual men and women.

Sexual orientation means an orientation towards a person of the same sex, the opposite sex or both sexes. It does not include sexual practices or sexual conduct.

6.2.3 Discrimination and harassment

Both sets of Regulations cover employees, contract workers, trustees and managers of pension schemes, office holders, the police, barristers, advocates, partnerships, trade organisations, qualifications bodies, providers of vocational training, employment agencies and institutions of further and higher education.[216]

Regulation 2(3) defines employment as meaning employment under a contract of service or of apprenticeship or a contract personally to do any work. Thus there is a broader definition of employment, adopting the same approach as the SDA 1975 and RRA 1976. A contract worker is someone doing contract work and the protection is against the 'principal'. This is a person who makes work available for doing by individuals who are employed by another person. Thus agency workers are protected against discrimination by the employer to whom they are sent to work by their employment agency.

Discrimination may take place:

- on the grounds of religion or belief, or
- by way of victimisation.

Regulation 3(1)(a) defines direct discrimination as

> For the purposes of these Regulations, a person (A) discriminates against a person (B) if –
> (a) on the grounds of religion or belief (sexual orientation) A treats B less favourably than he treats or would treat other persons.[217]

Thus there is a need to show less favourable treatment compared to another person of a different religion or belief (or sexual orientation). The relevant circumstances of the person discriminated against and the comparator need to be the same, or 'not materially different'.[218] A simple example of direct discrimination given in the Government explan-

---

[215] [2001] IRLR 669 CA.
[216] Regulations 8–20 of both sets of Regulations.
[217] The reference to religion or belief here does not include A's religion or belief; see regulation 3(2).
[218] Regulation 3(3) Religion or Belief Regulations and regulation 3(2) Sexual Orientation Regulations; the Government guidance accompanying the Regulations suggests that this means that the relevant circumstances need not be identical.

atory notes on religion or belief[219] is if an employer refused to allow a prayer break for Muslim employees at certain times. This would not amount to direct discrimination if the employer refused breaks for all employees at that time.[220]

The protection is against discrimination on the 'grounds of religion or belief' (or sexual orientation). Thus a person who is not a Jew, for example, but is discriminated against because the employer perceives him or her as being Jewish is equally protected. Similarly a person who is not gay but is discriminated against because the employer perceives him or her as being gay is also protected. There is no defence of justification in direct discrimination as there may be for indirect discrimination.

Indirect discrimination is provided for in regulation 3(1)(b). Thus discrimination occurs when:

(1) A applies to B a provision, criterion or practice which A applies equally to other persons not of the same religion or belief (or sexual orientation) as B, but
(2) which puts persons of the same religion or belief (or sexual orientation) as B at a particular disadvantage when compared with others, and
(3) which also puts B at a disadvantage, and
(4) A cannot show it to be a proportionate means of achieving his or her legitimate aim.

Thus the stages in showing that A's application of the provision, criterion or practice amount to indirect discrimination, are, first, that there needs to be a 'particular disadvantage' suffered by the group who share B's religion or belief or sexual orientation. This is different to the 'considerably smaller' definition used in the SDA 1975 and the RRA 1976 and is intended to be less reliant on statistical evidence than those measures concerned with sex and race discrimination.[221] The second stage is then to show that the complainant, B, is also put at that disadvantage. Clearly this has to be the same disadvantage suffered by the group in the first stage, but it does mean that cases can only be brought by people who suffered the disadvantage themselves. There is then an opportunity for the employer to show that the application of the provision, criterion or practice is justified because it concerns achieving a legitimate aim by proportionate means. An example might be an advertisement for a leader of a playgroup for Muslim children, which specifies that applicants must be familiar with the teachings of the Koran. A Jewish applicant might be able to show a group disadvantage, in that this would disadvantage all Jews, as well as an individual disadvantage to him or herself. It would then be for the employer to show that this provision, criterion or practice had a legitimate aim and was a proportionate means of achieving it.[222]

The second means by which discrimination can take place is by way of victimisation.[223] In this case a person, A, discriminates against another person, B, if he or she treats B less

---

[219] See www.berr.gov.uk.
[220] It might, however, amount to indirect discrimination if not justified.
[221] DTI explanatory notes; see now www.berr.gov.uk.
[222] DTI guidance; see now www.berr.gov.uk.
[223] Regulation 4.

favourably than he or she treats or would treat other persons in the same circumstances because B has:

(1) brought proceedings against A under the Religion or Belief (or Sexual Orientation) Regulations;
(2) given evidence or information in connection with any proceedings brought against A under the Regulations;
(3) done anything else to A or any other person under the Regulations;
(4) alleged that A or any other persons have committed an act contrary to the Regulations.

The same applies if A treats B less favourably because B plans to do any of the above. Thus workers will be protected from less favourable treatment for taking action under the Regulations, even if any allegations made or information given are later shown to be false, so long as the allegations were made in good faith.

The definition of harassment is the same as that contained in other anti-discrimination statutes and regulations. Harassment on the grounds of religion or belief is defined as unwanted conduct which has the result of either violating a person's dignity or creating an intimidating, hostile, degrading, humiliating or offensive environment for the worker. Thus it is unwanted conduct, although it is clear that the worker need not express the view that the conduct is unwanted whenever it happens. There will be conduct which is self-evidently unwanted. The harassment does, however, need to be on the grounds of religion or belief. If a person is bullied for some other reason, it may not be possible to show that it took place because of an individual's religion or belief.

6.2.4 Discrimination and employment

Part II of the Religion or Belief (or Sexual Orientation) Regulations deals with discrimination in employment and vocational training. It is unlawful for an employer, at an establishment in Great Britain, to discriminate against applicants on the grounds of their religion or belief (or sexual orientation):

(1) in the arrangements made for the purpose of deciding who should be offered employment;
(2) in the terms of the offer;
(3) by refusing to offer, or deliberately not offering, employment.[224]

It is also unlawful for an employer to discriminate against employees, employed at an establishment in Great Britain:

(1) in their terms of employment;
(2) in the opportunities afforded for promotion, a transfer, training or in receiving any other benefit;
(3) by dismissing the employee or subjecting the employee to any other detriment.[225]

---

[224] Regulation 6(1).
[225] Regulation 6(2).

This includes constructive dismissal as a result of the employer's conduct.[226]

An example may be whether an employer needs to consider whether his or her pay arrangements, which include double pay on Sundays, are discriminatory. Such an arrangement might constitute indirect discrimination if not justified, as they may disadvantage employees whose faith recognises Sunday as a day of rest.[227] *Azmi v Kirklees Metropolitan Borough Council*[228] concerned a school support worker who was a devout Muslim. She was used to wearing a long dress and a veil which covered all her head and face apart from her eyes. After much consultation she was instructed not to wear the veil in school as it restricted the visual signals that children would normally receive from a person not wearing a veil. Her claim of direct discrimination failed because she was held not to have been treated less favourably compared to another person, who was not a Muslim, but who had her face covered.

Regulation 6(3) also provides that it is unlawful for an employer to harass applicants or employees. There is, however, no requirement for the employer to ask an applicant or employee about their religion or belief (or sexual orientation), especially as many individuals may regard the matter as a private one which they do not wish to discuss with the employer or potential employer.

Acts committed after the employment relationship has ended will also be unlawful if the discrimination or harassment arises out of, or is closely connected with, that employment relationship.[229] Anything done 'in the course of employment' shall be treated as if it was done by the employer, whether the employer had knowledge of the act or not. As in other areas of discrimination law the employer will have a defence if the employer can show that all steps as were reasonably practicable were taken to prevent the employee from doing the act, or, at least, from doing the act during the course of employment.[230]

There are some exceptions from Part II. These are, in the Regulations on Religion or Belief:

(1) national security – regulation 24 provides that an act done for safeguarding national security, so long as it was justifiable in that context, is not unlawful;

(2) positive action – this may be taken where it reasonably appears to prevent or com- pensate for disadvantages linked to religion or belief suffered by persons of that particular religion or belief;[231]

(3) special arrangements for Sikhs working on construction sites. If the employer has no reasonable grounds for believing that the Sikh worker would not be wearing a turban at all times, then the application of any provision, criterion or practice that stops the Sikh worker from doing this will not be one which can be shown to have a propor- tionate means of achieving a legitimate aim.[232]

---

[226] Regulation 6(5)(b).

[227] See DTI guidance; see now www.berr.gov.uk.

[228] [2007] IRLR 484.

[229] Regulation 21.

[230] Regulation 22; regulation 23 deals with aiding unlawful acts, so an agent or employee acting as an agent for the employer or other for whom the employer is liable will be assumed to be doing the act itself unless the agent or employee reasonably relies on a statement from the principal that the act is not unlawful under the Religion or Belief Regulations.

[231] Regulation 25.

[232] Regulation 26(1).

In the Regulations on Sexual Orientation the exceptions are:

(1) national security – regulation 24 provides that an act done for safeguarding national security, so long as it was justifiable in that context, is not unlawful;

(2) marital status – anything that prevents or restricts access to a benefit by reason of marital status is not unlawful, so it is perfectly lawful to discriminate in favour of married persons for access to some benefits;[233]

(3) positive action – this may be taken where it reasonably appears to prevent or compensate for disadvantages linked to sexual orientation suffered by persons of that particular sexual orientation.[234]

6.2.5 Genuine occupational requirement

In relation to applicants and employees, the provisions concerning discrimination do not apply if there is a genuine and determining occupational requirement for being of a particular religion or belief and it is proportionate[235] to apply that requirement in the particular case.[236] Thus there are a number of factors:

■ it must be a **requirement** of the job, which means that it must be essential for a person to be able to carry out the job;

■ it must be a **determining** requirement; something that is crucial to the job;

■ it must be an **occupational** requirement, meaning a close connection with the job in question;

■ it must be a **genuine** occupational requirement and not one just created to try and avoid the Regulations or because the employer does not like people of a particular religion or belief or specific sexual orientation.[237]

This may justify dismissal from a post where, for example, an employee changes their religion or belief (or sexual orientation) and this change means that he or she can no longer perform the functions of the post. If, on the other hand, an employee changes their religion or belief (or sexual orientation) and this has no effect upon performing the job functions, then the change in orientation would not be a justification for dismissal. There are likely to be only rare genuine occupational requirements for a person to be of a particular religion or belief or sexual orientation.

The above rules apply to any employer, but there are similar rules which apply if the employer has an ethos based on religion and belief.[238] This situation will relate to a limited number of employers. The differences are that:

■ the employer will need to show that they have an ethos based upon religion or belief;

■ the genuine occupational requirement will need to have regard to that ethos; and

■ the genuine occupational reason does not have to be the determining requirement.

---

[233] Regulation 25.
[234] Regulation 26.
[235] Proportionate, according to the guidance, means the appropriate means of achieving the aim in question.
[236] Regulation 7(1) and 7(2).
[237] See Government guidance.
[238] Regulation 7(3).

Thus it is a broader exception because the employer does not need to show that the genuine occupational requirement is a determining factor. It will still have to show that the genuine occupational requirement for an employer with a particular religious ethos applies to the particular job. *Glasgow City Council v McNab*[239] concerned a teacher who was turned down for an interview as acting principal teacher of pastoral care in a Roman Catholic school. It was established that had he been a Roman Catholic he would have been given an interview. The education authority failed to establish that being a Roman Catholic was a genuine occupational requirement as the post had not previously been covered by an agreement to reserve certain posts. The education authority also claimed that it was an employer which had an ethos based on religion or belief in accord with regulation 7(3) as it was responsible in part for schools which did have that ethos. This claim was also unsuccessful because such an authority, according to the EAT, could be one which had responsibility for schools with a number of different and possibly contradictory ethos at the same time.

One important issue here may be a potential clash between the protection given under the Sexual Orientation Regulations (see below) and those concerned with religion or belief. What is the situation if an organisation has a religious ethos that excludes homosexual people because it is against its ethos? Regulation 7(3) provides that if the employment is for an organised religion, then the employer may be permitted to apply a requirement related to sexual orientation:

- so as to comply with the doctrines of the religion, or
- to avoid conflicting with strongly held religious convictions of a significant number of the religion's followers.

In this latter case the exception refers to the nature of employment and the context in which it is carried out. This suggests that the exception applies to jobs whose purposes are to do with religion, rather than the religious organisations as such. Therefore it will be permissible for an exception to be made with the appointment of imans, priests, rabbis, etc., but perhaps not for all jobs within a religious organisation.

6.3 Equal pay

The Equal Pay Directive[240] built upon Article 141 EC and established that the principle of equal pay meant:

> . . . for the same work or for work to which equal value is attributed, the elimination of all discrimination on grounds of sex with regard to all aspects and conditions of remuneration.[241]

Pay is given a broad definition and actions which have been held to be discriminatory include when retired male employees receive travel concessions not available to female retirees;[242] when part-time employees do not receive pay during sickness when it was paid

[239] [2007] IRLR 476.
[240] Council Directive 75/117/EEC of 19 February 1975 on the approximation of the laws of the Member States relating to the application of the principle of equal pay for men and women OJ 1975 L45/19.
[241] Article 1 Directive 75/117/EEC.
[242] Case 12/81 *Garland v British Rail Engineering Ltd* [1982] IRLR 111 ECJ.

to full-time employees;[243] and when men and women receive different payments, including pensions, resulting from compulsory redundancies.[244]

The Equal Pay Act was passed by Parliament in 1970, but there was a long introductory period before it came into effect in 1975. Although one cannot doubt that the legislation has had an impact on the relative pay of men and women, a significant gap still remains. In 2005, as stated above, female employees who worked full-time earned 83% of the average gross hourly earnings of male full-time employees. This is an improvement, however, on the situation when the EPA was passed. In 1971 women earned only 63% of the average hourly earnings of full-time male employees.[245]

Section 1(1) EPA 1970 implies an equality clause into all contracts of employment which do not already contain one. An equality clause, according to section 1(2) EPA 1970, is a provision relating to the terms, not just pay, of a contract under which a woman is employed. The clause has effect where a woman is:

(1) employed on like work with a man in the same employment;
(2) employed on work rated as equivalent with that of a man in the same employment;
(3) employed on work which, not being work in (1) or (2), is, in terms of the demands made upon her, of equal value to that of a man in the same employment.[246]

In these situations any term of the woman's contract, apart from the equality clause, that is less favourable to the woman than the comparable man should be modified so as to be not less favourable. Similarly, if the woman's contract does not contain a term conferring a benefit on her that is contained in the comparable man's contract, then the woman's contract shall be deemed to include the term.[247] Equal pay must, therefore, be calculated not on the basis of the worth of the overall contract in comparison with the man's contract, but on the basis of each individual item taken in isolation. In *Brunnhofer*,[248] for example, two bank employees were employed in the same grade and on the same basic salary. The comparable man, however, was paid a higher supplement than Mrs Brunnhofer. This was subsequently justified on the grounds that the man carried out more important functions and was said to do work of a higher quality. The higher supplement, however, was paid from when they were recruited. It was not possible to justify the differences in pay by factors that became known only after the employees had taken up their employment and had been assessed.

These rules establish the need to make a claim based upon an inequality of terms between the complainant and a male comparator and not on the concepts of direct and indirect discrimination contained in the Sex Discrimination Act 1975.[249] The principle of equal pay presupposes that the men and women whom it covers are in comparable

---

[243] Case 171/88 *Rinner-Kühn v FWW Spezial-Gebäudereinigung GmbH* [1989] ECR 2743 ECJ.
[244] Case C-262/88 *Barber v Guardian Royal Exchange Assurance Group* [1990] ECR 1–1889 ECJ.
[245] See Equal Opportunities Commission, *Women and Men in Britain – At The Millennium* (2000).
[246] The Equal Pay Act 1970 was amended by the Equal Pay (Amendment) Regulations 1983, SI 1983/1794 in order to ensure that the ability of an employee to claim equal pay for work of equal value was not dependent upon an employer consenting to a job grading system.
[247] Section 1(2)(a), (b) and (c) EPA 1970.
[248] Case 381/99 *Brunnhofer v Bank der Österreichischen Postsparkasse AG* [2001] IRLR 571 ECJ.
[249] See *Ratcliffe v North Yorkshire County Council* [1995] IRLR 439 HL.

situations.[250] Succeeding in a claim will entitle the female complainant to receive the same terms as that comparator.[251] This, in itself, may not always seem fair. *Evesham v North Hertfordshire Health Authority*[252] was an appeal against the remedy awarded by an employment tribunal as a result of a long-running claim by speech therapists that their work was of equal value to that of a district clinical psychologist. The claimant was a district chief speech therapist with six years' experience in her post. The comparator was a newly appointed clinical psychologist in his first year and near the bottom of the pay scale. Ms Evesham argued that she should be placed at a point on the incremental scale that reflected her experience. The Court of Appeal held that to do this would be to entitle her to pay in excess of that received by the male comparator, with whom she had established equal value. The EPA 1970 requires an identified comparator with whom the value of the applicant's work can be compared. It was a comparison between the work of individuals, rather than a comparison between what speech therapists do and what clinical psychologists do.[253]

6.3.1 The comparator

The comparator needs to be selected by the complainant[254] and be in the same employment as the claimant. This does not mean that the claimant can just choose an artificial or arbitrary group, although, in principle, the comparison should be between the advantaged and the disadvantaged group.[255] The considerations in establishing this are:

(1) Both the claimant and the comparator must be 'employed', which means being employed under a contract of service, a contract of apprenticeship or a contract personally to execute any work or labour.[256] However, in *Allonby v Accrington and Rossendale College*[257] the ECJ held that the word 'worker' in Article 141 has a Community meaning and cannot be defined by Member States. For these purposes a 'worker' is a person who performs services for and under the direction of another for which they receive remuneration. In this case the requirement of having a contract of employment as a precondition of membership of a pension scheme set up by statute had to be disapplied unless it was objectively justified. This was because a much higher percentage of women fulfilled all the conditions of membership except that of having a contract of employment as defined by national law.

---

[250] See Case 218/98 *Abdoulaye v Régie Nationale Des Usines Renault* [1999] IRLR 811 ECJ, where employees absent through pregnancy were held to have occupational disadvantages which entitled them to an extra payment.
[251] According to *Hayward v Cammell Laird* [1988] IRLR 257 HL it is each item contained in the contract of employment that should be the same, not the overall terms and conditions.
[252] [2000] IRLR 257 CA.
[253] The ECJ held, in Case 236/98 *Jämställdhetsombudsmannen v Örebro Läns Landsting* [2000] IRLR 421 ECJ, that the proper comparison between the two groups is the basic monthly pay, excluding supplements; no account is to be taken of different working hours, although these might constitute reasons unrelated to sex.
[254] See *Ainsworth v Glass Tubes and Components Ltd* [1977] IRLR 74, where an employment tribunal was held to have erred by selecting the comparator they wished to use.
[255] See *Cheshire & Wirral Partnership v Abbot* [2006] IRLR 546.
[256] Section 1(6)(a) EPA 1970.
[257] [2004] IRLR 224.

(2) Two or more employers may be treated as associated if one has control, directly or indirectly, over the other or both are subject to direct or indirect control by a third person.[258]

(3) The comparators need to be employed by the same employer as the claimant at the same establishment or other establishments in Great Britain which, including the one at which the claimant is employed, have common terms and conditions of employment generally or for particular relevant classes of employees.[259] This appears to be interpreted widely, so if there is a sufficient connection in a 'loose and non-technical sense' between the different employments then this might be sufficient. In the *Allonby* case (above) the ECJ confirmed that Article 141 was not limited to situations in which men and women work for the same employer. It may be invoked in cases of discrimination arising directly from legislative provisions or collective agreements, as well as in cases where work was carried out in the same establishment or service. However, where the differences cannot be attributed to a single source there is no body which could restore equal treatment and Article 141 does not apply.[260]

(4) The applicant and the comparator do not need to be doing equal work for the same employer contemporaneously.[261] Thus an applicant may be able to rely on Article 141 EC to claim equal pay with either a predecessor or successor.[262]

6.3.2 Like work

A woman is to be regarded as employed on like work with a man if her work is of a 'broadly similar nature' to his.[263] It may not be enough that the two groups being compared appear to do identical work. In a case that considered a health authority which employed both graduate psychologists and medical doctors as psychotherapists, the ECJ held that a difference could be identified between the two groups even though they carried out similar functions. In treating their patients both groups drew upon their training and experience. The doctors had a very different training and experience. That, combined with the ability to employ doctors on a greater range of duties, was sufficient to justify a difference in treatment in their remuneration.[264] The level of responsibility, together with the severity of the consequences of one's actions, may be a factor that distinguishes two jobs where the work may otherwise be identical. In *Eaton Ltd v J Nuttall*,[265] for example, although the complainant and the male comparator were employed on like work, the consequences of an error by the male comparator were much more serious than the consequences of an error by the female complainant.[266]

---

[258] Section 1(6)(c) EPA 1970.
[259] Section 1(6)(c) EPA 1970, added by the SDA 1975.
[260] See now *Robertson v DEFRA* [2005] IRLR 363.
[261] *McCarthys Ltd v Smith* [1980] IRLR 210 ECJ.
[262] See *Diocese of Hallam Trustee v Connaughton* [1996] IRLR 505.
[263] Section 1(4) EPA 1970.
[264] Case C-309/97 *Angestelltenbetriebsrat der Wiener Gebietskrankenkasse v Wiener Gebietskrankenkasse* [1999] IRLR 804 ECJ.
[265] [1977] IRLR 71.
[266] See also *De Brito v Standard Chartered Bank* [1978] ICR 650 which also compared a trainee to more experienced employees.

Often jobs done are not precisely similar and employment tribunals have been called upon to assess the importance of small differences which might distinguish the job of the applicant from that of the complainant. It may be necessary to examine what individuals actually do, rather than what their contract of employment obliges them to do, if different.[267] There is likely to be a two-stage approach:

(1) an examination to decide whether, generally, the work that a complainant does is the same or broadly similar to the work done by a male comparator;
(2) if it is work of a similar nature, are the differences between the things she does and the things he does of practical importance in relation to the terms and conditions of employment.

Without this approach a tribunal may fail to recognise that, although a woman and a man may be doing work of a broadly similar nature, they may not actually be employed on like work.[268] All the duties done by a complainant and a comparator need to be examined and it is unlikely that some duties could be ignored even if they take only a little time.[269] Nevertheless, the final conclusion may be based upon a broader view:

> It is clear from the terms of the subsection that the work need not be of the *same* nature in order to be like work. It is enough that it is of a similar nature. Indeed, it need only be broadly similar. In such cases where the work is of a broadly similar nature (and not of the *same* nature) there will necessarily be differences between the work done by a woman and the work done by the man.[270]

6.3.3 Work rated as equivalent

A woman is to be regarded as employed on work rated as equivalent with that of a man only if her job has been given an equal value as his job in a job evaluation study undertaken with a view to evaluating the jobs in an undertaking or group of undertakings.[271] Alternatively it would have been given an equivalent rating if the evaluation system was not flawed by having a system which gives different values for men and women under the same heading. The factors used in the assessment of any job under a job evaluation system need to be objective. The criteria used should be common to both men and women, but must also not be such as to discriminate against women. This does not necessarily mean that criteria involving physical strength, viewed as a male characteristic, should be excluded. If a job is seen objectively as requiring a certain amount of strength, then this may be included as a criterion. It is important, however, to view the overall picture to ensure that any particular attributes, conventionally seen as female, needed for the job are also taken into account. Not to do this and leave, as part of the criteria, a factor associated with one sex might open the door to a discrimination claim.[272]

---

[267] *E Coomes v Shields* [1978] IRLR 263; see also *Redland Roof Tiles Ltd v Harper* [1977] ICR 349, which took into account the fact that the male comparator was also a trainee manager and, for five weeks in a two-year period, acted as a supervisor.

[268] *Waddington v Leicester Council for Voluntary Service* [1977] IRLR 32.

[269] In *Dance v Dorothy Perkins Ltd* [1978] ICR 760 the EAT held that, where a comparator was chosen as a representative of a wider group, then it was important to examine the duties in the context that they were a representative.

[270] *Capper Pass Ltd v Lawton* [1977] ICR 83.

[271] Section 1(5) EPA 1970.

[272] See Case 237/85 *Rümmler v Dato Drück GmbH* [1987] IRLR 32 ECJ.

There is a problem when jobs are just slotted in against benchmark jobs and given a consequent grading. It might be possible to claim that such jobs have not properly been considered against the various criteria. The onus is upon the employer to show that there had been a job evaluation study which satisfied the requirements of section 1(5) EPA 1970.[273]

In *O'Brien v Sim-Chem Ltd*[274] the three appellants complained that a job evaluation study had given their jobs an equal rating with that of their male counterparts. Apparently because of a Government incomes policy the employer did not apply the new job grade or salary range to the individuals in question. Although a job evaluation study required the co-operation of both employees and an employer, the consequences of a study were that, where jobs were found to be rated as equivalent, there should be a comparison of the respective terms and conditions. The job evaluation system does not, in itself, determine any terms of the women's contract. This is done in the subsequent comparison. Even where the results of the job evaluation study are not entirely accepted by the parties to the study, the existence of a *prima facie* valid job evaluation study would be enough for an employment tribunal to be bound by section 1(5).[275]

6.3.4 Work of equal value

This category applies if a woman is employed on work which, not being work falling into the categories of like work or work rated as equivalent, is nevertheless, in terms of the demands made on her, of equal value to that of a man in the same employment. Examples given in section 1(2)(c) EPA 1970 include demand under headings such as 'effort, skill and decision'. It will not be enough for an employer to cite the presence of workers, amongst the comparators, who fall into the categories of section 1(2)(a) or (2)(b) EPA 1970 in order to argue that they therefore cannot fall into section 1(2)(c). This is the situation that existed in *Pickstone v Freemans Ltd*[276] where female warehouse operatives claimed work of equal value with male warehouse operatives. To deprive the female employees of their right to a comparison for these reasons would be to deprive them of their rights under Article 141 EC.

If a complaint is made to an employment tribunal, then that tribunal has the option of appointing an expert from an independent panel to prepare a report on the equal value issue.[277] Section 2A(1A) EPA 1970 allows an employment tribunal to determine the question of equal value itself and the circumstances in which the parties can choose to

---

[273] See *Bromley v H and J Quick Ltd* [1988] IRLR 249 CA.

[274] [1980] IRLR 373 HL.

[275] See *Greene v Broxtowe District Council* [1977] ICR 241.

[276] [1988] IRLR 357 HL.

[277] Section 2A(1) EPA 1970; this was inserted by the Equal Pay (Amendment) Regulations 1983, SI 1983/1794 and amended by the Sex Discrimination and Equal Pay (Miscellaneous Amendments) Regulations 1996, SI 1996/438. The ECJ had held that section 1(5) EPA 1970 provided for equal pay for work of equal value, but only where there was a job classification system. The introduction of such a system was dependent upon the employer's agreement. Thus without the employer's consent there was no way that an employee could show that their post was of equal value to another. This, according to the ECJ, meant a denial of their rights and a conclusion that the EPA 1970 did not comply with the Equal Pay Directive; see Case 61/81 *Commission v United Kingdom* [1982] IRLR 333 ECJ.

adduce expert evidence are restricted. Section 2A(2) and (2A) EPA 1970 provide that if a job evaluation study has attributed different values to the work of the claimant and the comparator, the tribunal must conclude that the work is not of equal value unless it has reasonable grounds to suspect that the study discriminated on the grounds of sex or that there are other reasons why it is unreliable.[278]

6.3.5 Material factor defence

Section 1(3) EPA 1970 provides a 'material factor' or 'material difference' defence to an equal pay claim. This defence will assist an employer if they are able to show that the difference in pay is genuinely due to a material factor which is not the difference of sex.[279] In cases involving like work or work rated as equivalent, the factor 'must' be a material difference between the woman's case and the man's. However, in equal value claims the material factor 'may' be such a material difference.

Glasgow City Council v Marshall[280] concerned an equal pay claim between instructors and teachers in certain specialist schools. A number of female instructors claimed that they were employed on like work with male teachers and a male instructor claimed that he was employed on like work with a female teacher.[281] After a long hearing, over some 52 days, the instructors won their case at an employment tribunal. The employers appealed against the tribunal's decision on their defence under section 1(3) EPA 1970. Their case was based upon the fact that the sets of employees had their terms and agreements settled by different collective bargaining structures. The employers also, with the help of statistics, sought to show an absence of sex discrimination. This latter argument was not appealed against. It was this presumed lack of sex discrimination that undermined the instructors' case, however. The House of Lords held that to exclude matters of sex discrimination would mean that the EPA 1970 was concerned with one employee being paid less than another, rather than with arguments about whether a female employee was paid less than a male comparator. Lord Nicholls stated:

> The scheme of the Act is that a rebuttable presumption of sex discrimination arises once the gender based comparison shows that a woman, doing like work or work rated as equivalent or work of equal value to that of a man, is being paid or treated less favourably than the man.

The burden of proof, according to the court, then passes to the employer who needs to show that the reason for the differences is not tainted with sex. In order to satisfy the employment tribunal the employer must show that:

(1) the explanation or reason offered is genuine, and not a sham or pretence;
(2) the less favourable treatment is due to this reason, i.e. it is a material factor;

---

[278] See Employment Tribunals (Constitution and Rules of Procedure) (Amendment) Regulations 2004, SI 2004/2351, Schedule 6 which sets out the procedural rules which apply in equal value cases.
[279] See *Ministry of Defence v Armstrong* [2004] IRLR 672.
[280] [2000] IRLR 272 HL.
[281] Section 1(3) EPA 1970 applies the Act to a reverse situation where a male employee may make a claim against a female comparator.

(3) the reason for the difference is not the difference of sex. In order to do this, the employer will need to show that there is an absence of direct or indirect sex discrimination. Finally, the employer will need to show that the factor relied upon is a 'material difference', i.e. a significant and relevant difference between the woman's case and the man's case.[282] If there is evidence of sex discrimination the employer will need to show that the difference in pay can be objectively justified. If, however, as in this case, the employer shows an absence of sex discrimination, then the employer will not be required to justify the pay disparity.[283]

A material factor is said to be a 'significant and relevant' factor which is 'material' in a causative sense, when considering a pay difference.[284] Thus an employer can establish a section 1(3) defence by identifying the factors causally relevant to the pay disparity and showing that they are free of sex discrimination. One result of this was the somewhat surprising decision of the ECJ in *Cadman*[285] where the court held that where there was a disparity of pay between men and women as a result of using length of service as a criterion, then the employer did not need to establish specifically that using this criterion was appropriate in order to achieve a legitimate objective. The court did add that where a worker can show evidence that casts serious doubt as to whether recourse to the criterion of length of service was appropriate in the circumstances, then the employer may have to justify in detail how length of service leads to experience which enables the worker to perform his or her duties better. The problem of course is that generally women are often unable to achieve the same length of service as men, because it is women who are more likely to have career breaks as a result of caring responsibilities.

In *Strathclyde Regional Council v Wallace*[286] a group of nine female teachers claimed to be doing like work with higher paid principal teachers. They were part of a group which consisted of 134 teachers, comprising 81 men and 53 women. The difference in sex was not a factor that could be relied upon. The material factor was, amongst other matters, the financial constraints that the education authority found itself under. There is nothing, according to the court, in section 1(3) that requires the employer to justify the factors causing the disparity by showing that there was no other way in which they could have taken action to avoid the difference.

Nevertheless, if a sexually discriminatory practice is the cause of the disparity, the employer may still be able to rely on objective justification. In *Seymour-Smith*,[287] the effect of the, then, two-year continuous service qualification before a claim for unfair dismissal could be made was held to have had a disparate effect on women and amounted to indirect discrimination for the purposes of Article 141 EC. It could, nevertheless, be objectively

---

[282] See *McGregor v GMBATU* [1987] ICR 505 which considered that the work of the applicant was of equal value to the comparator, but that the comparator's long experience and exceptional knowledge was a material factor which justified the difference in pay.

[283] See *Nelson v Carillion Services Ltd* [2003] IRLR 428 and *Parliamentary Commissioner for Administration v Fernandez* [2004] IRLR 22.

[284] See *Rainey v Greater Glasgow Health Board* [1987] IRLR 26 HL.

[285] Case C-17/05 *Cadman v Health and Safety Executive* [2006] IRLR 969.

[286] [1998] IRLR 146 HL.

[287] *R v Secretary of State for Employment, ex parte Seymour-Smith and Perez (No 2)* [2000] IRLR 263 HL.

justified as a legitimate method of encouraging employers to recruit.[288] It will not be enough for the employer to show that they had no intention of discriminating against a woman on the grounds of her sex. Thus an employer who mistakenly placed a male employee at a point on a salary scale higher than that to which they were entitled could not use this mistake as evidence of a material factor when a female employee made a claim for equal pay.[289]

6.3.6 Enforcing equal pay

Any claim, including a claim for arrears of remuneration and damages, relating to equal pay may be made to an employment tribunal.[290] Compensation for non-economic loss is not recoverable in an equal pay claim, unlike claims under the Sex Discrimination Act. Thus there can be no damages for injury to feelings under the Equal Pay Act.[291] An employer may also apply to an employment tribunal, where there is a dispute about the effects of the equality clause in section 1(1) EPA 1970, for a declaration as to the rights of the employer and employees.[292] Section 2(4) EPA 1970 provides that claims must be lodged before a qualifying date. This is normally six months after the last day on which the claimant was employed. Where the proceedings relate to a period during which a stable employment relationship subsists, the qualifying date is six months after the day on which that relationship ended.[293]

The EA 2002 introduced a questionnaire procedure into equal pay claims, as already existed in those relating to sex, race and disability discrimination claims.[294] The questions and replies can be admitted as evidence in any subsequent employment tribunal proceedings. If the employment tribunal considers that the respondent deliberately, or without reasonable excuse, failed to reply to the questions in the time limit, then it can draw any inference that it thinks just and equitable.

Section 2(5) EPA 1970 had provided that a successful complainant could only be awarded remuneration or damages in respect of the two years prior to the time when proceedings were instituted. The limitation period was challenged and referred to the ECJ, who held that the two-year period was a restriction on the right to have a full and effective remedy for breach of Article 119 EEC (now 141 EC) and the Equal Pay Directive. The time

---

[288] See also Case 170/84 *Bilka-Kaufhaus v Weber von Harz* [1986] IRLR 317 ECJ where excluding part-timers from membership of a pension scheme was held to be justifiable on the grounds that the employer wished to discourage part-time recruitment; this decision would now have to take into account Directive 97/81/EC on part-time work; in Case 96/80 *Jenkins v Kingsgate (Clothing Production) Ltd* [1981] IRLR 228 the ECJ also stated that the differences between the pay of part-timers and full-timers was only contrary to Article 119 if it also amounted to indirect sex discrimination.

[289] *McPherson v Rathgael Centre for Children and Young People* [1991] IRLR 206 CA; it was suggested, *obiter*, that the employment tribunal might have considered whether the applicant was able to select an anomalous employee, rather than four other male employees who were on the same salary as her.

[290] Section 2(1) EPA 1970.

[291] *Council of the City of Newcastle upon Tyne v Allan* [2005] IRLR 504.

[292] Section 2(1A) EPA 1970.

[293] Section 2ZA EPA 1970. On the features which characterise a stable employment relationship see *Preston v Wolverhampton NHS Trust (No 3)* [2004] IRLR 96.

[294] Section 7B EPA 1970, introduced by section 42 EA 2002. See Equal Pay (Questions and Replies) Order 2003, SI 2003/722.

limit under the Sex Discrimination Act 1975, the Race Relations Act 1976 and the Disability Discrimination Act 1995 was six years. Section 2(5) EPA 1970 was, therefore, a unique restriction and the period for equal pay claims should also be extended to six years.[295] Sections 2(5) and 2ZB EPA 1970 now provide that sums can be awarded back to the 'arrears date' in respect of any time when there was unequal pay. Normally, the arrears date will be six years before the date on which the claim is made.

6.3.7 Code of Practice

The most recent version of the Equal Opportunities Commission Code of Practice on equal pay came into effect on 1 December 2003. A failure of any person to observe any provision of the Code will not render that person liable to any proceedings, but the failure will be taken into account in any proceedings before an employment tribunal.[296] Its purpose is to provide practical guidance and to recommend good practice to those with responsibility for the pay arrangements within organisations.

Further reading

Deakin, S. and Morris, G. *Labour Law* (4th edn, Hart Publishing, 2005), Chapter 6.

McColgan, A. *Discrimination Law: Text, Cases and Materials* (Hart Publishing, 2005), Chapters 6, 7, 9 and 10.

http://www.equalityhumanrights.com for the web site of the Commission for Equality and Human Rights.

http://www.berr.gov.uk/employment/discrimination/index.html for the Department for Business, Enterprise and Regulatory Reform web site on discrimination at work.

Visit **www.mylawchamber.co.uk/sargeant** to access legal updates, live web links and practice exam questions to test yourself on this chapter.

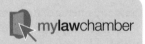

---

[295] *Levez v TH Jennings (Harlow Pools) Ltd (No 2)* [1999] IRLR 764.
[296] Section 56A(10) SDA 1975.

7

Age and Disability Discrimination

7.1 Introduction

Consideration of discrimination on the grounds of age and disability are considered separately from the grounds of sex and race because they are both more recent statutory innovations and because there is a close link between the two. The Disability Discrimination Act was not adopted until 1995 and the Employment Equality (Age) Regulations did not take effect until October 2006.

The likelihood of disabilities and chronic conditions increases with age. Older workers with disabilities have traditionally been more likely to lose their jobs in workplace re-organisations as a result of fewer opportunities to train and upgrade their skills. Age and disability are a barrier when trying to get a job, according to research carried out by the Ontario Human Rights Commission.[1] The number of people aged over 50 years who are long-term sick or disabled has been increasing. This is somewhat paradoxical because there has also been a continuing increase in life expectancy and in the health position of older people.[2] In the UK some 10.3% of working age men in the 20–24 years age band are disabled compared with 33.9% of men in the 50–64 years age group, suggesting a high correlation between age and disability.[3]

One paper by the European expert group on employment for disabled people reported as follows:[4]

> Disability is much more prevalent among older people: 63% of people with disabilities are older than 45. For non-disabled people the corresponding percentage is only 34%. So the disabled population is relatively old. This is particularly so in Germany, Greece, Italy and Spain.
>
> This pattern is mainly due to individuals' health condition deteriorating with age. Furthermore, many impairments leading to disability are acquired during a person's life. There may, in addition, be a 'generation factor', in so far as younger age groups experience better health and working conditions in their early working life and better health care and rehabilitation provisions, than their predecessors in older generations.

---

[1] See www.ohrc.on.ca

[2] House of Lords Select Committee on Economic Affairs, *Aspects of the economics of an ageing population*, November 2003, HL Paper 179–1, para 5.3.

[3] For further consideration of this see Malcolm Sargeant, 'Disability and age – multiple potential for discrimination' (2005) *International Journal of the Sociology of Law*, 33, 17.

[4] *The employment situation of people with disabilities in the European Union*, Executive Summary of Research Paper 2001; written by European Experts Group on employment for disabled people; commissioned by the DG Employment and Social Affairs.

People of working age with disabilities (%)

Men	Disabled	Not disabled
16–29	9.2	90.8
20–24	10.3	89.7
25–34	12.1	87.9
35–49	17.5	82.5
50–64	33.9	66.1
Total	19.3	80.7

Women		
16–29	8.4	91.6
20–24	10.6	89.4
25–34	13.6	86.4
35–49	19.5	80.5
50–64	33.6	66.4
Total	19.3	80.7

The Framework Directive on Equal Treatment in Employment and Occupation[5] included discrimination on the grounds of disability and age.

7.2 Age discrimination in employment

People of all ages can suffer from age discrimination, but it manifests itself mostly in discrimination against older people and young people. Article 1 of the Equal Treatment in Employment and Occupation Directive provides that the Directive's purpose is to lay down a general framework for combating discrimination in relation to a number of grounds including that of age. This is to be, according to Article 3, in relation to conditions for access to employment, access to vocational training, employment and working conditions and membership of employers' or workers' organisations. The approach is the same as other measures in relation to disability, sexual orientation, religion or belief. The Directive aims to introduce the 'principle of equal treatment' into all these areas, including age.

Article 4 provides for the possibility that a difference of treatment may be justified where there is 'a genuine and determining occupational requirement, provided that the objective is legitimate and the requirement is proportionate'. Article 6 refers to the justification of differences of treatment on the grounds of age. Differences in treatment on the basis of age may be justified if 'they are objectively and reasonably justified by a legitimate aim including legitimate employment policy, labour market and vocational treatment'. Examples given of such differences are:

- the setting of special conditions for access to employment and training, including dismissal and remuneration for young people, older workers and persons with caring responsibilities in order to promote their integration into the workforce;

---

[5] Directive 2000/78/EC.

- the fixing of minimum conditions of age, professional experience or seniority for access to employment or certain advantages linked to employment;
- the fixing of a maximum age for recruitment which is based either on the training needs of a post, or the need for a reasonable period before retirement.

It is interesting that it was felt necessary to spell out these exceptions to age discrimination in the Directive. It is perhaps symptomatic of the way that age discrimination is treated differently from other forms of discrimination. These provisions effectively state that some age discrimination is benign. There appears to be an economic or business imperative that suggests that more harm will be done if discrimination does not take place, rather than an imperative that states that age discrimination is wrong and can only be justified in exceptional circumstances. Effectively discrimination is not to be allowed to continue except those forms which are held to be for the economic good of business.

The Directive was due to be transposed into national law by December 2003, but there was a provision, in Article 18, for Member States to have an additional period of three years. The United Kingdom took advantage of this flexibility and finally transposed the Directive in October 2006 by adopting the Employment Equality (Age) Regulations 2006.[6]

7.2.1 The ageing population

Over the 25-year period between 1996 and 2021 the proportion of people in the United Kingdom over the age of 44 years will increase from 38% to 46%; the 45 to 59 age group will increase by almost one-quarter; the 60 to 74 age group will increase by over one-third and the 75 years and over group will increase by 28%. In contrast the 16 to 29 years age group will fall by 5.7%.[7] This process is a Europe-wide one, although the speed of the process is variable.[8] The number of people in the European Union aged between 50 and 64 years is projected to increase by 6.5 million during the next ten years.[9]

The relevance of these statistics here is that whilst the population is ageing and the proportion of older workers is increasing, there is also a decrease in the proportion of people who are economically active in the older age groups. Economically active is used here to describe those in work and those seeking work. Between 1966 and 1990 the labour force participation rate in the UK for workers aged 55 years and over declined from 53.8% to 36.5%.[10] Some 69% of those aged between 50 years and State Retirement Age (SRA) and 9% of those over SRA are in employment. This compares with an employment rate of 82% for those aged between 15 and 49 years. Older workers are more likely to work part time than the 25 to 49 age group, but less likely than the 16 to 25 years group. They are also more likely to be self-employed than any other age group. The average time spent unemployed was substantially longer for those over 50 than all ages. For example, those aged between

---

[6] SI 2006/1031.

[7] The immediate source was 'Tackling age bias: code or law?' *EOR* No 80 July/August 1998, although the ultimate source was ONS Monitor 10.3.98.

[8] See *Ageing and the Labour Market: Policies and Initiatives within the European Union*, Report of a European conference at the University of Twente, Netherlands, Eurolink Age, 1998.

[9] These and other statistics are available from Demographic Report, European Commission Office for Official Publications, September 1997, Luxembourg.

[10] See *Age and Employment*, Institute of Personnel Management, 1993.

55 and 59 spent an average of 44 weeks unemployed as opposed to 23 weeks for all ages. Two of the issues that are raised by these figures are, first, that older workers are likely to find it more difficult to obtain new employment and, secondly, that the proportion of economically active people declines the greater the age.

The Government consultation document on its Code of Practice on Age Diversity in Employment[11] concluded that 'it is clear that age discrimination against older workers does exist'. It is interesting to speculate at what age a person becomes an older worker. One study asked this question of organisations.[12] Five companies put 40 years as the starting point, four suggested 45 and five said 50 years. One company stated that anyone over 30 years was in the category of older worker. Further information suggested that these generalisations were qualified by consideration of occupation and gender. Forty-something was not necessarily old for a management position, but might be for another occupation. Similarly women seemed to become 'older' at an earlier age. One respondent suggested that when women returned to work after children in their mid-thirties that they might be classified as an older worker.

7.2.2 The Employment Equality (Age) Regulations 2006

7.2.2.1 The meaning of discrimination

As with the other Regulations protection is offered against direct and indirect discrimination, harassment and victimisation. The definition of direct and indirect discrimination is the same. The difference is that, unlike other forms of discrimination[13], it is permissible to directly discriminate on the grounds of age in some circumstances. There is a requirement to show that the less favourable treatment is a 'proportionate means of achieving a legitimate aim'.[14]

In 2005 the Government had proposed some examples where direct discrimination could be justified as a proportionate means of achieving a legitimate aim. These were, first, the setting of age requirements to 'ensure the vocational integration of people in a particular age group'. This might include, presumably, the lower rate of the national minimum wage paid to those under the age of 22 years. Secondly, the fixing of a minimum age to qualify for certain employment advantages in order to recruit or retain older people. Thirdly, the fixing of a maximum age for recruitment or promotion based on the training requirements of the post and 'on the need for a reasonable period in post before retirement'. All three of these exceptions are, of course, debatable, but they do effectively permit direct discrimination on the grounds of age in the interests of both diversity and, perhaps, acceptability.

The further matter for concern is that this was not an exhaustive list. The 2005 consultation document stated that 'we would not want to prevent employers or providers of vocational training from demonstrating that age-related practices could be justified by

---

[11] First published in 1999 and subsequently updated.
[12] Hilary Metcalf and Mark Thompson, 'Older workers: employers' attitudes and practices', Institute of Manpower Studies, Report No 194, 1990.
[13] Except in relation to genuine occupational qualification.
[14] Regulation 3(1).

reference to aims other than those in such a list'. An example contained in the 2005 consultation document was that 'economic factors such as business needs and considerations of efficiency may also be legitimate aims'. It is not conceivable that these exceptions would be allowed for sex, race or disability discrimination or on the grounds of sexual orientation or religion or belief.

7.2.2.2 Further exceptions

Part 2 of the Regulations deals with discrimination in employment and vocational training and provides that it is unlawful to discriminate against applicants and employees, including harassment, on the grounds of age. However, regulation 7(4) provides that applicants who would become employees[15] can be excluded from protection if they are older than the employer's normal retirement age or, if the employer does not have such an age, 65 years. It also excludes those who, at the date of application, are within a period of six months of such an age. The justification for this is that there would be little point stopping an employer discriminating on recruitment if the same employer could legitimately discriminate (without it amounting to discrimination) under regulation 30 (exception for retirement). All applicants over the age of $64^1/_2$ years may be turned down on the grounds of their age only. Difficulties in obtaining work are amongst the most common forms of discrimination suffered by older people and some discrimination in this area is allowed to continue under the new Regulations.

Part 2 also contains an exception, as do other grounds of discrimination, for genuine occupational requirement. The Government has stated that it was likely to be construed narrowly and in one consultation gave the example of the acting profession.

Part 4 of the Age Regulations is devoted to 'general exceptions to parts 2 and 3'.[16] These are in addition to those already mentioned in respect of direct discrimination. There are exceptions for complying with statutory authority, safeguarding national security and positive action.[17] There are also exceptions relating to the national minimum wage, certain benefits based on length of service, retirement, the provision of enhanced redundancy payments and the provision of life assurance to retired workers.[18]

Service related pay and benefits may include salary scales, holiday entitlement, company cars etc, all or some of which may be related to length of service. Without some action benefits linked to length of service may amount to age discrimination as younger people who have not served the necessary time required may suffer detriment. Regulation 32 provides that an employer may award benefits using length of service as the criterion for selecting who should benefit from the award. First, there is no need to justify any differences related to service less than five years. Where it exceeds five years it needs to fulfil 'a business need of the undertaking'

> for example, by encouraging the loyalty or motivation, or rewarding the experience, of some or all of his workers.[19]

---

[15] Which in this case means those defined in section 230(1) Employment Rights Act 1996 and Crown and parliamentary staff.

[16] Part 3 is concerned with 'Other Unlawful Acts' including aiding unlawful acts and the liability of employers and principals.

[17] Regulations 27–29.

[18] Regulations 30–34.

[19] Regulation 32(2).

The argument is that having pay scales of a certain length is justified to recognise experience and, perhaps, seniority. It can also be argued strongly that workers who have been with an employer for five years should receive some preferential treatment compared to those who have just joined an organisation. These are, however, exceptions to a rule requiring the principle of equal treatment.

There is also a general exemption concerning the national minimum wage so that employers can pay the lower rate for those under 22 and under 18 years without it amounting to age discrimination.[20] It is, of course, age discrimination against the younger person, but he or she will be prevented from claiming this. The intention is to help younger workers to find jobs, by making them more attractive to employers. One question is whether such a measure is a proportionate response to the problem. In *Mangold v Helm*[21] the European Court of Justice considered a German law which restricted the use of fixed-term contracts, but did not apply these restrictions to those aged 52 years and over. The court accepted that the purpose of this legislation was to help promote the vocational integration of unemployed older workers and that this was a 'legitimate public-interest objective'. It is not only the objective that needs to be legitimate, but the means used to achieve the objective need to be 'appropriate and necessary'. The problem with the German law was that it applied to all workers of 52 years and above, whether unemployed or not. The result was that a significant body of workers was permanently excluded from 'the benefit of stable employment' available to other workers. The court then stated:

> In so far as such legislation takes the age of the worker concerned as the only criterion [for the application of a fixed-term contract of employment], when it has not been shown that fixing an age threshold, as such, regardless of any other consideration linked to the structure of the labour market in question or the personal situation of the person concerned, is objectively necessary to the attainment of the objective [which is the vocational integration of older workers], it must be considered to go beyond what is appropriate and necessary in order to attain the objective pursued.

There must be a question about whether the application of a universal lower minimum wage for younger people is an appropriate and necessary response to the problem of youth unemployment.

One of the difficult issues for the Age Regulations was the question of what to do about the age related aspects of redundancy payments. The Government had proposed removing these and paying a uniform rate for all. Presumably when faced with the prospect of levelling upwards, so that no group would be worse off, the Government decided that the age related aspects can be objectively justifiable. The lower and upper age limits to entitlement are to be removed and employers are to be allowed to enhance payments.[22]

7.2.2.3 Retirement

The Framework Directive does not say a great deal about retirement ages. Paragraph 14 of the Preamble states that the Directive shall be 'without prejudice to national provisions laying down retirement ages'. Article 6.2 allows for the fixing of ages for invalidity and

---

[20] Regulation 31.
[21] Case C-144/04 [2006] IRLR 143.
[22] Regulation 33.

retirement schemes, and the use of ages for actuarial calculations, without it constituting age discrimination. Article 8.2 provides that any measures implementing the Directive shall not lessen the protection against discrimination that already exists in the Member State.

The UK, in implementing the Directive, adopted a default retirement age of 65 years. Retirement below the age of 65 years will need to be objectively justified and presumably this will be entirely possible and proper in some cases. Section 98 of the Employment Rights Act 1996 was amended to add another fair reason for dismissal which will be 'retirement of the employee'. There is, however, no requirement to go through any statutory dismissal procedure. This is replaced by a statutory retirement procedure as outlined in new sections 98ZA to 98ZF of the Employment Rights Act.

For retirement to be taken as the only reason for dismissal, it must take place on the 'intended date of retirement'. There is still the opportunity for the employee to claim that the real reason for dismissal was some other reason and that the planned retirement would not have taken place but for this other reason, or if the dismissal amounts to unlawful discrimination under the Regulations. The operative retirement date is 65 years unless there is an alternative date which is the normal retirement age, in which case it is that date.[23] There is then a procedure in which the employer and employee must participate. Failure on the employer's part in this regard may render the dismissal unfair.

The statutory retirement procedure comprises a duty on the employer to consider a request from the employee to work beyond retirement.[24] There is a duty upon the employer to inform the employee of the intended retirement date and the employee's right to make a request. There is then a statutory right for the employee to request that he or she be not retired on the intended retirement date. The employer then has a duty to consider this request. This is done by holding a meeting with the employee, unless not reasonably practicable. There is also an appeal procedure for the employee if turned down and timescales for meetings and decisions. Most notably there is an absence of criteria to be used by the employer in their consideration of the employee's request. Their only duty is to follow the procedure and consider it.

Thus the situation will be that where there is no consensual retirement, the employer may dismiss the employee and this dismissal will be a 'fair' dismissal provided it takes place on the retirement date and the employer has followed the statutory retirement procedure for consideration of any request from the employee not to retire. The most likely outcome of any decision by the employer not to require the employee to retire at the intended retirement date is for the employer to agree a new date. In effect this will allow the employee to continue his or her contract for a fixed term.[25]

Thus older workers, i.e. those over 65 or the normal retirement date, will continue to be discriminated against. This will be as a result of the Age Regulations which were, perhaps ostensibly, intended to stop age discrimination. Older workers will have no security, knowing that their employer can legitimately dismiss them at each new retirement date,

---

[23] Sections 98ZA–98ZE Employment Rights Act 1996 as amended.
[24] Schedule 6 to the Age Regulations; Schedule 7 makes provision for transitional arrangements.
[25] Schedule 6 to the Age Regulations.

provided a procedure of information and consideration is followed. The Government has promised to review the need for a default retirement age by 2011.

7.3 Disability discrimination

The Framework Directive on Equal Treatment in Employment and Occupation included proposals to combat discrimination on the grounds of disability 'with a view to putting into effect in the Member States the principle of equal treatment'.[26] In particular it provided[27] that employers should have a duty of 'reasonable accommodation'. This means that employers are obliged to take steps, when needed, to ensure that a person with a disability could have access to, participate in, have advancement in and undergo training. The only possible exception to this duty, according to the Directive, is if this places a 'disproportionate burden' on the employer. Thus the Directive permits, in certain circumstances, positive discrimination in favour of the disabled employee or applicant.

The Disability Discrimination Act 1995 (the DDA 1995) was the first measure to outlaw discrimination against disabled people in the United Kingdom and included an obligation upon the employer to make adjustments (see below).[28] The Act, which preceded the Framework Directive, gives disabled people rights in employment and other areas. The Act provided originally for a National Disability Council,[29] whose task was to advise the Government 'on matters relevant to the elimination of discrimination against disabled persons and persons who have a disability'. One of the criticisms of the Act was that this was an advisory body, which did not have the powers of investigation and enforcement held by the Equal Opportunities Commission and the Commission for Racial Equality. The position was changed with the Disability Rights Commission Act 1999 (DRCA 1999), which abolished the National Disability Council and replaced it with a Disability Rights Commission[30] (see below). The Disability Rights Commission itself has now been absorbed into the new Commission for Equality and Human Rights, which was established by the Equality Act 2006. The DDA 1995 was further amended by the Disability Discrimination Act 1995 (Amendment) Regulations 2003,[31] much of which took effect from 1 October 2004, and the Disability Discrimination Act 2005, which included a duty on public authorities to have regard to the need to eliminate disability discrimination in the carrying out of their functions.[32]

The need for action is illustrated by the fact that there are over 6.8 million disabled persons of working age in Great Britain,[33] who account for nearly one-fifth of the working age population in Great Britain, but only for one-eighth of all those in employment. When employed they are more likely than non-disabled people to be working part-time or as self-employed. Disabled people are over six times as likely as non-disabled people to be out of

---

[26] Council Directive 2000/78/EC OJ L 303/16.
[27] Article 5.
[28] The approach prior to the DDA 1995 had been to establish quotas of disabled people in an employer's workforce: see Disabled Persons (Employment) Act 1944; this approach failed.
[29] Section 50 DDA 1995.
[30] Section 1 DRCA 1999.
[31] SI 2003/1673.
[32] Section 49A DDA 1995.
[33] Disability Rights Commission Disability Briefing January 2004 (figures compiled from the Labour Force Survey). See now www.equalityhumanrights.com.

work and claiming benefit. Employment rates do, however, vary with the type of disability. Some types, such as those concerned with diabetes, skin conditions and hearing problems, are associated with relatively high employment rates. Other types, such as those associated with mental illness and learning disabilities, have much lower employment rates.

One survey on the effectiveness of the employment provisions of the DDA 1995 shows that, at the time of the report, only 23% of the claims disposed of at employment tribunal hearings were successful. Those claimants who were legally represented did better with a 39.7% success rate for those represented by a barrister and 32.1% for those represented by a solicitor. In contrast only 15.6% of applicants in person were successful. Of all the DDA cases, some 68.6% concerned dismissal compared with 9.2% which concerned recruitment. Medical evidence was considered in just over 50% of cases. In 33.9% of cases where it was claimed that the employer should have made a reasonable adjustment (see below), the adjustment in question was a transfer to an existing vacancy.[34]

Section 53A provided for the Disability Rights Commission to give practical guidance on how to avoid discrimination in relation to the DDA 1995 and to promote equality of opportunity. The current Code of Practice was issued by the Disability Rights Commission and took effect in October 2004 (hereafter referred to as the DRC Code of Practice; now taken over by the Commission for Equality and Human Rights).[35] Failure to observe the provisions of the Code does not in itself make a person liable to proceedings, but any provision of the Code that appears to be relevant to any question arising in any proceedings will be taken into account.[36] In addition further clarification is given in the Disability Discrimination (Meaning of Disability) Regulations 1996 and the Disability Discrimination (Employment) Regulations 1996.[37]

7.3.1 Meaning of disability

A disabled person is a person who has a disability,[38] or has had a past disability.[39] According to section 1(1) DDA 1995 a person has a disability if he or she has a

physical or mental impairment which has a substantial and long-term adverse effect on his ability to carry out normal day to day activities.

Thus the tests are, first, that there must be a physical or mental impairment; secondly, that it must have a substantial adverse effect; thirdly, that it must have a long-term adverse effect and, finally, this adverse effect must relate to the ability to carry out normal day to day activities. Schedule 1 DDA 1995 provides some meaning to these terms. Certain addictions and conditions are not to be treated as impairments for the purposes of the DDA 1995. These include:[40]

---

[34] Incomes Data Services, *Monitoring the Disability Discrimination Act 1995. First Interim Report to the DFEE,* March 2000.
[35] The Disability Discrimination Codes of Practice (Employment and Occupation, and Trade Organisations and Qualifications Bodies) Appointed Day Order 2004, SI 2004/2302.
[36] Section 53A(8) and (8A) DDA 1995.
[37] SI 1996/1455 and SI 1996/1456.
[38] Section 1(2) DDA 1995.
[39] Section 2 and Schedule 2 DDA 1995.
[40] See SI 1996/1455 above.

(1) addictions to alcohol, nicotine or any other substance, unless the addiction was originally the result of medically prescribed drugs or treatment;

(2) a tendency to set fires, to steal or to physical or sexual abuse of other persons;

(3) exhibitionism and voyeurism;

(4) seasonal allergic rhinitis (asthma), although it can be taken into account where it aggravates other conditions;

(5) severe disfigurement which results from tattooing or piercing.

In *Goodwin v The Patent Office*[41] the EAT held that the DDA 1995 requires the employment tribunal to look at the evidence by reference to four different conditions or questions:

(1) Whether the applicant has a mental or physical impairment. 'Mental impairment' includes an impairment resulting from or consisting of a mental illness only if the mental illness is a clinically well-recognised illness.[42] One route to establishing the existence of a mental impairment is to show proof of a mental illness classified in the World Health Organisation International Classification of Diseases (WHOICD). Many parts of its classification require specific symptoms to manifest themselves over a specified period. Thus just claiming 'clinical depression' without further clarification is unlikely to be sufficient.[43] Similarly a failure to establish that back pain was the result of a physical or mental impairment put it outside the scope of the DDA. The word impairment is to have its ordinary and natural meaning and may result from an illness or consist of an illness. The onus is on the employee to show an impairment.[44] *Greenwood v British Airways plc*[45] considered a complaint from an employee who was told that one of the reasons for a failure to gain promotion was the employee's sickness record. The employee suffered flashbacks which could prevent him from working and affected his ability to concentrate. After a failure to gain promotion the employee was absent through depression. The employment tribunal decided to look only at matters at the time when the employee was rejected for promotion. The tribunal held that the applicant was not disabled at the time of the act complained of. The EAT concluded that the employment tribunal had erred in law and had wrongly decided that events subsequent to the act complained of were not relevant. The EAT concluded that one needed to look at the whole period up to the employment tribunal hearing to assess whether a person had a long-term impairment. Considering the whole period does not necessarily mean an investigation of the causes of the disability. In *Power v Panasonic UK Ltd*[46] an areas sales manager had the geographical area for which she was responsible expanded, following a reorganisation. She became ill and was eventually dismissed after a long period of absence. It was not disputed that during her long

---

[41] [1999] IRLR 4.

[42] Schedule 1 paragraph 1(1) DDA 1995.

[43] *Morgan v Staffordshire University* [2002] IRLR 190.

[44] *McNicol v Balfour Beatty Rail Maintenance Ltd* [2002] IRLR 711; in this case a trackman claimed that the vehicle that he was driving had gone over a pothole and jolted his back. He could not, however, show a mental or physical impairment that was the cause of the back pain that he then continued to suffer.

[45] [1999] IRLR 600.

[46] [2003] IRLR 151.

absence she was both depressed and drinking heavily. The tribunal concerned itself with whether the drinking or the depression came first, but the EAT stated that it was not necessary to consider how the impairment was caused. What was relevant was to discover whether the person had a disability within the meaning of the DDA at the relevant time. Even if the applicant were not held to be disabled under section 1(1) DDA 1995, then he or she could be held to have had a past disability in accord with Schedule 2 DDA 1995. Schedule 2 paragraph 5(2) provides that where an impairment ceases to have a substantial adverse effect, then it may be treated as continuing if the effect recurs. This modifies Schedule 1 paragraph 2(2) which provides that where an impairment ceases to have a substantial adverse effect on a person's ability to carry out normal day to day activities, it is still to be treated as continuing to have that effect if it is likely to recur.[47]

(2) Whether the impairment affects the applicant's ability to carry out normal day to day activities. The fact that an applicant can still carry them out does not mean that the individual's ability has not been impaired. If the individual can only carry them out with difficulty, then there may be an adverse effect. An impairment is said to have an effect upon a person's ability to carry out normal day to day activities only if it affects mobility; manual dexterity; physical co-ordination; continence; the ability to lift or move everyday objects; speech, hearing or eyesight; memory or ability to concentrate, learn or understand; perception of the risk of physical danger.[48] This will include the impairments that affect the individual's ability to carry out duties at work, particularly if they include these 'normal day to day activities'.[49] In *Hewett v Motorola Ltd*[50] the complainant, an engineer, was diagnosed as having autism in the form of Asperger's Syndrome. He argued that, without medication or medical treatment, his memory would be affected and he would have difficulties in concentrating, learning and under-standing.[51] The EAT held that one had to have a broad view of the meaning of under-standing and that any person who had their normal human interaction affected might also be regarded as having their understanding affected. What is 'normal' may be best defined as anything that is not abnormal or unusual. It does not depend upon whether the majority of people do it, for example, there may be some activities that only women usually do and the fact that men do not do them does not stop them being 'normal day to day activities'.[52] The DRC Code of Practice gives guidance as to what constitutes 'day to day' activities,[53] but this guidance is intended to be illustrative and not exhaustive. It is for the employment tribunal to arrive at its own assessment, rather than relying too much on this or medical opinions about what constitutes such activities.[54]

---

[47] Schedule 1 paragraph 3 provides that an impairment consisting of a severe disfigurement is to be treated as having a substantial adverse effect, although this does not include a tattoo which has not been removed or a non-medical piercing of the body – see SI 1996/1455.
[48] Schedule 1 paragraph 4 DDA 1995.
[49] *Law Hospital NHS Trust v Rush* [2001] IRLR 611, where the work of a nurse was stated to include some normal day to day activities.
[50] [2004] IRLR 545.
[51] See Schedule 1 paragraph 4g to the DDA 1995 which includes in the list of day to day activities 'memory or ability to concentrate, learn or understand'.
[52] *Ekpe v Commissioner of Police* [2001] IRLR 605.
[53] Appendix B.
[54] See *Vicaray v British Telecommunications plc* [1999] IRLR 680.

(3) Whether the adverse effect is 'substantial'. If an impairment is likely to have a substantial adverse effect upon the ability of the person concerned to carry out normal day to day activities, but does not do so because of measures taken to treat or correct it, it is still to be treated as having the adverse effect.[55] Such measures can include counselling sessions for an individual who was suffering from a form of depression. This was held to be the case in *Kapadia v London Borough of Lambeth*[56] where an employment tribunal failed to find that a person was disabled within the terms of section 1(1) DDA 1995, despite uncontested medical opinion. The EAT held that the employment tribunal had erred in doing so and had arrived at a judgment based on how the complainant seemed when giving evidence, although in *Goodwin* the EAT stated that this was something that the employment tribunal could take into account. The Court of Appeal, in this case, confirmed this approach and held that just because the symptoms are kept under control by medication, this does not stop a person suffering a substantial adverse effect on their day to day activities,[57] although there is a need for the individual to show that he or she would suffer from this effect without the medication or treatment.[58] The DDA 1995 was amended by the DDA 2005 to ensure that those suffering from a progressive condition, specifically cancer, HIV infection or multiple sclerosis, are deemed to have a disability. This means that they would not, as previously, need to show that it had a substantial adverse effect on their ability to carry out day to day activities.[59]

(4) Whether the adverse effect was long-term. According to Schedule 1 paragraph 2(1) DDA 1995, the effect of an impairment is long-term if it has lasted at least 12 months or is likely to be at least 12 months or if it is likely to last for the rest of the affected person's life. *Cosgrove v Caesar & Howie*[60] concerned a legal secretary who had been absent from work for over a year due to depression, prior to her dismissal. The question was whether she had been treated less favourably for a reason related to disability. The EAT held[61] that the questions to be asked were, first, to determine the material reason for a person's dismissal, secondly, is the material reason related to her disability and, finally, would the employer have dismissed some other to whom the material reason did not apply? The material reason for the employee's dismissal was her absence on medical grounds, which amounted to a disability, and there would have been no reason to dismiss someone to whom the reason did not apply.

There is also an important issue concerning 'associative' discrimination. *Attridge Law v Coleman*[62] concerned a legal secretary who had a son suffering from disabilities. She alleged that she had suffered discrimination under the DDA as a result of being a carer for her

---

[55] Schedule 1 paragraph 6(1) DDA 1995; see *Abadeh v British Telecommunications plc* [2001] IRLR.
[56] [2000] IRLR 14.
[57] [2000] IRLR 699 CA; see also *Leonard v Southern Derbyshire Chamber of Commerce* [2001] IRLR 19 where the EAT held that a tribunal should concentrate on what a person could not do or had difficulty doing.
[58] *Woodrup v London Borough of Southwark* [2003] IRLR 111 where an individual failed to produce medical evidence that the discontinuation of her psychotherapy treatment would have a substantial adverse effect.
[59] See para 6A Schedule 1 DDA 1995.
[60] [2001] IRLR 653.
[61] Following *Clark v TDG Ltd t/a Novacold* [1999] IRLR 318 CA.
[62] [2007] IRLR 89.

disabled son. She was not disabled herself. She argued that the Framework Directive offered protection from discrimination on 'the grounds of disability' and that the DDA 1995 should be construed broadly so as to implement this, and thus provide her with protection. The issue was referred by the tribunal to the European Court of Justice.

7.3.2 Discrimination

Part II of the DDA 1995 concerns employment. Prior to 2004 there was an exemption for small employers, employing fewer than 15 employees. This has now been removed.[63] Employment is defined as being under a contract of service or apprenticeship or a contract personally to do any work.[64] Thus there is a wider definition than just employee, following the approach in the SDA 1975 and the RRA 1976.

It is unlawful for an employer to discriminate against a disabled[65] person in:

(1) the arrangements which are made for the purpose of determining who should be offered employment;[66]
(2) the terms in which that person is offered employment; and
(3) refusing to offer, or deliberately not offering, employment.[67]

It is also unlawful for an employer to discriminate against a disabled person who is employed in, first, the terms of employment offered; secondly, in the opportunities afforded for promotion, transfer or training; thirdly, by refusing, or deliberately not affording, any such opportunity; and, finally, by dismissing the individual or subjecting them to any other detriment.[68] These provisions apply in relation to an establishment in Great Britain.[69]

In *British Sugar plc v Kirker*[70] an individual selected for redundancy claimed that they had been discriminated against because of a visual impairment, suffered since birth. The employers had carried out an assessment exercise in order to select those to be dismissed. This had consisted of marking employees against a set of factors. The complainant claimed that the marks attributed to them were the result of a subjective view arising out of the disability. The employee had scored 0 out of 10 for promotion potential and 0 for performance and competence. The EAT observed that such marks would indicate that the employee did not always achieve the required standard of performance and required close supervision. Yet the employee had never been criticised for poor performance and did not have any supervision. There was no need to consider the scores of other employees as the

---

[63] Regulation 7 Disability Discrimination Act 1995 (Amendment) Regulations 2003, SI 2003/1673.

[64] Section 68 DDA 1995; see *South East Sheffield Citizens Advice Bureau v Grayson* [2004] IRLR 353 where CAB volunteer workers were held not to be employees and thus the employer fell outside the scope of the DDA 1995 under the old rule that exempted employers with fewer than 15 employees.

[65] It is also unlawful to instruct or pressurise another person over whom the employer has authority to discriminate or harass on the grounds of a person's disability: section 16C DDA 1995.

[66] Section 16B DDA 1995 also makes unlawful discriminatory advertisements.

[67] Section 4(1) DDA 1995.

[68] Section 4(2) DDA 1995; section 4(4) provides that subsection (2) will not apply to any benefits, including facilities and services, that are offered to a section of the public that includes the employee, when those benefits are different to those offered by the employer to employees.

[69] Section 4(6) DDA 1995; see also sections 68(4) and 68(4A) concerning the meaning of 'Great Britain'.

[70] [1998] IRLR 624.

DDA 1995 did not require comparisons. It was clear that this individual had been under-marked by reason of their disability. The fact that many of the relevant events took place before the coming into force of the DDA 1995 did not stop the employment tribunal from looking at them in order to help draw inferences about the employer's conduct.[71]

Similar provisions apply to contract workers.[72] It is unlawful for a 'principal', in relation to contract work, to discriminate against a disabled person. In *Abbey Life Assurance Co Ltd v Tansell*[73] the principal was described as the 'end user' in a situation where there was an unbroken chain of contracts between a person 'A' who makes work available for doing by individuals who are employed by another person who supplies them under a contract made with 'A'. In this case a contract computer person was employed by their own limited liability company which had a contract with a consultancy who supplied their services to an end user. Taking a purposive approach to the statute, the EAT and the Court of Appeal concluded that it was the end user who should be the target for the complaint as the agency would simply justify their actions by reference to the instructions of 'A'. Similar rules apply to office holders,[74] partnerships,[75] barristers and advocates.[76]

The DDA 1995 makes a number of forms of discrimination unlawful.[77] These are

- direct discrimination;[78]
- disability related discrimination;[79]
- victimisation;[80]
- failure to comply with a duty to make reasonable adjustments.[81]

7.3.2.1 Direct discrimination

Direct discrimination results from treatment of a disabled person when:

(1) it is on the grounds of the person's disability;
(2) it is treatment which is less favourable than that given to, or that would have been given to, a person not having that particular disability; and
(3) the relevant circumstances, including the abilities, of the person being used as the comparator are the same as, or not materially different from, those of the disabled person.

Thus the treatment must be on the grounds of the person's disability. There is no requirement for it to be a deliberate and conscious decision to discriminate. Indeed much discrimination may be the result of prejudices about which the discriminator is unaware.[82]

---

[71] See also *Kent County Council v Mingo* [2000] IRLR 90 where a redeployment policy that gave preference to redundant or potentially redundant employees, in preference to those with a disability, amounted to discrimination in accordance with the DDA 1995.
[72] Section 4B DDA 1995.
[73] [2000] IRLR 387 CA.
[74] Sections 4C–4F DDA 1995.
[75] Sections 6A–6C DDA 1995.
[76] Sections 7A–7D DDA 1995.
[77] See also Chapters 4 and 5 of the Code of Practice which gives a very good description of these types of discrimination with many examples, some of which are used here.
[78] Section 3A(5) DDA 1995.
[79] Section 3A(1) DDA 1995.
[80] Section 55 DDA 1995.
[81] Section 4A DDA 1995.
[82] The Code of Practice gives examples of this in its Chapter 4.

The comparator must be someone who does not have the same disability and may be someone who is not disabled. It is important, however, that the comparator's relevant circumstances, including his or her abilities, are the same as, or not materially different, to those of the disabled person. It is not necessary to identify an actual person to use as a comparator. Where one with similar relevant circumstances is not available, then a hypothetical comparator can be used.

An example of direct discrimination given in the DRC Code of Practice is one where a person who becomes disabled takes six months' sick leave because of his or her disability, and is dismissed by the employer. A non-disabled fellow employee also takes six months' sick leave, because of a broken leg, but is not dismissed. The non-disabled employee is an appropriate comparator because the relevant circumstances are the same, i.e. having six months' sick leave. Direct discrimination has occurred because of the less favourable treatment of the disabled person.

In relation to direct discrimination there is no justification defence for the employer. Treatment that amounts to direct discrimination cannot be justified, as it can in some other circumstances (see below).[83]

7.3.2.2 Disability related discrimination

Section 3A(1) DDA 1995 states that an employer discriminates against a disabled person when:

(1) it is for a reason related to his or her disability;
(2) the treatment is less favourable than the treatment given, or that would have been given, to others to whom the reason does not or would not apply, and;
(3) the employer cannot show that the treatment in question can be justified.

The phrase 'disability related discrimination' is not used in the Act, but is used in the DRC Code of Practice to describe discrimination that falls under section 3A(1) DDA 1995, but which does not amount to direct discrimination. It therefore has a wider scope and includes less favourable treatment which does not amount to direct discrimination. A good example of this is given in the DRC Code of Practice:[84]

> A disabled woman is refused an administrative job because she cannot type. She cannot type because she has arthritis. A non-disabled person who was unable to type would also have been turned down. The disability related reason for the less favourable treatment is the woman's inability to type, and the correct comparator is a person to whom the reason does not apply – that is, someone who can type. Such a person would not have been refused the job. Nevertheless, the disabled woman has been treated less favourably for a disability related reason and this will be unlawful unless it can be justified.

Importantly, this discrimination is not direct discrimination, because, in that case, the correct comparator would have been someone who did not have arthritis and who had similar disabilities, i.e. someone who could not type. This comparator would not have obtained the job either, so there would not have been less favourable treatment. In *O'Hanlon*[85] an employee who was disabled was affected by the employer's sick pay policy.

---

[83] Section 3A(4) DDA 1995.
[84] Chapter 4 DRC Code of Practice 2004.
[85] *O'Hanlon v Commissioners for HM Revenue & Customs* [2007] IRLR 404.

The employer paid for the first six months of sickness on full pay and a further six months on half pay in any one year, subject to a maximum of 12 months' paid sickness absence in any period of four years. In this case the employee had, in a four-year period, a total of 365 days' absence, some 321 of which related to her disability. One of the employee's claims was that the failure to pay her full pay amounted to a failure to make a reasonable adjustment. The additional pressure caused by the financial hardship added to the depression from which she suffered. Her claim was turned down by the Court of Appeal because the Court stated that it would be invidious for an employer to assess the financial hardship of the employee or the stress resulting from the lack of money. It had not been alleged that she was being treated in any different way from others who might be absent for a disability related reason.

Any justification under section 3A(1)(b) needs to be material to the circumstances of the case and substantial.[86] There are strict limitations to any justification defence. First, it cannot be used in cases of direct discrimination.[87] Secondly, it cannot be used to justify any failure in the employer's duty to make adjustments (see below).[88] There may be situations when the employer will still not be able to justify the treatment, even if there are material and substantial justifications for the less favourable treatment. This may occur if the employer has failed in the duty to make reasonable adjustments. The employer will, in such circumstances, need to show that the material and substantial circumstances would have applied even if the adjustments had been made.[89]

There is a need to establish a causal link between any discriminatory act and an employer's justification. Having no knowledge of a disability may not be a sufficient justification, given that the discriminatory act relates to the way in which the employer treats the employee.[90] In *London Borough of Hammersmith & Fulham v Farnsworth*,[91] an employer had failed to inquire further about an applicant's health record on the grounds of confidentiality. The EAT concluded that this failure was not relevant, but, in any case, the applicant had been examined by a doctor on behalf of the employer. This examination put the doctor into the position of being the employer's agent, so the doctor having knowledge was the same as the potential employer having it. The relationship between the disability and the treatment received by the employee is not a subjective one, i.e. based on what the employer perceived. It is an objective test as to whether there is a relationship between the treatment and the disability. If such a relationship exists the employer's knowledge, or lack of knowledge, is not relevant. Thus an employer who dismissed an employee after the individual had been absent for almost a year really ought to have considered the possibility of disablement, rather than claiming a lack of knowledge about the disability.[92]

---

[86] Section 3A(3) DDA 1995.
[87] Section 3A(4) and (5) DDA 1995 define direct discrimination as treating a disabled person less favourably than the employer treats or would treat a person not having that particular disability whose relevant circumstances, including abilities, are the same as, or not materially different from, those of the disabled person.
[88] Section 3A(6) DDA 1995.
[89] See Chapter 6 of the DRC Code of Practice 2004.
[90] See *Callagan v Glasgow City Council* [2001] IRLR 724.
[91] [2000] IRLR 691.
[92] See *HJ Heinz Co Ltd v Kenrick* [2000] IRLR 144.

The correct process for showing justification is, first, the disabled applicant shows less favourable treatment, such as dismissal, including constructive dismissal;[93] secondly, the employer shows that the treatment is justified if the reason for the decision is both material to the circumstances of the case and substantial, and that he has not, without justification, failed to comply with any duty under section 4A (duty to make adjustments). 'Material circumstances of the case' can include the circumstances of both the employer and the employee.[94]

Consideration of the statutory criteria may involve an assessment of whether there was evidence on the basis of which a decision could properly be taken by the employer. This may consist of appropriate medical evidence or undertaking a risk assessment. If the decision was not based upon such evidence or was irrational in some other way, the employment tribunal may hold the reason for the decision to be insufficient or unjustified.[95]

The Court of Appeal also stated that the function of employment tribunals under section 5(3) DDA 1995 is not very different from the task that they have to carry out with respect to unfair dismissals (see Chapter 5). In the latter they are required to adopt the range of reasonable responses test in deciding whether a dismissal was reasonable. In the case of section 5(3) they have to decide on the materiality and substantiality of the employer's decision. In both cases the employment tribunal might have come to a different decision themselves, but the need is to consider the opinion of the employer as to whether the decision was, in the one case, within the range of reasonable responses, and, in the other, whether the reason was both material and substantial.

7.3.2.3 Victimisation

An employer discriminates against an employee or another person if the employer treats that employee or other person less favourably than he treats or would treat other employees in the same circumstances because the employee or other person:

(1) brought proceedings against the employer or any other person under the DDA 1995, or
(2) gave evidence or information in connection with such proceedings brought by any other person, or
(3) otherwise does anything under the DDA 1995 in relation to the employer or any other person, or
(4) alleged that the employer or other person has contravened the DDA 1995.

Treating the employee or other person less favourably because the employer believes or suspects that the employee or other person has done or intends to do any of these actions is also unlawful.[96] Unlike the other forms of discrimination provided for by the DDA 1995, this form can be claimed by non-disabled people as well as disabled people. The treatment,

---

[93] Section 4(5) DDA 1995 provides a definition of dismissal which includes constructive dismissal; see also *Catherall v Michelin Tyre plc* [2002] IRLR 61, where the EAT held that giving an employee the choice of early medical retirement or redundancy effectively gave the employee no choice and could be said to amount to a dismissal.
[94] See *Baynton v Saurus General Engineers Ltd* [1999] IRLR 604.
[95] *Jones v Post Office* [2001] IRLR 384 CA.
[96] Section 55(1) and (2) DDA 1995.

however, will not amount to less favourable treatment if any allegation of the employee or other person was false and not made in good faith.[97]

There is also protection for ex-employees in a situation where there has been a relevant relationship between an employer and a disabled person and that relationship has come to an end. A relevant relationship is where there has been an employment relationship during which there was an act of discrimination or harassment. In such a situation it is unlawful for the ex-employer to discriminate or harass the disabled person concerned.[98]

7.3.4 Duty to make reasonable adjustments

The employer also discriminates against a disabled person if the employer fails to comply with a duty to make reasonable adjustments in relation to the disabled person.[99] A failure to make reasonable adjustments over a period of time would be almost bound to lead to a breach of the implied term of trust and confidence, which would then entitle the employee to treat it as a repudiatory breach of contract (see Chapter 4).[100] *Nottinghamshire County Council v Meikle*[101] concerned a local authority school teacher. Her vision deteriorated until she lost the sight in one eye and some vision in the other. She made a number of requests for adjustments, including to her classroom location, the amount of preparation time she was given, and that notices and written materials should be enlarged. There were delays in responses from the employer and eventually Mrs Meikle resigned. The Court of Appeal agreed with her that the continuing failure of the local authority to deal with the disability discrimination amounted to a fundamental breach of contract and that she had been constructively dismissed.

The importance of the need to make reasonable adjustments is shown in one survey,[102] which stated that over 25% of people who left their job because of their disability said that adaptations would have enabled them to stay in work, but less than 20% of these people were offered such changes. Thus, where the disabled person is placed at a substantial disadvantage compared to persons who are not disabled because of

- a provision, criterion or practice applied by or on behalf of an employer, or
- any physical feature of premises occupied by an employer,[103]

it is the duty of the employer to take reasonable steps, in all the circumstances of the case, to prevent the provision, criterion, practice or feature from having that effect.[104] This obligation applies in respect of applicants for employment as well as in respect of existing employees. There is, however, no obligation placed upon the employer if the employer

---

[97] Section 55(4) DDA 1995.
[98] Section 16A DDA 1995.
[99] Section 3A(2) DDA 1995.
[100] *Greenhof v Barnsley Metropolitan Borough Council* [2006] IRLR 99.
[101] [2004] IRLR 703.
[102] See Office for National Statistics, 'Disability and the Labour Market', *Labour Market Trends*, September 1999, p 467.
[103] Physical feature includes any feature arising from the design or construction of a building, approaches to it, access or exits, fixtures, fittings, furnishings, furniture, equipment or material in the building: section 18D DDA 1995.
[104] Section 4A(1) DDA 1995.

does not know, or could not have reasonably been expected to know, that the applicant or employee had a disability.

Provision, criterion or practice includes any arrangements.[105] The arrangements referred to include, first, the arrangements for determining who should be offered employment, and, secondly, any term, condition or arrangements on which employment, promotion, transfer, training or any other benefit is offered. The arrangements referred to are strictly job related. Employers are required to make adjustments to the way that the job is structured and organised so as to accommodate those who cannot fit into the existing arrangements. This appears to exclude providing assistance with personal arrangements and care so as to enable an individual to attend work.[106] Examples of steps which may need to be taken are[107]

(1) making adjustments to premises;
(2) allocating some of the disabled person's duties to another person;
(3) transferring the disabled person to an existing vacancy;
(4) altering his or her hours of work or training;
(5) assigning him or her to a different place of work or training;
(6) allowing him or her to be absent during working or training hours for rehabilitation, assessment or treatment;
(7) giving, or arranging to give, training or mentoring;
(8) acquiring or modifying equipment;
(9) modifying instructions or reference manuals;
(10) providing a reader or interpreter;
(11) providing supervision or other support.

The question of whether an employer had made sufficient arrangements in the light of their knowledge is one of fact for the employment tribunal. *Ridout v TC Group*[108] concerned an applicant with a rare form of epilepsy who may have been disadvantaged by the bright fluorescent lighting in the interview location. The EAT held that no reasonable employer could be expected to know, without being told, that the arrangements for the interview might place the applicant at a disadvantage. The EAT held that the DDA 1995:

> requires the tribunal to measure the extent of the duty, if any, against the assumed knowledge of the employer both as to the disability and its likelihood of causing the individual a substantial disadvantage in comparison with persons who are not disabled.

The extent of the adjustments needed is subject to a reasonableness test. This first requires an employer to carry out a proper assessment of what is needed to eliminate a disabled person's disadvantage. This might include a proper assessment of the individual's condition, the effect of the disability on her and her ability to perform the duties of the post and the steps that might be taken to reduce or remove the disadvantages to which she was

---

[105] Section 18D DDA 1995.
[106] See *Kenny v Hampshire Constabulary* [1999] IRLR 76.
[107] Section 18B(2) DDA 1995.
[108] [1998] IRLR 628.

subjected.[109] In deciding whether it is reasonable for an employer to have to take a particular step regard may be had to the nature of the employer's activities and the size of the undertaking, as well as the extent to which the step would prevent the effect or barrier that existed and the practicability of taking the step in the first place. It may mean creating a new job for an individual, such as in *Southampton City College v Randall*[110] where a reorganisation of work would have enabled the employer to create a new job for a lecturer whose voice had broken down. The employers were guilty of disability discrimination because they did not consider this option and others as possible reasonable adjustments.

The size of an employer's resources are also important because regard needs to be had for the financial and other costs, the possible disruption of the employer's activities, the extent of the employer's financial resources and the availability of any financial or other help.[111] Failure to comply with the duty to make adjustments is not in itself actionable. It is a duty imposed for the purpose of determining whether an employer has discriminated against a disabled person.[112]

A further example of the scope of the duty to make reasonable adjustments arose in *Archibald v Fife Council*.[113] This concerned an employee of Fife Council who was employed as a road sweeper. As a result of a complication during surgery she became virtually unable to walk and could no longer carry out the duties of a road sweeper. She could do sedentary work and the Council sent her on a number of computer and administration courses. Over the next few months she applied for over 100 jobs within the Council but she always failed in a competitive interview situation. Eventually she was dismissed as the redeployment procedure was exhausted. The issue for the court was the limits of the duty to make reasonable adjustments. It was agreed that the DDA 1995 required some positive discrimination in favour of disabled people, but did this include finding them another job if their disability stops them from performing their current one? The court held that the DDA 1995, to the extent that the provisions of the Act required it, permitted and sometimes obliged employers to treat a disabled person more favourably than others. This may even require transferring them to a higher level position without the need for a competitive interview.[114]

7.3.5 Harassment

It is unlawful for an employer to harass a disabled employee or a disabled job applicant.[115] Harassment has the same meaning as in other regulations concerning discrimination on the grounds of sexual orientation and religion or belief (see Chapter 6). A person subjects

---

[109] *Mid Staffordshire General Hospitals NHS Trust v Cambridge* [2003] IRLR 566.
[110] [2006] IRLR 18.
[111] Section 18B(1) DDA 1995.
[112] Section 18B(6) DDA 1995.
[113] [2004] IRLR 651 CA.
[114] This was one of the problems for the employer. Most positions were at a higher level than that of a road sweeper and the local authority assumed that it had an obligation to make all promotion interviews competitive.
[115] Section 4(3) DDA 1995.

a disabled person to harassment if he or she engages in, in relation to the disability, unwanted conduct which has the purpose or effect of:

(a) violating the disabled person's dignity, or
(b) creating an intimidating, hostile, degrading, humiliating or offensive environment for him.[116]

Conduct will be seen as harassment only if, having regard to all the circumstances, especially the perception of the disabled person, it can reasonably be considered as having the effect of harassment. Thus, although there is a reasonableness test, it is not necessarily an objective test as the view of the disabled person affected by the conduct is important.

7.3.6 Enforcement and remedies

When a person considers that they may have been discriminated against in relation to Part II DDA 1995 that person may question the respondent, or potential respondent, by using prescribed forms for this purpose.[117] The questions will be admissible in evidence only if they are raised within a period of three months beginning when the act complained of was done.[118] If it appears to the employment tribunal that the respondent deliberately, and without reasonable excuse, failed to reply within a period of eight weeks or that the respondent's reply was 'evasive or equivocal', it will be free to draw inferences including that the respondent has contravened the employment related part of the DDA 1995.[119]

Like the SDA 1975 and the RRA 1976, anything done by a person in the course of their employment is to be treated as also being done by the employer, whether or not it was done with the employer's approval,[120] although it will be a defence for the employer if they can show that they took all steps as were reasonably practicable to prevent the employee doing the act or doing such acts in the course of their employment.[121] Similarly, according to section 57(1) DDA 1995 a person who knowingly aids another person to do an act made unlawful by the DDA is to be treated as doing that act themselves. The defence is that they reasonably relied upon a statement from that other person that the act done was not unlawful in terms of the DDA 1995.[122]

A person may make a complaint to an employment tribunal within three months of the act complained of.[123] A tribunal may consider an out of time complaint if it is 'just and equitable' to do so.[124] Where the complainant proves facts from which the tribunal could conclude, in the absence of an adequate explanation, that the respondent has acted in a way which is unlawful within the terms of the Act, then the tribunal can uphold the complaint,

---

[116] Section 3B DDA 1995.
[117] Section 56 DDA 1995 and Disability Discrimination (Questions and Replies) Order 1996, SI 1996/2793.
[118] Article 3(a) Disability Discrimination (Questions and Replies) Order 1996, SI 1996/2793.
[119] Section 56(3) DDA 1995.
[120] Section 58(1) DDA 1995.
[121] Section 58(5) DDA 1995.
[122] Section 58(3) DDA 1995, but section 58(4) provides that a person who knowingly or recklessly makes the statement which is false or misleading is guilty of an offence.
[123] Schedule 3 DDA 1995; the time limit applies equally to attempts to amend existing claims by adding on a complaint related to disability discrimination; see *Harvey v Port of Tilbury London Ltd* [1999] IRLR 693.
[124] See Schedule 3 paragraph 3 DDA 1995; section 9 DDA 1995 provides that any term in the contract of employment that contravenes any provisions of the Act is void, but also contains rules for conciliation and compromise agreements regarding proceedings.

unless the respondent proves that he or she did not act in the way complained of. The tribunal may make a declaration as to the rights of the complainant and the respondent, order the respondent to pay compensation[125] to the applicant and/or recommend action to be taken by the respondent, within a specified period, for the purpose of obviating or reducing the adverse effect on the complainant.[126] If the respondent fails, without reasonable justification, to comply with the recommendation, then the tribunal may award compensation or increase the level of compensation already ordered.[127]

Further reading

Deakin, S. and Morris, G., *Labour Law* (4th edn, Hart Publishing, 2005), Chapter 6.

McColgan, A., *Discrimination Law: Text, Cases and Materials* (Hart Publishing, 2005), Chapter 8.

Sargeant, M., *Age Discrimination in Employment* (Gower Publishing, 2006).

Sargeant, M., 'The Employment Equality (Age) Regulations 2006: A Legitimisation of Age Discrimination in Employment' (2006) 35(3) *Industrial Law Journal* 209.

Sargeant, M., 'Disability and age – multiple potential for discrimination' (2005) 33 *International Journal of the Sociology of Law* 17.

http://www.equalityhumanrights.com for the web site of the Commission for Equality and Human Rights.

http://www.berr.gov.uk/employment/discrimination/index.html for the Department for Business, Enterprise and Regulatory Reform web site on discrimination at work.

Visit **www.mylawchamber.co.uk/sargeant** to access legal updates, live web links and practice exam questions to test yourself on this chapter.

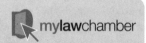

---

[125] See *Buxton v Equinox Design Ltd* [1999] IRLR 158 which considered the care that needs to be taken in assessing compensation where the amount is uncapped as in cases relating to the DDA 1995.

[126] Section 17A(2) DDA 1995; according to section 17A(4), compensation can include injury to feelings.

[127] Section 17A(5) DDA 1995.

8

Time and Pay

8.1 Working time

The arguments about the degree to which the working time of individuals should be regulated encapsulated the arguments about the extent to which Governments should intervene in the employment relationship and the extent to which such regulation should originate with the EU. The British Government, in *United Kingdom v Council of Ministers*,[1] argued that such matters were an issue of subsidiarity and should be settled within Member States rather than by the Community. The Council argued that the justification for the Working Time Directive[2] was a health and safety one and that the Community had competence in this field. In the event, the United Kingdom finally transposed the Directive into national law some two years late.[3]

The actual average number of hours worked each week in the EU is just over 40. There is a significant divergence between countries in the hours worked. The United Kingdom has the highest figures in this respect with an average week of 44.9 hours, whilst the lowest was in France with 38.2 hours.[4] For women the weekly average hours ranged from 42.5 in Latvia to 36.4 hours in Italy (40.6 hours in the UK).[5]

8.2 Young Workers' Directive

The Working Time Regulations include the transposition of parts of the Young Workers' Directive[6] into national law. This Directive came into effect on 22 June 1996, but the United Kingdom was permitted to delay this process. The final parts of the Directive were transposed into national law in 2002.

This Directive was also adopted under Article 137 EC concerning health and safety. It applies to any young person under the age of 18 years who has an employment contract or an employment relationship. Subject to minor exceptions, the Directive prohibits the

---

[1] Case C-84/94 [1997] IRLR 30 ECJ.
[2] Council Directive 93/104/EC concerning certain aspects of the organisation of working time OJ L307/18 13.12.93. This was significantly amended by the European Parliament and Council Directive 2003/88/EC.
[3] Working Time Regulations 1998, SI 1998/1833.
[4] *Working time developments 2003* European Industrial Relations Observatory: www.eiro.eurofound.ie.
[5] According to a study carried out for the International Labour Organisation in 1999 workers in the United States work the longest hours of the industrialised nations. They work some 1,966 hours per annum (in 1997). This compared to 1,883 hours worked in 1980. This increase is against the trend in the rest of the industrialised economies, where there has been a reduction in working hours.
[6] Council Directive 94/33/EC on the protection of young people at work OJ L216/12 20.8.94.

employment of children. These are defined as persons of less than 15 years of age, or the minimum school leaving age, whichever is higher. The minor exceptions include work experience, work in the theatre and light work.[7]

Articles 6 and 7, which describe the general obligations placed upon employers and the prohibition of certain types of employment of young people, were implemented by the Health and Safety (Young Persons) Regulations 1997.[8] Those parts concerning the employment of children were implemented by the Children (Protection at Work) Regulations 1998.[9] The provisions on working hours, night work, rest periods, periodic and annual breaks are included in the Working Time Regulations.[10]

The number of young people working is significant, despite the expansion of numbers in further and higher education. According to the Labour Force Survey[11] there were 1,370,000 individuals between the ages of 16 and 18 years inclusive employed during the summer of 1999. Of this number some 549,000 were in full-time education. Many of these will be part-time workers helping to finance their education.[12] The TUC commissioned a survey of school-age children carried out by MORI in the autumn term of the 1996/97 school year. One-quarter of the sample reported having a paid job at the time of the survey, although the occupations mostly involved babysitting and newspaper rounds. However, there were significant numbers who were employed in shop work, catering and cleaning. Of most concern is that 23% of under-13s reported having a paid job. Until the 1997 and 1998 Regulations such employment was impermissible under the Children and Young Persons Act 1933.

According to the Management of Health and Safety at Work Regulations 1999 (MHSW Regulations 1999),[13] an employer of a young person[14] must carry out a risk assessment which takes particular account of a number of factors.[15] These are:

(1) the inexperience, lack of awareness of risks and immaturity of young persons;
(2) the fitting-out and the layout of the workplace and the workstation;
(3) the nature, degree and duration of exposure to physical, biological and chemical agents;
(4) the form, range, and use of work equipment and the way in which it is used;
(5) the organisation of processes and activities;
(6) the extent of the health and safety training provided or to be provided to young persons;
(7) the risks from agents, processes and work listed in the annex to the Young Workers' Directive.

---

[7] Articles 4–5 Young Workers' Directive.
[8] SI 1997/135.
[9] SI 1998/276.
[10] There were also provisions relating to young people working on sea-going ships, which were dealt with by the Fishing Vessels (Health and Safety) (Employment of Children and Young Persons) Regulations 1998, SI 1998/2411.
[11] Reported in Office for National Statistics, *Labour Market Trends*, November 1999, p 577.
[12] See Chapter 3 on the Part-time Workers Regulations 2000.
[13] SI 1999/3242.
[14] Young person means any person who has not attained the age of 18 years; see regulation 1(2) MHSW Regulations 1999.
[15] Regulation 3(5) MHSW Regulations 1999.

Regulation 10(2) of the MHSW Regulations 1999 provides that, before employing a child,[16] any employer must provide a parent[17] of the child with 'comprehensible and relevant information' on any risks to the child's health and safety that have been identified by the risk assessment and the preventive and protective measures that have been taken.

Employers have a general responsibility for protecting young persons from any risks to their health and safety which are:

> a consequence of their lack of experience, or absence of awareness of existing or potential risks or the fact that young persons have not fully matured.[18]

The Children (Protection at Work) Regulations 1998[19] amended the Children and Young Persons Acts 1933 and 1963 to give effect to the Young Workers' Directive. They impose restrictions on the working hours and the type of work that can be undertaken by individuals under the compulsory school leaving age.

8.3 Working Time Directive

The justification for the Working Time Directive in 1993 was Article 118a EC (now 137), which stated at the time that:

> Member States shall pay particular attention to encouraging improvements, especially in the working environment, as regards the health and safety of workers, and shall set as their objective the harmonisation of conditions in this area, while maintaining the improvements made.

It was also justified, in the preamble to the Directive, by the following extract from the Community Charter of the Fundamental Social Rights of Workers:[20]

> The completion of the internal market must lead to an improvement in the living and working conditions of workers in the European Community. This process must result from an approximation of these conditions while the improvement is being maintained, as regards in particular the duration and organisation of working time . . .

Thus the measure was intended to harmonise the approach of Member States to 'ensure the safety and health of Community workers'.[21] One problem for the United Kingdom in this harmonisation process was that many other Member States of the Community already had statutory rules on weekly and daily hours, which preceded the Working Time Directive. Belgium, France, Greece, Ireland, Italy and Portugal all had existing rules which limited working hours.[22]

One of the consequences of using Article 118a EC (now 137) was that it could be adopted using the 'co-operation procedure' in Article 189c EC (now 252). This needed only a qualified majority by the Council of Ministers to adopt a common position with

---

[16] Someone who is not over compulsory school leaving age.
[17] A parent is someone who has parental responsibility according to section 3 Children Act 1989; the same definition as in the Maternity and Parental Leave etc. Regulations 1999; see Chapter 9.
[18] Regulation 19(1) MHSW Regulations 1999.
[19] SI 1998/276.
[20] Adopted on 9 December 1989 by all the then Member States with the exception of the United Kingdom.
[21] The preamble states 'Whereas, in order to ensure the safety and health of Community workers, the latter must be granted minimum daily, weekly and annual periods of rest and adequate breaks . . .'.
[22] *European Industrial Relations Review* 280, May 1997, p 18.

regard to the proposal. In the event the United Kingdom abstained, but indicated that it would challenge the legal basis for the Directive.

The subject matter of the Directive related to minimum periods of daily and weekly rest, breaks in work, annual leave, maximum weekly working time and patterns of work, such as night work and shift work. Subject to certain derogations permitted in Article 17, the Directive applies to the same public and private sectors as the Health and Safety at Work Directive.[23] There were a number of specific exceptions to this, which included sectors concerned with air, rail, road and sea, as well as the activities of doctors in training.[24]

The Directive was due to be transposed into national law by 23 November 1996 but, partly because of the United Kingdom Government's legal challenge, it came into effect with the Working Time Regulations in October 1998. This challenge[25] was through proceedings for annulment of the Directive, or of certain parts of Articles 4, 5, 6 and 7. The action was brought under Article 173 EC (now 230), which gives the ECJ jurisdiction in actions brought by Member States or certain EU institutions, to review the legality of acts of the EU:

> on grounds of lack of competence, infringement of an essential procedural requirement, infringement of this Treaty or any rule of law relating to its application, or misuse of powers.

The UK action was based on four claims. These were that:

(1) The Directive had a defective legal basis, i.e. it should have been adopted on the basis of Article 100 EC (now 94) or Article 235 EC (now 308), which required unanimity in the Council of Ministers.

(2) The Directive did not comply with the principle of proportionality, because its provisions went beyond the minimum requirements permitted under Article 118a EC (now 137). Specifically, overall reductions in working hours or an overall increase in rest periods were not 'minimum requirements', the desired level of protection could have been attained by less restrictive measures and the proposed measures were not justified by scientific research. Additionally, it had not been shown that the Directive's objectives could be better achieved at Community level, rather than at Member State level.

(3) The Directive contained a number of measures which were unconnected with its purported aims and were, therefore, a misuse of powers.

(4) Finally, it was claimed that there was an infringement of essential procedural requirements. This arose because there was a failure to show a causal relationship between the proposals and health and safety, which meant that it had failed to state the reasons on which it was based. Alternatively, it was argued, the reasoning was flawed as there was a failure to explain that many of the measures were concerned with matters other than health and safety.

The United Kingdom lost on every point, except where the ECJ annulled a proposal that, in principle, the weekly rest period should be on a Sunday. The ECJ held that the

---

[23] Council Directive 89/391/EEC on the introduction of measures to encourage improvements in the safety and health of workers at work OJ L183/1 29.6.89.

[24] Article 1 Working Time Directive; see below for current exclusions.

[25] Case C-84/94 *United Kingdom v Council of Ministers* [1997] IRLR 30 ECJ.

principal purpose of the Directive was the protection of the health and safety of workers and that it was, therefore, adopted under the correct part of the Treaty and that it was not in breach of the principle of proportionality. It stated that the concept of 'minimum requirements' is not about setting minimum standards but refers to the individual State's ability to impose more stringent standards than that set by Community action. The Council also dismissed the claims of misuse of powers or inadequate reasoning.

As a result of this case, there was a period when the United Kingdom had failed to transpose the Directive. In *Gibson v East Riding of Yorkshire Council*[26] a local authority employee claimed that she could rely on Article 7[27] of the Directive having direct effect (see Chapter 2) during the period between 23 November 1996, the date by which it should have been implemented, and 1 October 1998, the date when the Working Time Regulations came into effect. She was an employee of an emanation of the State and the EAT held that she could rely on the protection of the Directive, as Article 7 in particular met the requirements for having direct effect[28] by being sufficiently precise and unconditional. The Court of Appeal disagreed with this approach, however, and allowed the appeal.[29] The court held that certain provisions were not sufficiently precise, especially the definition of working time itself. The court stated:

> The first basic question for the national court is: what is the period of 'working time' for which the worker must have worked before he becomes entitled to annual leave under Article 7? Annual leave is leave from 'working time'. The concept of 'working time' is not precisely defined. To what period of 'working time' does the specified period of annual leave relate? The question is not answered by Article 7 itself or by any other provisions in the Directive. How then is it possible for a national court to decide which workers are entitled to annual leave?

8.4 Working Time Regulations

The Working Time Regulations 1998 have been amended on a number of occasions.[30] One effect of these amendments is to weaken the 1998 Regulations even further, making it much easier for the employer and the worker to agree to exclude the provisions of the maximum weekly working time of an average of 48 hours. There were also fresh exclusions from certain provisions for those whose working time is not measured or predetermined.

8.4.1 Scope and definition

The 1998 Regulations, which apply to Great Britain, offer protection to workers who are defined, in regulation 2(1), as those having a contract of employment or any other contract where the individual undertakes to do or perform personally any work or services for

---

[26] [2000] IRLR 598 CA.
[27] Concerning annual leave; see below.
[28] See also *R v Attorney General for Northern Ireland, ex parte Burns* [1999] IRLR 315 which also considered this issue in relation to night work.
[29] *Gibson v East Riding of Yorkshire Council* [2000] IRLR 598 CA.
[30] The Working Time Regulations 1999, SI 1999/3372; the Working Time (Amendment) Regulations 2001, SI 2001/3256; the Working Time (Amendment) Regulations 2003, SI 2003/1684. The 2003 Regulations are concerned with finally implementing the working time provisions of Directive 94/33/EC on the protection of young people at work.

another party. The effect is to ensure that the regulations cover the wider category of worker rather than just employees.[31] 'Young worker' is someone who is over the compulsory school age but is under 18 years of age.[32] Regulation 36 Working Time Regulations 1998[33] specifically provides for agency workers to be included. Where an individual is provided by an agency to do work for another, unless there is an agreement to different effect between the agency and the principal, the person who pays the agency worker in respect of the work is to be treated as the employer for the purposes of the regulations.[34]

The following three conditions must be satisfied for a period to constitute 'working time':

(1) any period during which the worker is working;
(2) any period when the worker is at the employer's disposal; and
(3) any period when the worker is carrying out his or her duties and activities.

The definition of working time also includes any period during which the worker is receiving relevant training.[35] Relevant training is defined as meaning work experience which is part of a training course or programme, training for employment, or both of these. It does not include work experience or training provided by an educational institution or a person whose main business is the provision of training or courses provided by such bodies. Presumably this is conditional upon the employer's relationship with the training provider. If an institution provides a training course, defined by the employer as relevant to work, on the employer's premises and during normal working hours, it is difficult to see how this could not be 'relevant training', even though provided by this third party.

Lastly, working time means any additional period which is to be treated as working time under a 'relevant agreement'.[36] A 'relevant agreement' is any workforce agreement or any contractually binding part of a collective agreement or any other legally enforceable agreement between the worker and the employer (see below).

8.4.2 Exclusions

The 1998 Regulations follow the Directive closely in listing the exceptions to its coverage. Regulation 18 (as amended) excludes certain categories entirely. These are seafarers covered by Directive 1999/63 and those on board a sea-going vessel or a ship or hovercraft 'employed by an undertaking that operates services for passengers or goods by inland waterways or lake transport'. In addition, mobile staff in civil aviation who are covered by Directive 2000/79 and those performing mobile road transport activities who are covered by Directive 2002/15 are excluded from certain provisions. Other special categories are

---

[31] See section 230(3) ERA 1996. See *Byrne Brothers (Formwork) Ltd v Baird* [2002] IRLR 96 and *Redrow Homes Ltd v Wright* [2004] IRLR 720.
[32] On the position of children see *Addison v Ashby* [2003] IRLR 211.
[33] Regulations 37–43 Working Time Regulations 1998 concern the position of other groups of workers, such as those in Crown employment and the armed forces and the police service.
[34] Regulation 36(2) Working Time Regulations 1998.
[35] Regulation 2(1) Working Time Regulations 1998.
[36] Regulation 2(1) Working Time Regulations 1998.

doctors in training[37] and those occupations where the characteristics of the activities are likely to be in conflict with the regulations, such as the armed services or the police.[38]

8.4.3 The 48-hour week

Regulations 4 and 5 are concerned with placing a 48-hour limit on the average amount of time worked per week. Unless an employer has first obtained the worker's agreement in writing to perform such work, a worker's working time (including any overtime) in any reference period shall not exceed 48 hours for each seven days.[39] Nevertheless, until 31 July 2009 the maximum hours of doctors in training will be 56 hours per week.[40]

Regulation 2(1) defines a day as a period of 24 hours commencing at midnight. The fact that working time is averaged over a period means that it is possible for workers to be obliged to work long hours for sustained periods. In *King v Scottish & Newcastle*,[41] an individual was required to work for between 50 and 60 hours over the Christmas period, but there was no breach of the regulations as her hours were to be averaged over the reference period. The reference period is normally 17 weeks. It can be varied by a collective or workforce agreement up to a maximum of 52 weeks.[42] This extension must be for 'objective or technical reasons'. It is not clear what these are likely to be but regulation 4(2) imposes an obligation on employers to take all reasonable steps 'in keeping with the need for health and safety of workers' to ensure that the limit specified is adhered to.[43] The obligation in regulation 4(2) is a separate obligation from the limit of 48 hours imposed by regulation 4(1). This was discussed in *Barber v RJB Mining (UK) Ltd*[44] where a trade union asked the High Court for a declaration that its members need not work again until their average working week fell to the 48-hour level. The trade union succeeded because the right in regulation 4(1) is a contractual obligation upon the employer.

The reference period can also be lengthened to 26 weeks for a number of special cases contained in regulation 21. These are situations where, for example, continuity of services needs to be maintained such as in hospitals or airports, or where there are peaks of work, such as in agriculture or tourism, or where the workers' activities are affected by events or accidents outside the control of the employer. Finally, for new workers, who have worked for less than the reference period, the period to be counted will be the actual time worked.[45]

The 1998 Regulations provide a formula for calculating the hours worked for each seven days during a reference period.[46] They are calculated as

$$\frac{A + B}{C} = \text{average hours per week during reference period}$$

---

[37] On doctors' maximum hours see below.
[38] On emergency workers see *Pfeiffer v Deutsches Rotes Kreuz* [2005] IRLR 137.
[39] Regulation 4(1) Working Time Regulations 1998.
[40] Regulation 25A Working Time Regulations 1998. On dealing with time spent 'on call' see the ECJ's approach in *Landeshaupstadt Kiel v Jaeger* [2003] IRLR 804.
[41] IDS Brief 641, 10 May 1999.
[42] Regulation 23(b) Working Time Regulations 1998.
[43] It does mean that annualised contracts are catered for within the 1998 Regulations.
[44] [1999] IRLR 308.
[45] Regulation 4(4) Working Time Regulations 1998.
[46] Regulation 4(6) Working Time Regulations 1998.

The purpose of this formula is not to count the days that are not worked during the reference period, but to include an equivalent number of days from the next period in order to make up for those lost days. In this formula:

A is the aggregate number of hours in the worker's working time during the course of the reference period.

B is the aggregate number of hours in the worker's working time in the period immediately after the end of the reference period, equivalent to the number of days excluded in A.[47]

C is the number of weeks in the reference period.

Example: An individual has two periods of employment during the 17-week reference period as follows: working ten hours per day for five weeks, then a break of two weeks before a further period of eight hours per day for ten weeks (working a five-day week). In the next reference period the individual works an average of nine hours per day. Thus A = (10 hours × 5 days × 5 weeks) + (8 hours × 5 days × 10 weeks) = 650 hours worked; B = 9 hours × 5 days × 2 weeks = 90. The formula is now

$$\frac{650 + 90}{17} = 43.53 \text{ hours}$$

If the employee has agreed in writing to perform their work outside the scope of the regulations, then this formula cannot apply. If there is agreement to exclude for a limited period of time, then that period will count as excluded days.

According to regulation 5, the agreement may apply for a specific period or for an indefinite period. It may also be subject to termination by the worker via the giving of notice, subject to a maximum of three months. If there is no such provision, then regulation 5 applies a seven-day notice period by default.

Prior to the 1999 amendments, there were requirements for the employer to maintain records of those who had opted out, specifying the numbers of hours worked during each reference period. All that an employer must now do is to keep up-to-date records of the employees who have signed such an agreement.[48]

8.4.4 Night work

Regulations 6 and 7 are concerned with limits on night working and related obligations placed upon the employer.[49] As with the rules on the 48-hour average week, there is an obligation upon the employer to take all reasonable steps, in keeping with the need to protect the health and safety of workers, to ensure that the limits specified are complied with.[50] Night work is defined as being work during 'night time'. Night time has a specific

---

[47] Regulation 4(7) Working Time Regulations 1998; excluded days means days taken for the purposes of annual leave, sick leave, maternity leave and any days in which the limit does not apply as agreed in writing between employer and worker; see below.

[48] See Working Time Regulations 1999, SI 1999/3372.

[49] Regulation 6A Working Time Regulations 1998 deals with young workers.

[50] Regulations 4(2) and 6(2) Working Time Regulations 1998.

meaning, which is a period of at least seven hours that includes the period between midnight and 5 am. There are two alternative meanings given to the term night worker:

(1) An individual who, as a normal course, works at least three of the normal daily working hours during night time. 'Normal course' means if the individual works such hours on the majority of days on which the individual works. This is said to be without prejudice to the generality of the expression, which suggests that there might be circumstances when 'normal course' can mean something else, such as working for at least three hours every day, rather than just the majority of days.
(2) A worker who is likely, during night time, to work at least such a proportion of annual working time as may be specified in a collective or workforce agreement.[51]

In *R v Attorney General for Northern Ireland, ex parte Burns*[52] the High Court in Northern Ireland considered the meaning of the term 'normal course' as defined in article 2(4) of the Working Time Directive. The employee concerned had been asked to change to a shift system, which meant working a night shift between 9 pm and 7 am one week in three. The court held that the requirement for someone to work at least three hours during night time as a normal course meant no more than that this should be a regular feature of their work. According to the court, it was inconceivable that the protection should be confined to someone who works night shifts exclusively or predominantly.

In any applicable reference period, a night worker's normal hours shall not exceed an average of eight hours for each 24 hours. There is a default reference period of 17 weeks in the course of employment and it is possible to agree to successive periods of 17 weeks[53] via a collective or workforce agreement, Where the individual has worked for the employer for less than 17 weeks, the reference period is the period since they started the employment.[54]

There is a formula for calculating a night worker's average normal hours of work for each 24 hours during a reference period. It is:

$$\frac{A}{B-C} = \text{average normal hours for each 24 hours}$$

A is the number of hours during the reference period which are normal working hours for that worker.

B is the number of days during the reference period.

C is the total number of hours during the reference period comprised in rest periods spent by the worker in pursuance of entitlement under regulation 11,[55] divided by 24.[56]

Example:[57] A night worker normally works four 12-hour shifts per week. With a 17-week reference period, A is 17 × (4 days × 12 hours) = 816 hours. B is 17 × 7 days = 119 days. The number of 24-hour weekly rest periods to which the worker is entitled under

[51] Regulation 2(1) Working Time Regulations 1998.
[52] [1999] IRLR 315.
[53] Regulation 6(1) and (3) Working Time Regulations 1998.
[54] Regulation 6(4) Working Time Regulations 1998.
[55] Weekly rest periods; see below.
[56] Regulation 6(5) Working Time Regulations 1998.
[57] Taken from the DTI guidance to the regulations.

regulation 11 is 17; thus C is $(17 \times 24 \text{ hours})$ divided by $24 = 17$. The formula will now look like this:

$$\frac{816}{119 - 17} = 8 \text{ hours}$$

The important difference between this formula and that applied to the 48-hour average is that this one is concerned with a worker's normal hours, rather than their actual hours.

8.4.4.1 Special hazards

There is an additional obligation on an employer contained in regulation 6(7) and (8). This is that the employer must ensure that no night worker whose work involves special hazards or heavy physical or mental strain works for more than eight hours in any 24-hour period in which the worker does night work. This is a return to control of actual hours rather than normal working hours. A worker is to be regarded as being involved in such hazards and strain either if it is identified as such in a collective or workforce agreement which takes into account the specific effects and hazards of night work, or it is recognised in a risk assessment carried out in accordance with regulation 3 MHSW Regulations 1999.

8.4.4.2 Health care

The other aspect of an employer's obligations with regard to night work relate to the worker's health and well-being. An employer must not assign an adult worker to night work unless the employer has ensured that the worker will have the opportunity of a free[58] health assessment prior to taking up the assignment, unless the worker has had a health assessment on a previous occasion and the employer has no reason to believe that it is no longer valid. The employer also has an obligation to ensure that each night worker has the opportunity for a free health assessment at regular and appropriate intervals.[59] Young workers are entitled to a free assessment of their 'health and capacities' before being assigned to work during the restricted period,[60] unless they had one on a previous occasion and the employer had no reason to believe that it was no longer valid[61] and unless the work is itself of an exceptional nature.[62] It is not clear if there is intended to be a difference between 'health assessment' and an 'assessment of health and capacities'. Health assessment does not appear to mean the same as a medical examination. In its guidance to the Working Time Regulations 1998, the DBERR suggests that a health assessment should take place in two stages. First, workers should be asked to complete a questionnaire which asks specific questions about their health which are relevant to the type of night work which they will be doing. Second, if the employer is not certain that they are fit for night work following the questionnaire, the worker should be asked to have a medical examination.

There is an obligation of confidentiality associated with the health assessment. There is to be no disclosure of an assessment, apart from a statement that the worker is fit to be

---

[58] Free means being of no cost to the workers to whom it relates: regulation 7(3) Working Time Regulations 1998.
[59] Regulation 7(1) Working Time Regulations 1998.
[60] The restricted period is between 10 pm and 6 am: regulation 7(2)(a) Working Time Regulations 1998.
[61] Regulation 7(2) Working Time Regulations 1998.
[62] Regulation 7(5) Working Time Regulations 1998.

assigned to or continue with night work, to anyone but the worker to whom the assessment relates. The only exception is if the worker has given permission for disclosure.[63] If a registered medical practitioner advises an employer that a worker is suffering from health problems associated with night work then the employer is under an obligation to transfer the worker. There are two conditions attached to this obligation. First, it must be possible to transfer the worker to work which is not categorised as night work and, secondly, it must be work to which the worker is suited.[64]

The employer must keep adequate records relating to regulations 4(1), 6(1), (7), 7(1) and (2).[65] These records must relate to each worker employed and must be kept for a minimum of two years from the date that they were made.[66]

8.4.5 Time off

In regulation 8 there is a general obligation for an employer to give workers adequate rest breaks where the pattern of work is such that the health and safety of the workers may be put at risk, in particular if the work is monotonous or the work rate is predetermined. Apart from this general obligation on an employer, regulations 10–17 Working Time Regulations 1998 give the worker a number of specific entitlements to different types of breaks. These are entitlements only and there is no obligation upon the worker to take advantage of them.[67]

8.4.6 Daily rest periods and rest breaks

According to regulation 10(1) Working Time Regulations 1998 an adult worker is entitled to a rest period of at least 11 consecutive hours in each 24-hour period during which the worker works for the employer.[68] The 24-hour period rather than an 11 hours per day rule means that, if necessary, the 11 hours can be over two working days. There is special provision for young workers who are entitled to a rest period of 12 consecutive hours in any 24-hour period that the young worker works for the employer, although this period may be interrupted in the case of activities that are split up during the day or are of short duration.[69]

Additionally, where an adult worker's daily working time exceeds six hours, then the worker will be entitled to a rest break which can be spent away from the workstation if they have one.[70] This break can be agreed by a collective or workforce agreement but, in default of such an agreement, it will be for 20 minutes. The rules for young workers are that where

---

[63] Regulation 7(6) Working Time Regulations 1998.
[64] Regulation 7(6) Working Time Regulations 1998.
[65] Maximum weekly working time, length of night work, length of night work involving special hazards or strain, health assessments for adult and young workers.
[66] Regulation 9 Working Time Regulations 1998; regulation 25 excludes this requirement in relation to workers in the armed forces.
[67] On the status of official guidance see *European Commission v UK* [2006] IRLR 888.
[68] On the impact of periods spent 'on call' see *McCartney v Overley House Management* [2006] IRLR 514.
[69] Regulation 10(2) and (3) Working Time Regulations 1998.
[70] See *Gallagher v Alpha Catering Services Ltd* [2005] IRLR 102 on the difference between 'downtime' and rest breaks.

their daily working time is more than four and a half hours[71] they will be entitled to a rest break of at least 30 minutes. This break should be continuous, if possible, and can be spent away from the workstation. Interestingly, and perhaps impracticably, there is a provision that where the young worker works for more than one employer, then the daily working time should be aggregated for the purposes of determining the entitlement to a rest break.[72]

8.4.7 Weekly rest periods

Adult workers are entitled to an uninterrupted rest period of not less than 24 hours in each seven-day period during which they work for an employer.[73] Subject to the employer's decision, this can be taken as one uninterrupted period of 48 hours in each 14-day period. Young workers are entitled to a rest period of not less than 48 hours in each seven-day period that they work.[74] Unlike adult workers, this period is not required to be uninterrupted. According to regulation 8, the period may be interrupted in the case of activities involving periods of work that are split up over the day or are of short duration and may be reduced where it is justified by technical or organisational reasons.[75]

The 7- or 14-day periods can begin on a day established by a relevant agreement. If there is no such agreement, then at the beginning of the week (or every other week) beginning at the start of the week in which employment began.[76] A week starts at midnight between Sunday and Monday.[77] Note that there is no requirement for a Sunday to be part of the rest period.

8.4.8 Annual leave

The Working Time Regulations 1998 introduced, for the first time, a statutory entitlement to paid annual holidays. One survey, conducted a year after the regulations came into effect, found that some 36% of organisations surveyed had introduced new paid holiday provisions for certain groups of workers.[78] A worker is entitled to 4.8 weeks' paid[79] leave per year.[80] The leave year begins on the date on which employment starts and subsequent anniversaries, unless otherwise agreed by a relevant agreement.[81] If a worker joins during

---

[71] Note that there is no requirement for these hours to be consecutive.

[72] Regulation 12 Working Time Regulations 1998.

[73] This is not to include any rest periods to which the worker is entitled under regulation 10(1) (daily rest periods) unless justified by objective or technical reasons concerning the organisation of work: regulation 11(7) Working Time Regulations 1998.

[74] Regulation 11(1)–(3) Working Time Regulations 1998.

[75] It may not be reduced for technical or organisational reasons to less than 36 consecutive hours.

[76] Regulation 11(4) and (5) Working Time Regulations 1998.

[77] Regulation 11(6) Working Time Regulations 1998.

[78] Conducted by IRS Employment Trends; see 'Beating the Clock', *IRS Employment Review* 692, November 1999, p 6.

[79] Regulation 16 Working Time Regulations 1998 specifies that a worker is entitled to be paid in respect of their annual leave. Sections 221–224 ERA 1996 apply for the purpose of determining a week's pay, except for any references to a maximum limit. See *Sanderson v Excel Ltd* [2006] ICR 337 and *Evans v Malley Ltd* [2003] IRLR 156 where a sales representative's commission payments were not included in the calculation of a week's pay.

[80] Regulation 13 Working Time Regulations 1998. This will rise to 5.6 weeks in April 2009 as a result of the Working Time (Amendment) Regulations 2007, SI 2007/2079.

[81] Regulation 15A Working Time Regulations 1998.

the leave year, they have a pro rata entitlement. The leave may be taken in instalments but cannot be replaced by a payment in lieu.[82] Any statutory leave in excess of four weeks can be carried over into the following year.[83] It should be noted that there is no statutory entitlement to bank or public holidays in addition to the leave arrangements in the Working Time Regulations 1998. Thus it is possible for an employer to count bank or public holidays against the entitlement to leave. However, a unilateral decision by one employer to reduce the hourly rate of its employees in order to assist in meeting the costs of paid holidays introduced by these regulations was held not to be permissible by the EAT.[84] In *Caulfield v Marshalls Products*[85] it was accepted that a contractual provision for 'rolled up' holiday pay, which identifies an express amount or percentage by way of addition to basic pay, does not infringe the regulations. According to the Court of Appeal, there is nothing in the Directive which imposes an obligation to pay workers in respect of their holiday at the time it is taken. Nevertheless, a reference was made to the ECJ for its opinion. In the subsequent case of *Robinson-Steele v RD Retail Ltd*,[86] the ECJ ruled that 'rolled up' holiday pay was precluded by the Directive. However, it suggested that such payments could be offset against a worker's entitlement if the employer could prove that the sums were paid transparently and comprehensibly.

A worker may take their leave entitlement when they wish by giving notice to the employer. This freedom is subject to the employer being able to give notice to the worker when to take leave or not to take leave.[87] A notice given by the worker or the employer must fulfil three conditions. These are that:

(1) it may relate to all or part of the leave to which the worker is entitled in a leave year;[88]
(2) it shall specify the days on which leave is to be, or not to be, taken;
(3) it shall be given to the employer, or the worker, by the 'relevant date'.[89]

The 'relevant date' is a date which is twice as many days in advance of the earliest day specified in the notice as the number of days or part-days to which the notice relates. If the notice relates only to the employer requiring the worker not to take leave, then this notice needs to be given as many days in advance of the earliest day specified as the number of days or part-days to which the notice relates.[90] It should be noted that employers are not required to consult with a worker before refusing a request for leave.

Agricultural workers are excluded and the whole notice period may be varied or excluded by a relevant agreement.[91] If a worker is entitled to a rest period, rest break or

---

[82] But see the transitional arrangements under the Working Time (Amendment) Regulations 2007, SI 2007/2079.
[83] See *FN v SDN* [2006] IRLR 561 and the Working Time (Amendment) Regulations 2007, SI 2007/2079.
[84] See *Davies v MJ Wyatt (Decorators) Ltd* [2000] IRLR 759.
[85] [2004] IRLR 564; see also *Smith v Morrisroes Ltd* [2005] IRLR 72.
[86] [2006] IRLR 386.
[87] Regulation 15(1) and (2) Working Time Regulations 1998. See *Sumsion v BBC Scotland* [2007] IRLR 278 and DBERR's 'Your guide to the Working Time Regulations'.
[88] Leave entitlement does not continue to accrue where the individual is on long-term sick leave: see *Commissioners of Inland Revenue v Ainsworth* [2005] IRLR 465.
[89] Regulation 15(3) Working Time Regulations 1998.
[90] Regulation 15(4) Working Time Regulations 1998.
[91] Regulation 15(5) and (6) Working Time Regulations 1998.

annual leave under the provisions of the Working Time Regulations 1998 and also has a contractual right, the worker may take advantage of whichever right is more favourable.[92]

8.4.9 Special cases

Regulation 19 excludes those employed as domestic servants in a private household from the provisions on the maximum working week and those concerning night work and health assessments for night workers.

Those whose working day is not measured or predetermined or determine their own hours are also an excluded category.[93] Examples of this last group are managing executives, family workers or those officiating at religious ceremonies in churches and religious communities. Also included are those who partly determine their own hours and partly have them determined for them. This group only have that part of their work which is predetermined counting against the provisions of the Working Time Regulations 1998, which seems to undermine the protection afforded.

There are a number of situations, in addition to the other exclusions, for which the regulations concerning night work, daily rest periods and weekly rest periods do not apply.[94] These exclusions are subject to compensatory rest periods being given.[95] There are six such situations:

(1) Where the worker's activities are such that the place of work and the place of residence are distant from each other, or there are different places of work which are distant from each other.
(2) Where the worker is engaged in security and surveillance operations, requiring a permanent presence to protect property and persons. Examples of this may be security guards or caretakers.
(3) Where the worker's activities require a continuity of service or production. This results in a large number of exceptions.[96]
(4) Where there is a foreseeable surge in activity, such as in agriculture, tourism and the postal services.
(5) Where the worker's activities are affected by unusual and unforeseeable circumstances, exceptional events, accidents or the imminent risk of accidents.
(6) Where workers work in railway transport and their activities are intermittent, they spend their working time on board trains or their activities are limited to transport timetables and to ensuring the continuity and regularity of traffic.

Regulation 22 provides that shift workers changing shift are excluded from the provisions on daily and weekly rest periods when it is not possible for them to take such

---

[92] Regulation 17 Working Time Regulations 1998.
[93] Regulation 20 Working Time Regulations 1998.
[94] Regulation 21 Working Time Regulations 1998.
[95] Regulation 24 Working Time Regulations 1998.
[96] Regulation 21(c) Working Time Regulations 1998 states that this is in relation to services provided by hospitals, residential establishments and prisons; work at docks or airports; press, radio, television, cinema, postal and telecommunications services and civil protection services; gas, water and electricity production, transmission and distribution; household refuse collection; industries that cannot be interrupted on technical grounds; research and development; agriculture.

rest between those shifts.[97] Neither do these rest periods apply to workers whose activities involve work split up over the course of the day. An example of this may be cleaning staff.[98]

In addition the rules concerning daily rest periods and rest breaks for young workers[99] can be varied if the employer requires a young worker to undertake work for which there is no adult worker available[100] and the need is the result of unusual or unforeseeable circumstances beyond the employer's control or occasioned by exceptional events which could not have been foreseen. Additionally, the need for the young worker's services must be immediate and of a temporary nature. In such circumstances the employee is entitled to compensatory rest to be taken within the following three weeks.

8.4.10 Relevant agreements

Regulation 2(1) defines 'relevant agreement' as a:

> workforce agreement which applies to him, any provision of a collective agreement which forms part of a contract between him and his employer, or any other agreement in writing which is legally enforceable as between the worker and the employer.

The term is therefore an umbrella term which includes collective and workforce agreements as well as any other written agreements such as the contents of the contract of employment. A collective agreement is one within the meaning of section 178 TULRCA 1992 and is an agreement between an employer and an independent trade union within the meaning of section 5 of that Act.[101] In a move opposed by the TUC, but supported by the CBI, the 1998 Regulations introduced the concept of workforce agreements, the requirements for which are set out in Schedule 1 (see Chapter 10). The importance of these requirements is that regulation 23 provides that collective or workforce agreements may modify or exclude the application of certain regulations. These are:

- regulation 4 – the possible extension of the reference period to a maximum of 52 weeks;
- regulation 6 – length of night work;
- regulations 10, 11 and 12 – minimum daily and weekly rest periods and breaks in relation to adult workers.

Regulation 24 provides for compensatory rest when rest periods or breaks are excluded or modified.

8.4.11 Enforcement

The provisions of the Working Time Regulations 1998 which impose obligations upon employers[102] are generally to be enforced by the Health and Safety Executive.[103] An

---

[97] Regulation 25(2) and (3) Working Time Regulations 1998 also exclude, subject to compensatory rest, young workers serving in the armed forces.
[98] Regulation 22(1)(c) Working Time Regulations 1998.
[99] As in regulations 10(2) and 12(4) Working Time Regulations 1998.
[100] Regulation 27 Working Time Regulations 1998.
[101] Regulation 2(1) Working Time Regulations 1998.
[102] Regulations 4(2) (48-hour week), 6(2) and (7) (night work and special hazards), 7(1), (2) and (6) (health assessment provisions), 8 (pattern of work) and 9 (record keeping).
[103] Regulation 28(2) Working Time Regulations 1998; although, in relation to workers employed in those premises for which local authorities are responsible, by the Health and Safety Commission issuing guidance to the local authorities.

employer who fails to comply with any one of the relevant requirements will be guilty of an offence and subject to a fine. The Health and Safety Executive has wide powers for their inspectors to enter premises and investigate and it is an offence to obstruct them in their investigations.[104]

A worker may present a complaint to an employment tribunal relating to an employer's refusal to permit the exercise of those parts of the Working Time Regulations 1998 which provide entitlements to workers,[105] or an employer's refusal to pay for all or any part of the annual leave entitlement.[106] The complaint must be presented within three months,[107] or such further period as the tribunal considers reasonable, beginning with the date on which the exercise of the right should have been permitted or payment made.[108] Where the employment tribunal finds such a complaint well founded, it will make a declaration and award compensation or order the employer to pay the worker the amount the tribunal finds is due to the individual in relation to annual leave. The amount of compensation will be such as the employment tribunal finds just and equitable and will take into account the employer's default in refusing to permit the worker to exercise the right and any loss sustained by the worker in relation to the matters complained of.[109]

Any agreements to exclude or limit the operation of the regulations, including limiting the right of a worker to bring proceedings before an employment tribunal, will be void unless it results from action taken by an ACAS conciliation officer under section 18 Employment Tribunals Act 1996 or it meets the statutory requirements for compromise agreements.[110]

8.4.12 Protection from detriment

Section 45A ERA 1996 provides that a worker has the right not to be subjected to any detriment by any act, or failure to act, by the employer on a number of grounds. These are:

(1) that the worker refused, or proposed to refuse, to comply with a requirement imposed by the employer in contravention of the Working Time Regulations 1998;
(2) that the worker refused, or proposed to refuse, a right conferred by the 1998 Regulations;
(3) for failing to sign a workforce agreement, or any other agreement, with the employer in relation to the 1998 Regulations;
(4) for performing, or proposing to perform, any of the functions or activities of an employee representative for the purpose of the 1998 Regulations;

---

[104] See regulation 29 Working Time Regulations 1998 referring to parts of section 33(1) HASAWA 1974.
[105] These are the provisions concerning daily and weekly rest periods, rest breaks and annual leave; for a detailed summary see regulation 30(1) Working Time Regulations 1998.
[106] Regulation 30 Working Time Regulations 1998.
[107] Six months for members of the armed services.
[108] This period is extended if regulation 15 of the Employment Act 2002 (Dispute Resolution) Regulations 2004 applies. Workers must first submit a statement of grievance to their employer: see paragraphs 6 and 9 Schedule 2 Employment Act 2002.
[109] Regulation 30(3)–(5) Working Time Regulations 1998.
[110] Regulation 35 Working Time Regulations 1998; see also Chapter 5.

(5) that the worker brought proceedings against the employer to enforce a right conferred by the 1998 Regulations;

(6) that the worker alleged that the employer had infringed such a right.

If the detriment is dismissal within the meaning of Part X ERA 1996 and the person is an employee, then those who are qualified must claim unfair dismissal rather than claiming a detriment under section 45A. Dismissal for relying on the rights conferred by the regulations as an employee or an employee representative will be an automatically unfair dismissal.[111] Otherwise a worker may complain to an employment tribunal that they have been subjected to a detriment.[112] If the claim is well founded, the employment tribunal will make a declaration and award compensation. If the claim relates to the termination of a worker's contract, which is not a contract of employment, then the compensation must not exceed the maximum amount that can be awarded to an employee under Part X ERA 1996.[113]

8.5 Statutory right to time off from work

There are a number of reasons for which an employee is entitled to time off work, sometimes with pay. These are, apart from time off for trade union duties and activities and for being a union learning representative, contained in Part VI ERA 1996.

8.5.1 Time off for public duties

There are a large number of statutory bodies that rely on part-time contributors. This in turn relies upon the ability of employees to obtain leave of absence from their employer in order to take part in the activities of these bodies. As a matter of public policy and to help ensure a mixture of individuals that reflect the makeup of the population, it must be in the interests of Government to ensure that it is possible for individuals to take time off work to perform public duties.

Section 50(1) ERA 1996 provides that an employer must permit an employee who is a Justice of the Peace to take time off during working hours to carry out any of their duties. There are no conditions as to length of service with an employer before an employee may take time off during working hours but there is no right to be paid for this activity. Working hours are defined as any time, in accordance with the contract of employment, that the employee is required to be at work.[114] Section 50(2) describes other bodies whose members qualify for time off. These include members of a local authority,[115] a statutory tribunal, a police authority,[116] a board of prison visitors or a prison visiting committee, a relevant health authority,[117] a relevant education authority[118] or the Environment Agency.

---

[111] Section 101A ERA 1996; similarly section 105(4A) makes selection for redundancy on these grounds an unfair dismissal.
[112] Section 48(1ZA) ERA 1996. Workers must first submit a statement of grievance to their employer: see paragraphs 6 and 9 Schedule 2 Employment Act 2002.
[113] Section 49(5A) ERA 1996.
[114] Section 50(11) ERA 1996.
[115] Section 50(5) ERA 1996 offers a definition of a local authority.
[116] Someone appointed under Schedule 2 Police Act 1996: see section 50(6) ERA 1996.
[117] A National Health Service Trust or Health Authority: see section 50(7) ERA 1996.
[118] The managing or governing body of an educational establishment: see section 50(8) ERA 1996.

The time off in relation to these bodies is for certain specific purposes. These purposes are: (i) the attendance at a meeting of the body or of any of its committees or sub-committees; (ii) the doing of something approved by the committee or body for the purpose of the discharge of the functions of the body or committee.[119] Section 50(10)(a) provides the Secretary of State with the power to add organisations to the list in order to bring attendance at their meetings and other work into these provisions.

The amount of time off that an employee is to be permitted to take is that which is reasonable having regard to all the circumstances; in particular, to how much time is required, how much the employee has already been permitted under sections 168 and 170 TULRCA 1992,[120] and the circumstances of the employer's business and the effect of the employee's absence on the running of that business.[121] In *Borders Regional Council v Maule*[122] the EAT considered the situation of a school teacher who was a member of a number of public bodies, including the Borders Social Security Appeal Panel. During the previous year she had taken 22 days' leave of absence for such duties and 24 days in the year preceding that. The employer tried to regulate and limit the absences to two days a month. During one month when she had already taken two days, her request for an extra day to attend training was turned down. The EAT held that all the circumstances needed to be taken into account, including the number and frequency of other absences permitted by the employer, in order to assess whether the employer was in breach of the statute. The EAT also observed that where an employee was undertaking public duties, to which the statute applies, there should be a discussion between the employer and the employee to establish a pattern of absences by agreement. An employee who was undertaking a number of such absences also had a duty to plan their level of commitment and produce a pattern that was reasonable in the circumstances.

An employee may present a complaint to an employment tribunal that an employer has failed to permit them to take time off. The complaint needs to be made within three months beginning with the date on which the failure occurred, unless it was not reasonably practicable to do so. If the tribunal finds the complaint well founded, then it will make a declaration to that effect and award compensation.[123] The amount of compensation will take into account the employer's default and any attributable loss suffered by the employee.[124]

8.5.2 Time off to look for work or arrange training[125]

An employee who has been given notice of dismissal by reason of redundancy is entitled to take reasonable time off during the employee's working hours[126] for the purpose of looking

---

[119] Section 50(3) ERA 1996.
[120] Time off for trade union duties and activities.
[121] Section 50(4) ERA 1996.
[122] [1993] IRLR 199.
[123] It may not make conditions about what time off an individual may be permitted to have in the future: see *Corner v Buckinghamshire County Council* [1978] IRLR 320.
[124] Section 51 ERA 1996.
[125] Section 52 ERA 1996.
[126] Defined in the same way as for time off for public duties: see section 52(3).

for new employment or making arrangements for training for future employment. This applies to employees who have two years' continuous service at the time the notice was due to expire or would have expired if given in accordance with section 86(1) ERA 1996.[127]

An employee who has time off under section 52 ERA 1996 is entitled to be paid at the appropriate hourly rate. The hourly rate is arrived at by taking the amount of one week's pay divided by the number of normal working hours in a week for that employee under the contract of employment in force at the time notice of dismissal was given. If the working hours vary from week to week, then the average over a 12-week period, ending with the last complete week before the day on which notice is given, is taken.[128]

If the employer unreasonably refuses to allow an employee to take time off from work, the employee is entitled to make a complaint to an employment tribunal within three months of the date on which time off should have been given. The tribunal, if it finds the complaint well founded, may make a declaration and order the employer to pay the employee an amount equal to the remuneration they would have received if they had taken the time off, provided that this does not exceed 40% of a week's pay for the employee concerned.[129]

8.5.3 Time off for ante-natal care

A pregnant employee is entitled to time off during working hours if she has, on the advice of a registered medical practitioner, a registered midwife or a registered health visitor made an appointment for the purposes of receiving ante-natal care. The woman may be required to produce a certificate from one of the above stating that she is pregnant as well as an appointment card or some other document showing that an appointment has been made.[130] This evidence is not required for the first appointment during the pregnancy. A woman is entitled to be paid by her employer during the period of absence from work.[131] It is important that pregnant women are not treated less favourably than others in the period before maternity leave begins. In *Pederson v Kvickly Save*[132] the ECJ considered a situation in Denmark where employees absent from work through pregnancy-related sickness prior to their maternity leave were paid less than other workers who were absent for non-pregnancy-related illnesses. The court held that to treat pregnant women in this way was contrary to Article 141 EC (ex 119) and the Equal Pay Directive and was to be regarded as treatment based upon the pregnancy and was therefore discriminatory.

If time off is refused or if the employer fails to pay the whole or any part of any amount to which the employee is entitled, then the employee may complain to an employment tribunal. This complaint must be made within three months of the appointment, or longer if an employment tribunal is satisfied that it was not reasonably practicable for the complaint to be presented within the three-month deadline. The tribunal may award compensation equivalent to the amount that the woman would have received if she had

---

[127] Minimum levels of notice to be given.
[128] Section 53(1)–(3) ERA 1996.
[129] Sections 53(4), (5) and 54 ERA 1996.
[130] Section 55(1)–(2) ERA 1996.
[131] Section 56(1) ERA 1996.
[132] Case C-66/96 [1999] IRLR 55 ECJ.

taken the time off, or an amount equal to the non-payment or under-payment of remuneration due.[133]

8.5.4 Time off for dependants

Clause 3 of the Framework Agreement on parental leave[134] states:

> Member States and/or management and labour shall take the necessary measures to entitle workers to time off from work, in accordance with national legislation, collective agreements and/or practice, on grounds of *force majeure* for urgent family reasons in cases of sickness or accident making the immediate presence of the worker indispensable.

The provisions to implement this requirement are contained in sections 57A and 57B ERA 1996.[135] They permit an employee to take a 'reasonable' amount of time off during working hours to deal with specified emergencies in relation to designated people. No definition of the word 'reasonable' is offered by the new legislation and it is likely that the reasonableness of the amount of time taken off will vary according to circumstances.

Many employers will allow employees time off in such circumstances as a matter of routine. The difference now is that the employee has a statutory right to the time off. There is also no indication in these provisions as to whether this time off should be with pay or without pay. There is also no requirement to keep records of the time taken off by employees. However, employers might feel that it is wise to do so because such records might be of assistance in showing that the amount of time taken was reasonable or not.

Section 57A ERA 1996 refers to employees being permitted to take a reasonable amount of time off 'in order to take action which is necessary'. Generally the right is for the care of dependants, although this is given a generous meaning within the Act. For these purposes dependants are: a spouse; a child; a parent; a person who lives in the same household as the employee and is not the employee's employee, tenant, lodger or boarder; any person who reasonably relies on the employee either for assistance on an occasion when the person falls ill or is injured or assaulted, or relies on the employee to make arrangements for the provision of care in the event of illness or injury. Section 57A(6) also makes it clear that illness or injury in the above definitions includes mental illness and injury.

8.5.4.1 Situations which qualify

The ERA 1996 specifies a number of situations which, if they occur to a dependant, entitle the employee to be permitted time off by the employer.[136] These are:

(1) to provide assistance when a dependant falls ill, gives birth or is injured or assaulted;
(2) to make provision for the care of a dependant when they fall ill or are injured;
(3) as a result of the death of a dependant;[137]

---

[133] Sections 56–57 ERA 1996.
[134] See Chapter 9.
[135] Added to the ERA 1996 by Schedule 4 Part II ERELA 1999.
[136] Section 57A(1) ERA 1996.
[137] See *Foster v Cartwright Black* [2004] IRLR 781.

(4) to deal with unexpected disruption or termination of care arrangements made for a dependant; and

(5) to deal with any incidents involving a child of the employee whilst at school.

The DBERR has given examples of situations that are likely to qualify. For example, when a dependant falls ill or has been involved in an accident or assaulted, including where the victim is hurt or distressed rather than injured physically, or when a partner is having a baby, or to make longer-term care arrangements for a dependant who is ill or injured.

It is clear that the Government's view was that such a right to time off should be linked to genuine emergencies, rather than a need to deal with more mundane domestic issues such as awaiting the arrival of a plumber to carry out repairs. During the report stage of the Employment Relations Bill, Lord Sainsbury stated on behalf of the Government:

> The statutory right will be restricted to urgent cases of real need. The emergency must involve a dependant who is either a family member or someone who relies upon the employee for assistance in the particular circumstances.

He then gave some examples of what the right to time off was intended to cover:

> We intend the right to apply where a dependant becomes sick or has an accident, or is assaulted, including where the victim is distressed rather than physically injured . . . reasonable time off if an employee suffers a bereavement of a family member, to deal with the consequences of that bereavement . . .
>
> Employees will be able to take time off in the event of the unexpected absence of the carer, where the person is a dependant of the employee. So if the childminder or nurse does not turn up, the employee will be able to sort things out without fearing reprisals at work . . .
>
> Employees may have to take time off to attend to a problem arising at their children's school or during school hours . . .
>
> A father will have the right to be on hand at the birth of his child . . .[138]

The ERA 1996 gives no indication about the length of time that should be permitted. It is likely to vary according to the type of incident and the only condition is that the employee is entitled to a 'reasonable' period of time off work. There will clearly be difficulties for employers in defining what is reasonable and whether each incident needs to be looked at on its merits or whether one can take into account the number of absences taken by an employee.

8.5.4.2 Notice requirements

Employees qualify for time off to deal with these emergencies if they tell their employer the reason for the absence, as soon as is reasonably practicable, and also tell the employer for how long they plan to be absent.[139] Failure to allow an employee time off may result in a complaint to an employment tribunal. The employee must make a complaint within three months beginning with the date when the refusal occurred or longer if the tribunal considers that it was not reasonably practicable to do so.[140] If the employment tribunal agrees with the complaint it shall make a declaration to that effect and may award com-

---

[138] HL Report stage, HL Deb, 8 July 1999, cols 1083–1089.
[139] Section 57A(2) ERA 1996. See *Truelove v Safeway* [2005] IRLR 589.
[140] Section 57B(2) ERA 1996.

pensation to the employee, the amount of which will take into account the circumstances surrounding the employer's refusal and any loss sustained by the employee.[141]

8.5.4.3 Protection from detriment and dismissal

According to regulation 19 MPL Regulations 1999, an employee is entitled not to be subjected to any detriment[142] by any act, or failure to act, by the employer for taking time off under section 57A ERA 1996. Similarly, an employee who is dismissed when the reason (or the principal reason) for the dismissal is taking time off under section 57A ERA 1996 will be regarded as unfairly dismissed.

Similarly, if an employee is dismissed for reasons of redundancy and it is shown that the circumstances constituting the redundancy applied equally to one or more employees in the same business holding similar positions who have not been made redundant, and the reason (or principal reason) for the employee being selected for dismissal was connected with taking time off under section 57A ERA 1996, the dismissal will be regarded as unfair.

In *Qua v John Ford Morrison Solicitors*[143] the claimant was a single mother whose young son had medical problems. As a result she was away from work for 17 days until she was dismissed ten months after her employment started. According to the EAT, section 57A(1)(a) ERA 1996 is dealing with something unforeseen and does not allow employees to take time off in order to provide care themselves beyond the reasonable amount necessary to enable them to deal with the immediate crisis.[144] To determine whether action is 'necessary', factors to be taken into account include: the nature of the incident; the closeness of the relationship between the employee and the dependant; and the extent to which anyone else was available to assist. However, the EAT thought that for these purposes the inconvenience caused to the employer's business was irrelevant.

8.5.5 Time off for pension scheme trustees[145]

Employees who are trustees of the employer's 'relevant occupational pension scheme'[146] must be permitted time off during the employee's working hours[147] for the purpose of: (i) performing any of the duties of a trustee; (ii) undergoing training relevant to the performance of those duties.[148] The amount of time off and any conditions attached to it must be reasonable having regard to how much time is required for the performance of the duties and training, as well as the circumstances of the business and the effect of the employee's absence on the running of that business.

An employer who permits an employee to take time off under section 58 ERA 1996 must pay the employee for the time taken off, for which permission had been given, as if they

---

[141] Section 57B(4) ERA 1996.
[142] See section 47C ERA 1996.
[143] [2003] IRLR 184.
[144] Section 57A(1)(b) ERA 1996 permits reasonable time off to make longer-term arrangements for care.
[145] Sections 58–60 ERA 1996.
[146] Relevant occupational pension scheme is one defined in section 1 Pensions Act 1993 and established under trust: section 58(3)(a) ERA 1996.
[147] Working hours is any time, in accordance with the contract of employment, that the employee is required to be at work: section 58(4) ERA 1996.
[148] Training can be on the employer's premises or elsewhere: section 58(3)(c) ERA 1996.

had been at work. If the remuneration for the work which they would normally be doing varies with the amount of work done, the employee must be paid by calculating the average hourly earnings.[149] An employee may make a complaint to an employment tribunal that there has been a failure to allow time off or to pay for it within three months beginning with the date when the failure occurred, unless the tribunal decides it was not reasonably practicable. The employment tribunal may make a declaration and award compensation to be paid by the employer to the employee. The amount of the compensation will have regard to the employer's default and any attributable loss suffered by the employee.

8.5.6 Time off for employee representatives[150]

In certain circumstances, an employee elected for the purpose of representing employees in discussions with the employer has a statutory right to be paid reasonable time off during the employee's working hours for the purpose of carrying out the functions of an employee representative. Section 61 ERA 1996 provides that the employee representatives with whom an employer should consult when proposing collective redundancies[151] and a transfer of an undertaking[152] are entitled to such time off. Candidates for election as employee representatives also have such an entitlement. Similarly the Transnational Information and Consultation of Employees Regulations 1999 (TICE Regulations 1999)[153] provide that an employee who is a member of a Special Negotiating Body, a member of a European Works Council, an information and consultation representative, or a candidate in an election for any of these, is also entitled to reasonable time off with pay. The working hours of any employee are any time that the employee is required to be at work in accordance with the contract of employment.[154]

Employee representatives or candidates for election are entitled to be paid at the appropriate hourly rate for permitted time off. This rate is a week's pay divided by the normal working hours of the employee, according to the contract of employment in force on the day that leave is taken. Where there are no normal working hours or the number of hours varies, then the average over a 12-week period is taken. Where an employee has been employed for less than 12 weeks, then reference is made to the normal working hours of other employees of the same employer with relevant comparable employment.[155]

An employee may make a complaint to an employment tribunal that the employer unreasonably refused time off or failed to pay the whole or part of the remuneration to which the employee was entitled. The complaint must be made within three months of the day when time off should have been permitted, unless it was not reasonably practicable to do so. If the tribunal finds the complaint well founded, then it shall make a declaration to

---

[149] The average hourly earnings of the employee or of persons in comparable employment with the same employer; if none of these, then an average figure which is reasonable in the circumstances: section 59(4) ERA 1996.
[150] Sections 61–63 ERA 1996.
[151] See Part IV Chapter II TULRCA 1992.
[152] See regulations 10 and 11 Transfer of Undertakings (Protection of Employment) Regulations 1981, SI 1981/1794.
[153] SI 1999/3323 regulations 25–27; see Chapter 10.
[154] Section 61(2) ERA 1996; regulation 25(2) TICE Regulations 1999.
[155] Section 62 ERA 1996; regulation 26 TICE Regulations 1999.

this effect and order the employer to pay the employee an amount equal to that which would have been paid if the time off had been permitted, or, if the complaint is about not being paid, order the employer to pay the amount due to the employee.[156]

8.5.7 Time off for a young person for study or training[157]

Certain employees are entitled to time off with pay during the employee's working hours for the purpose of undertaking study or training leading to a relevant qualification. If the employee is someone supplied to another employer (the principal) to work in accordance with a contract between the employer and the principal, then the obligations under the regulations fall upon the principal.[158] The employee must: (i) be 16 or 17 years of age; (ii) not be receiving full-time secondary[159] or further[160] education; and (iii) not have attained such standard of achievement as is prescribed by regulations made by the Secretary of State.[161] A 'relevant' qualification is an external[162] qualification which would contribute to the attainment of the standard prescribed in the regulations issued by the Secretary of State and would be likely to enhance the employee's employment prospects (whether with their employer or otherwise). Where an employee is 18 years of age and began study or training leading to a relevant qualification before that age, then the provisions as described continue to apply.[163]

The amount of time to be permitted needs to be reasonable in all the circumstances, taking into account the requirements of the employee's study or training, the circumstances of the business of the employer or the principal and the effect of the time off on the running of the business.[164] Pay is to be at the appropriate hourly rate. This rate is a week's pay divided by the normal working hours of the employee, according to the contract of employment in force on the day that leave is taken. Where there are no normal working hours or the number of hours varies, then the average over a 12-week period is taken. If an employee has been employed for less than 12 weeks, then reference is made to the normal working hours of other employees of the same employer with relevant comparable employment.[165]

An employee may make a complaint to an employment tribunal that the employer or principal unreasonably refused time off or failed to pay the whole or part of the remuneration to which the employee was entitled. The complaint must be made within three months of the day when time off should have been permitted, unless it was not reasonably practicable to do so. If the tribunal finds the complaint well founded, it must

---

[156] Section 63 ERA 1996; regulation 27 TICE Regulations 1999.
[157] Sections 63A–63C ERA 1996.
[158] Section 63A(3) ERA 1996.
[159] Secondary as in the Education Act 1996.
[160] Further as described in Schedule 2 Further and Higher Education Act 1992.
[161] Right to Time Off for Study or Training Regulations 2001, SI 2001/2801; regulation 3 specifies standards of achievement.
[162] An external qualification is an academic or vocational qualification awarded or authenticated by a body as specified by the Secretary of State in the Schedule to regulation 4 Right to Time Off for Study or Training Regulations.
[163] Section 63A(4) ERA 1996.
[164] Section 63A(5) ERA 1996.
[165] Section 63B ERA 1996.

make a declaration to this effect and order the employer or principal to pay the employee an amount equal to that which would have been paid if the time off had been permitted, or, if the complaint is about not being paid, order the employer or principal to pay the amount due to the employee.[166]

8.5.8 Time off for trade union duties, activities and union learning representatives

Sections 168–170 TULRCA 1992 provide that an employer must permit officials and members of independent trade unions, recognised by the employer, to take time off during working hours for purpose of carrying out the duties[167] of, or taking part in the activities of, the trade union.[168] There is a distinction between carrying out trade union duties and carrying out trade union activities. The former relates to duties carried out by officials, whilst the latter is concerned with the activities of members of a trade union. The statutory provisions providing trade union officials with a right to a reasonable amount of time off with pay to carry out their trade union duties and to undergo trade union training originated in the Employment Protection Act 1975. The right for an employee who is an official of an independent trade union recognised by the employer to take time off during working hours[169] is now contained in section 168 TULRCA 1992. Official means either an officer[170] of the union, or of a branch or section of the union, or a person elected or appointed to be a representative of the members or some of them.[171] The right is to enable the official to carry out duties relating to the following circumstances:

(1) Those duties concerned with negotiations or matters related to collective bargaining[172] for which the trade union is recognised by the employer.[173] This appears to be a test of proximity, i.e. to what extent are the duties undertaken by the official related to negotiations or collective bargaining. In *Adlington v British Bakeries*,[174] union officials wanted time off to attend a workshop on Government proposals to repeal 1954 legislation which controlled working hours, etc. The employer had agreed to give them time off, but not with pay. The Court of Appeal held that the proximity of meetings to actual negotiations was a matter of degree and therefore a question of fact. In this case

---

[166] Section 63C ERA 1996.
[167] This includes accompanying workers, at their request, to disciplinary and grievance hearings: see section 10(7) ERELA 1999.
[168] The employee needs to ensure that a request for time off has been made and that the employer has refused the request, ignored it or failed to respond before they can establish a right to compensation: see *Ryford Ltd v Drinkwater* [1996] IRLR 16.
[169] Working hours are those hours when, in accordance with the contract of employment, the individual is required to be at work: section 173(1) TULRCA 1992.
[170] Officer means any member of the governing body of a trade union or any trustee of any fund applicable for the purposes of the union: section 119 TULRCA 1992.
[171] Section 119 TULRCA 1992.
[172] Section 168(2) TULRCA 1992. See *Beal v Beecham Group Ltd* [1982] IRLR 192 CA where duties connected with collective bargaining were held to include duties in preparation for that bargaining. See also *London Ambulance Service v Charlton* [1992] IRLR 510.
[173] See section 178 TULRCA 1992 and Chapter 12.
[174] [1989] IRLR 218 CA.

the purpose of the workshop was to acquaint union representatives with the implications of repeal, which would lead to negotiations, rather than any attempt to prevent the repeal. In contrast an unofficial preparatory meeting of shop stewards was held to be outside the scope of the statute. It was not convened or authorised by the trade union, neither did the union ask that its shop stewards be given leave to attend.[175]

(2) Those duties[176] connected with the performance, on behalf of the employees, of functions related to collective bargaining matters to which the employer has agreed. Section 199 TULRCA 1992 provides that ACAS has a duty to provide practical guidance on the time off to be permitted by an employer.[177] Paragraph 12 ACAS Code of Practice gives a number of examples of trade union duties for which time off should be given. These include functions connected with terms and conditions of employment, matters of discipline and the machinery for negotiation or consultation. However, time off to attend a conference about collecting information from employers may not fall within the terms of the legislation where there is already a means for obtaining that information.[178]

(3) Those duties[179] concerned with the receipt of information from the employer and consultation by the employer concerning collective redundancies and transfers of undertakings.[180]

(4) For the purpose of undergoing training in industrial relations.[181] This training needs to be relevant to the carrying out of the duties for which recognition is given and needs to be approved by the TUC or the union of which the individual is an official. The ACAS Code of Practice (see above) gives examples of the types of training that might be included, such as the structure of the union or the role of the official. The ACAS Code of Practice makes it clear that an official will be more effective if they possess the skills and knowledge that might come from this training.

The time off for officials is with pay on the basis that the individual should receive what they would have earned if they had worked during the time off.[182] The guidance given by ACAS[183] on this subject is that there is no statutory requirement to pay for time off where training is undertaken at a time when the official would not normally have been at work. This was a problem especially for union officials who were part-time employees or worked shifts as they appeared to be excluded from receiving pay for union duties during the hours when they were not at work. In *Hairsine v Kingston-upon-Hull City Council*[184] a swimming pool attendant was a shop steward and also worked a shift system. The individual was given time off with pay to attend a training course, only some of which clashed with the working

---

[175] *Ashley v Ministry of Defence* [1984] IRLR 57, where, in addition, a union/MOD advisory committee was held to be too remote from the actual negotiations.
[176] Section 168(2)(b) TULRCA 1992.
[177] ACAS Code of Practice on Time Off for Trade Union Duties and Activities 2003 which was brought into force on 24 April 2003 by SI 2003/1191.
[178] See *Depledge v Pye Telecommunications Ltd* [1981] ICR 82.
[179] Section 168(2)(c) TULRCA 1992.
[180] Section 188 TULRCA 1992 and Transfer of Undertakings Regulations 2006, SI 2006/246; see Chapter 10.
[181] Section 168(2) TULRCA 1992.
[182] Section 169 TULRCA 1992.
[183] Section 2 paragraph 128 ACAS Code of Practice.
[184] [1992] IRLR 211.

hours. This individual was unable to substitute the daytime hours spent on the course for the evening shift hours they were expected to work. However, part-timers are more likely to be protected.[185] *Davies v Neath Port Talbot Borough Council*[186] concerned a council employee who worked a 22-hour week. The individual was a health and safety representative who was given time off to attend two five-day courses run by the union. The employer agreed to pay for the usual working hours, not the 40 and $32^1/_2$ hours actually spent on the courses. In this instance the employee made an equal pay claim under Article 119 EC (now 141). The EAT agreed that part-time workers had a right, under Article 119, to be paid on the same basis as full-timers when attending union-run courses. As the great majority of part-timers are female, to do otherwise would amount to indirect sex discrimination. The EAT concluded that section 169(2) TULRCA 1992 which provides for the individual to be paid what they would have earned if they had been at work was, in so far as it applied to part-timers, in conflict with Article 119 and therefore could not be applied.[187]

8.5.8.1 Taking part in trade union activities

Section 170 TULRCA 1992 provides that employees who are also members of an independent trade union recognised by the employer are entitled to time off during working hours for the purpose of taking part in any activities of the trade union or any activities in relation to which the employee is acting as a representative of the union. This right excludes time off for activities in relation to industrial action, whether or not in contemplation or furtherance of an industrial dispute.[188] There is no statutory right to pay during this period of time off. Examples of trade union activities are contained in paragraphs 30–31 ACAS Code of Practice. They include attending workplace meetings to discuss and vote on the outcome of negotiations or voting in union elections. Examples of acting as a representative are attending branch, area or regional meetings of the union to discuss union business or attending meetings of official policy-making bodies, such as the union's annual conference. In some way the activity needs to be linked to the employment relationship and the trade union. Thus a TUC lobby of Parliament against an Education Reform Bill was not an activity which would entitle a number of teachers, who were members of the National Union of Teachers, to time off under section 170 TULRCA 1992. Such a lobby was to express political and ideological objections to the proposed statute and was not part of the employment relationship.[189]

Sections 168(3) and 170(3) TULRCA 1992 state that the amount of time off, and the purposes for which it is taken, should be 'reasonable in all the circumstances' having regard to the relevant provisions of the ACAS Code of Practice. In *Wignall v British Gas Corporation*[190] the EAT held that each application need not be looked at in isolation. It would be reasonable for an employer, when considering a request for time off, to consider

---

[185] See the Part-time Workers Regulations 2000 (Chapter 3 above).
[186] [1999] IRLR 769.
[187] The EAT also refused to follow *Manor Bakeries v Nazir* [1996] IRLR 604, which had held that attendance at a union conference was not 'work' under Article 119.
[188] Section 170(2) TULRCA 1992; see Chapter 12.
[189] *Luce v London Borough of Bexley* [1990] IRLR 422.
[190] [1984] IRLR 493.

this in the light of time off already taken. The Code states that trade unions should be aware of the variety of difficulties for employers and take into account the size of the organisation, the number of workers, the production process, the need to maintain a service to the public and the need for safety and security at all times. Equally, employers should be aware of the difficulties for trade unions in ensuring effective representation for a variety of workers, such as those who are shift workers, part-timers, employed at dispersed locations and workers with particular domestic commitments.[191] Trade union officials and members requesting time off should give as much notice as possible, giving details of the purpose of the time off, the intended location and the timing and duration of the time off.[192]

The remedy for employees is to present a complaint to an employment tribunal.[193] The complaint needs to be made within three months of the date when the failure occurred, unless the tribunal finds that it was not reasonably practicable to do so.[194] If the tribunal finds the complaint well founded, it may make a declaration and award compensation. This compensation will be such as the tribunal decides is just and equitable and will take into account any losses suffered by the employee as a result of the employer's actions, including unpaid wages.[195]

8.5.8.2 Union learning representatives

Section 168A(1) TULRCA provides that an employee who is a member of an independent trade union recognised by the employer, must be given time off with pay to perform the duties of being a union learning representative (ULR).[196] The employer has this obligation if notice has been received from the trade union that the employee is a ULR and has undergone (or will undergo) sufficient training for the role.[197] The employee is also to be permitted time off to undergo training for the role.[198]

The functions of a ULR are, in relation to members of the trade union and others, to:

(1) analyse learning or training needs;
(2) provide information about learning or training matters;
(3) arrange learning or training; and
(4) promote the value of learning or training.

This will include consultations with the employer about carrying on these activities and any preparations necessary for carrying on these activities.[199]

8.6 Protection of wages

One of the major aspects of the relationship between the worker and the employer is the payment for the work carried out, or time spent at the employer's disposal. Section 27

---

[191] Paragraphs 35–36 ACAS Code of Practice.
[192] Paragraph 39 ACAS Code of Practice.
[193] Sections 168(4), 169(5) and 170(4) TULRCA 1992.
[194] Section 171 TULRCA 1992.
[195] Section 172 TULRCA 1992; see *Skiggs v South West Trains Ltd* [2005] IRLR 459.
[196] The ACAS Code of Practice on Time Off for Trade Union Duties and Activities includes guidance on time off for union learning representatives.
[197] Section 168A(3) TULRCA 1992.
[198] Section 168A(7) TULRCA 1992.
[199] Section 168A(2) TULRCA 1992.

ERA 1996 provides a statutory definition of the meaning of wages etc. Wages are to include any fee, bonus,[200] commission,[201] holiday pay,[202] or other emolument relating to the employment, whether or not payable under the worker's contract. It can also include statutory sick pay[203] and statutory maternity pay.[204]

8.6.1 Unauthorised deductions

Workers have a right not to suffer deductions of pay by their employer, unless the deduction is authorised by statute,[205] a relevant provision of the worker's contract or by the worker previously signifying their agreement to the deductions in writing.[206] A 'relevant provision' of a contract is a term of the contract which has been notified to the worker prior to the employer making the deduction.[207] In *Kerr v The Sweater Shop (Scotland) Ltd*[208] it was held that an individual need not agree in writing to the deduction because it was possible for the agreement to be given through continuing to work once the change had been brought to the individual's attention.

The deduction in wages is to be treated as the difference between the amount owed to the worker[209] and the amount actually paid.[210] This can be considered on each occasion that wages are paid. Thus where a person is paid a regular salary, each occasion that the salary is paid can be considered for the purposes of whether there has been an unlawful deduction of wages.[211] The conditions needed to show that the worker has given their consent to the making of a deduction are: (i) that there must be a document which clearly states that the deductions are to be made from wages; (ii) it must be clear that the worker agrees to the deduction being made.[212]

---

[200] See *Farrell Matthews and Weir v Hansen* [2005] IRLR 160 where the EAT held that an employee suffered an unlawful deduction when the employer refused to pay the balance of a non-contractual discretionary bonus which was payable in monthly instalments.

[201] See *Kent Management Services Ltd v Butterfield* [1992] IRLR 394, which held that the withholding of commission was an unlawful deduction, even though the commission might be on a discretionary and non-contractual basis.

[202] See *Campbell & Smith Construction Group Ltd v Greenwood* [2001] IRLR 588, where an employer's refusal to give an extra day off with pay following the Government's announcement that there was to be an additional public holiday, on 31 December, to celebrate the millennium was not held to be an unlawful deduction of wages. It was a day that the employer gave off with pay every year.

[203] See *Taylor Gordon Ltd v Timmons* [2004] IRLR 180.

[204] For a full list of what is included and excluded see section 27 ERA 1996.

[205] For example, income tax and national insurance contributions.

[206] Section 13(1) ERA 1996; section 15(1) ERA 1996 is similarly concerned with the rights of employees not to have to make payments to an employer.

[207] Section 13(2) ERA 1996; 'to the worker' means some written notification, not just the displaying of a notice; see *Kerr v The Sweater Shop (Scotland) Ltd* [1996] IRLR 424; also see section 15(2) on 'relevant provision' concerning the right not to have to make payments to an employer.

[208] [1996] IRLR 424.

[209] This can be what is 'properly payable' in terms of employee expectations.

[210] Section 13(3) ERA 1996.

[211] See *Murray v Strathclyde Regional Council* [1992] IRLR 396, where a deduction in one month for a series of alleged overpayments was held to be a deduction in salary in terms of the statute.

[212] See *Potter v Hunt Contracts* [1992] IRLR 108, which concerned the deduction of the balance of a loan made to the employee from wages due on termination of employment.

Section 14 ERA 1996 provides a list of deductions which are excluded from section 13 ERA 1996.[213] These are if the deduction:

(1) is a reimbursement of overpayment of wages or expenses[214] paid by the employer;[215]
(2) is made as a result of disciplinary proceedings resulting from a statutory provision;[216]
(3) is as a result of a statutory requirement to deduct sums and pay them over to a public authority;
(4) is where there is prior contractual agreement, or other prior written agreement, for the deduction of money to be paid over to a third person, after notification by the third person of the amount due from the worker;
(5) is as a result of the worker taking part in industrial action;[217]
(6) is a deduction, made with prior written consent of the worker, resulting from the order of a court or tribunal.

There are special provisions for dealing with cash shortages and stock deficiencies in retail employment.[218]

It is not permissible to make a complaint about a threatened deduction from wages.[219] Section 23(1) ERA 1996 states that a worker may present a complaint to an employment tribunal that the employer *has made* a deduction from wages in contravention of section 13 ERA 1996 or received a payment in contravention of section 15 ERA 1996.[220] The complaint must be made within three months of the date of the deduction or payment. This date is the last date on which the payment could have been made in accordance with the contract of employment, rather than from the date when it was actually made.[221] Where the complaint relates to a series of deductions or payments, then it must be within three months of the last deduction or payment, subject to the employment tribunal being satisfied that this was not reasonably practicable.[222] If the tribunal finds the complaint well founded it may issue a declaration and order the employer to repay the unauthorised deductions or payments to the worker.[223]

A failure to make a payment in lieu of notice is unlikely to be treated as a deduction in wages, although it might amount to a breach of contract. In *Delaney v Staples t/a De Montfort Recruitment*[224] the House of Lords considered a case where an employee was

---

[213] Section 16 ERA 1996 provides similar exceptions concerning the right of an employee not to have to make payments to an employer.

[214] Expenses are not to be subject to too much scrutiny; if there is a profit element in expenses, this would not necessarily stop the whole amount from being expenses; it is not the tribunal's job to try and apportion sums in order to be precise about what are expenses and what are not: *London Borough of Southwark v O'Brien* [1996] IRLR 420.

[215] See *Murray v Strathclyde Regional Council* [1992] IRLR 396.

[216] It has been suggested that this provision refers not to private employers, but to such services as the police or fire service: see *Chiltern House Ltd v Chambers* [1990] IRLR 88.

[217] See *Gill v Ford Motor Company Ltd* [2004] IRLR 840.

[218] Sections 17–22 ERA 1996.

[219] See *Mennell v Newell & Wright (Transport Contractors Ltd)* [1997] IRLR 519 CA.

[220] An employer shall not receive a payment from a worker employed by them unless it is required by statute or has the worker's prior agreement in writing.

[221] See *Group 4 Nightspeed Ltd v Gilbert* [1997] IRLR 398; also *Taylorplan Services Ltd v Jackson* [1996] IRLR 184.

[222] Section 23 ERA 1996. See *List Design Ltd v Douglas & Catley* [2003] IRLR 14.

[223] Sections 24–26 ERA 1996.

[224] [1992] IRLR 191 HL.

summarily dismissed and given a cheque as payment in lieu of notice. The employer subsequently stopped the cheque, claiming that the employee had taken confidential information with her. The employee then claimed an unlawful deduction had been made from her wages. The court held that a payment in lieu was not wages where it relates to the period after employment. Wages are payments in respect of rendering services during employment. All payments relating to the termination of the contract are excluded unless expressly provided for in the legislation. However, payments paid after termination in relation to work done before the termination are wages. In *Robertson v Blackstone Franks Investment Management Ltd*[225] the payment of commission earned during employment but paid after the employee had left was held to be wages within the meaning of the Act.

Any variations in contractual terms to allow deductions does not give authorisation to the making of a deduction until the variation takes effect.[226] If there is a variation in pay resulting from a change in work patterns permitted by the contract, then a related variation in pay may not be treated as a deduction. Thus when there is a change in shift patterns, permitted by the contract of employment, which results in the payment of a lower shift premium, this reduction in payment could not be treated as an unauthorised deduction from wages.[227] If the variation in a contract is as a result of a unilateral decision of the employer, then any resulting reduction in wages may contravene section 13 ERA 1996. In *McCree v London Borough of Tower Hamlets*[228] the employer introduced a new bonus system which absorbed a previously paid supplement to an employee. The unilateral abolition of this supplement was held to be a breach of the legislation.[229]

Where the employer makes an error in calculating the gross amount of pay due to a worker, the shortfall is not to be treated as a deduction.[230] For these purposes, an error is not one that is based upon a misunderstanding of the law. In *Morgan v West Glamorgan County Council*[231] an employee was demoted for disciplinary reasons and suffered a reduction in salary. The employer wrongly thought that they had the contractual authority to do this. This error was not an error in terms of section 13(4) ERA 1996, but rather the result of a deliberate decision by the employer to demote and reduce salary. Thus the shortfall in salary was to be treated as a deduction for the purposes of the statute.[232]

8.6.2 Normal working hours and a week's pay

Sections 220–229 ERA 1996 define a week's pay. For such purposes as the basic award of compensation for unfair dismissal[233] and the calculation of protective awards resulting

---

[225] [1998] IRLR 376 CA.
[226] Section 13(5) ERA 1996.
[227] See *Hussman Manufacturing Ltd v Weir* [1998] IRLR 288.
[228] [1992] IRLR 56.
[229] See also *Bruce v Wiggins Teape (Stationery) Ltd* [1994] IRLR 536, where there was a unilateral reduction in overtime rates; the EAT stated that no distinction was to be drawn between a deduction and a reduction in wages.
[230] Section 13(4) ERA 1996.
[231] [1995] IRLR 68.
[232] See also *Yemm v British Steel* [1994] IRLR 117, which also concerned a mistaken belief that the employer could change contractual duties with a resulting reduction in pay.
[233] Section 119 ERA 1996.

from a failure to consult in collective redundancy situations,[234] a week's pay is subject to a maximum. This was set at £310 per week for 2007.[235]

Normal working hours are usually determined by reference to the contract of employment. If the contract stipulates a minimum number of fixed hours, then those are to be taken as the normal working hours.[236] If the contract requires overtime to be worked, these may become part of the normal working hours provided that there is an obligation by the employee to work the hours and those hours are guaranteed by the employer.[237] It is not enough to show that an employee regularly worked extra hours. There needs to be an obligation upon the employer to pay for the hours and a duty on the employee to carry them out. This was the situation in *Lotus Cars Ltd v Sutcliffe and Stratton*[238] where employees were expected to work a 45-hour week but contractually had a basic working week of 40 hours. They were paid a premium rate for the extra five hours worked each week. The court followed *Tarmac*[239] and concluded that the element of obligation was absent for these purposes.

The calculation date depends upon the purpose of the calculation.[240] There are a number of different categories where the approach to the calculation of a week's pay may differ:

(1) If the employee's remuneration for employment in normal working hours does not vary with the amount done in that period, then the amount of a week's pay is the amount payable by the employer under the contract of employment in force on the calculation date if the employee works the normal working hours.[241] There are additional rules for those who do not have regular hours of work or are not paid according to the time they work (see below).

(2) In cases where the amount of remuneration varies in relation to the amount of work done, the amount of remuneration will be calculated by using the average hourly rate paid by the employer in respect of the 12 weeks ending with the last complete week before the calculation date or, if the calculation date is the last day of the week, then that week. This can include those whose remuneration includes commission or similar payment which varies in amount, but will exclude overtime premium rates.[242]

(3) Where the normal hours worked vary from week to week, perhaps as a result of shift work, then the amount of a week's pay is the amount of remuneration for the average number of weekly normal working hours at the average hourly rate of remuneration. The average number of hours is to be calculated by totalling the number of hours worked over the previous 12 weeks and dividing by 12.[243]

---

[234] Section 190 TULRCA 1992.
[235] See section 227(1) ERA 1996.
[236] Section 234 ERA 1996.
[237] *Tarmac Roadstone Holdings Ltd v Peacock* [1973] IRLR 157 CA.
[238] [1982] IRLR 381 CA.
[239] [1973] IRLR 157 CA.
[240] See sections 225–226 ERA 1996.
[241] Section 221(2) ERA 1996.
[242] Section 221(3)–(4) ERA 1996; see *British Coal Corporation v Cheesebrough* [1990] IRLR 148 HL.
[243] Section 222 ERA 1996; the hourly rate and calculation date is as for section 221(3) above; if there has been no pay in any of the weeks for the purposes of sections 221 and 222, then earlier weeks are to be used to bring the total to 12, but any overtime hours included will not take into account any premium rates paid: see section 223.

(4) Where there are employments with no normal working hours, then the weekly pay will be the average weekly remuneration in the period of 12 weeks ending with the calculation date, which is the last complete week before the calculation date or, if the date is the last day of the week, then that week. No account is to be taken of weeks when there was no remuneration. In such cases earlier weeks will be used to bring the total to 12.[244]

(5) If an employee does not have sufficient service to calculate the 12 weeks, then there are a number of factors to help in the calculation of an amount 'which fairly represents a week's pay' contained in section 228 ERA 1996. Those employees who have retained continuity of employment may use time served and remuneration earned with the previous employer if necessary.[245]

8.6.3 Guarantee payments

An employee is entitled to be paid an amount by the employer for any day,[246] or part of a day, during which they would normally be required to work in accordance with the contract of employment, and they have not been provided with work. The workless days must be as a result of:

(1) a diminution in the requirements of the employer's business for work of the kind that the employee was employed to do, or

(2) any other event affecting the normal working of the employer's business in relation to such work.[247]

There is a statutory maximum payable to an employee, which makes the provision of little value to many people. The maximum daily figure set in 2007 was £19.60[248] and the maximum number of days for which payment must be made is five in any three-month period.[249] This right does not, however, affect any contractual rights to payment and any such payment can be offset against the statutory requirement.[250] In practice, this provision is of most use to those who have a contract of employment which allows them to be laid off without pay or those who are paid by the amount of work that they produce (piece workers, commission-only workers).

There are a number of exceptions to this entitlement:[251]

(1) an employee must have been continuously employed for at least one month ending with the day before the day for which a guarantee payment is claimed;

---

[244] Section 224 ERA 1996.
[245] Section 229 ERA 1996.
[246] Section 28(4) ERA 1996; day means the 24-hour period between midnight and midnight; see also section 28(5) dealing with situations where the day extends through midnight.
[247] Section 28(1) ERA 1996.
[248] Section 31(1) ERA 1996.
[249] Section 31(2)–(6) ERA 1996; see section 30 for guidance in calculating the amount due, subject to this maximum.
[250] Section 32 ERA 1996.
[251] Sections 29 and 35 ERA 1996.

(2) employees are not entitled to payment for 'workless days' if the failure to be provided with work results from a strike, lock-out or other industrial action[252] involving any employee of the employer or associated employer;

(3) if the employee has been offered suitable alternative work by the employer for that day and has unreasonably refused that offer;

(4) if the employee has not complied with reasonable requirements of the employer ensuring the employee's availability for work;

(5) situations where there is a collective agreement or an agricultural wages order concerning guaranteed payments and the Minister to whom an application is made issues an order excluding the obligation under section 28 ERA 1996.

An employee may complain to an employment tribunal if the employer fails to pay all or part of the entitlement. The complaint must be made within three months of the failure to pay unless the tribunal accepts that it was not reasonably practicable to do so. In the event of the tribunal finding the complaint well founded, it may order the employer to pay to the employee the amount due.[253] There are no provisions for any sanctions to be applied to the employer as a result of the failure to pay.

8.6.4 Suspension from work on medical grounds

There is a right for an employee to be paid by the employer if they are suspended from work on medical grounds.[254] An employee is suspended on medical grounds if the suspension is as a result of a requirement or provision imposed under any enactment, or a recommendation in a code of practice issued or approved under section 16 Health and Safety at Work etc. Act 1974.[255]

This suspension, with the right to remuneration, is subject to a maximum of 26 weeks. An employee is to be regarded as suspended only for as long as employment with the employer continues and the employer does not provide work or the employee does not perform the work normally performed before the suspension.[256] Exclusions from this right are:

(1) employees who have not been continuously employed for at least one month ending with the day before the suspension begins;

(2) there is no entitlement to payment in respect of any period during which the employee is incapable of work because of a disease or other physical or mental impairment;

(3) there is no entitlement if the employee has been offered suitable alternative work and has unreasonably refused that offer;

(4) where the employee does not comply with reasonable requirements imposed by the employer to ensure that the employee is available for work.[257]

---

[252] 'Other industrial action' is to be given its natural and ordinary meaning, e.g. it can include a refusal to work overtime: see *Faust v Power Packing Casemakers Ltd* [1983] IRLR 117 CA.

[253] Section 34 ERA 1996.

[254] Section 64(1) ERA 1996. On maternity grounds see Chapter 9.

[255] Section 64(2)–(3) ERA 1996; the Health and Safety Commission has the power to issue or approve codes of practice relating to health and safety regulations.

[256] Section 64(5) ERA 1996.

[257] Section 65 ERA 1996.

Complaints about a failure to pay the whole or part of the amount due may be made to an employment tribunal within three months of the failure, unless the tribunal accepts that this was not reasonably practicable. Where the tribunal finds the complaint well founded it will order the employer to make the payment. There are no provisions for any other sanctions against the employer.[258]

8.7 National minimum wage

Section 1(1) of the National Minimum Wage Act 1998 (NMWA 1998) places an obligation upon employers and provides that any person who qualifies should be remunerated, in any pay reference period, at a rate which is not less than the national minimum wage. The pay reference period is one month, or a shorter period if the worker is paid at shorter intervals.[259] Employers are defined in section 54 NMWA 1998 as the person by whom the employee or worker is employed, but there are provisions to ensure that a superior employer is identified as the real employer.[260] The Act was brought into effect on 1 April 1999 with the adoption of the National Minimum Wage Regulations 1999 (NMW Regulations 1999).[261]

The Act established the Low Pay Commission,[262] which is given the responsibility for advising the Government on the amount to be paid. However, it is HM Revenue & Customs which has the role of enforcing the payment and prosecuting offenders (see below). The hourly rate was set at £5.52 per hour from October 2007, although there is a lower rate for young workers and those undergoing training (see below).[263]

8.7.1 Who qualifies for the national minimum wage

An individual qualifies for the national minimum wage (NMW) if they are a worker[264] who is working, or is ordinarily working, in the United Kingdom under a contract and who has ceased to be of compulsory school age.[265] However, regulation 12(1) NMW Regulations 1999 specifies that workers who have not reached the age of 18 years do not qualify for the NMW. Agency workers and home workers qualify. In the case of agency workers, if there is confusion as to who is the employer because of the lack of a contract between the worker and the agency or the principal, the person providing the wages or salary has the responsibility for paying the NMW.[266] Home workers are defined as individuals who contract to carry out work in a place not under the control or management of the person with whom they have contracted.[267]

---

[258] Section 70(1)–(3) ERA 1996.
[259] Regulation 10(1) NMW Regulations 1999, SI 1999/584; financial arrangements when a worker's contract terminates are assumed to be done in the worker's final pay reference period: regulation 10(2).
[260] Section 48 NMWA 1998; see also section 34 NMWA 1998 on the employer of agency workers.
[261] SI 1999/584.
[262] Sections 5–8 NMWA 1998.
[263] Most benefits in kind, apart from living accommodation, are not to be treated as payments to the worker for the purposes of calculating the NMW: regulation 9 NMW Regulations 1999.
[264] Worker is defined in section 54(3) NMWA 1998 and is given the same meaning as in section 230(3) ERA 1996.
[265] Section 1(2) NMWA 1998.
[266] Section 34 NMWA 1998.
[267] Section 35(2) NMWA 1998.

Apart from those workers under the age of 18 years, there are a number of other groups who do not qualify. These are:

(1) Workers who are under 26 years of age, who are employed under a contract of apprenticeship[268] and who are either within the first 12 months of that employment[269] or under 19 years of age.[270]

(2) Workers participating in schemes to provide training, work experience or temporary work, or to assist them in finding work.[271]

(3) Workers attending a higher[272] education course who are required before the course ends to complete a period of work experience not exceeding one year do not qualify for the NMW for work done as part of that course, e.g. sandwich students who spend part of their course gaining work experience.[273]

(4) Workers who are homeless or residing in a hostel for the homeless, are eligible for income support and are participating in a voluntary or charitable scheme.[274]

(5) Share fishers.[275]

(6) Workers employed by a charity or a voluntary organisation, or similar, who only receive expenses in respect of work done. These expenses can include subsistence income for the worker concerned.[276]

(7) Workers who are residential members of religious or charitable communities in respect of work done for those communities. Exempt from this are communities which are independent schools or those that provide courses in further or higher education.[277]

(8) Workers who are prisoners do not qualify for the NMW in respect of any work done in pursuance of prison rules.[278]

Work is also defined as excluding any work relating to the employer's family household if the worker lives in the employer's family home, is treated as a member of the family, does not pay for the living accommodation and, if the work had been done by a member of the employer's family, it would not have been treated as being work.[279]

---

[268] Contracts of apprenticeship include Modern Apprenticeships: regulation 12(3) NMW Regulations 1999; further definition is given by regulation 4 NMW Regulations 1999 (Amendment) Regulations 2000, SI 2000/1989 (NMW Amendment Regulations 2000); see *Edmunds v Lawson QC* [2000] IRLR 391 CA.

[269] If there is a change of employer and continuity is preserved, then a worker does not need to start the 12 months over again: regulation 12(4) NMW Regulations 1999.

[270] Regulation 12(2) NMW Regulations 1999.

[271] Regulation 12(5) NMW Regulations 1999.

[272] Higher education course as in Schedule 6 Education Reform Act 1988: regulation 12(9) NMW Regulations 1999.

[273] Regulation 12(8) NMW Regulations 1999, as amended by the NMW Amendment Regulations 2000.

[274] Regulation 12(12) NMW Regulations 1999.

[275] Section 43 NMWA 1998.

[276] Section 44 NMWA 1998.

[277] Section 44A NMWA 1998.

[278] Section 45 NMWA 1998.

[279] Regulation 2(2)–(4) NMW Regulations 1999; work by members of the family is not defined as work if the worker lives in the family home and shares in the tasks of the family or participates in the running of the family business.

Two groups of workers qualify for the NMW at a reduced rate. First, those workers who have attained the age of 18 years and are less than 22 years old.[280] The second group are those workers who:

(1) have attained the age of 22 years;
(2) are within the first six months after the commencement[281] of employment with the employer;
(3) have not previously been employed by that employer or an associated[282] employer; and
(4) have entered into an agreement with the employer requiring the worker to take part in accredited[283] training on at least 26 days between the start of employment or of the agreement and the end of the six-month period.[284]

The reduced rate for these workers will be £4.60 per hour from October 2007. Since October 2007 there has been a £3.40 per hour minimum for 16- and 17-year-old workers who have ceased to be of compulsory school age but are not apprentices.

8.7.2 Calculating the hourly rate

The hourly rate paid to a worker in the pay reference period is calculated by finding the total remuneration paid in that period and dividing it by the total number of hours of time work, salaried hours work, output work and unmeasured work worked in the pay reference period.[285]

The total remuneration in a pay reference period is calculated[286] by adding together:

(1) all money paid by the employer to the worker in the pay reference period;
(2) all money paid in the following reference period that relates to the pay reference period;
(3) any money paid by the employer later than the following reference period in respect of work done in the pay reference period;[287]
(4) any amount permitted to be taken into account for the provision of living accommodation.[288]

Then various reductions are to be made, before the final figure can be arrived at, in accordance with regulations 31–37 NMW Regulations 1999. These include money paid during absences from work and during industrial action[289] and any money payments made

---

[280] Regulation 13(1) NMW Regulations 1999.
[281] When there has been a change of employer and continuity is preserved, then the worker does not commence employment again: regulation 13(4) NMW Regulations 1999.
[282] See regulation 13(5) for a definition of an associated employer.
[283] Accredited training is a course of a description mentioned in Schedule 2 Further and Higher Education Act 1992; regulation 13(3)(d) NMW Regulations 1999; see regulation 13(6) for the meaning of a relevant course.
[284] Regulation 13(2) NMW Regulations 1999.
[285] Regulation 14 NMW Regulations 1999.
[286] Regulation 30 NMW Regulations 1999.
[287] There are further conditions related to whether a worker is obliged to complete records of the amount of work done: regulation 30(c)(i)–(iii) NMW Regulations 1999.
[288] Defined in regulation 36 NMW Regulations 1999.
[289] Regulation 31(1)(b)(i) NMW Regulations 1999.

by the employer representing tips and gratuities paid by customers, but not paid through the payroll.[290]

The hours which are to be divided into this total are themselves put into four different categories. These are time work, salaried hours work, output work and unmeasured work.

8.7.2.1 Time work[291]

Time work is when workers are paid[292] for the number of hours that they are at work. It is also when a worker is on a contract to do a particular job, but is paid for the hours done each week or month. Time work can also be when a person is doing piece work, but is expected to work a certain number of hours per day. Whatever the level of the piece work, the worker must receive, on average, at least the NMW for each hour during the pay period.

Time work includes[293] time when the worker is available at or near the place of work (other than at home) for the purpose of doing time work. Regulation 15(1A) provides that if the worker is permitted to sleep, by arrangement, at or near the place of work, it is only the hours when they are awake for the purpose of working that counts as time hours. This does not apply to situations where an employee is required to be on the premises for a specific number of hours and who may sleep, if he or she chooses to, when the designated tasks have been completed. It only applies where the employer gives specific permission to the employee to take a particular amount of time off for sleep.[294] Similarly, in *British Nursing Association v Inland Revenue*[295] staff providing a night-time booking service from home were entitled to have the entire period that they were available to answer the phone counted as time work. This was so even though they were able to undertake other activities during these hours, such as watching TV or reading. The Court of Appeal stated that it would make a mockery of the national minimum wage to conclude that the employees were only working when they answered the telephone and that all the time spent waiting for a call should be excluded. Time spent travelling can also be time work, unless it is incidental[296] to the worker's duties or is concerned with travelling to and from work. Travelling to an assignment or between assignments might be time work.[297] Time work does not include periods when the worker is absent or taking part in industrial action. According to the DBERR guide to the NMW, most workers who are not on an annual salary will be on time work.

---

[290] Regulation 31(1)(e) NMW Regulations 1999. On deductions for gas and electricity in tied accommodation, see *Revenue & Customs v Leisure Management Ltd* [2007] IRLR 450 CA.

[291] Regulation 3 NMW Regulations 1999.

[292] Regulation 8 NMW Regulations 1999 provides a definition of payments as being payments made before deductions, except for a limited number of payments including advances, pension payments, court or tribunal awards, payments relating to redundancy and payments as an award for a suggestions scheme.

[293] Regulation 15 NMW Regulations 1999.

[294] *Scottbridge Construction Ltd v Wright* [2003] IRLR 21.

[295] [2002] IRLR 480 CA.

[296] Travelling is incidental unless the worker needs to travel for the purposes of work, e.g. a bus driver or a catering worker on a train: regulation 15(3) NMW Regulations 1999.

[297] Assignment work is time work if it consists of assignments of work to be carried out at different places between which the worker is obliged to travel that are not places occupied by the worker's employer: regulation 16(3)(b) NMW Regulations 1999.

8.7.2.2 Salaried hours work

Salaried hours work is where a worker is paid under a contract for a set number of hours worked per year, is entitled under the contract to an annual salary and is paid in equal weekly or monthly instalments during the year regardless of the number of hours worked. Variations in pay as a result of the payment of a performance bonus, a pay increase, excess hours payments or because the worker left part-way through the week or month do not stop the hours being salaried hours.

The provisions relating to salaried workers are similar to those for time workers[298] except that absences count if the worker is paid the normal pay during the absence. Absences such as lunch breaks, holidays and sickness absence count if they form part of the worker's basic minimum hours. Periods paid at a lesser rate do not count, for example, when the worker is absent as a result of long-term sickness; neither do periods of unpaid leave and time on industrial action.[299] The basic number of hours for a salaried worker are the basic number of hours in respect of which a worker is paid, under the contract, on the first day of the reference period.[300]

8.7.2.3 Output work

Output work is work that is paid for by reference to a worker's output, be it the number of tasks performed or the value of sales made.[301] It is sometimes known as piece work or can be work that is paid for by commission. Time travelling can be included except for travelling to the premises from which work is done and, in the case of a home worker, the premises to which the worker reports. Again, time spent in taking industrial action does not count.[302]

There are two ways in which the hours of an output worker can be calculated. These are: (i) by counting the number of hours spent in output work,[303] or (ii) by applying a complicated system called 'rated output work'. This requires employers to give their workers a notice containing specified information and to test them to identify 'the mean hourly output rate'. The number of hours taken by a worker in producing the relevant pieces or performing the relevant tasks during a pay reference period is deemed to be the same number of hours that a person working at the mean hourly output rate would have taken to produce the same number of pieces or perform the same number of tasks during the pay reference period. Employers must pay their workers producing that piece or performing that task an amount per piece or task which, given that the workers are deemed to have worked at the mean hourly output rate, is at least equivalent to the hourly national minimum wage. Since April 2005, the number of hours spent by a worker on rated output work has been treated as being 120% of the number of hours that a person working at the mean hourly output rate would have taken.

---

[298] Regulation 16 NMW Regulations 1999.
[299] Regulation 21(3)–(4) NMW Regulations 1999.
[300] Regulation 21(2)–(3) NMW Regulations 1999; regulations 22 and 23 are concerned with determining the salaried hours when the basic hours have been exceeded and when the employment terminates.
[301] Regulation 5 NMW Regulations 1999.
[302] Regulation 17 NMW Regulations 1999.
[303] Regulations 24–26 NMW Regulations 1999.

8.7.2.4 Unmeasured work

Unmeasured work is work that is not time work, salaried hours work or output work. It is work that has no specified hours and the worker is required to work when needed or when work is available, for example, work as a carer.[304] There are two methods of identifying the number of hours to be worked and for which the NMW should be paid. These are, first, to pay the NMW for every hour worked. The second is for the employer and the worker to come to a 'daily average' agreement, to determine the average number of daily hours the worker is likely to spend on unmeasured work. The agreement must be made before the start of the pay reference period that it covers, be in writing, set out the average daily number of hours, and ensure that the daily average is realistic.[305] Where there is a dispute about the number of hours worked, no account will be taken of hours for which the worker has not submitted records, if that is what is required before payment can be made.[306]

8.7.3 Record keeping

An employer of a worker who qualifies for the NMW has a duty to keep records.[307] These records need to be sufficient to establish that the worker is being remunerated at a rate at least equal to the NMW. They must also be kept in such a way that the information relating to a worker in a pay reference period can be produced in a single document. In addition, the employer is required to keep copies of any agreements entered into with the worker concerning regulations 13(2) (accredited training), and 28(1) (unmeasured work).[308] These records must be kept for at least three years beginning with the day upon which the pay reference period immediately following that to which they relate ends.[309] The records may be kept on computer.[310]

If workers believe, on reasonable grounds, that they are being remunerated, in any particular reference period, at a rate less than the NMW, they have the right to request that the employer produce any relevant records and have the right to inspect those records.[311] This right to inspection can be by the worker alone or by the worker accompanied by another person of the worker's choice. The request to inspect records must be done by the worker giving a production notice to the employer requesting the production of relevant records[312] relating to a specific period. If the worker is to be accompanied this must be stated in the production notice. When this notice has been given the employer must give the worker reasonable notice of the place[313] and time when the records will be produced.

---

[304] Regulation 6 NMW Regulations 1999. See *Walton v Independent Living Organisation* [2003] IRLR 469.
[305] Regulations 27–29 NMW Regulations 1999.
[306] Regulation 29A NMW Regulations 1999 as amended.
[307] Section 9 NMWA 1998 and regulation 38 NMW Regulations 1999.
[308] Regulation 38(3) NMW Regulations 1999.
[309] Regulation 38(7) NMW Regulations 1999.
[310] Regulation 38(8) NMW Regulations 1999.
[311] Section 10 NMWA 1998.
[312] Relevant means those records which will establish whether or not the worker has been remunerated at a level equivalent to the NMW in any pay reference period: section 10(10) NMWA 1998.
[313] The place must be the worker's place of work, any other place that is reasonable for the worker to attend or any further place agreed with the worker: section 10(8) NMWA 1998.

However, the records must be produced within 14 days of the employer receiving the production notice unless otherwise agreed with the worker.[314]

If the employer fails to produce some or all of the records requested or fails to allow the worker to inspect the records or be accompanied by another person of the worker's choice, then the worker may make a complaint to an employment tribunal.[315] The complaint must be made within three months of the end of the 14-day period allowed for the production of the records, or at the end of any other period agreed by the worker and the employer according to section 10(9) NMWA 1998, unless the tribunal accepts that this was not reasonably practicable. Where an employment tribunal finds the complaint well founded, it may issue a declaration and make an award that the employer pays the worker a sum equal to 80 times the amount of the NMW in force at the time.

8.7.4 Enforcement

HM Revenue & Customs has the task of ensuring that workers are remunerated at a rate at least equivalent to the NMW. Officers of HM Revenue & Customs are given wide powers to inspect records, require relevant persons to provide information[316] and to enter any relevant premises for the purpose of exercising their powers.[317] According to section 14(4) NMWA 1998, a relevant person can be the employer or the employer's agent, the supplier of work to the individual workers or the workers themselves. Relevant premises means the premises at which the employer carries on business or premises that the employer, or employer's agent, uses in connection with the business.[318]

Section 19 NMWA 1998 allows HM Revenue & Customs officers to issue an enforcement notice to ensure that the employer remunerates at the NMW level and pays sums due from previous failures to remunerate at the required level.[319] The recipient of the enforcement notice has four weeks in which to appeal. Such appeals must go to an employment tribunal, which has the power to rescind the notice or rectify it.[320] If an enforcement notice is not complied with, HM Revenue & Customs are able to take civil proceedings for the recovery of the money or present a complaint to an employment tribunal, on behalf of the worker, that there has been an unlawful deduction of wages in contravention of section 13 ERA 1996 (see above).[321] In such proceedings the burden of proof is on the employer to show that the worker was remunerated at the appropriate level.[322] Additionally, a failure to comply with an enforcement notice can result in a financial penalty. The amount of the penalty is twice the hourly NMW for each worker that the enforcement notice relates to for

---

[314] Section 10(9) NMWA 1998.
[315] Section 11 NMWA 1998.
[316] Although no person may be required to provide information that will incriminate themselves or their spouse: section 14(2) NMWA 1998. On disclosure of information by officers see section 16A NMWA 1998.
[317] Section 14(1) NMWA 1998.
[318] Section 14(5) NMWA 1998.
[319] Section 17 NMWA 1998 provides that workers who have been under-remunerated have an entitlement to the amounts by which they have been underpaid.
[320] See section 19(4)–(10) NMWA 1998.
[321] Section 20 NMWA 1998.
[322] Section 28 NMWA 1998.

each day that there is a failure to comply.[323] An employer may appeal against the penalty notice to an employment tribunal, which will have the power to rescind or rectify it.[324]

A failure to comply with certain requirements of the NMWA 1998 can lead to prosecution for a criminal offence and can result in a fine. The offences in question are a refusal or wilful neglect to pay the NMW; failing to keep NMW records; keeping false records; producing false records or information; intentionally obstructing an enforcement officer; and refusing or neglecting to give information to an enforcement officer.[325]

8.7.5 Right not to suffer detriment

Section 104A ERA 1996 provides that the dismissal of an employee shall be unfair if the reason, or the principal reason, for the dismissal is the entitlement to the NMW or any reason related to the enforcement of it. It is immaterial as to whether the employee has the right or whether the right has been infringed. It is important, however, that any claim is made in good faith.

Section 23 NMWA 1998 provides that workers have the right not to be subjected to detriment because of entitlement to the NMW or any reason related to the enforcement of it. Again good faith is required for complaints and it is immaterial whether the worker has the right or whether it has been infringed. Detriment here will include workers who are not protected from unfair dismissal by Part X ERA 1996. The complaint to an employment tribunal must be made within three months beginning with the act, or failure to act, that is to be complained of, unless the tribunal considers that it was not reasonably practicable to do so.[326] If the tribunal finds the complaint well founded it may make a declaration and award compensation.[327]

Further reading

Collins, H., Ewing, K. and McColgan, A., *Labour Law: Text and Materials* (Hart Publishing, 2005), Chapter 4.
Deakin, S. and Morris, G., *Labour Law* (4th edn, Hart Publishing, 2005), Chapter 4.
Simpson, R., 'The National Minimum Wage Five Years On' (2004) 33 *Industrial Law Journal* 22.
www.acas.org.uk
www.lowpay.gov.uk
www.tuc.org.uk

Visit **www.mylawchamber.co.uk/sargeant** to access legal updates, live web links and practice exam questions to test yourself on this chapter.

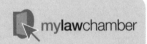

---

[323] Section 21 NMWA 1998.
[324] Section 22 NMWA 1998. On the withdrawal and replacement of enforcement notices see sections 22A–22F NMWA 1998.
[325] Sections 31–33 NMWA 1998.
[326] Again claimants must first submit a statement of grievance to the employer: paragraphs 6 and 9 Schedule 2 Employment Act 2002.
[327] Sections 48–49 ERA 1996.

9

Parental and Maternity Rights

9.1 The Pregnant Workers Directive[1]

The Pregnant Workers Directive identified pregnant workers and workers who have recently given birth, or who are breastfeeding, as workers who face particular risks in the workplace. The Directive makes such workers a particular case for protection and makes provisions regarding the health and safety of this group, and adopted certain employment rights connected with pregnancy.

All Member States of the European Community already had laws for the protection of pregnant workers prior to this Directive. In the United Kingdom, for example, there had been a long tradition of offering such protection: for example, section 34 Employment Protection Act 1975 provided that a dismissal would be unfair if the reason or the principal reason for the dismissal was pregnancy or a reason related to that pregnancy.

One of the purposes of the Directive was to create minimum standards throughout the Community. Before its introduction, there was considerable variation between the Member States on measures taken. As a result of the Directive there were a number of changes, although the variety remains. There were changes such as increases in maternity leave in Portugal and Sweden. In the United Kingdom there was a reduction in the qualifying period for maternity leave. There were amendments to Irish legislation and the introduction of paid time off for ante-natal examinations in Austria, Belgium, Denmark, Finland and Ireland.

9.1.1 Definition

The Directive[2] defines a pregnant worker as a woman who informs her employer of her condition, in accordance with national laws and practice. Most Member States require the worker to inform her employer of her pregnancy, or of the fact that she has recently given birth or is breastfeeding, before the protective measures can begin. In Belgium, Finland, France and the United Kingdom, for example, there is no general requirement for a woman to inform her employer that she is pregnant, but it is unlikely that there would be an entitlement to maternity rights and protection until the employer is informed. In Spain it is enough for the employer to be aware of the pregnancy, even though not officially

---

[1] Directive 92/85/EC on the introduction of measures to encourage improvements in the health and safety at work of pregnant workers and workers who have recently given birth or are breastfeeding OJ L348 28.11.92 p 1.

[2] Article 2(a) Pregnant Workers Directive.

informed. In Luxembourg a woman needs to send a medical certificate to her employer by registered post, whilst in Austria the Labour Inspectorate needs to be informed, as well as the employer, of the pregnancy. There is a similar diversity in how long a woman can be defined as breastfeeding and, as a result, receive special protection. In Ireland women receive protection for six months for breastfeeding; in Spain it is nine months and in Greece it is one year.

A refusal to employ results in direct discrimination when the most important reason for the refusal applies only to one sex, rather than to employees, without distinction, of both sexes. Only women can be refused employment because of pregnancy, so a decision not to employ someone because they are pregnant is directly discriminatory against the woman concerned. *Dekker*,[3] which was a reference to the ECJ from the Dutch Supreme Court, concerned a woman who had applied for a post of training instructor in a youth centre. She was pregnant when she applied and she informed the selection committee of this. The committee recommended her as the most suitable candidate, but the board of the youth centre declined to employ her. The reason given was that their insurer would not compensate them for payments which would be due to Ms Dekker during her maternity leave. The ECJ concluded that the refusal to employ had been a reason connected with the pregnancy and that this was contrary to the Equal Treatment Directive (see below). As only women can be refused employment because of pregnancy, the fact that there were no male candidates for the post was not seen as relevant.

9.1.2 Risk assessment

The employer is required to complete an assessment of the risk of exposure to a non-exhaustive list of agents,[4] processes or working conditions and then to inform the worker or her representatives of the results and the measures intended to be taken concerning health and safety at work.[5] All countries have health and safety legislation which takes particular account of pregnant workers and a variety of means of informing them of those risks. In most countries it is the responsibility of the employer alone, but in some Member States statutory bodies become involved, such as Finland, where occupational health experts carry out an investigation, and Ireland, where the National Authority for Occupational Safety and Health has a role in ensuring employee awareness. There should not be measures, however, that go so far in their attempt to protect pregnant women that they breach the Equal Treatment Directive.

9.1.3 Night work

There are various approaches to issues related to night work in the Member States. The Directive[6] ensures that pregnant workers should not be obliged to carry out night work if it is detrimental to their health or safety. If there is such a risk then the woman concerned

---

[3] Case C-177/88 *Dekker v Stichting Vormingscentum voor Jonge Volwassen* [1991] IRLR 27 ECJ.
[4] Article 4 Pregnant Workers Directive.
[5] A failure to carry out a risk assessment amounts to sex discrimination: *Hardman v Mallon* [2002] ICR 510.
[6] Article 7 Pregnant Workers Directive.

should be moved to day work or given leave from work, if day work is not possible. Some countries had a policy of not allowing such workers to work at nights at all. In *Stoeckel*,[7] an individual was the subject of prosecution for infringement of a section of the French labour code which prohibited the employment of women on night work, except in certain situations. The ECJ ruled that a provision that banned women from performing night work, when there was no such provision for men, was contrary to Article 5 of the Equal Treatment Directive.[8] Most countries require a medical certificate to show that working at night would be bad for the worker's health, although the certificate is not needed in Denmark or Greece. In Germany, Austria, Italy and Luxembourg there are still restrictions against night work which make it very difficult for such workers to work at nights at all.

9.1.4 Maternity leave

Workers must be permitted to take, as a minimum, at least 14 weeks' continuous maternity leave with at least two weeks' compulsory leave taken before or after confinement.[9] The duration of maternity leave in practice varies from 90 days in Portugal to 16 weeks in Greece and Austria and 20 weeks in Italy. Denmark has 14 weeks with a further ten weeks which either parent can have or share between them. In some countries, such as France, the leave entitlement is longer if the woman already has children. During maternity leave, entitlement to pay may vary from 100% of salary, as in Belgium, Germany, Greece, Spain, Luxembourg, the Netherlands, Austria and Portugal, to 90% in Denmark, 84% in France, 80% in Italy and 70% in Ireland. Most countries impose rules for entitlement to benefits.[10]

In *Ulrich Hofmann v Barmer Ersatzkasse*[11] the ECJ was asked to consider a claim that the giving of leave to women alone did not accord with the terms of the Equal Treatment Directive. The claimant was a man who looked after a child whilst the mother returned to work as a teacher shortly after the birth. He was denied a claim for maternity benefit by the German social security service. The argument, in the legal proceedings that followed, was that the introduction of maternity leave was concerned, not with the protection of the mother's health, but exclusively with the care that she gave to the child. If this argument was correct, it was said, then the leave should be available to either parent and become a form of parental leave. The ECJ rejected this approach and stated that the Equal Treatment Directive was not intended to 'settle questions concerned with the organisation of the family'. If national legislation had been only concerned with the care of the child, then it ought to be non-discriminatory. The court held that maternity leave came within the scope of Article 2(3) Equal Treatment Directive, which 'seeks to protect a woman in connection with the effects of pregnancy and motherhood'. Thus maternity leave could legitimately be reserved for the mother, as it is only she that is likely to suffer from undesirable pressures to return to work prematurely.

---

[7] Case C-345/89 *Criminal proceedings against Alfred Stoeckel* [1991] ECR-1 4047 ECJ.
[8] Directive 76/207/EEC on equal treatment for men and for women with regard to access to employment, vocational training and promotion, and working conditions OJ L39 14.2.76 p 40; see also Case 158/91 *Ministère Public et Direction du Travail v Levy* [1994] ECR 4287 ECJ.
[9] Article 8 Pregnant Workers Directive.
[10] European Commission, *The Regulation of Working Conditions in the Member States of the European Union*, 1999.
[11] Case 184/83 [1984] ECR 3047 ECJ.

9.1.5 Protection against dismissal

Member States are required to 'take the necessary measures to prohibit the dismissal of workers ... during their pregnancy to the end of their maternity leave ... save in exceptional cases not connected with their condition ...'.[12] As a result all countries provide protection against dismissal for pregnant workers or those that have recently given birth, although much of this protection emanated from previous anti-sex discrimination legislation. One issue for the national courts was whether there was a necessity to compare a pregnant woman's absence with that of a man to show that discrimination had taken place. *Webb v EMO*[13] was a case where an applicant was employed initially to cover for another employee who was to go on maternity leave. It was envisaged that the new employee would continue to be employed after the pregnant employee returned from her maternity leave. Shortly after starting work, the new employee discovered that she was pregnant also and the employer dismissed her. She complained of sex discrimination contrary to section 1(1) Sex Discrimination Act 1975. When the case reached the House of Lords it was referred to the ECJ for a decision on whether the dismissal constituted sex discrimination. The ECJ held that it was contrary to the Equal Treatment Directive and that one could not compare a pregnant woman who was not capable of performing the task for which she was employed with a male who was absent through sickness and incapable therefore of carrying out his tasks.

In the Danish case of *Hertz*,[14] the male comparator was of importance, however. Ms Hertz was a part-time cashier and saleswoman. She gave birth to a child after a difficult pregnancy during which she was mainly on sick leave. When her statutory maternity leave period ended she returned to work. After a further period of about six months she was ill and was absent for 100 days. The illness had arisen out of her pregnancy and confinement. Eventually her employers dismissed her on the grounds of repeated absence due to illness. A question for the ECJ was whether this dismissal contravened Article 5 of the Equal Treatment Directive as the illness had resulted from the pregnancy. The court held that dismissal because of absence during maternity leave would constitute direct discrimination. With regard to an illness that appears some time after, however, there was no reason to distinguish between an illness that had its origin in pregnancy or from any other cause. If such sickness absence would have led to the dismissal of a male worker under the same conditions, then there is no discrimination on the grounds of sex.[15]

In a number of countries the contract of employment is regarded as being suspended during the period of maternity leave, whilst in others, such as in Austria, Germany and Italy, there are periods when it is not permissible to dismiss a woman within a period of the birth, unless the dismissal is unconnected with the pregnancy.

---

[12] Article 10 Pregnant Workers Directive.
[13] Case C-32/93 *Webb v EMO Air Cargo (UK) Ltd* [1994] ICR 770 ECJ.
[14] Case 179/88 *Handels og Konturfunktionærernes Forbund i Danmark (acting for Hertz) v Dansk Arbejdsgiverforening (acting for Aldi Marked A/S)* [1991] IRLR 31 ECJ.
[15] See Case 394/96 *Brown v Rentokil Ltd* [1998] IRLR 445 ECJ, which also distinguished between the protected period during pregnancy and maternity leave compared to the period after that leave.

9.1.6 Employment rights during maternity leave

Article 11(1) Pregnant Workers Directive provides for rights under the employment contract including the maintenance of a payment whilst a woman is granted leave from work because of risks to her health or that of her baby, or when she is granted leave from night work. Article 11(2) provides similar rights for workers during maternity leave as exist for health and safety reasons. The case of *North Western Health Board v McKenna*[16] at the ECJ concerned a sickness scheme which guaranteed full pay for the first 183 days of sickness in any one year and half pay for the remaining period. The scheme also expressly stated that sickness related to maternity related illness prior to the taking of maternity leave would be treated in the same way as sickness for any other reason. Mrs McKenna was absent because of maternity related sickness for virtually the whole of her pregnancy and also after her maternity leave. She spent some time, as a result, on half pay. She claimed that this was sex discrimination. The Court of Justice did not agree with this and stated that Community law does not require the maintenance of full pay for absences related to maternity related illness, providing that the payment is not so low as to undermine the Community law objective of protecting female workers, especially before giving birth.

9.2 The Parental Leave Directive[17]

The Parental Leave Directive implemented a Framework Agreement on parental leave reached by the social partners. The social partners are the European representatives of employer and trade union organisations.[18] As part of a process called the 'Social Dialogue', these representatives were invited by the European Commission to reach an agreement on parental leave. This agreement, called the Framework Agreement, was subsequently adopted in its entirety as a European Directive.

The proposals for having Community rules on parental leave had been in existence for some time. They were first introduced as a proposed Directive in 1983,[19] but the British Government opposed them and was able effectively to veto them as adoption required a unanimous vote in the Council of Ministers. In 1994 the proposals were again put forward, but this time under the Social Chapter, from which the United Kingdom had excluded itself. These led to the Framework Agreement which was adopted by all the other Member States (excluding the United Kingdom) in 1996. After the 1997 general election, and a change of government, the United Kingdom 'signed up' to the Social Chapter. As a result Directive 97/75/EC was adopted on 15 December 1997 extending the Parental Leave Directive to the United Kingdom. In order to comply the Maternity and Parental Leave etc.

---

[16] Case C-191/03 [2005] IRLR 895.
[17] Council Directive 96/34/EC on the Framework Agreement on parental leave concluded by UNICE, CEEP and the ETUC OJ L145 19.6.96 p 4; applied to the United Kingdom by Directive 97/75/EC OJ L10 16.1.98 p 24.
[18] The organisations are UNICE, the European private employers' federation, CEEP, the European public employers' federation and the ETUC, the European trade union confederation; see Chapter 2.
[19] Proposal for a Directive on parental leave and leave for family reasons COM(83) 686 as amended by COM(84) 631.

Regulations[20] and sections 57A and 57B Employment Rights Act 1996 came into effect on 15 December 1999.[21]

9.2.1 Scope of the Directive

Men and women workers are given the individual right to parental leave on the grounds of the birth or adoption of a child,[22] in order to enable them to take care of that child, for at least three months, until an age of up to eight years. The actual age was left to individual Member States. Article 2(2) states that, in principle, these rights should be given on a non-transferable basis. Thus one parent could not transfer their right of up to three months' leave to the other parent, even if they had no intention of making use of the right.

The detailed rules and qualifying conditions on parental leave have been left to individual Member States to decide. This may include, for different countries, rules on the minimum length of service required to qualify, the arrangements for taking leave and the employer's ability to postpone leave for operational or other reasons. There is no requirement in the Directive that leave should be paid and any decisions on financing or social security arrangements are left to the individual Member States.[23] There are also provisions for countries to:

(1) protect workers against dismissal for taking parental leave;
(2) ensure that workers are able to return to the same job, or an equivalent, at the end of their leave period;
(3) ensure the maintenance and continuation of rights accrued to the start of the leave period;
(4) define the status of the contract of employment during the leave period.

In the *Hofmann*[24] case, the European Commission pointed out that a number of Member States were moving towards the granting of parental leave which, they stated, was 'to be preferred to leave which is granted to the mother alone'. Rules on parental leave have existed in other countries for many years, making the impact of the Directive substantially less than its possible impact in the United Kingdom.

9.2.2 Force majeure

Clause 3.1 of the Framework Agreement, implemented by the Parental Leave Directive, provides that Member States should take measures to entitle workers to time off from work on grounds of '*force majeure* for urgent family reasons in cases of sickness or accident making the immediate presence of the worker indispensable'. This led to the rules on the right to time off for dependants being introduced in the Employment Relations Act

---

[20] SI 1999/3312; subsequently amended by the Maternity and Parental Leave (Amendment) Regulations 2002, SI 2002/2789.
[21] See Employment Relations Act 1999 (Commencement No 2 and Transitional and Savings Provisions) Order 1999, SI 1999/2830.
[22] Clause 2(1) Framework Agreement on parental leave.
[23] Clause 2(8) Framework Agreement on parental leave.
[24] Case 184/83 [1984] ECR 3047 ECJ.

1999.[25] Thus an employee is entitled to take a reasonable amount of time off in order to take action which is needed:

  (i) to provide assistance when a dependant falls ill, gives birth, is injured or assaulted;
 (ii) to make arrangements for care for a dependant who is ill or injured;
(iii) as a result of the death of a dependant;
 (iv) as a result of the unexpected disruption of arrangements for the care of a dependant;
  (v) to deal with unexpected incidents resulting from a child being at school.[26]

The definition of dependant is restricted to a spouse, a child, a parent or a person living in the same household as the employee who is not an employee, lodger, tenant or boarder.[27] There is an obligation for the employee to tell the employer the reason for the absence and the likelihood of its length as soon as is reasonably practicable.[28] Complaints for a failure to grant reasonable time off are made to an employment tribunal within three months of the date the refusal was made, unless not reasonably practicable. The tribunal may make a declaration and award compensation that it considers just and equitable.[29] *Qua v John Ford Morrison Solicitors*[30] concerned a legal secretary who had a large number of absences during a relatively short period of employment. She stated that most of these absences were due to medical problems experienced by her son. The EAT held that there was no statutory maximum to the number of occasions that an employee could be absent in accordance with section 57A ERA 1996, but there was no entitlement to an unlimited amount of time off. The right to time off was to deal with the unexpected. When it was known that the employee's dependant was suffering from a medical condition which was likely to result in regular lapses, then it no longer came within the provisions of section 57A, because it was no longer unexpected.

9.3 Maternity leave in the United Kingdom

Special measures to benefit pregnant women and women who had recently given birth were first introduced in the United Kingdom during the post-Second World War period. The National Insurance scheme, in 1948, introduced a maternity allowance for women contributors who gave up work to have a baby. This was paid for 13 weeks. The period was increased to 18 weeks in 1953. In 1975 the Employment Protection Act introduced six weeks' maternity pay for women who contributed to the Maternity Fund. This maternity pay equalled 90% of normal weekly earnings less the amount of the maternity allowance. Maternity allowance and maternity pay were amalgamated in 1987 and became statutory maternity pay.[31] This is paid by employers, who then recover their costs by deductions from their tax and National Insurance contributions. Small employers can claim an additional amount in respect of such pay.[32]

---

[25] Now contained in sections 57A and 57B ERA 1996.
[26] Section 57A(1) ERA 1996.
[27] Section 57A(3) ERA 1996.
[28] Section 57A(2) ERA 1996.
[29] Section 57B ERA 1996.
[30] [2003] IRLR 184.
[31] See House of Commons Research Paper 98/99, *Fairness at Work*.
[32] See Statutory Maternity Pay (Compensation of Employers) (Amendment) Regulations 1999, SI 1999/363.

The Employment Protection Act 1975 also introduced the right to return to work for up to 29 weeks after confinement for women who had been employed for two years continuously with the same employer. In 1994, changes were made as a result of the Pregnant Workers Directive. These changes concerned the right for women to have at least 14 weeks' maternity leave, regardless of their length of service or hours of work. Two weeks of this were to be compulsory. They also concerned the payment to women of an 'adequate allowance', equal at least to State rules on sickness benefit, during their maternity leave period, although this could be limited to those with at least one year's continuous service. The changes were made in sections 23–25 Trade Union Reform and Employment Rights Act 1993 and various regulations.[33]

Prior to the Employment Relations Act 1999 and the Maternity and Parental Leave etc. Regulations 1999 all women were entitled to 14 weeks' maternity leave, although confusingly they were also likely to be entitled to 18 weeks' maternity pay. Some, with two years' continuous employment, were also entitled to extended maternity leave. One of the aims of the Government in making the changes contained in the 1999 legislation, and subsequently, was to remove some confusion, especially with respect to the procedures for giving notice, arrangements for return to work and the definition of remuneration. Importantly, the number of women likely to benefit is large. It is estimated that there are about 370,000 pregnant employees in any one year in the United Kingdom.

9.4 Maternity and Parental Leave etc. Regulations 1999

The Maternity and Parental Leave etc. Regulations 1999,[34] were amended in 2002,[35] and again in 2006[36] (the MPL Regulations). Further provision was also made by the Work and Families Act 2006. These provide for three types of maternity leave: ordinary maternity leave, compulsory maternity leave and additional maternity leave. These are periods of leave, before and after childbirth, to which a pregnant employee, or one that has recently given birth, is entitled. The dates of leave are calculated as being periods before or after the 'expected week of childbirth'. Regulation 2(1) MPL Regulations defines this as the week, beginning with midnight between Saturday and Sunday, in which it is expected that childbirth will occur. This regulation also defines childbirth as 'the birth of a living child or the birth of a child whether living or dead after 24 weeks of pregnancy'. This means, of course, that a woman who gives birth to a stillborn child after 24 weeks of pregnancy will be entitled to the same leave as a person who gave birth to a live child.

Similar rules exist for ordinary and additional adoption leave and are contained in the Parental and Adoption Leave Regulations 2002.[37]

---

[33] Maternity Allowance and Statutory Maternity Pay Regulations 1994, SI 1994/1230 and Social Security Maternity Benefits and Statutory Sick Pay (Amendment) Regulations 1994, SI 1994/1367.
[34] SI 1999/3312.
[35] SI 2002/2789.
[36] The Maternity and Parental Leave etc. and the Paternity and Adoption Leave (Amendment) Regulations 2006, SI 2006/2024.
[37] SI 2002/2788, as amended by the 2006 Regulations – see above.

9.4.1 Statutory maternity leave[38]

The rules on maternity and parental leave apply to employees only. Regulation 2(1) MPL Regulations defines an employee as an individual who has 'entered into or works under (or, where the employment has ceased, worked under) a contract of employment'. A contract of employment is further defined as a 'contract of service or apprenticeship whether express or implied, and (if it is express) whether oral or in writing'. This is the same definition as in section 230(1) and (2) ERA 1996 and is narrower than the definition of worker. It is the narrower definition that applies in the case of maternity or parental leave.

The MPL Regulations define employer, simply, as the person by whom an employee is (or, where the employment has ceased, was) employed.[39] The regulations also define associated employer, which assumes importance in certain respects, such as rights in a redundancy situation during maternity leave (see below). Two employers are treated as associated if one is a company of which the other (directly or indirectly) has control, or both are companies of which a third person (directly or indirectly) has control.[40]

An employee may be entitled to ordinary and additional maternity leave if she satisfies certain conditions. These are:[41]

(1) No later than the end of the 15th week before her expected week of childbirth she notifies her employer of her pregnancy, the expected week of childbirth and the date on which she intends to start her ordinary maternity leave. If it is not reasonably practicable to inform the employer by that time, then she must inform the employer as soon as is reasonably practicable.

(2) The employee must give this notice in writing if the employer so requests.[42] The employee is entitled to change her mind about the date for commencement of her maternity leave, provided she notifies the employer at least 28 days before the new date or the date varied.[43]

(3) The employer is able to request, for inspection, a certificate from a registered medical practitioner or a registered midwife stating the expected week of childbirth, and the employee is required to provide it.

(4) As a response to the notice the employer must, within 28 days, notify the employee of the date when her additional maternity leave will end.[44]

(5) If the leave period commences because of absence from work on a day after the fourth week before the expected week of childbirth (see below),[45] then the employee is not expected to have given the required notice, but she will lose her entitlement if she does

---

[38] Regulation 2(1) of the MPL Regulations states that statutory maternity leave means ordinary and additional maternity leave.

[39] Regulation 2(1) MPL Regulations.

[40] Regulation 2(3) MPL Regulations.

[41] Regulation 4(1)(a) MPL Regulations.

[42] Regulation 4(2)(a) MPL Regulations.

[43] Regulation 4(1A) MPL Regulations.

[44] Regulation 7(6) and (7) MPL Regulations.

[45] See Case C-411/96 *Boyle v Equal Opportunities Commission* [1998] IRLR 717 ECJ, which held that a rule which required a woman who is absent on a pregnancy-related illness within six weeks of the expected date of childbirth should take paid maternity leave, rather than be given sick pay, was not precluded by the Pregnant Workers Directive.

not inform her employer as soon as is practicable that she is absent from work wholly or partly because of her pregnancy.[46] This notice must give the date upon which her maternity leave now commences and must be in writing if the employer requests it.

(6) If the leave period commences on the day which follows the childbirth (see below), then she is not required to give the specified notice in order to keep her entitlement. Whether or not she has given that notice, however, she is not entitled to ordinary or additional maternity leave unless she notifies the employer as soon as is reasonably practicable after the birth that she has given birth and the date on which this took place.[47] This notice must be in writing if the employer requests it.

Ordinary maternity leave can be started in a number of ways.[48] First, the employee may choose the start date, providing the notice requirements are met and providing that she does not specify a date earlier than the beginning of the 11th week before the expected week of childbirth.[49] Secondly, if the employee is absent from work on any day after the beginning of the fourth week before the expected week of childbirth, for a reason wholly or partly because of the pregnancy, then the ordinary leave period will automatically begin on that day. Thirdly, when the child is born. If the ordinary maternity leave period has not begun by this time, then it will begin on the day after childbirth occurs.

Ordinary maternity leave continues for a period of 26 weeks from its commencement, or until the end of the compulsory maternity leave period, whichever is later.[50] This period can be further extended if there is a statutory provision that prohibits the employee from working after the end of the ordinary maternity leave period, for a reason related to the fact that she had recently given birth. The period of leave may end early if the employee is dismissed during the period of her leave. In the event of such a dismissal, the period ends at the time of that dismissal.[51]

An employee's additional maternity leave period commences on the day after the last day of her ordinary maternity leave period and continues for 26 weeks, meaning that all affected employees are entitled to a total of 52 weeks' leave.[52] The period of leave may end early if the employee is dismissed during the period of her leave. In the event of such a dismissal, the period ends at the time of the dismissal.[53]

9.4.2 Compulsory maternity leave

Section 72 ERA 1996 provides that an employer must not allow a woman who is entitled to ordinary maternity leave to work during the compulsory leave period. The compulsory leave period is for two weeks commencing with the day on which childbirth occurs.[54] These two weeks fall within the ordinary maternity leave period, so are part of the 26 weeks

---

[46] Regulation 4(3)(b) MPL Regulations.
[47] Regulation 4(4)(b) MPL Regulations.
[48] Regulation 6 MPL Regulations.
[49] Regulation 4(2)(b) MPL Regulations.
[50] Regulation 7(1) MPL Regulations.
[51] Regulation 7(5) MPL Regulations.
[52] Regulation 6(3) MPL Regulations.
[53] Regulation 7(4)–(5) MPL Regulations.
[54] Regulation 8 MPL Regulations.

permitted for such leave. An employer who contravenes this requirement will be guilty of an offence and liable to a fine if convicted.[55]

9.5 Employment rights before and during maternity leave

Certain special rights are accorded to pregnant workers and those who have recently given birth or are breastfeeding.

9.5.1 Time off for ante-natal care

Sections 55–57 ERA 1996 provide that an employee who is pregnant and has, on the advice of a registered medical practitioner, registered midwife or registered health visitor, made an appointment to attend at any place for ante-natal care is entitled to time off with pay during the employee's working hours in order to keep the appointment.

9.5.2 Suspension from work on maternity grounds

Regulation 3(1) Management of Health and Safety at Work Regulations 1999 (MHSW Regulations 1999)[56] requires an assessment by the employer of the risks to health and safety of employees and others. Regulation 16(1) MHSW Regulations 1999 requires special attention in the event of there being female employees of childbearing age. The assessment is to decide whether the work is of a kind which would pose a risk, by reason of her condition, to the health and safety of a new or expectant mother or that of her baby. The obligation to carry out this risk assessment is not confined to situations where the employer has a pregnant employee. The employment of a woman of childbearing age should be enough to set off the need for such an assessment.[57] If it is reasonable to do so, the employer can change the working hours or working conditions in order to avoid the risks.[58] If it is not reasonable to do so then the employer must suspend the pregnant employee for as long as the risk persists. This suspension can only take place where a risk cannot be avoided. Avoiding risk does not mean the complete avoidance of all risks, but their reduction to the lowest possible level.[59]

Sections 66–68 ERA 1996 provide that an employee who is suspended from work as a result of a statutory prohibition or as a result of a recommendation contained in a code of practice issued or approved under section 16 Health and Safety at Work etc. Act 1974, is entitled to be paid during that suspension, or offered alternative work. The alternative work needs to be both suitable and appropriate given the employee's circumstances and the terms and conditions offered to her must not be substantially less favourable than her previous terms and conditions.

---

[55] Section 72(3)(b) and (5) ERA 1996.
[56] SI 1999/3242.
[57] See *Day v T Pickles Farms Ltd* [1999] IRLR 217.
[58] Regulation 16(2) MHSW Regulations 1999.
[59] See *New Southern Railway Ltd v Quinn* [2006] IRLR 267, where managers became concerned about the safety of an employee who had been appointed to the post of station manager. The tribunal stated that the managers had jumped to the conclusion that the employee could not continue in this role because of their personal feelings and had then attached a health and safety label to it.

Failure to provide alternative work and/or remuneration[60] can lead to a complaint to an employment tribunal by the employee. *British Airways (European Operations at Gatwick) Ltd v Moore and Botterill*[61] concerned cabin crew who could not fly during their pregnancies and who succeeded in their claim for their full allowances whilst employed on alternative work. They were employed on alternative ground-based work, but were not given the flying allowances to which they had previously been entitled when working as cabin crew. If a statutory prohibition were to prevent the employment of a pregnant woman from the outset and for the duration of the pregnancy, then that prohibition might be held to be discriminatory.[62]

The complaint about pay is required to be made within three months, unless not reasonably practicable, of the day on which there was a failure to pay. Complaints about not being provided with alternative work need to be made within three months, unless not reasonably practicable, of the first day of the suspension.[63] The amount of compensation to be paid will be such as the tribunal decides is just and equitable in all the circumstances.

9.5.3 The contract of employment during maternity leave

The status of the employment contract during maternity leave has not always been clear. *McPherson v Drumpark House*[64] was a case that concerned an employee who went on maternity leave without fulfilling all the statutory requirements for taking such leave and returning afterwards. When she indicated to her employers that she was returning to work, they informed her that, in their view, she was no longer employed under a contract of employment. The issue for the EAT was whether the contract of employment continued during the period of maternity leave. The EAT concluded that it was not clear and that the payment of maternity pay was not in itself enough to show a continuation of the contract without some express or implied agreement to that effect.

9.5.3.1 Work during the maternity leave period

An employee may carry out up to ten days' work for her employer during her statutory maternity period (excluding the compulsory maternity period[65]) without bringing her maternity leave period to an end.[66] This is part of a policy designed to encourage employers and those on maternity leave to keep in touch with each other and, of course, to ease the moment of return to work. Any work carried out on any day shall constitute a day's work and the work can include training or any activity designed for the purpose of keeping in touch with the workplace.[67] Regulations 12A(6) MPL Regulations makes it clear that this

---

[60] See Case C-66/96 *Handels og Kontorfunktionærernes Forbund i Danmark (acting for Høj Pedersen) v Fællesforeningen for Danmarks Brugsforeninger (acting for Kvickly Skive)* [1999] IRLR 55 ECJ, which held that national legislation which permitted the sending home of a pregnant woman, in such a situation, without paying her salary in full was contrary to the Equal Treatment Directive; legislation that only affects pregnant employees is in breach of Article 5 of the Directive.

[61] [2000] IRLR 296.

[62] Case C-207/98 *Mahlberg v Land Mecklenburg-Vorpommern* [2000] IRLR 276 ECJ.

[63] Section 70 ERA 1996.

[64] [1997] IRLR 277.

[65] Regulation 12A(5) MPL Regulations.

[66] Regulation 12A(1) MPL Regulations.

[67] Regulation 12A(2) and (3) MPL Regulations.

does not mean that the employer has the right to require this work or that the employee has a right to work. It clearly needs to be a mutually agreed option, but one which many employers and those on maternity leave may be interested in using. The period spent working does not have the effect of extending the total duration of the maternity leave period.[68]

9.5.3.2 Ordinary maternity leave

Section 71(4) ERA 1996 provides that an employee on ordinary maternity leave is, first, entitled to the benefit of the terms and conditions of employment which would have applied had she not been absent. This does not include terms and conditions about remuneration,[69] although regulation 9 MPL Regulations limits the definition of remuneration to sums payable to an employee by way of wages or salary.[70] A failure to reflect a pay increase in calculating earnings-related statutory maternity pay, for an employee on maternity leave, was likely to be a breach of Article 141 EC on equal pay and the employee would have an entitlement to make a claim for unlawful deduction from her wages.[71]

Secondly, the employee is bound by obligations arising out of those terms and conditions, and, thirdly, she is entitled to return from leave to the job in which she was employed before her absence (for discussion on the right to return to work, see below).[72] Indeed, where the contract of employment continues during pregnancy, to afford a woman less favourable treatment regarding her working conditions during that time would constitute sex discrimination within the terms of the Equal Treatment Directive.[73]

9.5.3.3 Additional maternity leave

The rules are slightly different for the period of additional maternity leave. Section 73(4) ERA 1996 provides that those on such leave are entitled to the benefit of the terms and conditions which would have applied had they not been absent, and are bound, subject to any regulations, by obligations arising under those terms and conditions and entitled to return to a job of a prescribed kind. In this case terms and conditions are defined as matters connected with the employment regardless of whether they arise from the contract of employment, but they do not include remuneration. There are no regulations to define further the meaning of remuneration in this case, suggesting that it will have a much broader meaning than during ordinary maternity leave.

There are further contractual terms stipulated by the MPL Regulations for those who are taking additional maternity leave. These are:

(1) the employee is entitled to the benefit of her employer's implied obligation to her of trust and confidence and any terms and conditions of employment which relate to

---

[68] Regulation 12A(7) MPL Regulations.

[69] Section 71(5) ERA 1996.

[70] Case C-333/97 *Lewen v Denda* [2000] IRLR 67 ECJ where a voluntarily given Christmas bonus was held to be 'pay' within the meaning of Article 119 EC (now 141); thus an employer may not take into account periods when a mother was prohibited from working in order to reduce proportionately the amount awarded.

[71] See *Alabaster v Woolwich plc and Secretary of State for Social Security* [2000] IRLR 754.

[72] Following section 17(2) EA 2002, this is changed to the right to return 'to a job of a prescribed kind'.

[73] See, e.g., Case C-136/95 *Caisse National d'Assurance Vieillesse des Travailleurs Salariés v Thibault* [1998] IRLR 399 ECJ, where a woman on maternity leave was not given an annual appraisal and was, as a result, deprived of a merit pay award.

notice of termination of the contract of employment, compensation in the event of redundancy or disciplinary or grievance procedure;

(2) the employee is bound by her implied obligation of good faith and any terms and conditions relating to notice of termination of the contract of employment, the disclosure of confidential information, the acceptance of gifts or other benefits and the employee's participation in any other business.

All contracts of employment have an implied term of mutual trust and confidence which the employee and employer have a duty to maintain. This continues during the period of additional maternity leave.[74] The authors of the regulations obviously had a concern that employees might use periods of additional maternity leave or parental leave to participate in rival businesses (see Chapter 3). These provisions ensure that contractual obligations restricting this continue during the period of absence, as well as the employer's and the employee's rights and obligations concerning notice periods.

9.6 Protection from detriment

Regulation 19 MPL Regulations provides that an employee is not to be subjected to any detriment by any act, or failure to act, by her employer[75] for a number of specified reasons. It is important to note that deliberately failing to act can also be a detriment, such as giving benefits to employees, but failing to give those benefits to persons included in the categories below. The specified reasons include that the employee is pregnant, has given birth to a child, took, or sought to take, the benefits of ordinary maternity leave, took, or sought to take, additional maternity leave or failed to return after a period of ordinary or additional maternity leave and undertook, considered undertaking or refused to undertake work that is allowed (see 9.5.3.1 above) during the maternity leave period. (According to regulation 19(6) if the act that leads to a detriment in this case takes place over a period of time, then the date of the act is the last day of the period. A failure to act takes place on the date it was decided upon.[76])

In *Abbey National plc v Formoso*[77] an employee was held to have suffered detriment when her employer proceeded to hold a disciplinary hearing without the attendance of the employee, who was absent on a pregnancy-related illness. The employee had given notice of the date when she wished her maternity leave to begin, whilst she was absent through pregnancy-related sickness. The employers wished to resolve the matter prior to the maternity leave and proceeded with the hearing even though the employee's doctor considered that she was unfit to attend the meeting and would be so until the end of her pregnancy. The EAT confirmed the employment tribunal's view that pregnancy was the effective cause of the disciplinary hearing and that her treatment had amounted to sex discrimination. Similarly, in *Gus Home Shopping Ltd v Green and McLaughlin*,[78] two

---

[74] Regulation 17 MPL Regulations.
[75] See section 47C ERA 1996.
[76] Regulation 19(7) MPL Regulations states that, in the absence of any other evidence, a failure to act is when the employer does an act which is inconsistent with doing the failed act or, if no inconsistent act takes place, when the period expires in which the employer might reasonably have been expected to do the failed act.
[77] [1999] IRLR 222.
[78] [2001] IRLR 75.

employees who were absent from work because of their pregnancy were held to have been discriminated against when they did not receive a discretionary loyalty bonus payable to all employees who remained in their posts until a business transferred to a new location. The different treatment meant that they had been unlawfully discriminated against on the grounds of sex.

9.7 Protection from dismissal

9.7.1 Redundancy

It may be that, during an employee's ordinary or additional maternity leave periods, it is not practicable for the employer to continue to employ her during her existing contract of employment, by reason of redundancy (see Chapter 5). If this happens then the employee is entitled to be offered any suitable alternative vacancy before the end of her employment under a new contract of employment, which takes effect immediately upon ending employment under the current contract. This applies to vacancies with the employer, their successor or an associated employer (see above). The new contract of employment must be such that the work to be done is of a kind which is both suitable in relation to the employee and appropriate for her to do in the circumstances, and the terms and conditions of employment and the capacity and location in which she is to be employed is not substantially less favourable than had she continued to be employed under her previous contract of employment.[79] If the employee is not offered available alternative employment then she may be regarded as being unfairly dismissed for the purposes of Part X ERA 1996.

Regulation 20(2) MPL Regulations provides that if an employee is dismissed for reasons of redundancy and it is shown that the circumstances constituting the redundancy applied equally to one or more other employees in the same undertaking who held similar positions to the dismissed employee, and those other employees have not been dismissed, and the reason, or the principal reason, for the employee being selected for dismissal was related to her pregnancy (as in protection from detriment above), then the dismissal will be unfair for the purposes of Part X ERA 1996 (unfair dismissal).

9.7.2 Unfair dismissal

There are a number of relevant reasons for dismissal which will be regarded as unfair. If the reason, or the principal reason, for the dismissal is:

(1) the pregnancy of the employee or the fact that she has given birth to a child, during her ordinary or additional maternity leave period, or
(2) the application of a relevant requirement, or a relevant recommendation in accordance with section 66(2) ERA 1996 (see suspension from work on maternity grounds above), or
(3) the fact that she undertook, considered undertaking or refused to undertake work in accordance with Regulation 12A (see section 9.5.3.1 above),[80] or

---

[79] Regulation 10(2)–(3) MPL Regulations.
[80] Regulation 19 MPL Regulations.

(4) the fact that she took or availed herself of the benefits of ordinary maternity leave, or the fact that she took additional maternity leave,

then the dismissal is unfair.[81] A dismissal during pregnancy for reasons connected with the pregnancy is likely to amount to direct sex discrimination. In *Brown v Rentokil Ltd*[82] the employers dismissed a female employee for sickness absences related to her pregnancy. The employer was applying a rule which meant that any male or female employee could be dismissed if absent for more than 26 weeks. The ECJ held that the situation of a pregnant worker absent because of her pregnancy could not be equated to the absences of a male worker due to incapacity for work.[83]

9.8 The right to return to work

An employee who wishes to return early from her additional maternity leave period must give her employer at least eight weeks' notice of the date on which she intends to return. If the employee tries to return early without giving this notice, then the employer may delay her return for eight weeks.[84] 'Job' is defined, in relation to a person returning to work after additional maternity leave, as meaning 'the nature of the work which she is employed to do in accordance with her contract and the capacity and place in which she is so employed'.[85]

An employee's right to return from leave to the job in which she was employed before her absence[86] means that she has a right to return both with her seniority, pension and other similar rights intact, as if she had not been absent, and with terms and conditions no less favourable than those that would have applied had she not been absent.[87] Except where there is a genuine redundancy situation leading to the dismissal, an employee who takes additional maternity leave is entitled to return to the job in which she was employed before her absence.[88] If it is not reasonably practicable for an employer to permit her to do so, then she may return to another job which is both suitable and appropriate for her in the circumstances. This right to return is to return on terms and conditions no less favourable than would have been applicable had she not been absent from work at any time since the beginning of the ordinary maternity leave period. This includes returning with her seniority, pension rights and similar rights as if she had been in continuous employment during the periods of leave and not any less favourable than if she had not been absent through taking additional maternity leave after the ordinary maternity leave period.[89] There is not necessarily a right to return to a different job or to a job with different hours. Women of newly born children might need, for example, flexible working arrangements or part-time hours. Except in so far as they are affected by the Part-time Workers Regulations

---

[81] Regulation 20 MPL Regulations.
[82] Case 394/96 [1998] IRLR 445 ECJ.
[83] See also Case C-32/93 *Webb v EMO Air Cargo (UK) Ltd* [1994] IRLR 482 ECJ.
[84] Regulation 11 MPL Regulations.
[85] Regulation 2(1) MPL Regulations.
[86] Section 71(4)(c) ERA 1996.
[87] Section 71(7) ERA 1996.
[88] Regulation 18(2) MPL Regulations.
[89] Regulation 18(5) MPL Regulations.

2000[90] or the Flexible Working Regulations 2002[91] the legislation does not provide this flexibility as a legal right. An example of the problems experienced in the past is that contained in *British Telecommunications plc v Roberts and Longstaffe*,[92] which concerned two full-time employees who wished to return to work after their maternity leave on a job-share basis. They were unable to comply with an 'operational requirement' that the work should include Saturday mornings, and complained of indirect sex discrimination. On the issue of whether they had a right to return to work on a job share arrangement, it was held that this was not covered by the special protection given to women during their pregnancy and maternity leave. When a woman returns to work the statutory protection is ended.

If the employer offers an alternative post with an associate employer and this is unreasonably turned down by the employee, then the employee is likely to lose her protection from unfair dismissal under these regulations. In both these cases, the onus is on the employer to show that the provisions in question were satisfied in relation to any individual in question.[93]

If an employee has a statutory right to maternity leave as well as a contractual right, in her contract of employment, to such leave, then she is able to take advantage of whichever right, in any particular respect, is the more favourable.[94] Employees are not permitted to take advantage of the statutory right in addition to the contractual right. The regulation does suggest, however, in the use of the term 'in any particular respect', that an employee is able to select those aspects in each which are most favourable to her.

Regulation 22 MPL Regulations also provides an amendment to Part XIV Chapter II ERA 1996 in respect of a week's pay. When, for the purposes of that section, a calculation is being made on the basis of 12 weeks' average pay, then weeks in which the employee is taking ordinary or additional maternity leave and is paid less than her normal entitlement will be disregarded for the calculation purposes.

9.9 Flexible working

Section 47 EA 2002 amended the ERA 1996 to make provision for flexible working arrangements for the care of children. A qualifying employee may apply to his or her employer for a change in the terms and conditions of employment, in relation to:

(1) the hours that are required to be worked;
(2) the times when work is required;
(3) whether the work should take place at home or the place of business;
(4) any other aspect that might be specified in regulations.

The purpose of the application must be the care of a child.[95] Such an application must be made before the day on which the child reaches the age of six (or 18 if the child is

---

[90] See Chapter 3.
[91] Flexible Working (Eligibility, Complaints and Remedies) Regulations 2002, SI 2002/3236.
[92] [1996] IRLR 601.
[93] Regulation 20(7)–(8) MPL Regulations.
[94] Regulation 20(2) MPL Regulations.
[95] Section 80F ERA 1996.

entitled to a disability living allowance).[96] No more than one application every 12 months is permitted and the rules specifically exclude their application to agency workers, which may seem surprising in a wider context of making non-standard work attractive (see Chapter 3).

An employee is entitled to request a contract variation to care for a child if he or she has been continuously employed for a period of not less than 26 weeks and is either the mother, father, adopter, guardian or foster parent of the child, or is married to or a partner or civil partner[97] of one of these.[98] The request must be in writing, be dated and state whether a previous application has been made to the employer and, if so, when.[99] Within 28 days[100] of the request, the employer, unless he or she agrees to the request, must hold a meeting with the employee to discuss the application.[101] The employee has the right to be accompanied by another employee of the same employer. This companion has the right to address the meeting and confer with the applicant employee during the meeting.[102] After this meeting there are a further 14 days for the employer to give the employee notice of the decision reached. This decision needs to be in writing and can either be an agreement to the employee's request, specifying the contract variation which is to take place, or a rejection of the request. In the latter case the employer must give the grounds for refusal together with a sufficient explanation. *Commotion Ltd v Rutty*[103] concerned an individual who was employed as a warehouse assistant. After she became legally responsible for the care of her grandchild she made an application to work three days a week instead of five. Her request was turned down on the grounds that it would have a detrimental impact on performance in the warehouse. The EAT, however, supported her claim that the employer had failed to establish that they had refused the request on one of the grounds permitted by section 80G(1)(b) ERA 1996. Tribunals were entitled to investigate to see whether the decision to reject the application was based on facts and whether the employer could have coped with the change without disruption. In this case the EAT found that the evidence did not support the employer's assertion and the employer had not carried out any investigations to see whether they could cope with what the claimant wanted.

Regulation 3B[104] introduced an entitlement to request a contract variation for the care of an adult. Thus an employee can request such a variation for a person over the age of 18 years if the employee has been continuously employed for a period of not less than 26 weeks and is, or expects to be, caring for a person in need of care who is either married

---

[96] Regulation 3A Flexible Working (Eligibility, Complaints and Remedies) Regulations 2002.

[97] Regulation 2 defines partners as a man and a woman who are not married to each other but are living together as if they were husband and wife or two people of the same sex who are not civil partners of each other but are living together as if they were civil partners.

[98] Regulation 3 Flexible Working (Eligibility, Complaints and Remedies) Regulations 2002.

[99] Regulation 4 Flexible Working (Eligibility, Complaints and Remedies) Regulations 2002.

[100] All the periods referred to here can be extended by mutual agreement between the employer and the employee: Regulation 12 Flexible Working (Procedural Requirements) Regulations 2002, SI 2002/3207.

[101] Regulation 3 Flexible Working (Procedural Requirements) Regulations 2002.

[102] Regulation 14 Flexible Working (Procedural Requirements) Regulations 2002.

[103] [2006] IRLR 171.

[104] Added by the Flexible Working (Eligibility, Complaints and Remedies) (Amendment) Regulations 2006, SI 2006/3314.

to or the partner or civil partner of the employee, a relative of the employee, or living at the same address as the employee. In this case 'relative' means:

> a mother, father, adopter, guardian, special guardian, parent in law, step parent, son, step son, daughter, step daughter, brother, step brother, brother in law, sister, step sister, sister in law, uncle, aunt or grandparent, and includes adoptive relationships and relationships of full blood or, in the case of an adopted person, such of those relationships as would exist but for the adoption.

One of the oddities resulting from this much-needed amendment to the regulations is that the only people now for whom one cannot make a statutory request for flexible working are those between the ages of 6 years and 18 years. The parents of such an age group might feel that this is unfair as most people between these ages are still in need of adult care.

Section 80G(1)(b) ERA 1996 provides that an employer may refuse such a request only if one or more of the following grounds applies:

- the burden of additional costs;
- detrimental effect on ability to meet customer demand;
- inability to reorganise work among existing staff;
- inability to recruit additional staff;
- detrimental impact on quality;
- detrimental impact on performance;
- insufficiency of work during the periods the employee proposes to work;
- planned structural changes;
- such other grounds as may be specified by regulations.

An employee is entitled to appeal against any refusal by the employer. This appeal needs to be in writing, set out the grounds for the appeal and be dated. It must be done within 14 days after the date of the employer's notice giving the decision on the original application. Again within 14 days of this meeting the employer must give the employee a decision. If the appeal is dismissed, then the employer must state the grounds for dismissal and give a sufficient explanation as to why those grounds apply.[105]

Failure of an employer to respond in relation to one of these grounds or a decision by an employer to reject the application on incorrect facts may lead to a complaint to an employment tribunal and the award of compensation of up to eight weeks' pay.

9.10 Parental leave

Two important features of parental leave are, first, that it is available to fathers as well as mothers and, secondly, that it is unpaid.[106] This latter feature affects the take-up of the benefit, especially amongst those who cannot afford the cost of taking time off from work on an unpaid basis. The European Commission published a survey in 2004 on attitudes towards parental leave throughout the EU.[107] This showed that generally the level of awareness amongst men was quite high. Some 75% of male respondents were aware that

---

[105] Regulations 9 and 10 Flexible Working (Procedural Requirements) Regulations 2002.
[106] See 9.11 below for provisions relating to paid paternity leave.
[107] Directorate General Employment and Social Affairs, *Europeans' attitudes to parental leave*, May 2004.

men could take parental leave. There were some variations between countries. In Sweden, for example, some 97% of men were aware of this, whilst the figure fell to 57% for Irish and Portuguese men. Some 84% of male respondents, however, replied that they had neither taken parental leave not were thinking of doing so. This figure did not fall below 70% for any country except Sweden and Finland. At the other extreme were the Spanish male respondents where 95% said that they had not taken and were not thinking of taking parental leave. When the survey looked at the reasons stopping fathers from taking parental leave, the main responses were: insufficient financial compensation (42%); not enough information about parental leave (34%); and careers would be affected (31%). Some 13% of men gave a fear of having to do housework as a reason for not taking up the benefit! This included some 21% of German male respondents, but only 5% of the Greeks and Italians.

The issue of sufficient finance is not, of course, a male preserve. The average duration of extended maternity leave (which preceded the MPL Regulations 1999) actually taken was less than 30 weeks (40 weeks' entitlement). The main reason given for women returning to work early was that they needed the money (73% of those returning).

9.10.1 Entitlement

Certain employees are entitled to parental leave. This is in addition to any entitlement to statutory maternity or paternity leave. The employees who qualify for parental leave are those who have been continuously employed for a period of not less than one year, and have, or expect to have, responsibility for a child.

The second condition raises the question of who has responsibility for a child. A 'traditional view' of children with a male and a female parent sharing responsibility for a child is not an acceptable model. The MPL Regulations go some way towards offering a definition. Regulation 13(2) states that an employee has responsibility for a child if they meet one of a number of tests. These are:

(1) if the employee has parental responsibilities for a child;
(2) if the employee has been registered as the child's father under any provision of sections 10(1) or 10A(1) Births and Deaths Registration Act 1953 or of section 18(1) or (2) Registration of Births and Deaths and Marriages (Scotland) Act 1965.

9.10.2 Meaning of parental responsibility

Parental responsibility is defined in section 3 Children Act 1989. Section 3(1) provides that:

> ... parental responsibility means all the rights, duties, powers, responsibilities and authority which by law a parent of a child has in relation to the child and his property.

Section 2(1) Children Act 1989 states that where a child's father and mother were married to each other at the time of the birth, they shall each have parental responsibility for the child. Thus parental responsibility is automatically acquired by both parents if married at the time of birth. It can also be automatically acquired by both parents if they marry subsequent to the birth.[108] Where they are not married the mother has parental responsibility, unless the father acquires that responsibility in accordance with the provisions of the Act.[109]

Section 4 Children Act 1989 deals with the acquisition of parental responsibility by the father. Where the child's father and mother were not married to each other, parental responsibility can be achieved by the father on an order of the court resulting from an application by the father, or by entering into a parental responsibility agreement with the mother, which provides for the father to have parental responsibility for the child.

Parental responsibility is therefore automatically acquired by the mother, but this cannot be said of the father, if not married to the mother at the birth or subsequently.

Parental responsibility does not necessarily mean that a father is making day-to-day decisions about a child or, indeed, having the same responsibility for a child's welfare as the mother may have. It suggests, as stated by Lady Justice Butler-Sloss[110] in a case concerning a father's application for a parental responsibility order:

> A father who has shown real commitment to the child concerned and to whom there is a positive attachment, as well as a genuine *bona fide* reason for the application, ought in a case such as the present, to assume the weight of those duties and cement that commitment and attachment by sharing the responsibilities for the child with the mother. This father is asking to assume that burden as well as that pleasure of looking after his child, a burden not lightly to be undertaken.

As the MPL Regulations make clear, this includes having responsibility for an adopted child or a child who is placed with the employee for the purposes of adoption.

9.10.3 Leave entitlement

An employee is entitled to 13 weeks' leave in respect of any individual child and 18 weeks in respect of a child who is entitled to a disability living allowance.[111] The leave entitlement is of 'any individual child', so that an employee/parent of multiple-birth children will be entitled to 13 weeks in respect of each. Similarly employee/parents with more than one child, of differing ages, will be entitled to 13 weeks' leave in respect of each child. Section 76(1) ERA 1996 states that the absence from work is with the 'purpose of caring for a child'. Although the ERA 1996 suggests that the regulations may 'specify things which are, or are not, to be taken as done for the purpose of caring for the child',[112] they do not. It is, presumably, left to the employer and employee to decide.

A week's leave has different meanings in different circumstances. First, it can mean that where the employee is required, under the contract of employment, to work the same period each week, then a week's leave is equal in duration to that period. Thus if an employee works from Monday to Friday each week, then a week's leave will be a period from Monday to Friday. Secondly, where the employee is required, under the contract of

---

[108] See section 1 Family Reform Act 1987.
[109] Section 2(2) Children Act 1989.
[110] *Re S (A Minor) (Parental Responsibility)* [1995] 3 FCR 225.
[111] Regulation 14(1) MPL Regulations and regulation 14(1A) added by the Maternity and Parental Leave (Amendment) Regulations 2001, SI 2001/4010.
[112] Section 76(5)(a) ERA 1996.

employment, to work different periods in different weeks, or works in some weeks and not others, then a week's leave is calculated by adding the total periods that the employee is required to work in a year and dividing by 52. Thus, for example, if an employee works for five days every alternative week, then a week's leave will be 5 × 26, divided by 52, making it 2.5 days.[113] If an employee takes leave in shorter periods than a week, according to the definitions, then an employer will need to total the leave taken to aggregate it into weekly periods.

The entitlement to 13 weeks' leave is dependent upon one year's continuous employment with the same, or an associated, employer, so, if an individual changes employers, that individual will be required to establish one year's continuous service with the new employer before being able to acquire rights to parental leave again. This raises the question of transferring the balance on an employee's entitlement between employers. If an individual, for example, takes four weeks' parental leave with employer A and then moves to employer B, they will have a balance of nine weeks' leave to which they will be entitled after one year's continuous service with employer B. The problem for employer B is to know how much of an entitlement the individual has left. This information can only come from employer A or from the employee. There is no requirement for employers to keep records of parental leave taken, although it will surely be a matter of good practice to do so.

9.10.4 When there is entitlement to parental leave

The entitlement to parental leave is in respect of a child who is less than five years old. When the child reaches its fifth birthday the entitlement ceases in respect of that child. The three exceptions to this are, first, when there are adopted children or children placed with an employee for adoption. In these cases the entitlement ceases on the fifth anniversary of the date on which the placement began. In such cases the upper age of five years cannot apply. The regulations provide an absolute upper age limit of the date of the child's 18th birthday. Secondly, an employee with a child who is entitled to a disability living allowance will be able to use their leave over a longer period, until the 'child' is 18 years of age.[114] Disability living allowance is defined as the disability living allowance provided by Part III Social Security Contributions and Benefits Act 1992.[115] Thirdly, if an employer exercises their right to delay parental leave (see below) and this results in the child passing the fifth birthday, the entitlement can still be taken at the end of the period for which leave had been postponed, even though the child will now be over five years old.

9.10.5 Procedural rules[116]

If there are no contractual rules to the contrary or any collective or workforce agreements affecting the procedures, then the MPL Regulations lay down a number of default

---

[113] Regulation 14(2)–(3) MPL Regulations.
[114] Regulation 15(1)–(3) MPL Regulations.
[115] Regulation 2(1) MPL Regulations.
[116] Schedule 2 MPL Regulations.

procedures which apply before the employee can take their parental leave entitlement. There are essentially three conditions that an employee needs to comply with before their parental leave may commence. These are the evidence condition, the notice condition and the post-ponement condition. It should be noted that, under the default arrangements, employees may not take leave in periods of less than one week, except where the child is entitled to a disability living allowance. To fulfil the evidence condition an employer may request from the employee such evidence as may be reasonably required of the employee's responsibility or expected responsibility for the child in question, the age of that child or, if the request for leave is in connection with a child entitled to a disability living allowance, then evidence of that entitlement. It is interesting that the employee is not required to show any evidence of leave previously taken in respect of that child.

To fulfil the notice condition employees are required to give notice to the employer specifying the dates on which the period of leave is to start and finish. This notice is to be given to the employer at least 21 days before the start date. There are special rules for certain employees. The first applies to an employee who is the father and wishes his parental leave to commence on the date on which the child is born. In this situation the employee must give at least 21 days' notice before the beginning of the expected week of childbirth, specifying when the expected week of childbirth is and the duration of the period of leave. The second is where the leave is in respect of a child to be placed with the employee for adoption; then the notice needs to specify the week in which the placement is expected to occur and the duration of the leave. It needs to be given to the employer at least 21 days before the beginning of the placement week, or, if that is not reasonably practicable, as soon as is reasonably practicable.

Employers are able to postpone parental leave, except in relation to the leave requested in the special cases above, once the employee has given the required notice. The employer may take such action:

> if the employer considers that the operation of his business would be unduly disrupted if the employee took leave during the period identified in his notice.

This is an important safeguard for employers who may be faced with a number of employees wishing to take time off at the same time of the year (for example, school holidays). The employer may postpone leave for up to six months as long as, at the end of the postponement period, the employee is permitted to take the same length of leave as originally requested. The employer is required to give notice to the employee of the postponement, in writing, stating the reasons for the delay and specifying the dates on which the delayed leave may commence and end. The employer's notice of postponement must be given to the employee not more than seven days after the employee's notice was given to the employer. This means, of course, that employees will have a minimum of 14 days' notice of the employer's decision to postpone the leave.

9.10.6 Limitations on parental leave

There are two important limitations contained in the default procedures. First, an employee may not take more than four weeks' leave in respect of a particular child in any one year and that leave must be taken in periods of at least one week, unless the child in respect of whom leave is taken is entitled to a disability living allowance.[117] This is rather an inflexible approach and can mean that a person will need to take a week's parental leave when they actually need less. This happened in *Rodway v South Central Trains Ltd*[118] where an employee needed a Saturday off in order to look after his son. His application for parental leave was turned down because of the lack of available cover. In the event he took the day off anyway and was subsequently disciplined. The EAT held that the individual could not have suffered a detriment because of a reason related to parental leave, because such leave could only be taken in periods of one week and not just for one day.

A week is here defined as in regulation 14 (see above). The definition of a year is interesting. It is a 12-month period commencing with the date, except in certain cases, on which the employee first became entitled to parental leave in respect of the child in question. This presumably means, for example, 12-month periods from the birth of a child. Alternatively, where a period of continuous employment is interrupted, then at the date when the employee newly qualifies after a further period of continuous employment.

It is important to note that these procedural rules can be varied by agreement between employers and employees or their representatives, in the form of collective or workforce agreements.[119]

9.10.7 Complaint to an employment tribunal

Section 80(1) ERA 1996 provides that an employee may complain to an employment tribunal if the employer has unreasonably postponed a period of parental leave or has prevented, or attempted to prevent, the employee from taking parental leave. The complaint needs to be made within three months beginning with the date of the matter complained about, or such further period as the tribunal agrees if this was not reasonably practicable. If the tribunal agrees with the complaint it may make a declaration to that effect and award compensation to the employee, having regard to the employer's behaviour and any loss sustained by the employee as a result of the matters complained of.

9.10.8 Employee rights during parental leave

An employee who is absent on parental leave is entitled to the benefit of the terms and conditions of employment which would have applied if they had not been absent. This includes any matters connected with the employee's employment, whether or not they arise under the contract of employment, except for matters relating to remuneration.[120] The employee is also entitled to the benefit of the employer's implied obligation of trust and confidence and any terms and conditions of employment relating to notice of the termination of the employment contract by her or his employer, compensation in the event of redundancy, disciplinary or grievance procedures.

---

[117] Schedule 2, paragraphs 7–8.
[118] [2005] IRLR 583.
[119] For collective agreements, see Chapter 12.
[120] In Case C-218/98 *Abdoulaye v Régie Nationale des Usines Renault SA* [1998] IRLR 811 ECJ, the trade unions claimed that new fathers should be entitled to the same bonus given to women taking maternity leave; this view was rejected by the ECJ who held that they were not comparable situations.

The absent employee is bound by any obligations arising under their terms and conditions of employment. Additionally regulation 17(1) MPL Regulations states that the employee is bound by an implied obligation of good faith and any terms and conditions of employment relating to notice of the termination of the employment contract by the employee, the disclosure of confidential information, the acceptance of gifts or other benefits, or the employee's participation in any other business.[121]

There may be a problem in differentiating between when the employee is on parental leave and when occupying their own spare time. Generally, the spare time activities of employees are no business of the employer, although it may be possible to prevent employees working for competitors during their spare time if it can be shown that the employer's business would be seriously damaged. In *Nova Plastics Ltd v Froggat*[122] the EAT rejected the argument that there was a general implication that any work for a competitor should be regarded as being a breach of trust or a failure to give loyal service. The intention to set up in competition with the employer is not necessarily a breach of the implied duty of fidelity, although the renting and equipping of premises, in an employee's spare time, and arranging financial backing to set up in competition may be construed as a breach.[123]

9.10.9 The right to return to work

There are important differences in this right, depending upon the length of leave taken:

(1) An employee who takes parental leave for a period of four weeks or less, other than immediately after additional maternity leave, is entitled to return to work to the job in which they were employed before the absence.
(2) An employee who takes more than four weeks' parental leave is also entitled to return to the job in which they worked prior to the absence. If, in this latter case, it is not reasonably practicable to return to that job, then an employer must permit the employee to return to another job which is both suitable and appropriate in the circumstances. The exception to this will be as a result of a redundancy situation.
(3) An employee who takes parental leave of four weeks or less immediately after additional maternity leave is entitled to return to the job in which she was employed prior to the absence, unless it would not have been reasonably practicable for her to return to that job at the end of her additional maternity leave, and it is still not reasonably practicable for the employer to permit her to return to that job at the end of parental leave. In such a situation she will be entitled to return to another job which is both suitable and appropriate in the circumstances. There is also an exception for redundancy situations.[124]

This right to return is on terms and conditions, with regard to remuneration, which are no less favourable than those which would have applied if the employee had not been absent from work on parental leave, with seniority, pension rights and similar rights

[121] Section 77(1) ERA 1996.
[122] [1982] IRLR 146.
[123] See *Lancashire Fires Ltd v SA Lyons & Co Ltd* [1997] IRLR 113 CA.
[124] Regulation 18(1)–(3) MPL Regulations.

preserved as if the employee had been in continuous employment. Otherwise on terms and conditions no less favourable than those which would have applied if there had been no period of absence.

The MPL Regulations also make provision for a person who takes parental leave immediately after the period of additional maternity leave. In that case they are entitled to return with all the above as if they had not been absent during the period of ordinary maternity leave, additional maternity leave and parental leave combined.

9.10.10 Protection from detriment and dismissal

An employee who has taken parental leave is not to be subjected to detriment by any act, or any deliberate failure to act, by the employer.[125] An employee who is dismissed for reasons connected to the fact that they took parental leave is to be treated as unfairly dismissed in accordance with Part X ERA 1996 (the provisions relating to unfair dismissal).[126] If there is a complaint of unfair dismissal and the question arises as to whether the reason, or principal reason, is related to the fact that the employee took, or sought to take, parental leave, then it is for the employer to show that the provisions have been complied with.[127]

An employee shall also be regarded as unfairly dismissed if the reason, or the principal reason, for their dismissal is that they were redundant and it can be shown that the circumstances causing the redundancy applied equally to one or more employees in the same business and holding similar positions to that held by the dismissed employee, and who have not been dismissed by the employer, and the reason, or the principal reason, for the selection of the employee for dismissal was that they had taken parental leave.[128] Thus an employee selected for redundancy, where it can be shown that other employees in similar positions were not selected for redundancy and the selected employee was chosen because of their parental leave, will automatically be entitled to make a claim for unfair dismissal. If, however, the employer, or an associated employer, offers the employee a position that is both appropriate and suitable, but the employee unreasonably turns it down, then the employee will lose any right to claim unfair dismissal by reason of taking parental leave.[129]

9.10.11 Additional provisions

If an employee has a statutory right to parental leave and also a contractual right, in their contract of employment, to parental leave, then they are able to take advantage of whichever right, in any particular respect, is the more favourable.[130] He or she is not permitted to take advantage of the statutory right in addition to a contractual right. The regulation does suggest, however, when it uses the term 'in any particular respect', that it

---

[125] Regulation 19(1) MPL Regulations.
[126] Regulation 20(1)(a) MPL Regulations.
[127] Regulation 20(8) MPL Regulations.
[128] Regulation 20(2) MPL Regulations.
[129] Regulation 20(7) MPL Regulations.
[130] Regulation 21(2) MPL Regulations.

is permissible to 'cherry-pick', i.e. pick out the best features of both schemes and take advantage of those.

Regulation 22 MPL Regulations also provides an amendment to Part XIV Chapter II ERA 1996 in respect of a week's pay. When, for the purposes of that regulation, a calculation is being made on the basis of 12 weeks' average pay, then weeks in which the employee is taking parental leave should be ignored.

9.11 Paternity leave

The Paternity and Adoption Leave Regulations 2002[131] provide the qualification rules for paternity leave. An employee is entitled to paternity leave if:

  (i) he has been employed for at least 26 weeks prior to the 14th week before the expected week of childbirth;
 (ii) he is either the child's father or, if not, is married to or a partner of the child's mother;
(iii) he is to have responsibility, along with the mother, for the upbringing of the child.

An employee will still have satisfied the requirements if the child is born before the 14th week before the expected birth, or if the child is stillborn after 24 weeks of pregnancy, or if the child's mother dies.[132] An employee may take either one week's leave or two consecutive weeks' leave. This must be taken before the end of a period of at least 56 days beginning with the date of the child's birth. In the event of multiple births only the first born will count for leave and date purposes.[133] Similar rules apply to the entitlement to paternity leave as a result of adopting a child, except that the key date is the date on which the child is expected to be placed with the adopter.[134]

Other rules, such as the evidential requirements and protection offered are similar to those concerned with parental leave (see above).

9.12 Adoption leave

The right to adoption leave was introduced by the Employment Act 2002 and the Paternity and Adoption Leave Regulations 2002. Some amendments were made by the 2006 Regulations, and in addition the Work and Families Act 2006 provided for regulations to introduce additional adoption leave under certain circumstances. An employee who meets the necessary conditions and complies with the notice and evidential requirements is entitled to adoption leave. As with maternity leave this is divided into ordinary and additional adoption leave, although, of course, there is no equivalent of compulsory maternity leave.

An employee is entitled to adoption leave if the employee, if he or she is the child's adopter, has been continuously employed for a period of not less than 26 weeks ending

---

[131] SI 2002/2788; these were amended by the Maternity and Parental Leave etc. and the Paternity and Adoption Leave (Amendment) Regulations 2006, SI 2006/2014.
[132] Regulation 4 Paternity and Adoption Leave Regulations 2002.
[133] Regulation 5(1)–(2) Paternity and Adoption Leave Regulations 2002.
[134] Regulations 8–11 Paternity and Adoption Leave Regulations 2002.

with the week in which the employee was notified of being matched with the child, and has notified the agency that he agrees that the child should be placed with him on the date of placement.[135]

An employee's entitlement to adoption leave is not affected by the placement for adoption of more than one child as part of the same arrangement.

Ordinary adoption leave and additional adoption leave will normally last for 26 weeks each. It may be less, of course, if the employee were dismissed before the end of this period. It may also end early if the placement is disrupted. The other matters concerning adoption leave are identical to those concerning maternity leave, which are outlined earlier in this chapter. These matters concern the right to return to work, notice periods for early return matters concerning terms and conditions during adoption leave, and contact between the employer and employee during adoption leave, including the right to carry out up to 10 days' work with the employer without bringing the statutory adoption leave period to an end.

Further reading

Deakin, S. and Morris, G. *Labour Law* (4th edn, Hart Publishing, 2005), Chapter 6.
http://www.berr.gov.uk/employment/workandfamilies/index.html for the Government web site on work and families which includes the topics in this chapter.

Visit **www.mylawchamber.co.uk/sargeant** to access legal updates, live web links and practice exam questions to test yourself on this chapter.

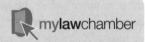

---

[135] Regulation 15(2) Paternity and Adoption Leave Regulations 2002.

10
Business Re-structuring

10.1 Introduction

One of the occasions when a worker is perhaps at his or her most vulnerable, in relation to work, is when the business is reorganised in some way. The reorganisation may be the result of a takeover by another employer, or because the worker's own employer has become insolvent or there is a perceived need to reduce the number of employees. In such situations a worker's security of employment and their terms and conditions are often at risk.

The European Community recognised this at an early stage. There was a concern that the development of the single market would lead to a large number of mergers and acquisitions as industry and commerce became more European based, rather than nationally based. In order to make these changes more acceptable to workers and their representatives, a number of initiatives emerged from the Community's Social Action Programme of 1974. These were initiatives concerned with consultation in collective redundancy situations, protection during transfers of undertakings and for those whose employer had become insolvent. In particular there were three Directives that have long been part of national law and provide some protection for employees as a result of business restructuring. These Directives were the Collective Redundancies Directive,[1] which is incorporated into Part IV Chapter II TULRCA 1992; the Acquired Rights Directive,[2] which was originally transposed by the Transfer of Undertakings (Protection of Employment) Regulations 1981;[3] and the Insolvency Directive,[4] which is incorporated into Part XII ERA 1996. Subsequently, the Community has adopted two directives concerned with information and consultation. These are the European Works Council Directive,[5] whose

---

[1] Council Directive 75/129/EEC on the approximation of the laws of the Member States relating to collective redundancies OJ 1975 L48/29; amended by Directive 92/56/EEC OJ L245/3; consolidated by Directive 98/59/EC OJ L225/16.

[2] Council Directive 77/187 on the approximation of the laws of the Member States relating to the safeguarding of employees' rights in the event of transfers of undertakings, businesses or parts of undertakings or businesses OJ L61/26; amended by Directive 98/50/EC OJ L201/88; now consolidated into Directive 2001/23/EC OJ L82/16 22.3.2001.

[3] SI 1981/1794; now the Transfers of Undertakings (Protection of Employment) Regulations 2006, SI 2006/246.

[4] Directive 2002/74/EC amended Council Directive 80/987/EEC on the approximation of the laws of the Member States relating to the protection of employees in the event of the insolvency of their employer OJ L 270/10 23.9.2002.

[5] Council Directive 94/45/EC on the establishment of a European Works Council or a procedure in Community-scale undertakings and Community-scale groups of undertakings for the purpose of informing and consulting employees OJ L254/64.

purpose was the establishment of formal consultation processes in transnational undertakings, and the Information and Consultation Directive[6] which provides for the establishment of information and consultation procedures in all undertakings employing at least 50 employees in one Member State. These Directives were transposed into national law by the Transnational Information and Consultation of Employees Regulations 1999 (TICE Regulations 1999)[7] and the Information and Consultation of Employees Regulations 2004 (the ICE Regulations).[8]

10.2 Consultation and information

The European Commission has a long history of introducing measures to encourage employee involvement and employee consultation in the enterprises in which they are employed. The Commission's attempts to adopt measures which included employee involvement, rather than measures aimed at consultation and information, have not been successful. The measures concerning employee involvement were associated with the Community's attempts to set up new legal instruments such as the European company statute.[9] This was one of a number of statutes aimed at setting up European legal entities, which would help organisations to carry out their business in different Member States within the Community without being hindered by a legal organisation based on the rules of just one Member State. Other entities included a European co-operative society and a European mutual society. The Commission included proposals for employee involvement in these organisations. Initially a German model of two-tier company boards was proposed, so that employee representatives would have membership of the supervisory board and have, therefore, some involvement in the running of the business. At various times since then the Commission has modified its proposals, but, as the Commission accepted, the proposals were never accepted because they were suggesting worker participation, rather than worker consultation.[10] It was only after, finally, adopting a much more flexible approach that directives were adopted, providing for a range of employee involvement in new legal entities, known as a European company (or Societas Europae)[11] and a European co-operative society.[12] The European Commission has two levels on which it has proposed to harmonise the approach of Member States to the issues of consultation of employees. These are, first, at the transnational level, as exemplified by the introduction of European Works Councils, and, secondly, at the national level, with the adoption of the Information and Consultation Directive.

---

[6] Council Directive 2002/14/EC establishing a general framework for informing and consulting employees in the European Community OJ L80/29 23.2.2002.

[7] SI 1999/3323.

[8] SI 2004/3426.

[9] See OJ C176 8.7.91.

[10] See Communication from the Commission on worker involvement and consultation COM (95) 547.

[11] Council Directive 2001/86/EC supplementing the Statute for a European company with regard to the involvement of employees OJ L294/22 10.11.2001.

[12] Council Directive 2003/72/EC supplementing the statute for a European Co-operative Society with regard to the involvement of employees OJ L207/25 18.8.2003.

10.3 The transnational model

The European Works Council Directive[13] (EWC Directive) was finally adopted after some 14 years of debate. It was originally adopted under the Agreement on Social Policy 1992 and so did not bind the United Kingdom. After the 1997 general election, and a willingness of the United Kingdom to accept the Social Policy Agreement, the Council adopted an extension Directive with a requirement for it to be transposed into national law by 15 December 1999.[14] The purpose of the Directive was:

> to improve the right to information and to consultation of employees in Community-scale undertakings and Community-scale groups of undertakings.[15]

A Community-scale undertaking is one that has at least 1,000 employees within the Member States and at least 150 employees in each of at least two Member States. A Community-scale group of undertakings is one where a group of undertakings[16] has at least 1,000 employees within the Member States with at least two group undertakings in different Member States employing at least 150 employees.[17] These measures were due to be transposed into the rest of the Community within two years and, perhaps, their lack of effectiveness was shown in the 'Vilvoorde' crisis in 1997. This was where the French car maker, Renault, announced the closure of its Belgian plant without any consultation whatsoever with its Belgian workers or its European Works Council. The Renault EWC met once a year, but was not called together until after the company had announced the closure. Although Renault subsequently agreed amendments to its EWC agreement to consult on future transnational structural changes, the whole process perhaps reflects the weakness of the requirements and of any potential sanctions. A similar lack of consultation appeared to take place when BMW of Germany sold its Rover car making subsidiary in the United Kingdom in 1999. Consultation appeared to take place with German workers represented on the company's supervisory board, but not with British workers represented by eight members of its EWC.[18]

On 20 December 2000 the Council of Ministers reached agreement on a Regulation establishing a European Company Statute. This gives companies operating in more than one Member State the option of establishing themselves as 'European companies' (Societas Europae or SE) operating under EU rules rather than a variety of national rules as at present. An SE can be established by the merger or formation of companies with a presence in at least two different Member States.

One concern in establishing this procedure was that companies previously based in countries with strong requirements for information and consultation might be able to avoid these requirements by establishing themselves as an SE, especially if they were

---

[13] Council Directive 94/45/EC on the establishment of a European Works Council or a procedure in Community-scale undertakings and Community-scale groups of undertakings for the purpose of informing and consulting employees OJ L254/64.

[14] Council Directive 97/74/EC OJ L010/22.

[15] Article 1(1) EWC Directive.

[16] Meaning a controlling undertaking and its controlled undertakings: article 2(b) EWC Directive.

[17] Article 2(a) and (c) EWC Directive.

[18] The workers employed at Luton by Vauxhall Motors also complained about the absence of consultation when the company announced the plant's closure in December 2000.

merging with companies from countries with weak consultation requirements. As part of this agreement, therefore, there is a Directive[19] establishing rules for information, consultation and, possibly, participation of workers employed by the SE.

Information is defined as informing the representatives of the employees:

> in a manner and with a content which allows the employees' representatives to undertake an in-depth assessment of the possible impact and, where appropriate, prepare consultations with the competent organ of the SE.[20]

Consultation is defined as:

> The establishment of dialogue and exchange of views between the body representative of the employees . . . and the competent organ of the SE, at a time, in a manner and with a content which allows the employees' representatives, on the basis of information provided, to express an opinion on measures envisaged by the competent organ which may be taken into account in the decision-making process within the SE.[21]

When the SE is created there will need to be a special negotiating body to discuss the arrangements for employee involvement. In the absence of any agreement there will be standard rules established by the Directive which will need to be followed. These require information and consultation on matters such as:

- the structure, economic and financial situation;
- the probable development of the business and of production and sales;
- the situation and probable trend of employment and investment;
- substantial changes concerning organisation, introduction of new working methods or production processes;
- transfers of production, mergers, cut-backs or closures of undertakings, establishments or important parts thereof;
- collective redundancies.

There are also provisions for employee participation for those SEs which include companies from countries where there are such rules. Participation can include the right to elect or appoint, or oppose the election or appointment of, members of the supervisory or administrative board.

10.3.1 Transnational Information and Consultation of Employees Regulations 1999

The EWC Directive was transposed into national law by the TICE Regulations 1999, which came into effect on 15 January 2000.[22] By this time many British employees were already represented in EWCs set up by multinational companies, influenced by the law of other Member States which had already transposed the Directive. The regulations do not have

---

[19] Directive 2001/86/EC.
[20] Article 2(i).
[21] Article 2(j).
[22] SI 1999/3323; the regulations are some 57 pages long, so what follows can only be regarded as a summary of the main points; the regulations themselves should be consulted for a more detailed understanding; see www.opsi.gov.uk and Chapter 1.

effect if there is already in existence an Article 6 or an Article 13 agreement, unless the parties have decided otherwise.[23] An Article 6 agreement is one that establishes an EWC in accordance with the Directive. An Article 13 agreement is one that established their own information and consultation procedures before the Directive was transposed into national law.

Consultation is defined in the TICE Regulations 1999 as meaning the exchange of views and the establishment of a dialogue in the context of an EWC or in the context of an information and consultation procedure.[24] The central management of an undertaking is responsible for creating the conditions and the means necessary for setting up an EWC, where the central management is situated in the United Kingdom; where it is situated outside the country, but has its representative agent based in the United Kingdom; or, if neither of these, has its biggest group of employees in the United Kingdom.[25] The number of UK employees is to be calculated by taking an average over a two-year period, with provision for counting some part-timers as a half number. The number of employees in undertakings in other Member States is to be calculated in accordance with whatever formula that State has adopted in its law transposing the EWC Directive. Employee representatives are entitled to information on these calculations so that they can decide whether the employer qualifies. If the information given to them is incomplete or inadequate, they may present a complaint to the Central Arbitration Committee (CAC).[26]

If central management does not act on its own initiative, the whole process of establishing an EWC can be started with a request from 100 employees, or their representatives, in two undertakings in two Member States. If there is a dispute as to whether a valid request has been made, this can be referred to the CAC for a decision.[27]

The first stage is the establishment of a special negotiating body (SNB), whose task is to negotiate, with central management, a written agreement covering 'the scope, composition, functions and terms of office' of an EWC or the arrangements for implementing an information and consultation procedure.[28] The SNB must consist of at least one representative from each Member State and there is a weighting formula to increase representation from bigger units in different States. The United Kingdom representatives are to be elected by a ballot of United Kingdom employees and any complaints about the ballot are to be made to the CAC. Where there is already an elected body in existence with whom consultation takes place, then that body can nominate the representatives from its membership.[29]

The contents of the agreement to be reached between the SNB and the central management are set out in Article 6 EWC Directive and are reflected in Part IV TICE Regulations 1999. The two parties are to negotiate in 'a spirit of co-operation with a view to reaching an

[23] Regulation 42 TICE Regulations 1999.
[24] Regulation 2 TICE Regulations 1999.
[25] Regulation 5 TICE Regulations 1999.
[26] Regulations 6–8 TICE Regulations 1999.
[27] Regulations 9–10 TICE Regulations 1999.
[28] Regulation 11 TICE Regulations 1999.
[29] Regulations 12–15 TICE Regulations 1999; the BMW EWC Agreement mentioned above, e.g., had a membership of eight German representatives, eight British representatives and four Austrian representatives.

agreement'.[30] They may negotiate an agreement to set up an EWC or to establish an information and consultation procedure.[31] The EWC agreement must include agreement on:

(1) the undertakings which are covered by the agreement;
(2) the composition of the EWC;
(3) the functions and procedures for information and consultation;
(4) the venue, frequency and duration of meetings;
(5) the financial and material resources to be allocated to the EWC;
(6) the duration of the agreement and the procedure for renegotiation.[32]

If the parties decide to establish an information and consultation procedure instead of an EWC, then this agreement must specify a method by which the information and consultation representatives[33] 'are to enjoy the right to meet and discuss the information conveyed to them'. The information conveyed to the representatives must relate in particular to 'transnational questions which significantly affect the interests of employees'.[34] If negotiations do not start within six months of a valid request by employees or fail to finish within three years from the date of that request, the regulations provide for a default agreement, which is contained in the schedule. These provide for an EWC of between three and 30 members, with at least one member from each Member State where there are undertakings. This representation is weighted according to the relative size of the undertakings in different States. The rules cover the election or appointment of United Kingdom delegates and provide that the EWC should meet at least once per annum.[35]

Complaints about the failure of the negotiating process, either because of lack of agreement or a failure to start the process, or because of a failure to keep to the agreement, are to be referred directly to the EAT. The EAT may order the defaulter to remedy the failure and impose a fine of up to £75,000. Central management will have a defence if they are able to show that the failure resulted 'from a reason beyond the central management's control or that it has some other reasonable excuse for its failure'.[36]

One concern related to statutory rights to information is the revealing by management of 'confidential' information. Regulation 24 TICE Regulations 1999 provides that central management is not required to disclose any information or document which, 'according to objective criteria', would seriously prejudice or harm the functioning of the undertaking concerned. It is interesting to speculate as to what this actually means. Would the sale of a subsidiary undertaking in one Member State be such information, if it would prejudice the price received, even though it might have important effects for employees? There is an obligation for a representative, or an adviser to a representative, not to disclose confidential information unless it is a protected disclosure under section 43A ERA 1996.[37] The CAC has

---

[30] Regulation 17(1) TICE Regulations 1999 which copies the wording in article 6(1) EWC Directive.
[31] Regulation 17(3) TICE Regulations 1999.
[32] Regulation 17(4) TICE Regulations 1999.
[33] Defined in regulation 2 TICE Regulations 1999 as a person who represents employees in the context of an information and consultation procedure.
[34] Regulation 17(5) TICE Regulations 1999.
[35] Regulation 18 TICE Regulations 1999.
[36] Regulations 20–22 TICE Regulations 1999.
[37] Regulation 23 TICE Regulations 1999.

the responsibility of settling disputes about confidentiality and can order information to be disclosed by management or order a representative not to disclose information.

Information and consultation representatives, members of EWCs, SNBs and candidates for relevant elections have certain rights. These are:

(1) the right to reasonable time off with pay during working hours;[38]
(2) protection against unfair dismissal; dismissal as a result of performing any of the functions or duties related to any of these bodies will make the dismissal automatically unfair in terms of Part X ERA 1996, the exception to this being where the reason or the principal reason for dismissal is a breach of confidentiality contained in regulation 23(1), unless the employee reasonably believed the disclosure to be a protected disclosure within the meaning of section 43A ERA 1996;
(3) the right not to be subject to detriment as a result of performing any of the duties or functions related to the bodies.

Complaints about any infringement of these rights are to be made to an employment tribunal.

10.4 The national model

Models of consultation vary between the Member States of the European Community. In many, works councils are an established way of channelling information, consultation and, sometimes, negotiation between management and employees.

In the United Kingdom, prior to the Information and Consultation with Employees Regulations 2004[39] (ICE Regulations), there were only a limited number of occasions during which there was a statutory requirement to consult. These included those concerned with collective redundancies and transfers of undertakings (see below). Prior to 1995 the only requirement was for this consultation to take place when there were trade unions recognised for the purpose. Following on from *Commission v United Kingdom*,[40] when the ECJ held this to be an inadequate application of the relevant Directives, this liability to consult was widened to include appropriate representatives.[41] Thus, in certain situations there is a requirement to consult even if there is not a trade union recognised for that purpose. A similar requirement is imposed by the Health and Safety (Consultation with Employees) Regulations 1996 (HSCE Regulations 1996).[42] Prior to these regulations there was a requirement for health and safety representatives nominated by the recognised trade union.[43] The 1996 Regulations were intended to provide for situations where there were no such safety representatives. The employer has a duty to consult, in good time, on a range of safety matters including the introduction of any measure at the workplace which

---

[38] Regulations 25–26 TICE Regulations 1999.
[39] SI 2004/3426.
[40] Cases 382/92 and 383/92 [1994] IRLR 392 ECJ and [1994] IRLR 412 ECJ.
[41] Collective Redundancies and Transfers of Undertakings (Protection of Employment) (Amendment) Regulations 1995, SI 1995/2587, as amended by regulations of the same name in 1999, SI 1999/1925.
[42] SI 1996/1513.
[43] Safety Representatives and Safety Committees Regulations 1977, SI 1977/500.

might substantially affect the health and safety of the employees.[44] The consultation must be with the employees directly or their elected representatives.[45]

The result of this approach has been extended to other regulations concerned with the transposition of Community law. These include the Working Time Regulations 1998[46] and the Maternity and Parental Leave etc. Regulations 1999.[47] In both sets of regulations there is a default agreement, one concerned with varying aspects of the rules on working time and the other concerned with the rules on parental leave. These default arrangements may be varied by a collective agreement or by a workforce agreement. The former occurs where there are independent trade unions recognised for the purpose. The latter occurs when there are employee representatives, either elected or appointed by the workforce.

Thus an employer has an obligation to consult employee representatives if they wish to adopt a more flexible approach to working time or parental leave. These consultations can result in workforce agreements.[48] An agreement is a workforce agreement if:

(1) it is in writing;
(2) it has effect for a specific period not exceeding five years;
(3) it applies to all the relevant members of the workforce or all those who belong to a particular group;
(4) it is signed by the representatives of the workforce; if the employer employs less than 20 workers, then there is the option for the majority of the workers to sign the agreement;
(5) before the agreement is made available for signature, the employer provides all of the workers to whom it is intended to apply with a copy of the agreement and such guidance as the workers might reasonably require in order to understand it fully.

The two Schedules also contain provisions for the election of employee representatives. These 'representatives of the workforce' are workers who have been elected to represent the relevant members of the workforce.[49] Thus, even prior to the 2004 Regulations there existed within the United Kingdom an alternative model for employee consultation. It applied to a very limited number of circumstances and was introduced as a result of the requirement imposed by the appropriate Directives to consult on specific issues.

10.4.1 The Information and Consultation Directive

Directive 2002/14/EC of the European Parliament and of the Council establishing a general framework for informing and consulting employees in the European Community[50] was finally unanimously adopted by the Council of Ministers in December 2001 after some

---

[44] Regulation 3(a) HSCE Regulations 1996.
[45] Regulation 4(1) HSCE Regulations 1996.
[46] SI 1998/1833.
[47] SI 1999/3312.
[48] See Schedule 1 Working Time Regulations 1998, SI 1998/1833 and Schedule 1 Maternity and Parental Leave etc. Regulations 1999, SI 1999/3312.
[49] Relevant members of the workforce are all those workers employed by a particular employer, excluding any worker whose terms and conditions of employment are provided for, wholly or in part, by a collective agreement: see Schedule 1 paragraph 2 Working Time Regulations 1998; paragraph 3 contains rules concerning the election of such representatives.
[50] OJ L80/29 23.3.2002.

years of debate. It suffered delays because of opposition from a number of countries, including the United Kingdom. The final version was much weaker than the original 1998 proposal, especially in terms of sanctions and of the implementation timetable. Nevertheless it is likely to have an important impact on employer/employee relations in the United Kingdom.

It is the first EU Directive to introduce a generalised requirement to provide information and to consult with employees or their representatives. All other information and consultation measures have been concerned with specific situations, such as collective redundancies, transfers of undertakings or in situations where companies have a European Works Council. The Directive applies to all undertakings with 50 or more employees. This represents less than 3% of all EU companies, but about 50% of all employees.

In the preamble to the Directive the European Commission provides the justification for the measure. Some of the reasons given are that:

(1) the existence of current legal frameworks at national and Community level concerning the involvement of employees has not always prevented serious decisions, that affect employees, from being taken and made public without adequate consultation;[51]
(2) there is a need to strengthen dialogue in order to promote trust within undertakings. The result of this will be an improvement in risk anticipation, making work organisation more flexible, and to facilitate employee access to training within the undertaking. It will also make employees more flexible in their approach and involve them in the operation and future of the undertaking, as well as increasing its competitiveness;[52]
(3) timely information and consultation is a prerequisite for successful restructuring and adaptation of undertakings to the needs of the global economy, especially through the new forms of organisation at work;[53]
(4) the existing legal frameworks for employee information and consultation are inadequate, because they 'adopt an excessively *a posteriori* approach to the process of change, neglect the economic aspects of decisions taken and do not contribute either to genuine anticipation of employment developments within the undertaking or to risk prevention'.[54]

There are perhaps some, even amongst those who support the aims of the Directive, who might be a little sceptical about such grand claims for the result of the introduction of employee consultation procedures. Nevertheless these justifications give rise to the purpose of the Directive. This is to establish minimum requirements for information and consultation, whilst not preventing Member States from having or introducing provisions more favourable to employees. The Directive only applies to undertakings with a minimum size of 50 employees or establishments with at least 20 employees. This is to avoid any action which might hinder the creation and development of small and medium-sized undertakings.[55]

[51] Preamble para (6).
[52] Preamble para (7).
[53] Preamble para (9).
[54] Preamble para (13).
[55] Preamble paras (18) and (19).

The purpose is set out as being to establish a general framework for the right to information and consultation of employees in undertakings or establishments within the European Community. The practical arrangements for defining and implementing this are to be left to the Member States, who must carry out their obligations in such a way as to ensure their effectiveness. In doing this the employer and the employees' representatives must work 'in a spirit of co-operation'.

There are some interesting definitions, particularly with regard to the distinction between undertakings and establishments.

An *undertaking* is a public or private undertaking carrying out an economic activity (whether or not for gain) which is located within the territory of the Member States. An *establishment* is a unit of business where an economic activity is carried out on an ongoing basis with human and material resources. It remains to be seen whether the UK Government further defines these definitions when it eventually introduces regulations to transpose this Directive into national law. It might be worth considering this in order to avoid the possibility of further litigation about the precise meaning of these terms.

Information means transmission by the employer to the employees' representatives of data to help them acquaint themselves with the subject matter and to examine it. *Consultation* means the exchange of views and establishment of dialogue between the employer and the employees' representatives.

The importance of the definitions of undertaking and establishment are relevant because the Directive will apply either to undertakings employing at least 50 employees in any one Member State or to establishments employing at least 20 employees in any Member State. The method for calculating the thresholds of employees is left to the Member State.

It may be possible to make special arrangements for political, religious and charitable bodies where special rules already exist in the Member State and, as ever, Member States may exclude crews of ships 'plying the high seas'.

As mentioned above, the practical arrangements are to be left to the individual Member State. There are, however, rules concerning what information and consultation will cover, when it is to take place and what its objectives are. The subject matter is to be:

(1) information on the recent and probable development of the undertaking's or establishment's activities and economic situation;
(2) information and consultation on the situation, structure and probable development of employment and on any anticipatory measures envisaged, especially those that threaten employment;
(3) information and consultation on decisions likely to lead to substantial changes in work organisation or in contractual relations (including those covered in Article 9 below).

Information shall be given at such time, and in such fashion, as to enable employee representatives to conduct an adequate study and, where necessary, prepare for consultation.

Consultation shall take place:

■ while ensuring that timing, method and content are appropriate;
■ at the relevant level of management, depending upon the subject under discussion;

- on the basis of information provided by employer and of the opinion of employee representatives;
- in such a way as to enable employee representatives to meet the employer and obtain a response, and the reasons for that response, to the employee representatives' opinion;
- with a view to reaching agreement on decisions within the scope of the employer's powers.

As with the European Works Council Directive, there is the opportunity for management and labour to negotiate their own information and consultation arrangements, providing that they meet the requirements of the Directive and national legislation. Thus any agreements existing at the transposition date of 23 March 2005 were able to continue as were any other agreements subsequently negotiated. Presumably the UK regulations will provide a framework for such individually negotiated arrangements.

Confidential information has always been an important concern of employers, and the question of what is confidential and what is not will be part of the interest in watching this Directive put into practice. There are two aspects to confidentiality. One is imposing an obligation upon the parties to maintain a confidence. The second is the decision as to what material is so confidential that it cannot be revealed at all. In dealing with the first of these, Member States may provide that employee representatives, and any experts who assist them, may not reveal information to employees or third parties if provided in confidence 'in the legitimate interest of the undertaking or establishment', unless that other party is bound by a duty of confidentiality. This obligation may continue after the expiry of a term of office.

Member States may also provide that the employer need not provide information or consult when the nature of the information or consultation is such that, 'according to objective criteria', it would seriously harm the functioning of the undertaking or establishment or would be prejudicial to it.

Member States shall provide for judicial review of situations where the employer requires confidentiality or does not provide information or consult in accordance with above. This is the case with the TICE Regulations implementing the European Works Council Directive. The independent body is the Central Arbitration Committee.

Article 8 obliges Member States to have suitable judicial processes in place to enable the obligations of employers and employees to be enforced. It also requires adequate sanctions to be available for infringement of the Directive. These sanctions must be 'effective, proportionate and dissuasive'. This is going to be an interesting provision of any UK regulations. There are potentially large sums of money which may be involved in, for example, a merger or an acquisition. If an employer decided that it wished not to consult the employees, is a fine of the sort contained in the TICE Regulations going to be a sufficient deterrent? If it is not, then there might be an issue related to a bigger fine as to whether it would be proportionate.

10.4.2 The Information and Consultation of Employees Regulations[56]

Although Article 11 of the Information and Consultation Directive stipulated 23 March 2005 as the deadline for transposition, there was an extension for Member States who did

---

[56] SI 2004/3426.

not have a general, permanent and statutory system of information and consultation, such as the United Kingdom. The ICE Regulations took effect over a period of three years. For employers with at least 150 employees in the United Kingdom they came into effect on 6 April 2005, for those with at least 100 employees the date was 6 April 2007 and employers with at least 50 employees are included from 6 April 2008.[57] There is a narrow definition of employee, so only those who work under a contract of employment are included.[58] The number of employees is worked out by taking the average number employed in the previous 12 months.[59] Employees, or their representatives, have the right to ask for the data on employee numbers[60] and if the employer fails to provide the information, or provides incorrect information, within one month, then the employee, or the employee representatives, can complain to the CAC. After this the CAC can order the employer to produce the information.[61] This information is, of course, crucial. It settles if and when the employer is covered by the regulations.

The regulations are complex and the process has a similar approach to that which is used in the statutory recognition of trade unions (see Chapter 12). The process can begin in one of two ways. Either the employer can initiate the process or it starts with a request from the employees. There is a duty of co-operation as stated in regulation 21:

> The parties are under a duty, when negotiating or implementing a negotiated agreement or when implementing the standard information and consultation provisions, to work in a spirit of co-operation and with due regard for their reciprocal rights and obligations, taking into account the interests of both the undertaking and the employees.

Stage 1 The request

At least 10% of the employees, either together or separately, need to make the request to the employer to open negotiations to reach an Information and Consultation Agreement in order for it to be a valid request. This 10% is subject to a minimum of 15 employees and a maximum of 2,500. Thus an employer with only 50 employees could require at least 15 employees to make the request, and, in larger organisations, of 25,000 or more, there is a cap on the numbers who need to be involved.[62] The request or requests must be in writing and sent to the employer's head office or principal place of business. It can be sent to the CAC if the employees wish to act anonymously.[63] If there is already an Information and Consultation Agreement in operation the employer may decide to hold a ballot of all employees to find out if they endorse the application for a new agreement.[64] In *Stewart v Moray Council*[65] the employer claimed that three existing agreements covered all employees, even though each only covered part of the workforce. The EAT accepted this argument but then stated that one of the agreements, that covering teachers, was not

---

[57] See Schedule 1 ICE Regulations 2004.
[58] Regulation 2 ICE Regulations 2004.
[59] Regulation 4 ICE Regulations 2004.
[60] Regulation 5 ICE Regulations 2004.
[61] Regulation 6 ICE Regulations 2004.
[62] Regulation 7(1), (2) and (3) ICE Regulations 2004.
[63] Regulation 7(4) ICE Regulations 2004.
[64] Regulations 8–10 ICE Regulations 2004; the employer can only initiate a ballot if less than 40% of the employees had endorsed the original request.
[65] [2006] IRLR 592.

detailed enough. Where more than one agreement is relied upon, each of them has to cover all the requirements of the regulations. In this case there was not sufficient information on one of the agreements concerning regulation 8(1)(d) where there is a requirement to set out how the employer is to give information and seek the views of the employee representatives.[66]

Stage 2 The negotiations

The employer may initiate negotiations without waiting for the employees to request action.[67] Whether it is done on his or her own initiative or as a result of an employee request the obligations upon the employer are the same. Regulation 14 sets out the procedure. As soon as is reasonably practicable the employer must make arrangements for the appointment or election of 'negotiating representatives'. The employees need to be informed of who these representatives are (in writing) and then invite the negotiating representatives to enter into negotiations to reach a negotiated agreement. All employees need to be entitled to take part in the appointment or election of representatives and all employees in the undertaking need to be represented by a representative.[68] As with the statutory recognition procedures for trade unions, there are strict time limits to be applied to the process. The negotiation must not last more than six months, unless both sides agree, from a time of three months after the employee request was made or the employer initiated the process.[69]

Stage 3 The negotiated agreement

A negotiated agreement must be in writing, be dated and cover all employees. It must set out the circumstances in which the employer must inform and consult the employees.[70] It must provide for the appointment of the Information and Consultation Representatives who are to be informed or consulted. Alternatively it may provide for the information and consultation of all employee representatives.[71] It must be approved by all the negotiating representatives signing it or at least 50% of them if a ballot of all employees is held which approves the agreement.[72]

10.4.2.1 Standard information and consultation provisions

If the employer fails to initiate negotiations then the standard provisions will apply from six months of the date the employee request was made or within six months of the date that representatives were appointed or elected (whichever is sooner). Similarly if the parties fail to reach agreement within the allowed time limit then six months from that time limit expiry the standard provisions apply.[73] In practice this means that the standard provisions

---

[66] In *Amicus v Macmillan Publishers Ltd* [2007] IRLR 378 the employers had a pre-existing agreement covering only one site. The CAC held that this could not be relied upon to meet the requirements of the Regulations.
[67] Regulation 7(1) ICE Regulations 2004.
[68] Regulation 15 ICE Regulations 2004 provides for complaints about these requirements to the CAC.
[69] This period does not take into account the delays caused by a ballot or by complaints to the CAC.
[70] Regulation 16(1) ICE Regulations 2004.
[71] Regulation 16(1)(g) ICE Regulations 2004.
[72] Regulation 16(2) ICE Regulations 2004; Schedule 2 specifies the electoral process for the election of representatives.
[73] Regulation 18(1) ICE Regulations 2004.

will normally be the minimum provisions agreed in any negotiated agreement. There is no need for the information and consultation representatives to agree to anything less as all they need do is wait for the period to expire and the standard provisions will automatically apply.

The standard provisions first itemise what information must be provided to the representatives.[74] These are:

(i) the recent and probable development of the undertaking's activities and economic situation;
(ii) the situation, structure and probable development of employment within the undertaking and on any anticipatory measures envisaged, in particular, where there is a threat to employment;
(iii) decisions likely to lead to substantial changes in work organisation or in contractual relations.[75]

Where there is a failure to comply with any of the terms of a negotiated agreement or a standard provision, a complaint may be made to the CAC within three months beginning with the date of the failure.[76] The CAC may then issue an order for compliance. Failure to carry this out within three months may lead to a further complaint, this time to the EAT which has the power to issue a penalty of up to £75,000.[77]

10.4.2.2 Confidential information
Regulations 25 and 26 deal with the issue of confidentiality. If the employer issues material to employees that is confidential, then the employee owes the employer a duty not to disclose the information.[78] This is always a difficult issue for employee representatives, when they are given information that they are not allowed to disclose to the people who elected or appointed them in the first place. If the recipient does not believe that it is genuinely confidential then he or she may apply to the CAC to decide whether it was reasonable for the employer to impose a confidentiality condition.

Similarly the employer need not disclose information at all where 'according to objective criteria, the disclosure of the information or document would seriously harm the functioning of, or would be prejudicial to, the undertaking.' Again any information and consultation representative or, where there are no representatives, any employee or their representative, may apply to the CAC for a declaration as to whether it is confidential or not.

10.4.2.3 Employee protection
An employee who is a negotiating representative or an information and consultation representative is entitled to reasonable paid time off during working hours.[79] Employees may take a complaint to an employment tribunal for an employer's failure in this regard within a period of three months beginning with the day of the alleged wrongdoing.

---

[74] Regulation 20(1) ICE Regulations 2004.
[75] The employer need not inform or consult under these regulations in relation to this section if the employer tells the representatives that he or she will be complying with the information and consultation obligations under section 188 TULRCA on collective redundancies or regulation 10 of the TUPE Regulations 1981 on transfers of undertakings.
[76] Regulation 22 ICE Regulations 2004.
[77] Regulation 23 ICE Regulations 2004.
[78] Unless the recipient reasonably believes the disclosure to be a 'protected disclosure' under section 43A ERA 1996.
[79] Regulations 27–28 ICE Regulations 2004.

A dismissal of any employee for carrying out activities in relation to the ICE Regulations will be an automatically unfair dismissal. The rules on minimum service or maximum age do not apply in these circumstances.[80] Similarly employees or representatives are protected from detriment.[81]

10.5 Collective redundancies

Redundancy is one of the potentially 'fair' reasons for dismissal listed in section 98(2) of the ERA 1996. It is therefore dealt with in Chapter 5.

Council Directive 98/59/EC on the approximation of the laws of the Member States relating to collective redundancies (the Collective Redundancies Directive) is a consolidation Directive. It consolidates Directives 75/129/EEC as amended by Directive 92/56/EEC on the same subject. The original Directive was adopted in 1975 and transposed into British law very quickly. It was included in the Employment Protection Act 1975 and has been part of national law, subject to various amendments, ever since. The provisions are now contained in Part IV Chapter II TULRCA 1992, which outlines the procedure for handling collective redundancies. The legislation has been targeted towards consultation and information, as distinct from negotiations, on the subject. The duty to consult rests upon an employer who is proposing to dismiss 20 or more employees at one establishment within a period of 90 days or less for reasons of redundancy.[82] This may include situations where the employer is proposing to dismiss a workforce and then immediately re-employ them as part of a reorganisation.[83] This consultation shall begin 'in good time' and in any event at least 30 days before the first dismissal takes effect, or at least 90 days before the first dismissal takes effect if the employer is proposing to dismiss 100 or more employees at one establishment within a period of 90 days.[84]

A debatable issue here, of course, is at what point in time is the employer 'proposing to dismiss'. It is likely that, except perhaps in a disaster situation, there is a period of time over which the decision to dismiss employees by reason of redundancy is reached. There is, perhaps, first the decision in principle to dismiss employees. There may be a second stage where the parts of the organisation in which the redundancies are to take place are identified, followed by a further stage when particular employees are identified. In *R v British Coal Corporation and Secretary of State for Trade and Industry, ex parte Price*[85] the court approved an approach to fair consultation which meant that it began when the proposals were still at a formative stage. Glidewell LJ cited the tests proposed in *R v Gwent County Council, ex parte Bryant*:[86]

---

[80] Regulation 30 ICE Regulations 2004.
[81] Regulation 32 ICE Regulations 2004.
[82] Section 188(1) TULRCA 1992; section 195 defines dismissal for redundancy as dismissals not related to the individual and there is a presumption of redundancy in any proceedings unless the contrary is shown.
[83] See *GMB v Man Truck & Bus UK Ltd* [2000] IRLR 636.
[84] Section 188(1A) TULRCA 1992. According to *Vauxhall Motors Ltd v TGWU* [2006] IRLR 674 this period of 90 days is only the starting point; it does not mean that the consultation should end within this period. In this case it extended over 22 months.
[85] [1994] IRLR 72.
[86] [1988] COD 19.

Fair consultation means:

(a) consultation when the proposals are still at a formative stage;

(b) adequate information on which to respond;

(c) adequate time in which to respond;

(d) conscientious consideration by an authority of the response to consultation.

The court in *Griffin v South West Water Services Ltd*[87] disagreed with this, expressing instead the view that the employer's obligation arose only when the employer was able to identify the workers and be in a position to supply the information required by the Directive.

This issue was considered in *Hough v Leyland DAF Ltd.*[88] This case concerned security staff at a number of the employer's premises. The security manager was asked to prepare a report on the possibility of contracting out the security function. The manager produced a report recommending that it should be contracted out. It was a further six months before the employer approached the trade union informing them of the employer's intention to contract out security services. The issue was at what stage the employers could be said to have been proposing to dismiss. The EAT held that this occurred at the time of the security manager making his report recommending the contracting out. The employers had argued that the proposals needed to be at a far more advanced stage before the statutory obligation to consult took effect. The EAT held:

> We agree that [s 99] read as a whole contemplates that matters should have reached a stage where a specific proposal has been formulated and that this is a later stage than the diagnosis of a problem and the appreciation that at least one way of dealing with it would be by declaring redundancies.

The EAT then went on to state that it would not be more helpful to seek a more precise definition because of the large variety of situations that might arise. Article 2(1) Collective Redundancies Directive states that consultation should begin when the employer is 'contemplating' collective redundancies. This was considered in *Re Hartlebury Printers Ltd.*[89] The court held that proposing redundancies cannot include merely thinking about the possibility of redundancies. Contemplating redundancies in the sense of proposing them meant 'having in view or expecting' them. It is, therefore, likely to be at an early stage, but not so early that it is merely an idea that the company is thinking about.[90] If, however, the employer's decision making has progressed to the stage of contemplating two options for the future, one of which is closing down the business and the other is selling it as a going concern, then the employer has reached the stage of 'proposing to dismiss as redundant'.[91]

---

[87] [1995] IRLR 15.

[88] [1991] IRLR 194.

[89] [1992] ICR 704.

[90] See also *National Union of Public Employees v General Cleaning Contractors Ltd* [1976] IRLR 362, which considered the position of a contractor who unexpectedly lost a contract on re-tendering. The industrial tribunal held that it was sufficiently early to begin consultations after news of the lost contract, not before, even though there was a possibility of losing a contract at re-tendering; see also *Association of Pattern Makers & Allied Craftsmen v Kirvin Ltd* [1978] IRLR 318 where the EAT held that proposing means a state of mind directed to a planned or proposed course of events; in this case on the appointment of a receiver.

[91] See *Scotch Premier Meat Ltd v Burns* [2000] IRLR 639.

The European Court of Justice[92] held that the notice of dismissals shall not take place until after some of the consultation had taken place. The court suggested that Article 2 meant that consultation with a view to reaching an agreement really meant 'negotiation'. Such negotiation would not be meaningful if it took place entirely after the notice period had commenced. This resulted in an amendment to section 193 TULRCA which ensures that notification of any proposals takes place prior to notice being given.[93]

10.5.1 Meaning of establishment

The obligation to consult rests upon 20 or more people being made redundant at one establishment. The ECJ considered the meaning of this term in *Rockfon A/S v Specialarbejderforbundet i Danmark*.[94] This case considered the Danish legal interpretation of the term 'establishment',[95] which provided that an establishment needed an independent management 'which can independently effect large-scale dismissals'. The ECJ held that the existence of such separate management was not necessary. The term applied to the unit to which the workers who have been made redundant are assigned to carry out their duties. This was further developed by the Court of Justice in a Greek case, *Athinaiki v Chartopoiia AE*,[96] where it was stated that an establishment

> may consist of a distinct entity, having a certain degree of permanence and stability, which is assigned to perform one or more given tasks and which has a workforce, technical means and a certain organizational structure allowing for the accomplishment of those tasks.

The link is not necessarily a geographical one, but one concerned with the employment relationship. In a much earlier case[97] the EAT had held that one should adopt a commonsense approach and use the word in a way in which ordinary people would use it. In this case this meant that 14 building sites administered from one base amounted to one establishment, rather than 14 separate ones. Establishment and employer are not synonymous, so if three distinct employers are making employees redundant, albeit at one location, the numbers cannot be aggregated to come within the terms of the statute.[98] In contrast, two field forces being restructured as a result of the merger of the two parent companies were held to be assigned to their branch offices, rather than to the field force as a whole. This meant that, when calculating whether the 20-person threshold had been exceeded, the establishment should be the field office rather than any other.[99]

10.5.2 Appropriate representatives

The employer must consult with the appropriate representatives of any of the employees who may be affected by the proposed dismissals or by any measures taken in connection

[92] Case C-188/03 *Junk v Kühnel* [2005] IRLR 310 ECJ.
[93] The Collective Redundancies (Amendment) Regulations 2006, SI 2006/2387.
[94] Case C-449/93 [1996] IRLR 168 ECJ.
[95] Used in article 1(1)(a) Collective Redundancies Directive.
[96] Case C-270/05 *Athinaiki v Chartopoiia AE v Panagiotidis* [2007] IRLR 286.
[97] *Barratt Developments (Bradford) Ltd v UCATT* [1977] IRLR 403.
[98] *E Green & Sons Ltd v ASTMS* [1984] IRLR 134.
[99] *MSF v Refuge Assurance plc* [2002] IRLR 324.

with those dismissals.[100] The appropriate representatives are the employees' trade union representatives if an independent trade union is recognised by the employer.[101] If there is no such trade union then they may be either employee representatives appointed or elected by the affected employees for some other purpose, but who have authority to receive information and be consulted about the proposed dismissals, or they may be employee representatives elected by the employees for the purpose of such consultation.

The choice of which of these two alternatives should be consulted is left to the employer.[102] Prior to 1995 there had only been a requirement to consult trade union representatives if they were recognised by the employer. Where there were no recognised trade unions, there had been no requirement to consult. This approach had been challenged by the European Commission in *Commission v United Kingdom*.[103] As a result the ECJ held that the United Kingdom had not adequately transposed the Directive. The legislation was then amended in 1995 to allow the employer to choose whether to consult a trade union or other appropriate representatives.[104] This was then amended again in 1999, so that an employer could choose between the alternative appropriate representatives only if there was not a recognised trade union with whom to consult.[105]

Section 188A TULRCA 1992 sets out the requirements for the election of employee representatives where this is necessary. The onus is on the employer to make such arrangements as are reasonably practical to ensure fairness. The election is to be conducted, so far as is reasonably practicable, in secret. The employer's duties include deciding on the number of representatives to be elected, what constituencies those representatives should represent and the term of office of those representatives. The term needs to be long enough to enable the information and consultation process to be completed. The candidates for election must be affected employees at the date of the election.[106] All affected employees have the right to vote and no affected employee must be unreasonably excluded from standing for election. Employees must be entitled to vote for as many candidates as there are representatives to be elected. The elected representatives are to be allowed access to the affected employees and given such accommodation and other facilities as are necessary.[107] They are also entitled to reasonable time off during working hours to carry out their functions as a representative or candidate, or in order to undergo training for the performance of these functions.[108] Where, after the election, one of those elected ceases to be a representative, then there may be a need for the election of a replacement.[109]

---

[100] Section 188(1) TULRCA 1992.

[101] The Secretary of State may, on the application of the parties, vary the statutory provisions in favour of a collective agreement concluded by the parties themselves: section 198 TULRCA 1992.

[102] Section 188(1B) TULRCA 1992.

[103] Case 383/92 [1994] IRLR 412 ECJ.

[104] Collective Redundancies and Transfers of Undertakings (Protection of Employment) (Amendment) Regulations 1995, SI 1995/2587.

[105] Collective Redundancies and Transfers of Undertakings (Protection of Employment) (Amendment) Regulations 1999, SI 1999/1925.

[106] They must also be employed by the employer at the time when they were elected: section 196(1) TULRCA 1992.

[107] Section 188(5A) TULRCA 1992.

[108] Section 61 ERA 1996.

[109] Note that section 47 ERA 1996 provides protection against detriment for employee representatives and section 103 ERA 1996 makes their dismissal unfair if it is related to their candidacy or position as an employee representative.

The consultation itself is to include consultation about ways of avoiding the dismissals, reducing the number of employees to be dismissed, and mitigating the consequences of the dismissals. It is necessary for the employer to consult on each of these three aspects and not on just some of them. Thus, if an employer genuinely consults with employee representatives about ways of reducing the numbers involved and mitigating the consequences of the dismissals, they will still have failed in their duty if they have not also consulted about ways of avoiding the dismissals.[110] There is an obligation for the employer to undertake such consultations with a view to reaching agreement with the appropriate representatives.[111] There is certain information that the employer must disclose in writing to the appropriate representatives. This information consists of:

(1) the reasons for the proposals;
(2) the numbers and descriptions of employees whom it is proposed to dismiss;
(3) the total number of employees of any description employed by the employer at the establishment;
(4) the proposed method of selecting those to be dismissed and the proposed method of carrying out the dismissals; and
(5) the proposed method of calculating payments if different to those required by statute. This information must be delivered to each of the appropriate representatives.[112] Whether sufficient information has been given is a question of fact for the employment tribunal to decide, although there is no rule that states that full and specific information under each of these heads should be given before consultation could begin.[113] It is not sufficient, however, for the employer to argue that the information can be gleaned from the surrounding circumstances and other documents and that any consultation would have had no effect upon the decision to close the workplace.[114]

10.5.3 Special circumstances

There are two 'escape' clauses for employers unable to comply with their obligations under section 188 TULRCA 1992:

(1) Where there are special circumstances which make it not reasonably practicable for an employer to comply with the consultation and information requirements, they are to take all steps towards compliance that are reasonably practicable in the circumstances.[115]
(2) Where they have invited affected employees to elect representatives and the employees have failed to do so within a reasonable time, then the employer must give all the affected employees the information set out above.[116]

---

[110] *Middlesbrough Borough Council v TGWU* [2002] IRLR 332.
[111] Section 188(2) TULRCA 1992.
[112] Section 188(4)–(5) TULRCA 1992.
[113] See *MSF v GEC Ferranti (Defence Systems) Ltd* [1994] IRLR 113.
[114] See *Sovereign Distribution Services Ltd v TGWU* [1989] IRLR 334.
[115] Section 188(7) TULRCA 1992.
[116] Section 188(7B) TULRCA 1992.

In *The Bakers' Union v Clarks of Hove Ltd*[117] the court held that there were three stages to deciding whether there was a defence in any particular case. First, were there special circumstances; secondly, did they render compliance with the statute not reasonably practicable; and, thirdly, did the employer take all the reasonable steps towards compliance as were reasonably practicable in the circumstances? In this case even an insolvency was not a special enough circumstance in itself to provide a defence against the lack of consultation.

The shedding of employees in an attempt by a receiver to sell the business was not a sufficient justification in *GMB v Rankin and Harrison*.[118] The fact that the business could not be sold and that there were no orders were common to insolvency situations and not enough in themselves to justify being special. Special circumstances means something out of the ordinary or something that is not common. In any complaint to an employment tribunal, the onus is upon the employer to show that there were special circumstances or that they took all reasonably practical steps towards compliance.[119]

10.5.4 Failure to comply

Where an employer has failed to comply with the requirements to consult, a complaint may be made to an employment tribunal.[120] If the tribunal finds the complaint well founded it will make a declaration to that effect and may make a protective award. A protective award to those who have been dismissed as redundant or whom it is proposed to dismiss and the protected period, up to a maximum of 90 days, begins with the date on which the first dismissals take effect or the date of the award, whichever is earlier. The length is that which the tribunal decides is just and equitable.[121] There is a time limit for complaints. They must be presented to the tribunal before the date on which the last of the dismissals takes effect, or during the three months beginning with that date, or within such further period as the tribunal considers reasonable if it is satisfied that it was not practicable for the complainant to present their complaint during that period.[122] During the protective period all the employees who are covered will receive a week's pay[123] for each week that he would have been paid by the employer during that period.[124] Parts of weeks are paid proportionately. Tribunals are required to state their reasons for the length of the award made.[125] Protective awards resulting from a claim by a trade union can only be awarded in respect of employees for which the trade union has been recognised. Other employees must make their own complaints.[126] The purpose of the award is to ensure that

---

[117] [1978] IRLR 366 CA.
[118] [1992] IRLR 514; neither were a local authority's financial difficulties a 'special circumstance' – see *Middlesbrough Borough Council v TGWU* [2002] IRLR 332.
[119] Section 189(6) TULRCA 1992.
[120] Section 189(1) TULRCA 1992; the onus of showing compliance with respect to questions about the election of appropriate representatives, or whether the employee representative was an appropriate representative, rests with the employer: section 189(1A)–(1B) TULRCA 1992.
[121] Section 189(2)–(4) TULRCA 1992.
[122] Section 189(5) TULRCA 1992.
[123] A week's pay as defined by Part XIV Chapter II ERA 1996.
[124] Section 190 TULRCA 1992; section 191 deals with certain situations, such as a fair dismissal and offers of alternative employment which might stop the employee continuing to receive payment.
[125] *E Green & Sons v ASTMS* [1984] IRLR 134.
[126] *TGWU v Brauer Coley Ltd* [2007] IRLR 207.

consultation takes place by providing a sanction against employers who fail to do so properly. The focus of the award is not on compensating the employees but on the seriousness of the employer's failure to comply with their statutory obligations[127] and the employer's ability to pay is not relevant.[128] An employee may bring a complaint to an employment tribunal if they have not been paid their protective awards in part or entirety. This complaint must be brought within three months of the last date on which the employee claims they were entitled to payment which is likely to be the last day of the protected period,[129] unless the period is extended by the tribunal if it considers that it was not reasonably practicable to do so. If the tribunal finds the complaint well founded it can order the employer to pay the award.[130]

Employers have an obligation to notify the Secretary of State of their proposals to dismiss employees for redundancy.[131] Proposals to dismiss 100 or more employees within 90 days or fewer are to be notified at least 90 days before any notice is given to employees in respect of any of the dismissals. Proposals to dismiss 20 or more within such a period require at least 30 days' written notice to the Secretary of State.[132] The written notice must contain details of where the employees are employed, identify the representatives to be consulted and when consultation with them began. The Secretary of State may give a written notice requiring more information.[133] There is also a special circumstances defence for the employer if it is not reasonably practicable for the employer to comply with these notification requirements. Failure of a controlling employer to provide the information does not constitute a special circumstance.[134] Failure to comply with these requirements may lead to a fine and individuals can be prosecuted if their actions had led to a corporate body not complying with these statutory requirements.[135]

10.6 Employer insolvency

Many redundancies and transfers of undertakings (see below) are likely to arise out of the insolvency of employers. The precise effect on employees will depend upon the action taken by creditors in order to secure their assets. If a winding up order is made by a court, the effect is, from the date of its publication, to bring the contracts of employment to an end with immediate effect. If the court were to appoint a receiver, the effect would be the same. Receivers appointed by creditors, by way of contrast, do not constitute a change in the legal identity of the employer and no automatic termination of the contracts of employment takes place. The effect of the appointment of an administrator is the same as

---

[127] *Susie Radin Ltd v GMB* [2004] IRLR 400 where the employers unsuccessfully argued that the tribunal should have taken into account a separate decision that consultation would have been futile anyway. The Court of Appeal stated that the futility of the consultation was not relevant to the making of a protective award.
[128] In *Smith v Cherry Lewis Ltd* [2005] IRLR 86 the employer was insolvent, but this was held not to be relevant in making the award.
[129] *Howlett Marine Services Ltd v Bowlam* [2001] IRLR 201.
[130] Section 192 TULRCA 1992.
[131] Requirements of articles 3 and 4 Collective Redundancies Directive.
[132] Section 193(1)–(2) TULRCA 1992 as amended by the Collective Redundancies (Amendment) Regulations 2006, SI 2006/2387.
[133] Section 193(4)–(5) TULRCA 1992.
[134] Section 193(7) TULRCA 1992.
[135] Section 194 TULRCA 1992.

a creditor appointed receiver. This is because they act as agents of the company and do not replace the legal entity.[136] Without statutory intervention such employees, if the insolvent business is not taken over or sold to a new employer, would merely join other creditors hoping to receive at least part of that which is owed to them.

Council Directive 80/987/EEC[137] on the approximation of the laws of the Member States relating to the protection of employees in the event of the insolvency of their employer (the Insolvency Directive) was the European Community's attempt to harmonise the approach of Member States. The purpose of the Directive was to add to employee protection by ensuring that each Member State had a guarantee institution which would guarantee, subject to limits, payment of employees' outstanding claims resulting from their contracts of employment and employment relationship.[138] Provisions providing this protection in Great Britain are contained in Part XII ERA 1996.

Section 182 ERA 1996 provides that employees may write to the Secretary of State to apply for payment of debts, owed to them by their insolvent employer, from the National Insurance Fund.

In *Everson and Barrass v Secretary of State for Trade and Industry and Bell Lines Ltd*[139] the ECJ was asked to settle the issue as to which country's guarantee institution should compensate the employees of an employer from a different Member State. In this case the Irish courts made a winding up order on the company in Ireland and the British employees of that company made a claim against the Secretary of State in Great Britain. In a previous case[140] the ECJ had held that it was the guarantee institution of the country of the parent company that was liable. This concerned employees who did not work from a registered office in the country where they were employed. In *Everson and Barrass* the ECJ held that, because the employees worked from a branch office from which all the employees worked, the guarantee institution of the country in which the branch was established should be liable for the payments.

The Secretary of State will need to be satisfied that the employer has become insolvent,[141] the employee's employment has been terminated and that the employee was entitled to be paid the whole or part of the debt. Section 183(3) ERA 1996 provides that an employer which is a company is to be treated as insolvent if:

(1) a winding up order or an administration order has been made, or
(2) a receiver or manager has been appointed or possession has been taken of any of the company's property by debenture holders, or
(3) there is a voluntary arrangement under Part I Insolvency Act 1986.

---

[136] See *In the matter of Maxwell Fleet and Facilities Management Ltd* [2000] IRLR 368 for an example of how administrators tried to use the Transfer of Undertakings Regulations 1981 in order to shed the employees and sell the business without inherited debts.

[137] Directive 2002/74/EC amended Council Directive 80/987/EEC on the approximation of the laws of the Member States relating to the protection of employees in the event of the insolvency of their employer OJ L 270/10 23.9.2002.

[138] Articles 3 and 4 Insolvency Directive.

[139] Case C-198/98 [2000] IRLR 202 ECJ.

[140] Case C-117/96 *Mosbæk (Danmarks Aktive Handelsrejsende) v Lønmodtagernes Garantifond* [1998] IRLR 150 ECJ.

[141] Section 183 ERA 1996 defines insolvency for employers who are individuals and for employers who are companies.

If the employee cannot show that one of these events has taken place, then it is unlikely that the individual will be entitled to payment from the National Insurance Fund. Even though, as in *Secretary of State for Trade and Industry v Walden*,[142] the employer is in financial difficulties and the company has been dissolved, this will not be enough in itself. The absence of any one of these three definitions was sufficient to stop the employee from successfully making a claim.

There is only liability for debts which the employee was entitled to receive from the employer.[143] The debts which are protected by statute are:[144]

(1) arrears of pay up to a maximum of eight weeks, although there is likely to be an entitlement to choose the best eight weeks;[145] this includes[146] guarantee payments, payments for time under Part VI ERA 1996[147] and for time off for carrying out trade union duties,[148] remuneration on suspension on medical grounds[149] and any amounts due from a protective award under section 189 TULRCA 1992;

(2) any amount payable to fulfil the statutory notice requirements in section 86 ERA 1996;

(3) any holiday pay outstanding at the appropriate date[150] from the previous 12 months, up to a maximum of six weeks;[151]

(4) any basic award of compensation for unfair dismissal;[152]

(5) any reasonable sum by way of reimbursing the whole or part of a fee paid by an apprentice or articled clerk.[153]

In addition, section 166(1)(b) ERA 1996[154] provides that employees whose employer is insolvent may apply to the Secretary of State for any statutory redundancy payments due.[155]

10.6.1 Occupational pensions

Article 8 of the Directive provides that Member States must ensure that all the necessary measures are taken to protect the interestes of employees and ex-employees at the date of the employer's insolvency in respect of rights under occupational pension schemes. This is

[142] [2000] IRLR 168.
[143] See *Mann v Secretary of State for Employment* [1999] IRLR 566 HL.
[144] Section 184(1) ERA 1996.
[145] See *Mann v Secretary of State for Employment* [1999] IRLR 566 HL.
[146] Section 184(2) ERA 1996.
[147] Time off for public duties, looking for work, ante-natal care, dependants, occupational pensions and for employee representatives.
[148] Section 169 TULRCA 1992.
[149] Section 64 ERA 1996.
[150] See section 185 ERA 1995 for the meaning of 'appropriate date'.
[151] This includes pay for holidays actually taken and accrued holiday pay: section 184(3) ERA 1996.
[152] Or an award under a designated dismissal procedure, so long as it is not greater than the basic award.
[153] A rare event in modern times.
[154] See generally Part XI Chapter VI ERA 1996 on the rules regarding these and other payments by the Secretary of State.
[155] See *Secretary of State for Trade and Industry v Lassman* [2000] IRLR 411 CA, where employees were mistakenly paid redundancy payments. This was held to break their continuity of employment and they were unable to claim for the same period again when their new employer became insolvent.

an important measure because it affects situations where not only the employer becomes insolvent, but also the pension scheme. *Robins v Secretary of State*[156] concerned two pension schemes which had a combined deficit of over £140 million. The pensioners therefore faced significant reductions in their pensions from these schemes. The question was whether the UK Government had an obligation, under Article 8, to make up the difference between what the funds would pay and what they would have been entitled to if they had not been in deficit. In the event the Court of Justice held that there was no requirement on the Government to provide a full guarantee. The Directive allowed a certain latitude to Member States. On the other hand, the amounts guaranteed in this case (between 20 and 49%) did not amount to the minimum degree of protection that the claimants were entitled to.

10.6.2 Controlling directors

One issue concerns individuals who are controlling directors of companies as well as having contracts of employment with those companies. If an individual can have an influence upon whether a company is insolvent or not, is it possible for that same individual to have a claim against the Secretary of State for redundancy pay and other contractual emoluments?[157] In *Fleming v Secretary of State for Trade and Industry*[158] an individual was refused a claim for redundancy and statutory notice payments on the grounds that he was not an employee. He owned 65% of the company's shares and, when the company got into difficulties, he had given personal guarantees to the company's two main suppliers and had elected not to take a salary for a time. This was enough for the employment tribunal to decide that he was not an employee. The appeal courts accepted that the decision as to whether an individual was an employee or not was a question of fact for the tribunal. The Court of Session held, therefore, that the tribunal was entitled to reach the decision that it did, but that the fact that a person was a controlling director was only one of the factors that should be taken into account. The significance to be given to that factor would depend upon the surrounding circumstances.

This view was supported in *Secretary of State for Trade and Industry v Bottrill*[159] which concerned the managing director of a company who held all the shares in that company. In this case he was also held to be an employee as the shareholding was only intended to be temporary. The court confirmed the approach that the controlling shareholding was only one of the factors to be taken into account. Other factors might be the degree of control exercised by the company, whether there were other directors and whether the individual was answerable to himself only and incapable of being dismissed.

---

[156] Case C-278/05 *Robins v Secretary of State for Work and Pensions* [2007] IRLR 271.
[157] See *Lee v Lee's Air Farming Ltd* [1961] AC 12 for the classic approach to the relationship between an individual as a controlling director and an individual as an employee; also *McMeechan v Secretary of State for Employment* [1997] IRLR 353 CA, where an employment agency worker established their employee status and were able to claim against the Secretary of State.
[158] [1997] IRLR 682.
[159] [1999] IRLR 326 CA.

10.6.3 Complaints to employment tribunals

The total amount payable in respect of any debt, where that debt refers to a period of time, is, currently, £310 per week[160] and even this is subject to deductions such as National Insurance contributions.[161] If the Secretary of State fails to make a payment that has been claimed, or only makes it in part, then the individual may make a complaint to an employment tribunal. This complaint needs to be submitted within three months, beginning with the date on which the Secretary of State's decision was communicated, or such further period as the tribunal considers reasonable. If the complaint is upheld, the tribunal may stipulate the amount that should be paid.[162]

Where a 'relevant officer' has been appointed in connection with the insolvency, then the Secretary of State may wait for a statement of the employer's debts to employees from that officer before making any payments. The relevant officer is a trustee in bankruptcy, a liquidator, an administrator, a receiver or manager, or a trustee under an arrangement between the employer and the creditors or under a trust deed.[163] The Secretary of State also has the power to require, by giving notice in writing, an employer, or any other person having control of the necessary records, to provide any information necessary for the Secretary of State to deal with the claim. Failure to co-operate or the provision of false information can lead to a fine.[164]

Once the Secretary of State makes a payment, then all the rights and remedies associated with that debt accrue to the Secretary of State. If, for example, an employment tribunal makes an award after the payment has been made, then the debt is paid to the Secretary of State.[165]

10.7 Transfers of undertakings

The Transfer of Undertakings (Protection of Employment) Regulations 1981 (the Transfer of Undertakings Regulations 1981)[166] were the Government's belated transposition of the Acquired Rights Directive[167] into national law. These regulations were amended on four different occasions.[168] The Directive itself was amended in 1998 and was subsequently consolidated into Directive 2001/23/EC. The 1981 Regulations were finally replaced by the Transfer of Undertakings (Protection of Employment) Regulations 2006 which came into effect in October 2006.[169]

---

[160] Section 186 ERA; this is the figure for 2007/08.
[161] See *Titchener v Secretary of State* [2002] IRLR 195.
[162] Section 188 ERA 1996.
[163] Section 187 ERA 1996.
[164] Section 190 ERA 1996.
[165] Section 189 ERA 1996.
[166] SI 1981/1794.
[167] Directive 77/187/EEC on the approximation of the laws of the Member States relating to the safeguarding of employees' rights in the event of transfers of undertakings; subsequently amended by Directive 98/50/EC and consolidated by Directive 2001/23/EC.
[168] SI 1987/442; section 33 Trade Union Reform and Employment Rights Act 1993; SI 1995/2587 and SI 1999/1925.
[169] SI 2006/246.

10.7.1 The meaning of a transfer of an undertaking

The application of the Directive has been much discussed at the European Court of Justice. The Court's decisions have been reflected in the consolidated Directive, but the British Government has gone further in some respects.

In *Spijkers*,[170] the seminal case on the application of the Directive, the European Court of Justice defined a transfer of an undertaking as the transfer of an economic entity that retained its identity. The court looked at the purpose of the Acquired Rights Directive and concluded that its aim was to ensure the continuity of existing employment relationships. Thus, if the operation that is transferred is an identifiable entity before and after the transfer then a relevant transfer is likely to have taken place. One needs to look at the situation before the transfer and identify an economic entity, then after the transfer to consider whether the economic entity has retained its identity.

The ECJ then gave further guidance as to factors which would help in the decision as to whether a transfer had taken place. It was necessary to take all the factual circumstances of the transaction into account, including:

(i) the type of undertaking or business in question;
(ii) the transfer or otherwise of tangible assets such as buildings and stocks;
(iii) the value of intangible assets at the date of transfer;
(iv) whether the majority of staff are taken over by the new employer;
(v) the transfer or otherwise of customers;
(vi) the degree of similarity between activities before and after the transfer;
(vii) the duration of any interruption in those activities.

The court stated that each of these factors was only part of the assessment. One had to examine what existed before the transfer and then examine the entity after the change in order to decide whether the operation was continued, but these factors might help that consideration.

This approach was further emphasised by the case of *Schmidt*,[171] which concerned the contracting out of a small cleaning operation. Mrs Schmidt complained about her dismissal and eventually her claim ended up in the national court (the Landsarbeits-gericht), which then referred the issue, of whether the transfer of a single person to an outside contractor could be a transfer of an undertaking, to the European Court of Justice. The bank, as well as the German and UK Governments, argued that the answer should be in the negative because the cleaning operation was neither a main function nor an ancillary function of the bank and that there was not a transfer of an economic entity. The fact that it was a small operation was held not to be relevant. What mattered was that there was a stable operation which retained its identity. This was indicated by the fact that before the transfer there was a cleaning operation and, again, after the transfer this continued or was resumed.[172]

---

[170] Case 24/85 *JMA Spijkers v Gebroeders Abbatoir CV* [1986] ECR 1119.
[171] Case 392/92 *Schmidt v Spar und Leikhasse der Fruheren Amter Bordesholm* [1995] ICR 237.
[172] See also *Dudley Bower Building Services Ltd v Lowe* [2003] IRLR 260.

In the United Kingdom this approach by the European Court of Justice resulted in the courts finding that contracting out of services, or outsourcing, could amount to a relevant transfer for the purposes of the Transfer Regulations. The case of *Kenny v South Manchester College*,[173] for example, concerned the provision of education services at a young offenders' institution. After a tendering exercise the contract was won by South Manchester College. The question was whether the undertaking had retained its identity. The High Court stated that 'the prisoners and young offenders who attend, say, a carpentry class next Thursday will, save those released from the institution, be likely in the main to be the same as those who attended the same class in the same classroom the day before and will doubtless be using exactly the same tools and machinery'. This was followed by other cases such as those involving the outsourcing of a local authority refuse collection contract[174] and the moving of a hospital cleaning contract from one contractor to another,[175] which were held to be relevant transfers.

It was then that the European Court of Justice appeared to have second thoughts about its approach. In *Süzen*[176] the court distinguished between the transfer of an entity and the transfer of an activity. As in the case of *Schmidt*, before the transfer there was a cleaning operation and after the transfer there was a cleaning operation. On the face of it, there was a relevant transfer because the entity appeared to retain its identity, as evidenced by its continuation and resumption. The ECJ, however, then stated that an entity could not be reduced to the activity entrusted to it. Thus the court distinguished between an entity that transferred and an activity that transferred. An entity, according to the court, was:

> an organised grouping of persons or assets facilitating the exercise of an economic activity which pursues a specific objective.

There has, therefore, to be something else, other than the activity taking place, which needs to transfer, such as assets or 'an organised grouping' of people. Without these, there appeared to be only the transfer of an activity. This was not enough to provide the protection of the Acquired Rights Directive.

It is from this point that many of the problems concerning the applicability of the Directive and the TUPE Regulations arose. *Süzen* set limits on the applicability of the Directive, but there has been confusion as to where these limits apply and the real difference between an entity and an activity. Both the *Schmidt* case and the *Süzen* case concerned the transfer of cleaning contracts, but in one the court held that an entity transferred and, in the second, it held that the cleaning contract only amounted to an activity and was therefore not protected by the Directive.

It is not surprising that many of those dealing with transfers became confused. The Court of Appeal tackled the problem in *RCO Support Services v Unison*.[177] This concerned the transfer of in-patient care from one hospital to another some three miles away. A new contractor won the cleaning and catering contract at the hospital to which the patients were being transferred. None of the staff at the original hospital transferred to the new one,

---

[173] [1993] IRLR 265.
[174] *Wren v Eastbourne District Council* [1993] ICR 955.
[175] *Dines v Initial Health Care Services and Pall Mall Services Group Ltd* [1994] IRLR 336.
[176] Case 13/95 *Süzen v Zehnacker Gebäudereinigung* [1997] IRLR 255 ECJ.
[177] [2002] IRLR 401.

so there was no transfer of assets or people involved in the change of contractor. Despite this the court held that there had been a relevant transfer of an undertaking. Although it was accepted that *Süzen* had placed limits on the applicability of the Directive, it did not exclude all occasions when none of the workforce transferred. In this case the other circumstances were sufficient to suggest that it was more than just an activity that transferred. Again, one had to adopt the multi-factorial test as in *Spijkers*.

The Government has decided to remove uncertainty in the public sector through administrative means (see below) whilst tackling the outsourcing sector with the application of the concept of 'service provision changes'.

Regulation 3(1)(a) of the 2006 TUPE Regulations states that the regulations apply, first, to a transfer where there is a transfer of an economic entity that retains its identity (the *Spijkers* test), and, secondly, to a service provision change. An economic entity is defined in regulation 3(2) as 'an organised grouping of resources which has the objective of pursuing an economic activity, whether or not that activity is central or ancillary' (the *Süzen* test). There has been an attempt therefore to clarify the meaning of a transfer, using decisions of the European Court of Justice, following Article 1 of the consolidated Directive.

Regulation 3(1)(b) provides that the TUPE Regulations 2006 also apply to a service provision change. These are relevant to outsourcing situations and are meant to ensure a wide coverage of the regulations. A service provision change takes place when a person (client) first contracts out some part of its activities to a contractor; when such a contract is taken over by another contractor (so-called second generation transfers); and when the client takes back the activity in-house from a contractor. Whereas, however, a relevant transfer consists of an 'organised grouping of resources', a service provision change requires there to be 'an organised grouping of employees, situated in Great Britain, which has, as its principal purpose, the carrying out of activities concerned'.[178]

The 2006 Regulations are introduced under powers given by section 2(2) of the European Communities Act and section 38 of the Employment Relations Act 1999. This latter power enables the Secretary of State to go beyond just the provisions of the Directive and extend the scope of the Regulations. It is the 1999 Act which allows the Secretary of State to include the provisions relating to service provision changes. Thus, for transfers other than those concerned with outsourcing, the Directive is to be followed. In outsourcing events, however, there appears to be a much broader interpretation so as to avoid the conflicts that have arisen in the past.[179]

10.7.2 Who is to be transferred

Regulation 4(1) of the 2006 Regulations provides that, except where an objection is made, a relevant transfer shall not operate to terminate any contract of employment of any person employed by the transferor and assigned to the 'organised grouping of resources or

---

[178] Regulation 2(1) provides that references to an 'organised grouping of employees' includes a single employee; nor does it apply to single specific events or tasks of a short-term duration: regulation 3(3)(ii).

[179] See Malcolm Sargeant, 'Transfers and Outsourcing' (2000) *Commercial Liability Law Review* 282 and Malcolm Sargeant, 'TUPE: the final round' (2006) *Journal of Business Law* 549.

employees that is subject to the relevant transfer'. In regulation 2(1) temporary assignments are excluded. An important addition here is the use of the word 'assigned'.

One problem that has occurred is in deciding who works for the part transferred, when only part of an organisation is transferred to a new employer. If, for example, a business decides to contract out its non-core activities and retain only those parts of the business that are concerned with its primary activities, or if only a part of the business is sold off, there are likely to be a number of employees, such as those in Human Resources, who work in the parts remaining, but whose jobs consisted of servicing those parts transferred. This may be the entire content of their jobs or only a part. If such staff remain with the transferor organisation, they may be faced with the loss of their jobs or, at the very least, a significant change in their job activities. The question then is whether these support staff have the right to transfer also.

It was in the case of *Botzen*[180] that the European Court of Justice first devised the assignment test to deal with such situations. The Advocate General[181] in the case proposed a test for deciding who should be transferred if only a part of a business was sold off:

> A basic working test, it seems to me, is to ask whether, if that part of the business had been separately owned before the transfer, the worker would have been employed by the owners of that part or the owners of the remaining part.

The Advocate General did admit that employees could be involved in work other than for the part transferred, but only on a *de minimus* basis.

Some people, of course, would not have been employed in either part if they were separately owned. It may have been because the whole was a certain size that they were employed. This may be especially true of HR departments as bigger organisations can perhaps have the capacity to employ more specialists, whereas a smaller organisation might demand more generalist abilities. The Court of Justice held that 'An employment relationship is essentially characterised by the link existing between the employee and the part of the undertaking or business to which he is assigned to carry out his duties'. All that is needed therefore is to establish to which part of the business or undertaking the individual is assigned. This unhelpful conclusion did not establish a satisfactory test because of the need to define what was meant by 'assign'.

Duncan Web Offset (Maidstone) Ltd v Cooper[182] concerned three employees who worked at the company's Maidstone office, but spent some of their time working at other offices which were part of the same group. Occasionally this meant a significant amount of time spent away from their office. When the business of the Maidstone office was sold by the receivers these three were not transferred. All three had spent at least 80% of their time on work connected with the Maidstone office. The EAT concluded that the whole of the Maidstone business had been transferred and, unless the employees were also transferred, their contracts of employment would come to an end because they would be left with no employment and no employer. They were, therefore, held to be protected by the TUPE Regulations and the Directive.

---

[180] Case 186/83 *Arie Botzen v Rotterdamsche Droogdok Maatschappij BV* [1986] 2 CMLR 50 ECJ.
[181] The Advocate General investigates cases, summarises the arguments and makes recommendations to the European Court of Justice.
[182] [1995] IRLR 633; see also *Michael Peters Ltd v (1) Farnfield and (2) Michael Peters Group plc* [1995] IRLR 190.

The Employment Appeal Tribunal declined to give guidance about when a person was assigned to an undertaking and when they were not. They accepted that there 'will often be difficult questions of fact for employment tribunals when deciding who was assigned and who was not'. It felt, however, that it could not give guidance because the facts may vary markedly from case to case. During the course of argument a number of indicators were suggested and the EAT accepted that they may well help future consideration by tribunals. These suggestions were: the amount of time spent on one part of the business or another; the amount of value given to each part by the employee; the terms of the contract of employment showing what the employee could be required to do; how the cost to the employer of the employee's services had been allocated between the different parts of the business.[183]

Regulation 4(3) also provides that it is only persons employed immediately before the transfer and who are assigned to such an organised grouping, or would have been had they not been unfairly dismissed, who are protected.[184]

10.7.3 Contract variations

The ability to vary contracts of employment at the time of transfer, even with the consent of the employees, was considered by the House of Lords in the joined cases of *Wilson v St Helens Borough Council* and *British Fuels Ltd v Baxendale*.[185] The first case concerned the transfer of a community home from Lancashire County Council to St Helens Borough Council. The County Council had decided that it could no longer afford to run the home and, as a result, gave the trustees of the home two years' notice that it would cease to be involved. St Helens Borough Council agreed to take it over, but only after substantial reorganisation. The result was a reduction in the size of the home and the number of staff needed to run it. Negotiations took place with the trade union concerned and staffing levels were reduced from 162 to 72. In addition, some of the 72 who transferred did so on reduced terms and conditions. All were dismissed for reasons of redundancy by the County Council prior to the move. Subsequently the employees claimed that the Transfer Regulations applied and that they should have been transferred on the same terms and conditions that they enjoyed when employed by Lancashire County Council.

The House of Lords concluded that 'the transfer of the undertaking did not constitute the reason for the variation'. The transfer itself was not the reason for the variation, although deciding when a variation in terms is as a result of a transfer and when it is not seems a difficult question. Lord Slynn, in delivering judgment, stated that:

> It may be difficult to decide whether the variation is due to the transfer or attributable to some separate cause. If, however, the variation is not due to the transfer itself it can in my opinion, on the basis of the authorities to which I have referred, validly be made.

In the *British Fuels* case, an existing subsidiary company was merged with a newly acquired organisation. The employees concerned were dismissed because of redundancy by the old

---

[183] This issue is not confined to large organisations only as was shown in *Buchanan-Smith v Schleicher & Co International Ltd* [1996] IRLR 547.
[184] *Litster v Forth Dry Dock and Engineering Ltd* [1989] IRLR 161 HL.
[185] [1998] IRLR 706.

company and taken on by the newly set-up business. They were offered a new contract of employment, which was accepted. The problem for the new enterprise was that the terms and conditions of the two sets of employees were different and the new employer wished to rationalise them. The employees subsequently claimed that their terms and conditions should have been protected. The House of Lords held that their original dismissals had been effective and could not be regarded as a nullity.

It is possible, therefore, to reorganise providing that the reason for the dismissal or variation is not connected with the transfer. Indeed the EAT has distinguished between changes that take place in connection with the transfer and changes that take place 'on the occasion' of the transfer.[186] This is not to say that an employee is barred from taking advantage of a more favourable variation if agreed with the transferee. According to the EAT the case law merely establishes that an employee may rely on the provisions agreed with the transferor. The employee can object to any matters that may be detrimental to him or her, but this will not stop him or her taking advantage of any more favourable provisions.[187]

The 2006 TUPE Regulations provide that it is not possible to vary a contract of employment if the sole or main reason was the transfer or any other reason that was not an economic, technical or organisational reason entailing changes in the workforce (ETO reason; regulation 4(4)). The employer and employee are able, however, to agree a variation if it is changed for an ETO reason or 'a reason unconnected to the transfer'.

10.7.4 Employee choice

The Directive was silent on the subject of whether an individual employee can decide that they do not wish to transfer. Initially it was left to the European Court of Justice to decide. In *Daddy's Dance Hall*[188] the court suggested that employees had no choice in the matter. Whether the individuals wished it or not there was a public policy reason for not allowing employees to opt out, because this alternative would normally be that they would be worse off by opting out. This position was considerably softened in *Katsikas*[189] when the Court of Justice held that to stop someone objecting to the transfer of his or her employment would undermine the fundamental rights of the employee who must be free to choose his employer and cannot be obliged to work for an employer whom he or she has not freely chosen. It followed, therefore, that the Directive does not oblige employees to transfer provided that they choose freely not to continue the employment relationship. It was then left to the Member State to 'decide the fate of the contract of employment or employment relationship with the transferor'.

The 1981 TUPE Regulations were amended by the Trade Union Reform and Employment Rights Act 1993, so that a person's contract of employment will not transfer if the individual informs the transferor or the transferee that he or she objects to becoming an employee of the transferee.

The problem for such an employee is that they are left in a sort of employment nether region with no claims against the transferor or the transferee. Regulation 4(7) of the 2006

---

[186] *Ralton v Havering College of Further and Higher Education* [2001] IRLR 738.
[187] See *Power v Regent Security Services Ltd* [2007] IRLR 227.
[188] Case 324/86 *Foreningen of Arbejdsledere I Danmark v Daddy's Dance Hall A/S* [1985] IRLR 315.
[189] Case 132/91 *Katsikas v Konstantidis* [1993] IRLR 179.

Regulations repeats that position so that an employee is not transferred if he or she objects to being so transferred. The current outcome is repeated in regulation 4(8) where the employee is then in a 'no man's land'; they have not been transferred, but the transferor cannot be treated as having dismissed the employee.

The question of how an employee objects to the transfer has also been considered. In *Hay v George Hanson*[190] the work of an employee was to be transferred from a district council to a private contractor. The question was whether there needed to be a clear and unequivocal statement from the employee objecting to the transfer. The EAT stated that the 'drafting of the Regulations leaves much to be desired'. In this case the employee was held to have objected. He unsuccessfully sought alternative employment with the council and he tried to obtain a redundancy package amongst other actions. This led the employment tribunal to conclude that, cumulatively, he had objected to the transfer. There was, therefore, no particular method by which an employee may object, but he or she is able to communicate their state of mind to the transferee by word or by action. It should not, according to the EAT, be difficult to distinguish between expressing concern, and protesting, about the transfer and withholding consent. It was a matter for the tribunal to decide in each individual case, but the EAT did state:[191]

> ... nor is there any requirement, which seems singularly unfortunate, that the employee intending to object should be informed of the consequences by the transferring employer, given the draconian nature of the result that reg. 5(4B) achieves.

This situation is unchanged by the 2006 Regulations.

10.7.5 Insolvency

Measures to deal with insolvency situations were absent from the original Directive and the problems resulting from this were recognised by the European Court of Justice at an early stage. The perceived problem was that the obligation, imposed by the Directive, upon the transferee enterprise to take over all the debts in relation to the insolvent organisation's employees and, indeed, to transfer all those employees at their current terms and conditions, would act as a disincentive to the 'rescue' of such enterprises.

In *Abels*[192] the ECJ tried to distinguish between different types of proceedings in deciding the applicability of the Directive. Mr Abels worked for a company which became insolvent and he and other staff were laid off. The liquidator eventually sold the business to another company which re-employed Mr Abels and others, but did not pay them for the time that they had been laid off. Mr Abels claimed that it was a transfer of an undertaking and that their contracts should have automatically passed to the buyer of the business. If this had happened, then they would have been entitled to continuing pay. The outcome of the case was that the court distinguished between those situations when the insolvency proceedings were aimed at liquidation of the assets and those situations when the aim, at an earlier stage, was to rescue the business. It was an unsatisfactory outcome because it left uncertainty about when the Directive applied.

---

[190] [1996] IRLR 427.
[191] See also *Senior Heat Treatment Ltd v Bell* [1997] IRLR 614.
[192] Case 135/83 *Abels v Administrative Board* [1987] 2 CMLR 406.

The consolidated Directive excludes, in Article 5.1, any transfers where the transfer is the subject of bankruptcy proceedings with a view to liquidation of the assets of the transferor. Article 5.2 of the consolidated Directive also gives Member States the option of excluding transfers of liabilities in other types of insolvency proceedings as well as giving them the option of agreed changes to terms and conditions of employees which are 'designed to safeguard employment opportunities by ensuring the survival of the undertaking, business or part of the undertaking or business'.

Unsurprisingly the TUPE Regulations 2006 take advantage of both of these options in regulations 8 and 9. Relevant insolvency proceedings for this purpose in the regulations repeat the definition stated in the Directive, namely that they are 'insolvency proceedings which have been opened in relation to the transferor not with a view to the liquidation of the assets of the transferor and which are under the supervision of an insolvency practitioner' (regulation 8(6)).

The outcome is that those elements which the Government would normally be responsible for under its statutory obligations towards the employees of insolvent employers do not transfer. This effectively amounts to a government subsidy to transfers in insolvency situations. The debts owed to employees by the transferor, to the limits of its statutory obligations, will be guaranteed by the Secretary of State. This, of course, includes some arrears of pay, notice periods, holiday pay and any basic award for unfair dismissal compensation.[193] Other debts owed to employees will transfer.

In addition to this subsidy there is provision in regulation 9 for the employer and employee representatives to agree 'permitted variations' to their contracts of employment. Permitted variations are those which are not due to ETO reasons entailing a change in the workforce and are designed to safeguard employment opportunities by ensuring the survival of the undertaking (regulation 9(7)).

Thus the method of dealing with the perceived problem of insolvency transfers is both to provide a potential subsidy and to lessen the protection available to employees. It is difficult to see what employee representatives can use as their case in resisting changes to terms and conditions when they are negotiating under the threat of unemployment arising from the employer's insolvency.

10.7.6 Information and consultation

Regulations 13 to 15 TUPE Regulations 2006 replace regulations 10 and 11 of the 1981 Regulations. The obligations to inform and consult employees remain the same apart from the introduction of joint liability between the transferor and the transferee for any compensation awarded as a result of a failure to inform and consult (regulation 15(8) and (9)).

Information should be provided 'long enough before[194] a relevant transfer to enable the employer of any affected employees to consult all the persons who are appropriate representatives of any of those affected employees'. The High Court, in *Institution of Professional and Civil Servants v Secretary of State for Defence*,[195] decided that the words

---

[193] See, for example, Part XII of the Employment Rights Act 1996.
[194] Regulation 13(2) TUPE Regulations 2006.
[195] [1987] IRLR 373.

'long enough before' a transfer to enable consultation to take place meant as soon as measures are envisaged and *if possible* long enough before the transfer. The court held that the words did not mean as soon as measures are envisaged and *in any event* long enough before the transfer. This case concerned the introduction of private management into the Royal dockyards at Rosyth and Devonport; a measure which was opposed by the trade unions. Before consultation could take place there needed to be some definite plans or proposals by the employer around which consultation could take place.

The information to be provided should consist of:

(1) the fact that a relevant transfer is to take place, approximately when it is to take place and the reasons for it;
(2) the legal, economic and social implications for the affected employees;
(3) the measures which are envisaged to take place in connection with the transfer, in relation to the affected employees or the fact that there are no such measures envisaged.

The rules on who are appropriate representatives and the requirements are identical to those rules concerning the appointment of appropriate representatives for the purposes of consultation in collective redundancies (see above). The representatives are the independent trade union which is recognised by the employer. If there is no such trade union, then there are employee representatives[196] to be elected or appointed by the affected employees, whether for the purpose of these consultations or for some other purpose.

It is, of course, both the transferor and the transferee that need to consult and there is an obligation upon the transferee to provide the transferor with information about their plans, so that the transferor can carry out their duty to consult.[197] Where the employer actually envisages taking measures in relation to any of the affected employees, then the employer must consult the appropriate representatives 'with a view to seeking their agreement to the measures to be taken'.[198] In the course of these consultations the employer will consider the representations made by the appropriate representatives and, if any of those representations are rejected, the employer must state the reasons for so doing.[199]

There is a special circumstances defence for the employer if it renders it not reasonably practicable to perform the duty to consult and inform. In such a case the employer must take all such steps as are reasonable in the circumstances.[200] There is also a defence for the employer if the employees fail to elect representatives. In such a case the duty to consult is fulfilled if the employer gives each employee the necessary information.[201]

---

[196] Regulation 13(3) TUPE Regulations 2006 states that employee representatives are either those who are elected for the purpose of consultation or elected for some other purpose and it is appropriate to consult them.
[197] Regulation 13(4) TUPE Regulations 2006.
[198] There is also a common law duty upon the employer to take reasonable care in any statements made to employees with regard to the transfer, to ensure that the information is accurate and that all intentions were capable of being fulfilled: see *Hagen v ICI Chemicals Ltd* [2002] IRLR 32 HC.
[199] Regulation 13(7) TUPE Regulations 2006.
[200] Regulation 13(11) TUPE Regulations 2006; the courts have traditionally construed special circumstances very narrowly; see collective redundancies above and *Bakers Union v Clarks of Hove* [1978] IRLR 366 CA and *GMB v Rankin and Harrison* [1992] IRLR 514, where the shedding of employees to make a sale more attractive was held not to be a special circumstance.
[201] Regulation 15(2) TUPE Regulations 2006.

Complaints to an employment tribunal may be made for a breach of the rules concerning consultation. Complaints must be made to the employment tribunal within three months beginning with the date upon which the transfer was completed.[202] If the complaint is well founded the employment tribunal may order appropriate compensation. Tribunals are expected to adopt a similar approach to that taken concerning failures in consultation concerning collective redundancies (see above). This means that awards should be concerned with punishing the employer rather than concerned with compensating the employee.[203]

There is a further issue related to information, especially the passing of information between contractors. This has been a particular issue especially for those involved in outsourcing. Regulations 11 and 12 of the TUPE Regulations 2006 concern the notification of employee liability information and now provide a statutory duty for the transferor to pass onto the transferee certain information. This includes the identity and age of the employee; their terms and conditions of employment (as required by section 1 of the Employment Rights Act 1996); disciplinary or grievance action over the previous two years and any details of any claims, cases or action brought in the last two years and any future actions that the transferor might have reasonable grounds to believe are possible. The 2006 Regulations provide for compensation to be paid to the transferee, with a normal minimum of £500 per employee.

10.7.7 Public sector

The Government has decided that 'employees in public sector organisations should be treated no less favourably than those in private sector organisations when they are part of an organised grouping of resources that is transferred between employers'. The chosen methods of implementing this policy are to be the application of the Statement of Practice on *Staff Transfers in the Public Sector*,[204] by applying any case specific legislation when necessary and by the use of section 38 of the Employment Relations Act 1999. There are a number of outcomes resulting from these principles. These are as follows:

(1) all contracting-out exercises with the private and voluntary sector and all transfers between different parts of the public sector will be treated as if the Transfer Regulations apply, unless there are exceptional reasons for not doing so;
(2) second generation transfers, i.e. when there is a change of contractor dealing with an outsourced public service, and transfers back into the public sector are to be treated as being covered by the regulations;
(3) there should be appropriate arrangements for the protection of occupational pensions, redundancy and severance payments to staff affected by these situations.

The Statement of Practice represents a willingness to apply the Transfer Regulations generally throughout the public sector with the result that they will still be applied even if there is no change of employer, such as transfers of functions within the civil service.

---

[202] Regulation 15(12) TUPE Regulations 2006.
[203] *Sweetin v Coral Racing* [2006] IRLR 252.
[204] Issued by the Cabinet Office January 2000.

10.7.8 Pensions

Article 3(4)(a) of the Directive provides for the exclusion of 'employees' rights to old age, invalidity or survivors' benefits under supplementary company or inter company pension schemes outside the statutory social security schemes in Member States'. The 2006 Regulations repeat this in regulation 10(1) by excluding occupational pension schemes, but state that any other provisions which do not relate to old age, invalidity or survivors' pensions should not be treated as part of the scheme (regulation 10(2)).

Further reading

Deakin, S. and Morris, G., *Labour Law* (4th edn, Hart Publishing, 2005) Chapters 3 and 9.
McMullen, J., 'An Analysis of the Transfer of Undertakings (Protection of Employment) Regulations 2006' (2006) 35(2) *Industrial Law Journal* 113.
Painter, R. and Holmes, A., *Cases and Materials on Employment Law* (6th edn, Oxford University Press, 2006), Chapter 9.
Sargeant, M., 'TUPE: the final round' (2006) *Journal of Business Law* 549.
http://www.berr.gov.uk/employment/employment-legislation/index.html for the web site of the Department for Business, Enterprise and Regulatory Reform on employment policy and legislation.
http://www.berr.gov.uk/files/file20761.pdf for a Government guide to the Transfer Regulations 2006.

Visit **www.mylawchamber.co.uk/sargeant** to access legal updates, live web links and practice exam questions to test yourself on this chapter.

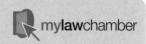

11

Trade Unions

11.1 Introduction

For much of its history the trade union movement in Great Britain has struggled to establish a position within the law which would enable it to organise and make use of the power that comes from size. In the nineteenth century the struggle was with the criminal law, which was used to control and limit the activities of workers' organisations, whilst in the twentieth century the struggle was with the civil law as the courts imposed new tortious liabilities upon them.

The Combination Act 1800, for example, made unlawful any contracts or agreements between certain groups of workers which had, as their purpose, the improvement of wages or working hours or almost anything that interfered with an employer's ability to run their own business. The severity of the oppression varied over time but there were important landmarks, such as the Trade Union Act 1871 which adopted the principle of non-intervention in trade union affairs. Section 2 of that Act provided that trade unions were not to be considered as criminal conspiracies just because their rules were in restraint of trade. Nevertheless, unions suffered a series of setbacks as the civil courts continued to regard them with suspicion. The Trade Disputes Act 1906 was adopted by the last Liberal administration and was partly a reaction to the *Taff Vale* case[1] which had the effect of limiting opportunities to take strike action and threatening the finances of trade unions. The 1906 Act provided trade unions with immunities from civil actions, for example the tort of inducing breach of contract when in contemplation or furtherance of a trade dispute.[2]

In more modern times the Conservative Government of 1971–74 introduced the Industrial Relations Act 1971, which repealed the 1906 Act and tried to set up a new legal framework for industrial relations. The National Industrial Relations Court was established to administer this process. It failed because of the lack of co-operation from the trade union movement and because the Government lacked the authority to enforce its will. The Trade Union and Labour Relations Acts of 1974 and 1976 repealed the Industrial Relations Act 1971 and returned to the system of immunities. After the 'winter of discontent'[3] the Conservative Government came to power in 1979 with an intention and a

---

[1] *Taff Vale Railway Co v Amalgamated Society of Railway Servants* [1901] AC 426.
[2] This is a very simplistic description. For those who wish a more serious historical analysis there is a wealth of material; see, for example, Paul Davies and Mark Freedland, *Labour Legislation and Public Policy* (Clarendon Press, 1993).
[3] The 'winter of discontent' was a description given to the winter of 1978/9, where there was a peak in industrial action by trade unions, especially within the public sector.

mandate to reform the trade union movement. Throughout the 1980s and the early 1990s there was a series of Acts of Parliament which limited the freedom of action of trade unions and their members. It is these legislative measures, mostly incorporated into the Trade Union and Labour Relations (Consolidation) Act 1992 (TULRCA 1992), which largely define the rules governing the right to association and the rights of members and trade unions in relation to each other. These rules have been amended only in a limited way by the Labour Government elected in 1997.

11.2 Freedom of association

An important part of the struggle by trade unionists in the past has been for the right to associate together in trade unions and not to be discriminated against by governments or employers as a result of doing so. In more recent times the trade union movement has declined in size and, perhaps, in influence. In 1979 it reached its peak membership of over 13.2 million members. By 2003, this had declined to some 7.75 million.[4] There is not enough evidence to prove a causal relationship between this decline and the policies of the Conservative Governments between 1979 and 1997, but it is safe to assume that they contributed towards that decline. More striking is the reduction in industrial action. In 1979, albeit an exceptional year for strike action,[5] some 29,747,000 working days were lost as a result of strikes. By 2006, this had declined to just over 7.6 million.[6]

The right to associate has been a concern of international organisations and is seen as a basic right of workers in a democratic society. For example, Article 11 European Convention on Human Rights (CHR) states that everyone has the right of peaceful association and freedom of association. This Article was incorporated into national law, from October 2000, by the Human Rights Act 1998. The European Charter of the Fundamental Social Rights of Workers,[7] 1989, stated:

> 11. Employers and workers of the European Community shall have the right of association in order to constitute professional organisations or trade unions of their choice for the defence of their economic and social interests. Every employer and every worker shall have the freedom to join or not to join such organisations without any personal or occupational damage being thereby suffered by him.

It is interesting that the freedom to join a trade union is linked with the freedom not to join. This dual freedom is reflected in the United Kingdom legislation and results from the perceived coercion resulting from the 'closed shop'. Until their existence became impossible as a result of legislation during the 1980s and 1990s,[8] there were two types of closed shop. These were the pre-entry and the post-entry closed shops. In the former there was a requirement for any applicants for job vacancies to be members of the recognised trade union or unions.[9] In the latter there was a requirement for successful job applicants

---

[4] Labour Market Trends, July 2004.
[5] The figure for 1978 was 9,405,000.
[6] Annual Report of the Certification Officer 2006–7.
[7] Signed by all the Member States of the European Community at the time, except the United Kingdom.
[8] Especially the Employment Acts 1980, 1982, 1988 and 1990.
[9] In some instances the trade union had the right to put up candidates from its own known unemployed members before any wider recruitment exercise.

to join a recognised trade union within a specific period of starting employment. This was a widespread practice and one not always opposed by employers. In 1978 about 23% of the workforce (about 5.2 million people) worked in locations where there was a closed shop. The advantage for the management of these companies was that they avoided multi-union situations. It was also seen as a source of abuse and as a means of making the trade unions too powerful. Professor Friedrich Hayek, admired by Prime Minister Margaret Thatcher, for example, reflected this view:

> It cannot be stressed enough that the coercion which unions have been permitted to exercise contrary to all principles of freedom under the law is the coercion of fellow workers . . . the coercion of employers would lose most of its objectionable character if unions were deprived of this power to exact unwilling support.[10]

Whether the 'negative right' not to join a trade union can be equated with the 'positive right' to join one is debatable. In *Young, James and Webster v United Kingdom*[11] three employees of British Rail lost their jobs for refusing to join one of the trade unions with whom British Rail had concluded a closed shop agreement. In total, 54 individuals were dismissed for refusing to join one of the trade unions, out of a total workforce of about 250,000. The European Court of Human Rights held that Article 11 CHR had been breached. The majority of the judges concluded that Article 11 did not put the 'negative' aspect of the freedom of association on the same footing as the 'positive' aspect, although a minority of six judges felt that:

> . . . the negative aspect of freedom of association is necessarily complementary to, a correlative of and inseparable from its positive aspect. Protection of freedom of association would be incomplete if it extended to no more than the positive aspect. It is one and the same right that is involved.[12]

This approach is incorporated into section 137(1) TULRCA 1992, which outlaws the refusal of employment on the grounds that a person is or is not a member of a trade union (see below).

11.3 Meaning of a trade union

Section 1(a) TULRCA 1992 defines a trade union as an organisation:

> which consists wholly or mainly of workers of one or more descriptions and whose principal purposes include the regulation of relations between workers of that description or those descriptions and employers or employers' associations.

Similarly it can be an organisation which consists of constituent or affiliated organisations which meet these criteria or an organisation of the representatives of such constituent or affiliated organisations.[13]

Thus a trade union is defined by its membership and its purposes. For example, in *Hopkins v National Union of Seamen*[14] the objects of the union were shown to include the

---

[10] *The Constitution of Liberty* (Routledge & Kegan Paul, 1960).
[11] [1981] IRLR 408 ECHR.
[12] *Ibid* at p 419.
[13] Section 1(b) TULRCA 1992. Section 122 TULRCA 1992 applies the same purpose to employers' associations.
[14] [1984] ICR 268.

promotion and provision of funds to extend the adoption of trade union principles and the improvement of the conditions and protection of the interests of all members of the union. According to the court, this might have been enough to justify payments to the National Union of Mineworkers during the miners' strike of 1984, the justification being either that keeping coal pits open might supply more work for seamen involved in transporting coal or that helping miners' families during the strike might have promoted trade union principles of solidarity.

A list of trade unions is maintained by the Certification Officer (CO)[15] and being on the list is evidence that an organisation is a trade union.[16] An organisation of workers can apply to be included in the list and will need to supply the CO with various materials, including a copy of its rules and a list of its officers.[17] If the CO is satisfied with the information, then the organisation will be added.[18] Conversely the CO may remove an organisation if the CO decides that it is not a trade union or if the organisation so requests it or if the organisation has ceased to exist (for example where two trade unions merge). The CO is required to give 28 days' notice of the intention to remove a name from the list.[19]

11.3.1 Independence

An advantage of being on the list maintained by the CO is that any trade union on it may apply to the CO for a certificate that it is independent.[20] The statutory benefits accruing to trade unions usually go to those that are independent. For example, workers cannot have action taken against them because they seek to join, have joined or have taken part in the activities of such a union (see below). The CO may withdraw the certificate if the CO is of the opinion that the trade union is no longer independent.[21] While in force, the certificate is conclusive proof of independence.[22] Section 5 TULRCA 1992 provides a definition of an independent trade union. There are two tests to be satisfied:

(1) the trade union is not to be under the domination or control of an employer or an employers' association or of a group of employers or employers' associations; and
(2) the trade union is not to be liable to interference by an employer, or any such group or association, which tends towards control.

An organisation that is refused a certificate or has one withdrawn may appeal to the EAT on a question of law.[23]

In *Blue Circle Staff Association v The Certification Officer*[24] the CO outlined the factors used in assessing the independence of an organisation. These were finance, and whether

---

[15] Section 2(1) TULRCA 1992; the CO publishes an annual report containing the list and size of membership; it is available free of charge.
[16] Section 2(4) TULRCA 1992.
[17] Section 3(1) and (2) TULRCA 1992.
[18] Section 3(3) and (4) TULRCA 1992.
[19] Section 4 TULRCA 1992.
[20] Section 6(1) TULRCA 1992.
[21] Section 7(1) TULRCA 1992.
[22] Section 8(1) TULRCA 1992.
[23] Section 9(1) TULRCA 1992.
[24] [1977] IRLR 20.

there was a direct subsidy from the employer; other assistance received, such as free premises, facilities and time off; employer interference; history and the extent to which it has grown away from being a 'creature of management'; rules and the extent to which the employer's senior employees are involved in running it; single company unions are more likely to be under the employer's dominance; organisation; attitude, such as a 'robust attitude in negotiation'. The newness of the Blue Circle Staff Association was a major factor in its failure to gain a certificate.[25]

Interference tending towards control might be as a result of providing financial, material or other support. It is not necessary to show that interference actually takes place, nor is it necessary for the CO to decide on the likelihood of such interference tending towards control. The question for the CO is whether there is a possibility of interference by the employer tending towards control. 'Liable to interference' means 'vulnerable to interference' or being 'exposed to the risk of interference'.[26] This was highlighted in *Government Communications Staff Federation v Certification Officer.*[27] Here a staff association was established at GCHQ after the Government withdrew recognition of the trade unions and banned GCHQ employees from union membership. The EAT concluded that the Staff Federation was equally vulnerable to interference and that its continuing existence depended upon the approval of the Director of the organisation. It therefore supported the CO's refusal to issue a certificate of independence.

11.4 Contract of membership

It is clear that when an individual joins a trade union they enter into a contract of membership. It has not always been entirely clear whether that contract is one that is between the trade union and its members or whether it is one between the members of the trade union. In *Bonsor v Musicians Union*[28] a musician was expelled from the Musicians Union and thereafter found it difficult to obtain work. It was held that, although the trade union was an unincorporated body, it was capable of entering into contracts and being sued as a legal entity, as distinct from its individual members. When Bonsor's application to join was accepted, a contract came into existence with the union. The trade union impliedly agreed that the member would not be excluded by the trade union or its officers otherwise than in accordance with the rules. When the trade union broke this contract by wrongfully expelling the individual, it could be sued as a legal entity. Thus there was no reason why Bonsor should not be granted all the remedies against the union which were appropriate for a breach of contract.

Section 10 TULRCA 1992 gives trade unions a 'quasi corporate status'. The trade union is not a body corporate, except that it is capable of making contracts and suing or being sued in its own name. Any proceedings for an offence alleged to have been committed by it may be brought against it in its own name. Section 11 TULRCA 1992 provides for an exclusion of common law rules on restraint of trade (see Chapter 12).

---

[25] See *Association of HSD (Hatfield) Employees v Certification Officer* [1977] IRLR 261, where an organisation was able to satisfy the EAT of its independence.
[26] See *The Certification Officer v Squibb UK Staff Association* [1979] IRLR 75 CA.
[27] [1993] IRLR 260.
[28] [1956] AC 104.

The contract of membership serves as the constitution of the trade union. The primary source of the contract is the union rule book, which is likely to cover the rights and obligations of individual members, the power and composition of various bodies within the union, the purposes for which union funds can be expended and the powers of union officers. The contract between all the members is embodied in the rules of the union. As was stated in *Wise v Union of Shop, Distributive and Allied Workers*,[29] which concerned a challenge to a decision of the union executive committee concerning elections:

> A decision which is inconsistent with the rules . . . is a decision . . . to which the member has not given his or her consent. The decision has been made or the election held in a manner which contravenes the contract into which the member has entered by joining the union. Accordingly, as it seems to me, the right of a member to complain of a breach of the rules is a contractual right which is individual to that member; although, of course, that member holds the right in common with all other members having the like right.

Thus, by joining a trade union, the member enters into an agreement and joins with all other members in authorising officers or others to carry out certain functions and duties on their collective behalf. The basic terms of the agreement are to be found in the union's rule book.[30]

As with other contracts the terms may be modified by custom and practice, although not so as to conflict with the union's rules, and terms can be implied with caution.[31] However, the rules are not to be treated as if they were written by parliamentary draftsmen:

> The rules of a trade union are not to be construed literally or like statute, but so as to give them a reasonable interpretation which accords with what, in the court's view, they must have been intended to mean, bearing in mind their authorship, their purpose, and the readership to which they are addressed.[32]

In *Iwanuszezak v GMBATU*[33] an individual tried to argue that a trade union had an implied obligation to use its collective strength to safeguard an individual member's terms and conditions. In this case a new agreement between employers and the trade union had rearranged work shift patterns to this individual's detriment. The Court of Appeal refused to imply the term, accepting the argument that where there was a conflict between collective and individual interests, then the collective interests must prevail. In every contract of membership there is also a statutorily implied right for a member to terminate their membership, subject to reasonable notice and reasonable conditions.[34]

There are three areas considered here where statute provides trade union members with rights which they may exercise in relation to their trade union. These are those rights relating to trade union membership and discipline; rights which may be exercised in the event of the trade union not complying with statutory obligations on ballots; and rights concerned with the application of funds for political objects.

---

[29] [1996] IRLR 609 at p 613.
[30] See *Heatons Transport (St Helens) Ltd v TGWU* [1972] IRLR 25 HL.
[31] See *Porter v National Union of Journalists* [1980] IRLR 404 HL.
[32] *Jacques v AUEW (Engineering Section)* [1986] ICR 683.
[33] [1988] IRLR 219 CA.
[34] Section 69 TULRCA 1992.

11.5 Rights in relation to trade union membership and discipline

Until the Industrial Relations Act 1971 there was little statutory regulation limiting a trade union's powers to admit, discipline or expel a member.[35] Section 65 of this Act introduced rules against arbitrary exclusions or expulsions and unfair or unreasonable disciplinary action. Although this section was repealed in 1976, it was reintroduced in the Employment Act 1980 as part of the Government's attack on the closed shop.

11.5.1 Exclusion and expulsion

Currently an individual may not be excluded or expelled from a trade union, except for four specific reasons.[36] (Note that exclusion means not being admitted to membership.[37]) These are:

(1) if the individual does not satisfy an enforceable membership requirement;
(2) if the individual does not qualify for membership on the grounds that the union only operates in a particular part or parts of Great Britain;
(3) if the union's purpose is to regulate the relations with one particular employer, or a number of particular employers, and the individual no longer works for any of those employers;
(4) if the exclusion or expulsion is entirely attributable to the individual's conduct (other than 'excluded conduct') and the conduct to which it is wholly or mainly attributable is not 'protected conduct'.

In the first of these exceptions, the 'enforceable membership requirement' means a restriction on membership as a result of employment being in one specific trade, industry or profession; or of an occupational description such as a particular grade or level; or of the need for specific trade, industrial or professional qualifications or work experience. 'Excluded conduct' means:

(i) being or ceasing to be, or having been or ceased to be, a member of another trade union or employed by a particular employer or at a particular place;
(ii) conduct to which section 65 TULRCA 1992 applies.

'Protected conduct' consists of the individual being or ceasing to be, or having been or ceased to be, a member of a political party. However, activities undertaken as a member of a political party are not protected.

These rules necessitated a revision of the 'Bridlington Principles'. These were a set of recommendations agreed at the 1939 Trades Union Congress which were designed to minimise disputes over membership questions.[38] They laid down the procedures by which the TUC dealt with complaints by one trade union against another and were designed to

---

[35] The Trade Union Act 1913 had established a requirement that a trade union could not refuse admission or discipline solely because of a refusal to contribute to the political fund.
[36] Section 174 TULRCA 1992.
[37] See *NACODS v Gluchowski* [1996] IRLR 252.
[38] For an example of a TUC disputes committee attempting to resolve issues under the Bridlington Principles, see *Rothwell v APEX* [1975] IRLR 375 CA.

stop inter-union disputes over membership and representation. In the light of the legislation to inhibit unions from excluding members, introduced by the Trade Union Reform and Employment Rights Act 1993, these principles were revised. These principles are that:

(1) each union should consider developing joint working arrangements with other unions to avoid such conflicts;
(2) no union should commence activities at an establishment where another trade union had a majority;
(3) there should be no industrial action in an inter-union dispute until the TUC had an opportunity to examine the issue.

Lastly, the revision criticised the Government amendments for removing the right of trade unions to refuse admission. The atmosphere at the time, however, was that trade unions were not to be trusted with such freedom and that legislative controls were necessary.

The courts have not always shared this hostility to trade unions deciding these matters. *Cheall v APEX*[39] involved an individual who was excluded from membership on the orders of the TUC's disputes committee. The relevant union rule stated that 'the executive committee may, by giving 6 weeks' notice in writing, terminate the membership of any member, if necessary to comply with a decision of the disputes committee of the TUC'. The House of Lords rejected the view that this was contrary to public policy. Lord Diplock stated that:

> freedom of association can only be mutual; there can be no right of an individual to associate with other individuals who are not willing to associate with him.

This was clearly not the view of the Government, as shown by its subsequent legislation.[40]

Individuals may present a complaint to an employment tribunal if they have been excluded or expelled in contravention of section 174.[41] The employment tribunal is unable to consider the complaint unless it is presented before the end of six months beginning with the date of exclusion or expulsion, unless the tribunal is satisfied that it was not reasonably practicable for the complaint to be presented in time.[42] Where an employment tribunal finds the complaint to be well founded it will make a declaration to that effect. A subsequent application for compensation can be made to an employment tribunal but, in order to give the trade union time to act, the complainant may not make the application for compensation until after four weeks beginning with the date of the declaration. There is also a limit of six months after which an application cannot be made.[43] If the applicant has not been admitted or readmitted, there is a minimum amount that will be awarded by the EAT of £6,600 (in 2007).

---

[39] [1983] IRLR 215 HL; see also *Edwards v SOGAT* [1971] Ch 354, where a person's right to work in a closed shop was supported by the court.
[40] In *ASLF v UK* [2007] IRLR 361 the European Court of Human Rights ruled that there is no general right to join the union of one's choice irrespective of the rules of the union.
[41] Section 174(5) TULRCA 1992.
[42] Section 175(a) and (b) TULRCA 1992.
[43] Section 176(3) TULRCA 1992.

Compensation can be reduced if the union member is partly at fault. In *Howard v NGA*[44] an individual was dismissed from a job, in a closed shop environment, for not being a member of a trade union. The EAT recognised four heads of compensation: loss of earnings during the period of unemployment, the net loss of earnings resulting from his dismissal, loss of earning opportunity generally as a result of being denied union membership, and non-pecuniary loss. However, the individual had contributed by taking the job in a closed shop organisation whilst an application for union membership was still under consideration. This resulted in compensation being reduced by 15%. In *Saunders v The Bakers, Food and Allied Workers Union*[45] an applicant resigned from the union over a disagreement about an unofficial strike. The individual later reapplied for membership and was refused. An appeal was made to the national executive committee in writing but the individual failed to attend. The application was rejected and, subsequently, an employment tribunal held this action to be an unreasonable refusal of membership. The EAT agreed with the employment tribunal when it stated that the individual could have done more to help themselves by attending the meeting of the national executive committee. Compensation was reduced as a result. Similarly, in *Day v SOGAT 1982*,[46] a member's failure to pay their subscription was not seen as capable of being conduct which contributed to the union's refusal to readmit into membership, so as to justify a reduction in compensation. However, the individual's failure to tell the union that he had a new job, which might have led to the return of the union card, had contributed to the situation and this led to a reduction in the amount of compensation.

It is the trade union's duty to put the member back into the position that they were in before the wrongful expulsion. This might include arranging for the employee to sign a further mandate to authorise the employer to recommence deductions of union subscriptions, rather than placing the onus on the employee to take the initiative.[47]

11.5.2 Discipline

The courts have the role of interpreting the application of union disciplinary rules, often in favour of the individual, especially where the offences are of a broad nature such as being 'detrimental to the interests of the union'. *Esterman v NALGO*[48] considered the application of a rule that stated that 'a member who disregards any regulation issued by the branch, or is guilty of conduct which, in the opinion of the executive committee, renders him unfit for membership, shall be liable to expulsion'. The member concerned had refused to obey an instruction not to help with local election organisation. The member successfully obtained an injunction against the union on the grounds that, in these circumstances, no committee could find the individual guilty of the offence. The court doubted whether the trade union had the power in the first place to stop people doing things outside their normal working hours, or from volunteering for duties.

---

[44] [1985] ICR 101.
[45] [1986] IRLR 16.
[46] [1986] ICR 640.
[47] See *NALGO v Courtney-Dunn* [1992] IRLR 114.
[48] 48 [1974] ICR 625.

Rules which appear to conflict with public policy can be struck out,[49] as can rules requiring action in breach of the rules of natural justice. In *Hamlet v GMBATU*[50] an unsuccessful candidate challenged the election results using an internal procedure. The individual claimed a breach of the rules of natural justice when an appeal committee was composed of some of the same membership as the committee against whose decision the appeal was being made. In this case the court held that the individual had expressly agreed to accept a tribunal with this membership and that an individual 'cannot therefore come bleating to the courts complaining of a breach of natural justice when the contract is carried out expressly according to its terms'. Similarly, in *Losinska v CPSA*,[51] a union president was able to stop the union's executive committee and its annual conference from discussing matters critical of themselves on the grounds that both played a part in the union's disciplinary process. They could not therefore be allowed to condemn the individual until that process had taken place.

Section 64(1) TULRCA 1992 states that an individual who is, or has been, a member of a trade union has the right not to be 'unjustifiably disciplined' by that trade union. A person is disciplined by a trade union if it takes place under the rules of the union or by an official of the union or by a number of persons which include an official.[52] Section 64(2) TULRCA provides a list of six meanings to 'disciplined'. These include expulsion from the union, payment of a sum to the union, depriving them of access to any services or facilities that they would be entitled to by virtue of belonging to the union, encouraging another union or branch not to accept the individual into membership, and subjecting the individual to some other detriment.[53]

Suspension of membership can mean depriving someone of access to the benefits of membership. In *Killorn*[54] an individual was suspended from membership for refusing to cross a picket line. The trade union also sent out a circular naming her, and others, as being suspended for strike-breaking. Both the suspension and the circular were held to be forms of unjustifiable discipline.

The meaning of 'unjustifiably disciplined' is set out in section 65 TULRCA 1992. This provides a list[55] of ten different items of conduct[56] for which any resulting discipline will be 'unjustified'. This conduct includes failing to participate in or support a strike or other industrial action,[57] or indicating a lack of support for, or opposition to, such action; asserting that the union, an official or a representative of it,[58] has contravened, or is

---

[49] 49 See *Lee v Showmen's Guild* [1952] QB 329, where the court could find no evidence that the members had agreed to a rule which gave an internal body exclusive jurisdiction.

[50] [1986] IRLR 293; see also *Radford v National Society of Operative Printers* [1972] ICR 484, where the failure to apply such rules was an issue.

[51] [1976] ICR 473.

[52] Section 64(2) TULRCA 1992.

[53] Section 64(2)(a)–(f) TULRCA 1992.

[54] *NALGO v Killorn and Simm* [1990] IRLR 464.

[55] Section 65(2)(a)–(j) TULRCA 1992.

[56] Conduct includes statements, acts or omissions; section 65(7) TULRCA 1992.

[57] See *Knowles v Fire Brigades Union* [1996] IRLR 617 CA, where the complainants failed to prove unjustifiable discipline because the pressure exerted on employers by the union did not amount to industrial action.

[58] Representative means a person acting or purporting to act in their capacity as a member of the union or on the instructions or advice of a person acting, or purporting to act, in the capacity of an official of the union: section 65(7) TULRCA 1992.

planning to contravene, a requirement under union rules or some other enactment or law;[59] or working with, or proposing to work with, individuals who are not members of the union or who are not members of another union.[60]

An individual who claims to have been unjustifiably disciplined may present a complaint to an employment tribunal within three months of the infringement, unless it was not reasonably practicable for the complaint to be presented in that time.[61] Additionally, if there is a delay resulting from an attempt to appeal against the discipline or have it reviewed or reconsidered,[62] the three-month limit may be extended.[63] This happened in *Killorn*[64] where a letter to the union branch chair, in which the complainant raised a series of questions about the suspension, was held to be a 'reasonable attempt' to appeal in accordance with this section. The EAT held that the statute did not lay down any specific method of appealing, so an employment tribunal should consider the reality of the events, rather than look for formal appeal proceedings. It is also necessary to wait until the union has made a final determination of some form of discipline, such as expulsion, before making the complaint to an employment tribunal. If there is only a recommendation to the general executive committee of a union that an individual be expelled, that cannot be seen as the final decision. It is not possible to make a claim in respect of an act that might never take place, no matter how much the individual thinks it is likely to happen.[65]

The employment tribunal may make a declaration that the complaint is well founded.[66] The applicant may then make an application to the employment tribunal for compensation and repayment of any money unjustifiably paid to the union.[67] The employment tribunal may award compensation in line with that for cases of expulsion or exclusion under section 174 TULRCA 1992 (see above).[68] This can include injury to feelings.[69] It should be noted that the complaint cannot be made before four weeks from the date of the tribunal's declaration and not more than six months beginning with that date.[70]

11.6 Rights in relation to statutory obligations on union elections

Strict statutory rules were introduced during the 1980s concerning the election of certain union officials. The rules stipulated which trade union offices were to be the subject of regular elections, but also laid down detailed rules about how those elections were to be conducted. The Government at the time stated its intentions:

---

[59] A person is not unjustifiably disciplined if the reason is that they made such assertions vindictively, falsely or in bad faith: section 65(6) TULRCA 1992.
[60] See *Santer v National Graphical Association* [1973] ICR 60, where a trade union expelled a member for working for a firm which did not recognise the union.
[61] Section 66(1) and (2) TULRCA 1992.
[62] In *McKenzie v NUPE* [1991] ICR 155 it was held to be an implied term of the contract between the union and the member that a disciplinary tribunal should be entitled to reopen it if new evidence came to light.
[63] Section 66(2)(b) TULRCA 1992.
[64] [1990] IRLR 464.
[65] See *TGWU v Webber* [1990] IRLR 462 and *Beaumont v Amicus* [2007] ICR 341.
[66] Section 66(3) TULRCA 1992; section 66(4) TULRCA 1992 prevents any further proceedings relating to expulsion being brought under this section and section 174 (see above).
[67] Section 67(1) TULRCA 1992.
[68] Sections 67(5)–(7) TULRCA 1992.
[69] See *Bradley v NALGO* [1991] IRLR 159.
[70] Section 67(3) TULRCA 1992.

There must also be a proper balance between the interests of the unions and the needs of the community . . . individual unionists themselves [are] . . . entitled to see minimum standards established to ensure that union power is exercised more responsibly, more accountably and more in accordance with the views of their members.[71]

Section 46(2) TULRCA 1992 lists those positions for which there is a duty to hold elections at least every five years.[72] However, there is no requirement for a ballot if the election is uncontested.[73] The positions are: (i) a member of the executive, or any position held as a result of being a member of the executive; (ii) president; and (iii) general secretary. The executive is defined as the principal committee of the union exercising executive powers.[74] However, a member of the executive includes any person who may attend or speak at meetings of the executive, excluding technical or professional advisers.[75]

According to section 119 TULRCA 1992, presidents and general secretaries are the people that hold those offices or the nearest equivalent to them. Those who hold the position of president on an annual basis and are not voting members of the executive or employees of the union and have not held the position in the 12 months before taking up the position, are excluded from the rules on elections.[76] Similarly, such office holders may stay in office for up to a further six months if they fail to be re-elected. This is a period which may 'reasonably be required' to give effect to the election result and aid the transition between office holders.[77]

No member of the trade union can be 'unreasonably' excluded from standing as a candidate, although the trade union is able to have rules that apply eligibility conditions which are applicable to all members. Thus there is a requirement for objective criteria to be applied in relation to eligibility. *Ecclestone v National Union of Journalists*[78] concerned a rule which provided that 'the NEC [National Executive Committee] shall prepare a shortlist of applicants who have the required qualifications'. The union argued that this rule gave the executive committee a discretion to decide on the qualifications appropriate to the post. In this case they imposed the qualification that the candidates should have the confidence of the NEC. According to the court, this amounted to the exclusion of a class of members which was determined by reference to whom the union chose to exclude. It was essentially a subjective test which was in breach of section 47(3) TULRCA 1992. Good practice requires that selection criteria be laid down in advance of applications so as to avoid arbitrary decisions on particular candidates.

---

[71] *Democracy in Trade Unions* (HMSO, 1983).
[72] Section 46(1)(b) TULRCA 1992, although there is an exception in section 58 for those within five years of retirement age.
[73] Section 53 TULRCA 1992.
[74] Section 119 TULRCA 1992.
[75] Section 46(3) TULRCA 1992. There is a definition of 'voting members of the executive' in section 46(5) TULRCA 1992.
[76] Section 46(4)–(4A) TULRCA 1992.
[77] See *Paul v NALGO* [1987] IRLR 43 CO, where a retiring president who continued on the executive for a further year was held to be covered by the transitional arrangements.
[78] [1999] IRLR 166; see also *Wise v USDAW* [1996] IRLR 609, where it was held that even if much of the rule governing the election of the general secretary was inconsistent with TULRCA, it would be wrong not to give effect to any of it.

No candidate directly, or indirectly, can be required to be a member of a political party.[79] Although it might be understandable for a Conservative Government to impose such a rule on trade unions, it does seem rather an odd one. Presidents or general secretaries of large trade unions are likely to play an active part in the political party to which their union is affiliated. Those trade unions that are affiliated to one political party are affiliated to the Labour Party.

Every candidate may provide an election address and the union will distribute it to all members entitled to vote in the election. This will be done at no expense to the candidates. The union can decide the length of the address, subject to a minimum of 100 words. All candidates are to be treated equally in this matter. Their material cannot be changed without their consent and it is the candidate that incurs any civil or criminal liability arising from the contents of the election address.[80]

The entitlement to vote should be accorded equally to all members, although the rules of the union can exclude certain classes, such as unemployed members, those in arrears with their subscriptions, new members and students, trainees or apprentices.[81] In *NUM (Yorkshire Area) v Millward*[82] an election result was challenged when a group called 'limited members', who were mostly people who had taken early retirement, were excluded from participating. The EAT held that their exclusion was permissible within the union rules, as they were not members for the purpose of voting in ballots. Although they were members of the union and received fringe benefits, they had no right to vote on decisions or stand for office and were only indirect beneficiaries of the purpose of the union.

The trade union will appoint an independent scrutineer[83] to supervise the production of the ballot papers and their distribution to those entitled to vote. As soon as is reasonably practicable after the end of the ballot period the independent scrutineer will make a report to the union.[84] In *Douglas v Graphical, Paper and Media Union*[85] the independent scrutineer issued a certificate stating that there were no reasonable grounds for believing that there had been any breach of statutory requirements relating to the ballot. Subsequently the scrutineer examined a complaint and decided that there had been a breach of the union rules which might have influenced the outcome of the ballot. The union then attempted to set the ballot aside and call a fresh election. The High Court held that in doing this the union was acting outside its powers. There was nothing in its rules that permitted it to do this. It was also doubtful whether it was possible to cancel a ballot once the scrutineer had issued their report approving the ballot.[86]

---

[79] Section 47(1)–(3) TULRCA 1992.
[80] Section 48(1)–(7) TULRCA 1992.
[81] Section 50(1)–(2) TULRCA 1992.
[82] [1995] IRLR 411.
[83] Section 49 TULRCA 1992.
[84] Section 52 TULRCA 1992.
[85] [1995] IRLR 426.
[86] See also *Brown v AUEW* [1976] ICR 147, where a union called a fresh ballot after some irregularities in the voting process. The new election resulted in a different outcome, but the election was held to be outside the union's powers to call.

There are detailed rules on the voting process contained within section 51 TULRCA 1992. The essential features are that it is to be done by marking a ballot paper; the ballot is, as far as is reasonably practicable, to be conducted by post; at no cost to the individual member; the ballot should, as far as is reasonably practicable, enable votes to be cast in secret. In *Paul v NALGO*[87] the union was held to be in breach of the rule that there should be no cost to the member. Arrangements were made for the ballot papers to be collected from the union district organisers. The responsibility of getting their completed ballot paper to the district organiser was placed on the individual member. If a member did not wish to use that system, then the cost of sending the vote in was left to that member.

The ballot is to be conducted so as to enable the result to be determined solely by counting the votes cast for each candidate.[88] This does not necessarily mean that those with the highest votes get elected. For example, if there are rules which state that there is a maximum number of elected representatives for each region, then it will be those with the highest votes in that region who are elected. It does not matter that an unsuccessful candidate in one region might have gained more votes than a successful candidate in another region.[89] In *AB v CD*[90] two candidates gained identical numbers of votes in an election using the single transferable vote system. The rules did not have any provision for such an eventuality. The court implied a term into the union's standing orders that the candidate with the most votes in the initial voting should be declared the winner.

The remedy for a failure to comply with the statutory requirements is for a person who was a member of the trade union at the time of the election, or a person who was a candidate in the election, to make a complaint, within one year of the election result being announced, to the Certification Officer (CO) or to the High Court.[91] If the application is to the CO,[92] in accordance with section 55 TULRCA 1992, then the CO has an obligation to ensure, so far as is reasonably practicable, that the matter is determined within six months.[93] On receiving the application the CO will make inquiries and give the applicant and the trade union the opportunity to be heard.[94] The CO may then make a declaration specifying where the trade union has failed to comply, giving reasons for the decision in writing.[95] This declaration may be accompanied by an enforcement order requiring a new election or rectification of the fault or a requirement to abstain from specified acts in the future.[96] A declaration or enforcement order made by the CO may be relied upon as if it were an order of the court.[97] Appeals on points of law arising from complaints dealt with by the CO are to the EAT.[98]

---

[87] [1987] IRLR 43 CO.
[88] Section 51(6) TULRCA 1992, although section 51(7) allows for the single transferable vote system to be used.
[89] See *R v CO, ex parte Electrical Power Engineers' Association* [1990] IRLR 398 HL.
[90] [2001] IRLR 808.
[91] Section 54(1)–(3) TULRCA 1992.
[92] Similar provisions concerning applications to the court are dealt with in section 56 TULRCA 1992.
[93] Section 55(6) TULRCA 1992.
[94] Section 55(2) TULRCA 1992.
[95] Section 55(3) and (5) TULRCA 1992.
[96] Section 55(5A) TULRCA 1992.
[97] Section 55(8) and (9) TULRCA 1992.
[98] Section 56A TULRCA 1992.

11.7 Rights related to the application of funds for political objects

The funds of a trade union cannot be used for the furtherance of political objects unless a political resolution is in force. The political resolution needs to be supported by a majority of those voting and needs to be approved at least every ten years.[99] The process of the ballot and the rules governing it are similar to those concerned with ballots for the election of union officials (see above).[100] An individual member of a trade union may give notice that they object to contributing to the political fund and section 84(1) TULRCA 1992 contains an example of such a notice. When a political resolution is adopted all members must be given notice of their right to be exempted and where they can obtain a form of exemption.[101] The employee can certify to their employer that they are exempted from such contributions, and the employer must then ensure that no deductions are made for that part of the subscription which applies to the political fund.[102]

There also need to be provisions in the union rules for the making of such payments out of a separate fund and for the exemption of any member of the union who objects to contributing to that fund.[103] Section 72 TULRCA 1992 provides some definitions of expenditure for political objects. These are:

(1) any contributions[104] to the funds of a political party, or the payment of expenses incurred directly or indirectly by a political party;
(2) the provision of any service or property for use by, or on behalf of, a political party;
(3) in connection with the registration of electors or the candidature of any person, including the holding of a ballot by the union in connection with any election;
(4) on the maintenance of any holder of a political office;[105]
(5) the holding of a conference or meeting by, or on behalf of, a political party, including any meetings whose main purpose is the transaction of business in connection with a political party; this includes, according to section 72(2) TULRCA 1992, any expenditure incurred by delegates to the conference or meeting;[106]
(6) on the production, publication or distribution of any literature, document, film, sound recording or advertisement concerned with persuading people to vote, or not to vote, for a particular candidate[107] or political party.

---

[99] Section 73 TULRCA 1992.
[100] See sections 75–81 TULRCA 1992.
[101] From the trade union or the CO; see section 84(2) TULRCA 1992.
[102] Section 86 TULRCA 1992; this applies only if the employer is deducting subscriptions on behalf of the trade union.
[103] Section 71(1) TULRCA 1992.
[104] Contribution includes affiliation fees or loans made to a political party: see section 72(4) TULRCA 1992.
[105] Political office means the office of Member of Parliament, Member of the European Parliament, or a member of a local authority or any position within a political party: see section 72(4) TULRCA 1992.
[106] See *Richards v NUM* [1981] IRLR 247, where this was held to include the cost of sending delegates and a colliery band to a lobby of Parliament organised by the Labour Party to protest at government cuts.
[107] Candidate also includes 'prospective candidates': see section 72(4) TULRCA 1992.

A number of these issues were tested in *ASTMS v Parkin*,[108] where decisions of the CO were appealed against. The appeals related to donations made by the trade union and are indicative of how strictly the line between the union's general funds and the political fund are drawn. The donations considered here were a contribution from the union's general fund towards the development of the property then used by the Labour Party as its headquarters and a donation from the general fund to the Leader of the Opposition's office at Parliament. The contribution towards the Labour Party offices was done at commercial rates and, the union argued, was a commercial investment. The EAT supported the CO's conclusions that, despite their commercial nature, they were still payments to a political party and fell within the political objectives as set out in what is now section 72 TULRCA 1992. Similarly, the EAT supported the CO in deciding that the donation to the Opposition Leader's office should not have been made out of the general fund. The maintenance referred to the legislation refers to the support of someone as a politician. The union had argued that this interpretation gave too wide a meaning to the term but the EAT held that maintenance covered expenses incurred in carrying out the functions of being a Member of Parliament. Thus a grant to an MP to enable them to conduct research for the purpose of carrying out parliamentary functions is maintenance as an MP and should come out of the political fund.

A trade union having its own views on political issues and campaigning for them may not be involved in political activities as defined in the statute. *Coleman v Post Office Engineering Union*[109] concerned an affiliation fee of £8 to a District Trades Council campaign against government cuts. The CO decided that 'political' meant 'party political'. It was difficult to draw the line between these two concepts but the legislation applied to support of some kind to a political party or to candidates of political parties.

A member of a trade union who wishes to claim that the trade union has misapplied its funds in breach of section 71 TULRCA 1992 may apply to the CO for a declaration to this effect.[110] Where the CO makes a declaration the CO may order for the breach to be remedied.[111] The CO's declaration may be relied upon as if it were a declaration of the court.[112] If the employer fails to comply with section 86 TULRCA 1992, the individual may make a complaint to an employment tribunal within three months of the date of the payment, unless the tribunal accepts that this was not reasonably practicable.[113] The employment tribunal may make a declaration and/or an order to remedy the failure of the employer. If the employer fails to comply with the order then the individual may make a further complaint to the tribunal after four weeks and before six months. The tribunal may then order the employer to provide the claimant with up to two weeks' pay.[114]

---

[108] [1983] IRLR 448.
[109] [1981] IRLR 427.
[110] Section 72A(1) TULRCA 1992.
[111] Section 72A(4) TULRCA 1992.
[112] Section 72A(7) TULRCA 1992.
[113] Section 87(1)–(8) TULRCA 1992.
[114] Subject to the definition of a week's pay contained in section 225 ERA 1996.

11.8 Breach of rules

Apart from any common law action for breach of contract, a member of a trade union[115] may apply to the CO for a declaration that there has been a breach, or threatened breach, of rules relating to certain matters.[116] The matters affected are:

(1) the appointment or election (or the removal) of a person from any office;
(2) disciplinary proceedings by the union (including expulsion);
(3) the balloting of members on any issue other than industrial action;
(4) the constitution or proceedings of the executive committee or any other decision-making committee;[117]
(5) any other matters specified by the Secretary of State.[118]

Specifically excluded are the dismissal of an employee of the union or any disciplinary proceedings against such an employee.[119] The application must normally be made within six months from the day in which the breach or alleged breach took place. Alternatively, if an internal appeals procedure is invoked, within six months of the end of that procedure or within one year of the invocation of that procedure.[120] A person may not make a complaint both to the CO and the court but may appeal to the courts against the CO's decisions[121] and to the EAT on points of law.[122]

The CO may decline the application unless satisfied that the applicant has taken all available steps to make use of the internal complaints procedure. Thereafter the CO may make whatever inquiries the CO thinks fit and give the applicant and the trade union the right to be heard. The CO may make a declaration with written reasons and may make an enforcement order to remedy the breach and take such action necessary to stop such a breach happening in the future.

11.9 Discrimination against members and officials

11.9.1 Compilation of lists of members

Section 3(1) ERELA 1999 enables the Secretary of State to make regulations prohibiting the compilation of lists which contain details of trade union members, or persons who have taken part in the activities of trade unions, with a view to being used by employers or employment agencies for the purpose of discrimination in relation to recruitment and treatment of workers. Worker is given a wide meaning and includes those who work under a contract personally to do or perform any work or services for another,[123] and specifically

---

[115] Or was a member at the time of the alleged breach: section 108(3) TULRCA 1992.
[116] Section 108A TULRCA 1992.
[117] Definitions are provided by section 108A(10)–(12) TULRCA 1992.
[118] Section 108A(2) TULRCA 1992.
[119] Section 108A(5) TULRCA 1992.
[120] Section 108A(6)–(7) TULRCA 1992.
[121] Section 108A(14) TULRCA 1992.
[122] Section 108B(9) TULRCA 1992.
[123] See section 230(3) ERA 1996.

includes agency and home workers.[124] A list includes any index or set of items whether recorded electronically or otherwise.[125] At the time of writing no regulations have been issued.

11.9.2 Refusal of employment

Part III TULRCA 1992 deals with refusal of employment related to membership of any trade union or membership of a particular trade union.[126] This part contains a number of measures designed to prevent employers or trade unions introducing measures related to a closed shop. Thus it is unlawful to refuse employment for belonging to, or not belonging to any trade union or a particular trade union. Pressure exerted by a trade union may also result in the union being joined to any employment tribunal proceedings and being liable to pay compensation (see below). Employment for these purposes means employment under a contract of employment.[127]

There is not a rigid dividing line between membership of a trade union and taking part in its activities. Thus an applicant who is refused employment because of trade union activities with a previous employer may have been refused because of their membership of a trade union.[128] Any requirements that a person must take steps to join a trade union or make payments in lieu connected with membership or non-membership are also unlawful.[129] Persons offered employment on these conditions who refuse it because they do not meet the conditions, or are unwilling to meet the conditions, are to be taken as being refused employment for those reasons.[130] Previous practices of putting trade union membership requirements in advertisements or recruiting from trade union nominations only are also unlawful.[131]

A person is taken to have been refused employment if, in seeking employment of any description, the potential employer: refuses or deliberately fails to entertain and process the application or inquiry; causes the person to withdraw or cease to pursue the application or inquiry; refuses or deliberately omits to offer employment of that description; makes an offer of such employment on terms which no reasonable employer would offer if they wished to fill the post (and the offer is not accepted); makes an offer of employment, but withdraws it or causes it not to be accepted.[132] Section 138 TULRCA 1992 applies similar rules in respect of employment agencies.

Where a person is refused employment for a reason related to trade union membership they may make a complaint to an employment tribunal.[133] The complaint needs to be made within three months of the date of the conduct which is complained about, unless the

---

[124] Sections 3(5) and 13 ERELA 1999.
[125] Section 3(5) ERELA 1999.
[126] Section 143(3) TULRCA 1992.
[127] Section 143(1) TULRCA 1992.
[128] See *Harrison v Kent County Council* [1995] ICR 434; also *Fitzpatrick v British Railways Board* [1991] IRLR 376 CA which concerned dismissal for previous trade union activities (see below).
[129] Section 137(1)(b) TULRCA 1992.
[130] Section 137(6) TULRCA 1992.
[131] Section 137(3) and (4) TULRCA 1992; section 143(1) gives a wide meaning to the term 'advertisement'.
[132] Section 137(5) TULRCA 1992.
[133] Section 137(2) TULRCA 1992.

tribunal accepts that it was not reasonably practicable to do so.[134] The date of various types of conduct is defined in section 139(2) TULRCA 1992:

(1) in the case of an actual refusal of employment, it is the date of that refusal;
(2) in the case of a deliberate omission to entertain or process the application, then the date is the end of a period in which it was reasonable to expect the employer to act;
(3) in the case of conduct causing the applicant to withdraw or stop pursuing an application or inquiry, the date is when that conduct took place;
(4) in the case when the offer was made and then withdrawn, the date is when it was withdrawn;
(5) in any other case where an offer is made, but not accepted, then the date is when the offer was made.[135]

If an employment tribunal finds that a complaint is justified, then it may award compensation and/or make a recommendation that the employer takes action within a specified period which appears to be reasonable to obviate or reduce the adverse effects on the complainant of the conduct complained of.[136]

11.9.3 Subject to detriment

Section 146 TULRCA provides for workers not to be subject to detriment by any act, or deliberate failure to act, if the act or failure to act takes place for the purpose of:

(1) preventing and deterring them from seeking to become a member of a trade union,[137] or penalising them for doing so;
(2) preventing or deterring them from taking part in the activities of the trade union or from making use of trade union services at an appropriate time, or penalising them for doing so;
(3) compelling them to be or become a member of a trade union, or a particular trade union.[138]
(4) enforcing a requirement that in the event of their failing to become, or their ceasing to remain, members of any trade union or a particular trade union or one of a number of particular trade unions, they must make one or more payments. For this purpose, any deduction from remuneration which is attributable to the employee's failure to become, or his or her ceasing to be, a trade union member will be treated as a detriment.

Where either party claims that the employer acted under pressure from a third party, for example, a trade union, they may request that the third party be joined to the proceedings. In these circumstances the tribunal may require that any compensation be paid by the third party.[139]

---

[134] Section 139(1) TULRCA 1992.
[135] Section 138 TULRCA 1992 applies similar provisions to actions and omissions by employment agencies.
[136] Section 140 TULRCA 1992; section 141 applies similar provisions in respect of employment agencies.
[137] In *Ridgway and Fairbrother v National Coal Board* [1987] IRLR 80 CA, it was held that this can mean either an individual trade union or any trade union.
[138] Section 146(1) TULRCA 1992.
[139] Section 142 TULRCA 1992.

It is not always easy to identify when the purpose of an act or omission falls within section 146. For example, *Gallagher v Department of Transport*[140] concerned an individual who was elected group assistant secretary of a trade union. The individual was a higher executive officer in the civil service, but, with the employer's approval, the trade union duties were effectively full-time. When the individual applied for promotion to the next grade, he was turned down. Previously, in an appraisal, the employee had been told of problems with management skills. As a result of being a trade union assistant secretary, it was said that there was no way of telling whether these skills had improved. The job also required more management experience than could be gained by being a trade union activist. The employment tribunal agreed that there had been discrimination on the grounds of trade union membership and activities. However, the Court of Appeal held that the tribunal had confused cause and effect. The purpose of the promotion procedure was to ensure that those promoted had management skills, not to deter the employee from continuing with trade union activities, although this may have been the effect.[141]

The detriment is to be interpreted as action against workers as individuals rather than as trade unionists. In *FW Farnsworth Ltd v McCoid*[142] an individual was derecognised by the employer as a shop steward. Mr McCoid claimed that this was action in breach of section 146(1)(b) TULRCA 1992. The Court of Appeal held that the words 'as an individual' were inserted into the legislation to exclude collective disputes from the scope of the section, neither did the words mean an individual in their capacity as an employee or a representative of a trade union. The complainant here was an individual who happened to be a shop steward and so the employer's action was held to be against him as an individual and thus unlawful.[143]

'Penalising' is given a wide meaning and is to be interpreted as subjecting an individual to a disadvantage.[144] Indeed, it is specifically provided that penalising a worker because an independent trade union raises a matter on the member's behalf (with or without the member's consent) falls within the ambit of section 146 TULRCA 1992. 'Activities' can mean the organising of meetings at an appropriate time. In *British Airways (Engine Overhaul) Ltd v Francis*[145] the employee was a shop steward whose members had an ongoing grievance concerning equal pay. They organised a meeting during their lunch break. It was not a formal meeting of the branch or of a committee of the union and the discussion was critical of the union. Nevertheless it was held to be an activity of an independent trade union. 'Trade union services' means the services made available to the worker by virtue of union membership and 'making use' includes consenting to the raising of a matter by the union on his or her behalf.[146]

---

[140] [1994] IRLR 231 CA.
[141] See also *Southwark London Borough Council v Whillier* [2001] ICR 142, where a union branch secretary was offered promotion, but no salary increase until she had taken up the new duties; this was held to be a detriment because the individual would have to give up her trade union duties in order to take on these responsibilities.
[142] [1999] IRLR 626 CA.
[143] See also *Ridgway and Fairbrother v National Coal Board* [1987] IRLR 80 CA, which was distinguished in this case.
[144] See *Carlson v Post Office* [1981] IRLR 158, where the withdrawal of a car parking permit was sufficient to penalise an individual.
[145] [1981] ICR 278.
[146] Section 146(2A) TULRCA 1992.

'Appropriate time' means either a time outside working hours or a time within working hours where 'in accordance with arrangements agreed with or consent given' by the employer, it is permissible to take part in union activities or make use of union services. 'Working hours' means any time, in accordance with the contract of employment, that the individual is required to be at work.[147] This does not necessarily require the express agreement of an employer and arrangements can be of an informal nature.[148] If workers are able to converse while working and discuss trade union membership and activities, there is no reason why an employment tribunal could not come to the conclusion that there was implied consent or implied arrangements for them to talk about trade union activities.[149] Additionally, being at work is not necessarily the same as working. An employee is entitled to take part in trade union activities whilst on the employer's premises, but not actually working.[150] Thus tea breaks might be occasions when an employee is being paid, but is not necessarily at work.[151]

A worker may make a complaint to an employment tribunal if they have been subjected to a detriment contrary to section 146 TULRCA 1992.[152] The complaint needs to be made within three months of the act or failure to which it relates. If there is a series of acts or failures, then the three months runs from the last of them.[153] There is the usual proviso that where the tribunal is satisfied that it was not reasonably practicable to do so, then the period may be extended.[154] In the absence of evidence to the contrary the employer shall be taken to have decided on a failure to act when they do an act inconsistent with the failed act or when a period expires when they might reasonably be expected to have done the failed act, if it was going to be done.[155] The burden of proof is on the employer to show the purpose of the act or the failure to act.[156]

If the tribunal finds the complaint well founded, then it may award compensation. Any compensation must have regard to any loss suffered by the complainant as a result of the act or failure complained of. This loss will include any expenses reasonably incurred as a result of the act or failure plus the loss of any benefit which the complainant may reasonably be expected to have received but for the act or failure. It may also include compensation for injury to feelings.[157] Compensation is to be seen as compensation to the employee for the injury sustained, not as a punishment of the person who commits the injury.[158] The complainant has a duty to mitigate their losses and the tribunal may take

---

[147] Section 146(2) TULRCA 1992.
[148] See *Marley Tiles Co Ltd v Shaw* [1978] IRLR 238.
[149] See *Zucker v Astrid Jewels Ltd* [1978] IRLR 385.
[150] See *Post Office v Union of Post Office Workers* [1974] IRLR 23 HL.
[151] *Zucker v Astrid Jewels Ltd* [1978] IRLR 385.
[152] Section 146(5) TULRCA 1992. However, this does not apply to employees who have been dismissed (see below).
[153] In *Adlam v Salisbury and Wells Theological College* [1985] ICR 786 continued weekly payments of a disputed settlement were held not to be a series of similar actions.
[154] Section 147(1) TULRCA 1992.
[155] Section 147(3) TULRCA 1992.
[156] Section 148(1) TULRCA 1992.
[157] See *London Borough of Hackney v Adams* [2003] IRLR 402 where £5,000 was awarded for injury to feelings after the withdrawal of an offer of promotion.
[158] See *Brassington v Cauldon Wholesale Ltd* [1977] IRLR 479.

into account any contributory action by the worker towards causing the act or failure complained of.[159]

11.9.4 Inducements relating to membership or activities

Employers may try to influence decisions of individuals, about joining a trade union, in other ways. One such interesting case was *Associated Newspapers v Wilson*,[160] where the employer ceased to recognise the trade union for negotiating purposes and encouraged employees to agree individual contracts. Those that did not agree were given a smaller pay rise than those that did. The question was whether this omission was action aimed at deterring employees from being members of a trade union. The House of Lords held that the action was not for this purpose but was designed merely to end collective bargaining. The European Court of Human Rights,[161] however, disagreed and held that:

> such conduct constituted a disincentive or restraint on the use by employees of union membership to protect their interests.

As a result there was a failure in a State's positive obligation to secure rights under Article 11 of the Convention.

Section 145A TULRCA 1992 now provides workers with the right not to have an offer made to them by their employer for the sole or main purpose of inducing them:

 (i) not to be or seek to become a member of an independent trade union, or
 (ii) not to take part in the activities of an independent trade union or make use of union services at an appropiate time, or
 (iii) to be or become a member of any trade union at a particular time.[162]

In addition, section 145B TULRCA 1992 gives members of independent trade unions which are recognised or seeking to be recognised the right not to have an offer made to them if acceptance of the offer would have the 'prohibited result' and the employer's sole or main purpose is to achieve that result. The 'prohibited result' is that any of the worker's terms of employment will not (or no longer) be determined by collective agreement. Claims under section 145A or 145B TULRCA 1992 must be brought within the usual three-month time period; and it will be for the employer to show the main purpose in making the offers.[163] If a complaint is upheld the employment tribunal must make a declaration to that effect and award £2,700 (in 2007) to the complainant. It is also provided that if an offer made in contravention of section 145A or 145B is accepted, the employer cannot enforce the agreement to vary terms.[164]

---

[159] Section 149 TULRCA 1992.
[160] [1995] IRLR 258 HL; section 298 TULRCA 1992 also defines act or action as including omission.
[161] [2002] IRLR 568 ECHR.
[162] 'Appropriate time', 'trade union services' and 'working hours' have the same meaning as in section 146 TULRCA 1992 (see above).
[163] Sections 145C and 145D TULRCA 1992. An employee must first submit a statement of grievance to the employer: paragraphs 6 and 9 Schedule 2 Employment Act 2002.
[164] Section 145E TULRCA 1992.

11.9.5 Dismissal on grounds related to membership or activities

A dismissal will be unfair if the reason or the principal reason for it was that the employee: (i) was, or proposed to become, a member of a trade union; (ii) had taken part, or proposed to take part, in the activities of a trade union or make use of union services at an appropriate time; (iii) was not a member of a trade union, or had refused or proposed to refuse to become a member; (iv) had failed to accept an offer in contravention of section 145A or 145B (see 11.9.4 above).[165] Similarly, if one of the reasons in section 152(1) TULRCA 1992 is a reason for an individual being selected for redundancy, then this is also likely to be an unfair dismissal.[166] The dismissal of an employee on the basis of trade union activities with a previous employer, when that decision was because of a fear by the employer of future trade union activities by the employee, may also be a breach of section 152 TULRCA 1992.[167]Another example of an employee suffering dismissal as a result of their trade union activities is an individual who spoke on behalf of the trade union at a company recruitment meeting and made derogatory remarks about the company.[168]

The reasons in section 152(1) are inadmissible for the purposes of Part X ERA 1996, therefore such a dismissal will be automatically unfair. Section 108 ERA does not apply so there is no requirement for a qualifying period of service.[169] Where there is a dismissal by virtue of section 152(1) or 153 TULRCA 1992, then there is a basic minimum award of compensation, before any reductions under section 122 ERA 1996.[170]

An employee who presents a complaint to an employment tribunal that they have been dismissed by virtue of section 152 may also apply to the tribunal for interim relief. This application must be made within seven days of the effective date of termination.[171] If the application is in connection with becoming a member of a trade union or taking part in the activities of a trade union[172] then the tribunal will require a certificate signed by an authorised official[173] stating that the individual was or proposed to become a member of the union and there appeared to be reasonable grounds for the complaint.[174] The tribunal has an obligation to determine the application for interim relief as soon as practicable after receiving it and, where appropriate, the certificate. The employer[175] will be given a copy of the notice and certificate at least seven days before the hearing.[176] The tribunal will ask the employer whether they will reinstate or re-engage the employee. If the answer is yes, the tribunal will make an order accordingly. If the employer fails to attend or refuses

---

[165] Section 152(1) TULRCA 1992. 'Appropriate time', 'working hours' and 'trade union services' have the same meaning as in section 146 (see above).
[166] Section 153 TULRCA 1992; see also *Driver v Cleveland Structural Engineering Co Ltd* [1994] IRLR 636.
[167] *Fitzpatrick v British Railways Board* [1991] IRLR 376 CA.
[168] *Bass Taverns Ltd v Burgess* [1995] IRLR 596.
[169] Section 154(1) and (2) TULRCA 1992.
[170] Section 156 TULRCA 1992 (£4,200 in 2007). If the dismissal is unfair by virtue of section 153, then section 156(2) (reduction for contributory fault) applies.
[171] Section 161(1) and (2) TULRCA 1992.
[172] Section 152(1)(a)–(b) TULRCA 1992.
[173] Authorised official is an official of the trade union authorised by it to act for these purposes: section 161(4) TULRCA 1992.
[174] Section 161(3) TULRCA 1992.
[175] And any party joined to the proceedings: section 160 TULRCA 1992.
[176] Section 162 TULRCA 1992.

to reinstate or re-engage, then the tribunal can make an order for continuance of the employee's contract of employment.[177] If the employer fails to comply, then the tribunal will award compensation to the employee having regard to the infringement of the employee's right to reinstatement or re-engagement and any loss suffered by the employee as a result of the non-compliance.[178]

Further reading

Barrow, C., *Industrial Relations Law* (Cavendish, 2002), Chapters 1–7.
Collins, H., Ewing, K. and McColgan, A., *Labour Law: Text and Materials* (Hart Publishing, 2005), Chapters 7 and 8.
Deakin, S. and Morris, G., *Labour Law* (4th edn, Hart Publishing, 2005), Chapters 8 and 10.
www.ilo.org
www.tuc.org.uk

Visit **www.mylawchamber.co.uk/sargeant** to access legal updates, live web links and practice exam questions to test yourself on this chapter.

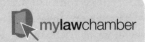

---

[177] Sections 163 and 164 TULRCA 1992.
[178] Section 166 TULRCA 1992.

12

Collective Bargaining and Industrial Action

12.1 The trade union role

Any discussion about the relevance, historical or otherwise, of trade unions will include an analysis of the inequalities of the relationship between employer and employee. Whilst the law of contract regards the parties to the contract as being equal and as having willingly entered into a contractual arrangement, the reality is somewhat different. It is only a privileged few that are able to negotiate and agree their terms and conditions of employment. For most the choice is represented by being offered a job by an employer, with associated terms and conditions of employment, and deciding whether to take it or leave it. For many, even this choice may be absent. If there is little alternative employment to be had, then the economic realities for individuals may mean that they have no choice but to accept the contract offered to them.

To some extent, the inequalities in the employment relationship are levelled out by workers joining trade unions that can negotiate with employers on equal terms:

> This system of collective bargaining rests on a balance of the collective forces of management and organised labour . . . However, the common law knows nothing of the balance of collective forces. It is (and this is its strength and its weakness) inspired by a belief in the equality (real or fictitious) of individuals; it operates between individuals and not otherwise.[1]

Perhaps because of the traditional influence of trade unions and the perceived importance of wage levels by governments in their attempts to regulate the economy, collective bargaining and the agreements that are reached are subject to statutory definition.

12.2 Collective agreements

Collective bargaining is a means of achieving a collective agreement. In statutory terms it means any agreement or arrangement made between trade unions and employers relating to a number of specific issues.[2] These issues relate to:

(1) terms and conditions of employment;
(2) engagement, non-engagement, termination or suspension of one or more workers;
(3) allocation of work or duties between workers;

---

[1] Otto Kahn-Freund, *Labour and the Law* (Stevens, 1972).
[2] Section 178(1) TULRCA 1992; the issues included are listed in section 178(2).

(4) matters of discipline;
(5) membership or non-membership of a trade union;
(6) facilities for officials of trade unions;
(7) the machinery for negotiation or consultation.

Sometimes these last two items are treated as a separate 'facilities agreement' between management and trade unions. It should be noted that a collective agreement may be as a result of negotiations in a formal setting or it might be the result of deliberations of a joint consultative committee or other committee which makes recommendations.[3]

12.2.1 Legal enforceability and incorporation

For historical reasons, trade unions have been suspicious of the intervention of the law in industrial relations and, although there is the opportunity for trade unions to enter into legally binding agreements with employers, few actually do so. Collective agreements are presumed not to be legally enforceable contracts, unless the agreement is in writing and contains a provision which states that the parties intend the agreement to be a legally enforceable contract.[4] Any agreement which does satisfy these provisions will be 'conclusively presumed to have been intended by the parties to be a legally enforceable contract'.[5] It is also possible to enter into an agreement where only part is designated as being legally enforceable. In such circumstances the part which is not legally enforceable may be used in interpreting the part that is.[6]

The intentions of the parties appear to be crucial and unless that intention to enter into a legally enforceable agreement is clear, then there is likely not to be such an agreement. The collective agreement needs to show that, at the very least, the parties have directed their minds to the issue of legal enforceability and have decided in favour of such an approach. Without this there will be an insufficient statement of intent for the purposes of the statute.[7] The court may take into account the surrounding circumstances and even the general climate of opinion about this issue when the agreement is made. In *Ford Motor Co Ltd v Amalgamated Union of Engineering and Foundry Workers*[8] the court found the generally unanimous climate of opinion as relevant. It cited (from Flanders and Clegg) an extract[9] which described the general view at the time:

> This appears to be the case with collective agreements. They are intended to yield 'rights' and 'duties', but not in the legal sense; they are intended, as it is sometimes put, to be 'binding in honour' only, or (which amounts to very much the same thing) to be enforceable through social sanctions but not through legal sanctions.

---

[3] See *Edinburgh Council v Brown* [1999] IRLR 208, which concerned a local authority joint consultative committee.
[4] Section 179(1) TULRCA 1992.
[5] Section 179(2) TULRCA 1992.
[6] Section 179(4) TULRCA 1992.
[7] See *National Coal Board v National Union of Mineworkers* [1986] IRLR 439, which concerned whether a 1946 agreement on consultation was legally binding; the court held that there would need to be evidence that the parties had at least directed their minds to the question and decided on legal enforceability.
[8] [1969] 2 QB 303.
[9] A. Flanders and H. Clegg, *The System of Industrial Relations in Britain* (Blackwell, 1954), p 56.

This view that collective agreements are binding in honour and are subject to social sanctions, rather than legal sanctions, still reflects the climate of opinion.

It is possible for the terms of collective agreements to become legally binding through the route of incorporation into the individual contract of employment (see also Chapter 4). This can be achieved expressly or impliedly. Express incorporation is most effectively achieved by including a term of the contract of employment which refers to the collective agreement.[10] If a collective agreement is not expressly incorporated in this way or by some other form of agreement, then the courts may be prepared to give it legal effect via implied incorporation. It is possible that this may be done on the basis of custom and practice but the collective agreement would need to be well-known and established practice and to be 'clear, certain and notorious'.[11]

Alexander v Standard Telephones & Cables Ltd[12] concerned a claim that a redundancy procedure had become incorporated into individuals' contracts of employment. The High Court summarised the principles to be applied in deciding whether there had been incorporation of a part of the collective agreement. These were as follows:

(1) the relevant contract is that between the individual employee and the employer;
(2) it is the contractual intention of these two parties that needs to be ascertained;
(3) in so far as that intention is found in the written document, then the document must be construed on ordinary contractual principles;[13]
(4) if there is no such document, or if it is unclear, then the contractual intention has to be inferred from other available material, including the collective agreement.

In *Kaur v MG Rover Ltd*[14] it was held that a provision in a collective agreement stating that there would be 'no compulsory redundancy' was not incorporated. According to the Court of Appeal, in conjunction with the words of incorporation, it is necessary to consider whether any particular part of the document is apt to be a term of a contract of employment. Looking at the words in their context, it was decided that they were expressing an aspiration rather than a right. However, the fact that a document is presented as a collection of 'policies' does not preclude their having a contractual effect if, by their nature and language, they are apt to be contractual terms. Thus a provision which is part of a remuneration package may be apt for construction as a contractual term even if couched in terms of information or explanation, or expressed in discretionary terms. Provisions for enhanced redundancy pay would seem to be particularly appropriate for incorporation.[15]

---

[10] See *Whent v T Cartledge* [1997] IRLR 153, in which the issue was whether the national agreement had transferred to a new employer as a result of regulation 6 Transfer of Undertakings Regulations 1981, SI 1981/1794 (see Chapter 10).

[11] *Duke v Reliance Systems Ltd* [1982] IRLR 347; in *Henry v London General Transport Services Ltd* [2002] IRLR 472 CA the court held that there is no requirement for 'strict proof' of custom and practice; the burden is on the balance of probabilities.

[12] [1991] IRLR 286.

[13] See also *Lee v GEC Plessey Telecommunications* [1993] IRLR 383, where the court considered whether consideration had passed from the employees for the enhanced redundancy terms contained in a collective agreement which was incorporated into the contract of employment.

[14] [2005] IRLR 40.

[15] *Keeley v Fosroc Ltd* [2006] IRLR 961.

Once the collective agreement has become incorporated into the contract it is not open to the employer unilaterally to alter it.[16] It is only when terms are altered by agreement that individual contracts of employment can be lawfully varied. If the collective agreement is unilaterally varied or the employer withdraws from it, the contracts of employment containing the provisions are likely to remain intact.[17] The possible exception to this is when there are provisions which allow the employer to vary the terms. If there is a collective agreement which allows an employer to vary part of the contents unilaterally, then the fact that it has become part of the contract of employment will not inhibit this option.[18] One issue here is whether the employer's authority is limited as a result of an agreement reached mutually with employee representatives. In *Cadoux v Central Regional Council*[19] an employer introduced rules after consultation with the relevant trade unions. This consultation was different from an agreement and the employers retained the right to alter their own rules.

Employees are assumed to know of the contents of a collective agreement negotiated with a trade union. In *Gray Dunn & Co Ltd v Edwards*[20] an employee was dismissed only three weeks after the signing of an agreement which included the provision that being at work whilst under the influence of alcohol was a serious misdemeanour which could result in summary dismissal. The EAT stated that there could be no stability in industrial relations if an employee could claim that an agreement did not apply to them on the basis that they had not heard of it or its contents. This suggests that the trade union is acting as the agent of the member in reaching an agreement with an employer that becomes part of the contract of employment. The problem with this approach is, of course, that non-union members would not be bound by such an agreement as the trade union could not act as their agent.[21] Such an approach has not been followed, but it does raise an interesting question in relation to employees who are not members of the trade union with whom the collective agreement is negotiated. In *Singh v British Steel Corporation*[22] a group of employees had not received any document which indicated that their system of working could be changed by the employer without consulting them or by consulting a trade union, whether or not they belonged to it. At the time that the employers negotiated a new shift arrangement these particular employees were not members of the trade union concerned. Neither did the employment tribunal find it possible to imply any term entitling the employer to vary the contract. Without an express or implied term binding the individuals to the collective agreement, the variation in working arrangements could not be said to apply to them. The effect is similar to an employer's unilateral variation.

In certain situations the courts are willing to be assertive in their remedies. *Anderson v Pringle of Scotland Ltd*[23] concerned a decision about whether an agreed 'last in first out'

---

[16] See *Gibbons v Associated British Ports* [1985] IRLR 376.
[17] See *Robertson and Jackson v British Gas Corporation* [1983] IRLR 302; also *Gascol Conversions Ltd v JW Mercer* [1974] IRLR 155 CA which concerned conflicting national and local agreements.
[18] See *Airlie v City of Edinburgh District Council* [1996] IRLR 516.
[19] [1986] IRLR 131.
[20] [1980] IRLR 23.
[21] See *Heatons Transport (St Helens) Ltd v TGWU* [1972] IRLR 25 HL.
[22] [1974] IRLR 131.
[23] [1998] IRLR 64.

redundancy procedure should be followed as a result of incorporation or whether the employer could introduce a different selection method. In order to stop the employees being made redundant under the new procedure the court was willing to grant an interdict (injunction) restraining the employers from changing the selection procedure, even though this might amount to an order for specific performance. In this case the court felt that there was still no lack of trust and confidence in the employee by the employer. There may also be some judicial reluctance to fill gaps in collective agreements. Thus where a collective agreement leaves a topic uncovered the inference is not that there has been an omission so obvious as to require judicial intervention. The assumption should be that it was omitted deliberately for reasons such as the item being too controversial or too complicated.[24]

12.3 Recognition

Recognition of a trade union or trade unions by an employer or employers is defined in section 178(3) TULRCA 1992. It means recognition for the purposes of collective bargaining and, therefore, is likely to be recognition in respect of one or more of the items listed in section 178(2) (see above). Recognition need not be for the purposes of all these items, but can be partial in the sense that it is only for specific purposes. It appears to require a positive agreement between the parties:

> An act of recognition is such an important matter involving such serious consequences on both sides, both for the employers and the union, that it should not be held to be established unless the evidence is clear upon it, either by agreement or actual conduct clearly showing recognition.[25]

It would be difficult for a trade union to claim implied recognition if the employer had expressly refused recognition for collective bargaining purposes. Recognition is not given because the employer responds to points raised by union representatives, neither is it to be implied from the fact that a union provides health and safety representatives or is a member of a national body, which is not the employer, that is concerned with terms and conditions of employment.[26]

Recognition implies that an employer is willing to recognise a trade union as the legitimate representative of the workforce. There are a number of benefits which accrue to the union as a result of this recognition. There are rights associated with: being given time off for trade union duties and activities;[27] consultation over a number of matters, for example, transfers of undertakings, collective redundancies and health and safety matters; and the disclosure of information for collective bargaining purposes.[28]

Prior to the ERELA 1999, the decision as to whether to recognise a trade union belonged to the employer.[29] Perhaps as a result of this the majority of workplaces in the United Kingdom have no coverage by collective agreement at all.

---

[24] See *Ali v Christian Salvesen Food Services Ltd* [1997] IRLR 17 CA.
[25] *National Union of Gold, Silver & Allied Trades v Albury Brothers Ltd* [1978] IRLR 504 CA at p 506.
[26] See *Cleveland County Council v Springett* [1985] IRLR 131.
[27] See sections 168–170 TULRCA 1992.
[28] See sections 181–184 TULRCA 1992.
[29] An exception to this is in the Transfer of Undertakings Regulations 2006, SI 2006/246, where regulation 6 provides for any trade union recognition by the transferor to be transferred to the transferee. This seems a rather strange requirement as it is then open to the transferee to exercise the right to derecognise the union.

12.3.1 A legal framework

There have been previous attempts at government intervention to ensure that recognition disputes were settled without disruption. The Industrial Relations Act 1971 was a Conservative Government's attempt to provide a comprehensive legal framework for industrial relations. It allowed employers, trade unions and the Government to refer recognition disputes to a Commission for Industrial Relations.[30] This body was able to make recommendations on whether a union should be recognised for a particular bargaining unit. The legislation largely failed because of the unwillingness of the trade unions to co-operate. The Employment Protection Act 1975, passed by a Labour Government, changed the approach. Section 11 allowed an independent trade union to apply to ACAS to resolve a recognition dispute. ACAS was allowed to organise a workforce ballot and then make recommendations for recognition.[31] Failure to follow an ACAS recommendation could lead to a referral to the CAC, which could then make an award on the terms and conditions that might have been agreed if those negotiations had taken place. This award would be incorporated into the contracts of employment of the employees concerned.[32] This process had only limited success. Between 1976 and 1980 there were 1,610 referrals to ACAS of which some 82% were resolved voluntarily without resort to the section 11 procedure.

A number of problems were associated with the Employment Protection Act 1975 and inhibited its success. First, some employers refused to co-operate. In one dispute, concerning Grunwick Processing Laboratories Ltd, the employers refused to supply ACAS with the names and addresses of their employees, which resulted in ACAS being unable to carry out its statutory duty under section 14(1) Employment Protection Act 1975 to ascertain the views of the employees. The result was that the recognition process was thwarted.[33] Secondly, there were difficulties in dealing with inter-union disputes, where more than one trade union claimed recognition on behalf of a group of workers. In *Engineers' and Managers' Association v ACAS*[34] there was just such a dispute between two unions. ACAS had deferred its decision on recognition and the House of Lords upheld its right to do so if the deferral would help promote good industrial relations. Thirdly, there were problems associated with defining acceptable bargaining units which would also help foster good industrial relations. ACAS had to deal with situations where there was a demand for representation within a particular unit, but fragmentation of larger units into smaller ones might not be conducive to better industrial relations.[35] Finally, there were problems associated with the length of time the process took[36] and with employers attempting to influence the outcome of the recognition ballots.

All these problems have been addressed in the statutory recognition procedures contained in Schedule A1 TULRCA 1992. An awareness of these potential problems is

---

[30] See *Ideal Casements Ltd v Shamsi* [1972] ICR 408 on the effect of the legislation in a dispute over recognition.
[31] Sections 14 and 15 Employment Protection Act 1975.
[32] Section 16 Employment Protection Act 1975.
[33] See *Grunwick Processing Laboratories Ltd v ACAS* [1978] 1 All ER 338 HL.
[34] [1980] ICR 215 HL.
[35] See *ACAS v United Kingdom Association of Professional Engineers* [1980] IRLR 124 HL.
[36] *Ibid.*

important in understanding the reasons for some of the procedures contained in the schedule.

12.3.2 Statutory recognition

Section 70A TULRCA 1992 gives effect to Schedule A1 which is concerned with the recognition of trade unions for collective bargaining purposes. Collective bargaining here has a more limited meaning than that contained in section 178 TULRCA 1992 (see above). For the purpose of statutory recognition, collective bargaining means, unless otherwise agreed by the parties, negotiations concerned with pay, hours and holidays only.[37] However, 'pay' does not include terms relating to a person's membership of or rights under, or the employer's contributions to, either an occupational or personal pension scheme.[38]

The schedule was brought into effect on 6 June 2000.[39] The procedures contained in it for claiming recognition are long and complex. Below is a summary of the essentials of part of the recognition process, which shows the underlying principles. The principles underlying the procedures are that:

(1) the measures apply to independent trade unions only (see Chapter 11);[40]
(2) trade unions will need to demonstrate 'baseline support';[41]
(3) the subsequent vote must demonstrate widespread support;[42]
(4) the bargaining unit needs to be clearly defined;[43]
(5) there are exceptions for small businesses;[44]
(6) there is a right to derecognition;[45]
(7) the time that the process will take should be clear.[46]

12.3.2.1 The request for recognition[47]

The process must begin with the trade union or unions seeking recognition making a request for recognition to the employer.[48] This request must be in writing, it must identify the union or unions concerned and the bargaining unit. It must also state that the request is made under Schedule A1.[49] However, an application is inadmissible if there is already in force a collective agreement under which the employer recognises another union as entitled to conduct collective bargaining on behalf of the workers concerned.[50] If more than one union is applying for recognition the applications will not be admissible unless

---

[37] Schedule A1 paragraph 3 TULRCA 1992.
[38] Schedule A1 paragraph 171A TULRCA 1992.
[39] Employment Relations Act 1999 (Commencement No 6 and Transitional Provisions) Order 2000, SI 2000/1338.
[40] Schedule A1 paragraph 6 TULRCA 1992.
[41] Schedule A1 paragraph 13(5) TULRCA 1992 for a description of 'the 10% test'.
[42] Schedule A1 paragraph 29 TULRCA 1992.
[43] Schedule A1 paragraphs 18–19F TULRCA 1992.
[44] Schedule A1 paragraph 7 TULRCA 1992.
[45] See Schedule A1 Part IV TULRCA 1992.
[46] See, e.g., Schedule A1 paragraph 10(6) and (7) TULRCA 1992.
[47] Derecognition is covered by similar provisions contained in Schedule A1 Parts IV–VI TULRCA 1992.
[48] Schedule A1 paragraph 4 TULRCA 1992.
[49] Schedule A1 paragraph 8 TULRCA 1992.
[50] See Schedule A1 paragraph 35 TULRCA 1992 and *R v Central Arbitration Committee* [2006] IRLR 54.

the unions show that they will co-operate with each other and that, if the employer so wishes, they will enter into collective bargaining arrangements which ensure that they will act together.[51]

Schedule A1 paragraph 7 provides the exception for small businesses. The employer, together with any associated employers, needs to employ at least 21 workers on the day the request for recognition is received, or an average of 21 workers over the 13 weeks ending with this day.

12.3.2.2 Parties agree

There are clearly defined periods of time in which events should take place, which are contained in Schedule A1 paragraph 10(6) and (7). The first period is one of ten working days commencing on the day after the employer received the request for recognition. The second period commences on the day after the first period ends and lasts for 20 working days or such longer time as the parties agree.

Thus, if before the end of the first period the parties agree on the bargaining unit and that the trade union is to be recognised, then there are no further steps to be taken under this schedule. If the employer informs the union, before the end of the first period, that they do not accept the request, but are willing to negotiate, then they may do so. Providing that they reach agreement before the end of the second period, no further steps will need to be taken under this Schedule.

12.3.2.3 Employer rejects request or negotiations fail

If, by the end of the first period, the employer has either failed to respond to the request or has rejected the request and refused to negotiate, then the union may apply to the CAC[52] for the determination of two questions. These are:

(1) whether the proposed bargaining unit is appropriate;
(2) whether the union or unions has or have the support of the majority of workers in the proposed bargaining unit.[53]

If the negotiations have not succeeded by the end of the second period, then the union or unions may apply to the CAC for the determination of the same two questions. Additionally, if the parties agree on the bargaining unit, but fail to agree on whether the union or unions should be recognised to represent it, then the union may only apply to the CAC for an answer to the second question on whether it has the majority support of the workers in that bargaining unit.[54]

There is some pressure on the trade union to negotiate as well as the employer. If, within the first period of ten days, the employer requests the help of ACAS during the negotiations and the unions reject that help or fail to accept the employer's proposal for the help of ACAS, then the union will lose its right to put the questions to the CAC.[55]

---

[51] Schedule A1 paragraph 37 TULRCA 1992.
[52] In the year 2006/7 the CAC received 64 applications concerning trade union recognition under Schedule A1 Part I. See CAC Annual Report 2006/7.
[53] Schedule A1 paragraph 11(1) and (2) TULRCA 1992.
[54] Schedule A1 paragraph 12(1)–(4) TULRCA 1992.
[55] Schedule A1 paragraph 12(5) TULRCA 1992.

12.3.2.4 Acceptance of application[56]

The CAC must give notice of receipt of an application. The CAC must decide, within the 'acceptance period', whether any of the applications received fulfil the 10% test, contained in Schedule A1 paragraph 14(5) TULRCA 1992. This test is satisfied if at least 10% of the workers constituting a relevant bargaining unit are members of the trade union applying for recognition. The acceptance period is ten working days from the receipt of the last application or such longer period as the CAC specifies, giving reasons. If the 10% test is satisfied by more than one applicant union or none of them, the CAC will not proceed. There is a clear message that there needs to be baseline support for one trade union and that the CAC is not the body to decide which union is to be given recognition where more than one meet this basic test. If the CAC decides that one union meets the test, then it will proceed with that union.

12.3.2.5 Appropriate bargaining unit[57]

Once the CAC has decided to accept an application it has an obligation to try to help the parties to reach agreement as to what the appropriate bargaining unit is, if they have not already agreed. This must be done within 20 working days, starting with the day after that on which the CAC has given notice of acceptance, or a longer period specified by the CAC by notice and with reasons.[58] After the end of this period the CAC has ten days in which it must decide on the appropriate bargaining unit, or a longer specified period by notice and with reasons.[59]

There is a set of criteria contained in Schedule A1 paragraph 19B (2)–(3), which the CAC must use in arriving at its decision. These are the need for the bargaining unit to be compatible with effective management and, so far as they do not conflict with that need:

(1) the views of the employer and the trade union or unions;
(2) existing national and local bargaining arrangements;
(3) the desirability of avoiding small or fragmented bargaining units within an undertaking;
(4) the characteristics of the workers falling within the proposed bargaining unit and any other workers the CAC considers relevant;
(5) the location of the workers.

It is expressly provided that the CAC must take into account the employer's view about any other bargaining unit it considers would be appropriate.[60]

In *Graphical, Paper and Media Union v Derry Print Ltd*[61] an application was made to the CAC seeking recognition for all production workers employed by the two different companies. Both companies had the same majority shareholder, operated in the same premises and interchanged employees. In considering the most appropriate bargaining

---

[56] Schedule A1 paragraphs 13–15 TULRCA 1992.
[57] Schedule A1 paragraphs 18–19F TULRCA 1992.
[58] Schedule A1 paragraph 18(2) but note also paragraphs 18(3)–(7) TULRCA 1992. Paragraph 18A introduced a duty on employers to supply information to the union.
[59] Schedule A1 paragraphs 19(2) and (4) and 19A(2) and (4) TULRCA 1992.
[60] Schedule A1 paragraph 19(4) TULRCA 1992. See *R v CAC ex parte Kwik-Fit Ltd* [2002] IRLR 395.
[61] [2002] IRLR 380 CAC.

unit, the CAC was faced with the choice of deciding whether there should be separate units or whether one should cover all the production workers of both companies. Despite 'employer' being referred to in the singular throughout the schedule, the CAC held that a bargaining unit that covered both employers would be appropriate. It concluded that the two companies had a long history of separate incorporation, but:

> We consider, however, that the power to lift the veil [of incorporation] in respect of a sham is not intended as a form of punishment but relies on the conclusion that the reality of unity is concealed by the technical appearance of separation . . . This is an exceptional situation, in which the two companies are managed in the interests of asset utilisation and are inextricably intertwined.

12.3.2.6 Union recognition[62]

Once the issue of the bargaining unit is resolved, the CAC may then move on to the question of recognition. If it is satisfied that the majority of the workforce in the bargaining unit are members of the union or unions, the CAC will issue a declaration that the union or unions are recognised for collective bargaining purposes.[63] However, this will not be done if any one of three qualifying conditions are met. These are that:

(1) a ballot will be in the interests of good industrial relations;
(2) the CAC has credible evidence from a significant number of union members within the bargaining unit that they do not want the union or unions to conduct collective bargaining on their behalf;
(3) evidence is produced that leads the CAC to conclude that a significant number of union members within the bargaining unit do not wish to be represented by the union or unions.[64]

If any of these qualifying conditions are met the CAC will give notice to the parties that it intends to organise a ballot to discover whether the workers in the bargaining unit wish the union or unions to conduct collective bargaining on their behalf. The cost of the ballot is to be borne half by the employer and half by the union or unions.

The ballot must be conducted by a qualified and independent person appointed by the CAC.[65] It will take place within 20 working days starting with the day after the independent person is appointed or longer if the CAC so decides. The CAC may decide whether to organise a workplace ballot or a postal ballot, or a combination of the two. It will determine the method by taking into account the likelihood of a workplace ballot being affected by unfairness or malpractice and the costs and practicality of the alternatives, as well as any other factors it considers appropriate.[66]

There are five duties placed upon an employer who has been informed that a ballot is to take place. These are:

(1) to co-operate generally in connection with the ballot, with the union or unions and with the person appointed to conduct the ballot;

---

[62] Schedule A1 paragraphs 20–29 TULRCA 1992.
[63] See *Fullarton Computer Industries Ltd v Central Arbitration Committee* [2001] IRLR 752.
[64] Schedule A1 paragraph 22(4) TULRCA 1992.
[65] See the Recognition and Derecognition Ballots (Qualified Persons) Order 2000, SI 2000/1306 which names a number of suitable persons, such as the Association of Electoral Administrators.
[66] Schedule A1 paragraph 25 TULRCA 1992.

(2) to give the union or unions access to the workforce constituting the bargaining unit for the purposes of informing them about the ballot and seeking their support. The Government Code of Practice recommends that the parties reach an access agreement which will include the union's programme for when, where and how it will access the workers and will also provide a mechanism for resolving disagreements;[67]

(3) to provide the CAC, within ten working days, with the names and home addresses of the workers concerned and to inform the CAC subsequently of the names and addresses of any new workers or those who cease to be employed;

(4) to refrain from making workers an unreasonable offer which has or is likely to have the effect of inducing them not to attend a meeting between the union and the workers in the bargaining unit;

(5) to refrain from taking any action solely or mainly on the grounds that a worker attended or took part in a meeting between the union and workers in the bargaining unit or indicated an intention to attend or take part in such a meeting.[68]

If the employer fails in any of these duties the CAC may order the employer to take steps to remedy the situation within a certain time. If the employer fails to comply with this order, then the CAC may cancel the ballot and declare the union or unions recognised for the purposes of collective bargaining in respect of the bargaining unit.[69]

Once the result of the ballot is known the CAC must inform the parties of the result. If the ballot result is that the union is supported by a majority of the workers voting and at least 40% of the workers constituting the bargaining unit, then the CAC will declare the union recognised. If the result is otherwise, the CAC will issue a declaration stating that the union is not recognised.

12.3.2.7 Consequences of recognition[70]

If the CAC has made a declaration for recognition, the parties have a 'negotiation period' to agree a method by which they will conduct collective bargaining. This negotiation period is 30 working days starting with the day after they have been informed of the declaration, or a longer period if the parties agree. If the parties do not agree in the period then they can ask the CAC for assistance. The CAC will assist for a period of 20 working days or longer, with the agreement of the parties, if the CAC so decides. After this period, if the parties still fail to agree, the CAC will specify the method.[71] Unless the parties agree otherwise, this specified method will have the effect of being a legally binding contract, which can be enforced through an order for specific performance. If, however, the parties negotiate and agree a method of collective bargaining between themselves and one party fails to keep to the agreement, then they may apply to the CAC for assistance. The CAC

---

[67] Code of Practice on Access to Workers during Recognition and Derecognition Ballots, issued under section 203 TULRCA 1992; the code imposes in itself no legal obligations, but any of its provisions may be taken into account in any proceedings before the CAC or any court or tribunal: section 207 TULRCA 1992.

[68] Schedule A1 paragraph 26 TULRCA 1992. See Schedule A1 paragraph 27A TULRCA 1992 on unfair practices in relation to recognition ballots.

[69] Schedule A1 paragraph 27 TULRCA 1992.

[70] Schedule A1 paragraphs 30–32 TULRCA 1992.

[71] In specifying the method the CAC will take into account in exercising its powers the method specified in the Trade Union Recognition (Method of Collective Bargaining) Order 2000, SI 2000/1300.

will then treat the parties in the same way as if they had failed to reach agreement in the first place.[72]

If the CAC has declared that the unions should not be recognised, then those same unions cannot apply again within a period of three years if the bargaining unit remains substantially the same.[73]

12.3.2.8 Changes affecting the bargaining unit

Schedule A1 Part II TULRCA 1992 is concerned with providing the CAC with similar powers for situations where the parties have entered into voluntary arrangements and agreed on recognition and the bargaining unit. Part III is concerned with the issue of a changing bargaining unit which can have important consequences for the recognition process. If the employer or the union or unions believe that the original bargaining unit is no longer appropriate they may apply to the CAC to make a decision as to what is an appropriate unit. The CAC will consider such an application only if it decides that the original unit is no longer appropriate because there has been: a change in the organisation or structure of the business; a change in the activities pursued by the employer; or a substantial change in the number of workers employed in the original unit. The CAC will then decide on whether the original unit is still appropriate. If it decides that it is not, then it will decide which new unit is appropriate. If necessary it will then repeat the process of assessing whether a union or unions passes or pass the membership test and proceeding to a new ballot.

12.3.2.9 Detriment and dismissal

Schedule A1 Part VIII TULRCA 1992 provides protection from detriment by any act, or failure to act, of the employer if it takes place, or fails to take place, on the grounds that the worker:

(1) acted with a view to obtaining or preventing recognition of a union;
(2) indicated support or lack of support for recognition;
(3) acted with a view to securing or preventing the ending of bargaining arrangements;
(4) indicated support or lack of support for the ending of bargaining arrangements;
(5) influenced, or sought to influence, the way votes were cast;
(6) influenced, or sought to influence, other workers to vote or abstain;
(7) voted in such a ballot;
(8) proposed to do, failed to do, or proposed to decline to do any of the above.[74]

A ground does not fall within these categories if it constitutes an unreasonable act or omission by the worker.[75] The only remedy is a complaint to an employment tribunal[76] within three months of the act or failure to act to which the complaint relates, or such

---

[72] See *UNIFI v Union Bank of Nigeria plc* [2001] IRLR 712.
[73] Schedule A1 paragraph 40 TULRCA 1992; the same rule applies to derecognition claims by employers: see Schedule A1 paragraph 121 TULRCA 1992.
[74] Schedule A1 paragraph 156(2) TULRCA 1992.
[75] Schedule A1 paragraph 156(3) TULRCA 1992.
[76] Schedule A1 paragraph 156(5) and (6) TULRCA 1992.

further period as the tribunal considers reasonable.[77] If the tribunal finds the complaint well founded it may make a declaration and award compensation, which may be reduced if the employee contributed in any way to the action complained of.[78]

The same grounds are contained in Schedule A1 paragraph 161 in relation to dismissal, with the same proviso that a reason does not fall within these grounds if it constitutes an unreasonable act or omission by the employee. Thus a dismissal for any of these reasons will be automatically unfair for the purposes of Part X ERA 1996. If a worker who is not an employee is dismissed, compensation would be subject to the same rules as those for employees who are unfairly dismissed.[79] Similarly, dismissal for reasons of redundancy will be an unfair dismissal if the grounds are any of those listed above.[80]

12.3.2.10 Training

If a trade union has become recognised as a result of the process in Schedule A1 and the method of collective bargaining has been specified by the CAC, then the employer is under an obligation to invite the trade union to send representatives to a meeting to discuss the employer's policy on the training of workers, together with training plans over the next six months, as well as reporting to them on training since the previous meeting.[81] These meetings are to take place at least every six months and there is an obligation to disclose information in advance[82] (see below on disclosure of information generally). The employer is also obliged to take into account any written representations about matters raised at a meeting, which are received by the employer within four weeks of the meeting.[83] Failure to fulfil these obligations in relation to a bargaining unit will enable the trade union to make a complaint to an employment tribunal. If it finds the complaint well founded, the tribunal may make a declaration and award compensation up to a maximum of two weeks' pay per individual.[84]

12.4 Prohibition of union recognition requirements

Despite these new rules enabling a trade union to obtain recognition against an employer's wishes, the provisions stopping recognition being a condition of a contract with a third party remain. Section 186 TULRCA 1992 provides that a term or condition of a contract for the supply of goods and services is void in so far as it requires recognition of a trade union or unions for collective bargaining purposes or to the extent that it requires the other party to negotiate with or consult an official of a trade union or unions. Neither is it permissible to refuse to deal with a supplier or prospective supplier on the grounds that the supplier will not recognise a trade union or negotiate or consult with one.[85] A person

---

[77] Schedule A1 paragraph 157 TULRCA 1992.
[78] Schedule A1 paragraph 159 TULRCA 1992.
[79] Schedule A1 paragraph 160 TULRCA 1992.
[80] Schedule A1 paragraph 162 TULRCA 1992.
[81] Section 70B(1) and (2) TULRCA 1992.
[82] Section 70B(3) and (4) TULRCA 1992.
[83] Section 70B(6) TULRCA 1992.
[84] Section 70C(4) TULRCA 1992; a week's pay is subject to the limit in section 227(1) ERA 1996.
[85] Section 187(1) TULRCA 1992.

refuses to deal with a supplier by failing to include them on a list of approved tenderers, or by excluding them from tendering, or by stopping them from tendering or by terminating a contract for the supply of goods or services.[86] The obligation to comply with this section is to be interpreted as owing a duty to the adversely affected party.[87]

12.5 Disclosure of information

A natural consequence of the recognition of a trade union by an employer is the need for both parties to have sufficient information about the undertaking for them to be able to bargain effectively. That there needs to be a statutory requirement, albeit a weak one, to ensure that information is disclosed to the trade union by the employer is an indication that not all employers have regarded it as important that the trade unions with whom they negotiate should be kept informed. One may equally surmise that there have been trade union negotiators who, at times, have not wished to know about the employer's financial position, in order to press their claims for a pay rise, regardless of the consequences for the employer.

Section 181(1) TULRCA 1992 provides a general duty for an employer, who recognises an independent trade union, to disclose certain information for the purposes of all stages of collective bargaining. The duty relates to the categories of workers for whom the trade union is recognised as representing for collective bargaining purposes. The information must be disclosed to representatives of the union, who are defined as officials or other persons authorised by the union to carry on such bargaining. According to *R v Central Arbitration Committee, ex parte BTP Oxide Ltd*[88] these provisions contemplate that there may be alternative types of relationship between employers and unions, rather than just collective bargaining that entitled a union to information. These alternatives might be:

- bargaining between employers and unions which does not amount to collective bargaining because it does not deal with matters referred to in section 181(2) TULRCA 1992;
- dealings between employers or unions which do not amount to collective bargaining because they cannot properly be called negotiations;
- collective bargaining which does not attract the right to information because it is not about matters in respect of which the union is recognised for collective bargaining. In this case the union concerned unsuccessfully asked for information about a job grading structure for which it had representational rights, rather than negotiating rights.

The information to be disclosed is that which relates to the employer's undertaking and is in its possession.[89] There is a twofold test to decide the relevance of the information. It must be:

(1) information without which the trade unions would be 'to a material extent impeded in carrying out collective bargaining';

---

[86] Section 187(2) TULRCA 1992.
[87] Section 187(3) TULRCA 1992.
[88] [1992] IRLR 60.
[89] Section 181(2) TULRCA 1992; employer also includes associated employers.

(2) information the disclosure of which 'would be in accordance with good industrial relations practice'.

There is an ACAS Code of Practice on the disclosure of information to trade unions for collective bargaining purposes.[90] Paragraph 11 of this Code provides examples of information which might be relevant in certain collective bargaining situations. These examples are information relating to the undertaking about pay and benefits, conditions of service, manpower, performance and finances. Although the ACAS Code is an important guide, it does not exclude other evidence that might be in accord with good industrial relations practice.[91] The request for information by the trade union must be in writing, if the employer so requests, as must the employer's reply, if requested by the trade union.[92]

An employer is not required to disclose information if the disclosure:[93]

(1) would be against the interests of national security;
(2) could not be disclosed without contravening a statutory prohibition;
(3) has been communicated to the employer in confidence;
(4) relates specifically to an individual, unless the individual has consented;
(5) could cause substantial injury to the undertaking, other than its effect on collective bargaining;
(6) is information obtained for the purpose of bringing, prosecuting or defending any legal proceedings.

This list of exceptions clearly undermines the effectiveness of the legislation. The confidentiality clause, for example, could result in important and relevant information not being disclosed to a trade union. In *Sun Printers Ltd v Westminster Press Ltd*[94] a widely circulated document about the future of a company was held not to be confidential, but it was suggested by Donaldson LJ, *obiter*, that the stamping of the word 'confidential' on the document would have been enough to allow wide circulation, whilst retaining confidentiality. Perhaps of more concern to trade unions is the difficulty in obtaining pay information concerning parts of a business that are put out to competitive tender. In *Civil Service Union v CAC*[95] a trade union was stopped from obtaining information about a tenderer's proposed wage rates on the basis that they were given in confidence and that it was information the lack of which could not be held to impede, to a material extent, the union's ability to carry out collective bargaining.

There are further limitations, on the obligations of employers to disclose information, contained in section 182(2) TULRCA 1992:

(1) an employer is not required to produce any documents or extracts from documents unless the document has been prepared for the purposes of conveying or confirming the information;

---

[90] Originally introduced in 1977; it was last updated in 1997 and was brought into effect by the Employment Protection Code of Practice (Disclosure of Information) Order 1998, SI 1998/45; for the effect of failing to comply with the Code, see section 207 TULRCA 1992.
[91] Section 181(4) TULRCA 1992.
[92] Section 181(3) and (5) TULRCA 1992.
[93] Section 182(1) TULRCA 1992.
[94] [1982] IRLR 292 CA.
[95] [1980] IRLR 253.

(2) the employer is not required to compile or assemble any information which would involve an amount of work or expenditure out of proportion to the value of the information in the conduct of collective bargaining.

All these exceptions place important limitations on the right of trade unions to make employers disclose information. Indeed, it is significant that during the period of the 1980s and early 1990s, when Conservative Governments were introducing legislation to limit the power of trade unions, this particular piece of legislation remained untouched.

The remedy for failure to disclose information to trade unions is to make a complaint to the CAC. The CAC will refer the matter to ACAS if it thinks that there is a reasonable chance of a conciliated settlement. If this fails, the CAC will decide whether the complaint is well founded. Where it does so, then the employer is given a period of not less than a week to disclose the information. If the employer still fails to disclose, then the trade union may present a further complaint to the CAC, who will decide if the complaint is well founded and specify the information in respect of which it made that decision.[96] The CAC may then make an award in respect of the employees specified in the claim. This award will consist of the terms and conditions being negotiated and specified in the claim, or any other terms and conditions which the CAC considers appropriate. These terms and conditions can only be for matters in which the trade union is recognised for collective bargaining purposes.[97]

The ineffectiveness of this legislation is illustrated by the fact that between 1976 and 1997 the CAC received 463 disclosure of information complaints, which was an average of 22 per annum. In the year to 31 March 2007 only 11 complaints were received.[98]

12.6 Industrial action – trade union immunities

It is not appropriate in this book to provide a history of the struggles of individuals and groups to be allowed to join trade unions. Nevertheless, it is worth remembering that, until the latter part of the nineteenth century, it was the criminal law that was used against employees who combined and/or took industrial action in defence of their collective rights. Employees were prosecuted for such offences as obstruction, intimidation and conspiracy. The turning point came in the 1870s with the passing of a number of statutes, notably the Trade Union Act 1871 and the Conspiracy and Protection of Property Act 1875, which protected members of trade unions from the common law doctrine of 'restraint of trade'.

The 1875 Act was a landmark in that it provided immunities from prosecution for those involved in trade disputes. Like subsequent legislation, it did not abolish the offences for which one could be prosecuted. Rather it provided immunity from prosecution if the 'offence' was committed 'in contemplation or furtherance of a trade dispute'. Subsequent protection has followed the pattern of providing immunities, rather than offering positive rights to individuals. In some other Member States of the EU, such as France and

---

[96] Section 184 TULRCA 1992.
[97] Section 185 TULRCA 1992.
[98] See CAC Annual Report 2006/7.

Germany, there are constitutions which provide a right for individuals to join trade unions and take part in industrial action. These 'positive rights' are to be contrasted with the 'negative rights' approach in the United Kingdom. Workers do not have positive rights to take part in industrial action; rather they have protection if they do so. The distinction is important because it has allowed the courts and various governments to remove or change the degree of protection provided.

A classic example of this was in *Taff Vale Railway Co v Amalgamated Society of Railway Servants*.[99] This case arose out of a strike in support of an individual alleged to have been victimised by the employer. The trade union organised pickets to stop the employer bringing in non-union labour. The employers applied to the court for an injunction against the union leaders and the union itself. This latter move was a novel one in that it had been assumed that the unions themselves could not be sued in this way for the actions of their officials. Lord Macnaughton stated:

> Has the legislature authorised the creation of numerous bodies of men capable of owning great wealth and acting by agents with absolutely no responsibility for the wrongs they may do to other persons by the use of that wealth and the employment of those agents? In my opinion, Parliament has done nothing of the kind.

Thus trade unions were immediately put at risk if they took industrial action. In this case, damages and fines on the union amounted to £42,000 which, in 1902, amounted to two-thirds of its annual income.

A Royal Commission in 1903 led to the Trade Disputes Act 1906, which provided protection for acts done in 'contemplation or furtherance of a trade dispute'. It provided, in section 4, that an action in tort could not be brought against a trade union for acts of its members or officials, even though carried out on its behalf. It also provided immunity for a person who induced another to break a contract of employment and immunity against a possible tort of interference with trade, business or employment of another person. This Act was to be the foundation of future legislation on industrial action.

12.7 Common law torts

The common law has traditionally regarded a strike as a breach of the contract of employment and the calling or organising of a strike as an inducement to another to breach the contract of employment. The courts have developed a number of torts to limit the actions of workers, both individually and collectively. One perspective is to regard the history of the law regarding industrial action as a series of steps by the courts to introduce new torts to make individuals and unions liable, with the State stepping in from time to time to limit the worst excesses of the judiciary by providing some statutory immunity to individuals and unions for actions in contemplation or furtherance of a trade dispute. These liabilities in tort include the following.

---

[99] [1901] AC 426.

12.7.1 Inducing a breach of contract

This tort derives from the case of *Lumley v Gye*.[100] It involved an opera singer, Miss Johanna Wagner, who was induced by a theatre manager to breach her contract with one theatre in order to appear at the defendant's own theatre. The court held that each party has a right to the performance of the contract and that it was wrong for another to procure one of the parties to break it or not perform it.

An inducement to breach an employment contract is when a trade union, for example, instructs its members to take strike action against their employer. Without further intervention the employer may have a case against the trade union for inducing its employees to breach their contracts of employment. A direct inducement to breach of a commercial contract is when A puts pressure on B not to fulfil a contract with C. Thus if trade union A were, for example, to apply pressure on employer B, in order to stop employer B making a delivery to employer C, then C, without further intervention, may be able to take action against B for breach of the supply contract. It is also possible for A indirectly to induce B to break its contract with C. If the trade union instructed its members to take strike action against employer B in order to stop them supplying employer C, then they might be liable for indirectly inducing that breach.

DC Thomson & Co v Deakin[101] concerned the delivery of bulk paper from a supplier to a printing firm. The employees of the supplier refused to deliver paper to the printer and an injunction was sought to stop the trade unions concerned from inducing the supplier to breach its contract with the printer. Jenkins LJ listed four categories where there was a direct interference by a third party with the rights of one of the parties to a contract.[102] The four categories were:

(1) 'a direct persuasion or procurement or inducement by the third party to the contract-breaker, with knowledge of the contract and the intention of bringing about its breach';[103]
(2) dealings by the third party with the contract-breaker which, to the knowledge of the third party, are inconsistent with the contract between the contract-breaker and the person wronged;[104]
(3) an act done by a third party with knowledge of the contract, which, if done by one of the parties to it, would have been a breach of that contract;[105]
(4) the imposition by the third party, who has knowledge of the contract, of some physical restraint upon one of the parties to the contract so as to make it impossible for the contract to be performed.

---

[100] (1853) 2 E & B 216.
[101] [1952] 2 All ER 361 CA; see also *Merkur Island Shipping Corporation v Laughton* [1983] IRLR 218 HL which approved this approach.
[102] The summing up of these categories by Neill LJ in *Middlebrook Mushrooms Ltd v TGWU* [1993] IRLR 232 CA is relied upon here.
[103] *Lumley v Gye* (1853) 2 E & B 216 is an example of this.
[104] Jenkins LJ gave *British Motor Trade Association v Salvadori* [1949] Ch 556 as an example of this.
[105] Jenkins LJ gave *GWK Ltd v Dunlop Rubber Co Ltd* [1926] 42 TLR 376 as an example, where the defendant's employees had removed the tyres from a car, which belonged to a rival, at a motor show.

According to Jenkins LJ, the conditions necessary to show that there had been an actionable interference with one of the parties to the contract were:

(1) the person charged with the actionable interference knew of the existence of the contract and intended to procure its breach;
(2) the person so charged did persuade or induce the employees to break their contracts of employment;
(3) the persuaded or induced employees did break their contract of employment;
(4) the breach of contract was a natural consequence of the employees' breaches of their contracts of employment.

In relation to this last point, it needs to be shown that, because of the employees' actions, their employer was unable to fulfil the contract.[106]

The difference between direct and indirect inducement to breach a contract is, according to Neill LJ,[107] one of causation. For direct inducement to take place, as in *Lumley v Gye*, the persuasion had to be directed at the parties to the contract. In *Middlebrook Mushrooms Ltd v TGWU*[108] the distribution of leaflets by dismissed employees outside a supermarket was aimed at persuading customers not to buy their ex-employer's produce. This amounted to indirect inducement on the parties to the contract, namely the supplier and the shop. There was also the question of knowledge of the contracts. Jenkins LJ concluded that there needed to be knowledge of the contract(s) and an intent to procure its breach.[109] In this case the court held that there was no evidence that contracts existed between the shop and the supplier. It may be possible to infer knowledge, but not in this case.

The knowledge needed, however, may be minimal.[110] In a rather bizarre case in the county court,[111] a railway passenger claimed damages from two rail unions for costs incurred as a result of industrial action. The action had been called without a ballot, resulting in the union being unable to rely on any statutory immunities (see below). The claim was successful because, not only did the union know of the existence of contracts between the railway company and passengers, their intention was to affect the plaintiff and other passengers in order to put pressure on the employer. The county court judge decided that the unions were reckless in their intent, as they knew the effect of the action on the plaintiff, but nevertheless pursued it. More recently, the House of Lords has ruled that for a person to be liable they must know that they are inducing a breach of contract.[112]

There is the possibility of a defence against this tort if the defendant can show that they have an equal or superior right to that of the injured party: for example, where the contract interfered with is inconsistent with a previous contract with the person intervening.[113]

---

[106] See *Falconer v ASLEF and NUR* [1986] IRLR 331 as an example of a court applying these four steps.
[107] Note 102 above.
[108] [1993] IRLR 232 CA.
[109] *DC Thomson & Co v Deakin* [1952] 2 All ER 361 CA.
[110] See *JT Stratford & Sons Ltd v Lindley* [1965] AC 269 HL.
[111] *Falconer v ASLEF and NUR* [1986] IRLR 331.
[112] See *Mainstream Properties Ltd v Young* [2007] IRLR 608.
[113] See *Smithie's case* [1909] 1 KB 310 HL.

12.7.2 Interference with a contract or with business

This tort is closely connected with the tort of inducing a breach of contract. *Torquay Hotel Co Ltd v Cousins*[114] involved an attempt by a trade union to stop the supply of heating oil to a hotel with whom there was a trade dispute. Lord Denning MR extended the principle expounded in *Quinn v Leathem*[115] that 'it is a violation of legal right to interfere with contractual relations recognised by law if there be no sufficient justification for the interference'. Lord Denning stated that there were three aspects to the principle:

(1) there needed to be interference in the execution of a contract;
(2) interference must be deliberate, meaning that the person interfering must know of the contract;
(3) the interference must be direct.

Indirect interference would not be enough and might, according to Lord Denning, take away the right to strike. The conditions were satisfied in this case, where there was direct and deliberate interference in the contractual relations between the hotel and oil supplier.[116]

A further example can be found in *Timeplan Education Group Ltd v National Union of Teachers*.[117] This concerned a teacher's union attempting to interfere with the advertising for recruits by a teachers' supply agency. The Court of Appeal held that, in order to establish the tort of wrongful interference with contractual rights, five conditions need to be fulfilled:

(1) the defendant persuaded or procured or induced a third party to break a contract;
(2) knowledge of the contract;
(3) intention to procure a breach;
(4) the plaintiff suffered more than nominal damages;
(5) the plaintiff can rebut a defence of justification.

In this case no tort was committed because there was a failure to show knowledge of contracts or intention to procure a breach of them.[118]

12.7.3 Intimidation

In its direct form[119] this is committed where an unlawful threat is made directly to the plaintiff with the intention of causing loss to the plaintiff. In its indirect form it is where

---

[114] [1969] 2 Ch 106 CA at p 510.
[115] [1901] AC 495.
[116] See also *Merkur Island Shipping Corporation v Laughton* [1983] IRLR 218 HL, where a ship was boycotted. Lord Diplock approved the principle laid down by Denning LJ that interference is not confined to a breach of contract, but includes the prevention or hindering from performing their contract, even though it is not a breach.
[117] [1997] IRLR 457 CA.
[118] See also *Messenger Newspaper Group Ltd v National Graphical Association* [1984] IRLR 397, which concerned pressure on a third party by the union in an attempt to enforce a closed shop and *Union Traffic Ltd v TGWU* [1989] IRLR 127 CA where picketing at a location other than the pickets' own place of work, in an attempt to bring it to a standstill, was considered.
[119] See also section 240 TULRCA 1992 regarding breach of contract involving injury to persons or property and section 241 on intimidation or annoyance by violence or otherwise.

C suffers as a result of action taken by B following an unlawful threat by A to B. An example of this can be seen in *News Group Newspapers Ltd v SOGAT '82*[120] concerning the breakdown of negotiations between the plaintiff and the union over the employment of union members at its new plant in Wapping – the unions called their members out on strike but they were then dismissed. This was followed by picketing, large-scale rallies and demonstrations outside the Wapping plant. According to the High Court, although the tort of intimidation is not complete unless the person threatened succumbs to the threat and damage results, in this case there were sufficient threats of violence and molestation to justify the granting of injunctive relief.[121]

Rookes v Barnard[122] was a landmark case which caused great alarm to trade unionists by deciding that a threat to breach a contract of employment, by threatening to go on strike, was unlawful for the purposes of a tort of intimidation. In this case an airline company had a closed shop agreement for a part of its operation. The union threatened the airline that it would call its members out on strike if they did not remove an individual employee who had resigned from the union. The House of Lords reacted by making it almost impossible to threaten a strike without being subject to the tort of intimidation. Lord Devlin stated that there was nothing to differentiate a threat of a breach of contract from a threat of physical violence or any other illegal threat. This decision undermined the immunities enjoyed by trade unions in certain circumstances since the 1906 Act. Strikes are often preceded by threats of industrial action which would have fallen foul of the *Rookes v Barnard* decision if immunity had not been restored by the Trade Disputes Act 1965 (see 12.8 below).

12.7.4 Conspiracy

There are two types of conspiracy. One is the conspiracy to injure and the other is the conspiracy to commit an unlawful act.

A conspiracy to injure occurs when two or more people combine to injure a person in their trade by inducing customers or employees to break their contracts or not to deal with that person, which results in damage to that person.[123] *Huntley v Thornton*[124] was about an individual member of a trade union who failed to support a strike. Thereafter there were various successful attempts made to prevent the individual finding other work, by circulating details to shop stewards and others at alternative places of work. The individual then successfully brought an action for damages and conspiracy against a number of members of the trade union, who were held to have combined to injure the plaintiff in his trade and the acts were not done to further the legitimate trade interests of the defendants. Those acts were held to be done without justification. Of importance is the real purpose of the combination. If the predominant purpose was an intention to injure the plaintiff, then the tort is committed, even if the means used to inflict the damage were lawful and not

---

[120] [1986] IRLR 337.
[121] See also *Thomas v National Union of Mineworkers (South Wales Area)* [1985] IRLR 136 which partly concerned the intimidatory effect of mass picketing at collieries.
[122] [1964] AC 1129 HL; see also *JT Stratford & Sons v Lindley* [1965] AC 269 HL.
[123] *Quinn v Leathem* [1901] AC 495.
[124] [1957] 1 WLR 321.

actionable. In *Crofter Hand Woven Harris Tweed Co Ltd v Veitch*[125] the courts recognised that no liability should be attached to a trade union in a genuine trade dispute. It was held that the real purpose of an embargo on Harris Tweed exported by certain crofters was to benefit the members of the trade union. This contrasts with *Huntley v Thornton* where the motives were deemed to be personal rather than in furtherance of a trade dispute.

A conspiracy to commit an unlawful act is when a combination of persons conspires to inflict damage intentionally on another person by an unlawful act. Even if the primary purpose were to further or protect some legitimate interest, it is enough that this was achieved by the use of unlawful means.[126]

12.7.5 Inducing a breach of a statutory duty

It is possible that industrial action may have the effect of applying pressure on an employer to breach a statutory duty imposed on either the employer or the employee. *Associated British Ports v TGWU*[127] concerned proposed industrial action resulting from the Government's decision to abolish the National Dock Labour Scheme. This scheme had the effect of preserving jobs in the docks for registered dock workers. Part of the scheme listed the obligations of workers, which included the requirement to 'work for periods as are reasonable in his particular case'. The issue was whether industrial action would be an inducement to the dock workers to breach a statutory duty to work. The Court of Appeal took the view that this was the case but the House of Lords held that this was incorrect because the relevant provision imposed a contractual duty rather than a statutory one.[128]

12.7.6 Economic duress

Economic duress is when one party is in such a dominant position that they can exercise coercion on the other party. The issue of economic duress has occurred in the context of the boycotting of ships and demands for money and payments to the union or members concerned. *Universe Tankships Inc of Monrovia v ITWF*[129] concerned the boycotting of a ship whilst in a British port and subsequent payments made by the ship owners to obtain the release of the ship. Lord Diplock stated that:

> The use of economic duress to induce another person to part with property or money is not a tort *per se*; the form that the duress takes may or may not be tortious. The remedy to which economic duress gives rise is not an action for damages but an action for restitution of property or money exacted under such duress . . .

This approach was developed in *Dimskal Shipping Co v ITWF*,[130] which also concerned a ship that was confined to port by an industrial dispute. The employers were forced to

---

[125] [1942] 1 All ER 142 HL.
[126] See *Lonhro plc v Fayed* [1991] 3 All ER 303 HL.
[127] [1989] IRLR 399 HL.
[128] See also *Barrets & Baird (Wholesale) Ltd v IPCS* [1987] IRLR 3, where it was argued that a series of strikes stopped the employer from carrying out their statutory duties. The argument was rejected as no statutory duty was identified.
[129] [1983] AC 366 HL.
[130] [1992] IRLR 78 HL.

issue their employees with new contracts with backdated pay as well as to make a payment to the union. As these payments were induced by illegitimate economic pressure, the employer was entitled to restitution.

12.8 Protection from tort liabilities

Protection is given against certain potential liabilities in tort by section 219 TULRCA 1992. The immunity from liability is on the grounds that the act (i) induces another to break a contract or interferes, or induces another to interfere, with the contract's performance and, (ii) secondly, consists in threatening these actions.[131] Any agreement or combination of two or more persons to do, or procure the doing of, an act in contemplation of furtherance of a trade dispute will not be actionable in tort if the act is one that would not have been actionable if done without any agreement or combination.[132]

There are three requirements in respect of this protection:

(1) the act done should be in 'contemplation or furtherance of a trade dispute';
(2) it must be a trade dispute between workers[133] and their employer;
(3) it must relate, wholly or mainly, to a number of specific issues. These are:
    (a) terms and conditions of employment,[134] including physical working conditions;
    (b) engagement, non-engagement, termination or suspension of employment or the duties of employment;
    (c) allocation of work or the duties of employment between workers;
    (d) matters of discipline;
    (e) membership, or non-membership, of a trade union;
    (f) facilities for trade union officials;
    (g) machinery for consultation and negotiation in connection with any of the above, including disputes about the right of a trade union to be recognised in representing workers for the purpose of negotiating any of the above.[135]

The phrase 'relates wholly or mainly to' requires a consideration of more than the event that caused the dispute and involves analysis of the reasons why it arose.[136] This means investigating the motives of a trade union and whether there are other reasons which might be perceived as the real ones.[137]

---

[131] Section 219(1)(a) and (b) TULRCA 1992.
[132] Section 219(2) TULRCA 1992.
[133] Section 244(5) TULRCA 1992 defines a worker as either someone employed by the employer or a person no longer employed by the employer, but who was terminated in connection with the dispute or whose termination is one of the circumstances leading to the dispute.
[134] Section 244(5) TULRCA 1992 provides that employment includes any relationship where one person personally does work or performs services for another.
[135] Section 244(1) TULRCA 1992.
[136] *Mercury Communications Ltd v Scott-Garner* [1983] IRLR 494 CA.
[137] Perhaps a wider political motivation. Such motivation was considered in *University College London Hospital v UNISON* [1999] IRLR 31 CA where the court held that it was possible to have a wider political objective and, simultaneously, a specific objective of alleviating adverse consequences in a particular situation. See also *UNISON v UK* [2002] IRLR 497 where the ECHR considered the impact of Article 11 of the European Convention on Human Rights.

The term 'in contemplation or furtherance of a trade dispute' requires a subjective judgment as to how widely it should be interpreted. For example, is the collection of information about an employer's business performance and the terms and conditions of their employees an act in contemplation or furtherance of a dispute? In *Bent's Brewery Co Ltd v Luke Hogan*[138] a union attempted to collect such information. The court held that the union was inducing employees to breach their contracts of employment by revealing confidential information. The union was not entitled to statutory protection, because there was no imminent or existing dispute. There was a possibility of a future dispute, but no certainty that such a dispute would arise. The court relied upon a judgment given in *Conway v Wade*,[139] where Lord Loreburn LC discussed the words 'in contemplation or furtherance':

> I think they mean that either a dispute is imminent and the act is done in expectation of and with a view to it, or that the dispute is already existing and that the act is done in support of one side to it. In either case the act must be genuinely done as described and the dispute must be a real thing imminent or existing.

A trade dispute needs to be related to the contractual or other relationship between workers and the employer. In *British Broadcasting Corporation v DA Hearn*[140] the trade union attempted to stop the employer broadcasting the football cup final via a satellite which would allow it to be seen in South Africa. The court held that this could not be seen as a trade dispute in itself. If the unions had requested a change in the contract of employment to include a term that the union's members would not be required to take part in broadcasts to South Africa, then a subsequent dispute about whether to include that term might have been interpreted as a trade dispute about terms and conditions of employment. Without such a link, the dispute could not qualify for protection.

According to the House of Lords, a dispute about the reasonableness of instructions from an employer can be a dispute about terms and conditions of employment.[141] In this case an individual was excluded from school for disruptive behaviour. The school governors allowed the mother's appeal and reinstated the pupil, and, subsequently, the headmaster issued an instruction that he should be taught in class. The trade union balloted its members and the union gave notice that it would not comply with the instruction. The court held that the reality was that the dispute was about the working conditions of teachers and therefore related to terms and conditions of employment.

The dispute must be between existing workers and their current employer. Thus it is not possible to conduct a dispute, within the protection of section 219 TULRCA 1992, about the contracts of employment of future workers. This unfortunate outcome was confirmed in *University College London Hospital v UNISON*.[142] Here the trade union balloted its members on a strike over the employer's refusal to guarantee the protection of the Transfer of Undertakings Regulations 1981[143] for the duration of a 30-year PFI[144] scheme. The Court

---

[138] [1945] 2 All ER 570.
[139] [1909] AC 506 HL.
[140] [1977] IRLR 273 CA.
[141] *P v National Association of Schoolmasters/Union of Women Teachers* [2003] IRLR 307.
[142] [1999] IRLR 31 CA.
[143] SI 1981/1794.
[144] Private Finance Initiative to build and run a new hospital.

of Appeal held that there were three requirements of a trade dispute: (i) that it must be a dispute between workers and their employer; (ii) that the dispute must relate wholly or mainly to one of the activities in section 244 TULRCA 1992; and (iii) that the act must be carried out in contemplation or furtherance of a trade dispute. This was a dispute about terms and conditions between workers and a future employer and about workers as yet to be employed. It is difficult to see how this latter point is different to all other industrial disputes, which not only protect the contracts of current workers, but also future ones yet to be employed.[145]

12.9 Exceptions to statutory immunity

There are a number of actions which will not qualify for the immunity provided by section 219 TULRCA 1992.

12.9.1 Picketing

As well as the economic torts, pickets are potentially liable for other torts. Possible torts include: trespass to the highway, which would need to be enforced by the owner of the soil; the tort of private nuisance, which suggests an unlawful interference with a person's right to enjoy or use land or some right in connection with it;[146] and the tort of public nuisance which consists of an act or omission which causes inconvenience to the public in the exercise of their common rights, such as the unreasonable obstruction of the highway.[147]

There is no immunity from actions in tort for acts done in the course of picketing unless they are done in accordance with section 220 TULRCA 1992.[148] This provides that it is lawful for a person, in contemplation or furtherance of a trade dispute, to attend at or near their own place of work for the purpose of either peacefully obtaining or communicating information, or peacefully persuading any person to either work or abstain from working. The same provision allows an official of a trade union to accompany, for the same purposes, a member of the union, whom the official represents, at or near their place of work.[149] There is no precise definition of what is meant by 'at' or 'near' the place of work. May LJ declined to give one as the number of circumstances that one might have to provide for were so variable as to make it impossible to lay down a test.[150] He suggested the use of a commonsense approach, as did Woolf LJ in *R v East Sussex Coroner, ex parte Healy*:[151]

---

[145] In *Westminster City Council v UNISON* [2001] IRLR 524 CA the court held that a dispute about a proposed transfer was a trade dispute because it was about the change in the identity of the employer, rather than about the public policy issue of privatisation.

[146] See *Thomas v NUM (South Wales)* [1985] IRLR 136, which considered mass picketing of collieries and held that the way in which it was carried out amounted to harassment of working miners in using the highway for the purpose of going to work; see also *Mersey Docks v Verrinder* [1982] IRLR 152.

[147] See *News Group Newspapers v SOGAT '82* [1986] IRLR 337, which discussed the torts of public and private nuisance.

[148] Section 219(3) TULRCA 1992.

[149] Section 220(1) TULRCA 1992.

[150] See *Rayware Ltd v TGWU* [1989] IRLR 134 CA.

[151] [1988] 1 WLR 1194.

The word 'near' being an ordinary word of the English language indicating a short distance or at close proximity is to be applied . . . in a common sense manner . . . it seems to me that it is not for the courts to define what is precisely meant by the word.

In *Rayware Ltd v TGWU*[152] the issue had been whether a group of workers picketing at the entrance to a private trading estate, about 7/10ths of a mile from the workplace, were 'at' or 'near' the place of work. According to the Court of Appeal, the word 'near' was an expanding word and not a restraining one, i.e. its meaning was to be expanded to give effect to the purpose of the legislation. This purpose was to give a right to picket. This right was not to be taken away by holding that the nearest point where picketing could take place, even though it was 7/10ths of a mile away, was not 'at or near'.[153]

If a person normally works at a number of different locations or at a location where it would be impracticable to picket, then the place of work can be any location at which that employee works or otherwise at the location from which the work is administered.[154] The same rules apply for ex-employees whose termination is related to the dispute. They may treat their last place of work as their location for picketing purposes.[155]

The legislation does not prescribe the number of pickets that are to be allowed at or near the place of work. However, the requirement is for the picketing to be peaceful and it may be that the presence of large numbers of individuals may be too intimidating for it to be seen as peaceful. In *Thomas v NUM (South Wales Area)*[156] there was mass picketing at the gates of a number of collieries in South Wales during the 1984 miners' strike. It was held to be tortious because of its nature and the way that it was carried out. It represented an unreasonable harassment of those miners who were working. Mass picketing by trying to block the entry to the workplace may be a common law nuisance. The court relied on the existing Code of Practice on Picketing[157] which recommended that the number of pickets should be limited to six and issued an injunction restricting the number of pickets to that number.

12.9.2 Action taken because of dismissal for unofficial action

An act is not protected if the reason, or one of the reasons, for it is in connection with the dismissal of one or more employees who are not entitled to protection from unfair dismissal by reason of their taking unofficial action.[158]

---

[152] [1989] IRLR 134 CA.
[153] In *Union Traffic v TGWU* [1989] IRLR 127 CA, picketing at a depot some 14 miles away was held to be too far, even though the 'home' depot had closed down.
[154] Section 220(2) TULRCA 1992.
[155] Section 220(3) TULRCA 1992; if a reason for the dispute is a change of work locations, ex-employees will not be protected if they picket at the new location where they have not worked; they are confined to the old location even if it has been closed down. See *News Group Newspapers v SOGAT '82* [1986] IRLR 337.
[156] [1985] IRLR 136.
[157] This Code was made by the Secretary of State for Employment and came into force on 1 May 1992; SI 1992/476.
[158] See below, section 237 TULRCA 1992.

12.9.3 Secondary action

Secondary action is not lawful picketing.[159] It is defined as an inducement, or a threat, to break or interfere with a contract of employment where the employer in that contract is not party to the dispute.[160] An employer shall not be regarded as party to a dispute between another employer and the workers of that employer; and where more than one employer is in dispute with its workers, the dispute between each employer and its workers is to be treated as a separate dispute.[161] Finally a primary action in one dispute, which is protected if in contemplation or furtherance of a trade dispute, cannot be relied upon as secondary action in another dispute.[162]

12.9.4 Pressure to impose a union recognition requirement

An act is not protected if it constitutes an inducement or an attempt to induce a person to incorporate into a contract a requirement to recognise or consult with a trade union[163] or is an act that interferes with the supply of goods and services in an attempt to achieve the same with the supplier.[164]

12.10 Ballots and notices of industrial action

Detailed rules on the need for trade unions to conduct ballots before taking industrial action were introduced by successive Conservative Governments during the 1980s and early 1990s. Currently section 219 TULRCA 1992 provides that if industrial action takes place without a ballot complying with the rules then there will be no immunity from actions in tort.

An underlying assumption on the need for such ballots was that many strikes were organised and led against the wishes of the majority of members of a particular trade union. Compulsory balloting of the membership would stop this happening. It would also reduce or eliminate 'wildcat' strikes.[165] It was intended to stop public voting at mass meetings where, it was suggested, individuals might feel coerced into showing solidarity and voting for industrial action. The arguments against formalised balloting procedures include: (i) the fact that once a ballot has been held which is in favour of industrial action, then that action may be given greater legitimacy; and (ii) negotiators may have less flexibility to come to a deal with the employer if there is a ballot result which is binding upon them. It is worth noting that, although a ballot is required before protected industrial action can take place, no ballot is required to stop the action.

---

[159] Section 224(1) TULRCA 1992.
[160] Section 224(2) TULRCA 1992.
[161] Section 224(4) TULRCA 1992.
[162] Section 224(5) TULRCA 1992.
[163] As in sections 186 and 187 TULRCA 1992; see above under '12.3 Recognition'.
[164] Section 225 TULRCA 1992.
[165] A wildcat strike is where members of a group of workers stop work and take industrial action without notice to the employer or, possibly, their own trade union.

Although there was an unsuccessful attempt to introduce ballots and 'cooling-off' periods in the Industrial Relations Act 1971, the current legislation stems from the Trade Union Act 1984.[166] The rules were added to and amended in the Employment Acts 1988 and 1990, with the current law contained in TULRCA 1992. There is also a Code of Practice on Industrial Action Ballots and Notice to Employers.[167]

One must be careful about introducing causal relationships where none may exist, but it is certainly true that the number of industrial disputes has declined significantly. In 1986 (after the 1980s' miners' strike) the number of working days lost through strikes in the United Kingdom was 1,920,000. This figure increased during the next three years, but then started to decline again. In 1991 the figure was 761,000 and by 1997[168] it had fallen to 235,000 working days lost. Perhaps more remarkable is the number of working days lost per 1,000 employees. In 1986 this figure was 90 working days, in 1991 it was 34 days and, by 1997, it had become 10 working days lost per 1,000 employees.[169]

A trade union will lose its protection under section 219 TULRCA 1992 if it induces a person to take part or to continue to take part in industrial action that is not supported by a ballot and the rules about notifying the employer about the ballot contained in section 226A TULRCA 1992.[170] This is so even if the inducement is unsuccessful, whether because the individual is not interested or for some other reason.[171]

A failure to hold a ballot will deprive the union of protection against legal action taken by members under section 62 TULRCA 1992; by employers, or customers or suppliers of that employer, relying on section 226 TULRCA 199; or by an individual deprived, or likely to be deprived, of goods and services under section 235A TULRCA 1992 but relying on section 62 or 226 TULRCA 1992. Section 62 TULRCA 1992 deals with the rights of members of a trade union who have been, or are likely to be, induced into taking industrial action, which does not have the support of a ballot.[172] Industrial action shall only be seen to have the support of a ballot if all the requirements of sections 226–234A TULRCA 1992 have been fulfilled (see below).[173] The member or members of the trade union concerned may apply to an employment tribunal. If the tribunal finds that the claim is well founded, it may make such orders as are necessary to ensure that the trade union stops inducing members to continue or take part in industrial action.[174]

---

[166] The Trade Union Act 1984 only withdrew immunity for disputes concerning contractual matters. If the action did not concern contractual matters then, it could be argued, no ballot was required. This was the argument unsuccessfully used by teachers in *Metropolitan Borough of Solihull v NUT* [1985] IRLR 211, who refused to cover for colleagues' absences and to cover school lunches amongst other actions. They claimed that these were of a voluntary nature and not contractual, so a ballot was not required.

[167] The current Code came into effect on 1 September 2005, SI 2005/2420.

[168] The year that the Conservative Government lost office.

[169] Office for National Statistics, *Labour Market Trends*, June 1998, p 299.

[170] Section 226(1) TULRCA 1992.

[171] Section 226(4) TULRCA 1992.

[172] In sections 226–234A TULRCA 1992, a reference to a contract of employment includes any contract under which one person personally does work or performs services for another; see section 235 TULRCA 1992.

[173] Section 62(2) TULRCA 1992.

[174] Section 62(3) TULRCA 1992.

12.10.1 Notifying the employer of the ballot

The trade union must take such steps as are reasonably necessary to notify the employer of persons entitled to vote in the ballot, that the union intends to hold a ballot and the date which the union reasonably believes will be the opening day of the ballot.[175] The notice, which is to be in writing, must also contain: a list of the categories of employee to which the employees concerned belong and a list of their workplaces; the total number of employees concerned, the number in each of the categories listed and the number at each workplace, together with an explanation of how these figures were arrived at. Alternatively, where some or all of the employees concerned have union deductions made from their wages, the union can supply 'such information as will enable the employer readily to deduce': the total number of employees concerned, the categories to which they belong and the number in each of the categories; and the number who work at the workplaces concerned.[176] This notice must be given not later than the seventh day before the opening day of the ballot.[177]

It is still unlikely, however, that the statement of an intention to hold a ballot amongst 'all our members in your institution' would fulfil the requirements of the legislation. This statement was contained in *Blackpool and Fylde College v NATFHE*[178] which involved the introduction of flexible contracts for new members of staff. Of the 330 members of staff, 288 were members of the union. Only 109 had subscriptions deducted through the payroll, so it was not possible for the employer to ascertain which employees would be entitled to take part in the ballot.[179] The rule now is that if the trade union possesses information as to the number, category or workplace of the employees concerned, that is the minimum information that must be supplied. The fact that it is not necessary to give names of individuals to an employer[180] is an important safeguard for employees, both in terms of privacy and in terms of protection from potential harassment by the employer.

Not later than the third day before the opening day of the ballot, the trade union must also submit a sample of the ballot paper to the employer of the persons likely to be entitled to vote.[181] If, for some reason, not all the ballot papers are the same, then a sample of all of the different versions must be given to the employer.[182]

12.10.2 Appointment of a scrutineer

Before the ballot takes place, the trade union needs to appoint a suitably qualified[183] person as a scrutineer. The functions of the scrutineer are to take all the steps necessary to prepare

---

[175] Section 226A(2)(a)–(b) TULRCA 1992.
[176] Sections 226A(2)(c) and 226A(2A)–(2C) TULRCA 1992.
[177] Section 226A(1)(a) TULRCA 1992; section 226A(4) defines the opening day of the ballot as the first day when a voting paper is sent to any person entitled to vote.
[178] [1994] IRLR 227.
[179] See also *National Union of Rail, Maritime and Transport Workers v London Underground* [2001] IRLR 228 CA, where the phrase 'all members of the union employed in all categories at all workplaces' was held not to comply with the Act's requirements; and *British Telecom v CWU* [2004] IRLR 58.
[180] Section 226A(2G) TULRCA 1992.
[181] Section 226A(1)(b) TULRCA 1992.
[182] Section 226A(2F) TULRCA 1992.
[183] Section 226B(2) TULRCA 1992 provides information on who is a qualified person.

a report on the ballot for the trade union stating whether the ballot was satisfactory or not and providing a free copy to employers and voters on request.[184] This report is to be made as soon as possible after the ballot and, in any event, not more than four weeks after the date of the ballot.[185] There is an obligation for the trade union to comply with all reasonable requests made by the scrutineer in relation to the ballot.[186]

There is an exception for small ballots, as there is no requirement for the appointment of a scrutineer where the number of members entitled to vote does not exceed 50.[187]

12.10.3 Entitlement to vote

The entitlement to vote is to be given only to those members of the trade union whom it is reasonable at the time of the ballot for the union to believe will be induced to take part in, or to continue to take part in, the industrial action. No one else has any entitlement to vote.[188]

Subject to exceptions, a separate ballot is to be held for each workplace. If there is a single set of premises, a person's workplace is the premises the person works at, or, in any other case, the premises to which the person's employment has the closest connection.[189] The exceptions to the requirement for separate workplace ballots include, first, if the entitlement to vote is limited to all those members who have an occupation of a particular kind or have any number of particular kinds of occupation; secondly, where the entitlement to vote is limited to members employed by a particular employer, or by any number of particular employers, with whom the union is in dispute.[190] In *University of Central England v NALGO*[191] the ballot covered a number of colleges, in which the union had members entitled to vote. As the negotiations were with an employers' association and the vote covered all the colleges concerned, it was held that there was no requirement for separate workplace ballots. The potential absurdity of the rules on separate workplace ballots is shown in *Inter City West Coast v NURMTW*.[192] In this case there were two railway companies owned by the British Railways Board occupying separate office sites. The dispute concerned train conductors who worked from Manchester Piccadilly station, but the employers claimed that two separate ballots should have been held. The court rejected their arguments and held that the conductors had one place of work, i.e. the railway station.[193]

---

[184] Section 231B TULRCA 1992 describes the contents of the scrutineer's report: it is to state whether the ballot met statutory requirements, that the arrangements for the ballot were fair and that the scrutineer has been able to carry out the required duties without interference.

[185] Section 226B(1) TULRCA 1992.

[186] Section 226B(2), (4) TULRCA 1992.

[187] Section 226C TULRCA 1992.

[188] Section 227 TULRCA 1992. In *RMT v Midland Mainline Ltd* [2001] IRLR 813 the union omitted to ballot a significant number of members in the grades concerned.

[189] Section 228 TULRCA 1992.

[190] Section 228A(1)–(4) TULRCA 1992; section 228A(5) defines who are the particular members of a trade union affected by different types of disputes.

[191] [1993] IRLR 81.

[192] [1996] IRLR 583.

[193] See also *RJB Mining (UK) Ltd v NUM* [1997] IRLR 621, where the union decided to hold an aggregate ballot, but then omitted one location.

Industrial action will not be regarded as having the support of a ballot if a member of a trade union, whom it was reasonable to assume would be induced to take part in the industrial action, was not accorded their entitlement to vote and was subsequently induced to take part in the action.[194] Small accidental failures in the process are to be ignored if the failure was unlikely to have an effect on the result of the ballot.[195] There are problems for trade unions in organising ballots that meet the statutory requirements. These are connected with maintaining a centralised register of members when membership can be in a state of flux. *London Underground v NURMTW*[196] involved the recruitment of some 600–700 new members after the ballot for industrial action had been completed. The employers were unsuccessful in their attempt to obtain an injunction, because the Court of Appeal accepted that industrial action was not the action of the individual who voted, but was a collective action in which the individual took part. It is the collective industrial action that must have the support of the ballot.[197]

12.10.4 The voting paper

We have seen that voting at mass meetings is no longer permissible. Every member entitled to vote must be given a voting paper which must state the name of the independent scrutineer and clearly specify the address to which it is to be sent and the date by which it must be sent. In addition it must have a unique whole number which is one of a series of numbers.[198] The voting paper must also contain at least one of two questions, depending upon the industrial action envisaged. The first question is whether the voter is prepared to take part in, or continue, a strike. The second is whether they are prepared to take part in, or continue, industrial action short of a strike.[199] If the union wishes to pursue both options, then they must ask both questions.[200] The questions need to be in such a form that the members can vote either yes or no. Prior to the ERELA 1999 the only definition of a strike was contained in section 246 TULRCA 1992, which defined it as 'any concerted stoppage of work'. In *Connex South Eastern Ltd v NURMTW*[201] this was held to include any refusal by employees to work for periods of time for which they are employed to work, provided it was 'concerted'. Concerted was taken to mean mutually planned. Such action could therefore include a ban on rest-day working and overtime when people might normally be working. The ERELA 1999 changed this view and included a section stating that, for the purposes of section 229(2) TULRCA 1999, an overtime ban and a call-out ban constituted action short of a strike.[202]

---

[194] Section 232A TULRCA 1992; see also *National Union of Rail, Maritime and Transport Workers v Midland Mainline Ltd* [2001] IRLR 813 CA, which concerned the missing out of some of those entitled to vote.
[195] Section 232B TULRCA 1992.
[196] [1995] IRLR 636 CA.
[197] See also *British Railways Board v NURMTW* [1989] IRLR 349 CA where the number of ballot papers issued appeared to be less than the membership of the union entitled to vote.
[198] Section 229(1) TULRCA 1992.
[199] Section 229(2) TULRCA 1992.
[200] See *West Midlands Travel v TGWU* [1994] IRLR 578, which considered that each question had to be voted on individually and the majority in respect of each question considered separately.
[201] [1999] IRLR 249 CA.
[202] Section 229(2A) TULRCA 1992.

In addition, the voting paper must also specify, in the event of a yes vote, who is authorised to call upon members to take industrial action.[203] The person specified must be one of those included in section 20(2) TULRCA 1992, which defines those whose acts are to be taken as being authorised or endorsed by a trade union. Finally, the following statement needs to appear on the ballot paper:

> If you take part in strike or other industrial action, you may be in breach of your contract of employment.
>
> However, if you are dismissed for taking part in strike or other industrial action which is called officially and is otherwise lawful, the dismissal will be unfair if it takes place fewer than eight weeks after you started taking part in the action, and depending on the circumstances may be unfair if it takes place later.[204]

The second paragraph, perhaps making it less intimidatory, was added by the ERELA 1999.

12.10.5 The ballot

There are also strict rules applied to the ballot itself. As far as is reasonably practicable, voting must be done in secret.[205] Every person who is entitled to vote in the ballot must be allowed to do so without interference from the trade union or its officials and must be able to do so, as far as is reasonably practicable, without incurring any direct costs themselves.[206] Members must have a voting paper sent to them by post to their home address, or any other address to which the individual has requested the union to send it.[207] *London Borough of Newham v NALGO*[208] involved a strike ballot which the trade union thought would take one month to organise and hold. The union funded a campaign, and provided speakers, to rally support for a yes vote. The courts held that the statute did not require trade unions to adopt a neutral stance. The union is perfectly entitled to be partisan so long as it complies with the legislation.

There is an obligation that the votes in a ballot are to be fairly and accurately counted, although this does not mean that inaccuracies in the counting will necessarily invalidate the result. So long as the inaccuracies are accidental and do not affect the result, they are to be disregarded.[209] As soon as reasonably practicable after the ballot, the union must inform both those entitled to vote and all the employers concerned of the result.[210] The scrutineer will also produce a report on the ballot.[211]

The ballot will cease to be effective if action has not been called, by a specified person,[212] or taken place within a period of four weeks from the date of the ballot. This period can be

---

[203] Section 229(3) TULRCA 1992.

[204] Section 229(4) TULRCA 1992; see 12.14 below.

[205] Section 230(4)(a) TULRCA 1992.

[206] See *Paul v NALGO* [1987] IRLR 43 CO. Although this case did not concern industrial action, it did show that even minor costs incurred, i.e. the cost of posting a ballot paper, would be sufficient to breach the requirement that there should be no direct costs falling upon the member.

[207] Section 230(1) and (2) TULRCA 1992.

[208] [1993] IRLR 83 CA.

[209] Section 230(4)(b) TULRCA 1992.

[210] Sections 231–231A TULRCA 1992.

[211] Section 231B TULRCA 1992; see above.

[212] See section 233 TULRCA 1992 which states that action will only be regarded as having the support of a ballot if called by a specified person; see above.

extended to a maximum of eight weeks if such an extension is agreed between the employer or employers concerned and the trade union.[213] If there has been legal action by the employer during this period, which has resulted in a court order stopping the trade union from calling or taking industrial action, then, when such an order lapses or is discharged, the union may apply to the court for an order that this period does not count towards the four weeks or longer.[214]

12.10.6 Notice to the employer

An act done by a trade union to induce a person to take part in, or continue, industrial action will not be regarded as protected unless the trade union gives a relevant notice to the affected employer or employers, within seven days of having notified the employer of the result as required by section 231A TULRCA 1992.[215] A relevant notice is one that is in writing and contains: a list of the categories of employee to which the affected employees belong and a list of their workplaces; the total number of affected employees, the number in each of the categories listed and the number at each workplace, together with an explanation of how these figures were arrived at. Alternatively, where some or all of the employees affected have union deductions made from their wages, the union can supply 'such information as will enable the employer readily to deduce': the total number of affected employees, the categories to which they belong and the number in each of the categories; and the number who work at the workplaces concerned.[216] The relevant notice must also state whether the action is going to be continuous or discontinuous; the dates on which continuous action will commence and, if relevant, the dates on which discontinuous action will take place.[217] Discontinuous action is that which takes place on some days only.[218]

One of the problems with the legislation prior to the ERELA 1999 was that the rules were so rigid that if a trade union wished to cease or suspend action in order to negotiate, they were then required to go through the notice provisions again in order to restart the whole process.[219] The ERELA 1999 added subsections (7A) and (7B) to section 234A TULRCA 1992. These additions have the effect of allowing a suspension of the action and therefore of the requirement to notify the employer again of intended action. These suspensions can take place so that the union can comply with a court order or undertaking or if the employer and the union agree to the suspension.

---

[213] Section 234(1) TULRCA 1992; the possible extension to eight weeks was added by the ERELA 1999, presumably to allow more time for a negotiated settlement.

[214] Section 234(2)–(6) TULRCA 1992; although there is an absolute maximum of 12 weeks after which the effect of the ballot is removed.

[215] Sections 234A(1) TULRCA 1992.

[216] Section 234A(3)–(3C) TULRCA 1992; see also section 234A(5A) which describes the information that must be given to the employer, although not giving the names of any employees is not a ground for holding that there has been a breach of the condition. This provision was added by ERELA 1999; for an example of the position before this amendment see *Blackpool and Fylde College v NATFHE* [1994] IRLR 227.

[217] Section 234A(3)(b) TULRCA 1992.

[218] Section 234A(6) TULRCA 1992.

[219] See section 234A(7) TULRCA 1992.

12.10.7 Industrial action affecting the supply of goods and services

Where an individual claims that, as a result of an unlawful act to induce any person to take part in industrial action, there has been a delay or failure in the supply of goods or that there has been a reduction in the quality of goods or services supplied, that individual may apply to the High Court for an order. An act to induce any person to take part in or continue such industrial action is unlawful if it is actionable in tort and does not have the support of a ballot. The High Court may grant interlocutory relief or make an order requiring that there is no further inducement to take part in industrial action and that no person should engage in conduct after the order as a result of inducement before the order.[220]

12.11 Union responsibility for the actions of their members

Where proceedings in tort are brought against a trade union on the grounds that it is inducing, or threatening to induce, another to break a contract of employment or interfere with its performance, then the union is to be treated as liable if it has endorsed or authorised the act in question.[221] One of the perceived problems that this measure attempts to solve is that of unofficial action, where individual groups or parts of a trade union take action without the express approval of their trade union.

Trade unions are to be taken as having endorsed or authorised an act if it was done, or was authorised or endorsed: by any person who is empowered by the rules[222] of the union to authorise or endorse such action; or by the executive committee or the president or general secretary of the union; or by any other committee or official of the union.[223] For the purpose of this latter category a committee of the union is any group of persons constituted in accordance with the union's rules and an act is to be taken as authorised or endorsed by an official if it was authorised or endorsed by a committee of which the official was a member and the committee had as one of its purposes the organising or co-ordinating of industrial action.[224] *Heatons Transport (St Helens) Ltd v TGWU*[225] discussed the derivation of a shop steward's authority in order to assess the union's liability for the shop steward's actions. The court concluded that such authority could come from the rules expressly or by implication; or may come under the rules by express or implied delegation; or by virtue of the office held; or otherwise by such means as custom and practice. There is no need to look for specific authority in a particular case if the authority to act has been expressly or impliedly delegated to different levels of the organisation. A court may grant an injunction requiring the union to ensure that there is no further inducement to take

---

[220] Section 235A TULRCA 1992.
[221] Section 20(1) TULRCA 1992. See *Gate Gourmet Ltd v TGWU* [2005] IRLR 881.
[222] Rules means the written rules of the union or any other written provision between members: section 20(7) TULRCA 1992.
[223] Section 20(2) TULRCA 1992; an official need not be employed by the union; see *Express & Star Ltd v NGA* [1985] IRLR 455 where the West Midlands Secretary was held to be an official for whose actions, in this respect, the union was vicariously liable.
[224] Section 20(3) TULRCA 1992.
[225] [1972] IRLR 25 HL.

part in industrial action and that no person continues to act as if they had been induced to take part.[226]

It is possible for a trade union to avoid liability for the actions of its members if the executive, president or general secretary repudiates the act as soon as is reasonably practicable after it came to their knowledge. For such a repudiation to be effective, the union must give, without delay, a written notice to the committee or official in question and do its best, without delay, to give the notice to every member that the union believes might be involved in the action and to the employer of every such member.[227] The notice must, according to section 21(3) TULRCA 1992, contain the following statement:

> Your union has repudiated the call (or calls) for industrial action to which this notice relates and will give no support to unofficial industrial action taken in response to it (or them). If you are dismissed while taking unofficial industrial action, you will have no right to complain of unfair dismissal.

It is only by following this procedure that the union can avoid liability for the act and its consequences. There is a requirement for strict compliance with a repudiation, for the union not to be held liable for further breaches. Section 21(5) TULRCA 1992 provides that an act will not be treated as being repudiated if, subsequently, the executive, president or general secretary of the union acts in such a way that is inconsistent with it. Thus it is not enough to issue a written repudiation and then continue as before. In *Richard Read (Transport) Ltd v NUM (South Wales Area)*[228] there was a failure to comply with an injunction stopping mass picketing. Although the union president had said that the union would comply, there was no evidence that instructions to pickets had changed at all. The court cited a statement by Sir John Donaldson to the effect that it was not sufficient, when complying with an injunction, to say that one had done one's best (unless that was what was required by the injunction). Strict compliance was necessary.[229] In *Read*, the officials had shown an indifference as to whether or not the injunction was complied with.[230] As a result the union was held liable and fined.[231]

The union will be held not to have repudiated if, within three months of the repudiation, there is a request from a party to a commercial contract (i.e. not an employment contract) whose performance has been, or is being, interfered with and who has not been given the necessary written notification, and the union has not provided written confirmation that the act has been repudiated.[232]

---

[226] Section 20(6) TULRCA 1992; the provisions relating to union liability above also relate to complying with court injunctions; proceedings against the trade union do not affect the liability of any other person in respect of the act: section 20(5) TULRCA 1992.

[227] Section 21(1)–(2) TULRCA 1992.

[228] [1985] IRLR 67.

[229] *Howitt Transport Ltd v TGWU* [1973] IRLR 25.

[230] See also *Express & Star Ltd v NGA* [1985] IRLR 455, where the relationship of the statutory provisions on repudiation and contempt proceedings for failure to abide by an injunction were considered.

[231] Section 22 TULRCA 1992 provides limits as to the amount of fines that can be levied on trade unions in actions in tort and section 23 provides that certain property of the union is protected with regard to the enforcement of fines.

[232] Section 21(6) TULRCA 1992.

12.12 Prohibition on use of funds to indemnify unlawful conduct

Section 15(1) TULRCA 1992 prohibits trade unions from using their property in the following ways. First, towards the payment of a fine imposed by a court for an offence or for contempt of court. Secondly, towards the securing of any such payment and, finally, towards indemnifying an individual in respect of such a penalty. This reflects a view of the courts that such payments or indemnities are against public policy. *Drake v Morgan*[233] concerned the ability of the National Union of Journalists to pay the fines that its members incurred on the picket line. The court refused to make a declaration that such payments were not lawful. The resolution indemnifying the pickets had been made after the event and could not be seen as a way of indemnifying future unlawful acts. Thus it was not contrary to public policy because it could not be seen as either an incitement to commit an offence or aiding or abetting the securing of an offence. By way of contrast, in *Thomas v NUM (South Wales Area)*[234] an injunction was granted to stop the union indemnifying pickets against possible future fines. According to the court, even this did not stop the union from considering individual cases of hardship if it was in the interests of the union and the members as a whole. The court distinguished *Taylor v NUM (Derbyshire Area)*,[235] where payments had been made to pickets and striking miners, on the grounds that the strike was not authorised and was in breach of the union's rules.

12.13 Remedies

The remedies that may be available to the courts include specific performance, injunctions and damages.

Specific performance is an order of the court which compels the party in breach of contract to fulfil its obligations under that contract. Like all equitable remedies it is discretionary and is unlikely to be used in the context of industrial relations. In fact section 236 TULRCA 1992 stops the courts making orders for specific performance in relation to the contract of employment. It establishes an important statutory principle that an employee cannot be made to work or attend at any place for the purpose of doing so. The dividing line between an order for specific performance and an injunction may sometimes be unclear. It is possible that an injunction stopping an employer from, for example, dismissing an employee with one month's notice, rather than the six months' notice to which they were entitled, has the effect of ordering the continuation of the contract of employment.[236]

Injunctions can be interim or permanent in nature. The advantage of interim injunctions is the speed at which they can be obtained, although section 221 TULRCA 1992 does place some restrictions on their availability. First, where there is a without notice application for an injunction and the likely defence is that the action was in contemplation or furtherance of a trade dispute, the court cannot grant the injunction unless it is satisfied

---

[233] [1978] ICR 56.
[234] [1985] IRLR 136.
[235] [1985] IRLR 99.
[236] *Hill v CA Parsons Ltd* [1972] 1 Ch 305 CA.

that all reasonable steps have been taken to give the other side the opportunity of being heard. Secondly, where there is an application for an interim injunction pending a full trial of the action, and the party against whom the injunction is sought claims that they acted in the furtherance or contemplation of a trade dispute, then the court is to exercise its discretion as to whether it will be possible to establish a defence. Issues to be considered are whether there is a possibility of establishing a defence under sections 219 and 220 TULRCA 1992; whether it can be established that there is a trade dispute;[237] whether there is a serious issue to be tried: where the balance of convenience lies between the plaintiff and the defendant; and whether the granting of an order is in the public interest.

The standard authority for the approach to be taken in granting interim injunctions is set out in *American Cyanamid Co v Ethicon Ltd*.[238] Lord Diplock stated that the object of such an injunction was to protect the plaintiff against injury for which there could not be sufficient compensation in damages, if successful at the trial. However, this protection had to be weighed against the defendant's need to be protected from injury resulting from being stopped from exercising their own legal rights. Thus the test to be used is the balance of convenience. In particular, the court needs to decide whether the granting of an interim injunction is tantamount to giving final judgment against the defendant.[239] The courts will also need to ask whether there is a serious question to be tried.[240] For example, in *Associated British Ports v TGWU*,[241] the employers failed to show that a strike by registered dock workers would be in breach of their statutory duty under the National Dock Labour Scheme. Having failed in this argument there was no serious issue to be tried, so there was no basis for granting an injunction.

An injunction must be complied with by the person to whom it is addressed and must be obeyed from the moment that the defendant knows of its existence. It is not enough to claim that the order was not formally served and therefore could not be followed, as this would open the door to abuse. A telephone call or letter informing the defendant should be enough.[242]

Most disputes are resolved at, or soon after, the interim injunction stage and it is rare for a dispute to go all the way to obtaining a permanent injunction. If proceedings do continue, the appropriate remedy by then is likely to be damages rather than an injunction. In *Messenger Newspapers v NGA*[243] the plaintiffs were awarded: sums for liquidated damages for all the expenditure that they had incurred as a result of the tort; compensatory damages for the loss of revenue; aggravated damages as a result of the injury being caused by malice or by the manner of doing the injury; and exemplary damages for the necessity of teaching the wrongdoer that tort does not pay.[244]

---

[237] See *University College London Hospital v UNISON* [1999] IRLR 31 CA, which set out three conditions for establishing whether there was a trade dispute (see above).

[238] [1975] AC 396 HL.

[239] *NWL Ltd v Nelson and Laughton* [1979] IRLR 478 HL, *per* Lord Diplock.

[240] See *Dimbleby & Sons Ltd v NUJ* [1984] IRLR 161 HL.

[241] [1989] IRLR 399 HL.

[242] See *Kent Free Press v NGA* [1987] IRLR 267, where such an event happened.

[243] [1984] IRLR 397.

[244] See *Rookes v Barnard* [1964] AC 1229 HL, *per* Lord Devlin.

12.14 Dismissals during industrial action

An employee who is sacked is only able to claim unfair dismissal in limited circumstances. The circumstances that need to be taken into account are: whether the action is official or unofficial; whether all or some of the employees taking part have been dismissed or re-engaged; and whether the employee is taking part in protected industrial action.

12.14.1 Unofficial action

An employee has no right to complain of unfair dismissal if, at the time of the dismissal, the employee was taking part in unofficial industrial action.[245] Industrial action is unofficial unless the employee is:

(1) a member of a trade union and the action is authorised or endorsed[246] by that trade union, or
(2) not a member of a trade union, but there are members taking part in the action whose union has authorised or endorsed the action.[247]

There are exceptions to this rule which include if the dismissals are for a reason related to pregnancy, maternity leave, parental leave, time off for dependants, health and safety, being or planning to be an employee representative, or making a protected disclosure.[248]

12.14.2 Official action

Where an employee has a right to complain of unfair dismissal during industrial action or a lock-out, the employment tribunal will not be able to entertain the claim unless:

(1) one or more of the relevant[249] employees has not been dismissed,[250] or
(2) a relevant employee has been offered re-engagement within a period of three months, beginning with the date of dismissal, and the complainant has not been offered re-engagement.[251] Re-engagement means the same job as before the dispute or in a different reasonably suitable job.[252]

Even a re-engagement made in error might be enough to bring these provisions into effect. In *Bigham and Keogh v GKN Quickform Ltd*[253] an employee working on a site was dismissed as a result of going on strike. Less than three months later he applied for and

---

[245] Section 237(1) TULRCA 1992.
[246] Authorised or endorsed in accordance with section 20(2) TULRCA 1992 – see note 223 above.
[247] Section 237(2) TULRCA 1992.
[248] Section 237(1A) TULRCA 1992.
[249] Section 238(3) TULRCA 1992 states that a relevant employee is an employee, at the establishment of the employer, who is taking part in the industrial action; in the case of a lock-out, a relevant employee is an employee who was directly interested in the dispute leading to the lock-out.
[250] The material time for deciding whether a relevant employee has not been dismissed is at the conclusion of the hearing determining jurisdiction of the complaint; see *P & O European Ferries (Dover) Ltd v Byrne* [1989] IRLR 254 CA and *Manifold Industries v Sims* [1991] IRLR 242.
[251] Section 238(1) TULRCA 1992.
[252] Section 238(4) TULRCA 1992.
[253] [1992] IRLR 4.

was successful in obtaining a job at the employer's main office elsewhere. He revealed his previous employment but not the dismissal. After two weeks the connection with the dismissal was made and the employee was dismissed from the new position. This was sufficient to bring into effect section 238(2)(b) TULRCA 1992 as the employer had constructive knowledge of the employee's previous employment, even though they had not connected this to the previous industrial dispute.[254]

There are the same exceptions to this rule as are applied in unofficial industrial action above.

12.14.3 Protected action

A person takes protected industrial action if that person commits an act, or is induced to commit an act, which is protected from action in tort by section 219 TULRCA 1992 (see above). Such a person will be unfairly dismissed[255] if the reason, or the principal reason, for the dismissal is that the individual took protected industrial action, provided that the dismissal takes place within a basic period of 12 weeks beginning with the day that the employee started to take protected action. This basic period can be extended by the number of days on which an employee is locked out by the employer.[256]

The provisions will continue to apply to dismissals that take place after the protected period if:

(1) the employee had stopped the industrial action during or before the end of the period;
(2) the employee had not stopped industrial action during that period but the employer had not taken 'such procedural steps as would have been reasonable for the purposes of resolving the dispute to which the protected industrial action relates'.[257]

The protection is linked to applying pressure to both parties to act in a way that might lead to the resolution of the dispute, because, in deciding whether an employer has taken such steps, regard is to be had as to whether:

(1) there had been compliance by the union or the employer with any procedures agreed in a collective agreement or other agreement;
(2) the employer or the union had offered or agreed to negotiate after the start of the protected action;
(3) either party had unreasonably refused, after the start of the protected action, a request for the use of conciliation services;
(4) the employer or union had unreasonably refused mediation services in relation to the procedures to be adopted for ending the dispute.[258]

---

[254] See also *Crosville Wales Ltd v Tracey* [1993] IRLR 60, which concerned the dismissal of an entire workforce and the recruitment of a new one on different terms and conditions; some of the old workforce were recruited into this new workforce.
[255] The rules on length of service do not apply in respect of dismissals for taking a protected action: section 239(1) TULRCA 1992.
[256] Section 238A(7A)–(7C) TULRCA 1992.
[257] Section 238A(4)–(5) TULRCA 1992.
[258] Sections 238A(6) and 238B TULRCA 1992.

The remedies for an unfair dismissal in respect of taking protected industrial action are as for other unfair dismissal cases, except that the remedies of reinstatement and re-engagement are not available until the end of the protected industrial action.[259]

Further Reading

Barrow, C., *Industrial Relations Law* (Cavendish, 2002), Chapters 8–17.

Brown, W. and Oxenbridge, S., 'Trade Unions and Collective Bargaining: Law and the Future of Collectivism' in Barnard, C., Deakin, S. and Morris, G. (eds) *The Future of Labour Law* (Hart Publishing, 2004), Chapter 3.

Collins, H., Ewing, K. and McColgan, A., *Labour Law: Text and Materials* (Hart Publishing, 2005), Chapters 8 and 9.

Deakin, S. and Morris, G., *Labour Law* (4th edn, Hart Publishing, 2005), Chapters 9 and 11.

Ewing, K., 'Laws against Strikes Revisited' in Barnard, C., Deakin, S. and Morris, G. (eds) *The Future of Labour Law* (Hart Publishing, 2004), Chapter 2.

Novitz, T., *International and European Protection of the Right to Strike* (Oxford University Press, 2003).

www.acas.org.uk

www.cac.gov.uk

www.ilo.org.uk

www.tuc.org.uk

Visit **www.mylawchamber.co.uk/sargeant** to access legal updates, live web links and practice exam questions to test yourself on this chapter.

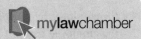 **my**lawchamber

---

[259] Section 239(4)(a) TULRCA 1992.

Index

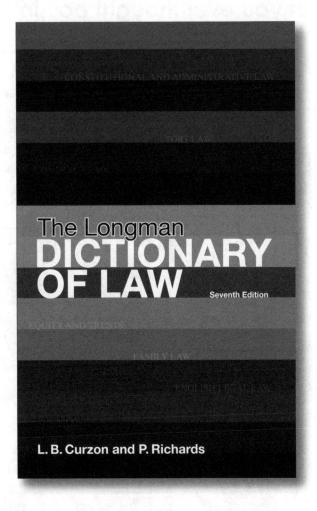

Get more support with study and revision than you ever thought possible ...

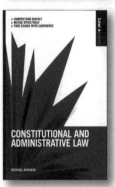
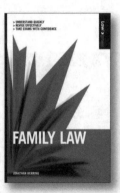

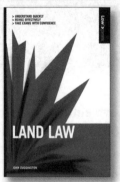